DICTIONARY
OF
AMERICAN
CHILDREN'S
FICTION,
1995–1999

DICTIONARY OF AMERICAN CHILDREN'S FICTION, 1995–1999

Books of Recognized Merit

ALETHEA K. HELBIG

AND

AGNES REGAN PERKINS

GREENWOOD PRESS
Westport, Connecticut • London

Library of Congress Cataloging-in-Publication Data

Helbig, Alethea.
    Dictionary of American children's fiction, 1995–1999 : books of recognized merit /
Alethea K. Helbig and Agnes Regan Perkins.
      p. cm.
    Includes bibliographical references and index.
    ISBN 0–313–30389–4 (alk. paper)
    1. Children's stories, American—Bio-bibliography—Dictionaries. 2. American fiction—
20th century—Bio-bibliography—Dictionaries. 3. American fiction—20th century—
Dictionaries. 4. Children's stories, American—Dictionaries. 5. Children's libraries—Book
lists. 6. Best books. I. Perkins, Agnes. II. Title.
PS374.C454 H45   2002
813'.54099282'03   2001023871
[B]

British Library Cataloguing in Publication Data is available.

Library of Congress Catalog Card Number: 2001023871
ISBN: 0–313–30389–4

First published in 2002

Greenwood Press, 88 Post Road West, Westport, CT 06881
An imprint of Greenwood Publishing Group, Inc.
www.greenwood.com

Printed in the United States of America

The paper used in this book complies with the
Permanent Paper Standard issued by the National
Information Standards Organization (Z39.48–1984).

10 9 8 7 6 5 4 3 2 1

CONTENTS

PREFACE

As university teachers of literature for children and young adults for more than thirty years, we are dedicated to the idea that books for children should be appreciated for their own sakes as imaginative literature, and many fine books are discussed in *Dictionary of American Children's Fiction, 1995–1999*. At the same time, we believe, as do many scholars, that literature for children and young people mirrors the times in which the books were written. If this is so, then sociologists, cultural anthropologists, historians, and students of literature, among other professionals, have much to gain by examining the books discussed in this volume, as well as from its immediate predecessors.

Whether the books are historical fiction or fantasy or set in the here and now, as a whole they continue the trend toward "reality" or "shock" programming prevalent in the last couple of decades on television, in movies, and in adult literature. The behaviors and attitudes of the characters can provide scholars with much to ruminate about as we embark on the new millennium.

Questions like these come to mind. Is this what our children and young people are really like? Is this, indeed, what most of our families are like? Are these the values that we hold dear? Is this the way in which we relate to one another? Do we want schools, churches, courts, other institutions to perpetuate these conditions? What do the intended audiences take away from their reading? What do these books tell us about the writers' interests and the narrative techniques that they employ to convey their ideas? What do they tell us about the criteria of the selection committees that have chosen them as the best in their respective years?

This book, *Dictionary of American Children's Fiction, 1995–1999: Books of Recognized Merit*, can serve as a starting point for exploration as well as a guide to pleasurable, imaginative reading. It contains critical comments on those books that authorities have singled out for awards or placed on citation lists during this period. It is the third of a projected series of five-year updates of our two volumes on American children's fiction from 1859 to 1984 and is intended, as are the earlier books, for the use of everyone who is concerned with children's literature in any way: librarians, teachers, literary scholars, researchers in comparative social history, parents, booksellers, publishers, editors, the children themselves—all those to whom literature for children and young people is of vital interest professionally or socially.

This *Dictionary*, which follows *Dictionary of American Children's Fiction, 1990–1994* and *Dictionary of American Children's Fiction, 1985–1989*, contains 759 entries on such elements as titles, authors, characters, and settings based on 245 books by 192 twentieth-century authors. It is also a companion to our earlier two volumes of American fiction for children and to *Dictionary of British Children's Fiction* (two volumes, 1989) and *Dictionary of Children's Fiction from Australia, Canada, India, New Zealand, and Selected African Countries* (1992).

Although we have dealt with the same awards and citation lists that we used in the previous volumes, this book contains about one-quarter more entries than the 1990–1994 volume based on fifty-six more books. Most of these books appear on only one or two lists, a factor that seems to indicate that there is less critical agreement about their literary value, perhaps that few are really outstanding, a matter that we also noted with *Dictionary, 1990–1994*.

The total number of authors is also greater than in *Dictionary, 1990–1994*, which has more than in each of our previous dictionaries. Although some of the authors have appeared in our previous volumes of American fiction, a few of them in several, like Eloise Jarvis McGraw, Mary Stolz, Katherine Paterson, and Robert Cormier, most of the writers in this five-year period appear for the first time. While in some cases this is the author's first published book, like Elizabeth Alder, author of *The King's Shadow*, a surprising number of them have published many books, some dozens, but these are the first to win awards or to be cited on selection lists. This may mean that publishers are reaching out to new authors, a commendable development, or that newer writers are finally being heard.

As critics trained in the study of literature as literature, we are convinced that books for children must be judged by the same criteria as those for adults, keeping in mind, of course, that children are the intended audience. The critical comments found in *Dictionary of American Children's Fiction, 1995–1999* judge each book as imaginative literature, not on other values, regardless of the particular emphasis of the award for which it was chosen.

The entries in this *Dictionary* are of several types, chiefly title, author, and character. A book's title entry gives the plot summary and a critical assessment of its literary value. Other entries about a book provide additional information. Taken together, they form a short essay, complete in itself for classroom or library use, and can serve as a good starting point for research.

Because our study is of fiction, not of illustration, we have followed the pattern of our earlier *Dictionaries* and have not included stories in picture-book form, since the texts of such books can seldom stand alone, and their analysis requires a consideration also of the illustrations. Somewhat artibrarily, we have set 5,000 words as a minimum; most books must be at least that long to develop a story that can function on its own. Books of more than 5,000 words are included, even if the illustrations are very prominent. Collections of short stories require a different sort of analysis and plot summary from those for novels and are also omitted, even if technically they are fiction. Retellings from oral tradition appear if the material has been developed like that in novels, as in *Ella Enchanted* and *Zel*. We have not included translations, books with awards given by strictly regional groups, or those issued by organizations to their members only. We have also excluded books chosen by children for awards, since children have limited critical experience.

In the entries about the authors, we have focused on those aspects of the authors' lives most relevant to children's literature and to their particular novels in this *Dictionary*. Although several other published sources give biographical information about writers, none considers all those whose books are in this reference. Having the information in the same volume is not only of convenience for researchers but also of particular value to libraries on limited budgets.

In presenting our entries, we have followed an arrangement convenient for a variety of users.

Title entries. These consist of bibliographical information; the subgenre to which the work belongs; a plot summary incorporating the plot problem (if any), significant episodes, and the conclusion; a note about sequels, if any; critical comments; and awards and citations in abbreviated form. (A list of the complete names of the awards and citations appears in the front of this book.) Entries vary in length. The number of words in an entry does not indicate the importance or quality of the book, since some plots can be summarized more briefly and critical judgments stated more succinctly for some books than for others.

A few books that appeared in one of our earlier *Dictionaries* have received additional awards during this five-year period. The entries for these books are briefer and refer readers to the more complete evaluation in the earlier volume.

Most readers will be acquainted with the terms that we have used for subgenres, but a few may need some explanation. By *realistic fiction*, we mean books in which events could have happened some time in the world as we know it, as opposed to an imaginary or fantastic world, and not necessarily that the action is convincing or plausible. *Historical fiction* includes those books in which actual historical events or figures function in the plot, as in *The Bomb* and *The Watsons Go to Birmingham—1963*, or in which the specific period is essential to the action and in which the story could not have occurred in any other time, as in *My Brother, My Sister, and I* and *The Ramsay Scallop*. Books that are merely set in a past time, like *The Barn* and *Gaps in Stone Walls*, we have called *period fiction*. Although all plots are driven by problems, we have used the term *problem novel* in its more recent sense to refer to those stories in which social, physical, or psychological concerns dominate, as in *The Midnight Club* and *Driver's Ed*.

Author entries. These consist of dates and places of birth and death, when available; education and vocational background; major contribution to children's literature; significant facts of the author's life that might have a bearing on the work; titles that have won awards; frequently titles of other publications, usually with brief information about them; and critical judgments where they can safely be made. Authors whose biographical entries have appeared in earlier volumes are again included, but usually with briefer sketches and references to the original entry.

Character entries. These include physical and personality traits for important, memorable, or particularly unusual characters who are not covered sufficiently by the plot summary. They focus on such aspects as how the characters function in the plot, how they relate to the protagonist, and whether the characterization is credible and skillful. Characters are classified by the name by which they are most often referred to or by the name by which the protagonist refers to them, for example, Uncle Hob, Mr. Larson, Ops. The name is also cross-referenced in the index under the most likely possibilities. If the character's surname does not often appear in the story, it usually does not appear in the index; when it is included, it is usually as a family name: Kirkle family, Hernandez family, and so on. If the plot summary gives all the significant information about characters, as with many protagonists, they are not discussed in separate character entries. All major characters, however, are listed in the index.

Miscellaneous entries. These include particularly significant settings and elements that need explanation beyond mention in the title entry.

Every book has title and author entries, with entries in alphabetical order for convenience. Asterisks indicate that the item has a separate entry elsewhere in the book. Entries are intended to supplement, not duplicate, one another, and when read together, provide a unified essay on the book.

A list of awards and their abbreviations appears at the front of the *Dictionary*. A list of books classified by awards is in the back of the volume. The index includes all the items for which there are entries and such elements as cross-references, major characters for whom there are no separate entries, specific place settings, settings by period, and such matters as themes and subjects, books of first-person narration, unusual narrative structures, significant tone, authors' pseudonyms, illustrators, and genres.

As in the two predecessors to this *Dictionary*, the majority of the works that we examined are contemporary realistic fiction, most of them problem stories and many of them laced with teenage angst. Few of them deal with simple domestic adventures, once a popular subgenre, two exceptions being *The Bones in the Cliff* and *Christie & Company Down East*. Most of these contemporary, realistic stories are ephemeral, although some, like the inventive puzzle-story *The View from Saturday*, may survive.

Both fantasy and historical fiction are represented by some fine books. Some were originally published for adults, like *Beggars and Choosers*, a futuristic novel concerned with gene alteration; *Finder*, about the area between Elfland and the human world; and *Pigs Don't Fly*, a picaresque story of a girl's travels with talking animals in a country rather like preindustrial Europe. Among those published for children, however, there are also strong novels, including *The*

Moorchild, about a changeling; *Mr. Was*, a complex time-slip story; *The Ear, the Eye, and the Arm*, a chilling adventure of three children in a Zimbabwe city of the future; *The Music of Dolphins*, about a feral girl captured and studied by scientists; *The Magic and the Healing*, a memorable Tolkienesque story in which veterinarian students venture into a remote Virginia valley to serve fantasy animals there; and *The Thief*, an amusing, adventurous mystery and hero-quest account set in a mythical land much like ancient Greece.

Historical and period novels are well represented, some of them of a very high order. In general, this genre is of two types: light, mostly humorous stories like *Alice Rose and Sam, Looking After Lily, The Great Turkey Walk*, and *The Ballad of Lucy Whipple*, all set in nineteenth-century America, and serious books of considerable depth. These range in time of setting from *Escape from Egypt*, which takes place at the time of Moses; *The King's Shadow*, of the eleventh-century Norman invasion of England; *The Examination*, in sixteenth-century China; and *The Revenge of the Forty-Seven Samurai*, in eighteenth-century Japan, to the mid-twentieth-century periods of *In the Time of the Butterflies*, concerning the dictatorship of Trujillo in the Dominican Republic, and *Come in from the Cold*, about the Vietnam War era. Among biographical historical fiction are two outstanding novels published for adults: *Pope Joan*, about the only known woman pope, and *Johanna*, about the van Gogh family as related by the wife of Vincent's brother, Theodoor, and one published for children, the amusing *Bandit's Moon*, about a Mexican-American bandit who terrorized California during gold rush times.

Ironically, in a period when family values have been widely touted, families in realistic novels are largely dysfunctional. Many mothers, in particular, are either alcoholic, as in *Toughing It* and *Hannah In Between*, or drug-addicted, as in *Forged by Fire*, or they are so preoccupied with their own concerns or ambitions for one child that their other children suffer neglect, as in *Missing the Piano, Spite Fences*, and *Keeping the Moon*. A few simply disappear, as in *The Cuckoo's Child, A Place to Call Home*, and *Don't You Dare Read This, Mrs. Dunphrey*. Strong, supportive families, when they appear, are likely to be unconventional, as in *Northern Borders, The Ornament Tree*, and *My Louisiana Sky*. Fathers (and live-in boyfriends) often do not come off well either. In *Choosing Up Sides*, the preacher-father is domineering and physically and psychologically abusive; in *Dancing on the Edge*, he also simply disappears; and in *Protecting Marie*, he is distant, demanding, and tyrannically fastidious.

We note again that while many of the novels are highly adventurous, being fast-paced and action-filled, few are of the "good, old-fashioned realistic adventure" or survival-story category, notable exceptions being *Far North*, which, set in the Canadian Northwest Territories, follows the classic Robinsonnade form, *The Maze*, and *The Cage*. While there are few stories in the old boarding-school mode, *Dave at Night*, which takes place during the Harlem Renaissance in a Hebrew orphanage with an abusive director, is ironically a lighthearted representative of the form. As in the past, many of the books take place in school settings, like the realistic *Bad Girls* and even the fantasy *Seven Spiders Spinning*, or employ school scenes, like *Deal with a Ghost*.

Mysteries remain a popular genre, and some of these are among the best books represented, considered both from the standpoint of technique and also from the sheer reading pleasure that they hold. In fact, as realistic fiction, they are a welcome relief from the "angst" mode. Published for adults, *Under the Beetle's Cellar* is a top-notch mystery-thriller with detective story aspects about the kidnapping of a school bus filled with children by a fanatic Armageddon cult leader. *The Clearing, Hawk Moon,* and *Prophecy Rock,* the latter two in which Hopi beliefs and ways influence the plot, are extremely high in entertainment value.

Some of the books tackle subjects previously not, or seldom, taken up, or avoided, like AIDS, as in *The Eagle Kite* and *Earthshine,* in which fathers die of the disease; assisted suicide, as in *Stone Water,* where a boy grants his grandfather's unspoken wish to die; as in *Petey,* about the callous way people with cerebral palsy were treated during the twentieth century; and, as in *The Facts Speak for Themselves,* where a young girl reveals that she encouraged and enjoyed the relationship that authorities deem rape and for which they have arrested and charged the man. A girl's gradual deterioration into mental illness is graphically traced in *Dancing on the Edge,* and several books are built around how poorly families cope with the loss of a child, among them *The Other Shepards,* in which a dozen years later the tragic deaths of the couple's older children dominate the lives of everyone in the house to the extent that the two younger children are losing their grip on reality. *While No One Was Watching* severely indicts social-services agencies for their inability or failure to maintain a safety net for the working poor, with devastating effects on the children.

A welcome change is the increasing number of books involving minorities. Many of these are contemporary, like *Me and Rupert Goody* (African Americans), *Dakota Dream* (Native Americans), and *Habibi,* which concerns the Arab-Israeli conflict from the Palestinian point of view. Of these, the strongest are historical fiction, among them *Under the Blood-Red Sun,* about Japanese Americans during the Japanese attack on Pearl Harbor, and *Bat 6,* about prejudice against Japanese Americans just after World War II. Altogether, more than 22 percent of the books examined involve minorities in a major way.

Substantively, some trends continue: single-parent families, usually headed by women, with *Flyers* being a notable exception, where the father copes well and has the respect and love of his two sons; live-in boyfriends; domestic abuse, one of these being *When She Was Good,* where an older sibling abuses a younger for years—a truly horrible situation; cold, uncaring, too-busy fathers; and children living with relatives, an old technique for getting children on their own, but with a modern twist—because their families no longer exist as a functioning unit and not because the parents are deceased. Some books inventively retell old stories, among them *Shadow Spinner,* which plays cleverly with the notion that Scheherazade has run out of stories.

Stylistically, as in the previous five-year period, the "I" person dominates the narratives, to such an extent that it has almost become a modern convention and tiresome because of its excessive use. Similarly, the very limited third person (which has the effect of first person) appears widely. More than half the books have female protagonists, also not a new trend. Trash talk, sex scenes, frank mention of birth control, erotic language, put-down one-liners—these and other conventions of the movies and television appear often. Welcome is the continuation of the departure from linear narrative like letters and journals, a mixture of presentations like newspaper reports, stream of consciousness, and flashbacks. Some books blend subgenres, for example, *Choosing Up Sides*, *Iceman*, and *Tangerine*, which are not only sports stories but also provide provocative looks at family life as well. *Holes* blends mystery, friendship, and social-problem forms.

As with books in any age, most of these novels will prove ephemeral and soon be forgotten. On the other hand, the Phoenix Award winners, which were selected from those published twenty years earlier, have retained their power and still seem fresh and undated. They are models of fine, imaginative literature for young audiences. While those interested in cultural history are perusing the books represented in this volume for values, behaviors, problems, and attitudes, students of literature might valuably examine the Phoenix list for the qualities and attitudes that have made the books endure.

As with the earlier American books and the companion volumes on British children's fiction and *Dictionary of Children's Fiction from Australia, Canada, India, New Zealand, and Selected African Countries*, we have read every book represented in this *Dictionary* and have done all the research and writing for it. We have had valuable assistance from a variety of sources. Specifically, we thank Brian Steimel and Margaret Best at the Eastern Michigan University Halle Library for their help in obtaining books not available locally, the staff of the Ann Arbor District Library Youth Room and the Loving Branch for their aid, and the staff at the Peters Branch of the Ypsilanti, Michigan, District Library for their assistance. We thank them all for their ongoing interest, support, and encouragement.

KEY TO AWARDS AND CITATIONS

Addams	Jane Addams Peace Association Children's Book Award
ALA	American Library Association Notable Books for Children
Boston Globe Honor	*Boston Globe–Horn Book* Award Honor Book
Boston Globe Winner	*Boston Globe–Horn Book* Award Winner
Christopher	Christopher Award
C. S. King Winner	Coretta Scott King Award Winner
Fanfare	*The Horn Book Magazine* Fanfare List
IRA	International Reading Association Children's Book Award
Jefferson	Jefferson Cup Award for Historical Fiction
Josette Frank	Children's Book Committee at Bank Street College Award (formerly the Child Study Award)
Lewis Carroll	Lewis Carroll Shelf Award
Newbery Honor	John Newbery Medal Honor Book
Newbery Winner	John Newbery Medal Winner
O'Dell	Scott O'Dell Award for Historical Fiction
Phoenix Honor	The Children's Literature Association Phoenix Award Honor Book
Phoenix Winner	The Children's Literature Association Phoenix Award Winner
Poe Nominee	Nominee for the Edgar Allan Poe Award Best Juvenile Mystery
Poe Winner	Winner of the Edgar Allan Poe Award Best Juvenile Mystery
SLJ	*School Library Journal* Best Books for Children
Spur	Western Writers of America Spur Award

Stone   George G. Stone Center for Children's Books Recognition
                                     of Merit Award
Western Heritage   Western Heritage Award

THE DICTIONARY

A

ABBY COOGAN (*Crash**), younger sister of Crash Coogan. Ten years old and in the fifth grade, she is self-possessed, aware, and determined to maintain certain politically correct stances. She wears T-shirts that display her antimall ideology, insists that the grass be allowed to grow in the backyard, and dismisses the ChemLawn man so that the Coogans can have a wildlife habitat. Like Penn* Webb, she is a vegetarian. Her action and words on behalf of her politically correct stances create humor, especially through the tension that they produce between her and her parents, while at the same time they are obviously didactic. Her love for her grandfather, Scooter*, and her low-keyed relationship with her brother, Crash, are among the book's best features.

ABELOVE, JOAN, received her B.A. from Barnard College and her Ph.D. in cultural anthropology from City University of New York. She lived in the Amazon jungle of Peru for two years in the early 1970s doing doctoral research and gaining experiences that she drew upon for her highly acclaimed first novel, *Go and Come Back** (DK Ink, 1998). She has also published *Saying It Out Loud* (DK Ink, 1999), about a family whose mother is dying from a brain tumor. Abelove has taught emotionally disturbed boys in a state hospital and anthropology at colleges in New York City and has been a technical writer. She lives with her husband, Steve Hoffman, and son in New York City.

ABEL'S ISLAND (Steig*, William, illus. William Steig, Farrar, 1976), castaway survival fantasy starring an elegant Edwardian gentleman mouse who, on an outing with his charming wife, is swept away by a sudden storm and deposited on a midriver island. Through his year alone, he learns self reliance and becomes a braver, stronger mouse. The formal, tongue-in-cheek style and clever illustrations make this an amusing parody of Victorian novels and the classical Robinsonnade. Phoenix Honor. For a longer entry, see *Dictionary, 1960–1984*.

*THE ABSOLUTELY TRUE STORY . . . HOW I VISITED YELLOWSTONE
PARK WITH THE TERRIBLE RUPES* (Roberts*, Willo Davis, Atheneum,
1994), humorous mystery told by fictional Lewis Q. Dodge, who is listed on
the cover as first author. When new neighbors move in next to their home in
Marysville, Washington, Lewis quickly becomes friends with Harry Rupe, 12,
just a year older than he is, and is delighted when the Rupes ask him along on
their vacation trip to Yellowstone Park in a large, rented motor home. Lewis'
twin sister, Alison, who has been feeling left out, is even more pleased to be
asked to accompany them, to help keep an eye on the two younger Rupes,
Ariadne, 2, and Billy, 4. She hopes to earn some money baby-sitting the youngsters and thinks that the trip will give her the opportunity to prove her reliability.
The Dodge parents assume that all will go well, because the Rupes seem solid
citizens, since they attend their church and Mr. Rupe is president of the bank.
Even before they leave home, there are signs of trouble. When Syd from the
rental company arrives with a different motor home, saying that a new employee
has delivered the wrong one, Mr. Rupe refuses to repack their excessive baggage
and abruptly backs out of the driveway, demolishing a small tree and almost
crashing into a neighbor's pickup. By the time that they are a block from home,
Lewis realizes that Mr. Rupe doesn't know how to drive the large rig and won't
listen to suggestions from anyone. At first the way that the Rupes live on junk
food munched anytime seems wonderful to Lewis, but he soon begins to long
for the healthful diet that his mother insists on, and he is incredulous that Harry
is uninterested in the scenic wonders or in reading about the interesting sights.
Alison is even more put off by the way the Rupe parents do nothing to control
their obstreperous and undisciplined children. Ariadne kicks and wets the bed
that they must share. Billy is continually running off and getting into mischief.
At the campground their first night, Lewis notices a man lurking around the
motor home and later sees him with another fellow in a blue Crown Victoria
with no trailer, a car that turns up everywhere they stop. Eventually, he recognizes the man as Syd from the rental place. In the meantime, Billy has kidnapped
a cat from the first campground by shutting it in their luggage compartment and
has displayed a $100 bill that he says he found. Lewis teaches both youngsters
to dog-paddle in the campground pools and begins to help Alison keep track of
them, since his sister is run ragged and Harry takes no interest in his siblings.
Before many days, both Dodges are thoroughly fed up with Mr. Rupe's rudeness
to other campers and are worried about the men in the Crown Victoria, who
keep lurking around. They figure that Syd and his partner, now identified as
Ernie, have something to do with the money, especially when Billy turns up
with another $100 bill but says he "forgot" where he found it. When Lewis
confides his suspicions to Harry, his friend shows his first real interest in the
trip, and together they do a bit of sleuthing. They also try to find the money
and to pressure Billy to tell where he got the bills, but he is uncooperative. The
mystery culminates on their last night in the park campground, when the Rupe
parents have gone into town for dinner with friends, leaving the five young

people behind. Thinking the motor home deserted, Syd and Ernie enter with a passkey and, astonished to find the children, shut them in the rear bedroom and drive the motor home off. By switching on an intercom that the men are unaware of, the children learn of their scheme. They have been swindling the rental business and stashed the money in the motor home, delivered by mistake to the Rupes. Now they are making a desperate getaway, heading north in Montana, obviously planning to drop the kids off, probably no longer living, in some remote area while they flee to Canada. Alison makes signs saying, "Help, we are being kidnapped," and tapes them on the windows with Band-Aids. When they stop for fuel, Lewis jumps out the window while the others slow Syd and Ernie by squirting shaving cream and hair spray into their eyes. Lewis alerts the serviceman, and, simultaneously, a police car pulls into the station. After a few tense minutes when Lewis fears that the policeman will believe Ernie rather than him, the true story comes out. Billy, who is always poking into things, admits that he found the money in the furnace vent and hid it in a bag of rotting lettuce in the refrigerator. Although he cries at losing his find, he is placated by being able to keep the cat, which the campground owner says was a stray, and by the promise of glasses after Lewis discovers that the child is even more nearsighted than he is and has been uninterested in the park animals because he could not see them. Arrogant Mr. Rupe and his careless wife are caricatures, and the antics of the two youngest Rupes get almost as tiresome for the reader as for the Dodge twins, but the story picks up with the kidnapping and has a plausible ending. The theme that the permissive lifestyle is not really desirable is overly obvious; the humor, however, keeps the story from seeming didactic. Poe Winner.

AESCULAPIUS (*Pope Joan**), highly respected and learned Greek scholar who enjoys the hospitality of the canon's* house on his way to Mainz and discovers Joan's aptitude for learning. He instructs her in spite of her father's opposition and later sends someone to usher her to the school at Dorstadt. The canon angrily refuses to let her go insisting that Aesculapius must have intended for her brother John to enroll at Dorstadt. Joan runs away from home and finds and joins John, an unlikely sequence of events, but nevertheless pleasing to the reader. Joan receives a terrible whipping from her father when he insists that she obliterate the Greek and Latin words from an edition of Homer that Aesculapius has given her and that she cherishes. Aesculapius represents a man in advance of his time, one who considers not the sex of his pupils but their aptitude for learning. Joan's other teachers, with the exception of Gerold* the knight, are not as enlightened as Aesculapius.

AIDEN TEAGUE (*Blood and Chocolate**), human youth with whom werewolf Vivian Gandillon falls in love and who returns her affection until he discovers that she is a werewolf. Aiden is sensitive, interested in magic and the occult, and talented at writing. Vivian first grows interested in him when she discovers that his poem, "Wolf Change," has been printed in the school literary magazine opposite a painting that she has done based on her own supernatural experiences. When they first meet, she paints a pentagram on his palm, a sign that she has claimed him for her own, a symbolism that he never really understands. Later, for her birthday, Aiden unwittingly presents her with a silver pentagram on a silver chain, an ironic gift since silver is the only metal with which werewolves can be killed. Like Vivian, Aiden is at odds with his parents, who regard his interests as satanic. At the end, on threat of death, her friend Gabriel* persuades Aiden not to tell anyone about their werewolf pack. Aiden behaves as expected for the genre; he cannot accept Vivian's dual nature because he is so firmly tied to his own as superior to all others.

AKI MIKAMI (*Bat 6**), sixth-grade Japanese-American girl who plays first base for the Bear Creek Ridge girls' softball team and who is deliberately injured by Shazam*, the center fielder for the Barlow Road team, because of her race. She and her family are presented sympathetically, because of their relocation experiences in World War II. They are almost stereotypes, because of their very retiring, highly courteous, almost abject behavior. The Mikamis did not return immediately after World War II, because they heard that other Japanese people were treated badly in their home communities. When they do return, the community of Bear Creek Ridge is uniformly welcoming, however, since apparently enough time has elapsed. The Mikamis' house is in very bad shape, having been rented to people who abused it. After the accident, which horrifies everyone, the community tries to help the family in various ways, including taking up a collection to defray medical bills.

ALAN YORK (*Rats Saw GOD**), father of Steve York. A highly respected astronaut, he is famous for his moon walk. Steve despises him. He thinks Alan spends too much time on his work and expects perfection from those around him, especially Steve. He blames Alan for the breakup of his parents' marriage. Steve hardly sees his father while he is living with the man in Houston, Texas, one notable exception being when his father discovers that Steve is having sex with Dub* Varner and informs his son that he wants nothing like that to go on in his house. Later Steve discovers Alan having sex with his wife-to-be. After Steve's sister, Sarah*, points out to Steve that their mother was involved with their stepfather before she was divorced from Alan, Steve realizes that his father regarded it as unseemly to contest the divorce and fought to keep Steve with him because he really thought living with Alan would be better for Steve. Steve also feels better about his father when at Alan's wedding, for which Steve is best man, there are no reporters, public officials, and business associates, no one to be impressed or courted. Steve also realizes that Alan feels that he had not spent the right kind of time with his first wife (Steve's mother) and is making an attempt to be more attentive and relaxed with his new bride. Alan is a complex character.

ALBERT (*Lily's Crossing**), World War II Hungarian refugee who becomes the friend and playmate of Lily Mollahan in the summer of 1944. When Lily first sees him, while she is spying on the Orbans, she thinks he is the "skinniest kid she had ever seen in her life." Albert has thick, curly hair and blue eyes and speaks with an accent. The two become friends when they rescue from the canal a small, red-orange kitten that an older boy had tossed in to drown. Albert is kind and generous, and, like Lily, lonely and friendless. He was sent to Canada two years earlier to be safe from the war, and during the school year, he lives with Mr. Orban's brother. He tells Lily that his father and mother ran a newspaper in Budapest, and because they wrote "bad things about Hitler and the Nazis," they were taken away by the Nazis and later were reported dead. Just before the Nazis came for Albert and his younger sister, Ruth, their grandmother smuggled them out through Austria and Switzerland into France, where Ruth, at that time about six years old, fell ill with a fever and was left behind. Albert wants more than anything else to be reunited with her, because she is all the family that he has now. Lily's father, serving in the U.S. Army in France, finds the girl in a convent, and she and Albert are together again.

ALBERT KIRKLE (*Beyond the Western Sea: Book One: The Escape from Home**; *Beyond the Western Sea: Book Two: Lord Kirkle's Money**), fifteen-year-old elder son of Lord Kirkle and elder brother of Sir Laurence Kirkle. Sir Albert engages the services of Mr.* Matthew Clemspool to frame Laurence as a thief and then, after Lord Kirkle has beaten Laurence for stealing, causes Laurence to run away to America and orders Mr. Clemspool to see to it that Laurence never returns. In fact, the implication is that Mr. Clemspool should bring about Laurence's death. Albert is determined to be his father's sole heir. When Lord Kirkle discovers what Albert has done, he tells Albert to go to America and find Laurence or never come home again. Albert arrives in Lowell, Massachusetts, after Mr. Clemspool does, the two connect, and new complications begin, since Albert is even more determined to see to it that Laurence dies. When last seen, Albert and Mr. Clemspool are aboard a ship bound for England, having been expelled from America as undesirable immigrants. Albert says that he will tell his father that Laurence has died, a lie that he blackmails Mr. Clemspool, so heavily guilty of misdeeds, to support. Hence, Albert fully expects to inherit the Kirkle fortune.

ALDER, ELIZABETH, teaches English in junior high school; lives in Ohio with her husband and five children. *The King's Shadow** (Farrar, 1995), set in England at the time of the Norman invasion, is her first book. A substantial historical novel, it received the International Reading Association Award and was cited by *School Library Journal*.

ALEXANDER, LLOYD (CHUDLEY) (1924–   ), born in Philadelphia, Pennsylvania; educated at West Chester State Teachers' College, Lafayette College, and the University of Paris (Sorbonne); author, freelance writer, and translator. He is best known for his spirited, humorous fantasies for children, in particular, the five frequently honored Chronicles of Prydain. The prolific, often acclaimed Alexander has also written novels of high adventure, political intrigue, and romantic adventures, among them *The Arkadians** (Dutton, 1995) and *The Iron Ring** (Dutton, 1997), as well as picture-book stories. He lives in Drexel, Pennsylvania. For additional information and titles, see *Dictionary, 1960–1984* [*The Black Cauldron*; *The Book of Three*; *The Castle of Llyr*; *The Cat Who Wished to Be a Man*; *The First Two Lives of Lukas Kasha*; *The High King*; *The Kestrel*; *The Marvelous Misadventures of Sebastian*; *Taran Wanderer*; *Westmark*]; *Dictionary, 1985–1989* [*The Beggar Queen*; *The Illyrian Adventure*]; and *Dictionary, 1990–1994* [*The Remarkable Journey of Prince Jen*].

ALICE ROSE AND SAM (Lasky*, Kathryn, Hyperion, 1998), rollicking mystery set in Virginia City, Nevada, at the time of the Civil War, the early 1860s. After her mother and newborn sister die, Alice Rose Tucker, 12, who hates the rough town and the barren countryside, decides to earn enough money to go to Boston to live with a very proper aunt. She starts designing and sewing a dress for the aging hurdy-gurdy girl Detta and soon has more customers than she can handle. Her newspaperman-father, Stan, who works for the *Enterprise*, is congenial but irresponsible and lets her do much as she pleases. Although she thinks she longs for more refinement, Alice Rose enjoys the freedom of this western boomtown and has many friends—the dancing girls, all the men on the *Enterprise*, Eilley Orrum, the wealthiest woman in town, Hop Sing from Chinatown, and a host of others. She soon meets and becomes friendly with Josh, whose real name is Sam Clemens, not yet having adopted the pen name Mark Twain. Because Chinese are forbidden from owning mining property, Alice Rose files a claim in her own name for Hop Sing, and they become secret partners. When she witnesses the shooting of Mutch, a good-natured drunk, Sam Clemens is the only person whom she can interest in investigating the killing. Together they find the murderer and uncover a conspiracy by the Society of Seven, a vigilante group headed by the local judge intent on illegally acquiring the most valuable interest in the Comstock silver mine and funneling the money to the Confederacy. Complications abound amid threats and narrow escapes. In the end Hop Sing is dead, and Alice Rose, though grieving for him, is wealthy, since their claim proves very valuable. Sam Clemens leaves for the East, but he has taught Alice Rose to see the beauty of the desertlike area and to love the rough, but exciting, community. The wildly improbable plot rips along at a fast pace, with a large cast of eccentric characters. Sam Clemens often discourses to Alice Rose about religion, truth, slavery, temperance, and other topics on which he has unconventional ideas that later appear in his books. Although the novel shows a good deal of research on Virginia City of this boom period, none of the action is to be taken seriously. Poe Nominee; Western Heritage.

ALIX PELDYRIN (*Stranger at the Wedding**), younger sister of Kyra Peldyrin. Kyra returns home from her training at the Citadel of Wizards, resolved to do what she can to prevent Alix from dying on her wedding night. Alix is beautiful and spoiled by doting parents, and since Kyra has been disowned, Alix is now her father's heir, and, a proud man, he spends enormous sums of money to marry her well. Alix, however, is madly in love with a handsome young pastry maker and poet, Algeron Brackett. The scene in which Alix and Kyra meet after having been apart for six years is a touching picture of a loving sisterly reunion. Alix is a bundle of contradictions, sometimes sweet and likable, at others a prattling minx. For a while, Kyra fears that Alix will take her life if she is unable to marry Algernon. Alix is an interesting, if stereotyped, figure.

ALLISON KIMBLE (*Rats Saw GOD**), along with Steve York, a National Merit Finalist in her senior year at Wakefield High School in San Diego, California. She and Steve become friends through their mutual achievement, and she helps him with some classes, since he is still adjusting after his hard times in Texas. Unlike Steve, she has clearly in mind what she wishes to do—go to a good college, get a good job, and take care of her ailing father. She and her father, who has been despondent since his wife and son were killed by a drunk driver, live in a run-down house in a disreputable neighborhood. Although Allison and Steve become very close friends, they decide to pursue independent paths after high school, she going to the University of California-Berkeley and he to the University of Washington. That Steve can continue his life without leaning on her is an indication of how he has matured and taken hold of himself.

ALVAREZ, JULIA (1950–   ), born in New York City but lived until she was ten years old in the Dominican Republic; poet, novelist, and teacher of English and creative writing. She attended Connecticut College and received her B.A. degree from Middlebury College and her M.F.A. from Syracuse University. She has served as poet-in-the-schools in Kentucky, Delaware, and North Carolina, as visiting writer at the University of Vermont and George Washington University, and as professor of English at the University of Illinois and Middlebury College. Among her writings are four books of poetry, her best-known novel, *How the Garcia Girls Lost Their Accents* (Algonquin, 1991), and *In the Time of the Butterflies** (Algonquin, 1994). She has made her home in Vermont.

AMBIADES (*The Thief**), good-looking, but disagreeable and snide, apprentice to the magus*, the scholar of King Sounis of Sounis. At first it seems that Ambiades is just stupid, unable, or, at the least, unwilling to put his mind to his learning. He verbally abuses Gen, whom he considers unworthy of any respect, and is generally at odds with Sophos*, another apprentice. On the journey to fetch the Hamiathes' Gift, he and Sophos are expected to practice their fencing, at which Ambiades is better than Sophos but about which he wants no suggestions or constructive criticism. On the way back from securing the Gift, the travelers realize that Ambiades has turned traitor and revealed to the Attolians the secret route through the mountains that they are following. Ambiades dies, pushed over a cliff by Pol* during a battle with the Attolians.

AMBUYA (*A Girl Named Disaster**), maternal grandmother of Nhamo, oldest villager, much respected by the people. When she was young, her husbnd worked at Nyanga in Zimbabwe on a tree plantation, but after he was killed on the road, she and her three little girls were turned out, and she had to return to her Mozambique village. Her eldest and favorite daughter, Nhamo's mother, was given a scholarship to the high school, but she became pregnant, married the father, and came back to the village. *Ambuya* is really responsible for Nhamo's having to run away. At the trading post, where most of the villagers have traveled to consult the *muvuki*, or medical spirit man, they are told they must wait for perhaps two weeks. In the meantime the *muvuki*'s spies have listened and pried to give him the right leads. *Ambuya*, drinking beer with the Portuguese trader, tells the whole story of how Nhamo's father murdered a man from another village, thereby giving the *muvuki* an idea of what to credit the cholera to and of negotiations that will make him a handsome profit. On the other hand, *Ambuya* is probably responsible for Nhamo's survival. She has concealed her partial recovery from a stroke so that her daughter, Aunt Chipo, will allow her to be alone with Nhamo so she can advise her to flee in the boat of Crocodile Guts and to dig up her bag of nuggets from under her sleeping mat, to give Nhamo. Also her love is the only affection that the girl has known, and the memory of her spirit helps Nhamo many times. She calls the girl "Little Pumpkin." At the end, her spirit seems to visit Nhamo, along with those of the girl's mother and father, so she is not surprised to learn that her grandmother is no longer living.

ANDERSON, LAURIE HALSE (1961–), born in Potsdam, New York; writer of novels and picture books. She grew up in Syracuse, New York, and lives in Pennsylvania, where she organized the fall conference of the Society of Children's Book Writers and Illustrators in Philadelphia. Among her published works are three picture books, *No Time for Mother's Day* (Whitman, 1999), *Turkey Pox* (Whitman, 1996), and *Ndito Runs* (Holt, 1996), and a novel for young adults, *Speak** (Farrar, 1999).

ANDIE MURPHY (*Mr. Was**), Andrea, girl in Memory, Minnesota, whom Jack Lund first meets when they are both thirteen. When Jack returns in 1941, after his mother's death, he works on the Murphy farm, where he tries to conceal his deep attraction to Andie because her father is very protective and their friend Scud* considers her his girlfriend and tells Jack he plans to marry her as soon as she is eighteen. Before he leaves for the service, Jack and Andie go for a walk one night, and she lets him know that she cares about him. When it seems that Jack has been killed on Guadalcanal, and Scud returns to Memory, Andie marries him, becoming Mrs. Skoro, since Scud has had his name legally changed to his mother's maiden name. They have one daughter, Elizabeth, who becomes Jack's mother in the later time period. Andie, therefore, is Jack's grandmother.

ANGELA FOSTER (*While No One Was Watching**), at six, the youngest of the three Foster children. A pretty child with curly brown hair, she is often the butt of the teasing and snide remarks from the playground children because she is dirty and unkempt. To compensate for their rejection and her unhappy home situation, she pretends that a broken yardstick is a magic wand and makes up stories that she tells with so much conviction that they often seem true. Through her Maynard* Glenn traces the stolen bikes and rabbit—she wears the sweatshirt that the boys found in Addie Johnson's yard and wrapped Spot the rabbit in when they stole him. Maynard recognizes it as one belonging to him.

ANNIE TAYLOR (*The Magic and the Healing**), one of four veterinarian students who travel with Sugar* Dobbs into the remote valley of Crossroads* to treat ailing animals. Since her religion is important to Annie, and they are cynics, Dave* Wilson and Sugar tease her about her beliefs. They appreciate her warmheartedness and thoughtfulness, however, and these qualities bring her success, among other tasks, with the sheep that she first tends. At the end, Annie forgoes routine practice and heads for the African nation of Chad to work with famine relief and upgrade the primitive agricultural program. Before she leaves, she solicits donations from the Western Virginia College of Medicine students, each of whom she thanks with a handwritten note of appreciation.

ANYA (*The Midnight Club**), one of the five teenagers with terminal cancer who gather every night at 12:00 in the hospice study to tell stories. Ilonka Pawluk's roommate, Anya, is a mixture of seemingly contradictory qualities. A once-pretty, socially active blond, she reads the Bible regularly, considers all the other patients imbeciles, is acerbic and very outspoken, and tells ghoulish, horrifying stories. She points out to Ilonka that Ilonka is in love with Kevin and is in denial about her impending death, statements that help Ilonka to face up to her situation. Anya thinks her loss of a leg from bone cancer is, in some way, connected to her being unfaithful to her old boyfriend, Bill. Because she wants to die with dignity, she and Spence* decide that Spence will assist her suicide by smothering her.

THE APPRENTICESHIP OF LUCAS WHITAKER (DeFelice*, Cynthia, Farrar, 1996), historical novel set for a few months in Connecticut in 1849. Having lost his father, uncle, little sister, and mother to consumption, earnest, dutiful farm boy Lucas Whitaker, 12, stands disconsolate and alone in his empty house when neighbor Oliver Rood arrives. Mr. Rood has heard of a cure for the dread disease that is decimating the countryside: dig open the grave of the first member of the family to die and render that person, now an "undead," powerless to continue sucking the life out of the remaining relatives. Feeling guilty because he has not thus saved his mother, Lucas leaves home with no destination in mind and wanders for two days until, dizzy with hunger, he arrives in the village of Southwick. He sees a Help Wanted sign, applies, and is hired by the local doctor, a kind, elderly man with tangled white hair and piercing blue eyes. Doctor Uriah Beecher, called Doc*, takes him on because he can read and write, knows horses, is not squeamish at the sight of blood, and is not afraid of the dead. As Doc's apprentice, Lucas is also handyboy to Mrs.* Cora Bunce, Doc's widowed sister and housekeeper, who presides over Doc's well-appointed house and insists that Lucas take regular baths. Lucas mixes medicines, sharpens instruments, and generally assists the physician, who, on the side, barbers, pulls teeth, amputates limbs, and even serves as town undertaker. One day young Lydia Stukeley arrives seeking Doc's help to save her sister, Sarah, who is dying from consumption. All Doc can do is prescribe tea and chest plasters, leaving Mr. Stukeley dissatisfied. He insists that his other children who died and Sarah, too, said that the first child to die, Thomas, had visited them after he died. Sometime later, Doc sends Lucas to the Stukeleys' house to see how Sarah is. Lucas helps as Mr. Stukeley opens Thomas' grave, cuts out the heart, and places it in the flames in his fireplace. After the smoke is fanned about the room so that Sarah can inhale it, the ashes are gathered and mixed with water to form a potion for her to drink. Sarah recovers, but when Lucas informs Doc of what the Stukeleys did, Doc said there is no scientific foundation for the cure. When townsman William Sheldon informs Doc that townspeople are holding a mass curing ceremony on the village green the next day and invites Doc to participate, the doctor refuses, calling the practice "pure and simple" superstition. Lucas, however, believes that the procedure saved Sarah and attends. Later, Doc sends Lucas to the house of Moll* Garfield, a wise old Pequot Indian herbalist, for materials to make medicines. When Lucas tells Moll about the curing ceremony and Sarah's cure, Moll indicates that she has no faith in the practice and tells Lucas that he should carefully consider the "end of the story," that is, see whether or not the cure holds up. On the way back to Doc's, Lucas stops at the Roods' house, where he learns that young Enoch Rood has died in spite of the cure, and visits his own old house, where, in an abrupt reversal, he realizes that he has been thinking wishfully and that no cure exists. Back at Doc's house, he learns from Doc that everyone who participated as a patient in the curing ceremony has died. Doc has also acquired a new instrument called a microscope, with which he can see very small creatures that he says are called animalcules and are thought by some people to cause disease. Lucas, who intends to train to become a doctor, sees possibilities for cures in scientific study. Characters are types but distinctive, the style undistinguished, and the plot holds no surprises. The book is underdone and didactic. Its sole memorability lies in its effective portrayal of the attitudes of the people of the day toward consumption (tuberculosis), the state of medical knowledge about it, and the graphic details of the curing scenes. The book was inspired in part by the experiences of the author's grandfather, who was apprenticed to a doctor at the age of twelve. ALA; SLJ.

THE ARKADIANS (Alexander*, Lloyd, Dutton, 1995), lighthearted, adventurous fantasy that plays with mythological material and is set in the fictitious land of Arkadia, a place that resembles ancient Greece. When King Bromios* consults the pythoness, Woman-Who-Talks-to-Snakes, at Mount Lerna and receives an oracular prophecy that he dislikes, he orders that she and all her kind be destroyed. Young Lucian*, a royal accountant who has inadvertently discovered an embezzlement, flees for his life with the help of a poet-turned-donkey, Fronto*, who himself is fleeing from a cruel master. Stolen by soldiers, Fronto is rescued by a spirited, wheat-haired, gray-eyed girl with magical powers and a persuasive tongue who calls herself Joy-in-the-Dance*, later to be revealed as the pythoness. She tells them that the Lady of Wild Things at Mount Panthea can help Fronto regain his true form and help Lucian decide what to do with his life. The three set out for the far north and the wisewoman's sanctuary. They gradually accumulate an unlikely assortment of traveling companions, whose tales of personal history are adaptations of ancient Greek myths. They first rescue a man stuck in a tree, Argeus Ops*. Then Lucian is knocked unconscious by a stone from the slingshot of an runaway youth, Catch-a-Tick*, son of Buckthorn Goat King, whose people dress to resemble goats. At a mountain pass, they meet creatures who appear to be half-human, half-horse, of whose tribe they are made members. Lucian and Fronto learn that one of them, Sees-Far-Ahead, is Joy's father and that her mother is the Lady of Wild Things. With Sees-Far-Ahead and a half dozen of his warriors, they arrive at the sanctuary, where the Lady informs Fronto that he can recover his human form by consulting the water maiden who lives on the island of Callista off the very southern shore of Arkadia. Lucian and Joy have fallen in love, but the Lady informs them that the girl is destined to remain a maiden. Lucian and Fronto set out alone for the village of Oudeis*, a mariner who can take them to Callista. They are joined by Catch-a-Tick, who has stowed away, and then by Joy and Ops. Their most harrowing experience takes place at the island of Tauros, where the king, Bolynthos, demands that they serve as substitutes for the hostages owed him by the king of Naxos and be sacrificed to bulls. They escape with luck and Joy's magic, sail onward, are shipwrecked on Arkadia, encounter King Bromios, now a tattered and torn fugitive, who says that his people have marked him for sacrifice and seeks forgiveness of the pythoness, and survive a palace fire in which Fronto's jackass exterior is burned away by the flames, and he is fully human again. The Lady arrives, establishes Joy as the teacher and pythoness in Metara, and helps Lucian see that his future is to be the master storyteller who writes down the tales that he has heard on the trip so that they will not be lost, a fitting occupation for one who has so eloquently embroidered on his own experiences to everyone whom they met along the way. Three weddings occur:

those of Lucian and Joy, the Lady having changed her mind about their marriage; Oudeis and his lost sweetheart, Mirina; and Ops and Laurel-Crown. In typical Alexander fashion, the narrative elements have been thrown into the creative pot, stirred with vigor, and served up with verve. The cast of characters is large and deliberately distorted for effect; most figures are unusually loquacious and excessively grandiloquent; events happen with great rapidity and fortuitousness; and style abounds with action words and arresting turns of expression. The whole is of no greater moment than to offer amusing reading, and the conclusion turns out as most readers would wish: the evil receive their comeuppance, and the lovers are united. The adaptations of such tales as those of Pandora, Odysseus, Atalanta, and Theseus and the frequent pseudomythological allusions provide added pleasure for those readers familiar with Greek myths. Occasional comments on the nature of poetry and story also seem aimed at more sophisticated readers. ALA.

ARM (*The Ear, the Eye, and the Arm**), tall, skinny mutant with extremely thin arms and legs, the main brain of the detective agency hired to find the Matsika children after they are abducted. Arm's mother, like those of Ear and Eye, drank water polluted by plutonium from a nuclear power plant and as a result produced the strange-looking person, so sensitive to emotions in other people that he has to be shielded by his colleagues when he walks in the street. In Resthaven, the area devoted to a re-creation of village life as it was in early Zimbabwe, Arm has the alertness to pretend that they are bogeymen, children of the chief's barren first wife, Myanda, and that they want to leave for some more hospitable area. A woman who once lived in the outside world, Myanda plays along with their story, denouncing their witchcraft and thrusting the newborn girl twin, named Sekai, at Arm so he will take her and save her from being murdered. So sensitive to others' feelings that he not only bonds with Sekai but shares his emotions with her, Arm is unable to care for her, although he adores the child. After he is badly injured in the fray at the Gondwannan Embassy, he loses much of his special skill and is able to reclaim the baby from the Mellower*, who has been caring for her.

THE ASHWATER EXPERIMENT (Koss*, Amy Goldman, Dial, 1999), realistic contemporary novel of family life and friendship. In her twelve years of life, narrator Hillary Siegel has attended seventeen schools. She and her near-hippy parents are nomads who cherish their simple life. Long-haired Ed, who believes in karma, chants, and similar ideas, and Ina, who is motherly and creative, move easily from place to place in their self-contained camper, leaving behind no trace, eking out all they need by selling at fairs, craft shows, and flea markets the "gizmos" that Ina creates out of found materials—a free, unencumbered way of life. When the story begins, the Siegels are in Florida, having just "escaped," Hillary says, from four months of Boston. Ed announces that he and Ina have accepted a house-sitting arrangement in Ashwater, California, for nine months. The idea of nine months in one place seems so totally unreal that Hillary wonders if anything in life is real except for her. Much of the book subsequently examines her notions about the nature of reality and human existence. She thinks maybe there are Watchers, beings who place her in certain situations to see what she will do, and that the Watchers may have planned life in Ashwater as a test or experiment. At school, Hillary soon classifies the students into the categories that she has encountered in other schools: Brian Moore, the class clown; Serena Montgomery, the pretty, popular girl; and the largest group of all, the sleep-walkers, the apathetic students who just go through the motions. Because she is good at math—she keeps the family books—her teacher, Mrs. Lew, asks her to tutor Brian and Serena, an activity that enables her to get to know Serena and the accumulated "Serenas," Serena's sycophantic followers, among them Meg, who snubs and derides Hillary. Later, Hillary discovers that Meg is jealous of her association with Brian and also that she has unwittingly supplanted Meg as math leader of her class. While Brian eventually passes math under her tutelage, Serena takes very little interest in her studies, a matter that her mother, Joan, blames on the school. Serena prefers roaming malls and beaches. Hillary notices, with misgivings, that Serena orders her mother around and that Joan seems to want Serena as a friend rather than her daughter. Impressed by a story that classmate Cass Davis wrote for class, Hillary engages her in conversation, and, although the Serenas expectedly deride Cass as ugly, klutzy, and generally un-desirable, Hillary discovers that Cass has broad interests, including growing plants, and often must care for her demented Great Grand. The two girls spend happy hours together making a garden in the Siegels' backyard. When, the school year almost ended, the homeowners indicate that they are returning early, Hillary discovers that she is reluctant to leave. She realizes that the extended associations have broadened her horizons. She has also learned that both Cass and Serena, in spite of the latter's shallowness, have questioned the nature of reality and sees that doing so is a natural part of growing up. Serena is more sober and independent, and even Joan has gained in maturity and has found a life for herself making and selling gizmos. Ina helps Hillary see that she has made friends of both girls and that henceforth she will look at life also won-dering how each would regard particular situations. The Siegels' way of life seems too deliberately contrasted with that of the Montgomery family, the Ser-enas too empty-headed and shallow, and Cass often too sober and mature. Hil-lary's ponderings and notations in her notebook are worthy, and she and her parents are thoroughly pleasant people who enjoy their abnormal way of life without condemning anyone else's. SLJ.

AUNT CASEY DAWSEY (*Dancing on the Edge**), sister of the deceased mother of protagonist and narrator Miracle McCloy. Tall, slim, stiff-legged in her pink spandex and too-high heels, Casey smokes excessively and is either fighting with her husband, Uncle Toole, or is "lovely-dovey" with him. Miracle does not like her at the beginning of the story. Later on, after she goes to live with her aunt and uncle, she sees other aspects of Casey's character and feels better about the woman. By the time that Miracle moves in with them, Casey and Toole are no longer getting along. Casey enrolls in college psychology classes and almost completely neglects Miracle, devoting most of her time to her studies and to making wigs for cancer patients. The wigs on the blank-faced mannequin heads frighten Miracle. After Miracle cracks up, Casey realizes that she has not done well by her. Dr. DeAngelis, however, praises Casey's ability as a student, which gives her confidence, and she does a lot to help Miracle learn the truth about herself and her family. Like the other characters, Casey is an eccentric, overdrawn figure, but she seems to have a stronger hold on reality than Gigi* McCloy does and is less self-engrossed.

AUNT EDNA TAYLOR (*The Window**), white aunt of African-American Elgin* Taylor, sister of Marcella* Taylor, daughter of Mamaw*, and great-aunt of Rayona Taylor, the eleven-year-old narrator. Aunt Edna is the only one of the three women to be employed outside the home, working in an office at an unspecified position. She likes to run things, enjoys art projects, like paint-by-number pictures and beadwork, and playing games like Monopoly. Aunt Edna plans an automobile trip to Tacoma. When she tells Marcella that the three women were in a rut until Rayona came along, Marcella wonders what they will do without the girl.

AVI (AVI WORTIS) (1937–   ), born in New York City and educated at the University of Wisconsin and Columbia University; resident of Providence, Rhode Island; librarian, storyteller, teacher of children's literature, and acclaimed, versatile, and highly productive author of some forty-five books, mostly for children and young people in several genres and a variety of approaches and tones. *The Barn** (Orchard, 1994), *Beyond the Western Sea: Book One: The Escape from Home**, and *Beyond the Western Sea: Book Two: Lord Kirkle's Money** (both Orchard, 1996) are period novels, while *Poppy** (Orchard, 1995) is a lighthearted animal fantasy. Recently, he published *The Christmas Rat* (Atheneum, 2000), about a boy, an exterminator, and a rat. For earlier biographical information and titles, see *Dictionary, 1960–1984* [*Emily Upham's Revenge*; *Encounter at Easton*; *No More Magic*; *Shadrach's Crossing*]; *Dictionary, 1985–1989* [*The Fighting Ground*; *Something Upstairs*]; and *Dictionary, 1990–1994* [*The Man Who Was Poe*; *Nothing But the Truth*; *The True Confessions of Charlotte Doyle*; *"Who Was That Masked Man, Anyway?"*].

B

BABA JOSEPH (*A Girl Named Disaster**), old African man who cares for the animals at the science compound of Efifi in Zimbabwe. *Baba* Joseph is a Christian of the *Vapostori* or Apostles sect. He and his followers meet every Saturday in the forest dressed in white and carrying poles with a crook at the top. They do not believe in Western medicine, but *Baba* Joseph does not seem to feel a conflict between his beliefs and the goal of Efifi to find a cure for the sickness carried by the tsetse fly. He performs an exorcism ceremony at night on a mountaintop to rid Nhamo of the spirit of Long Teats. Nhamo is convinced that this exorcism works, but when he also tries to drive away the *vadzimi*, or ancestor spirits, his followers go into shock and throw themselves down from the heights. Most are not seriously hurt, though one has to be hospitalized. Although she is a scientist, Dr. Masuku admits to Nhamo that she has to respect *Baba* Joseph and cannot completely reject the beliefs in spirits that she grew up with.

BABBITT, NATALIE (ZANE MOORE) (1932–   ), born in Dayton, Ohio; writer of fantasies for children. She is best known for her widely acclaimed novel *Tuck Everlasting** (Farrar, 1975), which received the Phoenix Honor Award of The Children's Literature Association in 1995 for a book published twenty years earlier that has stood the test of time. She has recently published *Ouch! A Tale from Grimm Retold* (HarperCollins, 1998), a folktale in picture-book form. For more information and title entries, see *Dictionary, 1960–1984* [*Goody Hall*; *Kneeknock Rise*; *Tuck Everlasting*; *The Search for Delicious*].

BACON, KATHARINE JAY, grew up on Long Island and attended Radcliffe College, which she left in 1948 to move to Paris, where she married, lived for five years, and became the mother of three children. Three more children were born after she returned to the United States. In 1976, about thirty years after leaving Radcliffe, she returned to college, receiving her degree from that institution in 1978. Her novel *Finn** (McElderry, 1998), about a psychologically scarred mute boy, was nominated for the Edgar Allan Poe Award. She has also published the novels *Pip and Emma* (Atheneum, 1986), about a brother and sister who spend the summer with their grandmother in Vermont, and its sequel, *Shadow and Light* (McElderry, 1987). She lives in Vermont.

BAD GIRLS (Voigt*, Cynthia, Scholastic, 1996), humorous school novel, which takes place entirely within a present-day fifth-grade classroom in September and October. Told almost completely in dialogue, the slim plot is less important than the relationships between the girl protagonists and between them and the class bully, Louis* Caselli. Margalo* Epps and Mikey* (Michelle) Elsinger are both new at Washington Street Elementary School. Although Margalo is slim, comes from a large, blended family, and likes to spread rumors, and Mikey is a short, chubby, opinionated singleton and crack soccer player, they share some traits that make them stand out: outspokenness, a desire to run things, the same initials, and feminism. Three threads unite the episodes: the growing friendship between the two girls, each of whom would like to be friends with the other but does not want to lose her individuality; their intense dislike for Louis; and, to a lesser extent, their curiosity about Mrs.* Chemsky, known to be the toughest, strictest teacher in school. Trouble starts on the very first day of school, when Mikey interjects herself into the fifth-grade boys' soccer game. Her action incites Louis to call her such names as Porky, Mee-Schell, and Blimpo and to torment her. The result is a drag-'em-out shoving and punching match with bloody noses and bruises all around, at the end of which the girls are added to the class team. Pet Day turns out to be a disaster. Margalo brings in a wild rat, which gets away when she suggests that the shoebox that Mikey brought contains a black widow spider, and the class goes wild with fear and excitement. When the coach disciplines Louis because he objects to girls' being added to the school team and then his love notes to classmate Lynnie are exposed, Louis furiously cuts off Mikey's foot-and-a-half-long braid. He is suspended for four days and switched to another class. Soon the children realize that they miss him and agitate for his return. Even Mikey speaks up on his behalf, admitting some culpability and offering him her hand to shake, the latter just to spite him. The two girls also ask to build models during activities period, another matter that infuriates Louis because making models has traditionally been reserved for boys. Nominations and speeches during class elections result in Louis' defeat for the presidency to Ira, a friendly, helpful boy, and Mikey gets angry at Margalo because she fully expected that Margalo would vote for her. Rhonda disparages Mikey before the whole class, saying that no one likes her. Her words so in-furiate Margalo that she substitutes a roadkill squirrel, garbage, and limburger cheese for Rhonda's lunches three days in a row, provoking Rhonda to emit "four-star screams" that disrupt the class. Mikey insists on accompanying Mar-galo to the office and sharing her punishment, and the book ends with the girls fast friends and planning to stay overnight together. Throughout, the class' cu-riosity about their teacher, Mrs. Chemsky, grows, mostly because Margalo leads the children to believe that Mrs. Chemsky is a witch and ponders openly about what happened to her husband—was he murdered, perhaps? Mrs. Chemsky remains largely an enigma to the end. The accurate conversations, the clear, vivid detail of action and attitude, the hyperbolic behavior, the cliquishness, the often cruel teasing, the descriptions of dress, the topical references—all these add up to a highly convincing picture of middle-grade life. Margalo and Mikey are more mischievous than bad, individualized and likable, in spite of their troublemaking. In an afternote, the author describes them: "Girls with an attitude. Girls up to no good," an obviously tongue-in-cheek, affectionate remark. Fanfare.

THE BALLAD OF LUCY WHIPPLE (Cushman*, Karen, Clarion, 1996), historical novel and girl's growing-up story starting in 1849 in California during the gold rush, narrated by bookish, nonadventurous California Morning (Lucy) Whipple, 12, whose great desire is to return to Massachusetts. After the death of California's father and her younger brother, Golden Promise, from pneumoia, Mama (Arvella) Whipple has sold the feedstore and the house and headed for California by sea with her remaining family to fulfill the dream that she shared with her husband for a new start in the West. The story opens after their arrival by ship to San Francisco, steamer to Sacramento, wagon to Marysville, and foot and mule to Lucky Diggins, a mining town where Mama has a job running a boardinghouse. Only, as California's jaundiced eyes see all too clearly, there is no real town, only a saloon and a general store in tents owned by Mr. Scatter and a cluster of other tents and lean-tos belonging to prospectors. Soon they are setting up a primitive boardinghouse in two tents lashed together. California writes long, discontented letters to her Massachusetts grandparents detailing the dirt, mice, gophers, and bugs and expressing her longing for houses, schools, and, most of all, libraries. Their first tenant is Jimmy Whiskers, a huge, hairy man who is hoping to find enough gold to replace his lost teeth. Others soon follow. California's brother, Butte*, fits in immediately, loving the rough, free life, and her little sisters, Prairie and Sierra, adjust easily, but California hates the work and the whole place and stops sulking only after she has done two things, changed her name to "Lucy" and started making and selling pies to collect enough money to get herself back to Massachusetts. Her ambition, however, is continually thwarted. Daydreaming one day while collecting wood, she allows the mule, Sweetheart, to stray, and Mama remorselessly takes its value from Lucy's savings. Another plan, to go east with Brother Clyde Claymore, who is planning to give up his ministry to the miners and return to New Hampshire because he has no converts, fails when he saves Butte, who has slipped into the swollen river and been swept downstream. In gratitude, all Lucky Diggins attends his prayer meeting, Amos Frogge, the blacksmith, finds religion, and Brother Claymore decides to stay in the West. Among the group of eccentric boarders are Mr. Percival Coogan, a man with no visible means of support, whom Lucy thinks is Rattlesnake Jake, the vicious desperado; Snowshoe Ballou, a man with enormous feet who walks with mail to San Francisco and back; the Gent, who wears a high, black silk hat and plays the fiddle; and Joe, a runaway slave, the first African American whom Lucy has ever seen, who is allowed to sleep in Sweetheart's old shed and to whom Lucy gives a name, Bernard Freeman. Besides her copy of *Ivanhoe*, which she brought with her, Lucy acquires a few books sent by her grandparents and her old teacher in Massachusetts, and she lends them to lonely and culture-starved miners. Two disasters nearly sink the family. Butte, who has never fully recovered from his fall into the river, dies, and, after a hard winter, fire sweeps through Lucky Diggins, burning everything on the west side of the river. Nearby miners show up and share their tents and blankets, but most of the inhabitants leave. Mama, who has been courted by all the men, decides to marry Brother Claymore and go with him to the Sandwich Islands. The younger girls are willing to join them, but Lucy decides to travel east with Mr. Scatter's daughter, Belle, and her husband, who are willing to take her to help mind their baby. While she waits for the wagon trail from Marysville to be cleared so they can start their overland trek, a hard-rock mining company representative comes to town and decides to make Lucky Diggins the headquarters. Gradually, miners have returned books that were borrowed and therefore escaped the fire. The story ends with a letter from Lucy to her mother, telling of her decision to stay in Lucky Diggins and start a lending library, signed with the name that she has readopted, Miss California Morning Whipple. The book has a long author's note about the gold rush, the women and childlren who were part of it, and the way that they started newspapers, theaters, operas, and libraries shortly after they arrived. Following is a bibliography. Despite these scholarly appendages, the novel is full of humor, partly in the point of view of Lucy, who is determined to be miserable, partly from the eccentric characters that people Lucky Diggins, partly from the lively, often exaggerated incidents. Lucy's gradual awakening of interest in the rough little town and her affection for some of the residents make her ultimate decision plausible. Descriptions include the cold, the mud, the drought, the dirt, and the vermin but also the beauty of the wild land. The colorful dialogue gives a flavor of profanity without actually using any objectionable words. SLJ.

BANDIT'S MOON (Fleischman*, Sid, illus. Joseph Smith, Greenwillow, 1998), hilarious, fast-moving, biographical tall tale of the historical Mexican-American bandit Joaquin Murieta, who terrorized Americans in California during the 1850s, as told by a girl who falls in with him. On the way to California from Louisiana, their widowed mother dies of fever, leaving Annyrose Smith, not yet twelve, and her brother, Lank, 17, to fend for themselves. As they make their way north from San Diego to the goldfields, Lank's pocket is picked of all their money. He leaves Annyrose, who has broken her ankle, with seemingly kind woman rancher O. O. Mary, who is, in reality, a viciously mean thief. Mary robs the girl of everything valuable, including her long blond hair, and locks her up. When Mary hears that the notorious bandit, Joaquin, is in the neighborhood, she releases Annyrose, telling her to flee, and then gallops off on her horse. Joaquin arrives with some of his gang, including equally notorious Three-Fingered Jack. He forces Annyrose to come out from hiding, thinking that she is his enemy, Billy Calico. He then befriends her, supposing her a boy. She accompanies him as he and his fellows make their way gradually northward toward Sacramento, visits his hideout (blindfolded, of course), and observes him and his gang hold up a stagecoach. She teaches the handsome, confident road-man to read English. He wants to be able to read the posters advertising for his head, and he also wants to teach his California Mexican people to read, so that they will no longer be taken advantage of by Americans, the Yankees, or gringos, as he calls them. He hates Billy Calico, because Billy stole Joaquin's gold claim, murdered his brother, and kidnapped his wife, and he hates Americans because they have passed laws discriminating against the Mexicans, who were already in the area when the Americans arrived and whose land and gold claims they usurp. Various complications ensue during which Annyrose has occasion to see a newspaper article reporting that a certain Lanky Lafayette Smith was killed during a stagecoach stickup. Angry because she is sure that Joaquin shot her brother, she turns him in to Sheriff Elwood (Iron Eyes) Flint, then discovers that Lank has left a letter for her indicating that he has joined the Rangers who are hunting for Joaquin. To save Joaquin from a mob aching to lynch him, she creates a clever diversion, but O. O. Mary and Billy Calico abruptly drive up in a buggy. Red-haired Billy, furious that Joaquin is still hunting him, shoots Joaquin, wounding him, and at the same time is himself shot dead by the Sheriff. Joaquin's gang turns up and rescues their leader, who rides off with his fellows. Lank arrives and, when his horse is stolen, is left behind by the Rangers, who catch up with Joaquin at Cantua Creek, where it is soon reported that he has been killed in a grand shoot-out. Later, at Stockton, Annyrose and Lank see a poster advertising an exhibit of Joaquin's head and Three-Fingered Jack's hand. When she sees the head, Annyrose realizes right away that it is not Joaquin's but that of an impostor and is pleased that Joaquin got away. His words, "Es destino," "It's destiny," flash through her mind. He had always said that it was his fate to hang from an oak tree, not to be shot to death. Annyrose is a strong and appropriately troubled character, torn between what she thinks is right and her gratitude to the likable, smart, clever, Robin Hood-type young man of twenty-two, who has been good to her but who breaks the law without compunction. The book stays close to the known facts, and throughout the reader is completely on the bandit's side. Hairbreadth escapes, nick-of-time rescues, outlandish names, incongruous situations like that of two whiskered miners, brothers who are ex-music professors from Boston, playing Mozart with highly polished violins on the streets of Jackson, and Joseph Smith's cartoonish, black-and-white drawings produce a hilarious mix. The novel gives a good sense of the period's turmoil and also of discrimination against the Hispanics. An author's note at the end gives historical background. ALA.

BANKS, RUSSELL (1940–   ), born in Newton, Massachusetts; attended Colgate University and received his bachelor's degree from the University of North

Carolina. During his more than twenty years of writing, he has often been honored for his poetry and many novels and short stories, mainly for adults. He has been a publisher and editor and has taught at Emerson College, University of New Hampshire, New England College, Princeton University, and New York University. *Rule of the Bone** (HarperCollins, 1995), a picaresque boy's growing-up novel set in upstate New York and in Jamaica, was chosen for its recommended list by *School Library Journal*. He has recently published *Cloudsplitter: A Novel* (HarperCollins, 1998), about John Brown's Raid, and *The Angel on the Roof: The Stories of Russell Banks* (HarperCollins, 2000). Banks lives in upstate New York and in Princeton, New Jersey.

BARB MCGUIRE (*Dakota Dream**), Floyd Rayfield's kind, caring social worker. When she first contacts Floyd, she tells him that she is not really a social worker yet but is still working on her degree. She is a widow whose soldier-son was killed in Lebanon and who has returned to school. She has a genuine interest in making life better for the boy and encourages him to ask for help and not just stoically endure conditions that he knows are not beneficial to him. She invites him to her house, lets him use the garage to work on the motorcycle, gets a large cottonwood log for him to convert to a canoe, and attempts to intercede with the authorities on his behalf. Floyd likes her a great deal and respects her for her continuing concern, but he is also afraid that the system will destroy her by forcing her into the callous social-worker mold that he has known all his life.

THE BARN (Avi*, Orchard, 1994), family novel set for a few months in 1855 in the Willamette Valley of Oregon Territory. Half-orphaned Ben (Benjamin), the nine-year-old narrator, tells how, not long after he is sent to school in Portland because he has a "particular fine gift of learning," Schoolmaster Dortmeister informs him that his father "has met with an accident" and that his sister, Nettie, 15, has come by buggy to fetch him home to the farm. His siblings need him, since much of the time Nettie and their brother, Harrison, 13, must care for the sightless, voiceless invalid, once a happy, joking man who now lies immobile, his increasingly frail body a deadweight, the stench from his bodily wastes often and revoltingly filling the tiny cabin. All three children know that if they do not work the claim for two more years, they will lose it, and if they do not care for Father, they will lose him. Ben helps Harrison in the fields, leaving Nettie to care for Father, but when Ben sees how much more land can be worked when Nettie helps Harrison, he suggests that he assume sole responsibility for Father. Ben's emotions about his tasks and his Father are mixed. He tries to study, he reads to Father from *The Pilgrim's Progress*, he tries conversing, and he feels guilty, cheated, angry, and overwhelmed by turns. Finally, in desperation he shouts that Nettie has told him that Father had been planning to build a barn and demands that Father close his eyes if that is true. Receiving the hoped-for response, Ben persuades Nettie and Harrison that Father wants them to build the barn, and the three spend much of the summer and the rest of the book on that enterprise. Ben promises Father the barn in exchange for Father's getting well and receives what he thinks is agreement from Father. He marks out the barn floor, employing principles that he learned in geometry. It takes eight weeks for the children to collect stones for the foundation and cut, haul, split, and trim the trees. Ben transports Father to the barn site in the wheelbarrow so that Father can watch the building progress. Two days before they start the actual construction, Father turns worse, and Ben presses for more urgent construction. They have the walls up in a week, mount the tree on the roof, and finish the structure, about two weeks' very hard and exhausting work in actual construction. During the night, Father dies. Ben is angry and distraught. He tells Nettie and Harrison that he wanted to give the barn to Father so Father would be grateful to Ben and realize that Ben was not different from the others as they keep telling him he is because of his ability to learn. But Nettie points out that Father knew the barn was finished because Father heard Ben say so. She says that Father accepted the barn and then died. Harrison, too, says that the barn was really Father's gift to Ben. They bury Father next to Mother on the hill overlooking the barn, but Ben says that Father's true place is in the barn. In the last, very brief chapter, Ben speaks seventy years later, saying that the barn is still standing and still strong, and as Father had once promised, it is "something fine to come home to." This tender, quiet story of devotion and sacrifice draws strength from its tone of reminiscence. The children steadfastly refuse all offers of help, even from Tod Buckman, Nettie's young fiancé. Tod summarizes the theme when he says that Father is very lucky to have such a family. As they give to one another, each to all, they symbolize the finest in family unity and dedication. ALA.

BAT 6 (Wolff*, Virginia Euwer, Scholastic, 1998), realistic period, school, and sports novel set during the school year of 1949 and revolving around a schoolgirl's hostile attitude toward the Japanese people, an attitude that derives from experiences in World War II. Twenty-one sixth-grade girls on two softball teams in the Oregon, fruit-growing small towns of Bear Creek Ridge and Barlow Road take turns describing their experiences leading up to and during their annual rivalry, the big game called Bat 6, which is canceled after one inning because a girl is severely injured. As a result, the girls, indeed their towns, have a deeper understanding of racial prejudice, individual responsibility, and the need for forgiveness. Each girl contributes to the narrative in first-person, detailed, often ungrammatical and awkwardly styled, "off-the-cuff" passages, ranging in length from two lines to several pages, at first alternating between schools but in the last one-third of the book in chapters that combine schools. Most characters are almost indistinguishable without the lineups given at the beginning of the book, and the author's introductory note helps with historical background. Students, teachers, and townspeople in both towns look forward eagerly to the traditional rivalry, begun in 1899 and played every year since at the end of May. The towns are economically on the edge, and the girls have mostly used equipment, but they have experienced, understanding, and inspiring coaches, whom they like and respect, and all do their best to keep up their grades, helping the less academically able and running and exercising regularly to build up their endurance. Two newcomers become the focus, self-effacing, polite Japanese-American Aki* Mikami of Bear Creek, who plays first and whose mother was Bear Creek's Most Valuable Player in 1930. The Mikamis have just returned from being relocated during the war. New in Barlow Road is unkempt, poorly clothed, aloof Shazam* (Shirley), who lives with her poverty-stricken grandmother while "her mother gets on her feet" and about whose illegitimacy of birth the town buzzes but is not unkind. Although she is a poor student, antisocial, and often abstracted, Shazam is big and strong, can hit, pitch, and field well, and is assigned to center field. Several players note that she seems disturbed when she sees Japanese people. During the big game, in running to first, she rams her elbow viciously into the side of Aki's head, severely injuring Aki, who is hospitalized and then must wear braces for weeks. It comes out that Shazam has never come to terms with the loss of her father, who was killed in the Japanese attack on Pearl Harbor, and that every time she sees a Japanese person, she relives the bombing all over again. As punishment, Shazam is assigned a community service project of helping to fix up the Mikami property, which had gone to ruin while they were gone. In doing so, she comes to terms, at least, with working with Aki's brother, Shig. Persuaded by a teammate, Manzanita, who teammates think is peculiar since she "got the spirit at a revival" and who is sure that Jesus has sent her to heal both girls, Shazam visits Aki and tells her that she is sorry. Aki accepts her apology graciously. Another teammate, in the concluding narrative, sums up what the girls collectively feel when she plaintively tells God that she still does not understand why all this happened. Although essentially a serious book, lighter times appear. The girls have parties, talk about fashions in clothes, go through chicken pox together, share opinions about their teachers, and show a great deal of community spirit, as do the townspeople, so that the sense of community life and ethic comes through very strongly. Although it is hard to adjust to the often-changing speakers and it seems contrived that two feuding fathers, one a World War II vet and the other a World War II conscientious objector, decide to put aside their differences because of the accident, a good feature is that the towns come together and that the teams become friends through their mutual concern over Aki and the Mikamis' financial problems owing to the medical bills. Addams; ALA; SLJ.

BAUER, JOAN, born in River Forest, Illinois; author of both realistic and fantasy novels for young adults. She has worked in advertising and marketing, as a writer for magazines and newspapers, and as a screenwriter. Her works are noted for humor in books with serious themes, among them *Squashed* (Delacorte, 1992), set in Rock River, Iowa; *Thwonk* (Delacorte, 1995), a fantasy set in Connecticut; *Sticks* (Delacorte, 1996), about a pool tournament; and *Rules of the Road** (Putnam, 1998), in which a teenage girl chauffeurs a wealthy old woman from Chicago to Texas and helps save her corporate empire. Bauer has made her home in Darien, Connecticut.

BEANS (*Wringer**), Arthur Dodds, nine-year-old bully when the story begins and leader of the four-boy gang to which Palmer LaRue is admitted on Palmer's ninth birthday. Beans is tough, argumentative, and mean. He looks forward to becoming a wringer—killer of wounded pigeons—and expects that his gang members will also become wringers. He is early described as having ugly teeth, "dull yellowish-brown fringed with green," which he swears he never brushes. The teeth are probably intended to be symbolic of his nature. He has a mean, yellow cat named Panther. Beans keeps the muskrat that Panther kills in the freezer and then hangs it on the door of Dorothy* Gruzik's house. He is terrible almost beyond belief.

BEAUTY (McKinley*, Robin, Harper, 1978), fictionalized retelling of "Beauty and the Beast," a fantasy novel set in a largely realistic, preindustrial period. The protagonist's real name is Honour Huston. After the fleet and therefore the wealth of her merchant father are lost at sea, the story follows the familiar folktale closely to the predictable ending. Phoenix Honor. For a longer entry, see *Dictionary, 1960–1984*.

THE BEEKEEPER'S APPRENTICE OR ON THE SEGREGATION OF THE QUEEN (King*, Laurie R., St. Martin's, 1994), mystery based on the unlikely premise that, after his retirement to keep bees in Sussex, Sherlock Holmes takes an American girl as his apprentice and, eventually, his partner. Supposedly a manuscript delivered mysteriously to the author, the story is ostensibly narrated in the late twentieth century by Mary Russell and tells how in 1915 as an American girl of fifteen she literally stumbles upon the great detective on the Sussex Downs, where she is walking while reading an engrossing book, and he is crouching, observing wild bees. A tall, awkward, nearsighted, and highly intelligent girl, Mary is an orphan since an automobile accident for which she was partly responsible killed both her parents and her younger brother. Although due to inherit a good deal of money, she is unhappily living with an aunt who underfeeds her and tries to bully her into conventional behavior. The friendships that she strikes up with Holmes and his housekeeper, Mrs. Hudson, who has moved from London with him, and later with Dr. Watson, who becomes "Uncle John" to her, mean a great deal to Mary, and she haunts the detective's cottage without realizing that he is systematically training her in the techniques of deduction, as well as chemistry, bee culture, and chess. In the next few years she is allowed to help in minor ways on several local cases, while she studies for Oxbridge examinations and enters a women's college at Oxford. Then they become involved in the search for kidnappers of six-year-old Jessica Simpson, daughter of an American senator, abducted from a family camping outing in Wales. With typical Holmes deduction, they narrow the possibilities of where the child could be held to an isolated house in a village, and, while Holmes, dressed as a gypsy, plays his violin and leads an impromptu Welsh chorus as a diversion, Mary ascertains that Jessica is indeed held in an upper room, climbs a tree to enter a second-story window, and with the child clinging to her, makes her way down the tree and to a place of safety. Although the kidnappers are apprehended, they have been hired anonymously for the job and do not lead police to the mind behind the crime. Back in Oxford, Mary concentrates on her studies until a series of bombings, the first of Holmes' beehive, one set in Mary's room but defused by Holmes, and one in Dr. Watson's lodgings, indicate that some malevolent and brilliant adversary is after Holmes, toying with him by stalking his friends and attempting to destroy whatever he values. There follow some tense escapes and a long trip to the Holy Land, where Holmes and Mary engage in cases unrelated to their major threat. By the time that they return to England, they realize that their enemy is a woman, and they have a plan. As in a devious chess game, they will appear to give up the Queen, that is, Mary, to throw their adversary off guard. Holmes and Mary stage a quarrel, an act both difficult and upsetting for Mary, who is genuinely hurt by Holmes' scathing scorn, even though she understands the purpose. The denouement occurs at Holmes' cottage in Sussex after Mary, by brilliant deduction, has realized that their adversary, the mind behind the kidnapping, is Patricia Donleavy, her math tutor at Oxford, who also turns out to be the daughter of Professor Moriarty, the master criminal for whose death Holmes was responsible years before. In the final confrontation, Miss Donleavy is killed, Mary is shot, her collarbone broken, and her spirit plunged into depression. A letter from Jessie Simpson, in her six-year-old cramped printing, saying that she is trying to be "brave and strong like you," helps Mary recover, and she joins Holmes for further adventures. As the protagonist develops from an awkward adolescent to self-confident, mature woman, her relationship to Holmes gradually changes to include a romantic element. Although no explicitly sexual scenes occur, the reader is left with the clear impression that their association will not continue platonic. Sherlockians will recognize several minor characters, including Mycroft Holmes and Inspector Lestrade. The slightly formal, Victorian style closely resembles that of A. Conan Doyle, and the technique of detection cleverly imitates that in his Sherlock Holmes stories, so that the somewhat implausible action is fun and thoroughly enjoyable. ALA; SLJ.

BEGGARS AND CHOOSERS (Kress*, Nancy, Tor, 1994), futuristic science fiction novel concerned with the problems caused by gene altering, set in the United States, mostly in a rural village of New York state in the years 2106 to 2115. It follows *Beggars in Spain*, which was first published as a novella, then expanded into a novel of 438 pages, telling of events from 2008 to 2091. Because expensive genetic modification in vitro has been possible for some years, there are now essentially four classes: ordinary, normal human beings, or Livers; people with some genetic changes, physical or mental, known as donkeys; a much smaller group who have been modified to function without sleep and their offspring, called the Sleepless; and about thirty children of Sleepless more extensively modified for intelligence, known as Super-Sleepless, the most powerful of all. Livers exist with almost no work, their food, clothing, entertainment, and other needs provided by the donkeys in exchange for their votes. Donkeys run the political establishment and most of the business, much of it operated by robots run on extremely cheap Y energy. Most of the Sleepless, who live evidently without aging since sleep, it has been proven, is actually harmful to organisms, have removed themselves to Sanctuary, a self-sufficient orbital where they experimented with in vitro modifications to produce the Supers. Before the year 2100 the twenty-seven Supers have thwarted a plan by the obsessive Sleepless leader to have Sanctuary secede from the United States and have holed up on an island called Huevos Verdes, which they built with their greatly advanced technology. The novel is told in first person by three characters: Drew* Arlen, a Liver who has been educated and, after an attack that left his legs paralyzed, gene-altered experimentally to become the Lucid Dreamer, giving holo-image concerts, a new art form that partly hypnotizes, partly creates dreams to entertain and influence huge audiences; Diana* Covington (later known as Vicki Turner), a donkey secretly trained to be an agent for the Genetic Standards Enforcement Agency (GSEA) but never employed, so her records are not in any database, now asked to trace the movements of Miranda* Sharifi, the leader of the Super-Sleepless; and Billy* Washington, a Liver in his sixties of the village of East Oleanta, New York, who is in love with ample Annie Francy, 35, of African-American descent, and devoted to her daughter, Lizzie*, 11. Disguised as a Liver, Diana attends a hearing in Washington, D.C., of the Science Court, which decides whether new technology can be licensed or even pursued, to hear Miranda propose the licensing of a new device called a "Cell Cleaner," invented in Huevos Verdes, which will destroy cancers, harmful viruses and bacteria, and any other dangerous bodily matter without hurting desirable elements. When Miranda's licensing request is turned down, as she seems to have expected, Diana trails her and loses her at East Oleanta. Because Lizzie has pneumonia, and the robotic medical unit has broken down, Billy lets Diana treat Lizzie, although Annie is highly suspicious. Diana, or Vicki as they know her, thinks that Billy may be able to lead her to Eden, a hidden facility to which she suspects Miranda has disappeared. Gradually, as other robotic devices—trains, food suppliers, water heaters, and so on—break down, Vicki, Billy, and the Francys join forces in a desperate struggle for survival. Not only have the ordinary services to Livers begun to fail, but it becomes apparent that they are deliberately sabotaged by technology from groups of militant terrorist Livers who consider themselves superpatriotic and are determined to kill all the "abominations," as they refer to the donkeys, whom they hate for being superior. In a series of exciting episodes these various forces confront each other and struggle over the basic question, "Who should control the advanced technology—the scientists, the government, the people, or the terrorists?" From untutored Billy comes the most revealing insight: "It only matters, who *can*?" Each new technological advance causes social disruption and can make some of the groups redundant, as the cheap Y energy has really made the labor of Livers useless, and Miranda's serum, which not only cleans cells but makes it possible for humans to "feed" through their skin by lying in mud, makes the donkey politicians' handouts and the donkeys themselves unnecessary. The value that seems to survive is simple human love, as felt by Billy, the Francys, and Diana/Vicki and as renounced or lost by Miranda and Drew. The action is compelling, and many of the minor characters are full-bodied and interesting, as well as the three narrators and young Lizzie. Although *Beggars and Choosers* is called "an independent sequel," it helps to have read the earlier book because the ideas and the relationships are complex, and the terminology can be confusing. SLJ.

BELLE BALL PRATER (*Belle Prater's Boy**), mother of Woodrow, a woman who never actually appears in the novel but whose past history and disappearance dominate the action. A plain girl, she was always compared unfavorably with her beautiful older sister, Love, although she was bright and an accomplished pianist. When, while Love was away at college, Amos Leemaster came to town, he and Belle fell in love and planned to marry. Then Love came home, and Amos dropped Belle for her. After a period of weeping and depression, Belle dressed up, went out, met Everett Prater in a bar, and ran off with him. Mostly estranged from her parents and sister, she lived far up an isolated hollow in a primitive house, unhappy in her marriage but devoted to her son, with whom she made up fantasies and stories from the personal ads that they read together. Although Woodrow has told the police, honestly, that none of her clothes or shoes is missing, he has failed to tell them that some of his own clothes and shoes, which would fit his mother, are gone. Woodrow reads the ads carefully every Sunday, thinking that she will send him a message, but he finally has to admit to himself that she must be getting on with her own life and not worrying about him.

BELLE PRATER'S BOY (White*, Ruth, Farrar, 1996), growing-up novel set in Coal Station, Virginia, in 1953, in which a boy and a girl, cousins, learn to face the fact that a parent deliberately left the family. Although she seems to have everything that a girl could want—beauty, brains, an attractive home, a loving mother—the narrator, Gypsy Arbutus Leemaster, 12, is plagued by a recurring nightmare of an animal with a horribly missing face. She also resents the time and care that her mother insists that she give her long, golden hair, wishing instead that she could be known for her expert piano playing and her ability to tell jokes. When her Aunt Belle* Ball Prater, her mother's sister whom Gypsy scarcely knew, disappears, Belle's son, Woodrow, 12, comes to live next door with their grandparents. Although the townspeople and even Gypsy are crassly curious about Belle's disappearance, Woodrow handles their rude questions well and soon is popular in school despite his crossed eyes and (or possibly because of) the outlandish stories that he tells. As they become close friends, he confides to Gypsy that on their farm, far up an isolated hollow, is a place where the air tingles, where two worlds meet, and that his mother stepped into it deliberately early one morning and now lives in another dimension. Gypsy doesn't know whether to believe the story or even whether Woodrow believes it. She notices that he always rises early on Sunday morning to get the newspaper first and carefully reads all the personal ads. He tells her that he and his mother used to make up stories about the people in them. Woodrow makes friends with Porter Dotson, Gypsy's stepfather, whom she used to like but whom she has rudely ignored since he married her mother, and with Blind* Benny, a derelict who picks over the trash at night, followed lovingly by all the town dogs. The only person who doesn't like Woodrow is Buzz Osborne, a bully in their class who is jealous of the attention that Woodrow is getting. When school starts in the fall, and they are introducing themselves to their new teacher with short autobiographical sketches, Gypsy says that her father, a volunteer fireman, was killed in a fire when she was five. Buzz shouts that it is a lie, that Amos Leemaster shot himself in the face because he was badly scarred in a fire and couldn't stand being ugly when he was married to the most beautiful woman in the hills. Gypsy's long-repressed memory of discovering her father's body with his face gone returns, and she runs home. Furious that he left her and her mother for such a trivial reason, she chops off her long hair, which was her father's pride. Woodrow beats up Buzz, and Porter intervenes to turn aside her mother's wrath. He takes Gypsy to the barbershop after regular hours to get a pixie cut, which Woodrow helps her pass off as a new style that she has coveted. Now that she has faced her demons, Woodrow admits to her that the tingly place was just a fantasy that he and his mother made up. He figures that his mother, unhappy in her marriage, just walked over the mountain dressed as a boy and started a new life. She also took the thirty dollars that they had saved toward an operation to fix his crossed eyes. He has thought that she might communicate with him through the personal ads but now gives up that hope. Porter's brother, the local doctor, investigates an eye specialist in Baltimore and arranges that he examine and possibly operate on Woodrow. Also Porter, with whom Gypsy now has a better relationship, arranges that she give a piano recital. Although the loose ends are tied up a little too neatly, the novel holds a reader's interest because Woodrow is a compelling character, given to wildly imaginative stories and pranks, like pretending to prim and proper Mrs. Cooper at the Annual Garden Party that he has added a little rum to her lemonade, so that she begins to act drunk through the power of suggestion. Gypsy is a less interesting figure, but minor characters, like the grandparents, the new male teacher, and patient Porter are well drawn. The social dynamics of a small Appalachian town are explored with a good deal of humor. ALA; Boston Globe Honor; Newbery Honor; SLJ.

BEN FINNEY (*Walk Two Moons**), classmate of Sal Hiddle and Phoebe* Winterbottom, a cousin of the wild, loud Finneys, with whom he lives, because, as Sal learns late in the book, his mother is in a psychiatric hospital. He likes to draw satirical cartoons. Early in their friendship, Ben seems to be romantically inclined toward Sal, brushing her with his lips and touching her hands. Gradually, Sal starts to like his attentions, and after she returns to Kentucky, he sends her a valentine in the middle of October with the first poem that he has ever written. She writes one for him that is equally sentimental and trite. Her relationship with Ben is a sign that she is growing up. On the trip to the university to locate the lunatic, Sal sees Ben visiting his mother at the hospital. The woman's meandering, unfocused behavior reminds Sal of the way that her mother acted after she returned from the hospital, having lost her baby.

BENITO (*A Sunburned Prayer**), Eloy's teenaged older brother. In Eloy's view at the beginning of the novel, Benito is a mean and disagreeable lout who smarts off and shouts at their parents, stays out late at night, and is interested only in girls and cars. Eloy likes to tease Benito but is careful to stay beyond arm's reach. He envies his brother's growing manhood, which he associates with Benito's pants being tight in the crotch. Eloy does not know until they arrive home from the pilgrimage that Benito deliberately provoked an argument with their parents on Good Friday morning to keep them from finding out that Eloy had left on the pilgrimage. Benito stayed home in order to drive *abuela* to the Santuario. He says that maybe the two of them, he and Eloy, can walk the Good Friday pilgrimage to Chimayo together next year. At the end of the story, Eloy thinks better of his older brother than he did when events began.

BENNETT, JAMES W. (1942–   ), teacher of creative writing; teaching assistant for mentally handicapped students at a Bloomington, Illinois, high school; and writer for young adults. He draws heavily on his personal experiences for his novels, which involve emotionally disturbed or confused high school-age protagonists like those with whom he works. He himself also suffered an emotional breakdown and, while convalescing, began to view writing as an avenue for raising awareness of the problems of people with mental or emotional disorders. His first novel, *I Can Hear the Mourning Dove* (Houghton, 1990), rose out of his acquaintance with a fellow patient. Other novels include *Dakota Dream** (Scholastic, 1994), *The Squared Circle* (Scholastic, 1995), and *Blue Star Rapture* (Simon & Schuster, 1998). After receiving his degree from Wesleyan University, he pursued graduate work at Illinois State University. He lives in Normal, Illinois.

BERYL FINDHAM (*The Cage**), young woman from Boston hired by a photography magazine for an expedition to take pictures of polar bears at the edge of Hudson Bay. A small person, she has been chosen mostly because she will fit into the cage from which, the plan is, she will take the still pictures of the bears at very close range, getting more authentic shots than a telephoto lens will give. She also is well known as a photographer of small animals, a reputation that she has achieved by her inexhaustible patience in waiting, unmoving, until the animal is at ease in her presence. A vividly imaginative person, she shares the emotions of her subjects and fantasizes dancing with the polar bears. Although she has had several relationships with men, they have all been brief, broken off because she feels her independence slipping away as they inevitably start telling her what to do. She takes the lead in lovemaking with Jean-Claude* Thibedeaux, who is nine years younger and inexperienced. On their terrible trek back to Churchill, she almost wrecks their chances of survival when she rescues David* Golding despite orders by Jean-Claude, who says anyone falling in the water must be abandoned. Still, against the expectations of all the others, she endures and may even get help in time to save Jean-Claude.

BETTY SKORO LUND (*Mr. Was**), mother of Jack, abused by her alcoholic husband. Although his drinking produces his violent rages and leaves her with blackened eyes and broken bones, her reaction often increases his fury, and Jack recognizes that her whiny tone and her inability to let go of a bad situation without trying to get the last word are complicitous behavior. When she finally does leave and goes to Boggs End with Jack, her husband follows her, is infuriated that she locks him out, and drives his Jeep crashing into and through the front door. In the ensuing scuffle he wrests away from Jack the baseball bat that the boy is trying to use to defend his mother and beats her to death with it. His comment is, "She made me do it." Afterward, although Jack doesn't find it out for many years, he cuts down the clothesline and hangs himself. In the end it is revealed that Betty was the daughter of Andie* Murphy and Scud*.

BEYOND THE BURNING TIME (Lasky*, Kathryn, Scholastic, 1994), historical novel of Salem Village at the time of the Massachusetts witch trials in the 1690s. Since her father's death, Mary Chase, 12, is so busy helping her mother, Virginia, with their small farm that she has no time to play at the "little sorcery" of fortune-telling and to catch the hysteria that afflicts many of the village girls. She is both fascinated and fearful when she hears of their accusations of being attacked by unseen spirits sent by witches, although her devout, but sensible, mother sees the whole business as nonsense. Her brother Caleb, 14, is now an apprentice carpenter at the shipbuilding yard in Salem Town and can come home only infrequently, but Gilly, the simple-minded hired man who was devoted to her father, helps out. At first the accusations of witchcraft are leveled at demented outcasts, like Sarah Good, but as the girls, now local celebrities, begin to name other women, some of them pious, churchgoing wives, a pattern emerges, with the wife and daughter of envious Thomas Putnam, especially, accusing those belonging to more successful families. Gossipy Goody Dawson keeps dropping by with scandalous tidbits to impart and is insulted when Virginia is scornful. The relative isolation of their house keeps them from being drawn into the village panic, but each Sunday at meeting they see the growing conviction of many of their neighbors that witches are at work in the area, and they are shocked by the arrests of respected neighbors and even four-year-old Dorcas Good. Gilly has transferred his devotion from Mary's dead father to her mother, but gradually it becomes a lecherous desire to see Virginia naked, and he climbs to the roof of the cattle shed and crouches where he can peer into the window of her room. When Caleb, returning after dark with Mary one night, catches him peeping, he throws the simpleton off the farm. Thereafter, Mary sees Gilly and Goody Dawson with their heads together, and not long afterward Virginia is arrested. Since the property of accused witches is forfeited to the state, and Caleb fears that Mary may also be named as a witch, he takes her to stay in the shipyard where he works. They are able to visit their mother three times, finding her in chains with sores on wrists and ankles where the fetters scrape but still vowing not to confess to a falsehood. She urges them to leave the area for Richmond, where they have an uncle, but instead they go to Boston, hoping to get the new governor Phips to intercede. Their interview with the governor, obtained because he is interested in shipbuilding, shows that he is uninterested in the spiritual problems and wants to solve the situation by hanging all the witches summarily. Caleb gets Mary a job in an inn near the wharves, where she meets Eli Coatsworth, captain of the sailing vessel *Raven*, who takes pity on her and works out a plan to rescue Virginia only to find that she has been moved to an undisclosed farm. Mary and Caleb ambush one of the accusing girls, Mary Warren, and threaten her until she reveals the farm where Virginia is being held. There they come upon Gilly, who is nearly insane with remorse. He helps them get back their two horses, which have been confiscated, and they ride after the cart carrying Virginia to her execution. They play upon the carter's superstitions, causing him to have a heart attack, whereupon they rescue Virginia. They escape on the *Raven* to Bermuda, where they live happily for some years, although Virginia's foot, infected by the leg-irons, has been amputated. An Epilogue, dated in 1779 and written by Captain Coatsworth, tells that, having married Virginia, he returned to Massachusetts with her and her two children, where in saner times they reclaimed the Chase farm and prospered. In a note at the end, set more than thirty years later, Mary finally faces the job of writing about the horrible time of her childhood, knowing that she is one of the few survivors to remember and record the true history. Although the Salem witch trials have inherent drama, the novel suffers from superimposing the fictional story of Mary Chase, her family, Gilly, and Captain Coatsworth on the historical events without weeding out unnecessary fact. For much of the novel Mary is an observer of the action; when she takes matters into her own hands at the end, too many coincidences and unlikely plot complications make the story implausible. Several earlier novels have told the story better. A long author's note at the end explains what is fact and what political and social conditions led to the witch-hunts. ALA; SLJ.

BEYOND THE WESTERN SEA: BOOK ONE: THE ESCAPE FROM HOME (Avi*, Orchard, 1996), intricate, Dickensian, realistic, period novel featuring a very large, colorful cast and filled with action, coincidence, and chance encounters. The first book in a set of two, the narrative occurs mostly in Liverpool, England, for two days in January 1851. The plot revolves around the efforts of two boys to leave their homes and sail for America. The story begins in famine-stricken Ireland in December with the nearly starving O'Connell family (timid mother, plucky daughter, Maura, 15, and impulsive son, Patrick, 12), whose father, Gregory, has emigrated, found work in a Lowell, Massachusetts, "cloth-making manufactory," and sent them money to join him. They get out just before the agent of wealthy English absentee landowner Lord Kirkle comes with constables and soldiers to "tumble" (completely destroy by knocking down) the rude huts in their village of Kilonny for nonpayment of rent. They reach Cork, where Mrs. O'Connell has a sudden change of heart, and the children proceed without her on a terrifying boat trip to Liverpool. There numerous, also terrifying adventures await the almost penniless pair before they embark for America. In late January, in his well-appointed London house, Lord Kirkle administers to his younger son, Sir Laurence, 11, a savage caning for insubordination to his snide and bullying older brother, Sir Albert (Albert Kirkle*), 15. Laurence runs away for America after stealing £1,000 from his father's desk. A patch-eyed London street thief soon steals almost all the money from the naive and frightened boy, who still manages to get to Liverpool. He manages to evade police and two men who pursue him, Mr.* Phineas Pickler, a private investigator hired by Lord Kirkle to find and bring him home, and Mr.* Matthew Clemspool (later accompanied by the thief, Mr.* Toby Grout), a shady figure hired by Albert to make sure Laurence gets to America and never returns. The two sets of characters become intertwined when Patrick encounters Laurence on the Liverpool dock, just after Laurence has been forced to attempt a robbery by another unsavory character, Ralph Toggs*, a street thief and con artist involved with one of the many Liverpool gangs, the Lime Street Runners Association run by Sergeant Rumpkin, a Fagin type. The two boys get lost in a fog and end up on the *Charity*, the chapel boat of the Reverend* Mr. Gideon Bartholomew, who feeds them and secretly writes a letter informing the police that he thinks Laurence is a wealthy runaway. The letter falls into the hands of the Lime Street gang, who are now in the pay of Mr. Clemspool and attempting to find the boy. Laurence has become entangled in a web of intrigue that will last many months and follow him to America. In related action, Toggs has taken Maura and Patrick to a seedy rooming house, run by grasping Mrs. Sonderbye, where they become friends with grandiloquent Mr.* Horatio Drabble, a down-on-his-luck Shakespearean actor. With Mr. Drabble's help they eventually get on the *Robert Peel*, and all three set sail with masses of other emigrants. Fred* No-name, another runner, smuggles Laurence on board the same ship, just in time to evade Mr. Pickler and Toggs, who are hot on Laurence's trail, and informs Patrick that his friend is inside a hat crate in the ship's hold. At the end of the story, Laurence, hungry, cold, and frightened, hopes that Patrick will soon be able to release him from the crate. Characters are an engaging mix of the one-dimensional innocents and villainous figures typical of the Victorian novel. The baroque plot (of which the preceding is indeed a minimalistic summary) supports a rich picture of teeming streets, docks, and ships; street urchins, peddlers, and pickpockets; drinkers; street players; honest and dishonest citizens—a breathtaking mix by day and foggy nights—and many evidences of class distinctions and crass inhumanity. One of the most graphic events involves the tumbling of the rude, ramshackle huts of the starving Irish, done with vicious disregard for all basic human needs. Mostly plot, the book unfolds in seventy-four snappy, cliff-hanger chapters and is a page-turner from gripping beginning to tension-filled finish. Although the conclusion is abrupt, and the story continues in a sequel, *Beyond the Western Sea: Book Two: Lord Kirkle's Money**, the book is complete in itself, and the expectation is that all will eventually work out for the main characters. ALA.

BEYOND THE WESTERN SEA: BOOK TWO: LORD KIRKLE'S MONEY (Avi*, Orchard, 1996), colorful, intricate, realistic, period novel, set on board the *Robert Peel*, an English emigrant ship bound for America, in Boston, and in Lowell, Massachusetts, from January 24, 1851, to March 8, 1851. Sequel to *Beyond the Western Sea: Book One: The Escape from Home**, the novel features the same protagonists and also overflows with duplicitous acts, chance encounters, near misses, sordid and grasping villains, naive innocents, and other conventions of the grandiose Victorian novel. The plot revolves around three interwoven story strands: (1) the efforts of the two Irish O'Connell children, Maura, 15, and Patrick, 12, to reach America and start a new life with their emigrant father, Gregory; (2) the efforts of English Sir Laurence Kirkle, 11, a penniless runaway and stowaway, to arrive safely, recover the £1,000 that he stole from his father and that was subsequently stolen from him, and evade the clutches of his avaricious, murderous, older brother, Sir Albert*; and (3) the efforts of fanatical Mr.* Jeremiah Jenkins to get revenge upon Mr.* James Hamlyn, who he feels has grievously wronged him, and to stir up the community against immigrants, especially the Irish. The O'Connells, accompanied by Shakespearean actor Mr.* Horatio Drabble, stoically endure the long, problem-filled voyage. In Boston, Mr.* Nathaniel Brewster, a cotton-mill worker, brings the sad news that Gregory has died of a heart attack. With Nathaniel's help, Maura finds a place to live in Lowell at the boardinghouse of the Hamlyns and work at the mill. Patrick, who rooms with Nathaniel, is soon accosted by Irish-hating hooligans, among them Jeb* Grafton, a shoeshine boy. Laurence has no luck while still on board in recovering his money from Mr.* Toby Grout, a one-eyed London street thief, also an emigrant, from whom, unbeknownst to Laurence, the money has been stolen by another passenger, Mr.* Matthew Clemspool, long a nemesis of Laurence. In America, having learned by chance that Albert has arrived, Laurence barely eludes his brother and Mr. Clemspool. Eventually, he inadvertently comes into possession of a safe-deposit box key belonging to Mr. Clemspool, who has placed Laurence's stolen money in a local bank. While all this is transpiring, Mr. Jenkins has been stirring up American laborers against the immigrants, specifically against the Irish and Mr. Hamlyn. At an evening meeting in early March, he incites a mob against Hamlyn and sets fire to the Hamlyn house. In the tumult that ensues, Mr. Drabble dies helping Maura escape, and Jenkins dies trying to find Hamlyn. For complicated reasons, the police throw Mr. Clemspool and Albert out of the country as undesirable immigrants. Laurence recovers his money, pays for Mr. Drabble's funeral, and distributes most of the rest of the money to his friends, reserving a small amount for himself to travel to the California goldfields along with Mr. Grout and Nathaniel. Like its predecessor, the book is long (about 400 pages, for a total for the two books of about 700 pages), fast-moving, and consistently entertaining. The plot is spun out with admirable invention and intricacy, and most characters get what they deserve as befits the genre, Mr. Drabble being an obvious exception. Some character development occurs with Mr. Grout and Mr. Drabble and especially with Laurence, who reveals greater pluck, resource, and moral resolve as his vicissitudes increase. An interesting aspect concerns the friendship between Patrick and Laurence, which almost founders when the Irish boy discovers the English boy's true identity as the son of the lord whose agent has thrown the O'Connells out of their home. Thus, Laurence's giving the stolen money to the O'Connells seems appropriate. Vivid, sensory word pictures illuminate life aboard ship and conditions in the mills, and the ranting sermons that Jenkins delivers against the immigrants connect ironically with socioeconomic matters of the late twentieth century. ALA.

BILLINGSLEY, FRANNY (1954–), raised in Chicago, where she currently lives with her husband and two children and is employed as a bookseller. She quit practicing law in 1983 and moved to Barcelona, Spain, where she began to write. Her first novel was *Well Wished** (Atheneum, 1997), a fantasy about a magic well. This was followed by another folkloric fantasy, *The Folk Keeper** (Atheneum, 1999), which was inspired by the Scottish ballads that her father sang. Both books were cited by *School Library Journal*.

BILLY (French*, Albert, Viking, 1993), period novel set in Deep South Banes County, Mississippi, from August 21, 1937, to February 28, 1938, involving murder and racial strife. On Saturday afternoon, two African-American boys, slender, quick, hot-tempered Billy Lee Turner, 10, and his slower, more timid chum, Gumpy (Roy) Thomas, 12, are poking around by the Catfish River and pick their way over to the pond that belongs to the white Pasko family. Redhaired, willful, tomboy Lori Pasko, 15, and her less aggressive, compliant cousin, Jenny, observe them in the pond and accost them, all the time yelling racial epithets at them. The stronger Gumpy gets away and flees, but Lori badly beats Billy, who pulls his small folding knife and plunges it into her ribs. The girl's death galvanizes the surrounding white community, which at first thinks that drifters were responsible for the deed and then, learning that the killer is a local black, fears a black uprising. The death also arouses fear among the blacks, some of whom can remember really bad times with the whites in the past. Sheriff* Tom, who to his credit attempts to maintain rule of law, his deputy, Cecil Hill, and other white men invade Patch, the black area, take Gumpy prisoner, and use dogs to track down Billy, who is hiding with Cinder, his mother, in the swamp in back of Patch. The Patch blacks are subjected to much verbal and some physical abuse, a house is burned, and the terrified boys are jailed. Reverend Sims, the black preacher, warns his congregation that "bad days are here." Although the Sheriff shows some small compassion, the boys are assumed to be guilty. As they are taken to the courthouse on the day of their arraignment, they are attacked and badly roughed up by townspeople, an incident that graphically depicts the intensity of white emotion. The local prosecutor handles the state's case, while aging Wilbur Braxton* is assigned to defend the boys. Gumpy is convicted of second-degree murder and sent to a juvenile prison camp, where he will serve until he is old enough to be sent to the men's camp. Braxton's plea that Billy is just a child and could not be aware of the potential seriousness of his deed is rejected. Billy, who has described how he stabbed the girl while she was beating him, is sentenced to be executed and taken to the state prison at Hattiesburg. During the months that he is on death row, he is surrounded by, but not physically intermingled with, assorted adult male murderers, among them a homosexual who propositions the boy even on his last night. Billy is befriended by a huge black prisoner, Sack Man, and the prison chaplain, Wilson Wagner, who shows true compassion. The execution, which occurs on the last day of February, is morbidly graphic and inhumane as described, the officials brutally carrying out orders. Occasionally, the narrative lapses into inept melodrama and purple passages, and the book cannot claim strength of plot, which is predictable, or characterization, since most figures are one-dimensional or types. Its grip on intellect and emotions arises from careful juxtaposing of white and black characters and specific scenes to point up racial attitudes. The very predictability of the action and the representative nature of the characters also set into stark relief the division between the races. The never-named narrator uses unschooled diction, and shifts from past to present tense heighten the drama. Certain scenes, like the search and the execution, are starkly memorable, and racial epithets, earthy language, and sexual references and innuendo appear frequently, much of it gratuitous. The conclusion is pessimistic. When, near the end, the black town handyman, Shorty, who has hitherto moved freely between white and black sectors, says that "things ain't never gonna be the same agins" and that "even them good white folks done change their ways," the reader knows that he is summarizing attitudes between the races for a long time to come and is prepared for the book's dismal last line: "Mississippi's sky stayed dark." ALA; SLJ.

BILLY (Roybal*, Laura, Houghton, 1994), psychological problem novel of a boy kidnapped by a father and the difficult adjustment of the boy when he is returned to his adoptive parents six years later. Billy Melendez, 16, nicknamed

Coyote, has a good life with his father, an ex-rodeo rider, near Monte Verde, New Mexico, where they live in a rough, but adequate, house up the canyon, across from the bar and general store owned by Sal Delgardo. Sal lets the boy practice calf roping with his horse and stock. Billy has friends, mostly Spanish Americans like him, a girlfriend, Dana Rodriguez, whom he is crazy about, and a good deal of independence, though he is expected to share the work around the place. After a ruckus at a dance, Billy and his friends are all arrested. Through his fingerprints, the officers discover that Billy is really William James Campbell, missing for six years from Davenport, Iowa. His father, Bill Melendez, is arrested, and Billy is held until the arrival of Dave Campbell, the man whom he considered his father for the first ten years of his life. The local marshal, Charlie Silva, an old friend, intervenes to make a deal with state authorities: Bill Melendez will not be charged with the kidnapping if Billy will return, without protest, to Iowa with Dave and have no communication again with his real father by letter or phone. The horrifying situation brings back the original kidnapping, six years earlier, which Billy has tried to erase from his mind. In italicized passages he relives that episode, the man whom he has known as "Jim" who volunteers to drive him home from Little League when he has been knocked out, the awakening in a strange motel, the weeks and months after that when they travel the rodeo circuit where his father's friends, thinking that he is a disturbed child rejected by foster parents, watch that he doesn't run away. Most of all, he is pained to recall his despair when he tries to phone his home in Iowa, only to learn that the number has been discontinued, and later when a letter that he writes is returned marked, "Not at this address." He has always known that his birth mother is his "aunt," Margaret Jane Trevor, and that Mrs. Campbell, the woman whom he thinks of as his mother, is her older sister. His father has told him that the Campbells took him out of a sense of obligation and that they probably moved away as soon as possible so he couldn't find them again. With the return of the letter, he has believed this. After an accident ended Bill Melendez's rodeo career, they moved to the canyon cabin near Monte Verde, and Billy has settled into the rough, but satisfying life of the Spanish-American community. Now, reunited with Dave Campbell, he is disoriented and deeply resentful of the way that he is whisked away from his father and all his friends without a chance to say good-bye. On the drive back to Des Moines, where the Campbells now live, he is sullen and uncommunicative. Momentarily, he is happy to see his mother and his sister, Cecilia, who is less than a year older than he is, but he feels no emotional connection to Dave Campbell. In the next weeks he continually runs afoul of the restrictive rules of the household, so different from the independent, hardworking life that he has known. Cecilia is the only one who acts normal to him, and she is mostly interested in television and visits to the mall, both of which he finds boring. At school he is an outsider, treated as a freak because he wears western clothes. His letters to Dana are not answered. Charlie sends him boxes of his possessions, including his rifle, which upsets the family, and his beautiful saddle, which the Campbells think is very strange and out of place. At school he makes one friend, a girl to whom he talks because her name appears on the attendance list mistakenly as Dana Rodriguez. Her real name is Diana, but he likes her. Dave Campbell disapproves, has him sent to an insensitive school counselor, and, without telling him, sells the truck that Billy left in New Mexico, into which he poured many hours of hard labor. He also sets unreasonable, rigid rules. Their disagreements culminate on the night of the school dance, when Billy gets home fifteen minutes after the curfew that Dave has set. His nerves raw from the explosion that follows, Billy punches another student at school and is expelled. In the family discussion later he and Dave finally air their misconceptions about each other and begin to reach some understanding. Dave gets Billy accepted back into school and finds him a part-time job at a riding stable. Billy looks forward to returning to New Mexico when he is eighteen and can reunite with his Melendez father before starting college. Although the ending is intended to show Billy's acceptance of life in Iowa and his Campbell family, the emotional impact of the novel is all on the side of his life in New Mexico. Even though Bill Melendez was clearly wrong to kidnap him, he has a much healthier relationship with the boy than Dave Campbell's tight-lipped insistence on discipline. Billy's best qualities are attributable to his independent life in the Southwest, and his fury at being treated like a naughty ten-year-old is a powerful element in the book. Cecilia is important only as a contrast, and the mother is a shadowy, unconvincing character. ALA; SLJ.

BILLY DAVIS (*Under the Blood-Red Sun**), the haole (white American) best friend of Japanese-American Tomi Nakaji. Staunch and loyal, Billy shares Tomi's love for baseball, and the two often practice together, Tomi catching Billy's fastballs and sharp curves. An ace pitcher, Billy's ambition is to join the New York Yankees. Although Billy's brother, Jake, is friends with Keet Wilson, the bully on whose family's land the Nakaji shack stands, Billy has no use for Keet (Billy's foil) and consoles Tomi when Keet mistreats him. Billy's father often takes the two boys to school in his car, Billy's mother, a nurse, also keeps a helpful eye on the Nakaji family, and all the Davises are a support to the Nakajis in the critical times after the bombing of Pearl Harbor. The Davises represent unprejudiced Americans during World War II.

BILLY WASHINGTON (*Beggars and Choosers**), 68, a Liver who remembers the times before donkey politicians bought votes by providing everything that people need, thereby doing away with productive work. A widower, Billy is crazy about ample, black Annie Francy and her skinny, highly intelligent daughter, Lizzie*. When Lizzie is very ill and the medunit, the medical robot, has broken down, Billy is so distraught that he brings Diana* Covington, who is using the name Vicki Turner, to Annie's apartment, simply because he can see despite her disguise that she is a donkey, and he hopes she has some medical skill. Even though Annie is suspicious, Billy is more open to "Dr. Turner's" interest in the child, but he is determined not to lead her to Eden, the secret laboratory of the Super-Sleepless, which he knows is in the woods. After the trains have broken down and the town is starving, he goes with a group of men through the snow to the next town to beg food and bring it back, an ill-fated mission on which they are attacked and robbed by young thugs, and he is injured. When Lizzie becomes deathly ill from some genemod virus manufactured by hate groups and spread by rodents and small animals, Billy reverses his decision about Eden and leads Vicki Turner, who carries Lizzie, and Annie there. Miranda* Sharifi injects them all with a serum that cleans their cells of all harmful elements and alters their metabolism so they can absorb nutrients from mud. Restored to youthful vigor by the serum, Billy becomes Annie's lover. Simple but wise, Billy embodies the best of Liver possibilities in his compassion and his devotion to Annie and Lizzie.

BINSTOCK, R. C. (1958–), born in Topeka, Kansas; novelist, short story writer, and technical writer in the computer industry in Massachusetts and California. He earned an A.B. degree from Harvard University in 1980 and has made his home in Cambridge, Massachusetts. Both his story collection, *The Light of Home* (Atheneum, 1992), and his novel set during the Japanese invasion of China in the 1930s, *Tree of Heaven** (Soho Press, 1995), achieved critical acclaim.

BJ VAUGHAN (*The Magic and the Healing**), veterinary student on large-animal service with Dr. Sugar* Dobbs, who helps to heal the creatures in Crossroads* and break the power of the evil forces of Morgan. BJ is recognized as an intelligent and conscientious student, but having just learned that her mother has committed suicide, she fails small-animal rounds with Dr. Truelove and is told she must repeat the course in order to graduate. Helping Dr. Dobbs in Crossroads restores her self-confidence, and she is able to retake the small-animal course and graduate. Her personal problem stays with her throughout most of the book, however. Her mother was suffering from Huntington's Chorea, a degenerative nerve disease, when she died, and BJ fears that she has inherited it. As she works in Crossroads, she notices that her clumsiness, what she has taken as a sign of the disease, is subsiding, and at the end she tests negative for the disorder. BJ's physical problem and the resulting emotional concerns are worked well into the plot.

BLACKWOOD, GARY L., playwright, amateur actor, and author of fiction and nonfiction for middle-grade readers and young adults. He grew up in rural Pennsylvania, where he attended one of the last one-room schoolhouses in the state. In his early teens, he began submitting stories to magazines and sold his first one when he was nineteen. Since then, he has published numerous stories and articles in journals and magazines and a dozen and a half novels and nonfiction books, in addition to having six stage plays produced. His nonfiction writings include *Life on the Oregon Trail* (Lucent, 1999), *Alien Astronauts*, and *Fatal Forebodings* (both Benchmark, 1999). Among his novels are *Wild Timothy* (Atheneum, 1987), about a father and son on a camping trip, which was recommended for reluctant readers by the American Library Association; *Beyond the Door* (Atheneum, 1991), an alternative-world fantasy; *Moonshine* (Cavendish, 1999), set in the Ozarks during the Great Depression; and *The Shakespeare Stealer** (Dutton, 1998), about the theater at the time of Shakespeare, which was cited by both the ALA and *School Library Journal*. He lives with his wife and daughter near Carthage, Missouri.

BLIND BENNY (*Belle Prater's Boy**), a man born with "hardly no eyes a'tall," who picks through the trash at night and collects discards that people leave for him on their porches. Woodrow Prater has made friends with Benny and brings him to Gypsy Leemaster's window while she is ill with measles. Later they walk with him one night, and he tells her that her birth father, Amos Leemaster, was his friend from their Kentucky community across the mountain where he was a sin-eater, a person in a backwoods area who is assigned to eat the food spread out on a coffin, where it absorbs the sins, leaving the newly dead and traveling to the eater. Amos had told him that this was superstitious nonsense, taken him to Coal Station, and given him a room above his hardware store, a commitment that Gypsy's mother, Love Leemaster Dotson, still honors. Blind Benny has a lovely voice and sings as he scavenges in the trash. Although he functions to illustrate the good side of Amos' ambiguous character, he is not a very believable figure.

BLOOD AND CHOCOLATE (Klause*, Annette Curtis, Delacorte, 1997), contemporary fantasy novel of werewolves and magic set from May to September in the town of Riverview, Maryland. Tall, tawny-haired, golden-skinned, exotically beautiful Vivian Gandillon, 16, can assume wolf form. She is often on the outs with her mother, Esme, widowed a year earlier when Vivian's father, Ivan, the pack leader, was killed in a fire set by angry townspeople in West Virginia. She is embarrassed that Esme is dating Gabriel*, a strong, handsome, self-assured man of 24, sixteen years Esme's junior, for whose affections Astrid, another pack member, is Esme's rival. Vivian worries about the future of the pack, now that they no longer have Ivan to make them obey the Law of the pack. She knows that adhering to the Law guarantees them protection through emphasizing the prohibition against revealing their identities and harming humans. Although every member of the Five, the only males her age in the pack, would eagerly mate with her, she yearns for more mature companionship and love. She thinks that she finds it in human Aiden* Teague and sets out to win him away from one of the girls in the Amoeba, the term by which the group of high school students with whom he runs call themselves. She and Aiden have good times together and hug and kiss with increasing passion. She "smarts off" at Esme when her mother repeats the pack's rule: "Don't date if you can't mate," a reminder that werewolves and humans are biologically incompatible. Her mother's words also bring up the unwelcome possibility that if Aiden discovers her real nature, he may react adversely, and the pack will be forced to leave, a clear foreshadowing of what transpires. Tension builds relentlessly after a full moon, the time during which werewolves cannot avoid changing into wolf form. The pack decides to choose another leader by Ordeal, the age-old way in which the adults contend physically. Gabriel emerges the victor and claims Vivian as queen, a position that the girl angrily refuses. Madly in love with Aiden, Vivian decides to "change" for him, that is, show him her wolf form, certain that he loves her enough to want to revel in her true nature, particularly during love-making, at which the wolves are far more passionate than humans. Aiden's revulsion for her is so strong, however, that she flees in terror, then is horrified to discover the next morning that she and her clothing are bloodstained. She believes that she has harmed him and possibly another human who has been found slain. Events so fall out that she is accused of that and still another killing in an anonymous phone call to police, murders for which Gabriel falsely provides her with an alibi. In the rushed, melodramatic conclusion, Aiden tries to kill her, and other humans die. Gabriel deals with Astrid, who has inspired the killings. Vivian decides to take her own life lest she be responsible for more deaths but is shot and trapped in her partially changed form. She is released from this terrible intermediate state by Gabriel's declaration of love and claim on her as his mate and queen. In the final, torrid love scene, the blood from his bites gives her the sensation of comforting chocolate, an allusion to *Steppenwolf.* Plot and atmosphere dominate the book, and most elements for determining the outcome lie on the surface. The many details of werewolf culture early capture the attention; they are clearly the book's best attribute. The wolves have a history, a mythology, a well-defined Law, and a pack sensibility well contrasted with that of the human young people. The writer never allows the reader to forget that Vivian and her kind have wolf instincts, motivations held in check by the wisdom of the Law, and also cleverly shows similar behaviors among the human Amoeba pack. Trash talk makes the book contemporary, and the sensory diction, both groups' keen awareness of their sexuality, and sexually explicit dialogue and inward thoughts produce an extremely erotic tone. In spite of the overabundance of sensationalism, the book raises serious questions concerning loyalty and responsibility to self and group. Quotations from Rudyard Kipling and Herman Hesse appear in the epigraph. SLJ.

BLOOR, EDWARD (1950–   ), born in Trenton, New Jersey; novelist, teacher, editor. He received his B.A. degree from Fordham University in 1973 and has taught middle school and high school in Winter Garden, Florida, where he has made his home. Since 1986 he has been a senior editor at Harcourt Brace School Publications in Orlando, Florida. Like the protagonist of his novel, *Tangerine**, (Harcourt, 1997), he is a soccer player.

BLUE (*Confess-O-Rama**), one of the art students at West Paradise High School with whom Tony Candelaria, the narrator, becomes friends. Blue's art, which wins prizes, goes on the wall. He wears only blue clothes, but not by choice. He is one of six children, each of whom has a color to make laundry easier for their mother. Blue encourages Jordan Archer to continue her kind of art and urges that Tony indulge her to keep her happy and hence a better artist. Blue is an engaging figure who pops in and out of the story, one of the many likable eccentrics who people the novel.

BOBBY YATES (*Tiger, Tiger, Burning Bright**), young rancher near Norbu, California. Since his spread is doing poorly, Bobby feels inferior to his hard-driving father, now disabled from a stroke, and hopes to restore the ranch to prosperity by persuading his neighbors to raise ostriches, which he sells. He also surreptitiously conducts big-game hunts for trophy seekers with old, pro-tected animals like the ancient tiger that Pappy* discovers in the Yates barn. Bobby stages, with great difficulty, an ostrich race down Norbu's main drag, in which the ostriches, Venus, Solomon, Diamond Lil, and Big Bad John, refuse to cooperate. Big Bad John even turns on Bobby and chases him down the street, all the while nipping at Bobby's backside. Jesse's mother, Bonnie, has no use for Bobby. A chiropractor, she relieved the pain of his sciatica, in return for which, she complains, "he stiffs me for four hundred and sixty-five dollars." She calls Bobby a "snake-oil salesman." When Pappy goes to Bobby's ranch to collect the IOU that Bobby gave him gambling, Pappy discovers the tiger in Bobby's barn.

BOGGS' END (*Mr. Was**), home of Jack Lund's Grandfather Skoro. It is a large house on a bluff, set apart from the town of Memory, Minnesota, and had been empty for some time when he bought it in the 1940s. Earlier it had been owned by Pincus Q. Boggs. In 1927 Boggs, his wife, and two children disap-peared, presumably back to the 1880s, since the time-slip door in the third-floor closet seems to work in segments of about fifty years. In the end the house burns down, destroying the passage into other time periods.

THE BOMB (Taylor*, Theodore, Harcourt, 1995), historical novel about the testing of the atomic bomb on Bikini Atoll of the Marshall Islands in 1946 and the events leading up to this disaster. The action starts in late March 1944, when Bikini, the northernmost atoll of the Ralik chain, is still held by Japanese soldiers as a weather observation station. The Micronesian people of Bikini have suffered under the occupation and are delighted when Americans in fighter planes machine-gun the weather station and three days later arrive in landing craft, only to discover that the Japanese defenders have committed mass suicide rather than be captured. Although their concept of the war is vague, Sorry Rinamu, 14, and all his family, including his mother, Ruta, his sister, Lokileni, 11, and his grand-father, Jonjen, have heard good things about Americans, and the first soldiers to arrive fulfill their hopes, acting friendly and allowing their chief, Juda, to distribute the food and equipment from the weather station to the villagers. Their teacher, Tara Malolo, who has been educated in a missionary college, has more understanding of the international picture, but not until the arrival by outrigger canoe of Sorry's uncle, Abram Makaoliej, who has served in the merchant marine and jumped ship, do they begin to follow the progress of the war, since he can speak English and understand the broadcasts that he picks up on the radio left by the Japanese. The islanders, therefore, are aware of the dropping of the atomic bombs on Hiroshima and Nagasaki and of the end of the war. Sorry, whose father was lost, probably killed by a shark on the barrier reef, bonds with his young, attractive uncle, and Tara and Abram develop a mutual attraction. Ruta worries that her brother has come home to die, in the island tradition, and he is observed taking pills, but he does not seem ill and remains active for some time. Early in 1946 a naval ship anchors in the lagoon, and the men begin to take soundings and blow up the coral heads, making the lagoon into a harbor. Eventually, they tell the people of Bikini that their atoll has been chosen for further bomb tests and that they will be removed to another island of their choice. Sorry, who has become a member of the council to replace his father, is chosen to accompany Chief Juda, Abram, and a couple of other council members to be flown in a four-engine aircraft in search of a new home. Because they have stipulated that their new island must not be inhabited, they tentatively choose Rongerik, but Chief Juda is so airsick that he will not even let them land and agrees to the island over the protests of Abram. The other islanders feel that they must honor their chief's choice and are philosophical, having been assured by the navy men that they will be able to return in two years. Abram is deeply suspicious of the whole enterprise and works out a protest. He takes Sorry with him to beg red paint from one of the navy vessels and, suffering from a heart attack on the way back, dies, but first he is able to tell the boy of his plan, to paint his canoe and sail red and to return to the lagoon on the morning of the test. Sorry and Lokileni become the unofficial guides to a scientist, Dr. John Garrison, who is collecting specimens of wildlife for comparison to determine the effects of radiation after the dropping of the test bomb. What they learn from him disturbs Sorry further. Newsreel crews descend on Bikini, making films claiming that the happy villagers are leaving willingly and being provided excellent accommodations for their new home. With the rest of the village, Sorry is removed to Rongerik, but he has already decided to carry out Abram's protest. When he lets Tara know, she insists on going with him, and Jonjen, a very religious man, joins them because "someone has to be there to pray." They sail to an island near Bikini and in the night before the test raise their red sail and move into the lagoon early in the morning. Their protest is futile, however, since they are not seen and the countdown to the bomb dropping has already started. An epilogue tells of the near starvation of the group on Rongerik and the disastrous return to Bikini in 1969 of some of the islanders, who are poisoned by radioactive material in the sand. Each chapter is preceded by a brief factual paragraph about the development of the bomb and the blind and insensitive plans for the bomb tests. While the whole history of Bikini Atoll is a powerful indictment of government atomic policy, the book is so clearly written to thesis that it lacks the compelling involvement for the reader found in good fiction. Sorry is pictured as a boy who has curiosity about the outside world and is potentially interesting, but the other characters are clearly chosen to illustrate various attitudes, and the result seems contrived. O'Dell.

BO MICHAELSON (*Flyers**), Gabe Riley's best friend and classmate, the producer of the films that Gabe writes and that they shoot together. Bo's father is an easygoing, absent-minded writer of books for children, and his mother is a formal, meticulous high school English teacher. Both are devotees of Transcendental Meditation and are determined to master the art of levitation and become *sidhas*, or flyers. Bo also meditates regularly, hoping that some day he, too, will be able to fly like the masters whose works he reads. Unlike diffident Gabe, Bo is a school leader, easy around girls and in large groups. He is also a good schoolboy painter, whose picture *The Second Flight of Icarus*, based on Breughel's painting, Ethan* Riley cherishes. Gabe has noted that Bo's Icarus is flying without wings, light and airy and happy. At the end of the novel, Gabe sees for the first time that Bo's plowman in the picture is not sinking into the dirt but rather is pulling himself up and out of it and straining to look up at the sky. Gabe sees him as symbolic of all who strive for better lives, that is, seek to become flyers.

THE BONES IN THE CLIFF (Stevenson*, James, Greenwillow, 1995), short, contemporary mystery novel for middle-grade readers set on the small seaside island of Cutlass, probably along the U.S. East Coast. Lonely, shy Pete, 11, the narrator, and Harry, his thin, alcoholic, easily agitated father, move often to avoid being found by a man whom Harry calls Looney Tunes. Since May they have been staying in a green bungalow, where Harry spends most of his time alone drinking. He instructs Pete to meet every ferryboat from the mainland and to phone Harry immediately if he spots a tall, husky man with a wig and a cigar. Pete does not know why Harry fears the man, nor does he know what his father did for a living, but he recalls an incident when his father drove the two of them to a big garage in the Bronx, from which he soon ran out, pursued and beaten by two men. Since then, Harry and Pete have been on the run. In the town souvenir shop one day, a skinny, black-haired, bubble gum-chewing girl about Pete's age strikes up a conversation. She says that her name is Rootie and that she comes every summer with her grandmother. The two become friends and go biking, hiking, and swimming together. Rootie is adventurous, imperious, and filled with ideas for activities. She takes Pete biking on the trail along the cliff to Blackbeard's Cove, where they observe bones protruding from the cliffside. Rootie says they are bones of Indians who died of smallpox and were buried in a mass grave many years before. Most of the episodes, like these, concern the children's activities together, sneaking into the old, abandoned Hyperion Theater and building a tree house called The Ship on Rootie's grandmother's property. Rootie tells Pete that her full name is Rosalie Ann Bowditch, that her parents are divorced, and that she now lives with her grandmother. Pete confides his story—that his mother is in a mental hospital, that he and his father are on the run, and that his father is extremely afraid of the cigar-smoking man. After that, the two children regularly meet the ferry together. One afternoon, while they are outfitting The Ship with items from Mrs. Bowditch's attic, Pete realizes that they have missed the six o'clock boat, races home, and finds his father being threatened by a "big slobby-looking guy" with a gun who he knows must be Looney Tunes. Pete sneaks into the basement for a gun that he knows should be there, makes a noise that attracts the gunman, flees, and races up the ladder into the tree house, Looney Tunes hot on his heels. The flimsy ladder breaks under Looney Tunes, and the man falls, hits his head on a rock, and lies there dead. A month later, after authorities have completed their questioning, Pete leaves with Rootie and Mrs. Bowditch to live with them in Manhattan until arrangements are made for Harry under the witness protection program. Tension grips immediately, as Pete tells the reader about his father's great fear, and escalates throughout. Characters and incidents are stereotypical, but the children's activities, while also typical, are individualized by the location and Rootie's lively imagination. Both children come from dysfunctional, single-parent families and are at the mercy of the adults on whom they depend. The circumstances of Pete's mother's mental illness are never explored, nor is there mention of Pete's having gone to school. The conclusion is open-ended, but since Pete's father is described as very thin and sickly, one wonders whether he will survive being a witness and whether Pete will ever be able to live with him again. The style is crisp, descriptive, and highly visual, and the subject matter is unusual for mysteries for middle graders. In addition to being gripping in its own right, the book shows how children's lives are affected for good or ill by their parents' behavior. The relationship between title and substance is unclear. Poe Nominee.

BONNER, CINDY (1953–   ), born in Corpus Christi, Texas, where she has continued to make her home; novelist with a wide variety of occupations in her background including yoga teacher, computer operator, real estate manager, blues/rock band manager, and co-owner of a wholesale nursery. Her novel *Lily* (Algonquin, 1992) was runner-up for the Western Writers of America award for the Best First Novel of the West. Its sequel, *Looking After Lily** (Algonquin, 1994), is a highly amusing parody of the traditional western.

BORDERTOWN (*Finder**), city on the edge of Elfland in which human runaways, elves, and halflings all congregate. Although it is a concrete place, the route there is not the same for any two people and can start in various parts of the world. To some of its inhabitants it seems to be inland, while others experience it as on the shore of a sea. Time also moves somewhat differently from that of either the World or Elfland. All the inhabitants agree, however, that through it runs a river whose water acts as a dangerously addictive drug on humans. Like any city, it has some upscale areas, like Dragonstooth Hill, populated mostly by pureblood elves, some middle-class areas, a large number of slums, and some dangerous, crime-ridden districts, where rival elf and human gangs often battle. Illusions and various forms of magic are common. The Border to Elfland, which is somewhere just beyond the edge of the city, is closed to humans, though elves can cross at will.

BOSSE, MALCOLM (1933–), born in Detroit, Michigan; professor of English, writer of a large numer of novels for adults and young adults. He received his B.A. degree from Yale in 1950, his M.A. from the University of Michigan in 1956, and his Ph.D. from New York University in 1969. He served in the U.S. Navy from 1950 to 1954 and also in the U.S. Army and Merchant Marine. Starting in 1969, he has been a professor at City College of the City University of New York, and he has been a novelist since 1959. Among his historical novels are *Captives of Time* (Delacorte, 1987), *Deep Dream of the Rain Forest* (Farrar, 1993), and *The Examination** (Farrar, 1994). Also for young people, he has published *The 79 Squares* (Crowell, 1979), *Cave beyond Time* (Crowell, 1980), and *Ordinary Magic* (originally titled *Ganesh*, Crowell, 1981). Bosse has traveled and lectured in India and in much of the Orient.

BRAXTON, WILBUR (*Billy**), aging white attorney assigned by the court to defend the African-American boys Billy and Gumpy. A longtime resident of Banes County, Mississippi, where his father was a major landowner, Braxton is a respected lawyer, known for his patient, humane ways and expertise. He knows that defending the boys will be difficult, probably futile, but accepts the case anyway. He first shows his sense of decency and great humanity by seeking out Cinder, Billy's mother, and promising her that he will do his best, but both know that he will probably fail. He goes beyond duty also in begging the judge to try Billy in juvenile court, a plea that the judge refuses, and at the trial he argues that what happened was a tragedy, not a vicious crime. His questioning of Billy when the boy is on the witness stand is a small masterpiece of appeal to logic and reason. What small triumph he achieves by his skill in this incident is soon negated by the prosecutor's emotionalism.

BROMIOS (*The Arkadians**), slow-witted, crude king of the land of Arkadia who consults the pythoness at Mount Lerna, receives an obscure prophecy that he does not like, and orders that she and her sanctuary be destroyed and that all similar wisewomen and healers be killed. His edict launches a reign of terror in Arkadia. Later the people decide to sacrifice him, but he is saved in the nick of time by Lucian*. His customary attire, before he is to be sacrificed, is a bearskin cloak, a bear's head helmet, and a necklace of bear's teeth and claws. At first he is a very unsympathetic figure, but his misfortunes and desire to be forgiven for his misdeeds redeem him in the eyes of the reader.

BROTHERS AND SISTERS (Campbell*, Bebe Moore, Putnam, 1994), adult, realistic, sociological problem novel set in Los Angeles in the early 1990s just after the Rodney King riots and involving racial and gender discrimination and corporate duplicity. Angel City National Bank intertwines several lives: Esther* Jackson, 34, well-educated, capable, black regional manager; white, blond, diffident Mallory* Post, 36, loan officer, who becomes Esther's friend and confidant; Preston* Sinclair, 53, white, toughly practical, opportunistic bank president; Kirk* Madison, ambitious head of lending operations; Tyrone* Carter, black Western Express deliveryman, who loves Esther; and Humphrey* Boone, suave, intelligent black man hired by Preston for a newly created executive position to promote diversity within the bank's operations. When Preston hires Humphrey for the new initiative, he stimulates emotions and actions that threaten the bank's stability. Kirk, in particular, resents Humphrey and conspires with hard-nosed, manipulative Bailey Reynolds, Preston's hatchet man, to scuttle both Humphrey and Preston. Both Esther and Mallory hope that Kirk can help them to promotions, but the prospect lessens as both Humphrey's and Preston's positions weaken. Humphrey and Preston grow close when Humphrey helps Preston's son, severely injured in an auto accident, out of a depressed mental state, and Preston informs Humphrey that he is grooming him for the presidency. Although both Humphrey and Esther hope that each can help the other, being a "brother" and "sister," and Esther entertains romantic notions about him, Humphrey sees her only as like the black women who have scorned him for his big lips and very dark skin. He makes advances to Mallory, who finds him attractive but refuses him. Kirk, meanwhile, steals from dormant accounts, a shortage blamed on Esther and a young black woman teller, LaKeesha. Humphrey graciously covers for them, and later they are proved innocent. Humphrey resigns under allegations of sexual harassment toward, and attempting to rape, Mallory, the second a charge trumped up by Reynolds and denied by Mallory. Humphrey accepts the presidency of Solid Rock National Bank, an institution newly established by a local minister specifically to help minorities, later to be joined by Esther and LaKeesha. Paralleling this professional plotline are several private-life stories: Esther's on-and-off love affair with Tyrone; Mallory's unfortunate romances with married men; the strong desire of a young Salvadoran teller, Hector Bonilla, to rise in position in order to help his family; LaKeesha's need to provide for her son and her family; Humphrey's need to provide for his family; his internal conflict over his relationship with Mallory; and his guilt over not helping Esther as he thinks a "brother" should. All characters are well drawn, even such minor ones as Vanessa, Esther's perennially optimistic, aspiring-actress friend. Especially well depicted are the lingering sense of racial tensions in the city; the search for love, success, and happiness on the part of all major figures; the slowly growing sense of trust between Esther and Mallory; the hopes and resentments that affirmative action inspires; and the reader's growing realization that all the main players share certain common traits and that these traits make them brothers and sisters in spite of the divisions of color, background, or ambition. At 550 pages, the book is longer and more detailed in emotions and motivations and contains more explicit love scenes than the usual teen fare. SLJ.

BROWN, MARY, author of highly inventive fantasies published in the paperback mass market. Her best-known novels are in a three-book series, starting with *Pigs Don't Fly** (Baen, 1994), a picaresque fantasy set in a preindustrial society peopled by knights, isolated villagers, cutthroat bandits, and talking animals. It is followed by *Master of Many Treasures* (Baen, 1995) and *Dragonne's Eg* (Baen, 1999). Among her other titles are *Strange Deliverance* (Baen, 1997) and *The Unlikely Ones* (Baen, 1999).

BUD, NOT BUDDY (Curtis*, Christopher Paul, Delacorte, 1999), realistic, picaresque period novel set in Michigan in 1936 during the Great Depression. The ten-year-old African-American narrator, smart, imaginative, resourceful, always introduces himself as Bud, not Buddy, Caldwell, since Bud is the name that his mother gave him. Since her death, when he was six, he has lived in an orphanage and a succession of foster homes in Flint. His dearest possessions are his memories of his loving mother and a picture of her as a child on a pony; Bud Caldwell's Rules and Things to Have a Funner Life and Make a Better Liar of Yourself, his memorized maxims for surviving; and a battered, cardboard suitcase holding a tattered blanket, a pouch with mysteriously inscribed rocks, and flyers bearing the picture of the man who he is sure is his father, Herman* E. Calloway, a handsome bass player and leader of a famous band, the Dusky Devastators of the Depression!!!!!! He runs away from his latest foster family, the cruel Amoses, and encounters a wide variety of people before he connects with Herman E. Calloway in Grand Rapids. He meets Bugs, another runaway orphan, with whom he becomes brothers by exchanging slob (spit) and with whom he almost hops a freight to Chicago; a family at a mission soup kitchen who pretend that he is their son so that he can get food; the library lady who shows him the atlas whereby he learns the route to Grand Rapids; a girl his age, Deza Malone, at the Hooverville shantytown outside Flint, who feeds him and gives him his first kiss; and Mr.* Lefty Lewis, a kind, grandfatherly gentleman who takes him home and then takes him to Grand Rapids, where the band is currently playing. Herman E. Calloway, the bassist and leader, who is older than Bud expected, disavows him, but the band members (Jimmy on horn, Thug Tennant on drums, Steady Eddie on sax, Chug Cross on trombone, and the only white man in the band, Dirty Deed Breed, on piano) soon develop a joking relationship with him and give him a recorder to play, a "professional name," Sleepy LaBone, and a room to sleep in. The beautiful vocalist, Miss Grace Thomas, is kind and motherly. When Bud shows Calloway the inscribed rocks, tells him his momma's name was Angela Janet, and shows him a childhood picture of her, Calloway grudgingly acknowledges him as, what the reader has suspected, his grandson, the son of his estranged daughter. Calloway was accustomed to giving his daughter inscribed rocks as tokens of his various gigs. At the end, the boys in the band give Bud an old saxophone to learn on, and he knows he now has a future, possibly as a musician if he works hard, and, what is more important, he has a home and family. Although the general plot and conclusion are what readers familiar with orphan stories expect, scenes have force: Bud imprisoned in the Amoses' shed, where he is terrified by what he thinks is a vampire bat hanging from the roof; life in Hooverville shantytown, which is viciously raided by Flint police; the warm and loving home life of Mr. Lewis' daughter; and Bud's sleeping under trees in his tattered blanket and suppressing his hunger. Bud employs unschooled, colloquial speech for the most part, which often seems forced, with such expressions as "writ," "ruint," "re-memorized," and "shucks" that recall Tom Sawyer. Since Bud tells the story in retrospect but is not writing it, the frequent comma splices are troublesome and unjustified and inhibit the flow. Bud is an attractive figure, plucky, tough, a survival sort, and the other major characters are plausibly drawn. Although the book is often poignant, there is a good deal of humor, mostly arising out of Bud's naive and melodramatic attitude and observations. References to people of the times, like Pretty Boy Floyd and J. Edgar Hoover, and to Great Depression economic difficulties, union movements, and such special problems that confronted black Americans at the time—limited job opportunities and laws against blacks' owning land—give a view of the period. To circumvent restrictions on landholding, for example, Herman E. Calloway always has a white man in his band, this time Dirty Deed Breed, to sign deeds and the like for him. C. S. King Winner; Newbery Winner; SLJ.

THE BUFFALO TREE (Rapp*, Adam, Front Street Books, 1997), realistic novel set in a brutal juvenile reform school, evidently in Illinois. The narrator, who goes by his last name, Sura, 12, has been arrested for "clipping hoodies," cutting hood decorations off expensive cars like Lincolns and Mercedes Benzes, for which there is an underground market, an activity at which he is especially good because he is a speedy runner. Although small and one of the few white boys at Hamstock Boys Center, he makes his way by being quick and by paying off the extortionist bullies, Boo Boxfort and Hodge, who dominate with the implicit approval of Mr. Rose, houseparent for Spalding Cottage, and the school dean, Mr. Petty, who beats the weaker boys with a heavy paddle until they bleed. In the yard at Hamstock is a dead tree with branches sticking up like a hand, referred to as the buffalo tree. One of the bullies' practices is to force a boy to climb the tree and sit in the branches while all the others watch, a sign of their dominance. Sura and his "patch" mate, Coly Jo, take turns sleeping so that Boo and Hodge won't steal from their room. Besides his growing affection for fat, slow Coly Jo, Sura is sustained by occasional visits from his mother, Mazzy, who has a new man named Flintlock, and a map, given him by a "juvy" who at sixteen has been sent to St. Chuck's (St. Charles), a facility for older offenders. The map shows an abandoned shed some three miles from Hamstock where he might hide out if he can escape. Flintlock, Mazzy tells him, owns a house and is fixing up a room for Sura when he gets out in four months, but looking ahead four months seem like a lifetime. When Coly Jo, accused of a vicious attack on another juvy really done by Boo and Hodge, goes berserk and hits Mr. Rose with a rickety side table, he is given three weeks in the Stink Hole, an unprecedented solitary punishment, and Sura gets a new patch mate, a white boy called Long Neck, who steals his clothes and, eventually, his map and breaks out. When Coly Jo is let out of the Stink Hole, he is almost catatonic, and he is put in an isolation room. Sura sneaks up at night, learns that Coly Jo is to be sent to St. Chuck's, and tries to persuade him to make a break that night, but Coly Jo is unable to focus, and Sura just sits holding his hand and patting his head. The next morning Coly Jo is found at the foot of the buffalo tree, frozen and broken, having dived off after leaving his clothes high in the dead branches. Sura is interrogated about Long Neck, and when he won't give any information, he is badly beaten. All he really knows about Long Neck is that his father blinded him in one eye with a kick, and he has sworn that when he gets out, he will shoot the man with a homemade gun that he has. Stunned by Coly Jo's suicide, Sura walks through the rest of his time at Hamstock in a daze. As he is being released, Dean Petty tells him that they found Long Neck, who tried to kill his father but blew his own hand to bits when his gun exploded and is now in maximum security at Cairo. Well away from Hamstock, Sura smiles at the picture of Dean Petty's pretty, blond daughter, which he has stolen from the man's desk. Before he goes home, he retrieves his bag of hoodies that he stashed before he was arrested and goes around taping them back onto the cars from which they came. This last bit seems highly unrealistic, but the novel as a whole is a convincing, if horrifying, picture of the juvenile reform system, all narrated in a street jargon that is at first difficult to penetrate but is very effective in showing all the action from the point of view of an essentially harmless victim. SLJ.

BULL, EMMA (1954–), born in Torrance, California; science-fantasy novelist, composer and singer with rock and blues bands, and co-owner of Steel-Dragon Press, which specializes in science fiction. She was graduated from Beloit College in 1976 and in 1981 married Will Shetterly, a well-known science fiction writer who, along with some other fantasy writers, has set various novels in Bordertown, an area between the World and Elfland, which is the setting for *Finder** (Tor, 1994). Among Bull's other novels is *War for the Oaks* (Ace/Berkley, 1987). She makes her home in Minneapolis, Minnesota.

BUNTING, (ANNE) EVE(LYN BOLTON) (1928–), born in Maghera, Northern Ireland; prolific author of both fiction and nonfiction for children and young people. Like the protagonist of *Spying on Miss Muller** (Clarion, 1995), Bunting attended a wartime boarding school in Ireland, an experience that contributed many authentic details to the novel. For earlier biographical information and title entries, see *Dictionary, 1985–1989* [*Is Anybody There?*] and *Dictionary, 1990–1994* [*Coffin on a Case*; *Our Sixth-Grade Sugar Babies*].

BUTLER (*The Cage**), naturalist on the Arctic expedition to advise the group about polar bears and write the article to accompany the pictures. A large, athletic man who never tells them his first name, he is confident of his own body and scornful of David* Golding for his small physique and because David is gay. Given to making rather crude remarks and putting his hands on Beryl* Findham, Butler makes her uncomfortable, and he is baffled and annoyed when she chooses Jean-Claude* Thibedeaux for a lover. Although he has insisted on the shortcut across the inlet that nearly kills them all, he shows his bravery and fortitude by rescuing both Beryl and David from the hole in the ice and supporting David the rest of the way across the ice. A day later, he is attacked and killed by a bear as they are packing the sled, and Beryl and Jean-Claude escape while his body is being eaten.

BUTLER, OCTAVIA E(STELLE) (1947–   ), born in Pasadena, California; noted for her novels and short stories of science fiction and fantasy that explore the effects of race and sex in futuristic societies. One of the few African-American writers to work in these genres, she has received prestigious honors such as the Hugo and the Nebula awards. After taking her associate of arts degree from Pasadena City College, she attended California State University and the University of California. She has been a freelance writer since 1970 and makes her home in Los Angeles. *Parable of the Sower** (Warner, 1995) and its sequel, *Parable of the Talents* (Seven Stories, 1998), focus on a strong black woman in a United States experiencing tremendous economic and social stresses. Her four "Patternists" novels concern telepaths: *Patternmaster* (Doubleday, 1976), *Mind of My Mind* (Doubleday, 1977), *Survivor* (Doubleday, 1978), and *Wild Seed* (Doubleday, 1980). Three in the "Xenogenesis" series involve aliens: *Dawn* (Warner, 1987), *Adulthood Rites* (Warner, 1988), and *Imago* (Warner, 1989). *Blood Child, and Other Stories* (Four Walls, 1995) is also highly regarded.

BUTTE WHIPPLE (*The Ballad of Lucy Whipple**), younger brother of California Morning (Lucy) Whipple, ten years old when they arrive at Lucky Diggins. A lively boy, he loves the rough, free life from the first and soon starts earning money sweeping out the saloon and fetching and carrying for the prospectors. For a while he is part of Lucy's pie-making business, since he is better at hiking around to the various claims to sell the pies that she makes, but he soon becomes too busy with his other interests. At one point, when their mother decides that he needs some book learning, Lucy tries to educate him, but he insists that he doesn't need her instruction, since he already knows forty-eight words for liquor (his ambition is to reach fifty), and, anyway, he plans to become a sea captain. During his long illness after he has been swept into the river, he talks to Lucy about dying. Just before he closes his eyes for the last time, he thinks up the forty-ninth word, and Lucy writes a fiftieth on a slip of paper to drop into his grave. In her letter explaining to her mother that she plans to stay in Lucky Diggins, she tells how she planted bulbs on Butte's grave and gave him his fifty-first word, antifogmatic, acquired from the hard-rock mining company representative.

BYRON (BY) WATSON (*The Watsons Go to Birmingham—1963**), at thirteen, the older brother of Kenny Watson and Joetta Watson. A bully, roughneck, and general troublemaker, By is the main reason that the African-American Watsons travel to Birmingham, Alabama, in the late summer of 1963 and become involved in the historical racist bombing of the local Baptist church. His parents are fed up with his skipping school, lighting fires, stealing change from Momma's purse, starting fights, joining a gang, and perpetrating various misfeasances. They decide that what he needs is a good dose of Granma Sands, who is a stickler for protocol and will tolerate no insubordination. Although mean, ornery, and sassy, Byron has a good side, which comes out at the end of book, perhaps too abruptly. In Alabama, he stays with sharp-tongued Grandma and with no-nonsense Mr. Robert, Grandma's friend, and for the first time begins to behave like a young man of a good family instead of the hoodlum Kenny reports he is. With Joetta's help, he saves Kenny's life from the whirlpool and later persuades Kenny that he was a great help to Joetta when the church was bombed, although the speeches that Byron delivers to cheer Kenny out of his despondency are too uncharacteristically articulate and moralistic. Not entirely credible as a character, Byron is still the most interesting figure in the book.

C

THE CAGE (Schulman*, Audrey, Algonquin, 1994), riveting adventure novel of a doomed contemporary Arctic expedition to photograph polar bears near Churchill, Manitoba, at the edge of Hudson Bay. Beryl* Findham, 29, whose professional expertise is in photographing small animals, accepts an assignment for *Natural Photography* intended to catch the bears in the fall as they wait for the ice to freeze so they can move out to stalk the seals that form the major part of their diet. In the meantime, they are near starvation, reduced to raiding the town dump and chewing on discarded tires and other rubbish. Beryl has been chosen mostly for her small size, since the plan is for the photographer to crouch in a small cage from which the bears can be filmed close-up, not through a telephoto lens. She practices sitting cross-legged in a cramped closet, about the dimensions of the cage, noting that she will have to keep her hands, feet, and equipment well away from the edges, where the bears can reach their claws and part of their paws between the bars. She flies from Winnipeg to Churchill with two other members of the expedition: David* Golding, an experienced nature photographer, also chosen for his small size, who will do the video filming, and Butler*, whose first name she never learns, a large, athletic naturalist who will write the article to accompany her still pictures. At Churchill they meet their fourth member, Jean-Claude* Thibedeaux, their guide, who, at twenty, already has six years' experience' and is respected for getting some groups out of extremely dangerous situations. A small, very taciturn man, he drives them to the dump every day, where they film bears while they wait for their specially designed vehicle to arrive. Beryl becomes friends with Maggie* Johnson, driver of the bear patrol car, and rides with her several nights, learning from her more about the Arctic and the bears. Before they leave Churchill, two important things occur. Beryl asks Jean-Claude whether her outfit from *Natural Photography* is adequate, and he, pronouncing it all wrong, lends her an Inuit double suit of caribou and wolfskin. One evening when Beryl steps out of the back door of the inn to meet Maggie, she is disoriented by the intense drop in temperature and the swirling snow and, only a few feet from the door, loses her way. Stumbling toward what she hopes will be a building, she comes on a bear mauling Maggie, and she literally crawls under it and butts her head against its testicles. Astonished, it veers off, and both women are able to get into the car. Maggie's injuries are superficial, but Beryl suffers frostbite and has two toes amputated. Still, she is determined to complete the assignment, and when their bus finally arrives, she is ready to go with the others. Their vehicle has been specially designed for the assignment. Its huge tires lift it high to ride over the rough terrain; an auxiliary fuel tank adds to the supply, which should last the whole month that they expect to be in the field; the interior is luxurious, like the most elaborate motor homes, with four bunks, each with closed doors for privacy; and its kitchen is stocked with a wide variety of canned goods. Bears surround them almost immediately. Flares and gunshots do not scare the animals, which have no experience with fire and are used to loud crackings of the ice. To get the cage into position, they have to play a Donny Osmond record, supplied for their leisure entertainment, at top volume through outside speakers. The bears back off slightly, and Beryl is able to enter the cage and lock the door. The plan that looked so good on paper, however, clearly will not work. The cold is so intense that the film cracks. Within a half hour she becomes so cold she can't think clearly. Even ten-minute periods prove too much. David can't stay more than five. The third morning Beryl wakes to disaster. The thermostat will not respond. Investigation proves that the bears, which can walk under the bus, have eaten through the fuel tanks. Efforts to rouse someone on the radio fail. A plane flying over does not respond to their flare. Jean-Claude assembles a five-foot sled that he has brought and gives them each snowshoes, remarking, "I always bring backups." They fashion other sleds from blankets to haul supplies and start the forty miles back to Churchill. On the excruciating trip, David and Butler both die. Jean-Claude and Beryl, by sheer persistence, get to within a couple of miles of Churchill when he collapses, telling her to get help. She staggers on, finally reaching a door and presumably safety. Jean-Claude's fate is unknown. The terrible physical adversity overcome is only part of the story. Conflicts and tensions in the little group make it clear the expedition probably would have failed even if their fuel had not been lost. Told in third person but entirely through Beryl's perceptions, the story is extremely sensory. The devastating cold is so well described that a reader's feet almost go numb. Beryl's reaction to the bears is full of both terror and sensual attraction. She is also attracted to Jean-Claude, with whom she makes love, and repulsed by Butler, who makes crude advances. She gets along better with David, who is gay, but Butler both scorns and fears him. They are all strongly drawn characters. It is ironic but seems inevitable that Beryl, a small woman of quiet stamina, is the only certain survivor. A vividly realistic novel. ALA; SLJ.

CALVERT, PATRICIA (1931–), born in Great Falls, Montana; novelist mainly for young adults, educator, laboratory technician. She received her B.A. degree and did graduate study at Winona State University and worked at the

Mayo Clinic in Rochester, Minnesota, first as a laboratory technician, then in the section of publications. Since 1980 she has published a large number of novels, mostly for young adults, among them *Glennis, Before and After** (Atheneum, 1996), a story of a young teenage girl whose family is broken up when her father is sent to prison for fraud, which won both the Christopher and the Child Study (now the Josette Frank) awards. Among her other recent titles are *Bigger* (Atheneum, 1994), *Sooner* (Atheneum, 1998), and *Michael, Wait for Me* (Atheneum, 2000).

CALVIN WIND SOLDIER (*The Grass Dancer**), decorated hero of the Korean War, husband of Lydia Thunder, father of Harley and Duane, and lover of Evie, Lydia's twin sister. Before leaving for Korea, he has a vision quest in the same pit in which Harley finds purpose in life thirty years later. Returned from Korea and haunted by the war, Calvin suffers from alcoholism, but after he is nearly frozen to death in the snow, overcome by liquor, and saved by Lydia, he stops drinking, becomes a respected member of the tribal police force, and marries Lydia, with whom he is very happy. The vengeful magic of jealous Anna Thunder, Lydia's mother, however, causes him to gravitate to Evie, by whom he fathers Duane. Although it is not clear, Anna probably brings about the auto accident in which both Calvin and Duane are killed. Harley is born after Calvin's death. As is true with most of the men in the book, Calvin is more acted upon than acting.

CAMPBELL, BEBE MOORE (1950–), African-American writer, best known for her fiction and nonfiction for adults, particularly on racism and divorce; former schoolteacher; commentator on National Public Radio; resident of Los Angeles. Her novels include *Your Blues Ain't Like Mine* (Putnam, 1992), about race relations in Mississippi; *Brothers and Sisters** (Putnam, 1994), a *School Library Journal* choice about racism and sexism in the Los Angeles banking world; and *Singing in the Comeback Choir* (Putnam, 1998), about an aging singer who makes a comeback in an unexpected way. *Successful Women, Angry Men: Backlash in the Two-Career Marriage* (Random House, 1986) is nonfiction, while *Sweet Summer: Growing Up with and without My Dad* (Putnam, 1989) is autobiographical. She has also written for radio and contributed to many periodicals. She has received, among other honors, the National Association of Colored People (NAACP) Image Award for outstanding literary work.

THE CANON (*Pope Joan**), cruel, brutal, demanding priest and husband of Gudrun and father of Joan, the protagonist, and her older brothers, Matthew and John. He brought Saxon Gudrun home to his Frankish village from a missionary trip after the Franks ravaged the Saxon lands. He feels no hesitation about beating Gudrun or the children, although he is easier on his sons. He is set against Joan's receiving an education and once whips her senseless because she refuses to obliterate the words from a treasured book given her by the scholar Aesculapius*, as he insists she do. He openly despises Gudrun, since she is foreign, and seems to feel no compunctions about forcing her to have sex with him. He appears to represent the prevailing attitude of the clergy toward women: they should be hardworking; respectful toward men; solicitous, indulgent mothers, in particular toward male children, of whom they should bear many, since girls are, in all other respects, useless; aware that learning is not needed for their lot in life; pious; and ready always to be willing bed partners. The canon dies of a stroke at the monastery in which Joan has been serving, a broken man.

CAPTAIN JOHN STEBBINS (*The 13th Floor: A Ghost Story**), Boston, Massachusetts, ancestor from the late seventeenth century of Buddy and Liz Stebbins of modern San Diego, California. Under the name of Stebbins, the captain is a respected seaman. On the high seas, however, he becomes the infamous Captain John Crackstone, wanted pirate. When Buddy meets him, he is on the way back to Boston on his ship, the *Laughing Mermaid*, fresh from capturing a treasure in jewels from a Grand Moghul in the Red Sea. The Stebbins family "death book" lists him as having been hanged for piracy. Buddy's time-travel experiences indicate, however, that it was Gallows Bird, the pirate who called himself Captain John Crackstone, who was really put to death. The end of the novel leaves open the possibility that Captain Stebbins benefited from his ill-gotten treasure. He buried it on Bedloe's Island, where the Statue of Liberty now stands. Although he no longer possessed the map, which Buddy brought into the twentieth century, he may have returned to the small island on a later voyage and dug up the treasure from memory.

CARLA PERKINS (*Coffee Will Make You Black**), best friend of Jean "Stevie" Stevenson through their last years of junior high and most of high school. Stevie becomes her friend by urging her teacher to let Carla sing in a chorus in her place, realizing how much this would mean to Carla. The gesture seems futile, since they are both excluded from the chorus, but Carla accepts Stevie for the first time. Much the more experienced of the two, Carla is continually urging Stevie into social and sexual situations beyond her depth by saying she's already tried it, later admitting that she was lying. Stevie's mother worries, with some reason, that Carla is a bad influence but is herself so inflexible that she is little help to her daughter. Carla is the fatherless child of a hairdresser, has two older sisters living at home with their illegitimate children, and seems destined to follow the pattern. She and her boyfriend smoke pot and have sex. When her period finally occurs, after being almost two weeks late, she is greatly relieved, but it seems only a question of time until she is pregnant.

CATCH-A-TICK (*The Arkadians**), rapscallion son of Buckthorn Goat King of the goat people tribe. The boy turns up at unlikely times and places to add amusing touches to the narrative. Twelve or fourteen, he immediately takes a great liking to Lucian*, looking up to the older youth as a hero and expecting always that Lucian has in mind a magnificent plan that will get them all out of whatever predicament they happen to be in. Most of the time, Catch-a-Tick's faith in his abilities leaves Lucian feeling ineffectual, but even when things turn out right in spite of Lucian's inability to manage them, Catch-a-Tick attributes the success to his hero. Catch-a-Tick teaches Lucian how to use the slingshot, a talent that Lucian uses to good effect, in particular, in rescuing Bromios*.

CATHERINE CALLED BIRDY (Cushman*, Karen, Clarion, 1994), novel set in medieval England concerned with a girl's efforts to assert herself in a society that treats her as a commodity, valuable only as a piece of property to be sold in marriage to the highest bidder. In Stonebridge, Lincolnshire, in 1290, Sir Rollo is a country noble who attempts to find a likely mate willing to forgo a dowry and pay handsomely to marry his daughter Catherine, called Birdy. Birdy, however, who has inherited his stubborn and assertive character, manages to thwart most of the unappealing arrangements until a more satisfactory prospect appears. Written as journal entries, the book gives a lively and realistic picture of life in the manor, village, and nearby abbey. The novel earlier was named to the Newbery Honor and SLJ Best Books lists. ALA; Fanfare. For a longer entry, see *Dictionary, 1990–1994*.

CAUGHT (Roberts, Willo Davis, Atheneum, 1994), mystery thriller for middle-grade readers set mostly in San Sebastian, California, in the contemporary era. Unable to bear the carping and criticism of her maternal grandmother, who is in charge of their Marysville, Washington, home while her mother is on a business trip, Vickie (Victoria Ann) Rakosi, 13, pries open her piggy bank and runs away to her father, Stavo, whose latest address is in San Sebastian. Unfortunately, Vicky's little sister, Joanie, 9, insists on going along. After a tedious bus ride that takes most of their money, they arrive at their father's apartment to find no one home. While her noisy bulldog, George, keeps up a frenzied din, the old lady who lives across the hall, Magda Kubelik, summons the apartment's also aging manager, Harold, who lets them in after exchanging friendly insults with Magda. Since they have thought no further than getting to their father, who is separated, but not divorced, from their mother, Vickie and Joanie are not sure what to do next. The apartment has only a little food, from which they make a meager dinner, and nothing to show where Stavo might be, but Vickie comes on a couple of disconcerting items: a pipe, though he abhors smoking, and a snapshot of a woman and a little girl. Since Joanie is already asleep, taking up the whole bed, Vickie finds a sheet and settles on the sofa, only to be terrified as a figure climbs in the window that she has just opened. To her relief, it is a boy of about fourteen whom they have glimpsed earlier, who introduces himself as Jake Ohanian from the apartment above and says that he just came down the fire escape to let the cat in to stop its yowling. Together they find some cat food, feed it, and discover from its collar that its name is Clancy. Vickie is glad for the cat's company in the strange apartment and with its comfort falls asleep but dreams that a large man unlocks the door, stands looking down at her for some time, moves around the apartment, and leaves. The next morning they make the disturbing discovery of blood stains on the windowsill and spots on the floor faintly pinkish and still damp, as if they have been recently scrubbed. Also, the pipe and the picture are gone. With the help of Jake, who likes being involved in a mystery, Vickie realizes that her night visitor must have been real. Other clues lead them to the conclusion that Stavo, who is an accountant, must be working for a local union and that he or someone in the apartment must be in the hospital. Further incidents involve a stranger who is prowling through the building with an empty briefcase and a bearded man who resembles their father lurking in the shadows behind the building. At one point both these men arrive at the door, and Vickie is forced to choose between pretending that the man really is her father or exposing him for a fraud. For some inexplicable reason, she trusts him more than the other stranger, who turns out to be Mr. Zeeman, president of the union for which Stavo now works. Both Mr. Zeeman and their father's look-alike are hunting for some papers, which Stavo evidently removed from the company office. Both George and Clancy are involved in a brouhaha that eventually exposes Zeeman as the bad guy, involved with another man in embezzling a large amount of money from union funds. Vickie, starting to tackle some of the mess, finds the missing papers, evidence for the fraud that Stavo has discovered, hidden in the vacuum cleaner. Although the bearded man tries to send the girls back to Washington on the bus immediately, Vickie insists on an explanation and on seeing her father first. He is, as they suspected, in the hospital under an assumed name, as is Zeeman's partner in crime who tried to kill Stavo but was himself injured. Both were taken out through the window to avoid alerting the other residents and possibly Zeeman, but the blood on the windowsill was missed in the hasty cleanup. Vickie is roundly scolded by her father, her grandmother, and her mother for running away, while Joanie is treated as an innocent victim. But Vickie thinks it all worthwhile, because her mother has invited Stavo to come live at home again while he recuperates, he is offered his old job back in Marysville, and Grandma, who despises Stavo and has caused most of the rift in the marriage, moves to Montana. Action is more important than character in the story, which is scary and fast-moving enough to grip the reader's attention and, while far-fetched, is plausible. The various figures in the run-down apartment building, both human and animal, are entertaining, eccentric without being extreme. Poe Nominee.

CAVANAGH, HELEN (1939–   ), born in Quincy, Massachusetts; novelist for both children and young adults. She attended Bay Path Junior College and worked in a variety of jobs, including reporter, feature writer, columnist, and teacher of creative writing. Her fantasy, *The Last Piper** (Simon & Schuster, 1996), set in Scotland, was a nominee for the Edgar Allan Poe Award. Among her more than a dozen other novels is *Panther Glade* (Simon & Schuster, 1993), a survival story set at an archaeological site in Florida. She has lived in Stotswood, New Jersey, and Marco Island, Florida.

CEZANNE PINTO: A MEMOIR (Stolz*, Mary, Knopf, 1994), historical novel of a young slave's flight to freedom in Canada and his attempts thereafter to build his life, beginning in 1860 and related in first person as a look back on childhood and youth from the vantage point of ninety years of age. Deucy has grown up on Gloriana, the Virginia plantation of Ol' Massa Clayburn, where he is saved from most of the brutality that other slaves must endure because he has a fine way with horses, especially a prized pinto named Shenandoah, of which Deucy becomes very fond. Deprived of his beloved Mam, who has been sold into Texas, Deucy runs away when he is about twelve, accompanied by tall, intelligent, determined Tamar*, the Clayburns' cook, who has been teaching him to read, write, and improve his English. He calls himself Cezanne Pinto, taking the first name from a child of the legendary black founder of Chicago and the last name from the horse that he has cherished but must leave behind. He takes along the harmonica given him by Cupid, the slave blacksmith, who has become his surrogate father, and Tamar takes food, a knife, her Bible, and a map to freedom that she previously copied from one that Harriet Tubman drew. Following the North Star, they connect first with the Underground Railroad at the farmhouse of the Quaker Forrest family, where they clean up and are given new clothes, food, and beds, the first beds and pillows that Cezanne has ever seen. Eventually, they arrive in Philadelphia, where the Vigilance Committee helps them and Cezanne works as an ostler and Tamar works in a laundry. They worry that they may be caught and returned under the Fugitive Slave Law, and Cezanne sees evidence of what will later be called Jim Crow prejudice. At Lake Erie, just before they board a boat for Canada, they realize that slave catchers have spotted them, even though they are disguised as father and son. They are rescued by Mr. Ramsey, an elegant Canadian gentleman, who pretends that Tamar is his coachman, and taken to Clive Court, the Ramsey home. Sheltered for four years by the Ramseys and tutored by Mrs. Ramsey, who has observed the boy's intelligence, and surrogate-fathered by the elderly coachman, Jim Maury*, Cezanne is happy and thrives. After Maury dies of a stroke or heart attack early in 1865, Cezanne feels compelled to join the Union forces. He takes the train to Washington, D.C., reading Dickens on the way, and falls in with a cavalry detachment just before war's end. After demonstrating his prowess with horses and skill as a kind of acrobatic rider, he is retained by the colonel to care for that officer's own horse. He also makes friends with brash Cal Trillo*, a Mex-Texan corporal, with whom, the war over, he goes to Trillo's widowed mother's ranch, the BoxK, near the Brazos River in the southern part of Texas. Finding that Trillo's mother is dead and that Trillo's brother, Jacob, has lost an arm fighting against the North and needs help with the ranch, Cezanne learns to rope and joins Ewen Frost's outfit, the RollingQ, on roundups and cattle drives for five years to help get the BoxK back on its feet. In the winter, he helps about the BoxK, teaches Jacob to read and write, reads Dickens to both brothers, and searches unsuccessfully for Mam. After five years of "trailing," he leaves for Chicago, where Tamar now teaches school, and becomes a family man. Told from the vantage of eighty years after events, the book succeeds as the memoir of a very old man, since incidents can convincingly remain undeveloped, and Cezanne can credibly comment on the progress of African Americans in their quest for civil rights after the emancipation of the war. The small cast of characters provides scope for developing them in dimension— especially Tamar, Cal Trillo, Jim Maury, and steady, sensible, proud Cezanne himself. The first part of the book recalls plantation and runaway slave narratives and offers few new views. The last part gives a limited, but keen, sense of the difficulties and challenges of rebuilding the western South, the beginning of the cowboy era, and the part that the freed blacks played in both and is clearly the book's strength. ALA; SLJ.

CHARLENE THUNDER (*The Grass Dancer**), granddaughter of Anna Thunder, the "witch," and daughter of Crystal Thunder and white Martin Lundstrom. Charlene is a fine powwow dancer and always wins the contests, probably because of Anna's magic. Charlene likes Harley Wind Soldier, who, however, is attracted to Pumpkin, the red-haired powwow dancer with the grass-dance costume. When Charlene's mother became pregnant with her, Anna claimed the baby. Crystal told Martin that their baby had died, and both moved to Chicago, leaving Charlene with Anna, who never told her about her parents. As she grows up, Charlene becomes increasingly remote, overly devoted to her studies, and isolated, certain that her grandmother will never let her go. Jeannette McVay, the white anthropologist and high school social studies teacher, helps her to locate and contact her parents. Charlene also knows how to use spells to accomplish what she wishes. Once having attracted too many boys, bruised and sore, she receives a vision in which her ancestor Red* Dress advises her to put such medicine behind her. Charlene dies on the way to Chicago and never meets her parents.

CHIEF BEAR-IN-CAVE (*Dakota Dream**), Donny* Thunderbird's uncle and leader of the group on Pine Ridge Indian Reservation in South Dakota to which Floyd Rayfield runs. Elderly, the Chief wears his gray hair in two long pigtails and has dark, leathery skin and a cataract in one eye. Floyd says that he has the "look of nobility." He listens to Floyd's story of why he ran away and of his dream with respect and invites him to participate in a vision quest. Floyd is amazed, because he knows that the ceremony is holy and realizes that the offer indicates respect and honor. After the ceremony, the Chief listens to Floyd's account of his vision and suggests that there probably is nothing wrong with the destiny that the boy thinks awaits him. Perhaps the only thing wrong, the Chief suggests, is wanting it too soon. The gentle, kind Chief contrasts with especially the school principal, who refuses to take the time to get to know the boy and simply accepts other people's impressions of him.

CHOOSING UP SIDES (Ritter*, John H., Putnam, 1998), boy's growing-up novel with sports-story aspects set in the spring of 1921 in the small town of Crown Falls, Ohio, on the Ohio River where it borders West Virginia. Luke Bledsoe, 13, describes his conflict with his rigid, Baptist-preacher father, Zeke*, and with himself over reverting to his natural left-handedness and playing baseball. From the time that he was very young, Zeke has refused to let Luke use his left hand, since he is firmly convinced that it is the "hand of the Devil." Zeke also feels that sports are godless activities that lead participants into dissolute lives. New in school, Luke is unaware of the local passion for baseball and of the school team's hope to become state champions this year. One day, while out checking his traps (trapping being a way by which Luke adds meat to the family's lean menu), Luke happens upon a practice game, picks up a hit ball, and heaves it back left-handed with all his might, astonishing everyone with his speed and accuracy. This "turning day" in his life launches Luke into arguments with his father, a close friendship with Skinny (Dexter) Lappman, 15, star hitter and aspiring major leaguer, and an acquaintance with pretty, perky, independent Annabeth Quinn, his age, both of whom encourage him to make the most of his talents. During the novel, Luke argues with himself about the right course, since the religious convictions passed on to him by the church and his father are very strong, among them, obedience, searching the Bible for answers to life's problems, and being alert for the Devil's temptations. His Uncle* Micah Barnes, ironically a sportswriter and editor, encourages him to use his talent, Skinny instructs him in delivering various pitches, and Annabeth urges him to do what she, being a girl, cannot do and also points out that he can make more money pitching, even as a teenager, than trapping. When he tries to explain to Zeke his need to follow his own destiny, Zeke flies into a rage, beats him severely, and tries to break his left arm. Luke decides to run away, possibly to live with Uncle Micah. Having gathered necessary supplies, he goes to his beloved Ohio River to set out in his boat, encounters Zeke, and explains that he is leaving "to be himself, use his left arm, and pitch." When Zeke angrily tries to strike him, Luke asks his father if that is what Jesus would do. Zeke stumbles over the tackle box and falls into the river. Not being a swimmer, he is rapidly carried away by the current. Despite his strongest efforts, even trying to use his badly injured left arm, Luke is unable to rescue Zeke and goes under himself. Two days later, when Luke regains consciousness, he learns that his father is dead, that Annabeth saved his life, and that he, his mother, and his little sister, Chastity, will be living with Uncle Micah. Although Zeke's drowning is too convenient a resolution to Luke's problems with his father, Luke's conflict is finely detailed and convincing. Zeke is a well-drawn figure—pivotal to the story—a man whom Luke loves, respects, and honors and who he believes wants what is best for him, until he realizes that Zeke picks and chooses the biblical rules that he follows, mostly stern ones from the Old Testament. Scenes have force, and details of place and colloquial style catch the flavor of the Ohio hill country and upper South. IRA.

CHRISTIANSEN, C. B., grew up in Washington state and received a bachelor's degree in psychology and a master's in education from the University of Washington. Her novel *I See the Moon** (Atheneum, 1994) is set in the Midwest, a story of an unwed teenage pregnancy in a Norwegian-American family. Christiansen is also the author of a highly acclaimed novel for young adults, *A Small Pleasure* (Atheneum, 1988), an illustrated chapter book, *Sycamore Street* (Atheneum, 1993), and picture books. She has made her home in Washington, both in Bellevue and on Vashon Island.

CHRISTIE & COMPANY DOWN EAST (Page*, Katherine Hall, Avon, 1997), realistic mystery-detective novel set on Little Bittern Island in Maine's Penobscot Bay one recent summer. Maggie Porter, 14, whose parents own the Blue Heron Inn, has eagerly awaited the arrival for a month's visit of her roommates and best friends from The Cabot School in Massachusetts, Bostonian Christie* Montgomery and Chinese-American Vicky* Lee, whom readers first met in *Christie & Company*. Their visit, she is sure, will be a pleasant relief from her troublesome younger brother, Willy, 10, and the recent irritability of her hardworking mother, Julia. Mrs. Porter wants to make a good impression on one guest in particular, Sybil Corcoran, a columnist who is doing a feature on the inn for *Gracious Living Magazine* and who is visiting with her nephew, Paul, a reclusive novelist. Peculiar happenings soon inspire the girls to draw again on their capabilities as detectives. On the drive to the inn from the ferry, they notice a stranger, a tall woman with long, heavy red hair walking by herself, seemingly aloof and abstracted. At breakfast the next morning, Sybil finds a dead mouse in her handbag, for which she loudly blames Mrs. Porter, and at dinner, someone substitutes red pepper for the paprika in Mrs. Porter's elegant stroganoff. A decapitated seagull is found on the front porch, and a masked person peers into windows, frightening guests. Somebody shoots out all the car tires on this part of the island, and a rifle is discovered missing. It seems that someone is attempting to put the Porters out of business. The girls briefly suspect old Caroline Griffith, who owns the big house on the water near by. She once owned the inn as Griffiths' Nest and is thought by some to be a witch. The girls overhear "Uncle Bob" Bishop disparage Maggie's father, Ned, to Hap Hotchkiss, an off-islander who is planning to develop a big piece of land into a controversial resort called Isle-Away. Old mainland friends of the Porters, Bob and Lucinda Bishop loaned the Porters money to start the inn and every year come as non-paying guests, this year with their snooty, newly married daughter, Bobbie, and her husband, Chad. Things come to a roaring climax on Fourth of July night, when the power goes out, and Willy cannot be found. A full-scale search is launched with the help of authorities. The girls search in Mrs. Griffith's area, on the way meeting the red-haired woman, who they have learned is Mrs. Griffith's estranged daughter, Diane. Diane tells them that her mother has disappeared. Looking inside the little pool shed, Maggie finds Mrs. Griffith huddling with Willy, who seems to be suffering from a concussion. The next day, the girls watch to see who might be leaving the island in a hurry and discover Paul in a rush to get to the ferry. He blurts out that Lucinda and Bob Bishop paid him to perpetrate dirty tricks in order to shut down the Blue Heron so that they might set up their daughter and son-in-law as proprietors as part of a proposed chain of resort hotels with Hap Hotchkiss. The girls are pleased that the inn has been saved for the Porters and that Diane Griffith, who is recognized as the famous Broadway actress, Persephone Hamilton, and her mother have been reconciled. The mystery builds carefully with gothic conventions, the girls are well drawn, the adults are flat but differentiated, and the sidebar mystery about the Griffiths—mother and daughter had a disagreement after which a terrible drowning tragedy ensued and further estranged them—complicates the already intriguing Porter mystery just enough. Descriptions of the terrain, social life, and interpersonal relationships give the island reality. Poe Nominee.

CHRISTIE MONTGOMERY (*Christie & Company Down East**), the tall, blonde, athletic one of the three roommates, along with Maggie Porter and Vicky* Lee, at The Cabot School, who make up Christie & Company, amateur detectives. Named for the mystery writer, Agatha Christie, she enjoys sleuthing and reading mysteries. Early in the novel, she wanders off to find a place along the coast, where, being a champion diver, she might practice. To her surprise, she happens upon a finely kept swimming pool beside a large house. The owner is elderly Caroline Griffith, whose family opened Griffiths' Nest on the site of the present Blue Heron Inn. Mrs. Griffith tells Christie that she may swim in the pool if she agrees not to tell anyone about it. After Christie meets Diane Griffith, Mrs. Griffith's estranged daughter, and learns her story, she tells Mrs. Griffith that Diane would like to be friends with her mother. When Mrs. Griffith rejects the idea, Christie angrily tells her that as a mother she has an obligation to make up with her daughter, an event that happens at the end of the book following Willy Porter's mishap.

CISNEROS, SANDRA (1954–), born in Chicago, Illinois, poet, author of Latina novels. Born of a Chicana mother and a Mexican father, an only daughter with six brothers, she often lived in Mexico during her childhood. In 1976 she received her B.A. degree from Loyola University and in 1978 her M.F.A. from the University of Iowa Writers' Workshop. She worked for Loyola as recruiter and counselor for minority students and has been author in residence at a number of universities, including Michigan, New Mexico, California at Berkeley, California at Irvine, and California State at Chico. In addition to her novel composed of vignettes of growing up in a Hispanic-American culture, *The House on*

*Mango Street** (Arte Publico, 1984) and a collection of short stories, *Woman Hollering Creek & Other Stories* (Random, 1991), she has published two acclaimed collections of poems.

CLARE HARRIS (*The Ornament Tree**), 12, granddaughter of Audra Devereaux. An impudent, almost bratty girl, Clare contrasts with Bonnie Shaster, orphaned daughter of Audra's cousin, who comes to live in the Seattle family house and is earnestly determined to be useful. Although not badly behaved by modern standards, Clare is first met swiping ice slivers from the delivery truck and often makes impertinent remarks or giggles at others' discomfiture. While she shares her room with Bonnie, she does so with poor grace and no effort to make the newcomer feel at home, yet they also share many of the same attitudes, including a fascination with blind Carson Younger, the new boarder, and infatuation with James, the young handyman. Though Bonnie manages to conceal her feelings, Clare hangs around the back gate to talk with James, despite her grandmother's disapproval. When her father, Jacob Harris, whom she hardly remembers, shows up, Clare is appalled at his crudeness, and later, when he returns and proposes taking her with him, hoping to get a claim on her inheritance, she is terrified. She admits to Bonnie that she tied a note to the ornament tree asking to have her father return, not believing her mother that he is a no-good rascal, and now is frightened that her wish has come true. Bonnie finds him in the house, stealing documents and Audra's pearls, and she calls the police, then grabs the papers from him, actions that lead to his arrest for an earlier fraud. Not until Bonnie is ready to leave for college does Clare finally break down and hug her, admitting that she will really miss her.

CLARK COLES (*The Wedding**), father of Liz* and Shelby* Coles, a doctor who married their mother, Corinne, mostly for social advantage. As a young man, he attended a conference in Washington, D.C., and met a student named Sabrina, with whom he fell in love. The older women, hostesses to numerous social events, initiated a deliberate campaign to pair him with Corinne, daughter of the college president, a girl as light-skinned as he was, and more through lack of forceful resistance than love or calculation he soon married her. Finding Corinne a cold and shallow woman and remembering Sabrina, he has turned to his office assistant, Rachel, a beautiful brown woman, for affection and, after a long-standing love affair, now plans to ask Corinne for a divorce and marry his mistress. Rachel's letter, which arrives on the morning of Shelby's wedding, tells him that, by the time he receives the letter, she will be the wife of a widowed city employee whom she has known for some time. Clark is confounded by the news. It makes him question all his assumptions, including Shelby's choice of a white man for a husband, fearing that it is the result of the family prejudice against dark skin and of his poor fathering. Clark is drawn as a well-meaning, but weak, man.

THE CLEARING (Miller*, Dorothy Reynolds, Atheneum, 1996), mystery novel set one mid-twentieth-century summer in a rural area of Pennsylvania. Looking back, Amanda describes how, when she is eleven and her parents are exploring a move to Minneapolis, she is sent to stay with her Aunt Sally and Uncle Cliff and their daughter, Elinor, her age. These relatives live about thirty miles away in a clearing surrounded by woods and containing about a dozen houses. Three interwoven problems drive the plot: trying to get along with bossy Elinor, learning the identity of the stranger who sits by himself in the woods, and discovering what happened to five-year-old Bucky Mead, who disappeared ten years earlier. Bucky is thought to have been kidnapped by reclusive Charles Wade, another neighbor, whom the kids call Spook. Resenting Elinor's picking on her and insisting that Amanda and the other children always do as she wants, Amanda persuades another cousin, Nelson, also her age, to stand up with her against Elinor and, when their effort goes awry, runs into the woods to nurse her hurt feelings. There she spies a tall, thin, pale young man who she is certain is Spook. She makes friends with "large and woman shaped" Cynthia Kennedy, 14, second eldest child in a big family of local ne'er-do-wells. She learns that Cynthia sometimes goes into the woods to be alone to write poems. Cynthia says that once she forgot a poem, and when she returned for it the next day, found that it had been replaced by a drawing that pictured its contents. This happened again several times. Although Amanda promises Cynthia that she will not tell anyone, she soon has misgivings about her promise and, swearing Nelson to secrecy, confides in him. Amanda quizzes Aunt Sally about Spook and learns that he is the autistic son of the now-reclusive old woman who had been Aunt Sally's sixth-grade teacher. Worried that something might happen to Cynthia if she continues to go into the woods and if the man is Spook, Amanda and Nelson discuss their concerns with Cynthia, who informs them that she knows that Spook did not harm Bucky. She is sure that the culprit was her older brother, Lander, now twenty-one and often drunk. She deduces from his drunken ravings that he confined the boy in an abandoned refrigerator just to scare him. A storm came up, toppling a tree on the refrigerator and killing the boy. All three children are now faced with a dilemma: should they tell and doom Lander, or should they let people continue to blame Spook falsely? Amanda and Nelson help Cynthia compose two letters, one to the mysterious young man thanking him for the pictures and another anonymously to Mrs. Mead, Bucky's aunt, informing her of what Cynthia believes to be the truth about Bucky. As they return from a pleasant interlude of four days at the beach, Amanda and her relatives observe a horrifying automobile accident. While driving drunk, Lander hit a tree and was killed. Because of the note to Mrs. Mead, the truth about Bucky's disappearance has come out. After the community heals somewhat, Spook, the stranger in the woods, is helped to come out of his psychic prison, and he eventually becomes a successful illustrator. Characters are a well-known mix of types—Cynthia, the pretty, artistic, overly responsible teenage daughter of a despised family; Nelson, the highly moral son of a minister; Spook, the maligned genius; Elinor, the brat who tones down and becomes friends with the cousin whom she has tormented; Mrs. Mead, the saintly neighbor; and the like. The accident seems an overly fortuitous solution to the problem of what to do about Lander, and the novel ends with a rosy-glow epilogue. Suspense is created and maintained well, and the children's dilemma is presented capably. Best are the depiction of childhood activities and attitudes, the overactive imaginations, the superstitions, the endless haggling over game procedures, bickering and back-biting, oaths, and the sometimes misguided desire for privacy and independence. The title has an obvious double meaning. Poe Winner.

CLEMENTS, ANDREW (1949–   ), born in Camden, New Jersey; writer, editor, educator. He was graduated from Northwestern University with a B.A. degree and from National Louis University with an M.A. degree in elementary education. For eight years he taught fourth grade, eighth grade, and English in high school in Illinois and since 1980 has been involved in publishing as editor and director for several different presses in Illinois and New England. In addition to *Frindle** (Simon & Schuster, 1996), which won a number of awards besides being named to the *Horn Book* Fanfare and the Christopher lists, he has published many picture books and reading-program books and another novel with a school setting, *The Landry News** (Simon & Schuster, 1999).

CLIFFORD (ROSENBERG), ETH(EL) (1915–   ), born in New York City; prolific author of more than eighty books for children, almost all under the pseudonym Eth Clifford, the most popular being humorous mysteries for middle graders. Typical is *Harvey's Mystifying Raccoon Mix-Up** (Houghton, 1994), in which Harvey, 12, and his cousin Nora bring counterfeiters to justice. Nominated for the Edgar Allan Poe Award, it is one of a series about the lively, undauntable pair. Clifford came to mystery/humor after doing stories for picture books and fictionalized history and biography. She turned to contemporary fiction with the *The Rocking Chair Rebellion* (Houghton, 1979), which was adapted for television. Other humorous series books of largely domestic adventures and lighthearted mysteries are those about sisters Jo-Beth and Mary Rose and the clever animal detective, Flatfoot Fox. Clifford has often been praised for her witty style, zany humor, lively plots, and distinctive, likable characters. She was from 1959 to 1970 an editor and writer for David-Stewart Publishing Co. in Indianapolis, a firm that she and her husband, David Rosenberg, founded and that produced a variety of books and educational materials. She makes her home in Florida, where she received an Artist's Fellowship Award in 1987 for the body of her work.

COFFEE WILL MAKE YOU BLACK (Sinclair*, April, Hyperion, 1994), novel of a girl's growing up in the 1960s on Chicago's South Side, recounting her often funny, often touching efforts to understand and come to terms with her feelings about race and her own sexuality. Starting when Stevie (Jean Eloise Stevenson) is eleven, it takes her through her last years of junior high, when she is baffled by a boy's question, "Are you a virgin?," since she thinks virgin means pure and spotless, until nearly the end of her junior year in high school, when she is sixteen and has decided to "do it" with her boyfriend, only to chicken out at the pain and the realization that she admires him but doesn't love him. Stevie's friends, most of them more worldly and experienced than she is, give her lots of bad advice, but what her mother tells her—"all men are dogs; some are just more doggish than others"—is no more helpful. Stevie's life story proceeds in a series of episodes, mostly involving her relationship to school friends, girls and boys. She pines to go to the birthday party of Carla* Perkins so much that she gets into trouble with her teacher by trying to give up her part in a program to Carla, then, when she is caught with Carla and other girls reading the steamy diary of one girl's sister, lies to keep her mother from knowing, endures a severe whipping from her mother, who finds out, and defies her by still wanting to go to the party. When her mother, to her surprise, lets her, she is dismayed at how dull the occasion is. With considerable reluctance she agrees to the request of her first real boyfriend, Yussef Brown, that she come into his backyard and pee with him, so that they can examine each other's equipment, not knowing that he has invited all his friends to watch through the window. She is saved from humiliation by nerdy Roland Anderson, whom she has previously rejected but who comes to warn her, having heard the boys discussing the plan in the lavatory. She looks forward to seeing again her closest friend, Terri Mathews, whose family moved away from Chicago and has recently returned. When Terri and her mother attend the annual church tea, they treat Stevie's mother and her Grandma* Dickens condescendingly and brag about their material possessions and country-club membership but do invite Stevie to join the Charisma Club, a group of Terri's upscale friends. When Terri confides in Stevie about the cruel trick that they plan to play on one of the girls, Stevie rejects the offer to join. Although the first half of the book concentrates on Stevie's relationships in her family and circle of school friends, events in the outside world gradually impinge on her life. Roland becomes a black militant, replacing his suit coat and tie with a dashiki and combat boots. When Stevie takes her proud father's forgotten lunch to him at the hospital where he is a janitor, she sees him shuffling and mumbling as his white supervisor chews him out. She backs off and waits a while; then they both pretend that the incident has not happened. After the assassination of Martin Luther King, she goes for comfort to her grandmother's business place, Mother Dickens' Fried Chicken Stand, where the presence of two University of Chicago students, a black man and a white woman, enflames the tense emotions of the crowd and almost causes a riot. Grandma controls the situation by demanding a moment of silence for the memory of Dr. King, then announcing that chicken sandwiches and dinners are on the house to all present, allowing time for the couple to scurry away. Stevie's own struggle with the problem of race coincides with her worries over sex. She realizes that she is much more attracted to Nurse Horn, the only white faculty member still at her high school, than to her current boyfriend, Sean. At the Afro-American Club she stands up for Miss Horn when the others demand that she be replaced by a black, and Roland backs her up. When she sees a book about lesbians in Miss Horn's briefcase, she fears that the nurse is "funny" and that she must be homosexual, too, to be attracted to her. At the end she has been rejected by Sean for not agreeing to intercourse and by Carla for possibly being gay, but Nurse Horn explains to her that many adolescents have crushes on a teacher at her age and that she is pretty young to be labeling herself. The question of her sexual orientation and even Miss Horn's is left open. Prejudices explored in the novel are not only white against black but also black against white and lighter- against darker-skinned people. Although the situations are not very different from that of many adolescent girls of the late 1960s, the language is distinctively African American, and Stevie's voice rings true. The conflicts between her rigid upbringing and bookish nature and her desires for experience, for an Afro, and for a place in a cool crowd are often hilarious but never condescending. This is one of the most convincing recent coming-of-age novels. ALA; SLJ.

COLE, BROCK (1938–   ), writer and illustrator of picture books and novels and illustrator of books for other writers. After receiving a bachelor's from Kenyon College and a doctorate from the University of Minnesota, he taught philosophy at the University of Wisconsin until 1975, when he turned to writing. After publishing five well-received, self-illustrated picture books, he attracted critical attention for his offbeat young adult novels, *The Goats* (Farrar, 1987), *Celine* (Farrar, 1989), and *The Facts Speak for Themselves** (Front Street, 1997), the story of a girl's surviving in a dysfunctional family, which was named to the *School Library Journal* list. He has also recently published *Buttons* (Farrar, 2000), a self-illustrated picture book. For earlier information and title entries, see *Dictionary, 1985–1989* [*The Goats*] and *Dictionary, 1990–1994* [*Celine*].

COMAN, CAROLYN, born in Evanston, Illinois; attended private, parochial, and public schools in Maryland, Connecticut, Indiana, New York, and New Jersey. She studied writing at Hampshire College in Amherst, Massachusetts, from which she was graduated. She operated her own bookbindery from 1975 to 1984, was an editor for Heinemann and a writing instructor at Harvard Extension and Harvard Summer School, and has served on the faculty of the M.F.A. Writing for Children Program at Vermont College. Among her novels are *Bee and Jacky* (Front Street, 1998), about incest, and *What Jamie Saw** (Front Street, 1995), about domestic abuse, which was a Newbery Honor Book and nominated for the National Book Award. For additional information, see *Dictionary, 1990–1994* [*Tell Me Everything*].

COME IN FROM THE COLD (Qualey*, Marsha, Houghton, 1994), novel of the protests against the Vietnam War and of the effects of that conflict upon

families and communities in the United States. In four parts, the novel, starting
in 1969, alternates between two high school-age protagonists, Maud Dougherty
in Minneapolis, whose story is told in the third person, and the first-person
narrative of Jeff Ramsey of the conservative small town of Red Cedar, Minnesota. On the same day, Maud's sister, Lucy, who has dropped out to become
an antigovernment activist, is killed in the bombing of a physics lab at the
University of Minnesota, where she delilberately returned to die in the blast,
and Jeff's popular brother, Tom, is killed in Vietnam. The first two parts concern
these events and the disorientation that they cause to the younger siblings. Maud
skips school, wanders around the university campus, and eventually meets a
young man named Ed, who had spent Lucy's last night with her and is delighted
to score with Lucy's sister, an initial sexual intercourse that is virtually meaningless to Maud. Jeff, who has infuriated many of his fellow townspeople by
pushing an antiwar resolution through his school's student council, attends a
party with Tom on his last leave, an affair where Jeff is ditched by both Tom
and the date whom Tom has arranged for him, but he meets Roger Heistad, a
minister working on a temporary assignment in Red Cedar, who recruits him to
help with various liberal projects and takes him to a protest demonstration in
Minneapolis. In the third section Maud and Jeff meet at a rock concert in Red
Cedar, which Maud is attending, somewhat unwillingly, as driver for her friend
who goes with the band's bassist. She sees Jeff being thrown out of the concert,
where he hoped to distribute announcements of a protest march, and his leaflets
consficated. Impulsively, she retrieves the leaflets and distracts the guard so that
Jeff can place them in the cars filling the parking lot. Because the band's van
has a breakdown, she stays over and attends the protest, at which Jeff is attacked
and badly injured by an irate antiprotester and is saved only by the violent
intervention of Gumbo*, his longtime neighbor and friend. Their romance develops despite their very different backgrounds. Maud's widowed father is a
professor; Jeff's divorced mother is a humorous, hard-drinking survivor who
works in a meatpacking plant and early in the story married Paul Sandborn, her
fellow worker. Both young people are alienated not only from the war-approving
establishment but also from the drinking and drugging culture of their peers.
The invasion of Cambodia and the shooting of students at Kent State by the
National Guard horrify both of them, and they become more disillusioned. Both
manage to finish high school, but Maud delays college and works in the child-
care program at a community center. Jeff starts college but finds it meaningless
and drops out to join a commune near Grand River, some of whose members
he and Maud met at a protest parade. In the final, briefest section, Maud and
Jeff are married at nineteen, living in the commune and looking forward to a
happy and useful life in the alternative society that they are building. Although
the history of failed communes since the Vietnam era makes the upbeat ending
somewhat suspect, the novel is strong in evoking the anger, frustration, and
resulting cynicism of young people of the period. While many of the scenes are
obviously contrived to illustrate various aspects of the social conflict, a number

of the people are more than cardboard figures. The parents are well-drawn, sympathetic characters. Maud's father is so overcome by the deaths of first his wife and then his elder daughter that he withdraws to his attic study, where he writes poetry and, though loving, does little to direct or help Maud. Jeff's mother has a hard-bitten practicality and grieves for Tom but is as supportive as she can be to Jeff, in whom she recognizes staunch idealism. Although clearly on the side of the young people against the war, the novel resists overindulging in antiestablishment rhetoric. ALA; SLJ.

CONFESS-O-RAMA (Koertge*, Ron, Orchard, 1996), contemporary boy's growing-up novel with school-story and family-life aspects set in the upscale Los Angeles suburb of West Paradise. The flavor and attitudes of midteen life take precedence over plot in this amusing assemblage of eccentric figures. As the school year begins, narrator Tony Candelaria, 15, a shy, gentle, intelligent boy, enrolls at West Paradise High, hoping to avoid attention and ride life out until the end of the semester, when he knows he will move again. He and his mother, Kathryn* Candelaria, who was recently widowed for the fourth time and of whom he is very protective, are occupying a relative's condominium until she decides what to do next with their lives. Outside of school, Tony mostly devotes himself to taking care of the place, consoling her, and seeing to the cooking, an activity that he especially enjoys and at which he is very good. On the first day, seniors attempt to terrorize him, among them Barry, the son of the local radio talk show personality, Larry* Deluxe of KGAB. He encounters Rochelle, an ex-art student who tries to persuade him to join Kids for Chastity, and art students Hector, an articulate boy in a wheelchair, Blue*, who wears only blue, and, most noticeable of all, flamboyant, exhibitionistic Jordan Archer, who affects tight black dresses fastened with padlocks and chains. On a telephone pole just outside school, Tony spots a flyer promoting Confess-O-Rama, a call-in service to which one can unburden one's self, and takes one of the attached tear-off telephone numbers. That evening after doing the laundry, cooking, and cleaning up, he calls the number and talks briefly to the anonymous tape machine, one of several times that he contacts the machine during the next few days. He learns that Jordan has fallen behind in her artwork, failing for some reason to complete projects, while Blue and Hector are forging ahead quite capably. He also learns that Larry is planning to do a weeklong high school talk show, focusing on West Paradise High. The reader gradually learns that, as Tony becomes more interested in Jordan and more involved with her and the other art students, he yearns to be free of having to take care of his mother and to have a father figure like his just-deceased stepfather, Bill, to talk to and maybe shoot baskets with. He learns also that Jordan feels responsible for her father, Drew*, a famous painter whose wife is deceased and with whom Jordan shares a duplex, he on one side, she on the other. Jordan wears to a party, to which Tony and his mother are also invited, a bra on top of her dress that lights up and flashes. Later, at Tony's suggestion, she makes exotic bras her art project.

Her garb leads to a school protest, chaired and aired by Larry, over censorship, when the school principal refuses to let her wear the bras to school. Just before the big art show at the mall, Tony discovers that Jordan is behind Confess-O-Rama and feels humiliated and betrayed. At the show, however, he discovers that she has artfully pieced together various voices to form an interesting commentary on contemporary life. By this time she has persuaded him to pursue his interest in cooking, and his mother has taken a job working for Larry's ex-wife, who runs a coffin business, and is less dependent on Tony. Since the cast of characters is large, events are hard to follow, and much of what happens and the attendant confusion are best taken as mirroring Tony's unstable reactions to this new life and his apprehensions about fitting in, taking care of his mother, and having a life of his own. The cast, for the most part, are the late twentieth-century equivalent of bohemians, and the book's best feature is the way it melds together this likable, if weird, conglomeration of characters and events. The dialogue is snappy with one-liners and quick cracks, mostly kind, although pointed and topical. SLJ.

CONLY, JANE LESLIE (1948–   ), born in Virginia; novelist, daughter of author Robert Leslie Conly (Robert C. O'Brien), whose fantasy *Mrs. Frisby and the Rats of NIMH* (Atheneum, 1971) was a Newbery Award winner. Besides writing two sequels to her father's book, Conly has published novels of her own, including *Trout Summer** (Holt, 1995). For earlier biographical information and a title entry, see *Dictionary, 1990–1994* [*Crazy Lady*].

COOK, KARIN, activist, health educator, and writer. Cook is a graduate of Vassar College and the Creative Writing Program at New York University. Her first novel, *What Girls Learn** (Pantheon, 1997), is a girl's growing-up story concerned with the adjustment of two sisters to their mother's new husband and how the death of the mother affects their relationship. Cook has worked in the development office at the Door, a multiservice youth center in New York City.

COOKIE GATES (*Like Sisters on the Homefront**), Constance Gates, sixteen-year-old cousin of Gayle Ann Whitaker and only child of the Reverend Mr. Luther Gates, a Georgia preacher, and his wife, Virginia, whom Gayle calls Miss Auntie, a strict, but loving, college professor. Gayle thinks tall, big-boned Cookie is gauche and ignorant about the important things in life: clothes, hairstyles, and, most important, sex, since Cookie is a virgin. Gayle urges her to hurry up and have sex, because she says that it is easier when young, and offers to get her "condos," that is, condoms. Cookie is a good student, does social service, carries out her household responsibilities with dispatch, participates in church youth activities and choir, respects her parents, never smarts off, and feels that sex belongs with marriage. Unable to believe ill of anyone, Cookie thinks that Gayle had a baby because she was raped or tricked. Cookie is capable of great patience and forbearance and seldom answers back to Gayle's jibes and then with gentle wit. Cookie's romance with Stacey Alexander brings the story to a climax, when Gayle prevents Cookie from running away to Stacey, an action grossly out of character for Cookie and also for Gayle. Cookie and Gayle are obviously foils.

COONEY, CAROLINE B., since 1978 a writer mainly noted for her young adult romances, for which she received the Romantic Book Award, Teen Romance Category, in 1985. Her first three books were mysteries, two for young readers, and the other, *Rear View Mirror* (Random House, 1980), an adult suspense novel, which was made into a television movie starring Lee Remick. After *An April Love Story* (Scholastic, 1981), she concentrated on romances. She has also written family stories like *What Child Is This?: A Christmas Story* (Delacorte, 1997); two companion problem and growing-up novels for young adults with a strong element of suspense, *The Face on the Milk Carton* (Bantam, 1990) and *The Voice on the Radio* (Delacorte, 1996); and *Driver's Ed** (Delacorte, 1994), a sociological problem novel about three young people who steal a stop sign and cause the death of a young woman, chosen by both the American Library Association and *School Library Journal.* She attended Indiana University, Massachusetts General Hospital School of Nursing, and University of Connecticut. Also a singer and organist, she lives in Connecticut.

COOPERSTEIN, CLAIRE (LOUISE) (1923–   ), born in Chicago, Illinois; poet, novelist, editor, artist. She has written fashion copy and feature stories and done interviews for local newspapers in Wisconsin and New York, exhibited painting and sculpture throughout the southeastern United States and in Washington, D.C., and contributed poems extensively to anthologies and periodicals. *Johanna: A Novel of the van Gogh Family** (Simon & Schuster, 1995) is an epistolary and journal-entry novel about the widow of Theodoor van Gogh and sister-in-law of the renowned painter, Vincent van Gogh. A combination of research, imagination, and skillful writing, the book justifiably earned a citation from *School Library Journal.* After attending the University of Illinois, she received a B.A. from Goddard College in Vermont and an M.F.A. in writing from Vermont College. Cooperstein studied painting and sculpture at various institutions, including the University of North Carolina at Chapel Hill, where she has made her home.

CORMIER, ROBERT (EDMUND) (1925–2000), born in Leominster, Massachusetts, novelist known for introducing pessimistic endings into novels for young adults, as in *I Am the Cheese** (Pantheon, 1977). This novel was named the Phoenix Award Winner in 1997 for a book published twenty years earlier that has stood the test of time. A more recent novel with Cormier's typical sociopathic adolescent character is *In the Middle of the Night** (Delacorte, 1995), a nominee for the Edgar Allan Poe Award. For earlier biographical information and title entries, see *Dictionary, 1960–1984* [*The Chocolate War; I Am the*

Cheese], *Dictionary, 1985–1989* [*Beyond the Chocolate War*], and *Dictionary, 1990–1994* [*Other Bells to Ring*; *We All Fall Down*].

COULOUMBIS, AUDREY, born in Illinois, has made her home in both Queens, New York, and upstate New York. Her first novel for young people, *Getting Near to Baby** (Putnam, 1999), was named to the *School Library Journal* list of Best Books for Children. It is a sensitive study of the effect that the death of an infant has on an entire family.

COUSINS IN THE CASTLE (Wallace*, Barbara Brooks, Atheneum, 1996), melodrama set in Victorian London, in New York, and on an ocean liner between the two cities. When news comes of her father's death in a hotel fire while he is on a business trip to the Near East, motherless Amelia Fairwick, 11, is forced to leave her father's fiancée, Felicia Charlton, and travel to live with cousins of her mother in America, people whom she has never seen or even heard of. Escorted by grim, unfriendly Cousin Charlotte, she has her own stateroom but is forbidden to converse with any of the other passengers. Although she is a well brought up and obedient girl, Amelia does break this rule when she meets Primrose Lagoon, a child her own age, on deck and takes her to be a princess because she was wearing a tiara as they boarded the ship. She is surprised when Primrose demands that she bring an apple for her the next day and later is astonished to discover that Primrose is not a princess at all but the Little London Canary, one of a theatrical troupe that entertains in the dining room. Still, she takes an apple from the abundant food provided to the first-class passengers, again meets Primrose, and learns that she is also an orphan, traveling with Mr. Alphonso Turk and Mr. Thessalonius Smeech, two abusive thespians. Amelia invites Primrose to her cabin, where they play jacks and exchange glimpses of the lockets containing pictures of their mothers that each wears secretly. Surprised by Cousin Charlotte, Primrose scoots away, and Amelia spends the rest of the ocean voyage virtually a prisoner. After the ship docks, they are approached by Mr. Pymm, the assistant purser, whom Cousin Charlotte accompanies to see to some problem about the trunks after ordering Amelia to stay where she is. Three hours later, Amelia is still waiting. As dusk approaches, a rosy-faced, kind-looking woman speaks to her, introduces herself as Mrs. Dobbins, and, learning of her predicament, summons her son Elmo, a stevedore, to make inquiries and takes Amelia with her through rough streets to a dim basement apartment where she feeds her and puts her to bed. In the morning Mrs. Dobbins is gone, as are Amelia's nice clothes, in their place hanging rough garments hardly more than rags. In the next few days Amelia is visited by a coarse woman, Mrs. Shrike, who gives her almost inedible food, imbibes from an ample supply of liquor, and locks the door as she departs, leaving Amelia alone in the rat-infested place. One day when Mrs. Shrike arrives already quite drunk, she collapses without locking the door behind her, and Amelia slips out, terrified, into the rough streets and, after considerable difficulty, makes her way to the Castle Theater, a low-class place where Primrose has told her she will be playing. She finds Primrose, who hides her in a broom closet and discloses that she is really Rosie, a boy masquerading as a young girl singer. He ingeniously finds her some boy's clothes, chops off her long hair, and, calling her Sam, persuades the theater manager to hire her to clean, since she is a bargain, asking only food and a place to sleep. Complications and revelations follow in rapid succession. Turk and Smeech, having learned of her cousin's last name, take her to the castlelike home of her Cousin Basil, thinking that they will get a large reward. On the contrary, they are turned out, and Amelia, at whom Cousin Basil refuses even to look, is sent to a tiny servant's room and warned not to wander about the house. The only friendly face she sees is that of Sarah, a very frightened young servant, until Rosie shows up, now a scullery boy, determined to discover the secrets of the house and free her from this new danger. In the end, Amelia's father arrives, not killed in the hotel fire but kept a prisoner and now married to Felicia. Evil Cousin Basil is arrested, along with his confederates, Mr. Quinge, who has acted as his butler, and Mr. Pymm, who is also not what he purported to be. Mrs. Dobbins, once Nanny for Charlotte and Basil, turns out to be true-blue; Cousin Charlotte, who has been kept prisoner in the attic, is a beautiful, kindly woman; Rosie turns out to be her son; and the good people all plan to live together in the castle with Sarah promoted to be a companion for Amelia. Just how Cousin Charlotte was persuaded to play the grim companion of the ocean voyage is not clear, but the motivation for Amelia's treatment is explained by Cousin Basil's gambling and need for her inheritance, which he expects to collect after he has sold her off, evidently into white slavery. The twists and turns of the final denouement are so outlandish that a reader need make no attempt to understand and believe them all. In spirit the novel is much like the Victorian parodies of Joan Aiken, but with less humor and no fantasy elements. Both the sumptuousness of the liner and the grime and bleakness of the rooms where Amelia is kept are described in graphic detail, and the breathless plot carries a reader on pell-mell to a satisfying, if implausible, conclusion. Poe Nominee.

COVILLE, BRUCE (1950–   ), born in Syracuse, New York, where he lives; highly prolific writer of mostly fantasies in both picture-book and novel form for middle-grade and early adolescent readers; playwright and lyricist for adult musical theater. After attending Duke University and the State University of New York at Binghamton, he received his B.A. from the State University of New York at Oswego in 1974 and taught elementary school for seven years before turning to writing. One of the lighthearted Magic Shop Books that feature the mysterious Mr. S. H. Elives, *The Skull of Truth** (Harcourt, 1997) tells of the misadventures of a boy who takes a skull from Mr. Elives' shop and henceforth is obligated to speak only the truth. The title appears on the *School Library Journal* list. Others in the set are *Jeremy Thatcher, Dragon Hatcher* (Jane Yolen, 1991) and *Jennifer Murdley's Toad* (Harcourt, 1992). Well known for his ability to tell a good story, Coville has also written the books in the A. I. Gang series, the humorous My Teacher series, the Alien series, and the Unicorn Chronicles set, compiled and edited many books of ghost, magic, monster, and generally scary tales, and retold stories from Shakespeare. He is cohost and coproducer of *Upstage*, a cable program promoting local theater, and is a frequent contributor to various publications.

CRASH (Spinelli*, Jerry, Knopf, 1996), amusing, realistic problem novel with sports-story aspects involving social discrimination and current ecological concerns, set in an unnamed Pennsylvania town in the late twentieth century. Brash, muscular, good athlete Crash (John) Coogan, the twelve-year-old narrator, tells in contemporary, sometimes wisecracking language and acute detail about his prowess as a seventh-grade football hero; his life with his parents and socially and politically aware sister, Abby*, 10, an elementary-school ecologist; his relationship with Penn* Webb, a small-for-his-age, dorky Quaker classmate; and his friendship with Mike Deluca. Crash and Penn met when both were six and Penn was new in town. Although both are excellent runners, Crash scorns Penn as awkward and naive, takes advantage of him at every turn, and derides his secondhand-store clothes, his lack of trendy toys, and his Quaker pacifism. Most of the book takes place the year both boys are in seventh grade, the momentous year that Crash establishes a Springfield Middle School football record by scoring six touchdowns in one game; Crash develops a crush on pretty Jane Forbes, who brushes him off as juvenile and crude; his maternal grandfather, Scooter*, an ex-navy cook, comes to live with the Coogans and suffers a stroke; Crash's mother, a real estate agent, helps to develop a new town mall; Abby turns the Coogan backyard into a wildlife habitat against her parents' wishes and, along with Penn and Jane, demonstrates against the proposed mall; and Penn becomes the school's first male cheerleader, a role that makes him the butt of jokes from the school's "regular" guys and girls. Crash develops a greater measure of respect for Penn after Scooter becomes ill and Penn brings him a box of Missouri mud, a precious family heirloom substance that, according to Webb family legend, has healing powers. Soon Crash becomes aware that Penn is sprinting by the Coogan house every night. When Mike Deluca swipes Penn's English essay and Crash recovers it, Crash learns that Penn is practicing his running so that he can participate in the annual Penn Relays that his great-grandfather once participated in. The old man is visiting Penn's family in order to attend the races. Although Crash defeats Penn at track in daily practice, when Crash sees Penn's great-grandfather in the audience at start time, Crash is not sure that he wants to win. Both boys race well and are even to the finish. Comfortable at feeling even, Crash shouts to Penn to lean against the string. Penn does so just enough to break the string before Crash does. Although at first Crash regrets his action, he is pleased knowing the satisfaction that Penn's great-grandfather obviously feels at his great-grandson's feat. Soon Crash and Penn are best friends. Crash rubs Scooter's toe in the Missouri mud, confident that it will help his beloved grandfather; his mother quits her job to stay home, care for Scooter and the family, and resume her painting career; Abby is happy with the wildlife-friendly backyard; and Crash's family is closer than it has ever been. Short sentences, snappy dialogue and repartee, humor both gross and subtle, and authentic scenes of family life, if exaggerated for good effect, are elements that play up to the middle-school set. The parents voice middle-class attitudes toward economic development and the need to maintain manicured yards, and the contrast between the conventional Coogans and the Quaker Webbs is didactically obvious. Crash's mother's decision to give up her job strikes a false note, and Crash's new tolerance and friendship for Penn lack motivation and believability, although they make for a pleasing ending. The warmth between Scooter and his grandchildren produces a good feeling, as does Crash's decision to make fish cakes for Abby's birthday, since he knows she likes them, even though he cannot make them as well as Scooter used to. The story of Crash's change from a self-centered jock to a young man with more serious, mature matters on his mind than football and leering sex, if not entirely credible, is still highly satisfying. SLJ.

CREECH, SHARON (1945–   ), born in Cleveland, Ohio; resident of Surrey, England, and Chautauqua, New York; teacher of literature; novelist; playwright; poet. She received her B.A. degree from Hiram College and her M.A. from George Mason University. After working for the Federal Theater Project Archives and as an editorial assistant for the *Congressional Quarterly*, she became a teacher of literature for TASIS (The American School in Switzerland) England School, a grade school in Surrey for the children of expatriate Americans, later taught for the same school in Switzerland, and married a headmaster, Lyle D. Riggs. Her first novel, *Absolutely Normal Chaos* (Macmillan [England], 1990; HarperCollins, 1995), involves a number of early teen issues. Similar themes of growing up, self-identification, dealing with death, and interpersonal relationships appear in her humorous, fast-paced Newbery Award-winning *Walk Two Moons** (HarperCollins, 1994), also an American Library Association choice. The ALA-cited *Chasing Redbird* (HarperCollins, 1997) is a similarly humorous observation of family life from the young person's perspective. She has also published poems and had a play produced in New York City, *The Center of the Universe* (1992).

CROSS, DONNA WOOLFOLK (1947–   ), born in New York City; professor and writer. After receiving her B.A. from the University of Pennsylvania, she worked as an editorial assistant for W. H. Allen & Co. in London and as an advertising copywriter for Young and Rubicam, took her M.A. from the University of California in Los Angeles, and has since been a professor of English at Onondaga Community College in Syracuse, New York, where she lives. Her first books, *Speaking of Words* (Holt, 1977), *Word Abuse: How the Words We Use Use Us* (Coward, 1979), and *Mediaspeak: How Television Makes Up Your*

Mind (Coward, 1981), argue that to be an effective citizen requires an understanding of language. After seven years of research and writing, she published the *School Library Journal* selection *Pope Joan** (Random House, 1996), an intriguing adult historical novel with a strong feminist slant set in the ninth century and revolving around the only woman pope.

CROSSROADS (*The Magic and the Healing**), magical, mythical kingdom located in a remote valley in western Virginia, to which the Western Virginia College of Veterinary Medicine students go to treat ailing creatures. There the students are also instrumental in helping the forces of good defeat the evil powers of Morgan, who seeks to overthrow King Brandal, otherwise known as the trader Owen*. Crossroads is much like the real world in mountainous topography and has a history; economy, mostly based on animals; political organization, in this case a monarchy; religion, in which a Stepfather God is revered; and a population made up of mythological beings and human beings, mostly refugees from war or tyranny. Maps of the land and the route into it appear in *The Book of Strangeways*, which is carefully guarded by the college librarian, Mrs. Sobell, but which nevertheless falls into evil hands. Owen tells the students of the origin of Crossroads and says that "whoever is lonely, or broken, or has no hope left, sooner or later will come to Crossroads." The beings of Crossroads take pride that people of all races and backgrounds live together peacefully.

CRUTCHER, CHRIS(TOPHER) (C.) (1946–   ), raised in Cascade, Idaho; received his B.A. degree in sociology and psychology from Eastern Washington State College; high school teacher, school administrator, mental health specialist, family therapist, and critically acclaimed writer of young adult novels. His books have been praised for their insights into the problems of young people, for their vitality of plot and character, and for the authority that comes from personal experience in working with the age group. He received the ALAN Award for Significant Contribution to Adolescent Literature. *Ironman** (Greenwillow, 1995), about a troubled young triathlete, was selected for the Fanfare list by the editors of *The Horn Book Magazine*. For more information and a title entry, see *Dictionary, 1990–1994* [*Staying Fat for Sarah Byrnes*].

THE CUCKOO'S CHILD (Freeman*, Suzanne, Greenwillow, 1996), novel of a girl's gradual realization and acceptance of her parents' death and her understanding that it was in her mother's character to abandon those who love her in her pursuit of new places and adventures. During all her three years of living in Beirut, Mia Veery has longed to return to the United States, to an American life of weiner roasts, Barbie dolls, school milk in small waxy cartons, and ten-cent movie matinees, all the things that make an ordinary life for a preteenage girl in 1962. When the boat that her mother, Jess, and her father are sailing disappears among the Greek islands, Mia and her half sisters, Bibi and Nell*, both high school age, go to Ionia, Tennessee, to live with Kit* Hanks, their mother's younger sister, an aunt whom Mia has never seen before. Feeling both disoriented, since the America to which she comes back is not that of her imagination, and guilty, since her wish, in coming true, seems to have required her parents' death, Mia engages in ritualistic behavior, bargaining with fate to make them return. Many of these compulsions are very troublesome or even disastrous to those around her. She climbs the nearby water tower, and when her family and neighbors assemble to talk her down, she seems to be told to jump. She breaks both arms of Kit, who tries to catch her. She must not unpack or wear any of her clothes from Beirut. She is prevented from eating an increasing number of foods, especially things that she likes. She has to get up every night and touch each number on the cuckoo clock in the kitchen. Her sisters fly to Boston to see their father, Morse Cooper. Kit, who has never been around children before, is well-meaning but baffled by Mia's strange behavior and irritated by the child's rudeness to her lover and fellow worker, Dan Flannery. Mia, who learns that he is married, breaks up the romance. Kit enrolls Mia in Vacation Bible School at the Church of Christ, where all the worst aspects of small-town life are played out. Mia is put in the Commandments group but can see clearly that the elite girls are in the Devotions group. Only one of the Commandments is friendly, a wild-haired girl named Sinclair Smith, who is given to odd enthusiasms, at the moment hoping to be a martyred saint. When the leader of the Devotions suddenly takes up with Mia, she is so happy to belong that she drops Sinclair and follows their lead in petty meanness. A man from the government comes to interview her about her parents' trip among the Greek islands, and she has hope that they will be found, not realizing that his leading questions indicate that he thinks that they might be political defectors. Mia's one stable influence is old Mrs. Swope, a neighbor for whom she does odd jobs and whose house seems a haven of normality. When Bibi and Nell return with Morse, who grew up in Ionia and is a technical writer, Mia resents him as an intruder and even bites his hand, a serious injury. After Bibi and Nell tell her that the government has called off the official search for their parents, Mia becomes more rude and mean and starts to steal things, knowing that she doesn't want to be so obnoxious but unable to stop herself. She resists the thoughtful and kindly advances by Morse, resenting his extended stay and his obvious interest in Kit, even though part of her wants to respond to him. Finally, on the last day of Bible School, when the Devotions have decreed that they will all wear dresses, she panics, unable to unpack and wear any of her own dresses. She finds a skirted outfit in Kit's closet, not discovering until she comes to the show for the parents that she is wearing an old gym suit that everyone recognizes. She shinnies up an oak tree, being used to climbing trees in Beirut, and defies the Devotions, who order her down. There she waits all through the program and watches everyone leave and the place grow dark. Then Kit, her sisters, and finally Morse all converge on the parking lot below her, having been out searching the streets and creek edges for her. Suddenly, she finds herself free of the compulsion that tells her not to come down and is able to give in to her love for all of them, understanding at last that they have all been abandoned by her mother but that they have each other and that a family doesn't have to fit the conventional pattern of her imagined America. Later she hunts up and apologizes to Sinclair, who has given up sainthood, taken up sketching, and found a boyfriend. Mia's distress and sense of abandonment are touching, at the same time that her behavior is annoying. Mrs. Swope, whose deceased husband was a bird-watcher, tells Mia about the cuckoo's practice of leaving its egg in another bird's nest but sensibly says that maybe the result is the best for everyone. The commands that Mia seems to hear are not the voices that torment schizophrenics nor holy words from on high, as Sinclair hopes, but inner orders summoned by her subconscious that tries to alter reality by a series of pacts, just as children ward off bad luck by avoiding cracks in the sidewalk. Kit's inexperience, her sisters' preoccupation with themselves, and the government man's suspicions all fail to provide the support that Mia needs. Only Morse has the kind of understanding that offers hope, and until the very end Mia resists his friendship. Scenes set at the Bible School are funny and scathingly satirical. Fanfare; Josette Frank; SLJ.

CURTIS, CHRISTOPHER PAUL (1954–), born in Flint, Michigan; African-American writer highly honored for his novels for early adolescent readers about African Americans. After high school, he worked on the assembly line at the Fisher Body Plant in Flint, attending the Flint branch of the University of Michigan part-time and receiving his degree in 1996. He has also been an aide to Senator Don Riegle, worked at Automatic Data Processing in Allen Park, Michigan, and been a maintenance man, a warehouse clerk, and a purchasing clerk. After receiving praise for a story that he wrote while a student, he was urged by his wife to take a year off to concentrate on his writing. The result was *The Watsons Go to Birmingham—1963** (Delacorte, 1995), which was named a Newbery Honor book and named to the Fanfare list. A situation-comedy, episodic family novel, set first in Flint and then in Birmingham, Alabama, it includes such period incidents as the racist bombing of the Baptist Church in Birmingham. Curtis' second book, *Bud, Not Buddy** (Delacorte, 1999), is an ironically humorous novel set during the Great Depression about a Flint orphan boy who is absolutely sure that a prominent entertainer is his father. It has also received high critical acclaim, being named a Coretta Scott King Winner, a Newbery Winner, and a *School Library Journal* choice. Curtis currently lives in Windsor, Ontario, with his wife and family.

CUSHMAN, KAREN (1941–), born in Chicago; novelist, museum studies specialist. When she was ten years old, she went west with her family and has lived in California most of her life. She received her B.A. degrees in both English and Greek from Stanford University, an M.A. degree in human behavior from International University in San Diego, and an M.A. in museum studies from John F. Kennedy University in Orinda, California. Her first three novels have received high acclaim: *Catherine Called Birdy** (Clarion, 1994) was a Newbery Honor book; *The Midwife's Apprentice** (Clarion, 1994) won the Newbery Medal; and *The Ballad of Lucy Whipple** (Clarion, 1996) was named to the *School Library Journal* Best Books for Children list. For earlier biographical information and a title entry, see *Dictionary, 1990–1994* [*Catherine Called Birdy*].

CYNTHIA GREY (*Penance**), lawyer nearing middle age who had defended John Brown, the drunk driver who killed private investigator Holland Taylor's wife and daughter. At first Taylor has little use for her, because she defends people whom Taylor regards with distaste. Later, when he notices that she devotes herself to cases whose defendants are unfortunate or unlikely to get adequate defense, he thinks better of her, and eventually, through their mutual concern over Brown's murder, they become romantically interested in each other. Cynthia grew up in foster homes, worked as a stripper, tried suicide, and after some time in a mental institution, changed her way of life, earned her high school equivalency diploma, worked her way through the university and law school, and became successful and respected in her profession. The end of the novel leaves open the possibility of a continuing romantic relationship between Cynthia and Taylor.

D

DAD (*Iceman**), father of Eric and Duane* and husband of Mom*. Dad, according to Eric, who tells the story, is a rabid hockey fan, having had a lifelong attachment to the Boston Bruins, and derives deep, vicarious satisfaction from his son's ability on the ice. He especially seems to gain pleasure when Eric plays rough. He hates his job at the public relations agency, is cool toward his wife, who is cool toward him, and is undergoing a midlife crisis, at least in the eyes of his sons. At the end, Duane tells him that Eric is quitting hockey before Eric has a chance to tell him. When Eric decides to continue playing, Dad is so happy with the decision that he accepts his son's less aggressive play. Dad is a character toward whom the reader feels mixed emotions.

DAD HERNANDEZ (*Parrot in the Oven: Mi Vida**), father of Manny (Manuel) Hernandez and Nardo* (Bernardo) Hernandez, his adolescent sons, and of daughters, Magda and Pedi, and husband of Mom* (Rebecca) Hernandez. Dad lost his job as a translator with the city because he has a drinking problem. Now he spends most of his time hanging around Rico's Pool Hall, gambling and drinking, to the frustration, in particular, of his wife. He often bullies her and his children and is usually irritable and hard to get along with. He is a proud man, however, and refuses to go to Welfare for help, even though Rebecca reminds him that his children need food. Near the book's end, he gets a job doing office work with a construction company. Although he is the stereotype of the Mexican-American father and husband, he is a strongly depicted figure.

DAKOTA DREAM (Bennett*, James, Scholastic, 1994), contemporary boy's growing-up novel lasting about two months at the end of the school year. Floyd Rayfield, 15, the narrator, who prefers to be known by the Native-American name of Charly Black Crow, arrives at the campground on the Pine Ridge Indian Reservation in South Dakota after an 800-mile trip, having run away from his Joliet, Illinois, foster home on a "borrowed" motorcycle and hitchhiked after the bike breaks down. He has had a dream in which he sees himself as a Sioux (Dakota) warrior and is convinced that his destiny lies with the Indians. Donny* Thunderbird, 19, college student and caretaker at the campground, listens to his story about the dream, introduces him to very, very old Delbert* Bear, respected elder, and takes him to Chief* Bear-in-Cave. The chief listens with respect to Floyd's story about the dream and running away. Convinced that the boy is truthful, the chief suggests that Floyd embark on a *hanblecheya*, the Dakota boy's traditional vision quest. With Delbert as shaman or medicine man performing the necessary rituals and Donny explaining what he is to do, Floyd engages in the sweat lodge ceremony and then is taken up into the hills to the cave where Black Elk, the much-respected, historical holy man, used to go. Floyd spends the next four days undergoing the ancient rite, fasting and alone. In the cave during his lucid moments, he writes in his journal the story of why he ran away. He says that he cannot remember his parents and has never lived in any one home for more than two years. When his latest foster mother can no longer keep him, he is placed by social workers at the Gates House group home, which is operated by sober, suspicious Mrs. Grice, and with a new social worker, Barb* McGuire, whom he immediately likes and who obviously likes him. He soon gets in trouble with all his authority figures for one reason or another except for Barb, partly because of his Indian propensities. He does not like his clinging, whiny roommate, Nicky, but develops a kind of friendship with the boy, whose ne'er-do-well family live nearby and whose brother has given him a broken-down Kawasaki motorcycle. Since Floyd learned about engines from his last foster father, the two boys fix the machine, mostly in Barb's garage. Floyd likes and respects Barb, but Floyd has grown so suspicious of The System, as he calls it, that he simply endures situations and takes refuge in his dream. A good writer, he submits to his English teacher a version of the traditional Indian Stone Boy legend. Encouraged when she accepts it, he enters in a young writers' contest an original story, "Mask," but she and the principal withdraw it as too psychologically disturbing for a high school entry. More trouble follows, and he is sent for psychological testing. Although Barb believes that he is being unfairly treated and wants to look for another placement, he feels that The System is against both of them and runs. On the last day of the vision quest, his mind numb from fatigue and hunger and in a kind of "mental zone," he sees the Stone Boy story. Having successfully completed the required four-day ritual and received a vision, he is called a "young man of honor" by the chief, who also says that the version of the legend that Floyd received is the "best Stone Boy tale" that he has ever heard. Barb arrives with the news that two possible new foster placements await him. The chief offers him a job on the reservation for the next summer and puts him on the tribal rolls as Charly Black Crow. Floyd understands himself better now and knows that he has a strong advocate in Barb, one who can help him make The System work for him. Although the journal is too detailed to be credible as a journal, and writing so much in such detail during the vision quest strains belief, the account of one boy's attempts to keep his self-respect and not knuckle under to a callous authority holds the interest all the way and moves to an acceptable conclusion. The details of Native-American Sioux (Dakota) rites and reservation life are engrossing. The teachers, group-home people, and social workers, except for Barb, are stereotypically insensitive, the attitudes that they project the antithesis of what those who work with young people should be. They are dramatically foiled by the Indians. ALA; SLJ.

DANCING ON THE EDGE (Nolan*, Han, Harcourt, 1997), contemporary, realistic problem novel with surrealistic aspects covering four years in the lives of a mentally ill Alabama girl and her dysfunctional family of eccentrics. The introverted, withdrawn narrator, Miracle McCloy, 10, spends a lot of time with her beloved father, Dane*, considered a prodigy because he published his first novel when he was thirteen, and her grandmother, Gigi*, a spiritualist. Gigi gave the girl the name Miracle because Gigi says she was delivered from the dead body of her mother who had been struck and killed by an ambulance. After a seance that Gigi conducts, Dane simply melts away on the floor of his basement room, leaving only a heap of garments behind. Miracle appropriates his bathrobe and wears it henceforth, constantly. Gigi moves back to Atlanta, Georgia, to live with her divorced husband, Opal*, a carpenter, and takes a job as a psychic at a gift shop. When Opal sees how skillful Miracle is at gymnastics and at improvising dances, he enrolls her in dancing lessons but orders her never to tell Gigi. One day, because her body is covered with bruises from falling at practice, their secret comes out. Gigi is greatly upset, driving Miracle more into a world of her own, a pleasant, beautiful one in nature, where she and Dane are close and he approves of her. At her 13th birthday party, a tornado strikes, depositing the house across the street and damaging it severely. Opal has a heart attack, a happening that Miracle thinks is also her fault. It is decided that Miracle will live with her Aunt* Casey Dawsey, her dead mother's sister, and Casey's husband, Uncle Toole. As before, Miracle has trouble in school and makes no friends. The students poke fun at her bathrobe and often laugh at her. When life gets bad, she drifts off to her safe place in nature. Gigi marries again and goes to Europe on her honeymoon. She sends Miracle a remarkable, gold-threaded shawl, which the girl wears to school. Miracle tells the students that it is a special shawl with which she can do love charms. Mildly successful in bringing young lovebirds together, she collects a bottle and candle for each ceremony that she performs. She intends to re-create Dane's old room, the dark basement place in which he kept bottle-candles burning. Then Uncle Toole and Aunt Casey split up, and a schoolmate accuses Miracle of being a fraud. Miracle puts on Dane's bathrobe, makes a circle of bottle-candles around herself and lights them, setting herself on fire and severely burning her legs. When she is healed enough to be moved to a psychiatric unit, she becomes the patient of Dr. DeAngelis, whose work with her intensifies after she cracks up reading Emily Dickinson's poem "I'm Nobody." Gradually, the doctor, with Aunt Casey's help, gets her to face the truth—that her relatives have never been a real family, have never given her love, have never even touched her or hugged her or accepted her as she is. In fact, they have made her feel inadequate because she is not the prodigy that they wanted her to be. She learns, for the first time, that her mother, who had been an outstanding dancer headed for New York, had committed suicide and that her father, smothered by Gigi's overprotectiveness, had simply run off. He did not melt away as she had been led to believe. Aunt Casey, however, offers her love and a home, and although Miracle can return to Gigi, if she wishes, she chooses to live with her aunt. All the characters are eccentricized types. While, on the one hand, it is easy to sympathize with Miracle, she does little to help herself, but perhaps by the time that the reader meets her, it is too late for her to do so. Although primarily serious in tone, the book has many humorous situations. By far its best aspect is the gradual, inexorable disintegration into mental illness of the protagonist's fragile personality. SLJ.

DANE MCCLOY (*Dancing on the Edge**), father of Miracle McCloy, the protagonist, and only son of Gigi* and Opal* McCloy. Considered a child prodigy, he published his first novel at thirteen and his second at fifteen. Gigi did all she could do to nurture his unusual ability, taking great pride in the talent that set her son apart from everyone else and isolating him from life. Opal, however, felt that Dane should also learn practical, everyday skills, like lawn mowing. Since the two parents differed so much about how to raise their son, Gigi divorced Opal and moved to Alabama, where Dane met and married Sissy, Miracle's deceased mother, while he was still in his teens. Dane became a withdrawn, reclusive man who talked to himself and spent many hours alone in his basement "cave," where he did his writing. Where he went after he "melted" is never disclosed. ·

DANGER ALONG THE OHIO (Willis*, Patricia, 1997), historical novel of three children who get separated from their father while traveling down the Ohio River in 1793. Although everyone on the flatboat knows that the Indians on the western side of the river are a great threat, they think that at Wheeling Island, just a stone's throw from the Virginia side, they are safe. While their father is ashore, Amos, 11, Clara, 12, and Jonathan, 7, asleep on the boat, are awakened by gunshots and the noise of Indians on the deck breaking open supply crates. The three pile hay around their cow, Queen Anne, hoping to hide her, then slip over the side and cling to the boat until the Indians leave. Clambering back onto the deck, they discover that the boat has been set afire and adrift. When they realize that their effort to fight the fire is in vain, Clara pushes Queen Anne into the water and, holding Jonathan's hand, jumps in after her, heading for the nearer western shore. Amos follows them. At first they are separated, but as daylight comes, they find each other, Jonathan having clung to the cow's tail in the river. Their options are limited. The only food that they have is a few strips of jerky in Clara's knapsack and the milk that Queen Anne is still giving. Amos has his pouch of marbles and his knife. They are afraid to try to return to

Wheeling Island, knowing that the Indians might be in charge there, and decide that their best bet is to try to walk to Marietta, a good-sized settlement probably several days away, even though they are on the Indian side of the river. One night Amos smells smoke and, creeping off to investigate it, almost stumbles on an Indian camp. Mosquito-bitten, cold, stiff, and too afraid to move, Amos waits until daylight, when the Indians abruptly rise and set off. Amos builds up the remains of their fire, then fashions a basket and lines it with sod to carry glowing embers back to Clara and Jonathan. While Jonathan catches frogs to cook, Amos explores the river for fish that he might spear and sees an Indian, clinging to a log, headed directly toward him. When the Indian, a boy not much older than he is, slips off the log and appears to be drowning, Amos impulsively jumps in and pulls him out. He sees that the boy has been shot, and persuades Clara, who is reluctant to help an Indian, to probe his wound for the bullet and contrive a poultice and a bandage. Laden with guilt for having accidentally shot and killed his best friend the year before, Amos is determined to give this boy a chance to live. Besides the frogs, they find some walnuts, Amos catches a Carolina parakeet roosting, and they continue to have milk, but they are always hungry, yet they share what they have with the Indian, whom they begin to call Red Moccasin. Their troubles increase when Clara comes down with a fever. Before they can move on, they are suddenly surrounded by Indians, obviously ones known to Red Moccasin. The old leader, who turns out to be Red Moccasin's grandfather, knows some English and questions Amos. He announces that they will all go to his village and become Shawnee. Amos tries to bargain with them: he will go willingly if they let Clara and Jonathan stay. The Indians leave the cow but force the children to accompany them. After a long day, their camp is attacked, and in the dark the three children get away and head toward Marietta again. Before they get back to the Ohio River, they are confronted by Red Moccasin pointing a gun at them, letting them know that his grandfather has been killed and that he intends to take them back to his village. Just then a white man emerges from the trees, his gun pointed at Red Moccasin. Determined to prevent conflict, Amos steps between them, soon joined by Clara and Jonathan. It turns out that the man has met their father, who is in Marietta, wounded but surviving, and he has been hunting for them. He also has found Queen Anne. Red Moccasin gives Amos back his pouch of marbles, which the Indians had taken from him, and in a return gesture of friendship, Amos gives the Indian boy his best shooter. He disappears into the forest, and the three children follow their rescuer toward Marietta. Although the ending is somewhat schmaltzy, and there is no exploration of how the family will fare with all their goods lost, the story is satisfying and does not gloss over the many difficulties that the children face. The incident that caused Amos to suffer from guilt is a clumsy addition to an interesting survival story, but it serves to explain why Amos allows his bossy sister to lead for most of their adventure. Spur.

DANZIGER, PAULA (1944–   ), born in Washington, D.C.; extremely popular writer of humorous novels for and about adolescents. Her first three books took the young adult (YA) audience by storm because of their catchy titles and their audacious content: *The Cat Ate My Gym Suit* (Delacorte, 1974), about a girl who uses that excuse to get out of suiting up for gym class; *The Pistachio Prescription* (Delacorte, 1978), about a girl with health problems and in conflict with her troubled parents; and *Can You Sue Your Parents for Malpractice?* (Delacorte, 1979), about a girl with both parent and boyfriend problems. The first two novels received many state and national citations and comments from critics about the attractive humor, strong dialogue, real-seeming, if superficial, characters, and vigorous style. A dozen and a half similar books later is *P.S. Longer Letter Later** (Scholastic, 1998), written with Ann M. Martin*, an epistolary novel cited by the American Library Association. Two former classmates send letters to one another describing their family, school, and romantic lives. Some critics complain that Danziger's books merely validate reader narcissism and do little to extend awareness beyond self, but all, even early ones, have retained their popularity as "quick reads." After receiving her bachelor's and master's degrees from Montclair State College, Danziger taught English in junior and senior high school until 1978, when she became a full-time writer.

DARING TO BE ABIGAIL (Vail*, Rachel, Orchard, 1996), novel of a girl's discovery of her real self after trying to change her personality at summer camp. Abby Silverman, 11, has decided to be Abigail at Camp Nashaquitsa, where she and her brother, Jake, 8, are going for the first time, because her deceased father preferred her full name, and she wants to become the lighthearted, daring daughter for whom he always wished. The book consists of episodes in which she attempts to project the new Abigail, punctuated by letters home to her mother that often give a brighter picture than the actual camp experiences. She reports, for instance, that Jake is getting along famously, while he actually is miserably homesick. Some of the girls in her cabin, including Tiff and Robin, were at the camp the summer before and seem enviably self-assured. One new girl, Dana, who desperately brags about her high IQ, her yellow belt in tae kwon do, and her first prize in Rhode Island for baton twirling, wants to be Abigail's friend, but Abby can see that Dana is doomed to be an outsider, and she opts for best friendship with Tracy, who wears a retainer. At the evening Brother-Sister Social, Abigail comforts Jake and acquires a boyfriend, Scott. At the getting-to-know-you session in the cabin, Abigail has rashly claimed that she never refuses a dare, thinking that her new personality requires this sort of bravery. This gets her into trouble, both minor and serious. Egged on by the other girls, she takes the initiative in kissing with Scott, and he breaks off with her. More disastrously, she accepts the dare to pee into Dana's mouthwash. As a result, she is called up before Uncle Gary, the camp director, and, after being grilled, is sent home. Jake, who by this time has found an odd-looking fat boy for a friend, opts to stay in camp. The book ends with a letter to her father, explaining that she tried, but she can't be the kind of girl whom he wanted, and signed "Abby." Although there are many amusing and satirical digs at camp life, including the dynamics of preteen boy-girl dating and the obsession of the girls to shave their legs, the novel ends without a sense of completeness. Abby has learned that she can't become Abigail by trying, but it is not clear whether she has understood the social forces that precipitated her meanness to Dana. She is left with no friends, a mother who can't believe her conduct, and a feeling of failure. While the point of view is mostly Abigail's, often quite clearly showing what is going on in her mind, it occasionally shifts joltingly to that of one of the other girls, thereby temporarily destroying the reader's identification with the main character. SLJ.

DAUGHTER OF SUQUA (Hamm*, Diane Johnston, Whitman, 1997), historical novel of the breakup of a Native-American village in Puget Sound and the love that will keep the family together. In the early 1900s, U.S. government policy demanded that Native-American peoples give up their old tribal ways and become "Americanized," specifically, the Suquamish on the Port Madison Reservation, where their land on the beach is to be taken over for a fort and the families given widely separated land allotments, some with no fresh water, most with no access to the salt water where fishing and clam digging have been their main food sources. Ida Bowen, 10, skips school to go with her maternal grandmother, Little Grandma, to fishing camp, not the all-community migration that it once was, but just the two of them, to build a temporary shelter, catch and dry salmon, and harvest cattail roots and stalks. When they return to Suqua, Ida's father, who works in a lumber camp many hours away, is home and leads a delegation to talk to Mr. Simpson, the white teacher and agent for the reservation, asking permission to build their new houses on the school land up the hill, thereby keeping the village together. Mr. Simpson, who is not totally unsympathetic, points out that this is not permitted and that if the families do not move to their allotments, the land will be taken from them. The rest of the book details the inexorable change that all this brings about: Mother must give up her plan to start a small village store, since the people will be too far apart to make trading there practical; Father takes leave from his job to start a house on their distant allotment; Tony Canavaro, ten years Ida's senior, whom she thinks she may some day marry, goes to Seattle, gets drunk, beaten up, and, when he returns to Suqua, arrested and jailed; worst of all, Ida is among the children who must go to Tulalip Indian School, a boarding school so far away that she will not come home until spring. In the time between these events, Ida learns more about her family and her people. David Jennings, an old man who still wears his hair in a braid and speaks Suquamish, was sold into the tribe as a child. When she was fifteen, Little Grandma was sold for three blankets to marry a Twana from the Skokomish Reservation. Later, after her daughter was born, her husband was jailed for having two wives, neither of whom he wanted to give up. To free him, Little Grandma had taken her daughter and returned to Suqua. She gives Ida the courage to leave on the steamer with the other children but to hold Suqua, like her Suquamish name, meaning Daybreak, in her heart and return when she can. In a simplified story intended for middle-school children, this misguided effort to stamp out a people's heritage is told from the point of view of a young girl, clearly and without polemics or undue sentiment. Ida's relationship to her grandmother, who exemplifies the traditional ways, is a strong element, as is the description of the beautiful island on which they live. A helpful map, an author's note, and a Foreword giving historical background open the novel. Western Heritage.

DAVE AT NIGHT (Levine*, Gail Carson, HarperCollins, 1999), humorous period, friendship, and orphanage-life novel set for a few weeks in New York City's Lower East Side and Manhattan in 1926 during the Harlem Renaissance. When eleven-year-old narrator Dave Caros' father, Abraham, a Sephardic Jewish immigrant from Salonika, dies of a fall, and Dave's stepmother, Ida, does not want him, Ida takes the now-completely orphaned boy to the Hebrew Home for Boys (HHB) on 137th Street and dumps him there. Filled with resentment that his older brother, Gideon, fourteen and thought smart, has not insisted that Uncle Jacob take Dave, considered troublesome, into his house, too, Dave is homesick, lonely, fearful, and soon cold and hungry besides. Scary Mr. Bloom, the HHB superintendent (the boys call him Mr. Doom), insists on being addressed as "sir" and often beats the boys madly with a yardstick; Mr. Meltzer, the prefect, is rough with Dave and calls him a brat; Dave's uniform is ugly and much too big; the place is freezing cold; and bullies grab his tiny portion of almost unpalatable food. Teacher Mr. Gluck (the boys call him Mr. Cluck), does very little instructing, just disparages the boys. Dave soon becomes fond of the other eleven-year-old boys (the elevens) with whom he lives and is gratified to see that they try to look out for one another, even sharing extra food if there is any. His best friends are spastic Mike, Eli, an organizer, and consumptive Alfie. One night unsuccessfully searching for the beautiful wood carving done by Abraham of Noah's Ark, all that now ties him to home but that was taken from him, he decides to run away, manages to scramble over the wrought-iron fence, and makes his way through the darkness across Saint Nicholas Park until he comes to a large building. He sees people entering and leaving, many of them African Americans, mostly well dressed and driving fancy cars. He is singled out by a grandfatherly old man, Solly* Gruber, who takes him inside and passes him off as his grandson. Solly enlists the boy in helping him and his parrot tell fortunes for the partygoers, which is the congenial old man's way of making a meager living. Dave thrills to the jazz music and savors the plentiful, elegant food. He meets Irma* Lee Packer, a black girl his age, adopted daughter of Odelia Packer, a well-known party-giver who invites him to a party at her house in a month. He gets caught sneaking back into the HHB and is taken to Mr. Doom, who beats him badly. When he discovers that Mr. Doom has the carving locked in his curio cabinet, he determines to recover it and run away for good. Complicating matters is that as days pass, he finds that he has become fond of the elevens and also his art teacher, Mr.* Hillinger, who recognizes that Dave has artistic talent. Many events and more forays outside HHB occur before Dave gets the key to the cabinet and takes the carving back, Solly gets Mrs. Packer involved in the home's affairs, the home's board investigates, and Mr. Doom is fired. The novel recalls nineteenth- and early twentieth-century orphanage stories but lacks their grimness because the tone is light. Exquisite use of detail gives life to the area and period—the clothes, the music, such historical figures as Langston Hughes, Countee Cullen, and W.E.B. Du Bois in the background, speakeasies, nightlife—the book teems with vitality. Dave's dreams of playing Robin Hood and freeing the elevens, his little boy's mingling of realism and idealism, his yearning for a real home, his finding that he has a true talent in drawing, his grit and determination—all these make him an attractive protagonist. While Irma seems incongruous, and most characters are one-dimensional, Solly Gruber almost overshadows the boy, so attractive a figure is he, almost like a fairy godfather who has magically appeared to take the boy into his care. In an Afterword, the author says that the book is based loosely on her own father's boyhood. SLJ.

DAVE WILSON (*The Magic and the Healing**), from tidewater Virginia, one of the four veterinarian students who travel with Sugar* Dobbs into the remote valley of the realm of Crossroads* to treat ailing creatures. At first he is a brash, arrogant young man, often cynical and troublemaking, but he becomes more thoughtful and helpful through his experiences. He eventually goes into research medicine. His first patient in Crossroads is the formidable Griffin*, whose case he fails to explain to Sugar's satisfaction but whose health he helps to restore and whom he works hard to care for at the vet hospital.

DAVID GOLDING (*The Cage**), video filmer on the *Natural Photography* Arctic expedition in northern Manitoba. He has been chosen partly because he is small enough to fit into the cage, from which they will take close-up pictures of polar bears. He has been on other assignments for the magazine and has agreed to this one mostly because he has been promised one later filming tree slugs in Venezuela. He hates the cold and talks incessantly about the tropics. Because David is gay, Butler*, the naturalist, treats him with scorn. David enjoys baiting Butler and watching his unease turn to apprehension. On the shortcut across the inlet, the ice breaks under him, and David slides into the water. Although Beryl* Findham manages to catch hold of his parka hood and hold on until Butler can pull them both out, he dies in the igloo that night.

DEAL WITH A GHOST (Singer*, Marilyn, Holt, 1997), ghost mystery-fantasy with girl's growing-up story aspects set in the town of Parkington somewhere in the United States in the late twentieth century. Flippant, saucy, underachiever Deal (Delia) McCarthy, about sixteen and new in town, is filled with resentment. Her mother, Renee, has taken her away from her friends and dumped her on aloof, rule-oriented Gram, Maureen Murray, a pharmacist, because Renee's new boyfriend does not want Deal living with them. Deal starts Blain Schott (called

Brain Rot by the students) High School in midyear, with little, she thinks, to look forward to except the Dating Game, which she also calls the Baiting Game, whereby she steals whatever boys she wants just to show that she can. The first day, she encounters a friendly boy, Laurie Lorber, whom she thinks of as nice but klutzy, "like an eager puppy," and who tells her that Brain Rot is haunted by a ghost—"she's a doozy." Within a few days, she and Laurie have been paired in glee club to sing "All the Things You Are" for the spring recital, and a friendship of sorts begins between the two. She also early meets the "center of the high school world," tall, blond athlete Mark Chelsom and his girlfriend, Tina Tchelichev, and their clique, decides that Mark is good prey, and, before many days have passed, has captured him. Still early in the semester, having forgotten her backpack one afternoon, she returns to the school, enters her home-room, which is also the music room, and hears someone playing the piano. She sees a slight, white-garbed figure bathed in a misty glow, the first of several sightings of the school ghost that she will have. Angry at Gram, she snoops in Gram's closet and finds a locked metal box, which later she opens. Inside is an old valentine, signed Marie. Out helping Laurie deliver pizzas, she learns that a certain Marie met her death at a particularly dangerous corner. Word of Deal's clandestine meetings with Mark gets out, and she is sorry for hurting Tina, who is thoroughly nice but feels unable to stop the game. When, on another occasion, the ghost says her name and asks for the heart, she feels that she must be going crazy. Details of the past gradually come out. Gram, now known as Maureen, used to go by her second name, Delia. She also liked to accumulate boys when she was young and stole her schoolmate Marie's boyfriend. When Marie tried to make up by sending him a valentine, Gram stole it. Deal realizes that although Marie's ghost was probably speaking of Gram, she might well have been ad-dressing Deal. She resolves to keep the terrible Game from continuing into her generation. When Gram learns what has been going on with the ghost, she almost faints, paramedics are called but arrive tardily, and it is learned that they have been tending Mark, who has been injured in a motorcycle accident at the corner where Marie died. Deal apologizes to Tina and tells her that Mark really loves her. Although learning to "deal with nice" may be a challenge, as Gram suggests, Deal resolves to stick with nice Laurie. Most characters are one-dimensional types and simply play their roles. Deal is an unlikable protagonist who excuses her immorality as the result of circumstances rather than taking responsibility for her actions. Mark, too, refuses to control his behavior, although he knows full well that Deal is toying with him. Gram's situations, past and present—she now has a man friend, who also is nice—parallel Deal's perhaps too patly, but they do add texture to the novel. They also raise the unanswered question of whether or not such behavior is inherited or fated. Similarly, whether the ghost of Brain Rot has been laid is never addressed. The ghostly appearances are the only fantasy elements. Discussing the Hamlet ghost in school seems too much of a coincidence. Poe Nominee.

DEFELICE, CYNTHIA, storyteller and author of stories for picture books and of critically acclaimed novels for later elementary and early adolescents. In addition to mystery and suspense fiction, among them *The Ghost of Fossil Glen** (Farrar, 1998), she has written historical novels, including *The Apprenticeship of Lucas Whitaker** (Farrar, 1996), about an apprentice surgeon during an epidemic of consumption in Connecticut in 1849, which was inspired by experiences of her grandfather. Both books were cited by *School Library Journal.* More recent are *Nowhere to Call Home* (Farrar, 1999), about a girl who hops a freight to live like a hobo, and *Death at Devil's Bridge* (Farrar, 2000), involving illegal drugs and murder on Martha's Vineyard. For additional information and an earlier title entry, see *Dictionary, 1990–1994 [Weasel]*.

DELBERT BEAR (*Dakota Dream**), aged Native-American Indian elder, so old that no one knows how old he is, who keeps memories of the Indian past alive by telling the traditional tales and stories of such important happenings as Crazy Horse's defeat of General Crook at the Battle of the Rosebud and the terrible Indian defeat at Wounded Knee. As he speaks, Floyd Rayfield takes notes on the stories in his journal. Delbert conducts the ceremonies for Floyd's vision quest, doing so, Floyd thinks, with whiskey on his breath.

DELIVER US FROM EVIE (Kerr*, M. E., HarperCollins, 1994), realistic problem novel set on a farm in eastern Missouri in recent years. Parr Burrman, 16, the narrator, tells how the lesbianism of his sister, Evie, 18, takes on importance in their family and attracts unfavorable attention in the claustrophobic farming community when she and beautiful, blond, private school-educated Patsy Duff, daughter of the wealthy local banker and community "boss," become friends, and rumor makes them lovers. Various attitudes about homosexuality, lesbians in particular, are voiced by different members of the family and community. A strength of the book is its keen sense of small-town and farming community life. ALA; Fanfare; SLJ. Earlier the book was cited by *School Library Journal.* For a longer entry, see *Dictionary, 1990–1994*.

DEMOUY, JEFF (*Rats Saw GOD**), earnest, caring counselor at San Diego Wakefield High School, former English teacher thirty years of age, who advises Steve York. He orders Steve to produce 100 typewritten pages on any subject that he cares to in any literary form he likes before the school year ends if he wishes to receive his diploma. DeMouy affects the nonchalant attitude and acerbic speech that contemporary high schoolers seem to expect and appreciate from the adults around them. Frequently harried-looking and often the target of disrespectful behavior from the students, he tells Steve that he nevertheless finds his work very rewarding. Although he misses the classroom, he says that he finds much satisfaction in helping students like Steve put their lives together and succeed. Of the few adults in the novel, he is the most likable.

DESSEN, SARAH, author of sensitive novels for young adults, including *That Summer* (Orchard, 1996), chosen for the American Library Association Best Books for Young Adults list. Two of her other novels, *Someone like You** (Viking, 1998) and *Keeping the Moon** (Viking, 1999), were named to the *School Library Journal* list of Best Books of the Year. All three novels have teenage girls as protagonists, each struggling for stability at a critical time in her life. Dessen lives in Chapel Hill, North Carolina.

THE DEVIL IN VIENNA (Orgel*, Doris, Dial, 1978), historical novel set in Vienna, Austria, in early 1938 during the Anschluss, the time that Germany annexes Austria and sentiment runs strongly against the Jews. Jewish Inge Dornenwald, 13, tells the story of the last weeks when her family live in Vienna and of her friendship with Catholic Lieselotte Vessely, which endures in spite of family disapproval and through which, ironically, the Dornenwalds escape to freedom. Chronology is difficult because flashbacks and letters interrupt the narrative, but with a realism born of personal experience, the author brings to life a troubled and terrifying period. Phoenix Honor. Earlier the novel received the Child Study (now Josette Frank) Award and was named to the Fanfare list. For a longer entry, see *Dictionary, 1960–1984.*

DEVORAH (*Escape from Egypt**), mother of Jesse* and wife of Nathan*. Devorah is a slim, serious, sometimes tart-tongued woman, respected for her deep religious beliefs and as the storyteller of the Hebrew tribe of Benjamin. When word goes around that Moses is to lead the enslaved Hebrews from slavery to freedom in Canaan, she tells how Joseph foretold their captivity but also predicted their release and return to Canaan. Although others complain about Moses, she staunchly supports him. She had lost two sons to the Egyptians before Jesse was born, and when her little girl, Shosha, is killed in the battle with the Amalekites, she becomes despondent and crazed with grief. She gradually declines in health until, tended solicitously by Jesse, she slips away in death, with her last words extracting a promise from Jesse to love his father.

DIANA COVINGTON (*Beggars and Choosers**), also known as Vicki Turner, a donkey, or person gene-modified for appearance and intelligence, who has dabbled in various enterprises and lived with a series of lovers, never really using her potential. At one point she was trained to be a GSEA (Genetic Standards Enforcement Agency) agent but failed to finish the course. She decides to go back to the GSEA and gets a secret assignment to follow Miranda* Sharifi, leader of the Super-Sleepless. After the Washington hearings, she trails Miranda to East Oleanta, New York, but doesn't check in with the GSEA, hoping to find the woman and get the credit herself instead of letting it go to her GSEA superiors. Involved at first with Lizzie* Francy in an effort to get Billy* Washington, who knows the woods, to lead her to the secret facility where she suspects Miranda is, Diana soon becomes interested in the little girl herself and enters into an unspoken competition with Lizzie's mother, Annie, to control and direct the child. Through the dreadful winter, in which she is saved from starving and freezing by Billy and Annie, Diana goes from feeling superior because of her donkey status to being dependent upon the good-heartedness and protection of the Livers with whom she shares a love for Lizzie.

THE DISAPPEARANCE (Guy*, Rosa, Delacorte, 1979), realistic mystery novel with boy's growing-up aspects, set for a few days at the time of publication among African Americans and West Indians in Harlem and Brooklyn, New York, one in a series. School dropout Imamu (John) Jones, 16, recently cleared of a murder charge, lives in a filthy Harlem apartment with his widowed, alcoholic mother. At the trial, socially conscious Ann Aimsley persuaded authorities to appoint her and her husband, Peter, Imamu's guardians. Although he hates to leave his mother, he yearns for an easier life in their neat home in Brooklyn. Adjustment is difficult, however, and the Aimsleys are not in complete agreement about being a foster family to the troubled boy. Peter, a former street kid himself, comes on strong with Imamu at first; Gail, 17, in college, and Ann try to be objective and welcoming, although Imamu thinks that Gail "pulls class" on him; cute little Perk, 8, turns on all her charm; and Dora Belle, a fortyish, well-endowed, former flame of Peter who owns several houses in the neighborhood, issues the invitation that she customarily extends to all men. One morning, as Imamu fixes his breakfast, he breaks one of Ann's crystal glasses and cuts his hand. Concerned about the bleeding, he goes to Dora Belle's house for help. Then Perk does not come home after school and is reported missing. Detectives, one white and one black, investigate. They soon fix on Imamu, especially when they discover blood in the kitchen and Dora Belle strangely does not completely substantiate his story about cutting his hand. Ann emotionally accuses Imamu, which hurts him deeply and drives him more into the street side of his already much-wounded personality. At the police station, reverting to street smarts, he withstands the beating that the detectives administer during the night. The next day, Gail, who regrets the family's behavior, comes for him, and soon thereafter also Ann. He goes home, however, with his mother, who has come to the station to fetch him. Three crises are in progress: the Aimsleys' with respect to where Perk might be and their suspicions about Imamu; Imamu's personal struggle about the disappearance and his attraction to both Gail and Dora Belle; and Imamu's with respect to his mother. Imamu and Gail take it upon themselves to investigate the mystery by interviewing neighbors. Seeking comfort and physical gratification from Dora Belle, Imamu goes to her house and walks in on her, to his amazement without her luxuriant hair, which he sees is really a wig. In a rage, she attacks him, but he gets away, then suddenly realizes what must have happened to Perk. Various other events occur before it is discovered that Perk had also come upon her godmother without her wig. Dora Belle accidentally killed her and then buried her under the basement floor of a rental house that she is fixing up. Imamu and the Aimleys come to respectful terms with one another, and he decides to go home and dedicate himself to fixing things there. He hopes to have a better life with both his mother and the foster family for whom he now feels affection and who now respect and feel affection for him. Characters are types, scenes are not well motivated, and the conclusion, where they all happen to be on the spot when Dora Belle assaults him as he finds Perk's grave, is too pat and melodramatic. Imamu's life with mother and on the street, the street-dude attitude that he affects, the African-American and West-Indian dialects, and the problems of the Harlem dwellers, especially the youth, are the book's best points. Phoenix Honor.

DOC URIAH BEECHER (*The Apprenticeship of Lucas Whitaker**), the kind, gentle, wise, small-town doctor to whom young, orphaned farm boy Lucas Whitaker is apprenticed. Doc cares to a fault about the people of his small town. Honest and fair, he tells Lucas that most of the time doctors do not really know what they are doing and that the state of medical knowledge is exceedingly impoverished. He says that the homegrown remedies of Pequot Indian herbalist Moll* Garfield may be at least as effective, and maybe even more, as those that he and his profession espouse. He tells Lucas that his experiences in the Philadelphia yellow fever epidemic of 1793 left him with the desire to learn more and to avoid arrogance. He hopes that such new instruments as the microscope that he has just bought will help doctors learn more and enable them to help their patients better. If stereotypically presented, Doc plays a strong role in the book and is more memorable than Lucas.

DOLLA BILL (*Ghost Canoe**), eccentric, enigmatic figure whom Nathan MacAllister finds sleeping inside the canoe that the Makah Indians are building. Dolla Bill wears a dark blue U.S. military jacket with bright brass buttons and circle tattoos on his face, two rows of them on his forehead. Of another tribe, he once lived among the Makah as a slave. During a smallpox epidemic that decimated the Makah, he was sold to a British ship's captain, with whom he sailed all over the world, and became a crack harpooner. Now returned to the Makah, he has great skill with sleight of hand and helps the Makah win in games against the Canadian tribe, the Nitinak, during the potlatch. Dolla Bill will do almost anything for money and becomes the tool of Jack Kane, the new trader and treasure seeker, who is behind the various acts of skullduggery that transpire. Dolla Bill dies a hero's death: taking a bullet intended for Nathan.

DONNY THUNDERBIRD (*Dakota Dream**), Native-American Indian Dakota youth of nineteen, a college student studying agriculture who works on the Pine Ridge Reservation of South Dakota in the summer as campground caretaker. He discovers and befriends Floyd Rayfield not long after the boy arrives. He is instrumental in helping Floyd sort out his options by introducing him to his uncle, Chief* Bear-in-Cave, and helping him with the sweat lodge and vision quest ceremonies. Donny realizes that the past should be important to the Indians and that they should not forget the old beliefs and ways. He also feels strongly, however, that they must adapt to the modern world. He tells Floyd that he has chosen his field of study because the Indians need to become more modern, especially in their agricultural practices. When Donny learns that Floyd likes to write and is good at it, he says that writing is another way through which the Indians can be helped. Donny is a positive influence on Floyd and contrasts with the troubled boys with whom Floyd lives in the group home.

DON'T YOU DARE READ THIS, MRS. DUNPHREY (Haddix*, Margaret Peterson, Simon & Schuster, 1997), novel in journal form tracing a girl's efforts to survive in her dysfunctional family and to protect her younger brother. With a strong chip on her shoulder, Tish Bonner, 16, starts the journal required for her sophomore English class, stating her scorn for school and her teachers, especially Mrs. Dunphrey, a newcomer so naive that she promises to respect any note of "Do not read" and to simply check that there is an entry. Tish marks all her entries "Do not read" and, after a trick to see whether the teacher is living up to her word, starts to write about her real life. Since the death of her maternal grandmother, in whose home the family lives, four years earlier, Tish has felt vulnerable to her abusive father, although he has been gone for almost two years. She rightly suspects that her mother, who weeps and pines for him, is borderline psychotic, and she worries about her brother, Matt, 7, who is timid and doesn't seem to be developing properly. Her after-school job at Burger Boy is complicated by her immediate supervisor, obnoxious Bud Turner, who wants her to go out with him and cuts her hours drastically when she refuses. She greets her father's sudden return, near the end of October, warily, not sharing the delight of her mother and Matt. For a few weeks he showers them with gifts, although he seems to have no job. Then he starts disappearing for a week or two at a time. When he returns on Christmas Eve, bearing elaborate gifts, Tish defies him, and he knocks her down, engages in a loud, screaming fight with Tish's mother, and takes off in his truck. For the next few weeks, Tish's mother, blaming her for her father's departure, seldom speaks to her, and Matt is totally confused. Then her mother departs, leaving a note to say that she has gone to find her husband and that she knows Tish can take care of Matt. At first it is almost a relief to have her constantly weeping mother gone, and Tish and Matt become even closer. Then difficulties begin to pile up: bills arrive, it becomes clear that their father's gifts had been charged to their mother's credit cards, Matt starts wetting the bed and catches a bad cold, and the grocery store where Tish's mother worked refuses to give Tish her last paycheck. Tish even resorts to shoplifting a package of hamburger, but is afraid to repeat this when two of her girlfriends are arrested for stealing in the mall. Hungry, exhausted, and increasingly scared, Tish is finally at her wit's end when she is laid off from her Burger Boy job, and the utilities company shuts off the electricity. With good reason, she has never had confidence in adults and has been desperate to keep anyone from knowing of her mother's absence. Now, unable to cope further and realizing that she would have a hard time explaining all her troubles in person, she writes a last entry, asking Mrs. Dunphrey, whom she has come to trust, to read the whole journal. The novel ends with a letter from Tish, in Florida, to Mrs. Dunphrey, telling about her new life with her paternal grandparents. They have also taken in Matt and Tish's mother, who has been hunted up and, having again been deserted by her husband, is in therapy. Even in this final letter, Tish's prickly personality keeps her from being smarmily grateful or even too hopeful about the future, but the strength that she has shown during her difficult year seems certain to help her succeed. The artificiality of the journal format is modified by Tish's determination to keep her teacher from reading her private thoughts, and her extensive entries are explained by her "academic potential," which she often refers to sarcastically, and her loneliness and confusion, so that the journal becomes a friend through which she can examine and discuss her thoughts. Through the worst of her spring, she returns to an orange afghan that her grandmother started her on, compulsively crocheting to counter her fears. What could have been a predictable, stereotyped novel is saved by Tish's strong characterization, a bright, irreverent, vulnerable girl truly devoted to her little brother. IRA.

DOROTHY GRUZIK (*Wringer**), neighbor and friend of Palmer LaRue from the time that the two were little more than toddlers. Up until he is nine, Palmer considers her his best friend but switches his allegiance because he wants to be in a group of boys. The group, which is headed by bully Beans* and comes to be known as Beans' Boys, torments Dorothy at every turn, yelling "fishface" at her, putting filth on her doorstep, and playing "treestumper," that is, blocking the sidewalk so she has to walk on the grass or in the street. Although Palmer does not participate in such acts with the intensity that the other boys do, Dorothy holds him responsible, turning to him one time with tears in her eyes and asking, "Why are you doing this to me?" Her words prick his conscience, and he resumes their friendship after a fashion. When the two play with Nipper, the pigeon in his room, he gets a good feeling from being with her again. She poses the book's major question in a simplified fashion, when she asks him why he just does not refuse to become a wringer, if he finds it morally distasteful and does not want to. When Dorothy and her family release Nipper in the unnamed city with railroad yards, she does not know that such cities are a major source of birds for the pigeon shoots. At the end of the story, the expectation is that Palmer and Dorothy will continue to be friends.

DORRIS, MICHAEL (ANTHONY) (1945–1997), born in Louisville, Kentucky; professor of anthropology and chair of the Native American Studies Department at Dartmouth College in New Hampshire; and writer of scholarly works, nonfiction, and novels for adults and young adults, some with his wife, Louise Erdrich. Individually, he published *Guests** (Hyperion, 1995), a young adult novel of a Native-American boy's growing up set at the time of very early contact with the Europeans, and *Sees behind Trees** (Hyperion, 1996), a blind Indian boy's coming-of-age story with fantasy aspects set in the sixteenth century. They were selected as best books by the American Library Association and *School Library Journal*, respectively. *The Window** (Hyperion, 1997), cited by both ALA and Fanfare, is a companion to the author's first and best-known adult novel, *A Yellow Raft in Blue Water* (Holt, 1987), and concerns Native-American Christine Taylor's daughter, Rayona. For additional information and titles, see *Dictionary, 1990–1994 [Morning Girl]*.

DRAGONWINGS (Yep*, Laurence, Harper, 1975), historical novel of the Chinese community in the San Francisco Bay Area during the first decade of the twentieth century. In 1903 Moon Shadow, 8, the narrator, leaves his native China to join his father, Windrider, in America. He encounters both prejudice and friendship from Americans, becomes involved in intrigue among his fellow expatriates in Chinatown, and learns to understand his idealistic and often impractical father. A sensitive boy's growing-up story, the book excels in conveying the immigrant experience against a background of innovation in aviation and the San Francisco earthquake. Phoenix Winner. Earlier the book received the following citations: Boston Globe Honor; Fanfare; IRA; Lewis Carroll; Newbery Honor. A longer entry appears in *Dictionary, 1960–1984*.

DRAPER, SHARON MILLS (1952–   ), born in Cleveland, Ohio; educator, novelist. She received her B.A. degree from Pepperdine University and her M.A. from Miami University of Ohio and since 1972 has taught junior and senior high school. In 1991 she won first prize in *Ebony* magazine's literary contest and since that time has had numerous stories and poems published. Both her novels, *Tears of a Tiger* (Simon & Schuster, 1994), and *Forged by Fire** (Simon & Schuster, 1997), were recipients of Coretta Scott King awards. She has also published a series of books for middle readers starting with *Ziggy and the Black Dinosaur* (Just Us, 1994). She has made her home in Cincinnati, Ohio.

DR. ELIZABETH BECK (*The Music of Dolphins**), research scientist at Boston University studying Mila, the feral girl who has been found living with dolphins in the Caribbean. An ambitious woman, Dr. Beck has won the right to use Mila as a subject from several competing groups, and she is fiercely determined to keep the girl safe until she can learn from her the language of dolphins. She is unable to comprehend that the language is not confined to words or sounds and that Mila can't translate the telepathic understanding that she had with her dolphin mother and cousins. Although Dr. Beck is always delighted at Mila's quick learning and at each new skill that she acquires, through most of the study she thinks of her as a subject. Only at the end, after Mila has stopped eating and begun to regress, as have all other feral children studied, does she see the girl as an individual with needs beyond those that she can supply in Boston. Her son, Justin*, tells Mila that his mother has a need to control. When

Dr. Beck finally gives up control of Mila, she begins to bond with her son in a positive way.

DREW ARCHER (*Confess-O-Rama**), father of Jordan Archer. He is a gifted and well-known artist who grieved a long time for his deceased wife. He has become a hypochondriac and is often seen popping pills or remedies of one sort or another. He sympathizes with Tony Candelaria's mother, who is recently widowed for the fourth time, compliments Tony on his cooking, and tells Tony that Tony needs a man, a father-figure, that is, in his life but says that he, Drew, is too weird to take on that role. When Tony receives the offer to work with a famous chef, Drew says that it is the result of "synchronicity," or opportunities coming along just when you need them. Another way that he explains such felicitously fortuitous happenings is that the "Universe" arranges them. Drew is a likable eccentric, as are most of the characters in the book.

DREW ARLEN (*Beggars and Choosers**), artistic young man, a Liver, who as a ten-year-old waif was taken in by Leisha Camden, one of the few Sleepless who have not retreated to the orbital, Sanctuary. Injured by one of Leisha's grand-nephews, Drew became wheelchair-dependent and, rebelling against the efforts to educate him among the donkeys, turned to petty crime and vandalism. He was kidnapped and experimentally altered in an illegal Mexican operation designed to reduce his aggression. Unexpectedly, it has enhanced his natural power to see in shapes and colors, and he has developed the ability to produce holograph programs that are hypnotic and can influence people's perceptions and emotions. Although he has imitators, his skill is unique, and as the Lucid Dreamer he has become wildly popular. For years he has been the lover of Miranda* Sharifi, the leader of the Super-Sleepless, a relationship far more intense on her side than on his. Returning after a series of concerts to the well-shielded island, Huevos Verdes, Drew is shot down in Georgia and captured by a renegade band of redneck Livers headed by James Francis Marion Hubbley and based on distortion of the ideas of the hero of the American Revolution, Francis Marion, known as the Swamp Fox. After his escape from Hubbley's underground bunker, Drew turns against Miranda and the other Super-Sleepless, since he knows that they could have rescued him if they had wished, and he doubts the morality of their program to let the local terrorists disrupt the social system of the United States so that they can step into the resulting anarchy and reshape the country by their own superior technology. By turning her in to the Genetic Standards Enforcement Agency, Drew has given up his childhood dream of owning Sanctuary, of which Miranda will be the eventual heir.

DRIES BONGER (*Johanna: A Novel of the van Gogh Family**), historical brother of the title figure and brother-in-law of Theodoor* van Gogh, who was the younger brother of the renowned Dutch artist Vincent* van Gogh. Dries, who is involved in the Paris art world, introduces Johanna to Theo and after their marriage, in particular, after Theo's death, reveals himself to be a loving, helpful brother. He advises Johanna on financial matters, even on occasion going over her accounts to make sound suggestions, gives her moral support when their father attempts to force Johanna to return home after Theo's death and to get young Vinnie*, Johanna and Theo's son, under his control, helps her crate, move, store, and show Vincent's paintings, and introduces her to Johan Cohen Gosschalk, the artist, art critic, and writer who eventually becomes her second husband and the true romance of her life. Dries' marriage to a wellborn young Dutchwoman proves disastrous, and the two separate, a happening that brings Johanna much sorrow.

DRIVER'S ED (Cooney*, Caroline B., Delacorte, 1994), realistic sociological problem novel set in a contemporary American city. Mr. Fielding, driver's education teacher, pays so little attention to his students that he does not notice that his students often switch name tags and talk openly about stealing street signs. Two students very eager for extra driving time are pretty Remy* Marland and handsome "hunk" Morgan* Campbell, both sixteen and romantically attracted to each other. One Thursday night near Thanksgiving, Remy and Morgan join their mutual friend, rat-faced, arrogant Nickie Budie, 17, regarded by schoolmates as a future criminal, pile into his Buick, and steal three signs, one that says MORGAN ROAD for Remy, THICKLY SETTLED for their friend Lark, and STOP, taken from a dangerous intersection, for Nickie. Remy and Morgan find the thefts thrilling and a romantic turn-on. The next night, television reporters describe a tragic accident: a Mrs. Denise Thompson, 26, the mother of a two-year-old boy, has been killed, her car struck broadside by a truck at the intersection where the STOP sign had been removed. The remainder of the novel focuses on Remy's and Morgan's actions and emotions as they gradually realize the implications of what they have done and come to terms with their guilt and their parents' anger and disillusionment. They deny to themselves any culpability, rationalize that "everybody's doing it," wallow in guilt, wonder how their parents' lives and careers (especially that of Mr. Campbell, a lawyer who has gubernatorial aspirations) will be affected, and worry what punishment awaits them if they tell or are found out. The sight of the crumpled death car is almost too much for them to bear. Nickie, however, is unaffected; he calls Mrs. Thompson's death "the ultimate cool." Their lives go on, but the very normalcy of their existence points up how the Thompson family can no longer share common family experiences. Fearing someone innocent will be charged, as she and Mr. Fielding leave the driver's license bureau, where, ironically, she has just been certified as a driver, Remy blurts out the truth to her teacher. Morgan owns up to his father, and the Campbells, the Marlands, and Mr. Fielding explore options and implications. Mr. Campbell outlines the possible penalties and informs them that, although a woman died because of their actions, they are not legally guilty even of manslaughter. Remy and Morgan visit Mr. Thompson to ask forgiveness, a hard task because of his deep grief and intense anger. The conclusion finds both families striving within themselves for the mutual love that they need to heal. Morgan and Remy hug, and Morgan tells Remy, "It's a wrap," meaning that what is past must lie in the past. The book sometimes seems didactic, and some scenes are melodramatic. The point of view shifts from Remy to Morgan to reveal their agony and gradual maturation. They change credibly, developing from air-headed hedonists and sexual fantasists to more socially responsible young people. Mr. Fielding's about-face and assumption of responsibility are also believable, especially when he makes the class face up to what they all are: "spoiled brats." The book's greatest force derives from its central controlling irony: these callous youths whose actions resulted in a woman's death come from homes with responsible, caring parents, are honor students, and have attended Sunday school and church regularly. They are society's "good kids." The reader realizes that what they did almost any middle-class kid might do under peer pressure and the desire to be cool. ALA; SLJ.

DUANE (*Iceman**), at seventeen the older brother of Eric and the son of Dad*, a public relations man dissatisfied with his job and life in general, and Mom*, a religious ex-nun, bent on "saving" her family. Duane, who had been a superstar at four sports, is the idol of Eric, a star hockey player. Duane abruptly gave up sports because he says that he could see no sense in them. He becomes proschool and very proficient on the guitar. Independent of mind, quick of tongue and thought, Duane is often abrasive and does not hesitate to go his own way, although he lives at home. His verbal sparring defeats his parents easily, and he even refuses to attend his grandmother's funeral, preferring to stay home and prepare the meal for the wake. He plays the guitar and sings at the wake in a way that thrills Eric but intimidates Mom. Conversations between the two brothers are often humorous and always project insights into contemporary family life, even though their home is dysfunctional. One subtly humorous passage that tells much about both of them reveals that Eric is romantically attracted to Little Martha, Duane's girlfriend. When Duane observes that nobody looks good without clothes, Eric asserts that surely Little Martha does. Whereupon Duane reiterates that nobody does, and adds "even Little Martha." Eric responds, "Jesus, Duane . . . this brutal honesty stuff of yours can be a real pain in the ass."

DUB VARNER (*Rats Saw GOD**), Wanda Varner, called Dub because she hates her first name and prefers to be known by its initial, W. This was shortened to Dub. Dub is in Steve York's grade in Houston, Texas, Grace High School and a fellow member of GOD* (Grace Order of Dadaists), a nonconformist school club. Dub is lively, filled with ideas, and iconoclastic. She and Steve fall in love and have sex frequently. After Sky Waters, their creative writing teacher, becomes the club adviser, Dub cools toward Steve, perhaps because she is jealous that Steve won a writing contest. She and Sky soon become lovers. After Steve finds out about their relationship, he moves to San Diego to live with his mother and becomes interested in Allison* Kimble.

DUNYAZAD (*Shadow Spinner**), a young woman of about fifteen, sister of Shahrazad*, the Sultan's consort. She discovers Marjan*, the novel's narrator, telling stories to children in the harem and sees an opportunity to help her sister, who is running out of tales to entertain the Sultan and thus save her life and the lives of other girls whom he might marry and kill. The beautiful, gray-eyed girl proves tough and resourceful in helping Marjan discover the end of the tale that Shahrazad is telling, an end that neither Shahrazad nor Marjan knows but that the Sultan once knew and has forgotten. At the end, Dunyazad is instrumental in getting Marjan and the vizier-storyteller out of prison and off to Samarkand, where they can live ever after in peace and splendor, as befits their good deeds. Dunyazad marries the Sultan's brother, a marriage that Dunyazad is willing to enter into so that she can protect her sister.

DUSTIN GROAT (*Reaching Dustin**), surly, unpopular sixth grader whom Carly Cameron must interview as a class assignment. Although Dustin has disagreeable habits, spitting, running a safety pin through skin on his knuckles and twisting it, jabbing into his ear with a pencil, he is also shown as sensitive and abused, both at his home and by his classmates. The school nurse removes a bug from his ear with her tweezers, but the other boys persist in thinking that it is still there and trying to look at it. The girls mostly shun him because he is crude and dirty, especially his boots, which are caked with mud from the swamp that surrounds the Groat compound. When he visits the Cameron farm with older Groat men and sees Carly and her little brother, Luke, peeking from the hayloft, he assumes that they are hiding from their father, as he hides in the tunnel from "them," obviously referring to his father and uncles. He often holds his left arm and winces, clearly having been injured, probably from blows. His sensitivity, rather overdrawn but effective in context, is shown in his concern for animals, a pet frog that he carries to school inside his shirt and a bat that he holds and untangles from a fish line, and by his love of music and amazing ability with his recorder and later with Luke's whistle. He carries messages between Noah and Julie, who is also abused, showing that he has a good relationship with his sister. He also alerts the school nurse when Alicia is hurt and calls 911 when Luke is shot and falls from the oak. At the end, when Carly assures him that her parents will go with him to the school authorities whenever he wants to, he doesn't answer at first, then whispers, "Tomorrow?"

E

THE EAGLE KITE (Fox*, Paula, Orchard, 1995), contemporary, realistic, sociological and personal-problem novel, lasting about one year, in which a son
comes to terms with his father's AIDS and sexual orientation. Liam Cormac,
14, lives in an apartment house in New York City with his mother, Katherine.
His father, her husband, Philip, has been living for a year in a small oceanside
cabin near Springton, New Jersey. Just after Liam's thirteenth birthday, Katherine tells him that his father is very ill, that his blood was tainted from a
transfusion that he received during an appendectomy three years earlier. Philip,
however, tells Liam that he has AIDS. Liam has mixed feelings. He fears losing
Philip, knows his mother has lied to him, worries about repercussions if the
neighbors find out, and lies to his friends. Liam realizes, too, but does not really
want to admit it, that he has known the truth for three years, since he saw his
father on a sand dune near the cabin embracing a blond young man named
Geoff Chaffee. At that time, he furiously broke the eagle kite that Philip had
given him for his birthday and buried it in the sand. His controlling, judgmental
Aunt Mary, Philip's sister, does not want Liam to visit his father, insisting that
Liam might catch the disease from casual contact. At Thanksgiving, Liam visits
Philip and is horrified to see how thin and weak he is, yet he notes that there
is an eaglelike strength to his father's face. He is amazed and shocked when
Philip discusses plans to visit Ireland or possibly North Carolina with Liam,
only gradually coming to realize that such planning gives Philip needed hope
and strength to confront the future. Liam asks whether Philip told Katherine
about Geoff and, when assured that she knew, admits that he himself has lied
by not telling her that he knew about his father's relationship with the young
man. He meets Mrs. Mottley, the old woman who visits Philip regularly, brings
him books from the library, and sees to it that he has what he needs. Liam
comes to see that adults are not always right or in control and to acknowledge
that Philip deserves love and respect simply because he is his father. While they
are shopping for Christmas, Mrs. Mottley calls to say that Philip is in the hospital. Katherine, Aunt Mary, and Liam leave immediately for Springton, where

Mrs. Mottley meets them. Katherine tends Philip until he dies, which is not long after they arrive. Liam weeps but also feels relieved. They have Philip cremated and hold a memorial service. The end of the story finds Katherine planning a trip for the two of them to Ireland, a symbolic act of acceptance of Philip's homosexuality and disease and a new lease on life for both of them. Chronology is difficult because the plot is often interrupted by flashbacks and memories. Ultimately, however, this disjointedness supports the sense that time is standing still for all of them as they wait for Philip to die. Characters are distinctively drawn. Liam's concerns enlist the reader's sympathies immediately. Philip is a landscape architect with a keen eye for form and beauty, especially in the out-of-doors, qualities supported by the many references to things in nature. Katherine is mostly subdued, except for occasionally standing up to bossy Aunt Mary. Mrs. Mottley seems almost too good to be true, serving as the antithesis of judgmental, acerbic Aunt Mary. The novel suggests that younger people like Aunt Mary and Liam's friend Luther, who uses street-talk terms for homosexuals, are not immune to homophobia and can be prejudiced against AIDS sufferers. The mood is static, as though one follows events through a haze or as reflections in a mirror, an atmosphere enhanced by the sharply realized visual imagery. ALA; SLJ.

EARL FOSTER (*While No One Was Watching**), eleven-year-old brother of Frankie*, 7, and Angela*, 5, both of whom he loves and feels responsible for. He is a cousin of tough, mean Wayne* Bonner, about seventeen, whom he fears but whom he also somewhat admires for the older boy's resourcefulness and daring. Earl is often sick to his stomach, probably from anxiety. His siblings notice that his eyes often have a kind of blank look, as though he is walling himself off from life. He is ashamed of stealing yet is afraid of what Wayne might do to him if he does not do what Wayne tells him. He also needs money to feed his siblings and himself. He remembers that in every letter home his father always admonishes the children to take care of one another. A good-hearted and fair boy caught in a terrible dilemma, he never blames his father for their plight—just bad luck, which he likens, in an ironically apt metaphor, to a kind of cancer.

THE EAR, THE EYE, AND THE ARM (Farmer*, Nancy, Orchard, 1994), futuristic novel set in 2194 in Zimbabwe, describing a boy's harrowing adventures when he escapes the stultifying protection of his prominent father's home. Tendai, 13, has never pleased his father, General Amadeus Matsika, chief of security for the country, who finds him imaginative and oversensitive, unlike his assertive sister, Rita, 11, or his fearless little brother, Kuda, 4. Life with Father is not only confining, because the children are seldom allowed outside the locked home enclosure at Mazoe, but also lonely and difficult, since Father has them privately tutored and imposes rigid military-style discipline on them. Mother, a chemistry professor, is kindly but preoccupied. Their best friend is the Mellower*, a professional Praise Singer employed full-time to lull away strong feelings with his hypnotic and fulsome flattery; he is a great storyteller but also lazy, impulsive, and cowardly. Because they want to get their Scout merit badges for exploring, the children persuade him to get Father, while he is under hypnosis, to sign permission for them to travel across the city and to provide the one-time-only pass cards to let them in and out of their locked enclosure. Because they have been so thoroughly insulated from the real world, the children are woefully unprepared and almost immediately fall prey to thugs called Fist and Knife, who abduct them and deliver them to the She* Elephant, an enormous woman who rules Dead Man's Vlei, a toxic waste site now inhabited by almost zombielike outcasts. Until she can make arrangements to sell them, the She Elephant puts them to work "mining" the trash for useful bits from earlier times, a job shared by the Vlei people, virtual slaves of the huge woman. After weeks of drudgery, Tendai finds a *ndoro*, a symbol of power from earlier times made of shell, which seems to confer courage on him, and he climbs up an abandoned well shaft, finds Rita and Kuda, and, with Kuda carried by a mental defective named Trashman* who has taken a liking to him, escapes from the Vlei. Trashman leads them to Resthaven, a closed area devoted to a village life like that of early Zimbabwe. At first, life in Resthaven seems idyllic, just what Tendai has always longed for. Gradually, he comes to see that the place is bound by superstitions and rigid social rules just as confining as the life that he left. In addition, Rita's lot is much worse, since girls are looked down upon, abused, and made to do the most grueling work. When she tries to save a newborn about to be killed because it is female and a twin, thought to be caused by witchcraft, and Tendai sticks up for her, they are both accused of being witches. They stand trial by ordeal, drinking a noxious fluid that makes them vomit, proving that they are normal, although the trial was meant to be rigged to prove them witches. In the ensuing commotion, they are evicted from Resthaven, along with Trashman, the only person free to come and go at will. Outside, they nearly encounter members of the dreaded Mask gang and escape on the subway, full of almost equally threatening characters. Since they have no money, they are put out at the next stop, Borrowdale, where Rita, who has a remarkable recall of numbers, remembers that the Mellower's mother lives at 25 Horsepool Lane. Although they have never met her and don't remember her name, Mrs. Horsepool-Worthingham, they make their way to her house, where she takes them in but also proves dangerous, holding them for a hoped-for reward. In the meantime, Father is extremely worried and blames himself, while Mother, just as concerned and more practical, hires the Ear, the Eye, and the Arm Detective Agency to find the children. This business is run by three strange-looking mutants who grew up near a nuclear energy site, each oversensitive in his own way: Ear, who has great, oversized ears, can hear the smallest sound; Eye can see a flea on a hawk's feathers; and Arm*, an extremely thin man with spiderlike limbs, is able to sense moods and emotions in others. They take on the case with some brilliant deduction but are always just one step behind the children. At Resthaven, they manage to rescue the unwanted girl twin as they pretend to be evil spirits and carry her with them as they leave. At Borrowdale, Tendai and Rita almost carry out an escape plan during a meeting of the Animal Fanciers' Society, but the yard is invaded by the She Elephant, who has traced them to Mrs. Horsepool-Worthingham's, and abducts them again, this time taking them to sell to the Masks, who need young people to torture and kill in their obscene rituals. In an exciting culmination, Ear, Eye, and Arm, along with Mother, invade the Embassy of Gondwanna, a threatening neighbor country whose officials actually make up the Mask gang and who are about to sacrifice Tendai. The She Elephant, gone berserk because they will not pay for the children, destroys a powerful Mask fetish, and the power of the evil group is overcome. Despite the title, Tendai is the true protagonist, and his maturing through his adventure is the main thrust of the story. Details of the three places where the children are held, though bizarre and very different, are convincing, as is their home compound at Mazoe. All the main characters and many minor ones are memorable. Although the Mellower is white, Arm is very dark, and most of the rest are shades of brown, differences of color are not emphasized, indicating that race is not a basis for tensions any more. Action is gripping, and the solution, though foreseeable in general outline, is both surprising and satisfying. ALA; Newbery Honor; SLJ.

EARTHSHINE (Nelson*, Theresa, Orchard, 1994), realistic, contemporary, sociological and physical-problem novel set in Los Angeles, concerning a family whose father is dying of AIDS. The story, told by the twelve-year-old daughter, shifts from scenes in a support group to views in the McGranahan home and back, with a few episodes set elsewhere. The book closes with the father's peaceful death and those closest to him scattering his ashes. Although the author avoids overt didacticism, the book seems more about AIDS than about people coping with the disease. Both poignancy and hilarity are used to advantage, and the tone is upbeat and hopeful. ALA; Boston Globe Honor; Josette Frank. Earlier the book was cited by *School Library Journal*. For a longer entry, see *Dictionary, 1990–1994*.

ELENOR (*The Ramsay Scallop**), Lady Elenor of Ramsay Castle, 14, the freckled, wild-haired, independent, spirited young woman who is betrothed to Thomas* of Thornham, also a noble. Since she is reluctant to marry Thomas, who intimidates her somewhat because he is a big, hulking, remote man and has been away so long on a Crusade that she hardly knows him, the priest of the castle, Father* Gregory, decides to send the two on a pilgrimage to the shrine of Saint James in Spain. He hopes that they can learn to know each other and something about human nature and hence will be better able to help the people of the manor after they marry. On the way, Elenor becomes less self-indulgent through, among other experiences, helping a young mother with three small children manage the difficult journey and locate her husband at Bordeaux. There Elenor sells her beloved horse, Mab, so that the little family can buy a house.

ELGIN TAYLOR (*The Window**), African-American father of triracial Rayona, the novel's eleven-year-old narrator. A temporary substitute mail carrier, Elgin is unreliable, irresponsible, and estranged from his wife, Christine, a waitress. Handsome, charming, and sweet-talking, he seems to have lady friends wherever he goes in Tacoma, Washington. Although she would like to associate more with her father, Elgin is seldom around when Rayona is home from school. When Christine enters treatment, he does not seem to consider having Rayona live with him, immediately seeking a foster home for her and, when that avenue does not work out, taking her to live with his women relatives. At the end, Rayona does not ask why he does not want his wife to know that he is half-white and has Irish ancestors. Although she says that she respects his need to have secrets, that does not seem to be a satisfactory reason for not asking.

ELIZABETH BURBANK (*What Girls Learn**), sister of Tilden, one year younger and very different in appearance and personality. While Tilden is dark, with her mother's features, Elizabeth is beautiful and fair, "the color of angels," Nick* Olsen says when he thinks both girls are asleep. She is taller than Tilden, long-legged and active, and makes friends easily. To the consternation of both sisters, she starts her menstrual periods before Tilden, causing them both to think that something is physically wrong until their mother takes them to a woman doctor who explains. In contrast to cautious Tilden, Elizabeth dives into new experiences, changes interests like a chameleon, and thinks little of the consequences of her actions. At one point, under the influence of an elderly neighbor, she becomes very religious, but she also experiments with beer and sex with a neighbor boy in the garage. Although she and Tilden are very different and fight frequently, they are extremely close at times, and their mother's death devastates both of them.

ELLA ENCHANTED (Levine*, Gail Carson, HarperCollins, 1997), fantasy novel retelling in an imaginative version the Cinderella story, set in the kingdom of Frell, where magic and fairies exist but which otherwise is much like early nineteenth-century England. At the funeral of her lively, fun-loving mother, the narrator, Ella, 14, weeps so loudly that her father, Sir Peter, sends her from the church, and she hides in the graveyard sobbing. She is found by Prince Charmont, 16, who tells her that he liked her mother but not her father, sentiments with which she agrees. He asks her to call him Char. At the reception afterward she meets Dame Olga, a rich, domineering woman, and her two daughters, mean, conniving Hattie and stupid Olive. She is appalled when, a short time later, her father, a sly merchant who has been away from home most of her life, decides that she will go to finishing school with the two girls. She is unable to resist because at her birth the foolish fairy, Lucinda, gave her a gift: that she will always be obedient. She is unable to resist a direct order. The cook, Mandy, who is revealed to be actually the fairy godmother of both Ella and her mother, is unable to reverse this gift, since it would involve "big magic," an activity that affects so much outside the immediate concern that all reputable fairies refuse to indulge in it. Lucinda's gift caused so many awkward situations when Ella was young that her mother ordered her never to tell anyone about it, leaving, after her mother's death, only Ella and Mandy aware of her compulsion to obey. Hattie, on the coach trip to the finishing school, discovers that she can make Ella do anything by ordering her, and she immediately takes the beautiful necklace that Ella inherited and continues to make her life miserable. In a magic book that Mandy gave her, Ella sees scenes from lives of distant people whom she knows and reads their letters, including one from Prince Char to the king, in which he says that he is delighted to be assigned to lead a patrol as his first military duty and mentions Ella, and one from Sir Peter to his bailiff, saying that he expects to attend the wedding ceremony of a pair of giants, hoping that he may pick up some valuable merchandise from fairies sure to attend. After her miserable time at the school, Ella realizes that while she had to obey her father's order to go to the school, he has not ordered her to remain there. She slips out at night, hoping to reach the site of the giants' wedding, find the fairy Lucinda, and persuade her to retract her gift. On her journey she has aids and obstacles, in the traditional quest pattern. Elves aid her. Ogres capture and plan to eat her. Ella's secret weapon is her ability with languages, many learned from the parrots in the royal menagerie. She is able to lull the ogres with their own language, with which they seduce their victims into cooperation, until Prince Char and his band arrive and rescue her. Char sends her on, escorted, to the giant wedding, where she finds Lucinda but cannot persuade her to take away her gift. In fact, the foolish fairy orders Ella to be happy to be obedient. For a while, this relieves Ella. She returns to her home with her father, who decides to marry her to a wealthy old earl, and she flirts obediently while Mandy fumes. Then her fairy godmother discovers what Lucinda has done and is able to reverse the order, since it does not involve big magic. Sir Peter, however, who is in dire financial straits, discovers that the earl is not really wealthy and, in need of immediate funds, decides to marry Dame Olga. From this point on, the plot follows the Cinderella story closely. With Dame Olga in charge and her father gone, Ella becomes a drudge to her stepmother and stepsisters. At first she is comforted by correspondence with Char, who has gone to spend a mandatory year in the province of Ayortha, letters sent to and from Mandy to bypass the scrutiny of Hattie and her mother. When he confesses to loving Ella in a letter and asks her to marry him, however, she has a sudden realization that her compulsion to obey could be a terrible threat to him and to the state if discovered by any unscrupulous power. Bravely, she writes a letter to Char, supposedly from Hattie, saying that Ella has eloped with a wealthy old man after ridiculing his letters from Ayortha. When he returns and gives them three great balls to survey the young women of his realm and choose a bride, Hattie and Olive prepare elaborately to attend. Lucinda, repentant after a year of being a squirrel, then an obedient child, provides the pumpkin coach and mice footmen for Ella, but her dress is one of her mother's saved by Mandy, and the glass slippers are a pair that Ella and Char found on the day of her father's wedding. When he brings the slipper, tries it on the scullery maid, realizes it is Ella, and says, "Say you'll marry me," she resists, out of love for him, and breaks the spell. On the familiar framework of the old tale, the novel builds a delightful story, full of clever twists and wry comments. Ella is a well-developed character, spirited, unimpressed by pomp and position. Char is charmed by her independence and her humor, which lightens the story throughout. The tone of the novel is amusing. ALA; Newbery Honor.

ELSWYTH (*Never Trust a Dead Man**), ugly, aged witch who bespells Farold, the dead man, as a bat, a goldfinch, and a duck and who gives Selwyn Roweson various disguises, so that Selwyn and Farold can find out who killed Farold. Elswyth's chief personality trait is her irritability, which she usually expresses by smacking Selwyn smartly on the side of the head with her hand. For helping him, she exacts years of servitude, eventually accumulating about nine and one-half years altogether. She encounters Selwyn when she goes into the burial crypt, because she needs materials from the dead to accomplish her spells. At the end, she has the appearance of a beautiful young woman, Farold has become a white duck, and Selwyn promises to serve her for a year. Elswyth forgives the rest of his servitude.

ELYA YELNATS (*Holes**), ancestor of Stanley Yelnats (Yelnats is Stanley spelled backward). In Latvia, to win the hand of a certain girl, Elya consults an old Egyptian woman, Madame Zeroni, who advises him to carry a pig repeatedly up a mountain and dip the pig in the river there until it is big enough to please the girl's father. Then he is to carry Madame Zeroni up the mountain, too. She says that if he fails to do this, he and his descendants will be doomed. When Elya fails to win the girl, he forgets about his promise to Madame Zeroni and leaves for America. His son is the first Stanley Yelnats, who makes a lot of money on Wall Street but loses it in a stagecoach robbery on his way to California. It turns out that Madame Zeroni was an ancestor of Zero*, whose real name is Hector Zeroni. In carrying Zero up the slope to Big Thumb several generations later, Stanley Yelnats "lays" the curse.

ENGLISH, KAREN, teacher, author. In addition to several picture books, including *Big Wind Coming!* (Whitman, 1996) and *Just Right Stew* (Boyds Mills, 1998), she has published *Francie** (Farrar, 1999), a novel of an African-American girl in the 1940s and her escape from the poverty and prejudice of Alabama. English has four children and has made her home in Los Angeles, California.

ENZO (*Stones in the Water**), Jewish friend of Roberto, the protagonist, kidnapped with him from Venice by German soldiers during World War II, and enslaved on building projects in Germany and Ukraine, where he dies of a beating. The boys early decide that for his protection he should call himself by the Italian name of Enzo rather than by his Jewish name of Samuele. On the whole, Enzo is an earnest fellow of about thirteen but with mischievous and daring moments. On the way to the theater, Sergio, Roberto's brother, grabs Samuele's armband, which identifies him as Jewish, and dumps it, an action that probably saves Samuele from immediate incarceration or death as a Jew. Nevertheless, Roberto is constantly frightened for both their lives, afraid that Enzo's Jewishness will be discerned because Enzo has been circumcised, and afraid for his own life because he has a Jewish friend. Roberto becomes keenly protective of Enzo, shielding him when he urinates and bathes. Even so, one of the other boys becomes suspicious and blackmails Enzo for food. As Enzo lies dying, he urges Roberto not to "ever let them win over the inside of you." Enzo is a convincing figure.

ERETH (*Poppy**), Erethizon Dorsatum, an elderly porcupine both literally and figuratively prickly, who enables Poppy the deer mouse to triumph over the villainous owl, Mr.* Ocax. Ereth is a flat-faced beast with a black snout and fierce grizzled whiskers who moves ponderously and exudes a stench so powerful that it gags Poppy. He speaks in high diction and alliteration. Although he is ugly and smelly, he ironically proves to be her savior. He drives away the fox that threatens to devour her and then escorts her through the dangerous woods to the New House area in return for Poppy's promise to bring him the salt block put out for the deer.

ERIK FISHER (*Tangerine**), older brother of Paul, evidently a sociopath from an early age, although his parents, especially his father, have denied and ignored his problems in favor of the Erik Fisher Football Dream, in which he is a high school grid hero, wins a scholarship to a prestigious university, and probably is drafted by a professional team. Paul has always feared him, with good reason, though he has blanked out the most serious occasion, when Erik held him, forced his eyes open, and had his sidekick spray white paint into them. There also was an incident that resurfaces in Paul's memory when Erik in a ski mask tries to bash him with a baseball bat from a moving car but misses because Paul dives from his bike just in time. Earlier, Erik has killed a neighbor dog and shown other indications of a deeply disturbed personality. At the same time, he can be charming and convinces adults and even many of his peers that he is the ideal all-American boy. In the various places where they have lived, he has always attracted a devoted follower, often as antisocial as he is, who does his dirty work for him. At Lake* Windsor Downs, he and Arthur Bauer are responsible for the death of Luis* Cruz and for the burglary of several houses while they are covered by exterminators' tents and filled with noxious gases. He is almost too evil to be believable, but because he is seen through the eyes of Paul, who has always known his brother's depravity and his parents' denial, he is a plausible character.

ESCAPE FROM EGYPT (Levitin*, Sonia, Little, Brown, 1994), historical novel that retells the biblical story of the ancient Hebrews' escape from slavery in Egypt, as seen from the perspectives of handsome, gentle Hebrew Jesse*, 16, and pretty, half-Syrian, half-Egyptian Jennat*. Two intertwined stories unfold: the slaves' escape and journey through the desert to Canaan and the romance between Jesse and Jennat, a relationship that forces them to clarify their religious beliefs. While apprenticed to a jewelry smith in the household of wealthy Egyptian In-hop-tep, Jesse is attracted to Jennat, the ward of In-hop-tep's wife. At the same time, the Hebrews hear that an old man, Moses, says that their god, Adonai, has sent him to free them from slavery. The reaction of the Hebrews to Moses' message is heated and remains so throughout the novel. Some, like Nathan*, Jesse's father, are adamantly opposed to what they think is an insane idea and question Moses' authority, while others, like Uncle Rimon*, the brother of Jesse's mother, Devorah*, and a highly respected religious leader, think that what Moses proposes accords with the traditional belief of return to their ancestral home of Canaan. On the night that Jennat is to be given to In-hop-tep as a concubine, the Nile River and other waters run red with blood, the first of a series of plagues sent by Adonai that will devastate the country because Pharaoh refuses to comply with Moses' request to release the people. While Jennat yearns to return Jesse's love, she is reluctant to adopt his god, whom she sees as cruel and unjust, and Jesse thinks that the Egyptians are cruel and worship hollow idols. At the same time, Jesse knows that his parents want him to marry sweet, pretty Hebrew Talia*. After Adonai slays the Egyptian firstborn sons, the Egyptians urge the Hebrews to leave. In spite of Jesse's pleading, Jennat refuses to go with him because she feels that her mistress needs her. The people gather behind Moses with their flocks and hastily collected belongings, follow the pillar of cloud by day and pillar of fire by night, cross the Red Sea, where hundreds of Egyptians die when the parted seas return, and move into the desert. To his amazement, Jesse discovers Jennat among a group of tattered strangers, a mixture of Egyptians and other tribes, who have attached themselves to the ex-slaves. Talia and Jennat argue over him, and Jennat leaves to join a traveling caravan. When the Hebrews are attacked by a marauding desert tribe, the Amalekites, Jesse is injured, and his little sister, Shosha, is killed. The book's most memorable scene occurs when the Hebrews meet Adonai at Sinai and accept the Ten Commandments and Adonai as their God and leader. Jesse is profoundly moved by the experience, and Jennat, who has returned, feels compelled to accept Adonai as her God. In the book's last chapter, a kind of epilogue, the reader learns that thirty-eight years have elapsed. Joshua has succeeded Moses as leader, Jesse has married Jennat, who is now an even more avid follower of Adonai than Jesse, and Jesse has been telling the story of his life to two of their sons on the eve of the Hebrews' crossing the Jordan River into Canaan. The book follows the biblical account closely, and biblical passages in italics introduce some chapters. Characters occasionally recite biblical speeches. Important scenes, like receiving the Ten Commandments at Sinai and dancing around the golden calf idol, are vividly depicted, and selective, descriptive details make the Hebrews' enslavement and journey credible. The many main figures are distinctly, if stereotypically, drawn, but the book bogs down in the middle with arguments and Jesse's romantic vacillations. Moses appears only briefly, and the emphasis throughout remains on the ordinary, everyday Hebrews who might have experienced the epic departure and journey. ALA; SLJ.

ESTHER JACKSON (*Brothers and Sisters**), black woman, 34, regional manager at Angel City National Bank in Los Angeles. Educated in private schools in Chicago, although from the city's black South Side, Esther is proud of her success and yearns to advance to lending but is unable to find a mentor. She also yearns to marry a black man of equal social and employment status and educational background. Although she deplores the lack of education of Tyrone* Carter, a black Western Express deliveryman, she appreciates his gentle ways and lively mind, and the two become lovers. She also has a conflicted attitude toward Mallory* Post, a beautiful blond loan officer. Esther and Mallory share job aspirations and personal confidences, but Esther never completely trusts white Mallory. When Humphrey* Boone "comes on" to Mallory, Esther believes that Mallory has encouraged him. Esther is a well-developed character who finally realizes that Tyrone is a good and worthy man.

ETHAN RILEY (*Flyers**), serious boy of eleven, younger brother of Gabe and son of Pop*. Older than his years in many respects, he is slow to take offense, likes to think situations through on his own, and is unusually well organized, keeping filmmaking paraphernalia in order for his brother and Bo* Michaelson and even straightening out Pop's office for him. Gabe recognizes his brother's essential niceness when he remarks that Ethan never tries to beat him when they are running, although the younger boy has become so good that he probably could. Ethan is the first to discover that Andy Foster is living in Mr. Lindstrom's house and provides clothes and food for him. Since Ethan, Gabe, and Pop are unusually close, it is not clear why Ethan helps Andy without confiding in Pop or Gabe.

THE EXAMINATION (Bosse*, Malcolm, Farrar, 1994), novel of a journey in sixteenth-century China made by two brothers from their village in Sichuan province to Beijing, where the elder is to take the extremely difficult examination for government service. A brilliant scholar, Lao Chen is unworldly and naive beyond his phenomenal knowledge of Confucius and other classics. His younger brother, Lao Hong, is just the opposite, a savvy, practical, capable boy whose main interest is in raising fighting crickets. Since he knows his brother's lack of peasant cunning and is dedicated to the memory of his mother, who was educated and cared deeply for Chen's scholarly success, Hong takes on the job of getting his brother first to the provincial examination in Chengdu and, when Chen passes in fifth place, on to the final examination in Beijing. Their trip is complicated by the need to carry and deliver letters entrusted to them, since there is no other mail system. One is from a retired soldier to his old commander, General Ma, who may be in the city of Suzhou. The village schoolteacher, a minor tyrant, gives Chen a sealed letter that he warns will cause trouble to them if it is intercepted. Chen feels a Confucian duty to respect the teacher, and, besides, the man has written him a recommendation saying that he is of a good family, even though they all know that the senior Lao is a drunkard who has squandered the family fortune. Both boys leave behind good friends, Hong his kite-flying and cricket-raising buddy, Wujiang, and Chen the daughter of a local noble, Daiyun. Since Chen has passed the county examination, he travels as a Flowering Talent, wearing a blue gown and winged cap that elicit respect and occasional discounts. While he takes the three-day provincial examination, Hong locates Ye Pan, the addressee of the schoolmaster's letter, with only the direc-tions, "Southwest Chengdu." The man turns out to be a barber and a member of the White Lotus, a secret revolutionary society dedicated to fight injustice, into which he draws Hong, recognizing the boy's wit and courage. After Chen passes fifth among the thousands of candidates, the brothers start for Beijing, a great distance off, with Hong carrying this time a coded message for the White Lotus society. They encounter a plague of locusts and floods and more than once are delayed as Chen is attracted to a girl. They take passage on a dilapi-dated river junk, the *Floating Lily*, down the Yangtze through sheer-sided gorges and dangerous rapids. Although an acquaintance is knocked overboard and drowned, the brothers have no personal trouble until they are attacked by river pirates. Chen is held for ransom, and Hong is taken to an army barracks captured by the pirates and, when he refuses to reveal the meaning of the coded message that he carries, is tortured with the Thousand Cuts, knife slits, small at first, over his chest and stomach, to be repeated and increased daily. Just before he passes out, he yells the secret White Lotus cry for help, "Fifteen." When he awakens, he is approached by Yao, a boy about twelve, who he learns is a White Lotus infiltrating the pirate group. Yao helps him escape with the message and the old soldier's letter but is himself caught and probably tortured and killed. Bleeding and very sore, Hong finds an army group and persistently insists on staying with them until they reach the headquarters of General Ma, where he can deliver the old soldier's letter. Since the army is seeking the pirate leader, Hong sticks with them, becoming very close to General Ma, until they trap the pirate and negotiate, letting him escape if he frees the hostages, among them Chen. Although there are other delays and adventures, the brothers finally reach Beijing. While Chen takes the municipal examination, Hong makes his White Lotus contact and learns that the message over which he was tortured was nonsense, simply a test of his dedication. Since he has passed, he is assigned a

contact that results in the assassination of a corrupt eunuch who has been usurp-
ing the emperor's power. Chen places second in the municipal examination and
first in all the country in the final palace examination. He is offered a variety
of positions and, after much hesitation, settles on becoming the Vice Secretary
of Rites Qufu, in charge of the temple and tomb of Confucius, a post that he is
offered because he not only has knowledge of the classics but actually believes
in them, a rare combination. Knowing that his older brother must some time be
on his own and learn to care for himself, Hong opts to return to General Ma
and seek a place in the military, a life that he found exciting. Although there
are many stirring, even breathtaking incidents, the main tension of the novel
comes from the contrast between the personalities of the two brothers, both
idealistic but Chen being intellectual, impractical, and ineffective while Hong is
full of drive and action, unimpressed by authority and class position. The wealth
of detail brings medieval China to life, with all its beauty, squalor, ritual behavior, and natural disaster. Especially interesting are the descriptions of the
examinations, which have no relevance to the duties for which they ostensibly
test the applicants. Maps on the endpapers are very helpful. ALA; SLJ.

F

THE FACTS SPEAK FOR THEMSELVES (Cole*, Brock, Front Street, 1997), realistic novel of family life and psychological and social problems set in recent years in Minnesota and Florida. Linda, 13, begins her first-person narrative by describing her responses to the myriads of questions posed to her by police and social workers as they investigate the murder of Jack Green, the realtor for whom Sandra, Linda's mother, works and with whom she has been sexually involved and with whom Linda also has been having sex, and the suicide of Frank Perry, her mother's erstwhile boyfriend. When authorities decide that the case is clearly murder-suicide and that Linda has been raped, Linda steals a look at the social worker's report and says that it makes her look ridiculous. She writes her own version of what led up to the event, a concise, factual, dispassionate report. An unusually capable, well-organized child, Linda has been the glue that has held together her exceedingly unstable household. She is the eldest of Sandra's three children—each by a different father. Never-married Sandra, a college dropout, is estranged from her affluent parents, the Hoeksmas, a physician and his wife. Linda is the child of Native-American activist Charles Taylor, who commits suicide. Before he dies, Sandra is already pregnant with Stoppard by a law student, Peter Hobbs, whose parents adamantly oppose their marrying. They live briefly with Sandra's parents until Sandra moves to Florida with wealthy widower Arthur Bloomberg, Dr. Hoeksma's friend. Sandra simply walks out on Arthur, Linda, and Stoppard when Arthur suffers a stroke and becomes disturbed, leaving Linda to cope. She returns to reclaim her children after she has taken up with another ne'er-do-well boyfriend, Frank Perry, with whom she is already pregnant. After Tyler's birth, she takes a position in Jack Green's office. Jack soon begins having sex with Linda, who finds their trysts exciting and a few moments of stability in her otherwise tumultuous life, her mother becoming more and more erratic and now drinking. Frank confronts Jack and shoots him, Linda a witness, on a parking lot ramp and then kills himself. Linda's account is bleakly factual, its dispassion enhanced by the lack of quotation marks for conversation and mostly short, simple sentences. Most characters are functionaries—the men being sex partners for unstable, immature Sandra, disappointing as providers, husbands, and fathers. While Linda's case is legally statutory rape (which is probably what authorities mean when Linda says they call it rape), Linda's relationship with Jack evidently has satisfied a deep psychological need. At the end, Linda is living in a center run by Catholic Charities, where the sisters are kind and understanding and where for the first time in her life she need be responsible only for herself. She is beginning for the first time to make friends her own age. Why Frank shot Jack is not explained, nor is the reader told what happens to Sandra and Linda's brothers. This is a shocking story, whose matter-of-fact tone intensifies its horror. SLJ.

FALCON'S EGG (Gray*, Luli, Houghton, 1995), lighthearted, contemporary fantasy involving magic and dragons set in New York City. While walking through the western edge of the Great Lawn in Central Park one Saturday in April, Emily Falcon Davies, 11, finds a hot, scarlet egg and carries it carefully home to her apartment building, where she shares her discovery with her dearest friend, African-American Ardene Taylor. Falcon then persuades her mother, Missy, a divorced book illustrator, who is often engrossed in her work and suffers from "Nerves" because of "Deadlines," to allow her to visit, with Ardene, her Great-Aunt* Emily Meade, in whose ability to direct matters she has great confidence. Emily calls on her friend Freddy* (Fernando) Maldonado, an ornithologist, for advice on caring for the egg. Calling themselves Friends of Egg, the four swear to keep Egg's presence secret and agree to keep it in Ardene's apartment until it hatches. As spring passes, Egg's heartbeat grows stronger, and its temperature rises even higher. After her exclusive Chapman School lets out for the summer, Falcon assumes responsibilty for her younger brother, Toody (Tudor), because Missy is working on another book. She shares the secret with Toody, who wraps Egg in the cherished snakeskin that their father sent him from Australia. In July, Egg hatches, coming out as a red, winged dragon six inches long, with dark blue eyes, gold claws, blue tongue, half-circle markings on its skin, and a crest down his back. Determined by Emily to be a girl, Egg eats anything except birdseed and especially loves edible flowers and boiling water. When Egg is about eight inches long, they move her to the aviary on the roof of Freddy's apartment building. Egg helps herself to Ardene's jewelry, and the Friends realize that she shares with all dragons the desire for her own private treasure hoard. As summer wears on, Freddy says that they will have to let her go because she is outgrowing her roof quarters. The thought so disturbs Falcon that she sneaks out at night, Egg on a collar and leash, to exercise her dragon friend. She continues this through fall, enjoying the park at night, which seems filled with magic. Egg is now the size of a beagle and extremely hot. After Thanksgiving, Egg scorches and devours Rothschild, Freddy's pet mallard. Freddy reminds the Friends that Egg is by nature a predator and proposes releasing Egg with a rites-of-passage ceremony. Falcon prepares invitations, including one for Missy, whom she finally tells about Egg. The Friends take Egg to Central Park on a cold, clear night. After steaming the snow with her warmth, Egg rises up into the night sky, glowing bright as a comet. Before she flies off, she drops a ring for Falcon as a keepsake. Because of Egg, Falcon has grown closer to her mother and brother, appreciates her friends more, and is more sure of her own worth. Although the story has no great moment, and almost everything is on the surface, the details about Egg are worked out convincingly, and Falcon's problems with Toody and her schoolmates seem typical of those that an older child might face in a single-parent household where the mother is employed at home in work that is by nature abstracting. Subtle and broad humor complement each other. Characters are eccentric but not satirized and form a pleasing mix. ALA; SLJ.

FARMER, NANCY (1941–), born in Phoenix, Arizona; scientist and author. She received an associate's degree from Phoenix College in 1961, a B.A. degree from Reed College in 1963, and later attended both Merrit College and the University of California at Berkeley. In the 1960s she was in the Peace Corps in India and later spent seventeen years in remote parts of Mozambique and Zimbabwe, working as a laboratory technician and entomologist for private companies and the University of Zimbabwe. More recently she has published several books set in Zimbabwe, including the amusing *Do You Know Me* (Orchard, 1993), and two Newbery Honor books, the highly inventive futuristic fantasy *The Ear, the Eye, and the Arm** (Orchard, 1994), and the realistic survival novel, *A Girl Named Disaster** (Orchard, 1996). Now a full-time freelance writer, Farmer makes her home in Menlo Park, California.

FAR NORTH (Hobbs*, Will, Morrow, 1996), tense survival and adventure novel set one recent winter mostly along the South Nahanni River southeast of Virginia Falls in the rugged Mackenzie Mountains of the Canadian Northwest Territories. Big, burly, half-orphaned Texan Gabe Rogers, 15, who tells the story, has come to boarding school in Yellowknife to be near his father, Tree, who is employed by an oil drilling company. Gabe's roommate, Raymond* Providence, is a tall, slim, handsome Slavey Indian from Nahanni Butte who is exactly Gabe's age, born on the same day and year. Because he wants Gabe to see the countryside, at the end of October Tree arranges for Gabe to accompany Clint, a young bush pilot, on a trip to fly two Indians to Nahanni Butte: Raymond, who is unhappy in school and homesick and has decided to drop out; and a frail elder, Johnny* Raven, who is Raymond's great-uncle and has been in the hospital. A restless, reckless man, Clint deviates from the flight plan and takes them west over Virginia Falls. When he lands on the Nahanni for a closer look at the falls, the engine stops, and the radio ceases to function. With Virginia Falls looming ahead, they paddle fiercely to shore and get some supplies out of the plane before the mooring rope breaks and Clint and the plane are swept downriver. Fortunately, the three survivors have warm clothing and such important supplies as some food, a rifle with a small amount of ammunition, a butane lighter, an ax, and some cable. Fortunately also, the old man is woods-wise. It will be five months before they see civilization again and then only after old Johnny has died and they have endured incredible hardships from the weather and the terrain. In temperatures that already on November 1 reach twenty-two degrees below zero, their fire has attracted no plane, and their food is running out. Gabe persuades them to build a raft and head downriver, but they almost crash against a wall of rock and lose most of their meat. Johnny leads them to a small trappers' cabin, where they hole up. Johnny makes snow-shoes and tells old Slavey stories about his namesake, the trickster Raven, stories that Gabe cannot understand because they are in Slavey but that Raymond can follow in part. On December 16, both boys celebrate their sixteenth birthdays, and on Christmas the gifts that they exchange are wishes for safety and good lives. When Johnny fails to return from hunting one day, the boys search and find him dead, apparently of a heart attack. Raymond grieves openly, they cremate the old man, and both must now face the inevitable: they, too, may not get out alive. Hiking out with a toboggan that they have fashioned proves un-successful, too, and they return to the cabin, which they find a wolverine has trashed. They try to go through a mountain pass into the Yukon, kill a mountain ram in a cave, and track wolves trailing a wounded moose, which leads them back to where they were. After many more hardships and close situations, for example, an encounter with a grizzly, Gabe manages to pull the more severely hurt Raymond out on the toboggan all the way to Nahanni Butte. After they recover from their wounds, they attend a potlatch in Johnny's honor on April 2 in the village, at which Raymond speaks in tribute to his deceased great-uncle. Somber and sober, Gabe whispers his good-bye and thank-you to Johnny, as both boys ceremonially toss straps of bear fat into a fire. The book overflows with excitement and follows the Robinsonnade formula for the wilderness sur-vival novel in characters and events. It is strongest in the skill with which the author includes native beliefs, in the careful details of survival in hostile terrain, and in its picture of the extremely rugged territory and incredibly demanding environmental conditions. The book reflects the author's experiences in explor-ing the Nahanni area by canoe and raft and uses weather and calendar details from *Dangerous River*, a book in which R. M. Patterson describes his experi-ences on the Nahanni in the 1920s. The cabin in which the boys spend part of the winter is the one built by Patterson and his partner. An outline map is helpful. ALA; Spur.

FATHER (*The Long Season of Rain**), cold, surly, often absent husband of Mother* and father of the narrator, Junehee, and three other daughters, and son of Grandmother*. He is a career army colonel and teaches in a military college in Seoul. Although he once was romantic with Mother, he has not been so for years evidently and pays little attention to her. She urges him to be more solic-itous to the girls, but he usually ignores what she suggests, leaving them to feel very let down and unwanted. He has high expectations for them in school and about the house but typically withholds approval when they comply. When, on one occasion, Grandmother criticizes his behavior, he breaks down and cries like a child, insisting that he cannot handle so much responsibility, a statement never explained. Although after Mother walks out, he is more attentive to her and the girls, Junehee's statement at the end that she is afraid that someone may bring home a son of his implies that all will not remain well between him and Mother.

FATHER GREGORY (*The Ramsay Scallop**), priest who serves the people at Ramsay Castle, the home of Lady Elenor*, who is betrothed to another young noble, Thomas* of Thornham. An elderly man who has devoted his life to these people, he is much loved and deeply trusted by them. While their men have been on Crusade with Thomas, some of the women have taken other men as husbands, borne them children, and assumed reponsibilities about the castle and estate that were once the prerogative of the men. To help the people atone for their sins, give Elenor and Thomas a broader view of how they can serve their people, and help the two become acquainted, Father Gregory sends them on a pilgrimage to the shrine of Saint James in Spain. He also instructs Thomas to pay attention to how people are living in France and in Spain so that he will be a better leader once he returns.

FENNER, CAROL (ELIZABETH) (1929–   ), born in Almond, New York, and raised in Brooklyn, New York, and Connecticut; illustrator and writer of novels for middle-grade and early adolescent readers. Although she received no formal training in either writing or illustrating, her earliest books, *Tigers in the Cellar* (Harcourt, 1963) and *Christmas Tree on the Mountain* (Harcourt, 1966), both self-illustrated, were well received by critics, who deemed them "poetic," "harmonious," and filled with "artless charm." Her next books, illustrated by others, were also praised, in particular, *Gorilla, Gorilla* (Random House, 1973). Of her novels, *Randall's Wall* (McElderry, 1991), about a boy who lives in poverty with an abusive father and uncaring mother; *The King of Dragons* (Simon & Schuster, 1998), in which a boy and his Vietnam vet father live in an abandoned courthouse; and *Yolanda's Genius** (1995), concerning the tender relationship between a bright, African-American fifth-grade girl and her little brother, have garnered the most critical attention, the latter being named a New-bery Honor book and cited by the American Library Association. Praised for her ability to create distinctive, memorable characters and vivid scenes, Fenner lives in Battle Creek, Michigan.

FENTON CALHOUN (*Moving Mama to Town**), proprietor of Fenton's Fine Establishment, a saloon and gambling and pool hall, which also sells food and is the largest of the few businesses in the tiny South Carolina town of Elderton. Fenton works very hard, to the point of exhaustion, and either drinks too much or is under so much stress that he suffers from a bleeding ulcer. Certainly, he is out to "make a buck" in any way that he can, honest or not so honest. One of Freddy James Johnson's responsibilities is to make Fenton a chocolate milk whenever he seems to need it. Fenton is a mixture of qualities. He seems clearly to want the best for the boy but at the same time works him hard and is not above exploiting him. Freddy likes and trusts him, for the most part, although he is aware that he is being used and realizes that he can learn a lot about building and running a business from Fenton.

FERGUSON, ALANE (1957–   ), born in Cumberland, Maryland; author of picture books and novels mostly for young adults. Her mystery novel *Poison** (Bradbury, 1994) was a nominee for the Edgar Allan Poe Award, as was a novel she coauthored with her mother, Gloria Skurzynski*, *Wolf Stalker** (National Geographic, 1997), one of a series of National Park Mysteries. For earlier biographical information and a title entry, see *Dictionary, 1990–1994* [*Show Me the Evidence*].

FIG PUDDING (Fletcher*, Ralph, Clarion, 1995), episodic novel of family life and domestic adventures for elementary and early middle-school readers. As the eldest of six children, the narrator, Clifford Allyn Abernathy III (known as Cliff), 11, frequently suffers from his parents' expectations that he will set a good example and keep his siblings out of trouble. Despite some rivalry, Nate, 10, is not his major problem, nor is Cyn (Cynthia), his only sister, but hyperactive second-grader Teddy is almost uncontrollable. In contrast, first-grader Brad is a sweet, gullible child, and the whole family dotes on baby Josh, not quite two. In a series of mostly amusing chapters set in the contemporary town of Ballingsford, presumably in New Hampshire, the various family members are distinguished. As Christmas approaches, Grandma Annie arrives to visit and make stollen, a job for which each child is assigned a task, while she tells them stories of her childhood. The holiday is almost spoiled when Josh must be rushed to the hospital with a sudden severe illness. While he is recovering on Christmas Eve, the others finally figure out what he has been asking Santa Claus to bring him, a "yidda yadda"—a little ladder, like the one leading to an upper bunk. All the family members, including Uncle Billy, combine efforts to build him a ladder that they can deliver to the hospital on Christmas morning. In other episodes, Cliff learns the pain of being selfish when he prevents his younger siblings from using his new fishing box, and Cyn, tired of being the only girl, decides briefly to join the family of her best friend. The light tone deepens when Brad, riding his bike, smashes into an ambulance and is fatally injured. The family struggles to adjust to his loss by spending the next Christmas at a resort hotel, a solution that satisfies none of them. Not until the gathering at Aunt Pat's for a New Year's feast does the family spirit begin to reassert itself. Dad has made a large bowl of his special fig pudding, a favorite of the extended family. As they scramble out of the car, Josh steps directly into the middle of the pudding bowl and loses his shoe when he pulls his foot out. Although Mom is appalled, Dad fishes the shoe out, smooths the pudding surface, and swears the children to secrecy. They choose various other desserts and manage to keep straight faces until Uncle Eddie declares that the fig pudding is the best ever and asks Dad whether he added some new ingredient. The other relatives are bemused at the hilarious response of Cliff's family, the first real laughter that they have enjoyed since Brad's death. After the humorous incidents, the little brother's death makes the novel more disjointed than merely episodic, but the description of the very different ways that the various family members grieve gives psychological depth to the otherwise light stories. ALA.

FIGURING OUT FRANCES (Willner-Pardo*, Gina, Clarion, 1999), realistic girl's growing-up and friendship novel set in the San Francisco Bay Area at the time of publication. Abigail Van Fossen, 10, and Travis Mooney, 11, whose mother and stepfather live next door to Abigail, have known each other for more than eight years. Abigail, who tells the story, considers Travis, even though he is a boy, her very best friend, better than Marlene, who is bossy and thinks she knows everything. Abigail and Travis enjoy hanging out together, exchange confidences, and even have pet nicknames for each other that only they know. When Travis' father, a geologist, is transferred for a year to Saudi Arabia, Travis leaves San Francisco and his Catholic school, moves in next door with his mother, and enrolls in fifth grade at Abigail's school. Abigail is hurt when Travis shuns her around his new friends, boys who are also crazy about basketball. He still comes over on weekends, but now he seems to be just another "moron," as Marlene describes boys. Abigail spends more and more time with Marlene, who, having five sisters, is more interested in girl things than Abigail has been. The growing relationship pleases Abigail's frazzled, demanding mother, with whom Abigail is often at odds. Abigail, however, does not mind helping out with her father's mother, Grandma Van Fossen. She loves the unpredictable, sometimes difficult old woman, who suffers from the early stages of Alzheimer's disease, although she wishes Grandma would not call her Frances, a name that means nothing to anyone in her immediate family but that Grandma persists in using. When her fourth-grade teacher assigns a mystery project—each student must try to unravel some mystery in her or his life—Abigail chooses to try to find out who Frances is. Her relationship with Travis begins to improve when, at a fourth- and fifth-grade overnight science camp, Travis confides during a campfire session that he feels sorry for having offended a longtime friend. Abigail realizes, however, that he will never really acknowledge his friendship with her, particularly around the guys. His remark that he had attended St. Francis Preparatory School triggers an idea for Abigail, and together they examine Grandma's high school yearbook. They learn that a boy named Francis X. McDermott, a fun-loving, bright youth who was killed in World War II, was a good friend of Grandma. Abigail concludes that Grandma calls her Francis because Abigail is funny and loyal as Grandma's friend was. At camp, she also comes to appreciate Marlene's desire to do active things, since she herself has enjoyed quieter pursuits. Later she comes to terms with her mother over junior aerobics, a class that her mother has enrolled her in without informing her ahead of time. They compromise by agreeing that Abigail will finish the class, since it is paid for, but can wear pink sweatpants rather than a pink leotard and tights. Abigail also decides that it is important to be herself and not make herself into what others want. She thinks she will look into pursuing some aspect of biology, maybe marine life, an ambition sparked by tide-pool investigations at camp. The first part of the book is slow, concerned with establishing the depth of the friendship between Abigail and Travis. Pace perks up with the mystery assignment. Occasional humor (the scene in which Abigail fakes a hurt leg in order to get out of junior aerobics is funny); her growing understanding that she needs to appreciate her friends and her mother for their best qualities; and the kind, gentle depiction of Grandma and her disease make for pleasurable reading for middle-grade girls. Unfortunately, the cover illustration gives the impression that the book is comic. Josette Frank.

FINDER: A NOVEL OF THE BORDERLANDS (Bull*, Emma, Tor Books, 1994), science fantasy set in Bordertown*, the city where the World and Elfland meet, peopled mostly by runaways who come from both sides for a wide variety of reasons. Orient, a Finder, was known as Richard Paul Weineman in the World, from which he fled as an adolescent to avoid a murder charge for killing a sexually predatory man. After a self-destructive period in Bordertown, he has been rescued by Tick-Tick*, a beautiful elf with incredible mechanical skills, and together they have a business using his equally incredible ability to find anything, as long as it is concrete and he or the seeker can visualize it. A female cop, Sunny* Rico, bullies him into helping her track down the killer of a small-time thug called Bonnie Prince Charlie, whom she knows to be involved with distribution of a drug that, by altering genes, causes the user to hallucinate, be euphoric, develop elflike characteristics, and then die. Still, its use is spreading through Bordertown with the promise that it will turn users into elves who can cross the Border, which is closed to humans but is the goal of every unhappy teenaged runaway. Taking Charlie's keys and asking where they belong, he is led to a boarded-up row house, where, as he and Sunny cautiously explore, a bomb explodes and nearly kills them. Another bomb destroys the building to which he traces Charlie's motorcycle. Various occurrences lead Sunny to suspect that the mastermind is one of her fellow cops. At the same time Sunny's partner, an elf named Linn, develops a mysterious, flulike illness that is spreading in epidemic proportions through Bordertown but affecting only elves, halflings, and the users of the new drug. Tick-Tick becomes ill and worsens while Orient and Sunny get closer to discovering the brilliant and ruthless designer of the drug and head of the distribution ring. It finally becomes apparent that in the alteration of the genetic composition of humans, some virus of Elfland has been loosed in Bordertown. At the end the development of a vaccine seems assured, but not in time to save Tick-Tick, whose widely diverse friends attend her unconventional funeral. Orient, whose relationship with Tick-Tick is a deeply loving friendship but not romantic, feels lost, but there is a possibility that the strong attraction that he feels for Sunny may be reciprocated. The book is fast-paced and compelling as Orient and Sunny struggle to discover the source of the lethal drug without tipping off the other police who may be involved. It is touching in the illness and loss of Tick-Tick. Although the novel is comprehensible by itself, it builds on a series of novels and stories about the Borderlands, a setting created by Terri Windling and picked up by various authors including Will Shetterly, author of *Elsewhere*, whose protagonist, now known as Wolfboy, is a minor character in *Finder*. ALA; SLJ.

FINN (Bacon*, Katharine Jay, McElderry, 1998), boy's physical and psychological problem novel set in recent years on an upland Vermont farm. Left with a broken leg, burned hand, scarred face, and the inability to speak from the plane crash that killed his parents and sister, Finn, 15, lives with his grandmother at Riverview Farm. Seeming not to understand that Gram, too, is grieving, he deliberately isolates himself and nurses his sorrow, except that after a fashion he resumes his friendship with lively Vietnamese-American Julia* Hatch, 13, from down the road. Unknown to Gram, Finn, and Julia, Jack the hired hand, also fifteen, is in league with two men, Pinky and Rafe, to secure and distribute drugs in the local high school. They are using an abandoned well in Gram's dense pine woods as a drop site. When Finn and Julia picnic at what they call their fort at the abandoned well, they release a severely injured dogwolf from a trap (an animal that in his previous existence as a human's pet bore the name of Toq). They later discover that Julia left her backpack behind. While Julia is at dance camp, Finn retrieves the pack and in so doing notices a little white packet on the ground. Sure that it contains cocaine, he takes it home. For days he is tempted to try it in order to forget his troubles. When Julia finds out, the problem is to get rid of it. A parallel story concerns the drug pushers, one of whom has become addicted and, to feed his habit without attracting attention, has been cutting the drug with "junk." The other two suspect him, however, and hope to catch him using or cutting. Julia decides to return the packet to the place where it was found and is spotted by Pinky, the user, who throws her into the well. Desperately needing a fix, he mistakenly uses the cocaine that he has cut, becomes ill, and sets the forest on fire with his lighted cigarette. On Belle, Gram's aged, faithful horse, Finn rides to the woods to look for Julia, suspecting that she is returning the packet and, with grateful, sensible Toq holding tight to his heels so he does not fall in, too, hauls her out of the well just in time (an unlikely sequence). During the rescue, Finn manages in his desperation to shout directions to Julia (also a fortuitous event), his need to help his friend breaking the influence of the trauma that had rendered him mute. It is expected that after the young people tell their story, the authorities will seek out and deal with the pushers. After a slow start, the pace picks up, and although cliched in characters and events, the story grips and holds, and the conclusion overflows with drama.

Julia is well drawn, and the little romance between her and Finn adds an appealing touch. The adult pushers are phony, and the didacticism is obvious. Finn's story comes out in italicized dreams and reflections. Although he is too immature and neurotic for his age, he and the level-headed Julia are effectively foiled. Details of farm life and the animals are good, and scenes have moment. The point of view is Finn's in third person, but occasionally it becomes Julia's. Poe Nominee.

FLEISCHMAN, PAUL (1952–   ), born in Monterey, California; poet, author of historical novels and short stories and, more recently, realistic novels for young people. Two very different novels of redemption through nature and hard work are *Seedfolks** (HarperCollins, 1997) and *Whirligig** (Holt, 1998), both of which received critical acclaim. For earlier biographical information and title entries, see *Dictionary, 1985–1989 [Rear-View Mirrors]* and *Dictionary, 1990–1994 [Saturnalia; The Borning Room; Bull Run]*.

FLEISCHMAN, SID (ALBERT SIDNEY) (1920–   ), born in Brooklyn, New York; former magician and newspaperman, writer popular for more than forty years for his tall-tale, fast-action novels for elementary-age children, especially the outrageous fantasies featuring Josh McBroom, his Newbery Award-winning *The Whipping Boy* (Greenwillow, 1986), and novels with an American historical background. *The 13th Floor: A Ghost Story** (Greenwillow, 1995), a humorous time-travel fantasy with period aspects involving pirates and high-seas adventure, was nominated for the Edgar Allan Poe Award. The American Library Association cited *Bandit's Moon** (Greenwillow, 1998), a hilarious, fast-moving, biographical tall tale of the historical Mexican-American bandit Joaquin Murieta. Father of Newbery Award Winner Paul Fleischman, he lives in Santa Monica, California. For additional information and title entries, see *Dictionary, 1960–1984 [By the Great Horn Spoon!; Chancy and the Grand Rascal; The Ghost in the Noonday Sun; Humbug Mountain; McBroom Tells the Truth; Mr. Mysterious and Co.]* and *Dictionary, 1985–1989 [The Whipping Boy]*.

FLETCHER, RALPH (1953–   ); educator, poet, novelist. He received his B.A. degree from Dartmouth and his M.F.A. degree in writing from Columbia University. He has traveled widely as a tour guide and as a consultant on the teaching of writing and has published books on the subject. He is also the author of picture books, several books of poems for young adults, and novels, mostly for middle school readers, including *Fig Pudding** (Clarion, 1995), *Spider Boy* (Clarion, 1997), and *Flying Solo* (Clarion, 1998). Fletcher has made his home in Durham, New Hampshire.

FLETCHER, SUSAN (CLEMENS) (1951–   ), born in Pasadena, California; media buyer, advertising copywriter, lecturer at Portland Community College in Oregon, and writer of novels mainly for young adults. After completing her undergraduate work at the University of California at Santa Barbara, she received her graduate degree from the University of Michigan. Fifteen years later, she published *Dragon's Milk* (Atheneum, 1989), the first in a trilogy about dragon-sayers, humans who communicate and interact with dragons in exciting, well-delineated situations. Selected by both the American Library Association and *School Library Journal*, *Flight of the Dragon Kyn** (Atheneum, 1993), the prequel to *Dragon's Milk*, is the action-filled account of how a young woman helps hunted dragons find a new home. The third book, *Sign of the Dove* (Atheneum, 1996), continues the quest for a safe haven for the dragons and again demonstrates the author's extraordinary ability to create setting. *Shadow Spinner** (Atheneum, 1998), placed in an ancient Persia-like kingdom and also cited by both ALA and SLJ, suspensefully, cleverly, and very credibly improvises upon the tale of Scheherazade. Author of two more novels and a frequent contributor to periodicals, Fletcher lives in Lake Oswego, Oregon.

FLIGHT OF THE DRAGON KYN (Fletcher*, Susan, Atheneum, 1993), suspenseful fantasy novel of magic and dragons set once upon a time in the mountains and fjords of the mythical kingdom of Kragland. Kara, a farmer's daughter, is regarded with suspicion because she can summon birds at will and, given up for dead at the age of three, was evidently restored to life by a dragon in the remote mountain cave to which her seemingly lifeless body was taken. When Kara is fifteen, Prince* Rog comes to her father's steading and fetches her for his brother, King* Orrik. Orrik wishes her help, she learns, in destroying the dragons that have ravaged the land of Signy, the woman whom he hopes to marry and whose kingdom he covets and whom, as Kara later discovers, Rog also desires. Although pleased at being treated royally and admired for skills that she had previously been scorned for having, Kara is uncomfortable at finding high-hall intrigues swirling about her. Orrick seems pleasant enough, but Rog, who has his own following, disparages his brother at every turn. Their imperious sister, Gudjen*, merely tolerates Kara, and Kazan, a shipwrecked fur trader from Vosland to the south, makes her uncomfortable with occasional attentions. She likes the little orphan boy Rath, however, grows to appreciate Corwyn, the skilled falconer and healer, and his little daughter, Myrra, and is pleased, if surprised, when Orrik presents her with a snowy gyrfalcon, Skava, which she tames. Kara's fears are realized when Orrik announces that they are embarking on a hunt to the northern mountains, where the dragon caves are known to lie. Although she protests, Kara is forced to accompany the men because the court believes that Kara can call dragons as well as birds. For an entire day, Kara attempts unsuccessfully to summon the dragons, but in the middle of the night, seemingly unbidden, a name comes to her mind, Flagra, which she realizes comes from her childhood healing experience. A huge bird-like dragon arrives and is summarily shot down. When Kara realizes, to her horror, that she can indeed command dragons, she pleads successfully with the dragons who follow Flagra to flee. In spite of the extreme cold, snow, and ice,

Kara escapes but falls on the mountain and eventually finds herself inside a huge cavern, where some forty dragons, adults and children, live. She learns that the dragons are searching for another home, having moved ever farther north to get away from humans. After Kara saves a wounded dragon, the others have enough confidence in her to consider her plan for saving them. Kazan has told her of a distant northern island to which Kara hopes Skava can lead the dragons. The plan goes awry when Rog rebels and sets out for Signy's realm, taking along Kara as a prisoner and Rath and Myrra as hostages to force Kara to call the dragons. Skava attacks him, however, he is slain, and Skava leads the dragons to their refuge. An Epilogue set at the king's steading seven years later shows the kingdom at peace. Kara and Kazan are married and have daughters, and the king's sons by Signy are being raised by the still-formidable Gudjen. Kara's first-person account is sure and polished in style and employs enough old speech to support the early Scandinavian-like setting, which is also augmented by bits of pithy Kragish folklore that introduce the chapters. Characters are one-dimensional types, easily recognized as good or bad. Kazan turns out to be the prince charming that the reader believes he is. Kara's dilemma is believable, the solution to the political problems credible, and the plentiful action holds the attention throughout. The details about the dragons are fascinatingly worked out. The word "kyn" means both kind, as in humankind, and kin, as in relatives. ALA; SLJ.

FLIP-FLOP GIRL (Paterson*, Katherine, Lodestar Dutton, 1994), novel of a troubled family life and an unusual friendship set in Brownsville, Virginia, in the 1990s. Vinnie Matthews, 9, is lonely and angry after her father's death necessitates her move with her mother and her brother, Mason, 5, to live with her eccentric stepgrandmother. Her only friend in her new school is Lupe Mahoney, a girl strangely dressed in a long skirt and flip-flops, whose father is in prison for the murder of her mother. Vinnie also resents the attention that Mason gets for no longer talking. When Lupe helps her save Mason from a dangerous railroad trestle where he has climbed, Vinnie takes responsibility for her acts of vandalism, which have been blamed on Lupe, and for her own involvement in Mason's inability to speak. The novel earlier was named to the SLJ Best Books list. ALA. For a more complete entry, see *Dictionary, 1990–1994*.

FLYERS (Hayes*, Daniel, Simon & Schuster, 1996), lighthearted, occasionally poignant, contemporary mystery set for a couple of weeks at the end of the school year in a rural area outside Wakefield, New York, just east of the Hudson River. For Gabe Riley, the sixteen-year-old narrator; his serious younger brother, Ethan*, 11; and his pals, intelligent school leader Bo* Michaelson, with whom Gabe often has philosophical discussions about transcendental meditation "flying"; acerbic Jeremy Wulfson; and fat, oafish Rosasharn* (Billy Rose), the mystery starts one night while they are filming a "campy, semi-horror piece," *Green Guy Gets Therapy*, down by Blood Red Pond for Bo and Gabe's Gifted and Talented Class. When Rosasharn, clad in his Green Guy swamp-monster outfit, leaps just for kicks onto the hood of neighbor Ray McPherson's old Buick, Ray sees something else in the shadows, too, and later describes the incident with dramatic embellishments to his drinking buddies. Gabe suspects that Ethan knows that something strange is going on. On several occasions Gabe misses jeans, shirts, and sneakers, and food disappears from the Riley refrigerator and from the boys' food hamper. Matters come to a head one night when Mr. Lindstrom, the old, misanthropic widower-farmer who lives next door and owns Blood Red Pond and the adjacent nature preserve, has a heart attack, apparently brought on by seeing what he thought was his dead son, Andy, and by a lawsuit alleging abuse filed against him by his estranged daughter. While Mr. Lindstrom is in the hospital, the boys clean his filthy house, and, except for postponing the messy upstairs, they leave the place spic and span. One night shortly thereafter, Gabe investigates a mysterious light in Mr. Lindstrom's upstairs and discovers that Andy's old room is exceptionally and suspiciously clean. After another strange occurrence, Gabe spies Ethan heading for the house and follows him. He discovers upstairs a frightened, desperate youth who is the image of Mr. Lindstrom's dead son and obviously acquainted with Ethan—Andy Foster, the son of Mr. Lindstrom's daughter. Fed up with his mother's ne'er-do-well ways, he has come to see whether he can get along with his grandfather. Pop* Riley, Gabe's lawyer-father, persuades Andy to accompany them to visit Mr. Lindstrom, which they do just before the old man dies. Pop buys the Lindstrom property, offering a good price so that Andy and his mother can put their lives together. When Mr. Lindstrom dies, Gabe and Ethan seem to sense his spirit, or some such inexplicable phenomenon, rising above them in the hospital room. Gabe concludes that maybe in some way we are all flyers, trying to transcend the limitations and unsatisfactory aspects of our existence and head off to a better life. Most episodes focus on the things that the boys do together, like filming, discussing how timid Gabe might get a date with pretty freshman Katie Lyons, and working on the Wulfson farm. Gabe and his friends are likable, respectful, and hardworking. Gabe and Ethan are unusually close to each other and to their single-parent father. The several gothic elements are carefully underplayed, with the result that the book is less a mystery than a picture of warm, integrated family life in a totally male household, as contrasted with the gone-awry one of Mr. Lindstrom. Local anecdotes add color, and some scenes are raucously funny, as when Jeremy is attacked by bees while the boys are stacking bales in Mr. Wulfson's haymow. Gentle, but pointed, satire appears with over-zealous antidrug social worker Emmett St. Andrews and school psychologist Mrs. Quinby, who is determined to get Gabe to admit to unhappiness with his home life that he simply does not feel. Best are the warm, real-seeming figures, Gabe's bouncy, occasionally facetious, always intelligent manner of speaking, and the bantering, wisecracking exchanges between the closely bonded boys. Also refreshing in a book for teens is the intellectual feature: regular guys like Bo and Gabe enjoy philosophical discussions and writers like Ralph Waldo Emerson. Poe Nominee.

THE FOLK KEEPER (Billingsley*, Franny, Atheneum, 1999), folkloric fantasy set once upon a time in an unidentified kingdom along a coastal area that sounds much like that of Scotland. Silver-haired, green-eyed, strong-willed, often vindictive Corinna Stonewall, 15, lives in the Cellar of the Rhysbridge Home for foundlings, serving as the Folk Keeper for the area. Disguised as a boy called Corin (because Folk Keepers are always boys), she keeps the ancient Folk calm by feeding and humoring them, lest they destroy animals and crops, and also maintains the Folk Record of what the Folk and she are doing. In her Folk Record from February through September, she records how Lord Merton, his wife, Lady Alicia, and his cousin, Sir Edward, come to Rhysbridge. Lord Hartley Merton offers her the position of Folk Keeper at Marblehaugh Park, the manor on Cliffsend, an island off the coast. Before Lord Merton dies, which occurs almost immediately, he tells her that she should remember the name Lady Rona. After his death, they travel by coach to the sea and then by ferry to the island, where Corinna assumes her responsibilities. On the way and after arrival, Corinna is strongly attracted to the sea, where she catches fish easily, is drawn to eat them raw, loses her normal clumsiness, and later realizes that she can control the waves. She is also drawn to Sir Finian Hawthorne, 21, the sea-loving, bearlike son of Lady Alicia by a previous marriage, who is to inherit Marblehaugh, to Sir Edward's great disappointment. On the walls of the Cellar of Marblehaugh Park manor house, where she spends most of her time, Corinna (still thought to be a boy) sees verses apparently written by a certain Rona, asking the viewer to pity her. In addition to dealing with the highly troublesome Folk, who are at their worst during the late winter and early spring storms that batter and bruise her, Corinna finds herself caught in manor intrigue. In searching for moldy earth to hold the Folk at bay, she explores the local cemetery and finds two graves hidden away, one the Lady Rona's and the other Lady Rona's baby, who died at birth. On Midsummer's Eve (which happens to be her birthday), Sir Edward imprisons her in the Caverns, where the Folk dwell and will, he hopes, destroy her. He reveals that she is the daughter of Lord Merton and Lady Rona. Lady Rona was a Sealmaiden, whose Sealskin Lord Merton refused to return, lest she rejoin her people in the sea, and who went mad. Her baby did not die but was taken by Lord Merton to the Rhysbridge Home. Since Corinna is the rightful heir to Marblehaugh Park, Sir Edward hopes the Folk will destroy her. Using her power of The Last Word, which is rhyming, Corinna staves off the Folk, emerging from her underground dungeon after six weeks. When Sir Edward threatens to burn her Sealskin, she uses The Last Word to compel his dog to attack him, but she and the Sealskin are badly burned. After a long illness, during which she is revealed as a girl and her proper identity otherwise disclosed, Sir Finian proposes, she declines, saying she wishes to join the Sealfolk, and then reverses her decision and agrees to live part of the time on land with him and the rest in the sea. The plot moves unevenly, not always logically, and holds few surprises, style is marred by overwriting, and characters are types. The book's best aspects are the gothic atmosphere and the descriptions of the

Sealmaiden aspects of Corinna's character and of her Folk Keeper duties. These are worked cleverly into the narrative. Boston Globe Honor; SLJ.

FORGED BY FIRE (Draper*, Sharon M., Atheneum, 1997), boy's growing-up novel of an African American in a dysfunctional family in Cincinnati, presumably in the late 1990s. "Framed by fire" might be a good description of the story, which starts when Gerald Nickelby, 3, left alone when his mother, Monique, goes out to buy drugs, plays with her cigarette lighter and nearly dies in the resulting fire and ends when he saves his little half sister, Angel, from a fire that kills his abusive stepfather. As a result of the original incident, Monique goes to jail, and Gerald is taken in by Aunt Queen (Queen Marie Antoinette Lincoln), her mother's aunt, a formidable, but loving, woman confined to a wheelchair. Although money is scarce, they have a happy life until Gerald's ninth birthday, when Monique reappears with a husband, Jordan Sparks, and a six-year-old daughter named Angel, born after she was jailed. Gerald is bitterly opposed to the suggestion that he go to live with his mother and Jordan, and Angel, a fragile child, seems unnaturally frightened but responds to the warm mothering provided by Aunt Queen, who hopes to take her in and raise her with Gerald. Before that plan can be implemented, however, Aunt Queen dies of a heart attack. Living with feckless Monique and abusive Jordan is difficult for both children but hardest on Angel, who is both terrified and ashamed that Jordan is sexually molesting her, threatening to kill her cat, Tiger, or even her mother if she tells. When Gerald realizes what is happening, he assumes the responsibility for protecting Angel and confides in Darryl Washington, the father of a school friend. After Mr. Washington has convinced the police that the problem is real, they surprise Jordan in the act and arrest him. Monique calls the children liars, but, supported, by Mr. Washington, they both testify at Jordan's trial, and he is sent to prison. In the six years that follow, Gerald does most of the housework and care of Angel, since Monique is irresponsible, but life is not too bad for them. Angel develops into a skilled dancer, and Gerald continues his friendship with Mr. Washington and enjoys being on the basketball team with his son, Rob. On the day that Angel gets the lead in a dance program, they return to the apartment to discover that Jordan has returned, supposedly rehabilitated. At seventeen, Gerald is muscular enough to stand up to his stepfather, but he cannot prevent him from visiting Angel. A nervous wreck, Angel vomits every time that Jordan has been near her, but he doesn't come to her dance recital, and she dazzles the audience. A short time later, Monique, after rushing out to buy Jordan cigarettes, is hit by a taxi and hospitalized briefly. Jordan begins supplying her with drugs to supplement her pain pills, and in a short time she seems to be on the road to a new addiction. Infuriated in a hot spell when his bedroom air conditioner is stolen, Jordan slaps Monique hard enough to knock her down and punches Gerald viciously in the face. For the first time, Gerald's mother seems to resent Jordan's treatment. Gerald has arranged that when he is not home, Angel will wait in the apartment of a neighbor.

He is playing basketball when Angel finds the neighbor gone and returns to the family apartment, where she is starting to boil a couple of hot dogs when Jordan comes in, drunk and intent on sexually molesting her. While she tries to fight him off, the pan boils dry and starts a fire. Gerald returns to find smoke pouring from the apartment. As he interrupts Jordan in his attack, Gerald is knocked down and his shin broken by the steel toe of Jordan's cowboy boot. Seeing the fire spreading, Jordan flees. With great effort, Gerald carries Angel into the doorway, where he falls over a large object and discovers that the air is clearer near the floor. Crawling toward the steps, he drags Angel but is nearly overcome by the smoke before firemen find him. They are too late for Jordan, who has slipped in the doorway and dies, unwittingly allowing the youngsters to escape. Although full of inner-city grimness, the novel is less moving than a plot summary suggests. Characters are one-dimensional, and most of the action is told, rather than shown. Opportunities for sensory details, as in Angel's dancing and Gerald's basketball games, are not developed. Action is predictable. C. S. King Winner.

FOR MIKE (Sykes*, Shelley, Delacorte, 1998), mystery novel in which dreams lead the protagonist to the discovery of his best friend's killer in an unnamed American town. After the disappearance of Mike Thayer, Jeff Owens begins to have dreams of their high school hallway in which Mike begs him, "Get Kirby and come get me." Jeff knows he is talking about Jerry Kirby, an older boy with whom Mike has recently become friendly, getting parts for an old car that he is fixing up from the junk car lot that Kirby's father owns. Having lost interest in Amy, his shallow girlfriend, Jeff turns to Berry Murphy, a junior a year younger than he is but whom he has known "forever" because both their fathers are policemen. Berry has an extensive library about paranormal experience and is receptive to Jeff's stories about his recurring dream, and is more likely to believe than Jeff that Mike is really trying to communicate. Neither father will give them any information about the search for Mike, so the two pair up to untangle the mystery. Jeff gets nowhere trying to find out anything from Kirby, who he knows drinks too much and suspects is into drugs, except when Kirby volunteers that Mike, a devout Catholic, once gave him a medal and said that he was praying for him. A number of clues lead to a deserted barn. When Jeff takes Mike's younger siblings there for a thrill on Halloween night, the oldest girl, Theresa, sees something that she thinks, for a moment, might be Mike. After Mike's body is found by hunters near the barn, Jeff and Berry turn their attention to finding the killer. Jeff realizes that the scapular that Mike always wore is missing and that he saw what might be one in Kirby's glove compartment. Kirby has told him that he is looking for Rick Whitman, who owes him some money. When Jeff confronts Kirby and discovers that he is wearing a scapular, they fight, and Berry calls the police. Kirby tears off before they arrive, but Jeff and Berry are both grilled by their fathers, who are disappointed and accusing and, predictably, skeptical about the dreams. Relieved at having at least told, Berry and Jeff start going out together more lightheartedly without trying to be detectives, but Jeff's dreams change to a more sinister message, "Watch out for Kirby." The final revelation comes in the cemetery, where Jeff is visiting Mike's grave and where Kirby, who has obviously been following him, turns up. Looking terrible from his weeks on the run, he confesses that he shot Mike by accident when he got his father's gun to drive off Rick Whitman, whom he discovered stashing drugs in the stolen cars that Kirby had let him store, for a fee, in the car lot. Mike showed up, and Rick attacked him. When Kirby threatened Rick with the gun, he grabbed it, and it went off, killing Mike. In panic, Kirby took Mike's body to the old barn and buried it nearby. Now he plans to kill himself. Jeff takes Kirby home and wakes his father, who hears the confession and goes with Kirby to the police station. The novel assumes that the reader will believe that Mike's spirit is sending Jeff the dreams, which contain most of the clues that he and Berry follow. Without them, the detection would not have gone far, though a case could be made for most of the ideas really coming from Jeff's own mind. The strongest elements are Jeff's depression and his concern for the Thayer family, where he is treated like another big brother. Tension and pacing are strong. Poe Nominee.

FORTY ACRES AND MAYBE A MULE (Robinet*, Harriette Gillem, Atheneum, 1998), historical novel set during the Reconstruction at the end of the American Civil War, mostly in Georgia. In April 1865, impulsive, capable, proud Gideon, 17, the older brother of steady, sensible, astute Pascal, 12, returns to the South Carolina plantation, from which he had run away several years earlier. He informs Pascal that all the slaves are now free and persuades the boy to leave with him to claim the "forty acres and maybe a mule" that every family of freed slaves can now receive under the law. Taking with them little Nelly, 8, a slave who had been assigned to the Big House along with Pascal, they walk many miles, avoiding whites who revile them and "night riders" whose aim is to return them to their former masters. They seek a Freedmen's Bureau office to make their claim, adding to their little company fellow travelers whom they meet along the way, notably, an old carpenter who calls himself Mr. Freedman, whose practical skills prove invaluable; his granddaughter, a beautiful young black woman named Gladness, with knowledge of healing; and the Bibb family from Tennessee, poor whites also seeking land and a better life. Arrived at the town of River Stop just over the Savannah River in Georgia, except for the Bibbs, the little group takes the last name of City (actually Gideon and Pascal's dead mother's second name) and declare themselves a family, so that Gideon can apply for land. They also discover a newly formed school for ex-slaves and illiterate whites, which the children later attend, a school that they all enjoy but in which supplies are not equal for both races. The City family's forty acres (they never get a mule), whose landmark is the Ghost Tree, lies a few miles away by a lake, a prime piece of land, in their eyes. Under Gideon's leadership and the practical common sense of Mr. Freedman and with the help of various people and others whom Gideon hires, sheer faith, and much hard work, they burn off the land, since they have no plow (Mr. Freedman tells them that this is the way that the Indians made the land ready), plant cotton, build a house, dig a well, and look forward to a good life at Green Gloryland, their name for their farm. Proud of what their hands have accomplished, they equate freedom with having their own place. Gideon and Gladness' wedding is celebrated with a party attended by people from all over the area. The City group is never too busy or uncaring to help those in need, among them the Bibbs, who suffer from typhoid, and others who pass by, either searching for kin or a place of their own or evading whites who seek to conscript them as laborers for white farmers or plantation owners. In the fall, however, white men come and put them off, a new law having been passed that assigns land in that area only to whites. With gold coins that they have fortunately (almost too fortunately!) discovered in a treasure box hidden under the Ghost Tree, they head east to start over on farmland that they have heard is available on the Georgia Sea Islands. Most characters are one-dimensional types. The impulsive Gideon and the clearer thinking, more clever Pascal are carefully foiled. The account is mostly dialogue and moves fast. Best is the depiction of the setting. The hardships that the ex-slaves faced during the period—hangings, fires (a whole black town is set ablaze), shootings, threats, and other attempts at intimidation, as well as the vagaries of the laws and the chicanery of those who executed those laws—all these come alive as epitomized by this little family. They start with nothing but hopes, dreams, and longings, at the same time trying to define what freedom really means. Pascal concludes that freedom is doing what is good and right regardless of the situation in which one finds one's self. At the end, it is not at all certain that they ever will have the farm for which they yearn. While this is a serious look at a turbulent period, there is occasional humor, and good times are also described. An author's note and a short bibliography appear at the end. O'Dell.

FOR YOUR EYES ONLY! (Rocklin*, Joanne, illus. Mark Todd, Scholastic, 1997), realistic problem and school novel told in journal entries and set in Los Angeles in recent years. As an assignment, Lucy Keane, 12, and her classmates write in the notebooks that their sixth-grade substitute teacher, Mr. Milledge Moffat, has given them, all the journals to be read by him alone. The book provides the entries written from the end of January through May by Lucy and her archenemy, Andy Cooper, the biggest troublemaker in the class. Lucy writes sometimes in response to, or in imitation of, the poems by usually well-known writers whose names Mr. Moffat writes on the chalkboard every Monday morning; about her inability to get along with her divorced mother; about her mother's boyfriend, Dylan, a chef whom she increasingly hopes her mother will marry; about the writing group that she and a few girls form called the Inky Pinkies; about her efforts to write poems herself; about visiting her father and fussy stepmother in their well-appointed home in San Francisco; and about how she handles her problems with Andy and learns that there may be reasons for his being so antisocial and belligerent. While Lucy's entries range in length, Andy's at first consist only of a few words and are expressively decorated with bellicose drawings of warplanes, bombs, and explosions, then gradually begin to lengthen and become reasonable essays. Eventually, they include well-composed drawings of the ducks that alight on the swimming pool at the Seaview Apartments where they both live—ducks that Andy becomes fond of. Andy's stepfather, Frank, a mean man who manages the apartment complex, says that the ducks are filthy, destroys the ducks' eggs, and beats Andy viciously because he objects. It comes out that Frank has been abusing Andy and his wife as well. A caseworker intervenes, and Andy and his mother move to Arizona to stay with Andy's grandparents. Lucy feels bad about her previous thoughts about Andy. All the while she "was hating him, [she] wasn't really seeing what was there." At the end, after Mr. Moffat has left, Lucy confesses to her friends, all of whom have enjoyed talking about boys they like, that all along her "SE-CRET LOVE" was Mr. Moffat. Until the last quarter of the book, in which the focus shifts to Andy's problems and the arrival and safety of the ducks, the novel is almost plotless. Interest comes from ordinary matters—the girls' discussions about school, boys, their writing, their parents—and Lucy's growing ability with words and increasing affection for poetry. Her writing becomes more skillful as the entries progress, as does Andy's. Characterization is minimal, and the abuse expected. Some humor arises from the children's naive perspectives. Although unexceptional, the book should appeal to middle-grade girls. SLJ.

FOX, PAULA (1925–), born in New York City; graduate of Columbia University; writer for forty years best known for her contemporary, realistic problem novels for middle-grade and early adolescent readers. In 1978 she received the Hans Christian Andersen Medal for her total work for young readers. Among her many other honors was the Newbery Medal for her historical novel about the slave trade, an anomaly among her books, *The Slave Dancer* (Bradbury, 1973). Named as a best book by both the American Library Association and *School Library Journal*, *The Eagle Kite** (Orchard, 1995) is a contemporary problem novel in which a son comes to terms with his father's AIDS and sexual orientation. More recently, she has published *Radiance Descending* (DK Ink, 1997), about a boy whose younger brother has Down's syndrome. For more information and title entries, see *Dictionary, 1960–1984* [*Blowfish Live in the Sea*; *How Many Miles to Babylon?*; *The King's Falcon*; *Maurice's Room*; *The Portrait of Ivan*; *The Slave Dancer*; *The Stone-Faced Boy*]; *Dictionary, 1985– 1989* [*The Moonlight Man*; *One-Eyed Cat*; *The Village by the Sea*]; and *Dictionary, 1990–1994* [*Monkey Island*; *Western Wind*].

FRANCES BURBANK (*What Girls Learn**), mother of Tilden and Elizabeth*, who takes them from the South to Long Island, New York, to live with Nick* Olsen. A beautiful woman who cares little about her appearance, Frances captivated Nick a year earlier when she met him at a wedding but has hesitated to marry him because of concern for her daughters. Evidently, her marriage was abusive, and she left her husband before Elizabeth was born, but she says nothing about it, considering it unproductive to look back. When Tilden asks about her father, Frances refuses to tell her, and even Uncle* Rand, Frances' younger brother, won't say anything about the man except that he didn't like him because of the way that he treated Frances. Neither of them seems to realize that this silence leaves a hole in Tilden's history of her life that she finds hard to cope with. When she develops breast cancer, Frances is at first hopeful, but after it is apparent that her condition is terminal, she tries, unsuccessfully, to commit suicide by taking an overdose of pills, knowing that her last weeks will be hard on all those whom she loves. Despite her unorthodox lifestyle, she is a strong role model for her daughters.

FRANCIE (English*, Karen, Farrar, 1999), realistic novel of an African-American girl's escape from the poverty and prejudice of Noble, Alabama, in the 1940s. The narrator, Francie Weaver, almost thirteen, lives with her mother and younger brother, Prez, 10, on Three Notch Road, waiting for their father, a Pullman porter living in Chicago, to send for them. She often helps her mother, who does day work for white people and well-off blacks like Miss Beach (who runs a boardinghouse for "colored"), handles the chores and cooks dinner most days, and does well in Booker T. Washington School, where her teacher, Miss Lafayette, encourages her. Although Francie knows that rural black people, like her family, are expected to be subservient to their "betters," she sometimes speaks or acts out in ways that make her mother, who is terrified of the possible consequences, beat her with a sweet-gum switch. She also has trouble with the even poorer African Americans, especially Augustine Butler, one of a large family of a drunken sharecropper, who resents her better grades and threatens bodily harm when Francie won't cheat for her. Two episodes especially upset her. In the Diller Drug Store, owned and patronized almost entirely by whites, she is accused of stealing the Nancy Drew book that she brought in with her, and when she suggests that Holly Grace, whom she has seen steal lipstick, might have taken one from the stand, Holly slaps her face, and Mr. Diller confiscates the book. Some days later, Clarissa Montgomery, who was present at the scene, gives her the book back, saying that she knew that Francie didn't take it so she bought it back for her. Francie thanks her and doesn't ask, though she wonders, why Clarissa didn't speak up for her at the time. More importantly, she becomes involved with Jesse Pruitt, 16, who comes to school unable to read. The overworked teacher sets Francie to teaching him, and, although he is reticent, she gradually learns something of his difficulties, with his mother dead and his father demanding that he work both before and after his six-mile walk to school. Jesse follows her toward home one day and saves her from Augustine, whom he has overheard plotting to set upon her. Jesse is a very quick student, but before he has mastered much, he disappears from school. Francie learns that he is working full-time at Early's farm, and soon after that he is wanted for attacking the foreman, Mr. Bellamy. Because she is almost sure that he is hiding in their woods, she swipes some jars of her mother's canning and leaves them partly concealed at the edge of the stream. In the next few days she becomes increasingly worried, as the sheriff's men start combing the area, and her mother discovers some of her jars missing. Prez, who has become her accomplice, and Francie admit to their mother that they left food for Jesse, and she frantically insists that they go retrieve it before the sheriff finds it and recognizes the labels as hers. Prez and his cousin, Perry, are apprehended by the tough Bascomb brothers, who say they are taking them to jail. Francie's aunt, who has just had another baby, is desperate, thinking that the boys will be lynched or at least seriously harmed. That night a long car rolls up quietly, and Clarissa Montgomery climbs out. Having seen the two boys hiding in her uncle's gazebo after they eluded the Bascombs, she has swiped her uncle's car and driven them home by back roads. The posse that has been searching the woods finally leaves. The next day, Jesse shows up, gaunt and dirty, having eluded the men and the dogs. Francie gives him food and a pair of her father's old shoes and hides him in their shed. In the morning, before another visit from the sheriff, he is gone, leaving no trace. Another letter from her father, which Francie must read to her illiterate mother, puts off their departure for Chicago until the next year. Francie senses a change in her mother but is astonished when she buys new clothes for all of them and tickets to Chicago with some money that she has "set by." Just before they leave, Francie gets a postcard from Jesse, addressed obviously by someone else. It is a picture of an orange grove, and she remembers his telling her that he wants to get to a place where oranges grow on trees. Strengthened by the realization that he has made it or at least taken a first step toward his goal, she has the courage to face whatever happens in Chicago. The conditions in pre–civil rights Alabama are presented realistically, without undue drama, and Francie's spunkiness is shown as both admirable and foolhardy. The strongest parts are the scenes of working in white households, where Francie and her mother are victims of continual, casual insults that they must ignore or be branded uppity. SLJ.

FRANKIE FOSTER (*While No One Was Watching**), at seven, the middle child of the three motherless Foster children, the one whom the others sometimes call Fat Frankie because he loves to eat. Frankie has longed for a pet. He refuses to leave the yard from which the other two boys have taken the bikes until they help him take the rabbit from the hutch. Spot the rabbit becomes his dearest possession, and he sacrifices in many ways to ensure its safety and good health. He keeps it in his basement room, where he ingeniously hides it from Angela*, his little sister with whom he shares the room. He has to provide for its needs, a difficult task since the Fosters have so little food and no money. He eventually returns the rabbit to its hutch in Addie Johnson's yard. He is a resourceful, sweet, winning child.

FRANKLIN HARRIS (*Under the Mermaid Angel**), schoolboy of thirteen in Ida, Texas, son of a doctor. He is so greatly disliked because he talks dirty, relishes gore, and plays such mean tricks that the other young people call him Frankenstein. Roxanne* (whom Jesse and the reader learn is Franklin's mother, who gave him up for adoption at birth) says that Franklin is just "battling testosterone," meaning that he will eventually grow out of his poor behavior. He is a bright boy and a talented artist, and most of the cartoons that he draws for *The Icon* are appropriate and clever, but on one occasion he substitutes an inappropriate one for the one that the editor had chosen. His trick causes an uproar, but the editor takes the blame in the interests of peace and keeping Franklin from being punished, banished from the editorial staff, and perhaps further harmed in personality. Jesse also helps in that regard when she offers to pay him for making sketches at Mr. Arthur's going-away party. It is discovered that Franklin feels bad about himself because he thinks that his mother "dumped" him, and Jesse, without giving away Roxanne's secret, tries to dispel that idea. Franklin's future seems hopeful at the end of the book because he returns the sketch money to Jesse and appears interested in looking into his Cherokee heritage for a series of articles for *The Icon*.

FRANKLIN, KRISTINE L., author of picture books and novels for middle-grade readers and young adults. In addition to *Lone Wolf** (Candlewick, 1997), a story set in the Minnesota Northwoods, she has published *Eclipse* (Candlewick, 1996) and *Dove Song* (Candlewick, 1999) for young adults and *Nerd No More* (Candlewick, 1996) for slightly younger readers. Among her picture book titles are *The Shepherd Boy* (Atheneum, 1994), *The Wolfhound* (Lothrop, 1996), *Iguana Beach* (Crown, 1997), and *The Gift* (Chronicle, 1999). Franklin lives in Minnesota.

FREDDY MALDONADO (*Falcon's Egg**), Fernando Maldonado, young ornithologist friend of Great-Aunt* Emily Meade, Falcon Davies' mother's aunt. A "clever young man" and "very nearly a bird himself," according to Emily, he writes for *Natural History* magazine. He is tall and skinny and has straight, floppy black hair and too-short pants, carries a stethoscope to determine Egg's growth, and takes notes on the little dragon's habits and progress. He comes up with practical suggestions, like housing the dragon on his roof and holding a rites-of-passage ceremony to ease Falcon's loss prior to releasing the dragon in Central Park. He is an engaging caricature.

FRED NO-NAME (*Beyond the Western Sea: Book One: The Escape from Home**), known as Fred No-name because, being a waif, he has no last name. Fred is about ten or eleven and the newest and youngest member of the Liverpool street gang known as the Lime Street Runners Association, ruled by Sergeant Rumpkin, a fat, ruthless man of about sixty. Fred is described as a "weasel-faced, sharp-nosed boy, with freckled cheeks and red hair." He is Ralph

Toggs'* rival for Rumpkin's esteem. Fred figures significantly in the novel at various points, one of the most important being that in which the Reverend* Mr. Gideon Bartholomew hires Fred to deliver a note to the police about his suspicions that Sir Laurence Kirkle is a wealthy runaway. Fred, being illiterate, cannot read and loses the note to Toggs, who can, realizes its importance, and takes it to Rumpkin. Fred also helps Laurence smuggle himself on board the *Robert Peel* in a hat crate. An orphan, Fred grew up in a workhouse, ran away as soon as he was able, and has lived on the streets ever since.

FREEMAN, SUZANNE, newspaperwoman, teacher of writing, book reviewer. Her highly acclaimed first novel, *The Cuckoo's Child** (Greenwillow, 1996), is about a girl who, after growing up in Beirut with an adventurous, but irresponsible, mother, at her death is shipped back with her two older half sisters to the United States to live with an aunt, a young woman well intentioned but poorly prepared to deal with a sudden family. Freeman has taught writing at the University of Virginia and made her home in Manchester, Massachusetts.

FRENCH, ALBERT (1944–   ), born in Pittsburgh; African-American writer of memoirs and novels for adolescents and adults. He saw service in Vietnam, where many of his friends were killed and where he was wounded. After recovery, he returned to Pittsburgh and worked as a photographer for the *Pittsburgh Post-Gazette* for thirteen years, leaving to establish his own magazine, *Pittsburgh Review*. When that failed, he experienced an emotional breakdown, which led him to write his memoir and then novels. His first book, *Billy** (Viking, 1993), selected by both *School Library Journal* and the American Library Association, is the grim and horrifying story of a young black boy in Mississippi in 1937 who, though innocent, is accused of murdering a white girl and executed. Its very matter-of-fact tone and sense of inevitability add to the atmosphere of racial prejudice, injustice, and the division between whites and blacks. Also about racial prejudice is *Holly* (Viking, 1996), set in World War II in North Carolina, about a young white woman and a black soldier who fall in love with devastating consequences. French has also published *Patches of Fire: A Story of War & Redemption* (Doubleday, 1996), his memoir, and *I Can't Wait on God* (Doubleday, 1999), an adult novel about the seamy side of Pittsburgh.

FRINDLE (Clements*, Andrew, illus. Brian Selznick, Simon & Schuster, 1996), amusing school novel of a contemporary fifth grader in Westfield, New Hampshire, whose effort to distract his teacher before she can give a homework assignment becomes a crusade in which he learns about the powers of imagination, persistence, and good teaching. From his various tricks and schemes in earlier years, everyone knows that Nick Allen has unusual ideas and energy to carry them out. As his fifth grade starts in Mrs. Granger's language arts class, he tries, experimentally, to keep the teacher talking about dictionaries until the bell rings and there will be no time to assign homework, but she is no beginner and, smiling sweetly, she assigns Nick an oral report on how words get into dictionaries. Nick is not easily put down. The next day he launches into his report, his enthusiasm carrying him nonstop until almost the whole period is used before Mrs. Granger shuts him off, and even then he sidetracks her by asking, "Who says that d-o-g means the thing that goes 'woof' and wags its tail? Who says so?" Although she manages to squeeze a homework assignment in before the end of the class, her answer to his question, "You do, Nicholas. You and me and everyone," gives him an idea. As he walks home with his friend, Janet Fisk, he picks up and hands her the pen that she has dropped, saying, "Here's your . . . frindle." The next day, in Mrs. Granger's class, he says he has forgotten his frindle, and his friend John, having been previously coached, announces that he has an extra frindle and will lend Nick one. A born organizer, Nick soon has all the fifth graders referring to their pens as frindles and asking for frindles in the nearby store, while pointing to the rack of pens. When the photographer comes to take the class picture and tells the kids to say, "Cheese," they all hold up pens and say, "Frindle!" The name catches on throughout the school. Mrs. Granger posts a notice that anyone referring to a pen as a frindle will have to stay after school and write 100 times, "I am writing this punishment with a pen." Soon it becomes a badge of honor to stay after school, and the clever youngsters vie to see how many times they can substitute "frindle" for "pen" without getting caught. Mrs. Granger shows Nick a sealed letter, which she promises to send him "when this is all over," and makes him sign and date it on the back so that he will know that it is the same letter. The battle heats up. The principal calls on Nick's parents, who defend his right to use the new word. A reporter, hearing about all the kids kept after school, writes a story for the local paper, illustrated with the class picture. It is picked up by television news; Nick is interviewed on various talk shows. Bud Lawrence, a local entrepreneur, starts marketing pens, T-shirts, and baseball caps, all stamped, "FRINDLE!," depositing a portion of the receipts in a college trust fund for Nick. As the excitement dies down, Nick is briefly discouraged, but he proves to be irrepressible and starts junior high by organizing a boycott of the cafeteria until they provide better food. Ten years later he gets an unexpected package. It contains a newly published dictionary, a note from Mrs. Granger directing him to look at page 541, and the letter that he signed when he was eleven. Page 541 contains a definition of "frindle" with the arbitrary derivation credited to him. The letter admits that he had a good idea and that it gave Mrs. Granger real satisfaction to see a student using his own intelligence and initiative, even though she had to play the villain to egg the scheme on. Although the information about dictionaries is a bit heavy in places, the idea of kids triumphing over represssive adults is so appealing that the didactic element is well disguised. Nick is a thoroughly likable and convincing character, the fifth grader who has driven most teachers crazy by his active brain and excessive energy, but the others are undeveloped figures, adequate for their parts. The brief book is geared for a reader Nick's age or younger. Christopher; Fanfare.

FRONTO (*The Arkadians**), talkative, good-natured poet-turned-donkey, who is a bit of a jackass in his thinking and behavior as well as in body and upon whom Lucian*, the feckless youth who becomes a hero in spite of himself, sometimes rides. Fronto often uses high-flown language to express himself, especially when he is discussing poetry. Seeking poetic inspiration, he drank of the pool of the oracular pythoness at Mount Lerna and found himself changed into an ass. He spends the entire book as a donkey, to be returned to his original shape when his donkey exterior is burned away during a palace fire. Sometimes wise, Fronto is the first to notice that Lucian is a natural storyteller.

G

GABRIEL (*Blood and Chocolate**), handsome, unusually strong young man of 24 who dates Vivian Gandillon's mother, Esme, and other marriageable women in their pack of werewolves. At first, Vivian perceives his behavior and attitude as arrogant but later sees that he is very self-assured and knowledgeable. He emerges as the pack leader after contending with the other males in the old pack tradition of Ordeal. Astrid, a she-wolf, insists on being allowed to participate in the Ordeal, since the Law specifies adults, not just males. Because Gabriel forbids Astrid and her little group of renegades from calling attention to the pack, Astrid initiates the killings. Gabriel decides that the pack must move from the area for their safety. At the end, he and Vivian mate. It appears that Gabriel will become a leader after the fashion of Ivan, Vivian's deceased father, strong, devoted, and highly respected.

GANTOS, JACK (JOHN BRYAN GANTOS) (1951–   ), born in Mount Pleasant, Pennsylvania; journalist, professor, and author of humorous books for elementary-age readers. After completing his graduate work at Emerson College, he joined the Emerson faculty as a professor of writing and literature. He has also been a visiting professor at Brown University and at the University of New Mexico. He is best known for his popular Rotten Ralph picture books, for which he received Best Book citations from the American Library Association, among other awards. His series of autobiographical story collections featuring his alter ego, Jack Henry, includes *Jack's Black Book* (Farrar, 1997). *Joey Pigza Swallowed the Key** (Farrar, 1998) involves a boy with attention-deficit hyperactivity disorder who causes trouble at every turn until a special education center caseworker helps him. Although often comic, the book treats Joey's problems with respect and understanding and received citations from the American Library Association and *School Library Journal*.

GAPS IN STONE WALLS (Neufeld*, John, Atheneum, 1996), realistic, period, murder-mystery novel set on Martha's Vineyard off the coast of Massachusetts for one week in October 1880. Merry Skiffe, 12, is one of the three surviving children of respected farmer Benjamin Skiffe. She, like many other islanders, her father included, has been deaf from birth. Although she is innocent, Merry knows that she may go to trial for the murder of wealthy, universally disliked Ned (Edward) Nickerson, who was thought to be rustling livestock from the islanders and whose dead body was found lying at the foot of the stone wall outlining the Vincent family farm. Merry, two men, and another young woman are the only islanders who have no alibis for the Saturday night on which he was killed. Merry is determined to leave the island, afraid for her life and for her family's reputation. On Monday, while the islanders are at Nickerson's place trying to identify their lost livestock, Mr. Fisher, the constable, tells Mr. Skiffe that he wants Merry and the other three suspects to come to the general store for a "test." Terrified, Merry runs away. She contacts her cousin Eleanor Norton, who is two years older than Merry and who knows that Nickerson once accosted Merry while she was sketching on the south beach. Merry learns that Eleanor and her boyfriend, Spaulding Mayhew, intend to elope to the mainland, leaving soon from the fairgrounds. Merry packs her bag, planning to hide out and leave with them. Simon Mayhew, who is romantically attracted to Merry, finds her, and the two conclude that the killer must be the stranger in a multicolored weskit whom they saw recently at Simon's father's store. Found by some children, Merry is put to the "test." Physically very strong, she picks up with ease the thirty-pound stone from the Vincent wall that is thought to have been the murder weapon. Simon, who also saw the accosting incident, urges Merry to run away. She does, hiding until the fair starts, when Spaulding finds her and warns her that the hunt is intense. At the time, the reader is apprised by way of being let in on Spaulding's thoughts that he was the one who had been stealing livestock for Nickerson. He hoped to elope with Eleanor and attacked Nickerson for the bag of money that he knew Nickerson was carrying. The stranger, the off-islander who runs the Dime Show at the fair, is shown not to be the killer, and it is decided that Nickerson's killer is still at large. Merry is evidently no longer a suspect and goes home. The lean plot peters out and ends inconclusively. Merry is the only developed figure. The intense turmoil of the girl's emotions is reported in vivid, clear, extensive, and convincing detail. Although her disability makes the audience more sympathetic to her, her deafness is a distinct disadvantage, since she is unable to understand situations as a hearing protagonist might. The book's strongest features, however, are the descriptions of the island's topography and of the way that the islanders live—their closeness; their gatherings, where those who cannot hear and speak are made aware by others who sign, since a large proportion of the islanders have hereditary deafness (an actual historical phenomenon); their ways of thinking about themselves and off-islanders; their moral code; their dress and transportation; and their social and economic life. The full-length novel is set up in forty-three short chapters, a technique that heightens the tension, and except for the portions in which Spaulding's thoughts and feelings are revealed, the point of view, though not in first person, is so severely restricted to Merry's vantage point that the effect is that of first-person narration. The dialogue in sign language is presented without punctuation marks, wave marks preceding and following the portions that would be spoken. An endpaper map helps in locating places and events, a note discusses the hereditary deafness that was prevalent on the island for generations, and a bibliography of books about Martha's Vineyard concludes the book. Poe Nominee.

GARLAND, SHERRY, writer of novels for middle-grade readers and young adults and of picture-book stories. She lives in Houston, Texas. Among her picture books are *The Lotus Seed* (Harcourt, 1993), in which a Vietnamese grandmother brings a lotus seed with her when the family emigrates to the United States, and *My Father's Boat* (Scholastic, 1996), in which a boy accompanies his father on their Vietnamese-American shrimp boat on the Gulf of Mexico. Both texts are expressive and nostalgic. *Indio** (Harcourt, 1995), recipient of a Spur Award, is a historical novel of Spanish contact with pit-dwelling Indians along the Rio Grande, in which the Indians are enslaved and taken to Mexico to work in missions and silver mines. Another period novel involving Indians is *The Last Rainmaker* (Harcourt, 1997), which has a Wild West Show setting and demonstrates vividly the problem of being biracial in a society that degrades and belittles the Indians. Garland's other novels include *Song of the Buffalo Boy* (Harcourt, 1992), *The Silent Storm* (Harcourt, 1993), and *Shadow of the Dragon* (Harcourt, 1993). While her plots are predictable and characters stereotypes, action is plentiful, issues are addressed, and substance is abundant and memorable.

GEROLD (*Pope Joan**), respected, brave Frankish knight in whose house Joan, the protagonist, stays while she is studying at the school in Dorstadt. He is always kind to her and encourages her in her studies, even giving her a book by the Roman author Lucretius. He also cautions her to be careful about what she says and to whom, because Joan tends to be outspoken and heedless. Although they are physically attracted to each other, neither encourages the other to become intimate. Gerold's wife, Richild, however, suspects that theirs may become more than mere friendship. Believing that Joan has been killed along with the rest of his family or kidnapped in the raid of the Norsemen, Gerold leaves to join Charlemagne's grandson, Lothar, and becomes embroiled in the power struggles and wars of the day. He eventually goes to Rome, where Joan is a priest and physician at the court of Pope Sergius. Although he and Joan declare their love, he never vigorously presses her to leave with him. Although not completely credible, Gerold is one of the few attractive figures in the book.

GETTING NEAR TO BABY (Couloumbis*, Audrey, Putnam, 1999), novel of what grief at the death of a baby does to a family and how they work through it. Set in Linden City, North Carolina, the story is told in the present tense by

Willa Jo Dean, 13, as she sits on the roof with Little Sister (JoAnn, nearly eight) beside her, and in long flashbacks to the happenings of the past months. Entirely fed up with Aunt Patty Hobson's fussy dictates, Willa Jo climbs out the dormer window in the attic to see the sun rise and is soon followed by Little Sister, still in her nightgown. A nosy neighbor points them out to Aunt Patty, who demands shrilly that they get down, and after that it seems impossible to go back inside, even after others spot them, and the sun gets hot. A couple of years earlier, Willa Jo's father lost his job and left the family, a move that upsets their mother, Noreen, more than it does the girls, who play with Baby (Joy Ellen) and watch their mother work on the greeting cards that she paints for a living. After a long, delightful, though hot and dusty, day at the carnival with Noreen and her friend, Milly, Baby sickens and dies, perhaps from contaminated water that she drank there. For some weeks the two girls huddle with their mother, none of them doing any housework or eating regular meals, sleeping most of the day, three in one bed, staying up through the night while Noreen paints a series of pictures of Baby among the angels. Little Sister completely stops talking. Aunt Patty, Noreen's older sister, finds them in what she considers a state of squalor and takes charge, directs a thorough cleaning, and insists on bringing the girls home to live with her. Although they try to be cooperative, and Aunt Patty means well, everything that she does is wrong. She packs away all their familiar clothes and buys them cute outfits and shoes that rub blisters on their feet. She invites Cynthia Wainwright, a most disagreeable girl, to come and play, mostly because Mrs. Wainwright is a social leader whom she'd like to know better. She tries to forbid the girls to play with the Fingers family across the road, an interesting group who, as Aunt Patty complains, are dirty, because, Willa Jo discovers, they are digging a tunnel into the woods. Worst of all, she enrolls them in a Bible school day camp where the teacher, Miss Pettibone, dislikes Willa Jo because she refuses to sit in the tick-infested grass. Finally, after Miss Pettibone has insulted Little Sister more than once for not talking, Willa Jo walks out with the younger girl. Aunt Patty is humiliated, but after several mothers complain about the ticks, Miss Pettibone is demoted. Though invited to return, Willa Jo refuses to go back. Liz, the eldest of the Fingers, turns out to be a good friend, and Isaac, one of the four younger brothers, becomes devoted to Little Sister, running through the yard with her, "flying" a June bug with a string attached to one of its legs, and learning to count, as she does, with a complicated set of finger signs. All the problems come to a head the evening that Aunt Patty wants them to go with her to meet some other suitable child to play with, and Willa Jo says they have plans with Liz and Isaac. Aunt Patty calls her uncooperative and says that she is fed up with her. Willa Jo points out that Aunt Patty doesn't want anyone to cooperate; she wants them to obey. The next morning, before sunup, Willa Jo goes out onto the roof, followed by Little Sister. In the middle of the day, Uncle* Hob, a mild-mannered man who seldom contradicts Aunt Patty, climbs out the dormer window with a jar of cool water, cheese sandwiches, an umbrella, and his guitar. He doesn't ask them why they are sitting there or urge them to go back in. He points out the roofs of various buildings and picks out a few melodies. Aunt Patty comes out into the yard looking for him and is appalled to see him with the girls on the roof. After protesting unsuccessfully, she goes inside to answer the phone and soon reappears at the dormer window, saying that it was the girls' mother. To their astonishment, she hoists herself up to the window and climbs out, getting stuck halfway but making it when they pull. She reports that Noreen wants the girls back and is coming to get them. In fact, she called from some-where nearby. Realizing that Aunt Patty is worried that Noreen will think that she has been neglecting them, Willa Jo is sorry for her for the first time and makes some tentative remarks toward reconciliation. Aunt Patty responds, not quite apologizing but making the gesture. They sing some, wave to neighbors, and watch the sun dropping. Finally, Aunt Patty asks them why they climbed out on the roof in the first place. Willa Jo says it was to see the sun rise. But Little Sister, speaking for the first time in months, says, "We were getting near to Baby." Pressed to explain why she has been quiet for so long, she says, "My voice was lost in sadness." Their mother, arriving with Milly, finds all four on the roof, waiting for the sunset. The novel does a remarkable job of expressing the point of view of Willa Jo, a good girl who is devoted to her little sister, grieves for Baby, misses her mother, and tries to please her aunt but is not willing to conform to foolish ways. Small southern town characters and attitudes are well evoked as background to a moving story. SLJ.

GHOST CANOE (Hobbs*, Will, Morrow, 1997), mystery novel set from April to September 1874, on the tip of Cape Flattery on the south shore of the Strait of Juan de Fuca in the very northwest part of Washington Territory. Nathan MacAllister, 14, is the assistant to his father, Zachary*, a former clipper ship captain who now keeps the lighthouse on Tatoosh Island off the cape. After a particularly hard April storm, they learn that a ship has gone aground and that the area Makah Native-American Indians have recovered fourteen bodies, dis-covered a man's tracks in the nearby sand, and found the captain's dead body, not drowned as expected but with a stab wound to the heart. Shortly afterward, Nathan and his mother move for her health to the Makah village. Nathan soon becomes good friends with Lighthouse* George, a Makah who regularly carries mail and supplies to the lighthouse by canoe. Nathan goes fishing with Light-house George and other Makah for salmon, halibut, seals, and whales, among other sea creatures, trips that he greatly enjoys and are excitingly described. Nathan also helps to build a dugout canoe and takes in the annual potlatch, the elaborate giveaway festival in which the Makah entertain the Nitinak from across the bay in Canada. He explores the mountains, cliffs, caves, and forests, on one such trip discovering high in a tree a burial canoe, called a ghost canoe, which contains a skeleton and artifacts, among them carved bone pieces. He meets Captain Bim, who has owned the local trading post for twenty-two years, a big, garrulous bear of a man. Bim urges Nathan to hunt for artifacts, which

Bim will buy for resale in the East. Captain Bim also tells the boy that there was once a Spanish fort in the area and that the commander is said to have buried a fortune in gold bullion somewhere on Cape Flattery. A number of strange occurrences follow: Nathan spots smoke rising from the cape; the murdered sea captain's brother is observed searching the area of the wreck; rumors spread of a "Hairy Man"; Captain Bim complains that he is being spied upon; Nathan encounters a strange Indian who calls himself Dolla* Bill sleeping by a half-constructed canoe; and Captain Bim reports the theft of the strongbox containing his savings. During the potlatch, a man with piercing blue eyes turns up, a natty dresser with a Panama hat and white suit and shoes, Jack Kane, who buys the post from Bim, a man who Bim is sure stole his strongbox. Kane is unusually interested in bone pieces of the kind that the Makah carve, the type that Nathan saw in the ghost canoe. It comes out that the ship's captain had acquired from a Spanish priest a bone piece containing half of a map showing the location of the Spanish treasure, the other portion of the map to be found in an identical bone piece somewhere among the Makah. Out of curiosity, Nathan retrieves the bone pieces from the canoe, which are immediately taken from him by Kane, who was the murderer, and Dolla Bill. In the fracas, Dolla Bill takes a shot that Kane intends for Nathan and dies. Kane locates the treasure of gold and flees with it by canoe down the coast, hotly pursued by the Makah. He throws all but three of the gold ingots into the sea, tries to scale a cliff with the remaining gold, and falls to his death on the rocks. When the doctor says that Nathan's mother must move to a warmer, drier climate, Zachary decides to buy a small farm in California, and the Makah give him one of the three ingots to help pay for it. Most characters are generic, and the plot is overly complicated and awkwardly motivated, but the pace is rapid, Nathan is a stalwart, sensible youth, and details of the murder and the treasure hold the attention. Descriptive passages vividly create the physical area, elaborating upon the map at the front of the book. Details about Makah life and history occasionally sound textbookish but are fascinating and sympathetic to these enterprising people and focus upon those practices that boys Nathan's age would find interesting. An author's note gives background. Poe Winner.

THE GHOST OF FOSSIL GLEN (DeFelice*, Cynthia, Farrar, 1998), ghost mystery novel set in Seneca Village near Lake Geneva in what is probably New York state beginning in April 1998. Allie Nichols, 11, is searching for fossils in the deep ravine called Fossil Glen not far from her house when she finds herself trapped on the cliff. A mysterious voice tells her how to get down. At home, while pulling mail from the family mailbox, she experiences a sort of electric sensation and hears the mysterious voice say that the time has come at last. Among the pieces of mail is a package, addressed only with her first name, containing a blank book with a red burnished leather cover. Allie decides to use the notebook for her school journal assignment. As she ponders what to write, she sees the unfamiliar face of a curly, black-haired girl about her age, who seems to be asking for help. Later, she finds the words "I am L" written on the first page. When she reports this strange happening to her parents, they say that she is just imagining things. Mrs. Nichols, who owns an antique shop, buys furniture from a man who is selling the contents of the old, empty Stiles house near Fossil Glen. Among the pieces is a desk, which she gives to Allie. For Earth Day, Allie's class cleans up Fossil Glen Cemetery. Allie and her best friend and classmate, Dub, a boy she has known since kindergarten, discover hidden off to one side the gravestone of a girl their age named Lucy Stiles, who died four years earlier. On a class trip to the library, the mysterious voice prompts Allie to investigate the newspapers, from which she learns that Lucy Stiles disappeared while looking for fossils in the glen. Her body was never found, but a gravestone was placed in the cemetery anyway. Allie accidentally discovers a secret compartment in the desk, in which she finds Lucy's diary. Lucy reports, among other things, that she is certain that her mother's boyfriend, Raymond Gagney, or Gag-Me, as she calls him, wishes to marry her widowed mother only for her money and is planning to forge her name to financial documents so that he can build houses on the land that Mrs. Stiles owns that adjoins the glen. Allie realizes that Lucy disappeared the night following the last journal entry. Sure that the R & G Enterprises now beginning to develop the area belongs to Gag-Me, Allie impulsively calls the company and warns Gagney away. Frightened for her own life now but feeling drawn to the glen, Allie returns, hears furtive noises, and is urged by the mysterious voice to run. On another field trip, she searches for Hoover, her teacher's runaway dog, finds that the dog has dug up some of dead Lucy's clothes, and then sees Gagney with a shovel. He threatens her, she starts to climb the cliff, he attempts to follow, and just as he is about to grab her, she hears him yell at someone, who he says is dead, to get away and falls to his death. It comes out that Gagney killed Lucy and stole Stiles' money to advance his development company. Mrs. Stiles, who now lives in California and had trusted him, dedicates the property as a nature preserve. Allie is an enterprising protagonist, courageous and determined, and her pal, Dub, is a sensible support. Her classmates, Karen and Pam, are typical sixth-grade sniping sorts, until she gains notoriety, when they think being friends with her would be advantageous. Extensive dialogue and fast action contribute to the attraction of this mystery for those who are just beyond chapter books. SLJ.

GIFF, PATRICIA REILLY (1935–), born in Brooklyn, New York; public school elementary teacher and reading consultant, children's bookstore owner, and writer of almost seventy books for the elementary age. Mostly humorous, lively stories at home and in school, they are easy to approach and read, and children can readily see themselves and their friends in them. Most of her books are in such popular sets as Kids of the Polk Street School Series, Polka Dot, Private Eye Series, Polk Street Special Series, and Ballet Slippers Series. Deviating from her usual form is *Lily's Crossing** (Delacorte, 1997), a period novel set during World War II in New Jersey, in which an American girl makes friends with a Hungarian refugee boy. It was a Newbery Honor book, a *Boston Globe-Horn Book* Honor book, and an American Library Association Best Book. Giff lives in Weston, Connecticut.

GIGI MCCLOY (*Dancing on the Edge**), eccentric, overprotective mother of Dane* McCloy, ex-wife of Opal* McCloy, and grandmother of narrator and protagonist Miracle McCloy. A large, flamboyant, strong-minded woman, Gigi is a devotee of the supernatural and believes that numbers and colors have special meanings. Miracle believes completely in what her grandmother says, enjoys being with her, and would like to help her with her psychic business at the gift shop by dancing appropriately, but Gigi refuses to let her participate. Gigi has taught Miracle from early childhood that Miracle is special because she was born from her mother's dead body. The girl believes, however, that she is a failure because she has shown no sign of becoming a prodigy as her father was. After Miracle is registered in the psychiatric unit, Gigi picks her up and takes the girl away with her, intending Miracle to live with her and her wealthy new husband in Tennessee. Miracle insists, however, that Gigi release her so that she can go back to Aunt* Casey Dawsey. Gigi drops the girl off at an unfamiliar bus stop, without giving the girl any money to get home. Miracle manages to get help in contacting Aunt Casey and thus returns to her aunt and the counseling that she sorely needs.

GILBERT, BARBARA SNOW (1954–   ), born in Oklahoma City, Oklahoma; attorney, mediator, and writer of novels for young adults. After graduating from Colorado College, she received her law degree from the University of Texas and since has been a practicing attorney and a member of various political staffs. In her first novel, *Stone Water** (Front Street, 1996), a fifteen-year-old boy wrestles with the moral issues of whether or not to assist his dying grandfather to commit suicide. The book, which was cited by *School Library Journal*, has been praised for confronting a thorny contemporary issue. She has also published *Broken Chords* (Front Street, 1998), about a girl who aspires to be a concert pianist.

A GIRL NAMED DISASTER (Farmer*, Nancy, Orchard, 1996), survival novel of a Shona girl of Mozambique in the 1980s who makes her way alone a great distance up Lake Cabora Bassa and eventually to Zimbabwe, where her father's family live. Nhamo, 12 or 13, whose name literally means "disaster," has been an orphan since her mother was killed by a leopard. She lives in a traditional village with her grandmother, or *Ambuya**, at the home of her Aunt Chipo and Uncle Kufa, kept not through any love or affection from them but because she is a useful worker. When a cholera epidemic kills many from the village and weakens Nhamo's cousin, beautiful Masvita, favorite of the whole family, it is determined by the medicine man, the *muvuki*, that the illness came because

Nhamo's father, Proud Jongwe, killed a man. To make reparations, Nhamo must become the third wife of the murdered man's brother, a brutal, diseased old man who will allow his first two wives to beat her and probably beat her himself. *Ambuya* tells Nhamo to run away, to take the only boat in the village, one that belonged to the fisherman Crocodile Guts, who died of cholera, and to leave in the night for Zimbabwe, where her father fled and where his family may take her in. Although Nhamo has never been alone before and is terribly frightened, she does as her grandmother tells her. Unfortunately, *Ambuya*'s idea of geography is sketchy, and a great dam has changed the course of the river since she returned from Zimbabwe when she was young, so that her advice is faulty. Although Nhamo does not realize it, she heads out into huge Lake Caroba Bassa, all the time looking for the bright lights that her grandmother says will tell her she is in Zimbabwe. After a number of near disasters, she comes to a large island, where she stays for months, her only companions a troop of baboons that are both threatening and in some way helpful, since they lead her to food and break up the devastating loneliness. Since Crocodile Guts' boat has cracked, she tries to make a new one but finally has to admit that it is a task too great for her. Throughout her stay on the island, she has a number of spirit companions, both helpful and threatening: Crocodile Guts himself, who frequently seems to be giving her advice, a wicked spirit named Long Teats, who follows and mocks her, water spirits or *njuzu*, who sometimes appear as snakes, the *vadzimu*, or ancestor spirits, mostly helpful, and, best of all, her mother's spirit, whom she has always idealized as the woman whom she saw pictured in a magazine, an ad, though she does not know it, for margarine. She also has some very real enemies, the chief being a leopard that lives on the far end of the island. She develops many skills, among them the ability to swim, something that her people did not do because of fear of crocodiles. Finally, realizing that she cannot last through the rainy season on the island, she figures out how to patch the boat and starts out again. After other difficulties, she stumbles, only half-conscious, into Efifi, a science camp where an Afrikaner, Dr. van Heerden, is studying the tsetse fly. Working with him, among others, is a Matabele woman named Dr. Everjoice Masuku, who Nhamo thinks is a reincarnation of her mother; Sister Gladys, a nurse; and *Baba** Joseph, an old man who practices a type of Christianity called *Vapostori*, or Apostles. Although no one knows quite what to do with Nhamo, they let her stay and soon find that she is very useful, quick to learn things, and skilled with the animals that *Baba* Joseph cares for. She learns to read but finds writing almost beyond her. Eventually, they find that Nhamo's uncle, Industry Jongwe, is manager of a chrome mine in Mtoroshanga, and Dr. van Heerden drives her there. Although they live in a Portuguese house and seem to have a lot of money, the Jongwes are about to reject Nhamo when the old great-grandfather announces that she looks like his first wife, and, having heard her story, that she obviously can communicate, as he can, with the spirit world. Since they cannot go against this elder's wishes, the Jongwes take Nhamo in and send her to school, which she likes, but it is not a happy life for the girl. Mostly she is ignored. Only the great-grandfather shows any interest in Nhamo, taking her once to a mine entrance in the mountains to show her the place where her father died and giving her a wedding picture of her parents, who were married in a Catholic church. When vacation comes, Nhamo returns to Efifi, where Dr. Masuku, who she now realizes is not her mother, shows her the bag of nuggets that she brought with her from *Ambuya*, which Nhamo has assumed those of Efifi took to pay for her food and clothes. She tells Nhamo that the gold is worth far more than her old grandmother could have known, and she arranges for the girl to start a bank account, pointing out that the Jongwe great-grandfather will not live forever and that the others might either throw her out or try to sell her for some high bride-price and that only if she has money will she be able to direct her own fate. While the ending is satisfactory, the most interesting part of the book is Nhamo's journey and solitary stay on the island. Her accomplishments are not too great for a girl raised in an isolated village, and she does not succeed in all her attempts. To comfort herself, she tells stories throughout the novel, first to her cousins in the village, then to the baboons or her mother's spirit on the island, and at the end to a little son of Industry by his second wife, who is ostracized by the other family members. The book is replete with aids: three maps trace Nhamo's journey and show where it fits into larger Africa; an extensive glossary lists and explains Shona words; two appendixes review the history and peoples of Zimbabwe and Mozambique and the belief system of the Shona; and a three-page bibliography lists sources. ALA; Fanfare; Newbery Honor; SLJ.

GLENNIS, BEFORE AND AFTER (Calvert*, Patricia, Atheneum, 1996), girl's growing-up novel, set mostly in Burnsville, Ohio, in the 1990s. When her father is sent to prison, and her mother suffers a nervous breakdown, Glennis Reilly, almost 13, opts to live with her Aunt Wanda in Burnsville, because that is the site of the Federal Detention Center where her father is incarcerated. Wanda, her mother's younger sister, is not considered the ideal parent-figure, having had three husbands and a rather wild life, but none of the others in the family really want Glennis, not her Reilly grandparents, who gladly take Vinnie, 17, thought of by himself and the family as the High School Hero, who reminds them of their son; nor her mother's friend, childless Ramona, who with her husband, Robert, is delighted to take quiet Louise, 15; nor her Uncle Roger and his wife, Helen, parents of two rambunctious junior high boys, who don't mind adding the two blond, blue-eyed twins, Allie and Missie, 6, to their family. Wanda, at present husbandless, has a seven-year-old son, Skipper, and works long hours to support him in their dilapidated house in a poor part of town. At first Glennis is buoyed up by her conviction that her father is trying to get a new trial to prove his innocence in a savings-and-loan fraud and her belief that he will call upon her to help him find the evidence. Faithfully, every Saturday, she boards the bus to the detention center and visits him, not certain that he is really happy to see her but determined to be the one who stands by him. She cheerfully lies to him and to Wanda that all is going well at school, whereas in reality she talks to no one and makes up an entirely fictional family to write about in her required journal for English class. Although she recognizes the regulars on the prison bus and makes up stories about their backgrounds, she neither looks at them nor talks to them. Then one day a boy about Vinnie's age leaves a notebook behind when he gets off. She picks it up, intending to return it, but she cannot find him and, knowing she shouldn't, looks inside, learns that his name is Cooper Davis, and reads a poem he has written about prisons and webs. Later, when she sees him feeding swans at a park near the prison, she returns the notebook and talks to him a bit, fantasizing that he is someone in whom she can confide. After her father, on her next visit, screws up courage to tell her that he committed every crime of which he was accused and that he wants her to make a life for herself, she seeks out Cooper and tells him, only to find out that he, too, is a criminal, serving a community service sentence, of which feeding the swans is part. He tells her not to look at people as all good or all bad, but some of each, trapped in the webs they spin for themselves. No longer willing to visit her father, Glennis turns her attention to little Skipper, whom she gets started in a peewee wrestling program and weans from his steady diet of packaged food and television by cooking from scratch, buying him a bluebird, his heart's desire, and enlisting him to help strip the peeling wallpaper in her room and walk a neighbor's dog. He is delighted with his first real taste of family life. Her efforts to rebuild her own family are less successful. She makes the long bus ride to Fair Haven, the mental institution where her mother is being treated, and finds her sweet and pale, with vague ideas of going to Albuquerque when she recovers. Contacts by letter and phone with her siblings show her that they are all busy with new lives. Her biggest effort goes into persuading Wanda to host the annual Memorial Day family picnic, held in past years at her parents' lavish home. Glennis organizes a much scaled-down version of the festivities, gets Skipper to help her make invitations, and waits anxiously as, one by one, they accept. Still not forgiving her father, she sends an invitation to him, writing across it, snidely, "Too bad you can't join us this year." He replies that, unfortunately, he has caught measles from his roommate's children, and they are both confined to their room. To her surprise, however, all the others come and seem to thoroughly enjoy the hot dogs and homemade ice cream in Wanda's tiny yard. Glennis even has her first real conversations with her grand-mother and with Vinnie, both of whom tell her that they have learned not to try to reconstruct a life that they expected to be perfect but to go ahead with whatever the future brings. Back at school, instead of giving her prepared speech for English class, Glennis has courage to talk about her own life and explain why she has held aloof from activities and friendships. The next Saturday she goes once more to the prison and reestablishes contact with her father. Walking home, she sees Cooper, who gives her a poem that he has written about her and tells her that he is through with his community service and is going to Wyoming to live with an uncle. She kisses him on the cheek and runs to Wanda's, which has now truly become her home. Although the plot is predictable, Glennis is developed as an interesting figure, and her turmoil in trying to accept her father's guilt is moving. Most of the characters, especially Cooper, are designed to fill parts, but little Skipper transcends his role and becomes a real child, whiny, scared, enthusiastic, and loving by turns. Christopher; Josette Frank.

THE GLORY FIELD (Myers*, Walter Dean, Scholastic, 1994), historical novel in six parts telling the story of an African-American family with the focus on the land that they work and later own on Curry Island, near Johnson City, South Carolina. The first, brief section set in 1753 starts off the coast of Sierra Leone, West Africa, where Muhammad Bilal, 11, suffers on a slave ship carrying him in horrible, squalid conditions to the New World. The second occurs in 1864, about a year before the end of the Civil War at Live Oaks Plantation, on Curry Island. Lizzy, 13, sneaks from the slave quarters at night to bring water to Lem, 16, one of Muhammad's descendants, who has tried to escape, been captured, suffered mistreatment, and is tied in the woods waiting to be whipped and possibly hanged or, more probably, sold in the morning. When the overseer catches and slashes her with his whip, he is attacked by Joshua, an older man who ran away with Lem and is hanging around, hoping to free him. It is clear that Lizzy, to save herself, must attempt to escape with them. After a terrifying chase, they stumble upon a Union camp, where Lem and Joshua join the Yankee army, and Lizzy follows. In the next segment, set in 1900, Moses Lewis dedicates the Curry Island field deeded to ex-slaves at the war's end as the Glory Field, a burying ground for the extended family, but the gathering is marred by the knowledge that they do not have thirty-five dollars for the pending taxes. Elijah Lewis, 15, son of Lizzy and Lem's brother, Richard, dares an almost suicidal boat trip with his cousin Abby in a storm to rescue the blind son of a local wealthy white man, then stands up to the man to collect the thirty-five dollars that he has promised for saving the child. That evening the sheriff warns the Lewises that a liquored-up group of men are coming to whip and possibly lynch Elijah for being uppity. While all the other African Americans sit in the dark with their guns across their knees, a relative drives Elijah and his girlfriend, Goldie Paige, to a rural station where he can board a train for Chicago. The next segment deals with Luvenia Lewis, 16, daughter of Elijah and Goldie. Brought up in Chicago, Luvenia has an ambition to attend college and is reluctant to join her parents, who have returned with her brother to Curry Island, where they have sent money over the years to buy up more of the land worked by their slave ancestors. The bank has agreed to lend Luvenia college money if her employer, Mr. Deets, will guarantee her a job for the four years. Luvenia decides to ask the Deetses' daughter, Florenz, who goes to the University of Chicago, to intercede with her father. Florenz, however, thoughtlessly involves Luvenia in a scheme to use her father's car, phoning him that Luvenia is pregnant and ill and that she has to take her across town to the Negro hospital. Mr. Deets not only refuses to guarantee Luvenia's job but fires her. At first devastated, she decides to start a business straightening and styling hair and, with the help of a rent party, thrown by her godmother, Miss Etta, sets out on the enterprise. In 1964, back on Curry Island, Abby's grandson, Tommy Lewis, is an outstanding basketball player. An important, wealthy white man offers him a scholarship to Johnson City State College as one of a small, select group of young people chosen to integrate the school. One condition is that he stay out of any civil rights demonstrations. Although his girlfriend and his family are part of a march, he stays away until a white boy who has joined them on principle is badly beaten by the White Citizens Council toughs. Tommy attends the press conference designed to cover up the incident and manages to shackle himself to the sheriff with the old slave chains handed down through the family, thereby guaranteeing publicity for the movement. Although he loses the chance for a scholarship to the previously white college, he gains in self-respect. The final section brings the story up to 1994, when Malcolm Lewis, grandson of Luvenia's brother Richard, is a musician in Harlem, working part time for Luvenia, who is a well-to-do woman and owner of a series of beauty shops and a wholesale beauty products business, and who is now is going into real estate development. She insists that he hunt up his cousin, Shep, and bring him to the family reunion on Curry Island. Shep, however, spends the ticket money for crack, and Malcolm has a terrible journey by bus and hitchhiking getting his sick cousin to Curry Island, where the family is taking in the last crop of sweet potatoes before turning the land over to become a resort, which Luvenia is financing. Bullied and goaded by old Planter Lewis, Tommy's father, Malcolm works three backbreaking days in the fields and watches the family rally around Shep, possibly starting him toward recovery. Although most of the difficulties faced over the years are predictable and familiar from other stories, each segment has well-developed characters who catch the interest and bring the family to life. The best sections are the more recent, which contain less stereotypical situations. Particularly strong are the details that distinguish life in South Carolina in the different periods and Chicago of 1930 from New York in the 1990s. Family trees at the first of each section help readers to stay oriented. ALA; SLJ.

GO AND COME BACK (Abelove*, Joan, DK Ink, 1998), realistic novel set in the mid-to-late twentieth century among a Peruvian Indian tribe, which contrasts American and Native attitudes and behaviors. According to narrator Alicia, about twelve, her people, the fictional Isabo, are atwitter with excitement when a canoe brings upriver to their remote upper Amazonian village of Poincushmana two New York City anthropologists, whom the "real people" refer to as "the two old white ladies." Outgoing, short, fat, blonde Joanna and often disapproving, tall, dark Margarita have selected this village in which to collect information for a year, Joanna about the children and Margarita about the agricultural practices. The Isabo receive the visitors with polite hospitality, share freely with them whatever they need, give them advice and suggestions, and build them a house. The novel is almost plotless, without tension or a clear problem, merely a series of episodes that provide contrasts and give the book a didactic flavor, occasionally relieved by humor. Alicia and other women, with whom the Americans mostly associate because the men are usually away hunting or cutting wood, gradually teach the outsiders their ways. The Isabo consider the women "stingy" and "stupid" because they do not share freely everything that they have as the Indians do; do not understand the importance of parties (and especially dispensing liquor generously); do not bathe their entire bodies, including their hair, every day; are ignorant of the value and importance of daughters; think sex should be with only one's husband (when all the Isabo know that it takes more than one man to make a healthy baby)—such aspects of life and belief are conveyed to the reader via brief situations that Alicia describes and conversations that she reproduces that are mostly in Spanish apparently but contain some Isabo words. A few scenes are more memorable— the Americans give away boxes of dental floss because the people explain the usefulness of the thin, very strong string; the Isabo women urge all the men to flee and then cover for them when the army boat comes upriver to conscript workers; and, when missionaries come and do not share with Joanna and Margarita, the two Americans finally understand the villagers' feelings about sharing whatever one has. Alicia, the character about whom most is revealed, adopts a baby from downriver whose father does not want her and cares tenderly for the child until the baby dies of the diarrhea that often takes the lives of the youngest villagers. By the time that the two women leave, they and the villagers have become fond of one another. As they board the plane, having given away almost everything that they have, they hear Alicia speak the Isabos' traditional parting words, an expression that indicates that they are accepted among these seemingly simple, but really very complex, people: "go and come back." Alicia tells the story in past tense, so the reader must accept the premise that she remembers all these details at some subsequent telling. Almost all the many characters have limited, functional dimension, and the slight story ambles on, the book's main draw being the revelation of the contrasting ways of life and outlooks. An author's note at the end says that the events and people are based on real life. ALA; Fanfare; SLJ.

GOD (*Rats Saw GOD**), the club at Grace High School in Houston, Texas, to which Steve York and Dub* Varner and about a dozen other iconoclastic high school youths belong. It is led, as much as the club has a single leader, by Doug Chappell, who later plays drums in a rising rock group. A kind of offshoot of Doug's previous anticlub, Skate or Die, GOD takes off on Dadaism and is intended to promote nonconformity among high school clubs. The acronym stands for Grace Order of Dadaists. The novel's title comes from the reverse of the slogan the group affects for an assembly, "Dog was star," the first assembly in which Sky Waters takes part as teacher-adviser of the club.

GRAM AND GRAMPS HIDDLE (*Walk Two Moons**), Sal Hiddle's colorful, life-loving grandparents. Sal's father thinks that they are irresponsible and lets Sal accompany them on the automobile trip to Idaho to keep an eye on them. They have offered Sal the trip as a gift because they want her to have a chance to "walk in . . . [her] mother's moccasins" to experience what she might have experienced on her last trip and thus to come to terms with her death. They call Sal "chickabiddy," and Gramps, the more assertive and outgoing of the two, calls Gram "gooseberry." Some of the book's most amusing and charming episodes involve them. For example, Gramps decides to help a woman at a rest stop whose car will not start and ends up with the "car-bust-er-ator" and "danged snakes" (hoses) scattered all over the pavement. He and Gram received an heirloom bed as a wedding present, a bed that they have used all their married life and with which Gramps compares unfavorably every motel bed in which they sleep. Gram never fully recovers from the water moccasin bite, being bothered henceforth by a raspy cough, and when they arrive at Coeur d'Alene, Idaho, she suffers a fatal stroke. Throughout the trip, her grandparents prompt Sal to tell them more about Peeby (Phoebe* Winterbottom), in whose story they become engrossed.

GRAM KITTREDGE (*Northern Borders**), Abiah, tiny, intense grandmother of Austen Kittredge, a woman of determined spirit who likes nothing more than to best her husband at any enterprise. An orphan, she was sent at thirteen along with her sister Helen, 11, and many other impoverished youngsters from the British Isles as Home Children to be household servants and hired hands in Canada. They soon escaped from the brutal Cape Breton sheep farmer to whom they were assigned and eventually made their way to Kingdom County. The steamship that brought them to North America was commissioned out of Cairo and, like many of that period, had a hold full of Egyptian mummies, to be burned for fuel. The sight of these relics made a lasting impression on the young girl, who ever after has revered things Egyptian and devotes a room of her house to a sort of museum to keep all the books, artifacts, and pictures that she can find concerning that country. Because she chose to see a resemblence between Austen as an infant and pictures of King Tutankhamen, she always calls him Tut. At her death, Gramp, who has seldom spoken to her directly in the more than eleven years that Austen has lived with them, goes to great pains to build her a sarcophagus, painted green and blue, labeled "Egypt," large enough to hold her body and all her most treasured Egyptian collection. Not until the next year, when Austen learns about his grandfather's youthful love for an Indian girl, does he discover that his grandmother knew about the girl and her child, who both died before Austen's grandparents met. Her existence, however, may explain, in part, Gram's scorn of the wanderlust in her husband's past, his "sashaying about the countryside."

GRAMMA HOUP (*Music from a Place Called Half Moon**), mother of Edie Jo Houp's father, who comes to live with the Houp family when her own house burns down. At first she feels very sorry for herself and grieves for her lost possessions, and she is uncomfortable in the family, where the parents are fighting and where she has displaced her granddaughter from her room. She tells Edie Jo that she thinks the Indians and mixed-bloods are "good in the sight of the Lord," but she sees no reason to be intimate with them. In the church meeting, however, she brings the rancorous argument to an end by climbing to the pulpit and starting a hymn. In other examples of her practical good sense, she stops bemoaning her lost articles of handwork, buys crochet string, and starts a new bedspread to replace the burned one, and she contributes what she gets from selling her land to build an additional room onto her son's house, a room with a whole wall of windows for Edie, who has been sleeping on a cot in the living room.

GRAMPA NAKAJI (*Under the Blood-Red Sun**), beloved grandfather of Tomi and Kimi, who still thinks of himself as Japanese in spite of living for many years in Hawaii. Until the bombing of Pearl Harbor, he insists that his family are Japanese. When first seen in September 1941, he has washed the Japanese flag with its blood-red sun emblem and has hung it out to dry on the wash line. His action both embarrasses and frightens Tomi, since anti-Japanese sentiment has been growing. Grampa also cherishes an heirloom samurai sword, and insists that Tomi keep and revere it. He also maintains a kind of altar in the living room, where he has placed his deceased wife's picture and above which is a picture of Emperor Hirohito. All his heirlooms are hidden after the Pearl Harbor bombing so that authorities will not become suspicious of the family. Since he had a stroke, Grampa can no longer work as a fisherman and raises chickens to help the family financially. After the bombing, food becomes scarce, and his chickens and eggs become an important food supply for the Nakajis. Grampa's behavior adds humor sometimes. For example, during the air raid, he waves the Japanese flag because he thinks that when they see it, the Japanese planes will not hit the Nakaji house. Whenever he is frustrated or feels that he must emphasize his words, he says, "Confonnit!" He is arrested by Federal Bureau of Investigation (FBI) agents in January in a sweep of Japanese-American men and taken to an unknown location.

GRAMP KITTREDGE (*Northern Borders**), Austen Kittredge, Senior, tall, taciturn, hardworking grandfather whom six-year-old Austen is sent to live with in northern Vermont. Before 1952, when electricity reaches Lost Nation, where Gramp has the last farm up the hollow, he runs a water-powered sawmill and contracts with the state to clear a section of the border with Canada every year. He keeps a cabin high on the ridge above the farm, which he calls "Labrador," and to which he frequently retreats for several days, especially when his Forty Years' Domestic War with his wife heats up. In his youth he traveled widely, going with a surveying crew as far north in Canada as the land had been mapped and taking part in the big log drives of the time. His highest form of praise for a man is that he "is a good fella to go down the river with." He also worked with a carnival in his youth. After his wife dies, and Austen is graduated from high school, Gramp, at seventy-two, organizes a trip by canoe and foot far into an uncharted area of Canada that is soon to be flooded by a huge lake. Not until they have struggled for weeks, often coming near death, does he tell Austen why he feels compelled to undertake this particular journey. When he was with the surveying crew, more than fifty years earlier, he met a "white Indian" girl whom he called Mira, one of a very small group of blue-eyed Beothuks possibly descended partly from Vikings, fell in love with her, and left the survey party to live with her people. She died the next year giving birth, and she and the baby were buried together on land that will be flooded. Gramp makes the terrible trip to dig up her bones and transport them to higher ground. Through the whole trip he carefully maps the land, even though it will soon be under water, and he sends the maps back with Austen, who flies out, even though he intends to stay and run a trap line with an Inuit whom he has met. In a novel full of interesting characters, Gramp is the most memorable.

GRAN (*The Wedding**), great-grandmother to Liz* and Shelby* Coles, a white woman born Caroline Shelby, daughter of the owner of the plantation Xanadu. After the Civil War, with the plantation lost and her menfolk dead, she and her daughter, Josephine, nearly starve and are kept alive largely by the tactful aid of the ex-slave Melisse, who was a girl with Caroline in the old days. When Josephine agrees to marry Hannibal, Melisse's son, since she is an old maid and sees him as someone who can at least feed her, Gran is appalled. Later, she responds to Josephine's plea that she is dying and wants to see her mother again and moves in with the couple to raise their child, Corinne, whom Josephine cannot bear to see or touch. Although Josephine lives some years a recluse in her room, Gran runs the household, treading a thin line between treating Hannibal as a slave and acknowledging him as a son-in-law. Gran outlives both Josephine and Hannibal and is still part of the household when Shelby is about to be married. She retains the prejudices of her youth, however, and will not touch Liz's brown-skinned baby, Laurie, until the death of Tina, the middle daughter of Lute* McNeil. Then Gran reaches for wailing Laurie and comforts her.

GRANDMA DICKENS (*Coffee Will Make You Black**), maternal grandmother to Jean "Stevie" Stevenson, a woman of strong personality and definite beliefs. She has become a successful businesswoman, owning and running Mother Dickens' Fried Chicken stand on Chicago's south side. She gives Stevie the warmth and affection that her own mother is unable or unwilling to give, and the girl naturally turns to her for comfort when she needs it. Disturbed by the attraction that she feels for Miss Horn, the white school nurse, Stevie asks her grandmother whether white and black women can ever be friends. Grandma Dickens tells her a heart-wrenching story of the hurt inflicted by the white girl who had been her continual companion in the South but rejected her in front of white friends and declares that there can be no interracial friendship except for prostitutes and "bulldaggers," lesbians. Stevie repeats this conversation to Miss Horn, who says she should tell her grandmother that the times, they are a' changing.

GRANDMA DOWDEL (*A Long Way from Chicago: A Novel in Stories**), big, strong, independent, commanding, taciturn, highly frugal old woman described by her grandson, Joey* Dowdel, as "tough as an old boot." She lives at the edge of her small country town, and although well acquainted and respected, she is not above being moved by local prejudices. She works hard taking care of her place, preserves her own food, despises rules that prevent helping those in need, and scorns pretentiousness. She goes out of her way to help the very old woman for whom she worked when she was a girl, when she was paid only in bed and board, and defies the sheriff to feed drifters, men down on their luck who ride the trains during the Great Depression. She is the central and best-drawn figure in the novel, the epitome of the best spirit of the times.

GRANDMOTHER (*The Long Season of Rain**), imperious mother of Father*; mother-in-law of Mother*; and grandmother of Junehee, the narrator, and her three sisters. Grandmother does not hesitate to control her family's lives as much as she can. A Methodist, she is inclined to pray long, involved prayers and looks down on Mother, who is Catholic. Although she can be cold and even cruel, particularly with respect to shielding her son, she also orders him around. She decides to bring the orphan boy, Pyungsoo, home, then insists that he not continue to live with them, even though she knows that Mother wants very much to keep him. Without consulting Mother, she takes the boy to live with her friend Mrs. Kim. This is the final straw for Mother, who leaves Father and her family and goes home to her mother, Grandma Min, who is the opposite of Grandmother, a warm, happy, approving woman. Late in the novel, Junehee reveals that years earlier Grandmother's husband abandoned her for another woman.

THE GRASS DANCER (Power*, Susan, Putnam, 1994), adult episodic period novel of Native-American Sioux (Dakota) on a North Dakota reservation that combines humor, tragedy, magic, and realism. The book employs a complicated narrative structure that moves gradually backward in chronologically uneven segments from 1981 to 1864 and then returns gradually to 1984, at book's end having completed a circle in time. The novel opens with a powwow and closes with another. Harley Wind Soldier, seventeen years old at the first powwow and nineteen at the second, searches for his center both literally and figuratively. Harley's father, Calvin* Wind Soldier, and older brother, Duane, were killed in an auto accident before Harley was born, leaving the boy with the sense of a gaping hole in his midsection. Although Charlene* Thunder, the granddaughter of Anna (Mercury) Thunder, the area "witch" who probably caused the accident, is attracted to Harley, Harley romances a visiting grass dancer, the beautiful, red-haired Menominee girl known as Pumpkin, 18, on the powwow trail for the summer. Harley gains some sense of self through the relationship, which ends when she dies in an auto accident. Throughout the book, however, Harley is closest to his mother, Lydia, who lost her voice and most of her desire to live when her husband and son were killed. The lives of these characters are touched by those of many other figures both past and present. Jeannette McVay, a white anthropologist and high school social studies teacher almost embarrassingly eager to learn Indian ways, tries to build the Indian students' self-esteem through getting them to share stories from their culture and about their families. Herod Small War, local medicine man who conducts ceremonies and finds lost objects, provides ballast for Harley and others throughout the book, sometimes offsetting the bad magic of Anna, who through her spells bends men, particularly younger ones, to her will and use. Margaret Many Wounds, the mother of Lydia and Evie, is widowed when her young husband, a Carlisle-school graduate, dies of tuberculosis. She falls in love with a Japanese-American doctor at a relocation camp and conceives Lydia and Evie, who remain ignorant of his existence and believe that they are fully Indian. When Crystal Thunder, daughter of Anna Thunder, marries white Martin Lundstrom and conceives a daughter, Anna demands the baby, Charlene, of whose birth Martin remains ignorant. Red* Dress, the maternal ancestor of some of these people, loves Ghost Horse, a warrior who is also a progenitor of some of them and becomes a *heyoka*, or sacred clown. At the ending powwow, many of these figures and others who have appeared previously in reality or in visions appear to Harley. He undergoes a sweat under the supervision of Herod, then enters the ritual pit for a vision quest, the same pit in which his father, Calvin Wind Soldier, had received his vision thirty years before. Harley sees Dakota warriors and people like Margaret Many Wounds, his brother, Duane, his father, Calvin, Ghost Horse, and finally Red Dress. These all join in magnificent song, and, in a final scene of reconciliation, acceptance, and completion, Harley's voice joins and then rises above theirs. It is unclear whether Harley or Pumpkin is the grass dancer of the book's title, but Herod explains to Harley at the end, when the young man dons a grass-dance costume, that the grass represents rebellion (here apparently against the inroads of white acculturation). Although Harley seems to be the focus, the book's many women are the most interesting figures, a narrative feature that underscores the importance of women in Sioux culture. The many interrelated and interacting characters and the varying points of view, sometimes third-, sometimes first-person, support well the Indian concept of contemporaneous time but may make the book difficult for unaware or inattentive readers. Cultural texture is high, and satire on the ways of both Indians and whites sets the basic story in relief. There are some hilariously comic scenes, such as that in which a bull charges the brand-new motorcycle that Archie Iron Necklace won at bingo and stomps it into the grass. Under the often light surface, however, this is an insightful view of a complex culture. ALA; SLJ.

GRAY, LULI (1945–), born in Buenos Aires, Argentina; resident for many years of New York City; freelance writer, food developer, writer of novels for middle-grade readers. After attending Boston College, she traveled extensively working at various jobs, including chef, caterer, and recipe developer, and currently contributes recipes to cookbooks published by Weight Watchers and to food magazines and writes food articles. *Falcon's Egg** (Houghton, 1995), cited by both the American Library Association and *School Library Journal*, is a lighthearted, contemporary fantasy novel in which a young girl faces a dilemma after she finds a mysterious egg in Central Park, from which hatches a tiny, red-winged dragon. Gray lives in Chapel Hill, North Carolina.

GREAT (*Like Sisters on the Homefront**), very old great-grandmother of Gayle Ann Whitaker and Cookie* Gates, bedridden, senile, and near death. Sometimes she simply rambles, while at others she seems right on target in her observations about people and matters. She is the repository of family history, which she passes on when she "tells" to Gayle just before she dies. She knows about herbs, folk medicines, love potions, and ways to make things happen that Uncle Luther Gates, a minister, disparages as voodoo. Great also has a kind of second sight about the future: she tells Gayle that she will straighten out and that Gayle's son, Jose, will become a preacher like the various men called Luther in the family.

GREAT-AUNT EMILY MEADE (*Falcon's Egg**), eccentric, knowledgeable, very old, almost deaf aunt of Missy, Falcon Davies' mother. Emily regards caring for Egg as a scientific emergency. After losing her fiancé in the Great War (as she calls World War I), she traveled the world as a foreign correspondent, picking up miscellaneous information and interesting friends as she went. She has a strong sense of wonder but tolerates no nonsense. She knows a lot about dragon habits and nature from personal experience with dancing ones. She suggests contacting Freddy* Maldonado, her young ornithologist friend, for help in managing Egg.

GREAT-AUNT LIZ (*Northern Borders**), Gramp* Kittredge's sister who ran away from home when she was sixteen and has had four husbands, mostly in the West. When she returns for a family reunion the summer that Austen is fifteen, wearing western garb and bringing two saddles, she enlists him to help her find a ring that she threw down a well when she left her first husband. As she admits, she never actually divorced her first husband, and, although he was lazy and unfaithful, she still loves him and has decided to go back to Butte, Montana, where she last saw him, and hunt him up again. She is widely thought to have robbed the local bank many years before, and a Federal Bureau of

Investigation (FBI) agent turns up to question her but gives up. She tells Austen, many years later, that one of her other husbands robbed the bank but that she retrieved the loot hidden under the windmill at old Fort Kittredge, a long-abandoned site on the border, found her first-and-fifth husband, and used the money to support him.

GREAT-AUNT MAIDEN ROSE KITTREDGE (*Northern Borders**), much elder sister of Gramp* Kittredge, who lives at the Home Place, a farm farther down Lost Nation Hollow from Austen's grandparents. For many years she was the teacher at Lost Nation Academy. A stubborn and difficult woman, she does not get on with many of her relatives, but she hosts big reunions at which she always presents a Shakespearean play, having coerced various relatives and locals to take part. At the memorable reunion when Great-Aunt* Liz returns, they present *The Tempest*. Two major skeletons from the family closet are imparted to young Austen by his "little aunts," his father's college-age sisters. One is that Gramp is a foundling, left in an orange crate on the doorstep with a note saying that he belongs in the family. Maiden Rose left college to care for the infant "brother," and the two girls assume that the baby may have been hers. The other secret is that the true love of her life was one of her pupils, April Mae Swanson, who lived with her for twenty years. The family and the community seem to have accepted this lesbian arrangement without criticism, respecting her right to live her life as she wishes.

THE GREAT TURKEY WALK (Karr*, Kathleen, Farrar, 1998), tall-tale, fast-action historical novel, similar to those of the celebrated practitioner of the form Sid Fleischman*. In 1860 the narrator, orphaned Simon Green, 15, is told by his teacher, pretty, kind Miss Rogers, in whose third-grade class he has been for four years, that she is graduating him. On the way home, he passes the turkey farm of Mr. Buffey, who tells Simon that he has too many turkeys for the depressed market and that turkeys are selling for five dollars apiece in Denver, Colorado. Far more astute than expected, Simon arranges to buy 1,000 of the big bronze birds from Mr. Buffey, staked by Miss Rogers' life savings, and walks the birds from the eastern Missouri town of Union to Denver, ending up with the princely sum of almost $6,000. He is also staked, for a fee, by his greedy uncle, aunt, and cousins (with whom he has been living) to a wagon, four mules, and corn. He hires as his mule skinner the town drunk, Mr*. Bidwell Peece, for a percentage of the proceeds, as suggested by Miss Rogers, acquiring also the services of the man's faithful terrier, Emmett. They set out on a perfect June day, with Mr. Peece handling the mules and Emmett happily nipping turkey tails. In old-story fashion, they have adventures along the way and acquire as traveling companions a runaway African-American slave Simon's age, Jabeth* Ballou, and late in the story, pretty Lizzie* Hardwick, 16, whose sodbuster family have died, probably of cholera. They also benefit on occasion from the help of Pottawattomie Indians, led by grandiloquent, sensible, obviously white-educated John Winter Prairie. They are faced with the daunting tasks of getting the turkeys across a river, surviving a grasshopper plague, and preventing the birds from being used as target practice by a bunch of unruly U.S. cavalrymen. Their biggest problem concerns Simon's long-lost father, Samson Green, who turns up as the strong man in a circus that Simon visits and who covets Simon's enterprise. Sam rides up with a con man friend, Cleaver, on the circus' fancy Arabian horses, which they have stolen, and, armed with a rifle and revolver, they briefly take the travelers captive but are soon outfoxed by them. On another occasion, Sam and Cleaver gallop up on circus camels that they have stolen, this time to be foiled by John Winter Prairie and his friends. Even in Denver, Sam tries to steal the birds. Accompanied by Cleaver, he arrives by stagecoach during the turkey auction and announces, guns in hand, that the birds are his property and that Simon rustled them, but both men are soon hustled off to jail for disturbing the peace. After the auction, Simon repays those who staked him for the journey, but Mr. Peece, Jabeth, and Lizzie refuse their share of the proceeds and join with Simon in establishing the Great Turkey Five Ranch (the fifth partner being Emmett the faithful dog) to raise turkeys for the obviously profitable western market. Characters are colorfully exaggerated, Simon's colloquial, often ungrammatical speech adds to the homespun, tongue-in-cheek humor, his incipient romance with Lizzie adds spice, incidents occur rapid-fashion, and some sense of history and geography lends credibility. The whole story is good fun from start to finish, a different sort of western. Events, as noted in an author's afterword, are based on an actual turkey walk from Missouri to Denver. SLJ.

GREENE, STEPHANIE, author of the popular series of amusing chapter books about the domestic and school adventures of second grader Owen Foote, including *Owen Foote, Second Grade Strongman* (Clarion, 1996); *Owen Foote, Soccer Star* (Clarion, 1998); the *School Library Journal* choice *Owen Foote, Frontiersman** (Clarion, 1999), in which Owen and his best friend, Joseph, emulate their hero, Daniel Boone, to outwit two older bullies; and *Owen Foote, Moneyman* (Clarion, 2000). The books are notable for their often hilarious humor, dialogue and point of view accurate for the age, and well-defined conflicts. Greene has also published *Show and Tell* (Clarion, 1998), in which a second grader has trouble with his student teacher and also with the kid across the street. Greene lives in Chapel Hill, North Carolina.

GRETA LUDOWSKI (*Spying on Miss Muller**), Jewish girl from Poland who has somehow been sneaked out and is at Alveara school in Ireland by special request, the first non-Christian girl ever admitted. Although the girls have been prompted to be kind to her and at first are willing, they find her unfriendly and scornful of their ignorance of real life. She left her parents in Poland and has since learned that her father was killed by the Nazis. Her bitterness focuses on Miss Muller, and she seems determined to get revenge by harming the half-

German teacher. Jessie Drumm is afraid that if Greta finds Miss Muller on the roof, she will push her off. Then Greta steals Jessie's sharp nail file, with which they cut the cake. Jessie is able to retrieve it, but Greta still destroys Miss Muller by reporting her tryst with Mr. Bolton to the headmistress. Greta is an unusual character for a children's book, not a poor, sympathetic refugee but an unapproachable, embittered girl intent on doing harm.

THE GRIFFIN (*The Magic and the Healing**), huge talking being, half lion, half eagle that lives in Crossroads* and enables the four veterinarian students and their professor, Sugar* Dobbs, to help defeat the evil Morgan. The students first encounter him when Sugar takes them into Crossroads valley so that student Dave* Wilson can diagnose and treat the creature. The task is a ticklish one, because the Griffin is characteristically stern and acerbic and makes sure everyone understands that he is, first and foremost, a dangerous predator. When the wyr (werewolves in service to Morgan) attack, the Griffin saves them but is so severely wounded that they must transport him back to the college of medicine hospital. Dave and BJ* Vaughan travel on Dave's motorcycle into Crossroads to get blood from other griffins for transfusions. After the battle against Morgan at Stein's* inn, the students learn that the Griffin is really the dreaded, legendary dispenser of justice in Crossroads known as the Inspector General. On the symbolic level, the Griffin exists to point out that justice must sometimes be not only blind but also cruel.

GRIFFIN, ADELE (1970–   ), born in Philadelphia, Pennsylvania; former editor for Clarion books, freelance manuscript reader, and writer of books for middle graders and early adolescents. She received her degree in English from the University of Pennsylvania. Her first novel, *Rainy Season* (Houghton, 1996), about a family living on an army base in the Panama Canal Zone in 1977 when resentment against Americans ran high, was well received by critics and audience. *Split Just Right* (Hyperion, 1997) examines in a lighthearted attitude the effect of divorce on a girl who longs to meet her father. Griffin's third book, *Sons of Liberty* (Hyperion, 1997), is a serious look at a family traumatized by a domineering father and was nominated for a National Book Award. The effect on the younger siblings when parents idolize siblings who died years before is the subject of *The Other Shepards** (Hyperion, 1998), a fantasy cited by both the American Library Association and *School Library Journal*. Griffin has won praise for writing in a fresh voice about difficult subjects and for capturing the essence of the adolescent perspective and relationships. She is a resident of New York City.

GROVE, VICKI, author of novels for young adults and older children. Among these are several concerned with friendships, *The Fastest Friend in the World* (Putnam, 1990), *The Crystal Garden* (Putnam, 1995), and *The Starplace** (Putnam, 1999), about a biracial friendship in Oklahoma of the still largely segregated early 1960s. Others deal with farm life, including *Good-bye, My Wishing Star* (Putnam, 1988) and *Rimwalkers* (Putnam, 1993). Dysfunctional families appear in *Reaching Dustin** (Putnam, 1998) and *Destiny* (Putnam, 2000). Most of Grove's novels are set in the South. She has made her home in Ionia, Missouri.

GROWCH (*Pigs Don't Fly**), nondescript, flea-ridden dog that accompanies Summer on her journey. On the pattern of the street-smart cockney urchin, he talks tough, swipes food, and makes scornful remarks about the others in the company, but he is intensely loyal and a number of times saves Summer from disaster. Never fond of Sir* Gilman, he recognizes Summer's infatuation for what it is and tries to talk her out of it. After Wimperling* turns into a full-grown dragon and flies off, Growch persuades Summer to return to the home of the merchant Matthew* Spicer because he craves the warmth and good food of the place. When Summer leaves him behind, however, he escapes and catches up to her to continue their travels.

GUDJEN (*Flight of the Dragon Kyn**), sister of King* Orrik and Prince* Rog of Kragland. Stern, imperious, unyielding, Gudjen runs the king's household of ladies and servants and takes charge of Kara as soon as the girl arrives. Gudjen's magical powers are first revealed when she takes Kara into the bathhouse and summons up a dragonlike creature in the steam. She informs Kara that it is commonly believed that dragons and birds are kin and that those who can summon birds, as Kara can, can also call dragons. Gudjen allies herself with Orrik against Rog, because she wishes Orrik to marry Princess Signy of Romjek and have sons, whom she, Gudjen, will then raise to be more forceful at ruling than their father. The Epilogue shows that she gets the chance to do just that.

GUESTS (Dorris*, Michael, Hyperion, 1994), realistic boy's growing-up novel set among an unnamed group of Native-American Indians in a forest village probably in New England at the time of very early contact. Moss, about twelve, resents being treated like a child while expected to act like an adult. Moss particularly resents his family's having as guests the white strangers whom his father has invited to their annual harvest dinner, following tribal custom to feed hungry newcomers. Sulking and disgruntled, Moss goes to the outskirts of the village, where he encounters Trouble*, a spirited, independent girl his age from another clan, in whom he finds a kindred, dissatisfied spirit. She points out that he cannot go into the woods on his "away time" (the period in which boys go alone into the forest to find direction for their lives and receive their adult names) because he has no knife, rope, or other aid. He impulsively runs into the forest to impress her with his bravery. He soon finds himself lost, or at least so disoriented that he feels lost, and simply runs until he is tired and falls asleep. When he awakens, he realizes that he has panicked and done everything wrong. He does not want to go back, because that would represent a step backward.

He decides to continue and "discover a new road that would belong to no one but me." He hears a gruff, crotchety, "old-lady" voice, which he determines comes from a porcupine in a raspberry thicket, and engages in a conversation with the animal entirely in his head. Among others, the porcupine leaves him with the puzzling idea that he is who he is. He realizes that he must behave like a man in the tribe if he wishes to be regarded as one. A little later, he wonders if the episode really happened, but as proof he finds two quills stuck in his shoulder. Soon he encounters Trouble who has run away to avoid her family's expectations for a girl. After listing their complaints and seeing that they are identical in kind, they burst into laughter, come to uncertain conclusions about their lives, and return to the village, from which they have been gone only a few hours. Moss regrets having caused his family concern and feels that he understands his father much better. He helps out at the dinner and later at another social gathering with the whites. Trouble has problems with her women relatives and is consoled by Moss' mother. When the matter of the away time comes up, Trouble says that Moss already has an adult name, Thunder. A pot-boiler, splintered plot, stereotypical characters, awkward dialogue, and too obviously foiled adolescents are among the book's negative features, while good points include the adolescents' rebellion and restlessness, which ring true to the age, the graphic style, the Indian customs, embedded stories, and sex-role expectations. ALA.

GUMBO (*Come in from the Cold**), longtime best friend of Jeff Ramsay, who lives across the street. While Jeff's opposition to the Vietnam War leads him to protests, Gumbo's disillusionment exhibits itself in his use of drugs and alcohol. Although often scornful of what he calls Jeff's puritanism, Gumbo defends his friend at the rally, where Jeff is attacked and injured. Gumbo is arrested but is released when Jeff agrees not to press charges against his attacker if Gumbo is not charged for injuring the man in his defense. When Gumbo's draft number comes up, he flees to Canada, illustrating one of the possible reactions of those who oppose the war.

GUY, ROSA, born in Trinidad, West Indies; at the age of seven immigrated with her parents and sister to Harlem, where she grew up; writer of picture books and novels for teens and adults. She became involved with the American Negro Theatre during World War II and, after attending New York University, began writing stories and plays, in which she also acted. In the late 1940s, she helped to form the Harlem Writers Guild. *The Friends* (Holt, 1973) was her first book for young adults and also the first in a trilogy about black young people, the other two being *Ruby* (Viking, 1976) and *Edith Jackson* (Viking, 1978). These books, in which Guy examines complex black interfamily relationships, were critically well received. They were soon followed by *The Disappearance** (Delacorte, 1979), a Phoenix Honor book of The Children's Literature Association. It tells of Imamu Jones, a sixteen-year-old Harlem high school dropout who is blamed when the daughter of his adoptive white family disappears and later is found murdered. Its successors are two more mysteries featuring Imamu, *New Guys Around the Block* (Delacorte, 1983) and *And I Heard a Bird Sing* (Delacorte, 1987). Guy lives in New York City.

GYPSY DAVEY (Lynch*, Chris, HarperCollins, 1994), contemporary realistic novel of family life and a boy's growing up set for one year in a large, unidentified urban area, perhaps New York City. The plotless narrative moves from chapter to chapter like snapshot pages in an album, alternating between twelve-year-old Davey's reflections on life with his mother, Lois, and sister, Joanne, and the author's third-person descriptions that contribute additional insights into the boy's life. When Davey is two, his mother turns him over to his older sister, Joanne, then seven, to raise, because, although Lois loves him, she considers him an encumbrance and finds it simply easier to let Joanne care for him. Lois drinks, enjoys lively parties, and often strikes and verbally abuses Joanne. Davey early learned to make himself invisible to avoid her anger and vindictiveness. Lois occasionally takes him when she goes dancing at a neighborhood bar, where, a silent "old kid," he is watched and given junk food by the indulgent barkeeper, while his mother is absorbed in "mating dances" with her latest boyfriend, who kisses and fondles her in front of the boy. Lois has an on-and-off relationship with their father, Sneaky Pete, a gambler who walked out some time ago and now lives in Florida, where Davey's older brother, Gary, is in prison. Having turned up on one of his brief visits, Pete gives Davey a mountain bike, on which the boy earns the nickname Gypsy for his long, rambling rides, once for twenty-four hours straight. Lois often berates Pete to his face or to her children for not sending support checks regularly and not indulging her as she thinks he should. Davey has mostly happy times with Pete, who takes the children to a carnival and loads them up with trinkets and junk food. After Joanne becomes Davey's surrogate mother, she lavishes love, attention, and gifts like second-hand games and toys on him. At nine, Joanne takes Davey along when she hangs with her gang and even fights tough Celeste to legitimate her brother's presence. At sixteen and a half and eight months pregnant, she marries Gus, a fruit dealer, in an elaborate wedding financed by Pete that is the biggest affair by far in the lives of Davey, his family, and their friends and provides some gross scenes involving mild pornography and excessive drinking. Not long after Joanne gives birth, Gus leaves her, and she soon passes Dennis, the baby, along to Davey's care. He is aware that Joanne is in some sort of trouble with social services and that the baby has what may be lead poisoning problems. He adores the baby, lavishing love and attention on Dennis exceeding even the love of Joanne for him. Although he gets involved briefly with a drug dealer who is later killed, his heart is with the baby, whom at the end Joanne takes away. Davey longs for a baby of his own and declares that the day will come when he will have his own "somebody" to love and love him in return. They will have babies together, and he will "love 'em like hell to pieces like nobody ever loved babies before." Davey is presented as a good kid, protective of his mother and sister but caught up in a way of life that seems to perpetuate itself without any effort on the part of the people involved. Davey's narrative of run-on sentences and fragments that repeat and turn back in on themselves shows that this young man, whom most people think is an inarticulate "retard," is capable of deeply felt emotions and perceptive thinking. The third-person passages are organized and low-keyed in comparison, their relative objectivity setting Davey's version of life in high relief. Although in places stark, the book is neither morbid nor depressing and is sometimes even humorous. It presents a picture of American life quite different from what most middle-class readers have experienced but one with which they are undoubtedly somewhat familiar from television and movies. ALA; SLJ.

H

HAAS, JESSIE (1959–   ), born in Putney, Vermont; graduate of Wellesley College; writer of more than twenty popular picture books and middle-grade novels, many involving horses. One such is *Unbroken: A Novel** (Greenwillow, 1999), a *School Library Journal* selection set in the Vermont hills about an orphaned girl whose life somewhat parallels that of her horse, Kid. Haas has also written the set of novels about Lily and her mare, Beware, among them *Beware and Stogie* (Greenwillow, 1998), and those about Barney, including *A Horse like Barney* (Greenwillow, 1993) and *Keeping Barney* (Greenwillow, 1982). *Fire! My Parents' Story* (Greenwillow, 1998) is a nonfiction chapter book that tells of a family tragedy. *Westminster West* (Greenwillow, 1997) is a period novel for young adults about two sisters in a post–Civil War Vermont community. Some of her books are self-illustrated. Critics praise her books as straightforward, well-plotted accounts of people facing problems of everyday existence.

HABIBI (Nye*, Naomi Shihab, Simon & Schuster, 1997), realistic novel of family life set at the time of publication mostly in Jerusalem, Israel, as seen from the vantage of the oldest child in the family, Liyana, 14. Since both Liyana and her brother, Rafik, 11, have long known that Palestinian Poppy (Dr. Kamal Abboud) yearns to return to his native land, which he left nineteen years earlier, they are not surprised when he and their mother, Susan, announce that he has accepted a position at a hospital in Jerusalem and that they will soon move. Still, Liyana has many regrets—leaving Sami the cat, grandmother Peachy Helen, the trees, flowers, and other features of their St. Louis landscape, and especially the boy from whom she recently received her first kiss. The family pitch in, however, and pack up and soon find themselves at the airport in Tel Aviv, where the Israeli guards are stern and unwelcoming. Poppy is sure that the formerly stressful political conditions are over, but he finds calling the country Israel difficult. To him it will always be Palestine. The Abbouds are greeted with tremendous joy and overwhelming hospitality by his very large extended family, headed by garrulous, warmhearted, chubby Sitti (grandmother). They live, for the most part, in the small Palestinian village of Ramallah a few miles north of Jerusalem. The Abbouds find an apartment in Jerusalem, and the children are enrolled in school, Liyana in the Armenian School in the Old City and Rafik in the Friends Girls [sic] School. Both settle in, Rafik more easily than Liyana, who often yearns for home. In addition to adjusting to the boisterous hospitality of their Palestinian relatives and to new school situations, they have other challenges: learning the language, getting around the city, adjusting to the customs (e.g., for Liyana, being restrained around boys, not wearing short shorts, always having to be conscious of what is "appropriate" for a girl), shopping, the foods, and the like, such matters as would be expected to call for adjustments if Americans were living in a culture so different from that of the United States. The family has many good times, among them when the children swim in the Dead Sea and visit a Bedouin encampment. Many tense moments occur, too, arising out of the continuing Arab-Israeli conflict. In a store, for example, Liyana is reviled by a Jewish man. Larger difficulties are more alarming. After public problems in the city, soldiers, searching for a young relative of Sitti thought to be involved, rampage through her house, viciously destroying her bathroom and damaging the rest of the place. In the refugee camp not far away, they demand a young friend of Rafik, and when he appears, they shoot him in the leg. When Poppy intervenes lest they hurt him further, Poppy is jailed. While most of the lengthy novel is concerned with everyday home and school events, the last part of the novel focuses on Liyana's relationship with an Israeli youth, Omer, whom she thinks of as the "cinnamon smelling" boy. She meets the good-looking, well-spoken youth in a ceramic shop during her lunch break one day, and at first she thinks he is Palestinian. Their friendship (which eventually finds expression in a low-keyed romance and chaste kiss) continues in spite of Susan and Poppy's reservations and gives the author the opportunity to voice hopes for peace. Omer visits Sitti and some of Poppy's family in Ramallah, where in spite of his ethnicity he becomes accepted because of his very obvious niceness and concern for the well-being of everyone. The book is almost plotless, and events, especially involving the Israeli soldiers, occur as expected. Except for Poppy, who has more dimension simply because he is the pivotal figure, the main characters are functionary types. Omer seems too friendly and open-minded to be true, but, since both he and Liyana are probably intended to suggest that hopes of peace and harmony between Jews and Arabs lie in the younger generation, he behaves just as the reader would like him to. Best are the descriptions of the region, vivid with sensory details, and of life and interpersonal relationships at Sitti's house. The title means darling or precious and refers not only to individuals but also to the way that Poppy thinks of the land. Addams; ALA.

HADDIX, MARGARET PETERSON (1964–   ), born in Washington Court House, Ohio; journalist, college instructor, novelist. She grew up on an Ohio farm, was graduated from Miami University of Ohio, and later worked as a reporter and copy editor in Indiana and as an instructor at a community college in Illinois. Her inventive first novel, *Running Out of Time** (Simon & Schuster, 1995), is about a tourist-attraction community where the children, at least, do not even know that the life of 1840 that they exemplify is not the actual time. Another well-received novel, *Don't You Dare Read This, Mrs. Dunphrey** (Simon & Schuster, 1997), is presented entirely in high school journal entries, which reveal that the sophomore writer is struggling to care for, and support, her younger brother after both parents have abandoned them. Other novels that have been named to young adult lists are *Leaving Fishers* (Simon & Schuster, 1997), about a religious cult, and *Among the Hidden* (Simon & Schuster, 1998), with a sinister futuristic setting. Haddix makes her home in Clarks Summit, Pennsylvania.

HAMBLY, BARBABA (1951–   ), born in San Diego; freelance writer of primarily sword-and-sorcery fantasies that often take place in alternative worlds and involve witches, magic, vampires, and the like. She studied medieval history for her graduate work at the University of California at Riverside, studied further at the University of Bordeaux, France, and worked as a research assistant, high school teacher, and karate instructor. Her novels show the influence of her background on the substance of her writings. Most of her three dozen books fall into several sets: the Darwath Series; Sun Wolf Series; Sun-Cross Series; the Windrose Chronicles; Star Trek Series; and Star Wars Series. Among her other books is *Stranger at the Wedding** (Ballantine, 1994), which describes a novice wizard's efforts to save the life of her sister, who is predicted to die on her wedding night. Deviating from Hambly's usual writing are *A Free Man of Color* (Bantam, 1997) and its sequel, *Fever Season* (Bantam, 1998), both mysteries about a free Creole surgeon trained in France who meets discrimination in nineteenth-century New Orleans.

HAMM, DIANE JOHNSTON (1949–   ), born in Portland, Oregon; teacher, artist, author. Her historical novel, *Daughter of Suqua** (Whitman, 1997), about the suffering caused to the Indians of Puget Sound by misguided government policies, received the Western Heritage Award. For earlier biographical information and a title entry, see *Dictionary, 1990–1994* [*Bunkhouse Journal*].

HAMMER LOGAN (*The Well: David's Story**), older brother of David Logan, who tells the story. From the beginning of the book, Hammer, 13, is presented as tough in mind and body, surly, proud, and self-assured. He is determined not to give the impression in any way that he is inferior to the Simms boys or to any other whites, for that matter, simply because he is African American. He feels that whites have no business taking water from the Logan well or even setting foot on Logan land. Because he thinks this way, he brings trouble to the Logan family the summer that the wells go dry. He is also quick and kind, and his finest hour occurs when he persuades Papa to hurry to the church to prevent

the Simms boys from playing dirty tricks on slow-witted African-American Joe*
McCalister. Hammer represents those African Americans who sometimes let
pride get in the way of prudence. He is a foil for diffident and sensible David,
who feels that one must weigh carefully what trouble one might take on before
courting it.

HANK THE YANK (*She Walks These Hills**), disc jockey and host of a radio
call-in show. In his real persona, Henry Kretzer, he is a nondescript, balding
man unlikely to be noticed, but on the air he is an articulate, friendly personality,
clever and able to project a certain flair that charms listeners. At first he exploits
the story of Harm* Sorley's escape from prison as a way to get listeners to call
in, but after a few days he becomes fascinated at the comments of the older
locals who seem to think of Harm as a hero. When he can find nothing revealing
in the old newspaper accounts or in the courthouse records about the crime that
sent Harm to prison thirty years earlier, he pursues the story for its own sake
and, convinced that the man was not given a fair trial, keeps trying to turn up
evidence. This search brings him to the mountain clearing where Harm lived
with his wife and baby daughter, and in the decrepit trailer Hank the Yank
discovers the body of Rita Pentland, once Harm's wife. A clever narrative device
to tell the reader a good deal about the community, Hank's character is also
interesting in itself.

HANNAH IN BETWEEN (Rodowsky*, Colby, Farrar, 1994), realistic problem
novel of the disruption and psychological strain on a family when the mother
becomes alcoholic. Hannah Brant, 12, relates events starting with her birthday
at Ocean Beach, Maryland, where her parents always rent a cottage near that of
her Granddad Brant and his second wife, Gloria. The summer month has been
marred by the erratic behavior of her mother, Katherine, which Hannah has
finally admitted to herself is caused by overdrinking but which she seems to be
the only one to notice. She agonizes over whether she should tell her father,
who solicitously puts his wife to bed, saying that she has a headache, or Gloria,
the one person who she thinks will understand, but she is afraid that she may
be mistaken and will humiliate her family needlessly. After they return to their
home in Baltimore, she observes more of her mother's drunkenness and is afraid
that her good friend Sam (Samantha) will notice, even making excuses to keep
Sam away from her house. When she accompanies Katherine, a professional
photographer, to a wedding, Hannah is impressed by her skill at managing her
subjects, but as the evening progresses, Katherine drinks more and more, leaning
on men she doesn't know, knocking over the wedding cake, and finally driving
a terrifying trip home. Even then, Hannah tells her father that her mother "has
a headache" and has gone to bed early. It is not until November, when Katherine
slams out of the house and doesn't return for the whole weekend, that Hannah
confronts her father, who admits that he has been pretending that she doesn't
know about her mother's drinking and that he doesn't know what to do about

it. Over Christmas Katherine seems better. Hannah gets a camera and a large supply of film, gifts that she doesn't particularly want. On New Year's Eve a big snow blankets the area, and a neighbor throws a spontaneous party. Although she is apprehensive, Hannah agrees when her mother suggests that Sam sleep over with her, and they talk until they hear her parents come in. As they pretend to be asleep, Katherine staggers into their room, knocks the dollhouse over, and stumbles around until Hannah's father comes in and steers her out. Although neither of them mentions the incident, Hannah is humiliated and wary, but Sam shows her friendship by deftly steering the conversation at school to safe topics. Shortly after that, Hannah finds her mother attempting to dismantle the Christmas tree, sitting on a ladder amid a chaos of broken decorations. Frustrated when the lasagna is frozen, Katherine storms out of the house. Later that evening, a call from the hospital reports that she has had a serious accident. After one hospital visit, when Katherine thinks Hannah is her mother, Hannah learns that her mother is suffering from delirium tremens and that she is not to visit her again. With the excuse that she and Sam are going to take pictures of the snow, Hannah sneaks into the hospital and stares, appalled, at the almost unrecognizable patient tied to the bed who is her mother. Suddenly furious at the whole situation, she starts taking pictures, snapping her mother's tangled hair and the grotesque way that her mouth hangs open. After Katherine gets home, still in denial, she finds Hannah's film and, thinking that it will be a nice surprise, develops it. The shock of seeing herself as they have seen her at first almost destroys her, but she pulls herself together and, finally, calls Alcoholics Anonymous to get help. The story skips rapidly through the next months, until she has an exhibit of artistic photographs, controls her urge to sample a bottle of gin that she has purchased, and follows a one-day-at-a-time pattern of sobriety. Hannah is hopeful enough to invite Sam to spend a month at Ocean Beach with them and celebrate her thirteenth birthday. Although the novel is written to thesis and predictable, it gives a good picture of the misery suffered by the child of an alcoholic and of the conspiracy of silence in afflicted families. Minor characters, among them Granddad Brant, who is a syndicated columnist, and Gloria, who is a strongly supportive stepgrandmother, are well drawn. ALA; SLJ.

HANNAH WELSH (*The Window**), best friend and helper of blind Mandy. Hannah is a lively, spunky, pretty high school girl, about Mandy's age. She is chosen to assist Mandy in finding her way to classes and in learning about the school. Hannah is a doer. She is in all the school clubs and volunteers for activities of every kind. She helps Mandy to socialize and encourages her to participate in the program in which the high school students befriend elementary children. She also suggests that Mandy control her prickly attitude. Hannah enjoys the warm atmosphere at Mandy's house, since the mood is stiff and the air tense at her own house. She confides to Mandy that her parents often fight, and she fears that they will get a divorce. When her mother leaves home, Hannah takes off, too, but Mandy finds her and persuades her to come back. Hannah seems tailor-made as Mandy's foil and is not as convincing as Mandy.

HARD LOVE (Wittlinger*, Ellen, Simon & Schuster, 1999), realistic boy's growing-up novel set at the time of publication in and near Boston, Massachusetts. Narrator John F. Galardi, Jr., 16, has, by his own admission, felt "invisible," that is, out of the mainstream of life, since his parents' divorce six years earlier. He has no friends his age, except for a classmate Brian, a long-suffering soul whom John puts down regularly. His neurotic mother sits alone in the dark, brooding on her unhappy marriage, and has not touched him, even for a hug, since the divorce. His egotistical publisher-father, who walked out on his family, dutifully takes John into his house in Boston every weekend but barely endures having dinner with him, preferring to spend his off-time with a succession of pretty, young women. John finds expression and escape in his newly created zine (self-published literary magazine) called *Bananafish*, which he writes under the name Giovanni and through which his considerable aptitude for writing is immediately evident. He is much drawn to a zine produced by someone calling herself Marisol*, decides to stake out her drop site at Tower Records in Boston, meets her, and is immediately attracted to her, although he knows that she is a lesbian. Since at this point he is unsure of his own sexual orientation, he just enjoys being with the tiny, dark, independent, intelligent high school senior, a Puerto Rican American named Marisol Guzman. When his mother makes plans to marry Al, the now-steady man in her life whom John barely tolerates, John is pleased that she seems happy but resents her letting Al touch her and also their decision to move to Al's house in another town. The junior prom marks an important stage in John's awareness of self and life. Pressured by Brian to accompany him and his girl to the dance, John, in turn, pressures Marisol to be his date and is surprised and pleased when she accepts. Things go fairly well until, carried away by circumstances and his almost unconsciously growing sexual attraction to her, he tries to kiss her. She leaves in anger, and they have a big fight. He has already invited her to accompany him to a zine conference at Provincetown. She calls to accept, thus patching up their rift, and raises his hopes because he now realizes that he is in love with her. Marisol's anger, however, and her assertion that he must face up to things and stop lying induce him to write letters setting forth his true feelings to his mother and father, although he does not mail the letters until they leave for the conference, which for both is an act of running away, or escape, as they call it, since they have set no time for return. At the conference John comes to terms with both Marisol and himself. Marisol finds several lesbians with whom she prefers to associate, but she and John decide to remain friends. Another zine writer, Diana Tree, an accomplished musician and singer, sings the pop/rock hit "Hard Love," the lyrics of which cause him to take stock of his behavior. He calls his mother, who has been frantic about his disappearance and the letter. She says that his action has forced her to take stock of her behavior toward him, and he thinks he better understands why she has been so aloof. In addition, Al says that they've decided not to move. At the end, possibilities seem open for a satisfying relationship between John and Diana, and he has identified his gender orientation. Although John suffers considerable angst, he is more honest and less self-pitying than most angst-laden adolescent protagonists. He knows much of his "suffering" is his own fault or a matter about which he can do something. He has not reached out, he has not tried to nournish relationships, and he has set himself up for failure. The end holds hope for him, his mother, and Al, but John Sr. opts out, which John now dismisses as his right. The style is crisp and controlled, selections from zines, lyrics from pop/rock songs, and poems add zest, the tone has a not unpleasing hard edge, and typography is heavy black—the whole holds the interest and seems appropriate to the turn of the century. SLJ.

HARM SORLEY (*She Walks These Hills**), actually named Hiram, convict who escapes from the Northeast Correctional Center at Mountain City, Tennessee, after serving thirty years for the ax murder of a prominent citizen and neighbor in the mountains near Hamelin. Harm suffers from Korsakoff's syndrome, a condition probably caused by drinking too much moonshine or jailshine and by injuries to his head that rob him of most of his near-term memory. He has no idea why he was incarcerated and, after he makes his escape in a garbage truck, soon forgets that he was in prison. He does remember, however, his wife, Rita, and their toddler-daughter, Charlarty, and he heads back to Mitchell County to the trailer where they lived. Like other victims of his condition, he makes up reasons to fill in the gaps of his memory. He decides that he must have been logging for a few weeks and worries that Rita will be missing him. He clings to his mother's Bible, from which he gets guidance by closing his eyes and concentrating, then opening it at random and pointing. On his trip home he breaks into cabins and takes food and clothes, and when he runs into Jeremy Cobb, lost and hungry, he offers the freeze-dried food that Jeremy earlier jettisoned to lighten his pack. While Jeremy goes for water, Harm forgets about him, picks up the backpack, and walks off, leaving Jeremy lost and stranded with no supplies. When he finally reaches his trailer, set afire by his daughter, Harm takes Charlarty for his wife, Rita, and, assuming that their child is in the trailer, plunges in to try to save her. It is finally determined that he killed Claib Maggard because the unprincipled man had, for a substantial profit, allowed toxic waste to be dumped on the Sorley land, but his trial had been perfunctory, and the story never came out. Despite his disregard for the law, Harm is a sympathetic character.

HAROLD GODWINSON, EARL OF WESSEX (*The King's Shadow**), historical figure who reigns briefly as King of England before he is defeated at the Battle of Hastings by William*, Duke of Normandy. He is the common-law husband of historical Lady* Ealdgyth Swan Neck, by whom he has children, and the beloved foster father of the fictional protagonist, Evyn. Golden-haired and mustached, he is a broad-shouldered man, calm, forceful, proud yet modest, brave in fighting, a good strategist, and a just and fair ruler. He defeats his younger brother, Tostig*, in battle at Stamford Bridge, and his younger brothers, Gyrth and Leofwine, die also in the battle against William. Evyn grows to respect and love him dearly and, at the novel's end, records the story of Harold's bravery and goodness so that they will never be forgotten.

HARVEY'S MYSTIFYING RACCOON MIX-UP (Clifford*, Eth, Houghton, 1994), realistic, lighthearted mystery-detective novel set at the time of publication in an unidentified middle-class American neighborhood. Narrator Harvey Willson, 12, is awakened at five in the morning by his often overly dramatic visiting younger cousin, Nora Jean Adams. Nora declares that a sinister figure is sneaking around outside his window. Together, they observe a tall, black-garbed, ski-masked prowler carrying a gun. Soon they hear shots, one of which shatters the window, while the other breaks the branch from the tree just outside in such a way that it falls into Harvey's room. While Dad, a traffic court judge, calls Oaty Clark, the chief of police, the children observe disentangling itself from the broken-off branch a small raccoon, with which Nora immediately falls in love and later names Buttons. Even before Oaty arrives, Mrs. Motley, their kindly, busybody, English-born, next-door neighbor arrives. When Harvey informs Oaty that the prowler was tall and thin, and Mrs. Motley is questioned about what she might have seen, she says that she saw the neighborhood "nurse person," who is tall and thin, but then says that the prowler could not have been the "nurse person" because the woman is never seen unless pushing her charge, chunky old Mrs. Grandy, in a wheelchair. Both women are new residents in the area. When the children clean up the mess in Harvey's room, they discover that Buttons is entranced by a shiny object, which Dad identifies as a plate for printing counterfeit twenty-dollar bills. They conclude that the prowler was shooting at Buttons to get the plate. Buttons slips out of the house with the plate and scurries up the tree. The "nurse person" unexpectedly arrives, attracted by the shots, she says, and points out that the raccoon is holding the plate. Frightened by the calls and cries from below, Buttons skitters under the eaves and into the attic. The children recover the raccoon and the plate, which Oaty identifies from certain misspelled words as the work of a counterfeiter named Wally Wurble, who is short and heavyset. Oaty also says that Wally works with a partner, Kookie Smith, who is long and lean. That night the children discover two intruders in the attic, one of whom threatens to wring the raccoon's neck. At this, Nora bites him and tells him that he will get hydrophobia, and the prowlers flee in terror. The children tell Harvey's parents that they are sure that the intruders were the counterfeiters. Mrs. Motley reports that a little earlier she saw the tall, thin nurse pushing the short, fat old woman in the wheelchair. Investigating, she found the wheelchair hidden under the hedge, empty, observed the two intruders as they fled from the house, took the wheelchair to her porch, and discovered the nurse's and old woman's garments on it. Even though the intruders have disappeared, Harvey points out that they must have been the counterfeiters, and Oaty is sure that they will soon be apprehended. Nora would like to keep Buttons but agrees that they should advertise for the owner, who turns out to be a girl about Nora's age delighted to have her Pumpernickel back. Pleasant, interesting, deftly contrasted main characters, lots of real-sounding dialogue, a transparent, uncomplicated plot with plenty of action, clues that are easy to follow so that readers can solve the mystery along with the children (including one given here that clearly identifies the nurse as one of the culprits)—these features combine for engrossing, fast-moving, light reading for those who are just beyond chapter books. Poe Nominee.

HAUGAARD, ERIK CHRISTIAN (1923–   ), born in Copenhagen, Denmark; writer of historical novels with a wide range of periods and settings. *The Revenge of the Forty-Seven Samurai** (Houghton, 1995) is based on an incident from feudal Japan. For earlier biographical information and title entries, see *Dictionary, 1960–1984* [*Hakon of Rogen's Saga*; *A Slave's Tale*; *Orphans of the Wind*; *The Rider and His Horse*; *The Little Fishes*; *Chase Me, Catch Nobody!*] and *Dictionary, 1985–1989* [*The Samurai's Tale*].

HAUTMAN, PETE (1952–   ), born in Berkeley, California; freelance writer of both fiction and nonfiction. He attended the Minneapolis College of Art and Design and the University of Minnesota in the 1970s and has lived in Minneapolis, the Sonora Desert near Vail, Arizona, and a small town on the shores of Lake Pepin in southwestern Wisconsin. His strange time-travel fantasy *Mr. Was** (Simon & Schuster, 1996) and *Stone Cold* (Simon & Schuster, 1998), about an incredibly successful teenage gambler, were both named to select lists for young adults. In addition, he has written novels for adults and, under the pseudonym of Peter Murray, many nonfiction books for young people.

HAWK MOON (MacGregor*, Rob, Simon & Schuster, 1996), contemporary murder mystery-detective novel with school- and sports-story aspects set in Aspen, Colorado. When Native-American Will Lansa, a half-Hopi, half-white high school senior and star football player, meets Myra Hodges in the ghost town of Ashcroft the night before the big game with Leadville, he has no way of knowing that that will be the last time that he will see her alive. The next day, just before the game, he learns from the principal and Myra's mother that Myra never returned home that night. During the game, in which he sets a new school record for rushing, Will suffers a head injury. While he lies unconscious, he sees a Hopi kiva ceremony involving the god Masau. After getting a postgame physical checkup, he makes inquiries about Myra at a party at the home of Paige Davis. Although he was not invited to attend, he discovers that all the school social movers and shakers and football stars are there. He discovers that some guests, who are behaving strangely, are using Chill, a Los Angeles designer drug currently in fashion. Soon gossip points to Will as Myra's murderer, and students and townspeople expect that he will be arrested momentarily, some even making bets on when it will happen. His knife is found with blood on it, traces of Chill appear in his bloodstream and on the floor of his locker, and Will can explain none of these matters. Rumor says that he was trying to break up with Myra. Taunting messages appear on his email, although theoretically no one else has his code. Since, however, Myra's body has not been found, and there is no tangible evidence that she is dead, the police cannot hold him. Will follows clues on his own behalf, determined to prove his innocence, and his divorced mother's father, burly old ex-miner Ed Conners, and Will's father, Pete Lansa*, a Hopi Reservation law enforcement officer, come to Aspen to help him. Complications ensue in abundance—two football teammates prove strangely unhelpful and unsympathetic; an email message suggests that Myra was thick with Will's mother's boyfriend, Tom Burke; a couple of mysterious strangers appear in town; police seem too eager to indict Will—the finger points variously, but Will remains the prime suspect. The breakthrough comes with a discovery by computer hack Corey Ridder, a biracial black-white girl new to Aspen who is attracted to Will since he is the only other biracial student. She learns that the police know all the students' email codes, having gained them during a crackdown on steroids. After Will has another Hopi-influenced dream in which a mine plays a prominent role, Will's grandfather Connors recalls that he sold a certain mine to Tom Burke. Will, Corey, Lansa, and Connors drive up to the mine, Corey picks the lock on the gate, and they discover sophisticated drug-producing paraphernalia and an empty grave. It turns out that a local drug ring has been operating there, involving Burke, two crooked Drug Enforcement Agency men, and local Sheriff Kirkpatrick. Also involved are the sheriff's son, Claude, a football player whom Will has regarded as his best friend, and Claude's girlfriend, Paige Davis. It comes out that Paige knifed Myra because Myra had found out about the drug operation and threatened to inform authorities. The grand climax comes when the "good guys" are captured and imprisoned in the mine, which the "bad guys" plan to demolish with a bomb. Will escapes through an opening in the ceiling; Corey, who managed to evade capture, summons help. Paige is killed in a shoot-out, the other culprits are captured, and Will is exonerated. He decides to return with his father to the reservation, where he can continue to benefit from the Hopi beliefs that appear to be strengthening him. The episodes at the mine seem trite and rushed, characters are usual for the genre, and one must read attentively to catch the plot pieces and find out what really happens at the end. The Hopi dream sequences, however, mesh well with the plot and occur at felicitous instances, and Will is a strong protagonist, who, if he makes mistakes, never lapses into self-pity or gives way to anger or self-destructive behavior. The book maintains a good pace and holds the attention well. The title, which refers to the time of the Hopi coming-of-age ceremony in which Masau appears, appropriately supports Will's maturing. Poe Nominee.

HAYES, DANIEL (1952–), born in Troy, New York; teacher, author of novels for young adults. He received his B.S. degree from the State University of New York at Plattsburgh and his M.S. degree from the State University of New York at Albany. Since 1975, he has taught English at Waterford Central High School and at Troy High School. His three books about thirteen-year-old Tyler McAllister, *The Trouble with Lemons* (Godine, 1991), *The Eye of the Beholder* (Godine, 1992), and *No Effect** (Godine, 1994), all are true to the psychology and school life of that age group. More recently, his novel *Flyers** (Simon & Schuster, 1996) has been well received. Hayes has made his home in Schaghticoke, New York.

HENKES, KEVIN (1960–), born in Racine, Wisconsin; popular, prolific writer and illustrator of lighthearted picture-story books and novels of family life and domestic adventures. Of his recently published novels, *Protecting Marie** (Greenwillow, 1995), a *School Library Journal* selection, is an almost episodic account of family life in which a temperamental professor-father and his sensitive, fearful daughter learn to get along with, and appreciate, each other. *Sun & Spoon** (Greenwillow, 1997), an American Library Association Notable Book, describes a family's slow progress in dealing with the death of their beloved Gram. Of Henkes' several picture books, *Owen* (Greenwillow, 1993) was a Newbery Honor book, and *Julius, the Baby of the World* (Greenwillow, 1990) and *Lilly's Purple Plastic Purse* (Greenwillow, 1996) are widely popular. Henkes is generally acknowledged to have remarkable skill at capturing the nuances of ordinary family life in an amusing, yet sensitive, fashion. For additional information and titles, see *Dictionary, 1990–1994* [*Words of Stone*].

HENRY (*Wringer**), George, called Henry by the gang to which he and Palmer LaRue belong. Like Palmer and Mutto, he never goes against the wishes of the gang's leader, Beans*. He is a tall, gangly boy of nine when the book begins, new in town. Palmer notes that, although Henry is the biggest boy in the group, he is also the meekest. The first scene in which Henry plays a major role shows his position in the group. Beans and Mutto attack him in the park, as though he were one of the pigeons to be destroyed in the town's annual Pigeon Day shoot. Palmer uncomfortably realizes that, while Henry is a member of the group, he is also its prey. Henry is the only real friend whom Palmer has in the group, which comes to be known as Beans' Boys.

HERMAN E. CALLOWAY (*Bud, Not Buddy**), the famous elderly bass player and bandleader who turns out to be Bud, not Buddy, Caldwell's curmudgeonly grandfather, the father of Bud's mother. Bud is disappointed when he sees the man, a "grouchy old bald-headed guy with a tremendous belly," not at all the way he looks in the pictures that his mother had, which were of Herman E. Calloway when he was much younger. When Calloway finds out about what happened to Bud's mother, he becomes very emotional in his grief. Evidently, Bud's mother ran away from home at a young age because her father was hard on her in ways not specified. Jimmy the horn man says that Calloway has always been hard on everyone around him and on himself as well. Herman E. Calloway is based on the author's father's father, Herman E. Curtis, a prominent bandleader of the time.

HESSE, KAREN (1952–   ), born in Baltimore, Maryland; writer of a number of distinctive novels for young people. Her sensitive story of life in the Oklahoma drought of the 1930s, *Out of the Dust* (Scholastic, 1997), written in free verse or a sort of prose poem, won both the Newbery Medal and the O'Dell Award. *Phoenix Rising** (Holt, 1994), which was earlier recognized for excellence by the *School Library Journal*, was named to the American Library Association list of Notable Books, and *The Music of Dolphins** (Scholastic, 1996), about a feral girl who has been raised by dolphins, also received literary acclaim. For earlier biographical information and title entries, see *Dictionary, 1990–1994* [*Letters from Rifka*; *Phoenix Rising*; *Sable*].

HICKMAN, JANET (1940–   ), born in Kilbourne, Ohio; received her B.S., M.A. (in education), and Ph.D. from Ohio State University; teacher in junior high school, instructor in children's literature at Ohio State; writer of novels. Although Hickman wrote four novels between 1974 and 1981, she made her name with her contributions to professional journals and her book *Children's Literature in the Elementary School* (Harcourt), which has gone to several editions. More recently she published *Jericho** (Greenwillow, 1994), a novel that was a *Boston Globe-Horn Book* Honor Book and named to Fanfare. It describes a girl's relationship with her senile great-grandmother, who longs for the friends, relatives, and town of her youth called Jericho. Another novel, *Susannah* (Greenwillow, 1998), tells of a girl who, after her mother's death, is taken by her father to live in a Shaker community in Ohio.

HILL, DONNA (1921–   ), born in Salt Lake City, Utah; librarian, painter, writer. She attended the Phillips Gallery Art School in Washington, D.C., and received her A.B. degree from George Washington University and her M.S. degree in library science from Columbia University. She has worked for the U.S. Department of State and in the U.S. Embassy in Paris, served in the New York Pubic Library and as head of the Hunter College Education Library, and taught in the Teachers Central Laboratory. Her paintings have been exhibited in Paris and in a United States Information Service (USIS) exhibit touring Europe. In addition to *Shipwreck Season** (Houghton, 1988), a novel of the New England lifesaving service, she has written picture books, reference works, and a biography of the Mormon leader Joseph Smith. She makes her home in New York City.

HITE, SID (1954–   ), born in Richmond, Virginia; raised near the small town of Bowling Green, West Virginia; novelist for middle grades and young adults. For several years after high school he traveled extensively in Europe, Asia, and South America, visiting twenty countries before returning to Virginia and the Blue Ridge Mountains that figure strongly in *It's Nothing to a Mountain** (Holt, 1994), about an orphaned boy of twelve who runs away from his grandmother's house to explore the mountains and falls in with a strange, almost feral youth. The book was named to both the American Library Association and the *School Library Journal* lists. He has been praised for his skill at blending colloquial humor and down-home philosophy with a good story. He has also published the novels *Dither Farm* (Holt, 1992), about peculiar events in an unusual southern Virginia family, and *Answer My Prayer* (Holt, 1995) and *The Distance of Hope* (Holt, 1998), both fantasies.

HOBBS, WILL, teacher of reading before becoming a full-time writer. He has published more than a dozen novels of mystery and adventure for middle grades and early adolescents. Born into an air force family, he lived in many places in the United States while he was growing up and attributes the years that he lived in Alaska to instilling in him the love of the natural world that is the hallmark of his books. After graduating from Stanford, he moved to southwestern Colorado, where he and his wife have lived for many years. Three recent books exemplify his work, which is filled with action and tense moments, projects a strong sense of physical setting, and is always highly entertaining. *Far North** (Morrow, 1996), winner of a Spur Award, describes how two boys, one of them a Slavey Indian, survive a winter in the rugged Mackenzie Mountains of the Canadian Northwest Territories. An Edgar Allan Poe Winner, *Ghost Canoe** (Morrow, 1997) is a period mystery set in 1874 in Washington Territory and also involves Native Americans. *The Maze** (Morrow, 1998), nominated for a Poe Award and also a boy's growing-up and adventure novel, is set in the Maze, a particulary rugged part of Utah's Canyonlands National Park. Two more books of the same genre set in the Colorado mountains involve a Ute-Navajo youth considered intractable who is sent to live with an old rancher-miner, *Bearstone* (Atheneum, 1989) and *Beardance* (1993). *Jason's Gold* (Morrow, 1999) and *Down the Yukon* (HarperCollins, 2000) are companion adventure novels also set in Alaska.

HOLES (Sachar*, Louis, Farrar, 1998), often humorous, complex, realistic mystery and friendship novel set on a dried-up lake bed in the Texas desert about the time of publication. Although innocent, obese, and often teased, Stanley Yelnats, perhaps twelve, is convicted of stealing a pair of sneakers that baseball star Clyde "Sweet Feet" Livingston has donated for a homeless-center fundraiser. Given the choice by the judge of eighteen months in jail or at Camp Green Lake, Stanley chooses camp, because, being poor, he has never been to camp. Neither he nor his parents are aware that the place is a penal facility in the desert. Every day in the torrid weather each boy prisoner must dig a hole five feet down and five feet across. Stanley attributes his misfortune to a curse placed on his Latvian immigrant "no-good-rotten-pig-stealing" great-great-grandfather, Elya* Yelnats, by an old Egyptian woman named Madame Zeroni back in the old country. Assigned to Tent D, Stanley, nicknamed Caveman, shares exceedingly spartan quarters with an ethnic and racial mix of boys, nick-named Zero*, X-Ray, Magnet, Squid, Armpit, Zigzag, and later one called Twitch. Their counselor, Mr. Pendanski, whom the boys call Mom, tends to be pompous and preachy, although he appears to want to treat his charges as hu-manely as the Warden* allows. The boys have almost no creature comforts and are given very little food and water. Their work area, from before light in the morning until each has finished his hole, is the dry lake bed. At first, Stanley finds the digging excruciatingly hard, but he persists, and gradually his body becomes tougher and leaner, his hands firmer, his determination stronger, and his self-esteem higher. Their orders are to inform Mom or Mr. Sir, a sadistic adult supervisor, of any "interesting" discoveries. Stanley unearths a golden tube with KB engraved at one end. The Warden, now revealed as a woman, excitedly organizes the boys into a digging expedition—for exactly what, the boys do not know. Stanley has been teaching Zero to read and write, for which Zero offers to do part of Stanley's digging. A brouhaha erupts, with the result that Zero hits Mom with his shovel and then simply walks off by himself through the desert toward the mountains. Stanley tries unsuccessfully to steal Mr. Sir's water truck and then runs off to seek Zero. He goes toward Big Thumb, a mountain peak where he is sure water exists and where an ancestor of his, the first Stanley Yelnats, son of Elya, presumably found refuge. Stanley's knowledge of family history leads him to suspect that the Warden seeks a treasure reputedly buried by Kissin'* Kate Barlow, a notorious outlaw. In spite of incredible odds, he locates Zero, gets them into the mountains, where they find water and onions to eat, and then gets them back to camp. Digging at night, they discover buried where Stanley found the tube a suitcase with, amazingly, Stanley's name on it. Evidently, it was stolen by Kissin' Kate from the first Stanley Yelnats, a Wall Street winner, in a stagecoach holdup on his way to California. Stanley's lawyer, Ms. Morengo, arrives, claims the suitcase for Stanley, and informs everyone that Stanley has been cleared by the court. The Attorney General initiates an investigation of the camp, which the Warden apparently organized to hunt for the treasure. Since the Warden has destroyed Zero's records, he cannot be held, and Ms. Morengo takes Zero away with her, too. Stanley's father, previously an unsuccessful inventor, has patented a remedy for smelly feet, which eases considerably the family's financial problems. Moreover, the suitcase contains securities of various sorts that yield an after-tax fortune of $2 million. The mystery is deftly strung out, and although most figures are one-dimensional functionaries or overdrawn to the point of caricature, Stanley is an attractive protagonist who emerges sounder in body and feeling better about himself. The story of Stanley's ancestor and Kissin' Kate is well meshed with Stanley's, the pace remains rapid, good and evil are clearly identified, the Cinderellas triumph, and problems of homelessness and the juvenile justice system are called to the attention. Offbeat, surrealistic, and comic elements, coupled with the triumph of the plucky hero, make for sure-fire appeal to middle graders. ALA; Boston Globe Winner; Christopher; Fanfare; Newbery Winner; Poe Nominee; SLJ.

HOLT, KIMBERLY WILLIS, born in Pensacola, Florida; writer of novels with southern settings for young adults. As a child, she lived in many different countries where her father was stationed in the United States Navy, but she considered Forest Hill, Louisiana, her home. *My Louisiana Sky** (Holt, 1997), a novel of a girl who parents are both retarded, is set in a small town much like Forest Hill. The small Texas town in *When Zachary Beaver Came to Town** (Holt, 1999) is an equally important setting. Another novel by Holt is *Mister and Me* (Putnam, 1998), about how a little African-American girl gradually accepts the man who is to become her stepfather. Holt has also published short fiction in literary journals, including the *Southern Humanities Review*. She makes her home in Amarillo, Texas.

THE HOUSE ON MANGO STREET (Cisneros*, Sandra, Arte Publico, 1984), girl's growing-up novel written in more than forty brief vignettes describing her family and neighbors, life in her run-down Latino neighborhood, and her own thoughts and longings. Esperanza (the name means "hope") sees the house on Mango Street as better than some places where they have lived, but not at all the white bungalow with a big yard that her parents have dreamed about and promised. With her little sister, Nenny, and sometimes her brothers Carlos and Kiki, she tours Mango and nearby streets, gets to know the bums, Gil, who owns the junk store, families with too many children, Puerto Rican Louie's older cousin, who tells them how a girl gets pregnant, and another cousin of Louie who comes in a yellow Cadillac, takes them all for a ride, is chased by police, and is arrested. She dances with her Uncle Nacho at her cousin's baptism and notices the changes in her own body like the development of hips. She gets her first job and is sexually asaulted by an older fellow worker. She dreams of getting away from Mango Street but knows that she will always return. There is an artlessness about the brief pieces, some less than a page long and seemingly random, but they add up to a picture of Hispanic life in a city, the expectations for girls growing up in the culture, and the struggle to assert themselves to achieve beyond what their mothers have. Small, memorable details ring true. Stone.

HOUSEWRIGHT, DAVID (1955–   ), born in St. Paul, Minnesota, where he also makes his home; freelance writer. He received his degree from the University of St. Thomas in St. Paul. After a seven-year career in journalism for the *Minneapolis Star Tribune* and other papers in Minnesota and North Dakota, where he covered, among others, the political and court beats, he returned to Minneapolis, where he worked in advertising for fourteen years, eventually forming his own company. Now in freelance advertising and writing, he drew upon his newspaper background for his several books about the fictional detective Holland Taylor, *Penance** (Norton, 1995), a nominee for the Edgar Allan Poe Award, and *Practice to Deceive* (Norton, 1997). In the first book, a murder investigation leads Taylor to the highest levels in Minnesota state government and into many ticklish situations. In *Practice to Deceive* (Norton, 1997), he must find both a killer and missing funds. *Dearly Departed* (Foul Play, 1999) continues Taylor's exploits. While offering nothing new in the detective-whodunit genre, these books have a sympathetic, regular-guy protagonist and offer never-fail good entertainment.

HUMPHREY BOONE (*Brothers and Sisters**), suave, elegant, well-educated young black man hired by Preston* Sinclair, president of Angel City National Bank, to implement affirmative-action and diversity sensitivity programs. When he arrives at Angel City Bank, he knows that he is resented and suspects that officers and personnel will work against him to get him ousted. This happens when Bailey Reynolds accuses him of attempting to rape Mallory* Post. Humphrey eventually resigns to take the presidency of the newly established church-supported Solid Rock National Bank. Humphrey has been working with youth in the church and is persuaded by the church's minister that he can make a significant contribution to the entire community. Humphrey is a personality in conflict: he would like to identify more with African-Americans but knows that money and power lie with establishing himself in the white corporate world.

I

I AM THE CHEESE (Cormier*, Robert, Pantheon, 1977), chilling novel of a boy who seems, at first, to be on a bicycle trip through Vermont but eventually is revealed to be the victim of either an underworld or a government conspiracy, or possibly both, that keeps him in a mental hospital, where his memory is continually probed to see how much he knew of his father's court testimony, which led to the family's being given a new identity. Very cleverly constructed, the novel is intense and rapid-paced. Phoenix Winner. For a longer entry, see *Dictionary, 1960–1984*.

ICEMAN (Lynch*, Chris, HarperCollins, 1994), contemporary boy's growing-up and sports novel set in Boston, Massachusetts, during one hockey season. Narrator Eric, 14, is a "rock-'em sock-'em" hockey player. He yearns to be as good as his brother, Duane*, 17, a high school superstar who abruptly quit sports, becoming "pro-school" and a talented guitarist. Eric has an uneasy relationship with Mom*, an ex-nun bent on "saving" everyone in the family, in particular, her younger son, but relishes the approval of his Dad*, a mediocre public relations man, ardent Boston Bruins fan, and his son's greatest hockey supporter. Dad encourages the rough play on the rink that often lands the boy in the penalty box, gains him applause, but also precipitates boos. Eric's coach praises him to the team as "the guy with fire in the belly," and the team calls him "Iceman," because he plays so heartlessly. Eric's only friends, besides Duane, are his Chinese water dragon, Mary, for whom he coldly kills mice, and strange, remote McLaughlin, the mortician's helper at nearby Gormely's funeral home. After his grandmother's funeral, Eric visits the graveyard near Gormely's, hoping unsuccessfully to see how real people "do it," mourn, that is, and, in a grotesquely humorous scene, even stretches out inside a newly dug grave for a few moments just to see how it feels down there. The novel is lean on plot, but Eric's changing attitude toward hockey provides cohesion. He is bewildered by the attitudes of his coach, his teammates, and the fans, who appreciate his skill but increasingly deplore his rough tactics. A crucial game in Montreal changes his thinking. He spears the goalie, whose brother, Rajan Houle, retaliates, precipitating a bloody fight that turns the crowd against Eric. Between periods, Houle magnanimously visits the locker room to see how Eric, badly bloodied, is faring, compliments him on his playing ability, and informs him that he thinks Eric hates the game. He observes that if Eric really liked the game, he would be a truly terrific player. Eric takes Houle's words to heart, and when Dad brings an ex-Bruin player home for dinner, the man's scarred face and generally sad existence confirm the boy's decision to quit hockey. He tells Duane that his ambition is to run a funeral home, but when he and Duane visit McLaughlin's workplace, the boys are horrified to see McLaughlin sleeping, his body curled around that of a dead woman. Despondent, Eric refuses to go to school and even hates getting out of bed, but he feeds his fish and the water dragon and goes to hockey practice. Since the season is nearly over, he decides to participate in the last game. To his surprise, Duane decides to go along. Although Eric does not play with his customary fire, he knows that he must get tough to survive, and, though eventually in terrible physical shape, he is encouraged by Duane, who says he is good enough so that he does not have to play with such "crap" to win. Taking Duane's advice, Eric feels good about himself on the ice for the first time. He enjoys how the crowd appreciates him when he simply plays well. He rescinds his decision to quit the sport, and, realizing that he can be more useful on the ice than in the penalty box, he decides that with a reformed attitude he may yet become a fine hockey player, respected for his ability. Humor, action, and poignancy blend for uneven, but compelling, reading about how a boy learns that he must decide for himself what is the morally right course. The family is dysfunctional but in a sympathetic way, and Eric's life is less filled with overt teenage angst than in most such stories. The funeral home aspects stretch credibility, even for a confused, seeking youth like Eric, but the hockey scenes are exciting, sexual references are subtle, and the boys' diction is handled with appropriate restraint. ALA; SLJ.

I HADN'T MEANT TO TELL YOU THIS (Woodson*, Jacqueline, Delacorte, 1994), realistic sociological problem novel set at the time of publication in Chauncey, Ohio, a predominantly middle-class African-American suburb of Athens and lasting about four months. Telling the story is African-American Marie, 13, daughter of a professor at Ohio University, whose manic-depressive wife walked out two years before the story begins, perhaps because, as Marie's father tells her, "sometimes you have to go away to live." After giving a capsule history of Chauncey, Marie describes how, three days after school begins in the fall, a poorly dressed, unkempt, somewhat aloof white girl named Lena Bright enrolls, and Marie is asked by their teacher to show her around. Marie learns that Lena lives with her father and younger sister, Dion, down by the dump, a place known to the blacks as the "whitetrash" area, and that Lena's mother died from breast cancer. Marie feels a kinship with Lena, because of their mutual losses and because Lena often looks as though she has a hard life. Marie shows her the postcards that her mother sends from exotic places. Lena enjoys their little poetic notes and points out how they always conclude with "Love, Me" and have a poignant alternative meaning if the comma is ignored. Marie's father has misgivings about the girls' friendship, being a former civil rights worker who was assaulted by whites and knows that "whitetrash" never stay in Chauncey long. After his divorce becomes final, he begins to date again, and, seeing that Marie and Lena are getting along, he relaxes about their relationship. Lena's slovenliness continues to puzzle Marie, as do some statements that she makes, like saying that sometimes you can get too much love. When taxed about her appearance yet again, Lena says that she and Dion have to get out of the house as fast as they can in the morning and then elaborates on that by saying that she has no privacy and her father "does things" to her. She also says that she often feels as though she is "the dirtiest, ugliest thing in the world" but makes Marie promise not to tell anyone. She fears that the authorities will find out and send the sisters to separate foster homes, as they did once before. Lena and Dion have hot chocolate and take bubble baths at Marie's house, which Dion says is the "most beautifulest house" she has ever seen, and the friendship deepens. Since Marie knows that Lena feels hopeless about the future, she suggests that Lena, a middling student, work hard and get a scholarship to some college. Lena replies that she cannot keep her mind on schoolwork, that her mind "goes off and does what it feels like." After appearing unusually nervous in school, Lena begins missing classes, then one day tells Marie that her father is "touching" Dion now and that she and Dion are leaving but will write to Marie some day. Later Marie finds outside their empty house a piece of notebook paper on which is written in Lena's handwriting: Elena Cecilia Bright and her sister Edion Kay Bright lived here once. Marie imagines the two walking hand in hand together, happy now. One morning, after dreaming about Lena, Marie thinks that Lena informs her that it is all right to tell Lena's story so that other girls can go through life not being afraid as Lena has been. Characters are one-dimensional, and the story's memoirlike quality supports the retrospective narration but lessens the emotional impact. The nature of the molestation is never specified, but Lena's behavior seems clinically correct. When Marie asks Lena if she is afraid that she will get pregnant, Lena replies that her father "doesn't do that." Even the girls' intimate conversations seem too brief and superficial to hold the interest as they should. The open-ended conclusion is troubling. Does Lena's whole family move away together? If so, is the reader to expect that the problems will continue? Or do the girls run away? If so, is that to be taken as the best way out of such a predicament? ALA; Fanfare; SLJ.

I-MAN (*Rule of the Bone**), easygoing, life-loving, elderly black man from Jamaica, the "homeboy and spiritual guide" who becomes a strong, positive influence on Chappie, the fourteen-year-old narrator. I-Man speaks in a mixture of Jamaican patois and personal philosophy-speak, liberally sprinkling his talk with mention of I-Self (with whom one must also get in touch) and Jah, his name for God (with whom one must also get in touch). I-Man wears dreadlocks, belongs to a Jamaican religious sect called the Rastafarians, and carries a Jah-stick, which seems to have some magical ability and of which people are afraid. He came to the United States to work as a laborer in New York state's apple orchards. He is well known in Jamaica, where he has a "squat," a place near Montego Bay to live and work, and a "groundation," a place up in the hills where he grows some sort of plant, perhaps marijuana, used for drugs. He has a Jamaican wife and children, to whom he pays little attention, and is heavily into the drug trade. I-Man's murder by an American drug dealer ironically helps put Chappie in tune with his I-Self, a state that I-Man had told him to strive for.

INDIO (Garland*, Sherry, Harcourt, 1995), historical novel of Spanish contact with Native-American Indian pit-dwelling farmers along the Rio Grande in southwestern Texas in perhaps the mid-seventeenth century. The small group of Indians to which Ipa-tah-chi belongs are called by the author Otomoacos, one of several riverside bands that have disappeared from history and about whom very little is known. When Ipa is ten and Apaches from the north raid her small village, kill her healer-grandmother, and carry off into slavery her older brother, Ximi, the Otomoacoan way of life continues. Four years later, just as Ipa is to be married to the son of the headman of a neighboring village, the Otomoacos cease to exist as a viable group. Spaniards invade and raid, killing or carrying off most of the people, including Ipa, her younger brother, Kadoh, and her cousin Xucate*, to northern Mexico, the men to labor in the silver mines, weak little Kadoh among them, and the women and children to work in the mission. The captives endure repeated beatings, starvation rations, and numerous indignities. Ipa proves of special value to the Spaniards because she learned healing from her grandmother. But Xucate, a year older and pretty, is taken as a servant by the cruel overseer of the mine, Juan Diestro, who beats, rapes, and impregnates her. Before she gives birth, she runs away. Kindly Fray Bernardo befriends Ipa, but even he is not able to rescue Kadoh from the mines before the boy's mind is deranged and his foot is maimed in an accident. Rodrigo, a Spanish soldier who had been attentive to Ipa when her village was raided, is assigned to the mine area, and a low-keyed romance ensues. When Diestro is found knifed to death, Ipa is imprisoned for murder. While she awaits execution, Rodrigo helps her escape and promises to come for her at her village and marry her. On the way home, she encounters Xucate, who dies giving birth to a baby boy. Ipa finds her village suffering from a smallpox epidemic, and more hardships follow, but eventually she leaves for Mexico City, with the expectation of marrying Rodrigo. The plot is familiar and the conclusion is overly optimistic, chauvinistic, and romantic, but well-drawn, detailed episodes of daily life both at home and at the mission reveal ways and attitudes well. Such scenes as the Apache raid, first contact with the Spaniards, and the Easter observance with Juan Diestro's playing Christ have power. Characters, too, are the expected ones, but Ipa, small, plain, enduring, wins sympathy as a worthy representative of her people. Most memorable is the effective contrast between the way of life and worldview of these peace-loving farmers and those of the Spaniards, who are ruthless, greedy, and contemptuous of the culture and the very beings of the *indios*, whom they regard as mere tools for grubbing wealth from the earth. In a Preface, the author indicates that she has based the novel on comparative archaeology, history, anthropology, and her imagination. Spur.

INGOLD, JEANETTE, born in Texas, raised in New York state, resident of Montana; educator, newspaperwoman, photographer, gardener, backwoods traveler, and writer of books for middle graders and young adults. An American Library Association choice, *The Window** (Harcourt, 1996) tells how a blind girl of fifteen copes with her disability, grows to love the elderly relatives with whom she lives, and discovers the truth behind the car accident that killed her mother. In *Pictures, 1918* (Harcourt, 1998), a period novel, a girl sees a beautiful camera, earns the money to buy it, and learns to take and prepare pictures. In *Airfield* (Harcourt, 1999), a girl seeks to learn from her pilot father details about her deceased mother.

IN THE MIDDLE OF THE NIGHT (Cormier*, Robert, Delacorte, 1995), mystery of suspense centering on a family harassed by phone calls accusing the father of being a murderer for his part in a theater disaster twenty-five years earlier. At the time of the accident, John Paul Colbert was sixteen, the assistant manager of the Globe Theater in Wickburg, Massachusetts, where a Halloween program for underprivileged children has filled the old building. His boss, hearing a strange noise in the rubbish-filled balcony, sends him up to investigate and gives him a book of matches to provide light. Afraid of rats, John Paul nervously drops the lighted matches, starting a fire just as the ancient balcony collapses, killing twenty-two children. Although the manager commits suicide, and investigators say that John Paul is not to blame, parents and survivors focus their fury on him, especially when he makes no statement to explain his part. The story picks up when his son, Denny, is sixteen, now living in Barstow, Massachusetts, the family having moved frequently but in vain to escape the harassment. His father has forbidden Denny to answer the telephone, but, alone in the house and greatly irritated by the incessant ringing, he impulsively answers, only to hear the sultry voice of someone called Lulu, who begins a seduction by phone that both fascinates and upsets the boy. This part of the novel is told in the third person. Interspersed with these sections are others in first person, narrated by a male who was a child of ten in the theater with his sister, Lulu, on that fateful day. Known only by her pet name for him, Baby, until almost the end of the book, he tells of his injuries and of his certainty, and hers, that she was killed and returned to life in the rubbish. The action culminates on Halloween night, after Denny by appointment waits on his corner, having been promised that he will meet Lulu. When he enters the car that stops, he is surprised that it is driven by Dave, a young man whom he has met and often talked to in the 24-hour convenience store in his neighborhood. In the back seat, although he cannot see her and recognizes her only by her voice, is Lulu. They drive him to their apartment, where with an increasing sense of terror, he discovers that Lulu is a disfigured cripple and that she has injected him with something that temporarily paralyzes him until she can give him a fatal injection in revenge on his father. Unable to move, he watches Dave prepare the needle, then turn it on Lulu. By this time Denny's muscles begin to work again, and he follows Dave's instruction to leave, knowing that he will inject himself after Denny leaves. Back in his own neighborhood, he calls anonymously to report the deaths. Although he has escaped the fatal poison, his life has been grievously damaged. Haunted by Lulu's voice, he cannot make himself respond to the overtures by a beautiful girl, Dawn O'Hearn, whom he has met on the school bus. Nor can he participate in school activities, having for all his life held off from friendships because of the shadow of the phone stalker over the family life. This downbeat ending is typical of Cormier's novels, as is the character of the young sociopath. Lulu's obsession for revenge is explained by her belief that she has seen the horror of death, a void of nothingness, and that her life has been ghastly ever since. Despite these elements, which have become clichés in the works of Cormier, the novel is cleverly written and keeps the reader's attention. Although withholding the identity of Baby as Dave is, in retrospect, an unjustified trick, it adds to the tension. Poe Nominee.

IN THE TIME OF THE BUTTERFLIES (Alvarez*, Julia, Algonquin, 1994), biographical novel of the Mirabel sisters, known as the Mariposas or Butterflies, three of whom were murdered on November 15, 1960, for their part in the opposition to General Trujillo, right-wing dictator of the Dominican Republic. Told in alternating chapters, each narrated by one of the sisters, it traces their lives, personalities, marriages, and involvement with the political opposition to the government from the time that they are girls to the death of the three, with an opening chapter, epilogue, and occasional other bits set in 1994 in the voice of Dede, the surviving sister. Of the four, Minerva, the third daughter, is the most rebellious in the restricted life of upper-class Latin women and the most ideologically committed to reform. Her great desire is to become a lawyer, and her constant harping on her need for an education finally makes her father agree to send her and her older sister, religious Patria, and later compliant Dede, away to Immaculata Concepcion School. Two friends whom Minerva makes there awaken her to political realities: Sinita Perozo, a charity student whose whole prominent family has been murdered at Trujillo's orders, and Lina Lovaton, a much-admired older girl who catches the dictator's attention and becomes his mistress, at first lavished with favors, then neglected as his ever-roving eye lights elsewhere. Eventually, Minerva finds herself the object of Trujillo's lust and risks the family's safety by rebuffing him. She does, however, bargain to be allowed to attend law school and finishes, only to have the dictator refuse her a license to practice. Early in her revolutionary activity Minerva is involved with Lio (Virgilio) Morales, but when he leaves the country, her father intercepts his letters to her asking her to join him. Not until she is twenty-nine, old maid by the standards of her culture, does Minerva marry Manolo Tavarez, another man whom she has met in the opposition movement. Patria, the eldest sister, seems to have a strong religious vocation, but as she develops, she realizes that she does not want to become a nun. At seventeen she marries Pedrito Gonzalez, a boy from a neighboring farm. When her third child is born dead, she questions God's will. Still, it is not until her son, Nelson, becomes involved with the underground and the priest to whom she turns for help reveals that he, too, is working against the government that she becomes politically involved. While she is attending a retreat in the mountains, an abortive insurrection occurs, and she sees a boy even younger than Nelson shot in the back. Although she clings to her religious faith through the arrest of her son and her husband and even that of two of her sisters, she is never a true believer again. Maria Teresa, called Mate, eleven years younger than Patria, is a romantic, caught up in her girlhood with thoughts of clothes and boys. When she is staying with Minerva in Monte Cristi, a young man known as Palomino delivers boxes of ammunition to the little house, and she falls in love and into the movement simultaneously. Within a few months, she and Palomino, really Leandro Rodriguez, are married. Most of her chapters are in the form of diary entries, the early ones revealing her frivolous interests but the later ones, written while she and Minerva are in prison, showing her emotional maturity. Dede, the second daughter, is the focal point of the novel, the only one of the sisters to survive, a situation for which she continues to blame herself. Her commitment to the movement is never as strong as that of her sisters. Early on, she falls in love with Lio, who seems to be Minerva's property, and settles for marrying Jaimito, a cousin who is good-natured and amusing at first but, after a number of business failures, becomes tyrannical. Partly out of fear of Jaimito, Dede never fully joins the underground organization, but her reluctance does not save her from the hardship, bitterness, and grief of the others. After Minerva, Patria, and Mate, traveling in the mountains to visit their imprisoned husbands, are waylaid and murdered, along with their driver, Rufina de la Cruz, Dede raises their children and becomes the unwilling spokesperson for their martyrdom. All of the sisters and their husbands, as well as many of the minor figures, are clearly delineated and well-developed characters. While the cruel and repressive regime is central to the story, the focus is on the young women themselves, their different personalities and reasons for being part of the movement and their varied reactions to crises. One interesting sidelight is Minerva's discovery of her father's mistress and second family, her later decision to send her half sisters to school, and the role that one of them plays in relieving some of the suffering that Mineva and Mate experience in prison. An author's note at the end explains that, while the author researched the historical background and what is known of the Mirabel sisters, much of the story is, necessarily, fiction. The role of the United States, which failed for many years to condemn the atrocities of the regime, is not white-washed, but it is not a major element in the novel. ALA.

IRMA LEE PACKER (*Dave at Night**), African-American girl of almost eleven with whom Dave Caros becomes friends. He meets her at the party to which Solly* Gruber takes him on the night he first runs away from the Hebrew Home for Boys. Irma, the adopted daughter of well-known party-giver Odelia Packer, is delighted to meet him, because it appears that she has no friends her own age. She explains to him that the party is called a rent party, because in Harlem when people cannot pay their rent, they have a party, and the quarter that the partygoers pay to get in goes to pay the needy person's rent. When she learns that Dave is looking for a place to live, she invites him to stay in her basement and even outfits the place for him. Both are disappointed when they learn that the adults will not allow this to happen.

IRONMAN (Crutcher*, Chris, Greenwillow, 1995), sometimes funny, often poignant contemporary boy's growing-up novel set in one school year in the university town of Clark Fork in eastern Washington state and revolving around domestic abuse. Events are presented partly in the form of letters from Bo (Beauregard) Brewster, 17, to Larry* King of the television show *Larry King Live* and partly in third-person omniscient. An on-and-off student but fine athlete, Bo excels at the triathlon (biking, running, and swimming) and is training for Yukon Jack's competition in the spring. A responsible youth, he also works two jobs, exercises his divorced mother's Siberian huskies in a five-mile run every day, and regularly delivers to and from school his younger brother. Bo smarts off once again at mean, sadistic Mr. Redmond, his football coach and English teacher, and faces expulsion unless he attends Mr.* Nakatani's (Mr. Nak) Anger Management Class. Although he considers the class, which he calls the Nak Pack, filled with "thieves and murderers" and other lowlifes, Bo attends at the urging of Mr.* Serbousek (Mr. S), his journalism teacher. To Bo's surprise, he grows to like and appreciate Mr. Nak's students. He finds that they are much like himself in having abusive homes, and, like him, they disguise their fears with anger. Interacting with him are Hudge, whose father shoots Hudge's dog because Hudge was tardy in feeding the animal; African-American Shuja*, who is incited by any comment or gesture that might be construed as racial; Elvis, who labors diligently to care for his younger siblings since his mother committed suicide and his abusive father ran off; and Shelly*, who is a large, athletic girl with whom Bo forms a sweet and gentle romantic relationship. Class discussions help Bo see that his irascibility stems from the demands of his tyrannical, controlling father. Mr. S, who coaches the university swim team, allows Bo to train with the university students, where Bo comes up against bullying Wryback. Presumably to teach Bo a lesson by causing him to lose, Bo's father arranges with Wryback to provide free for Wryback's team a top-flight racing bicycle, one much better than Bo's. On the day of the race, the team's top biker, knowing how Wryback obtained the bike and deeming the situation unfair, turns over his bike to Bo. Bo gives his all in the race. Spurred on at vital points by a tape recording made by the Nak Pack, who now call themselves the Stotans (a combination of Stoics and Spartans), he defeats Wryback's team. Bo and his father attend counseling sessions, Bo's father's grudging graduation gift to Bo at Bo's request, although how much their relationship can be repaired is left open. Bo has learned much about himself and about why his father is as he is (he was similarly abused by his father). Bo concludes that "no matter what happens, I'll survive, and I won't lead a desperate life." Bo writes to Larry King in sometimes high-blown, always literate, engaging style, asking for exclusive rights to an interview prior to the publication of the memoirs of Bo, the Ironman. The letters provide information not given in the third-person sections, as well as Bo's reactions to events in the other sections, an effectively ironic device. The third-person sections, related in present tense, have great immediacy. Teen talk, some of it trashy, contributes authenticity. Well-drawn school scenes; telling class sessions; a large cast of carefully developed, distinctive, expertly foiled characters; implied commentary on abusive teachers and parents and the cross-generational nature of abuse; anecdotes related by the Nak Packers about domestic life that rend the heart—the whole is a finely balanced, substantial, jigsaw puzzle account of one important year in the life of a proud, worthy boy rescued just in time from a life of trouble. Both Mr. Nak and Mr. S influence Bo positively, and he takes as his guide Mr. Nak's parting comment to the class that "mercy is the only medicine for our anger . . . hurt . . . desperation . . . [it] allows for all things." Fanfare; SLJ.

THE IRON RING (Alexander*, Lloyd, Dutton, 1997), mythological fantasy novel recalling the ancient epics of India, set in a far-off time of swords and spears and involving magic, miracles, talking animals, and demons. The hero undertakes a journey-quest, during which he learns that few things are what they seem to be and that honor, contrary to what he has been taught, is not more important than life itself. When young King Tamar, ruler of the tiny kingdom of Sundari, is bested in a dice game by his guest from far to the north, proud, wealthy, powerful King Jaya of Mahapura, Tamar is put under bond to obey the monarch, the symbol of his obligation being an iron ring that he discovers upon his finger. Unsure about whether the gaming event was actual or a dream, Tamar decides that his *dharma* or honor requires him to travel to Mahapura to settle the matter, although he has misgivings about what he owes to his own warrior code of conduct and what as their ruler he owes to his people. Leaving Darshan, his general, in charge, he sets out on a long and perilous journey accompanied by his teacher, Rajaswami, a *brahmana*, or sage and spiritual leader, and acquires other traveling companions as he proceeds, each of whom plays a role in what transpires. Among the most significant of these is a monkey, Hashkat, King of the Bandar-loka, the Monkey Realm, whom he rescues from a huge serpent, King Shesha, Prince of the Naga-loka, the Serpent Realm, then saves Shesha's life and is rewarded with a magnificent ruby with a lotus design called Fire Flower. Next to join his group is Mirri, a wise and beautiful *gopi*, or cowherd, with whom he falls in love and eventually marries; Garuda, a bedraggled eagle; Ashwara, a king whose realm has been usurped by a tyrannical kinsman, Nahusha; and Adi-Kavi, who was once a king's crier. All these and others who join the enterprise form a league against Nahusha, who treacherously launches an attack, in which Ashwara is slain, and Tamar is captured and taken to a paupers' burning ground, where he is claimed as a slave by a *chandala*, the lowliest of all the castes. From the *chandala*, Tamar learns the folly of revenge and begins to realize that every life, no matter how lowly or despised by others, is valuable. After Darshan arrives with Tamar's troops, and Mirri comes up with a trick that gains victory against Nahusha, the travelers advance to Jaya's realm, where, ironically, Tamar learns that the *chandala* is really Jaya and that everything that occurred was engineered by the *chandala* for the purpose of teaching Tamar the value and meaning of life. Now wiser, Tamar returns home with Mirri as his wife, wishing only that his people be happy, loving, and merciful to one other and that there be an end to the custom of caste. Dialogue employs high diction, and an exceptionally large number of characters people the action (the reader is grateful for the list of figures that opens the book). Comic characters, who suffer pratfalls, are often bad tempered and hurl insults seemingly at random, intermingle with serious ones, interjecting moments of levity or boorishness into what is essentially a serious exploration of the purpose of life. The action swirls across the landscape with incident piled upon incident broad-canvas fashion, improvising on ancient Indian epics and drawing morals. The slapstick humor, drama of battle and overt conflict, poorly motivated, but exciting, comic adventures, colorful banter, and cliff-hanger chapter endings are typical of Alexander. ALA.

I SEE THE MOON (Christiansen*, C. B., Atheneum, 1994), novel of an unwed teenage pregnancy in a Norwegian-American family in a small midwestern town in the contemporary period. The narrative is written to the baby, a niece whom she calls Isabella, by Bitte, 12, and sent to the child, we learn at the end, as a twelfth birthday present to give her an idea of the caring decisions that led to her adoption. Bitte asks her mother, "What is love?" and gets the unsatisfactory answer, "You will know it when you see it." Bitte thinks it must be what her sister, Kari, 15, and Kari's boyfriend, Angus, have, but Mamma doesn't like that suggestion. Because Bitte is the youngest, her family tries to keep her a child, excluding her from the secrets that preoccupy Kari, her brother Jorgen, and their parents. Bitte does know that Kari is pregnant and that shy Angus is the father, and she realizes that their small farm town could be cruel to an unmarried mother, but she is confident that Kari and Angus will soon marry, and she dreams of being an aunt as dear to Isabella as her own aunt, Minna, is to her. When Kari tells her that she has arranged to have the baby adopted, Bitte's dream explodes. Because she protests and tries to talk Kari into keeping the baby, her mother sends her off to stay with Uncle Axel, a brother fifteen years older than Mamma, husband of Minna. A visit to their attractive house on a pond would have pleased Bitte a year earlier, but her sense of rejection combined with the fact that Minna is suffering from Alzheimer's disease and is now in a nursing home makes her resent the move, and she feels shy with Uncle Axel, whose language is still sprinkled with Norwegian words and whose conversation is full of stories from Norway. In the weeks that follow, she begins to see the love that Axel exhibits in choosing the perfect bunch of bananas for visits to Minna and in his continued devotion, even while he must gradually give up his expectations for her. Before Bitte left, Kari pressed on her an album showing the adoptive parents, Hope and Jacob, whom she has chosen for her child with the help of a lawyer. At first Bitte will not look at it, but after Kari calls and asks her to try to understand, she takes up the album and has to admit that Kari has made a good choice. When the baby is about to be born, Axel drives Bitte to the hospital to join the vigil being kept by their parents, Jorgen, and, to her surprise, Hope and Jacob. Angus does not appear, but he has dropped off a stuffed toy for the baby, which turns out to be, as Bitte has predicted, a girl. Bitte's dream of holding the child is fulfilled for a few minutes. Then she takes her back to Kari, who wraps her in a quilt that she has made and hands her over to Hope and Jacob. Bitte understands that love is not the romantic notions in magazines but the bittersweet feeling that permeates the room as they do what is best for the tiny girl. Bitte is immature in her self-absorption and her unrealistic dreams of caring for the baby, but she does not seem to have suffered from taunts or derogatory remarks directed at her because of Kari's pregnancy. Although not much is made of the family's disgrace and the humiliation to which Kari is subjected to as she finishes her sophomore year in high school or how she will fare going back to school in the fall, she is pictured as strong in her realization that she and Angus are too young to marry or be single parents and her determination to find a good home for her child. The novel clearly comes down in favor of adoption over single motherhood but does not even mention the possibility of abortion. In spite of being written to demonstrate a thesis, the novel has some realistic characters with convincing emotions. The title comes from the song that Minna used to sing to Bitte. ALA.

IT'S NOTHING TO A MOUNTAIN (Hite*, Sid, Holt, 1994), realistic novel of family life and friendship set in the Blue Ridge Mountains of Virginia for about six months in 1969 beginning in April. After their parents are killed in a car crash, Lisette Sutter, 14, and her younger brother, Riley, 12, go to live with their kind and loving Sutter grandparents, Clara and Preston, in their large brick Revolutionary War-period ancestral home, Upper Place, high atop the plateau overlooking Sparkling River Valley. While Lisette often weeps and ponders where her parents are and the location of heaven (which Clara says is only a matter of belief not actuality), Riley grows weary of the constant stream of visitors voicing expressions of sympathy and runs off with camping gear to explore the mountains. He suffers a mishap while trying to pitch his tent and is helped by strange, almost feral Thorpe Greenwood, 15, a local youth who has been missing for a year. The friendship that the two strike up drives much of the rest of the book. After Thorpe swears Riley to secrecy, and the two become blood brothers, Riley spends the night in Thorpe's hidden cave home. As the school year draws to a close, Riley becomes more and more detached and often slips out to meet Thorpe, surreptitiously helping himself to such supplies for his new friend as flashlight batteries and peanut butter. Lisette gradually becomes more reconciled to their loss, gaining comfort from wearing her mother's little gold locket. She spends much of her summer vacation with Kissy Kidder, daughter of a friend of Clara, whom Clara feels will be good for her now-maturing, pretty granddaughter. After Lisette has a heart-to-heart talk with the Sutters' friend Phyllis Applegate, the wife of local Judge Applegate and a firm believer in guardian angels, Lisette comes to believe in the concept herself, sure that a guardian angel helped her and Kissy when they were lost in the forest. When Riley finds Thorpe lying ill in the cave and tends him, Thorpe explains that after his mother was sent to prison because she shot his abusive stepfather in the knees, he ran away to avoid having to live with the man. Riley decides to visit Thorpe's mother in prison, a courageous act that he accomplishes by bus. He learns that Nina Greenwood has divorced her husband, but he cannot tell Thorpe because Preston grounds him. He manages to sneak out at night, however, and leaves a cryptic note in the cave for Thorpe. Lisette suspects that he is friends with a mysterious boy who threw stones at two rowdy teenagers who harassed her and Kissy while they were swimming. She is sure that the same boy found the locket, which she lost at that time. After a terrible hurricane, Camille, devastates the area, causing landslides, Riley hunts unsuccessfully for the cave, within which Thorpe struggles to survive, eventually finding an escape route to the river, down which he is borne to the Applegates' backyard. Phyllis discovers him, bruised and battered, and gets him to a hospital, where he recovers. Judge Applegate leaves for Richmond to try to persuade the governor to release Mrs. Greenwood. Characters are shallow, suspense minimal, and events move much as a thinking reader expects that they will. Clara's statement that the Applegates have longed for children of their own is a clear tip-off to how Thorpe's problem will be solved. Thorpe's teaching Riley the "fundamentals of life on the lam" introduces the younger boy to experiences that help to mature him, and Thorpe's quiet crush on pretty Lisette is a sweet touch. Occasional remarks about ways, beliefs, and attitudes among the mountain people and the writer's philosophical comments add humor and dimension, but dialogue does not always fit the speakers. Chapters and sections of chapters are often introduced by descriptions of the region or bits of history, a narrative technique that underscores the idea conveyed by the title: the mountains persist and will continue to do so, regardless of the people who live there. ALA; SLJ.

IZZY PUGH (*Spite Fences**), Isabelle, discontented mother of Maggie, a product of the mean-spirited little town of Kinship, Georgia, which tolerates both racial and economic segregation. A violent woman, she beats and throws things at Maggie and berates the girl and her kind, ineffectual husband, Henry. Izzy has two goals that she pursues relentlessly: to be admitted to the United Daughters of the Confederacy (UDC), a membership that, in her eyes, will confer the social status she so obviously lacks, and to have her younger daughter, Gardenia, win the beauty pageants in which she enters her. When their redneck neighbor, Virgil Boggs, chops off Gardenia's lovely blond hair, her second goal seems impossible, but she gets Maggie to earn money for a wig for her little sister by cleaning for George Hardy, an African American whom Izzy previously had forbidden Maggie to see again. Her application to the UDC is returned with the information that her ancestor who fought in the Civil War was, actually, at different times, in both the Confederate and Union armies and that therefore she is refused membership. Maggie opens the letter first and although Izzy has never been kind or understanding to her, sets it aside until she can support her mother in her disappointment. Izzy's potential to be a better mother is shown in the way that she comforts Gardenia and sings to her after her hair is shorn and in her hard work, which keeps the family afloat after her husband loses his job.

J

JABETH BALLOU (*The Great Turkey Walk**), African-American slave boy of about fifteen, whom Simon Green encounters shortly after the trip to Denver begins, adds to his party, and eventually calls his friend. Jabeth's mother having died recently, he decides to run away from his master in Missouri and make his way to free territory. Jabeth works for Simon herding the turkeys, which he does badly at first because he has no boots and resists getting turkey dung on his feet. He keeps the party in provisions by hunting and fishing. Very clever with the bowie knife, he whittles a flute upon which he plays. He also shows great aptitude with the rifle, almost immediately becoming their sharpshooter. When they reach Kansas Territory, Simon, Mr.* Bidwell Peece, and Jabeth dance around joyfully to celebrate Jabeth's having achieved freedom. No longer do they have to fear that someone may claim him as a runaway, as they have up to this time. Jabeth develops in confidence and often rises to the occasion to help. At the end, he becomes a full partner in The Great Turkey Five Ranch. As a character, Jabeth is an effective foil for Simon.

JEAN-CLAUDE THIBEDEAUX (*The Cage**), local guide for the photography expedition to film polar bears near Churchill, Manitoba. A small, quiet man with a slight limp, he has been working as a guide since he was fourteen, and he usually looks older than his twenty years. Beryl* Findham thinks that he moves slowly and speaks very little as a result of having faced the extreme cold so much of his life. Although she makes love with him and shares her bunk with him for two nights in the bus, she realizes that she knows almost nothing about him. His foresight in bringing a sled and snowshoes, his knowledge of the terrain, and his ability to build igloos give them their only chance of survival.

JEB GRAFTON (*Beyond the Western Sea: Book Two: Lord Kirkle's Money**), boy of about twelve, small for his age and very poorly clothed who earns a meager living for his family by shining shoes and running errands. His father has been unemployed for some time, blacklisted by the Lowell, Massachusetts, cotton mills because he has been outspoken about speedups and other unfair management practices and the generally poor working conditions. Jeb's mother, Sarah, who suffers from cotton cough but has been the family's main support, is discharged from her mill job, her place taken ironically by Maura O'Connell. Because the Irish immigrants will work for lower wages, many American workers are laid off or discharged and replaced by Irish immigrants like Maura. Hence, Jeb has a special hatred for the Irish, bullies Patrick O'Connell, and accepts jobs from Mr.* Jeremiah Jenkins that advance Jenkins' anti-Irish movement. Jeb also accepts errand jobs from Mr.* Matthew Clemspool, among them breaking into the house of Mr. Ambrose Shagwell, owner of the Shagwell Cotton Mill, with whom Mr. Clemspool is staying. Jeb housebreaks to recover a particular key, which later, for temporary safekeeping, he ironically turns over to Sir Laurence Kirkle. It is coincidentally the key to the safe-deposit box in which Mr. Clemspool has placed the money that he stole from Mr.* Toby Grout, who had stolen the money from Laurence, who had stolen the money from his father, Lord Kirkle.

JENNAT (*Escape from Egypt**), beautiful, young half-Syrian, half-Egyptian girl with whom the Hebrew slave Jesse falls in love. Found as a four-year-old child trailing after a passing caravan, she is brought up by, and becomes a servant to, Memnet, the wife of the powerful Egyptian merchant In-hop-tep, in whose jewelry smith's shop she meets Jesse*, an apprentice there. Her mistress gives her to the elderly, ugly In-hop-tep as a concubine, a situation repulsive to the girl and one that colors her feelings toward men, even Jesse, until she realizes that Jesse truly loves her. She and Jesse often discuss their gods. She has trouble seeing Adonai as good as well as powerful, because she feels that Adonai visits harm on those not at fault as well as those who are. Nor does she understand Jesse's insisting that she relinquish her idol of Hathor, since she gets so much comfort out of simply holding the small statue close. Eventually, she accepts the Hebrew god, Adonai, marries Jesse, and accompanies him to Canaan.

JEREMY COBB (*She Walks These Hills**), young instructor working on his Ph.D. dissertation in ethnohistory. Utterly unprepared for an extended hike in a wilderness area, having never walked farther than from car to classroom building, he nevertheless decides to get in touch with his subject by retracing part of the trail followed by Katie Wyler, who, in 1779 after her capture by Shawnees, escaped and found her way hundreds of miles back to Mitchell County. After starting with far too much equipment, Jeremy gets lost, discards most of his food, his tent, his solar shower, and other things out of his pack and plods on with sore, bleeding feet. When Harm* Sorley walks off with his pack, Jeremy struggles on, too miserable to sit down and die. Meeting with Sabrina Harkryder seems to offer hope, but he really fails to communicate with her and simply follows where she directs out of fear of being again alone. When they arrive at the burning trailer, Harm Sorley assumes that they have set it afire and is about to shoot them with the gun from Jeremy's pack, but he is distracted by the arrival of Martha Ayers and his now-grown daughter, Charlarty, and Jeremy and Sabrina escape into the woods. There they stumble upon the remains of the old Wyler homestead and hear her voice, urging her young brother to try to make it to the river to escape the Indians, as he did. After Jeremy and Sabrina finally arrive at the mountain home of Nora Bonesteel, a woman with "the sight" who has seen Katie Wyler, Jeremy tells her the story, and she confirms that they have heard the long-dead Katie. Despite his misery and near-death experience, Jeremy feels that he has really come to understand and appreciate Katie's journey, and he knows that the experience has been invaluable.

JERICHO (Hickman*, Janet, Greenwillow, 1994), realistic, sociological problem novel with girl's growing-up story aspects. The book revolves around family life in the small town of Gatesville, once called Jericho, somewhere in the eastern United States, and is told as two separate, third-person stories with alternating and occasionally parallel episodes. That of Angela, 12, covers several summer weeks during the Reagan era, while that of her great-grandmother, Araminda, occurs much earlier in the twentieth century and lasts about twenty years, beginning when Araminda is about five. Angela and her family—mother, Carol; father, Jay; and older brother, Brian—have come to help Carol's mother, Gram, with Gram's mother, GrandMin (Araminda) Walters Dutton. Angela's specific task is to watch over the frail, senile, near-invalid, while the others paint, wallpaper, and otherwise prepare GrandMin's house for rent. Angela often chafes at the old woman's forgetfulness: GrandMin cannot remember who Angela is, complains that the others (her own family) have all left her, and wants to return to Jericho. Although her developing sexuality puzzles her, Angela's life becomes more exciting when she thinks that Tom Ferris, the boy who helps with the yard, may be interested in her, but after she sees him kissing another girl down by the creek, she does her best to avoid him. The family's visit is extended when GrandMin falls out of bed, much overworked Gram hurts herself trying to help GrandMin, and Carol investigates nursing homes. During a storm, Angela checks on GrandMin in her bedroom, is gratified to hear the old woman call her by name, and then notices that GrandMin has stopped breathing. GrandMin has returned to Jericho and her long-gone, loved ones. Angela's third-person story is related in the present tense, is so severely focused that it seems like first-person narration, and not only conveys a strong sense of her early adolescent emotions toward GrandMin, Tom, and herself but also highlights the problems that families encounter in caring for the aged infirm. Although both parts of the novel seem curiously truncated, Araminda's story is more engrossing, with less adolescent angst. Told in past tense, alternating episodes with Angela's story, it begins when Araminda Walters' mother has just died and moves through Araminda's marriage to a local farmer and the birth of their only child, Katy, Angela's Gram. The youngest of six children, Min is raised mostly by her sister Delia, about ten years older, who is a great comfort to the little girl but whose behavior in a kissing scene puzzles her. When Min is of an age to do day work, for which she yearns since she is no longer allowed to go to school, her other older sister, Lucy, usurps the position, as Lucy also later steals from Min the handsome, well-off nephew of Mrs. Blossom Clark, a woman for whom Min works. Min eventually accepts the proposal of Leo Dutton, an awkward, ungainly, but hardworking farmer about ten years her senior, who loves and cherishes her. The book ends when they finally have the child for whom they have longed. Several scenes are dramatically memorable: Delia's insistence on raising Min when a neighbor named Bagley asks to take her off her father's hands shortly after the mother's death; the poignant death of Delia's illegitimate little son, Sammy, from a fever; the hard birth of Min's own baby. Characters are satisfactory for their roles, and the style is rich with details and distinctive phrases, but the emotional aspects of GrandMin's death are glossed over, and the death of GrandMin and the birth of her baby, a scene concluded with the words that she feels "that she would live forever," seem too obvious and labored, too neatly juxtaposed. The novel's chief strength appears in the carefully constructed and artfully placed vignettes, which show how unlike and yet how alike were the lives of families and young girls in the two periods. Boston Globe Honor; Fanfare.

JESSE (*Escape from Egypt**), ancient Hebrew youth enslaved in Egypt and apprenticed to a jewelry smith who participates in the exodus under the leadership of Moses and who falls in love with, and eventually marries, a non-Hebrew girl, Jennat*. Jesse is a gentle, warmhearted young man who dislikes seeing anyone suffer, even those who have enslaved the Hebrews or are non-Hebrews. He is tender even toward the animals that he herds. He experiences great guilt over killing the Amalekites when that wandering tribe attacks the Hebrews on the way to Canaan. Jesse takes very seriously such family responsibilities as watching over his little sister, Shosha, and is devastated emotionally when she is killed in the Amalekite battle. He loves his mother, Devorah*, dearly and admires, respects, and grows very close to his Uncle Rimon* and wants to be just like him, but he resents his rude, surly father, Nathan*. He has difficulty resolving his feelings for Talia*, the girl whom his family wishes him to marry, and for Jennat. Although he never exploits either girl, he is not always a sympathetic protagonist because he seizes opportunities to kiss and embrace both of them. Jesse is a credible human figure, never a glorified hero.

JESS VEERY (*The Cuckoo's Child**), mother of Mia Veery and Nell* and Bibi Cooper. Although she never appears in the novel, she is a central figure, a romantic, adventurous woman who eloped with Morse Cooper at seventeen and later left him, just driving away from the mundane responsibility of marriage. Her second husband, Mia's father, is a geologist teaching in Beirut, a serious, rather pedantic man but evidently willing to follow her in impulsive schemes like their sailing trip around the Greek islands. Jess has no understanding of Mia's intense desire for normality. When Mia asks desperately what she should tell her friends who want to know her religion, Jess suggests that she say, "Unfettered," and then amends it to "Aesthete," both answers that the little girl knows will not be satisfactory. Jess loves her daughters, but, like the mother cuckoo, flies off and lets someone else take care of them.

JIP HIS STORY (Paterson*, Katherine, Lodestar/Dutton, 1996), historical novel set on a Vermont poor farm in 1855, in which a foundling discovers that he is a fugitive slave being hunted by the white master who fathered him. Since he fell off the back of a wagon when he was two or three and no one came to find him, Jip West has lived at the poor farm run by lazy, heavy-drinking Otis Lyman and his penny-pinching wife. Now, some eight years later, Jip at about eleven mostly manages things, handling the animals and, with the help of retarded Sheldon* Morse, plowing and putting in the garden. He sometimes wonders whether the Lymans' assumption is correct that the cart that left him on West Hill Road was a gypsy wagon—hence his name—but he is comparatively happy and not greatly worried about it. When a weaselly-looking stranger waylays him and asks questions about his origin, he is very uncomfortable. His life changes considerably when Mr. Flint, the Overseer of the Poor, brings a raving lunatic to be kept in a cage that Mr. Lyman has had Jip and Sheldon build. At first Jip is frightened, but he cuts the man's bonds and brings ointment to soothe the rope burns. Soon the man, Put* (Putnam) Nelson, becomes another of Jip's "pets," another creature that he is responsible for, being the only one able and willing to control him. Before long four more are added to the poor farm population, Mrs. Wilkins, a recent widow, and her three children, Lucy, about Jip's age, little Toddy, just beginning to talk, and a baby. At first Lucy is unfriendly, but Toddy soon follows Jip everywhere and loves Put, especially begging him to sing a hymn with the chorus, "All is well, all is well." To earn some money for the poor farm, Mr. Lyman rents Sheldon out to the quarry, where, as Jip has feared, he is unable to understand the work and is killed. Gradually, Lucy warms to Jip, and when the three-month school term starts and her mother wants her to go, she insists that Jip accompany her. Jip is reluctant, having tried once before and decided that he had no mind for letters. The new Teacher—she is never called by any other name—encourages him and, most important, starts reading *Oliver Twist* aloud during the last half hour. Both Jip and Lucy are fascinated, hoping the book will give them clues toward how to learn of Jip's origins. Put, who has some education, helps Jip at home when he isn't having a "spell." After the Christmas program, Teacher gets them a ride home with Luke Stevens, and when the brief term ends, she urges Jip to turn to Mr. Stevens if he should need help. At the local store, where he has gone for supplies, Jip sees the unpleasant stranger and with him a man whom the boy realizes he greatly resembles. Terrified, he drives the wagon at top speed away from the town and poor farm, ending up on Quaker Road at the Stevens' farm. There

Luke and his mother, abolitionists, explain that they have recently learned that the stranger is a slave-catcher now accompanied by the owner of a slave woman who attempted escape eight years earlier and was recaptured. The woman, however, set her toddler son, sired by the master, down on the road when her captor's wagon slowed for a curve and later swore that the boy had died on her trip north. Stunned, Jip refuses to be spirited off immediately, saying that he cannot leave Put behind. He returns to the poor farm and, after the others are asleep, lets Put out, and they start for the Stevens' farm. Although he tries hard, Put is too old and weak, and Jip has to leave him to get help from Luke. Luke hides the boy in a cabin farther up the mountain and promises to get Put. The old man, however, is ill, and although Mrs. Stevens tries to keep and nurse him, he breaks away and comes to Jip. The slavers are closing in, so Jip leads Put across the hills by night to the village, where the Wilkens family now lives, hoping to find sanctuary with them. Lucy warns him that her mother will turn him in for the reward. As a last resort, Jip heads for Deacon Avery's house, where Teacher rooms, but he is captured. When Put comes, singing his hymn, to try to save Jip, the slaver shoots him and tries to take the boy away. Teacher intervenes, reminding the sheriff that by law Jip is entitled to a trial, so he is taken to jail. There Teacher and Luke visit him. She proposes that she will swear in court that Jip is her child, product of a youthful indiscretion, and Luke says that he will claim to be the father. Rather than let them face this certain disgrace, Jip breaks the window in the flimsy jail that night, climbs out, and makes his way north to Canada. A brief coda in italics tells that he found the Reverend Ezekial Freeman, an ex-slave friend about whom Teacher had told him, grew up in his household, and now plans to return to the United States to join a Negro regiment in the Civil War. The book ends with the music and words of Put's hymn, "All Is Well." The novel is rich in events, characters, and sensory detail, from the beauty of the Vermont landscape to the hardships of the penurious poor farm. Although only the last bit set about eight years after the main story is in first person, the point of view is closely Jip's all through, and his love for the farm animals and for Sheldon, Put, Lucy, Toddy, and Teacher comes through strongly. The slaver's recognition of Jip because he looks so much like the white master is strongly ironic. ALA; O'Dell; SLJ.

JOANIE GILMORE (*Sun & Spoon**), little sister, 6, of Spoon Gilmore. Joanie has a high-pitched voice and, in Spoon's view, an annoying habit of turning up at inopportune times. She usually wears a red, hooded sweatshirt, which makes her look like an elf, and carries a small canvas suitcase in which she keeps her "bones," twigs that have some special interest to her. Like most little girls her age, she has an active imagination and frequently tries to enlist Spoon in escapades. Spoon often speaks sharply to her and tries to get rid of her, then, realizing how much he loves her, he feels guilty about not giving her the time and attention that she craves.

JOE MCCALISTER (*The Well: David's Story**), slow-witted African-American youth, a little older than David and Hammer* Logan and white Charlie and Ed-Rose Simms. Joe is the butt of a nasty joke that Charlie engineers. Knowing that Joe helps out at the church and is conscientious to a fault as well as gullible, Charlie tells Joe late one afternoon that the minister wants Joe to open the church for a service that night. Joe does, and when no one appears, he conducts the service himself, even preaching a sermon, while Charlie and his brother stand sniggering outside the window watching. Hammer Logan, who has discovered Charlie's intentions, Papa*, and David drive to the church, enter, and tell Joe that the reverend called off the meeting. After singing "Nearer My God to Thee" together, they all go home, having saved Joe's face and spoiled the Simms boys' joke. Joe later becomes the means for proving that Charlie is lying when he says that he and his brother did not foul the Logan well. As a character, Joe points up the innate meanness of Charlie Simms and also shows that Hammer has a warm heart and social conscience underneath his surly, intimidating exterior.

JOEY DOWDEL (*A Long Way from Chicago: A Novel in Stories**), the narrator and elder of Grandma* Dowdel's two grandchildren, the other being Mary* Alice, Joey's sister. Joey's character is less defined than Mary Alice's, but he reveals a sharp eye for details of everyday town life, for the few businesses that remain in town, and for the people and their social habits, for example, the gatherings in the sole restaurant, The Coffee Pot Cafe, with its framed picture of Franklin Delano Roosevelt, where the women discuss Roosevelt's marrying his cousin. He also picks up well on Grandma's attitudes and preferences. As he grows older, he is still expected to help about the place on visits, but his interests suitably change. He longs to ride in the barnstorming plane at the fair and to take driving lessons from Ray Veech, who is "seventeen and man-sized" and knows all about cars from working in the family garage. For Joey, it is "love at first sight, like I'd been waiting for her all my life . . . shimmering in her loveliness," when for the first time he sees a brand-new Hudson Terraplane 8.

JOEY PIGZA SWALLOWED THE KEY (Gantos* Jack, Farrar, 1998), humorous, realistic physical and psychological problem novel with school and family-life aspects, set near Pittsburgh in recent years. Joey Pigza, the narrator, 9 or 10, has one main, very troubling problem: He suffers from attention-deficit hyperactivity disorder (ADHD). His medications are "duds," he says, effective for only about half a day. Intelligent and quick, he knows the answers to the questions in class, but before Mrs. Maxy can call on him, his mind has taken off in another, completely different direction. He became more "messed up" after his father took off, when he was in kindergarten, his mother left to find his father, and Grandma, who obviously also suffers from ADHD, came to take care of him and further eroded his self-esteem by harping at him, disparaging him at every turn, and treating him quite literally like a small dog. After Mom, a hairdresser who drinks too much, returns, and Grandma leaves, the house is more orderly and far cleaner, but Joey's behavior is little better. He regrets repeatedly disappointing his teacher, principal, and Mom, but it seems that he simply cannot help getting into trouble. After he swallows his house key, Mrs. Maxy sends him to Mrs. Howard in the school's special education room for a while without discernible improvement. He creates an uproar on a field trip to an Amish farm, injuring his ankle. In school, after he wounds his finger trying to sharpen it in the pencil sharpener, he trips while carrying the teacher's sharp scissors, which he took without asking, and snips off the tip of classmate Maria Dombrowski's nose. He apologizes to Maria but is now considered a school hazard. He is enrolled in the Lancaster County Special Education Center, where his caseworker, astute and patient Mr. Ed Vanness ("call me Special Ed"), tells Joey that making bad decisions lands him in trouble. Special Ed also says that he and Joey "must look at the big picture," that is, that Joey's home situation must be evaluated, too. Joe and Mom take the bus to Pittsburgh, where Joey receives several medical tests, and the doctor tells him that his brain is fine (to Joey's relief). A patch is prescribed for more even delivery of medication, a better diet is recommended, and Mom is advised to stop drinking. At the end, Joey gets a dog, the reward that he had been promised for trying to do better. Joey thinks half-Chihuahua, half-dachshund Pablo Pigza, P.P. for short, is, just like Joey himself, messed up but still lovable. He feels much better about himself and life in general. Since the emphasis is upon exploring the effect of ADHD on one child, characters are types, and the overall plot proceeds as anticipated. Joey's rambling discourse gives a splendid sense of what it may be like to suffer from this disorder. His escapades are often comic, as are his explanations for how he gets into them, and are sure to appeal to the middle-grade set. One of the book's really good points is the warmth and patience with which Joey's teachers treat him, in spite of the extremely exasperating disruptions that he causes. ALA; SLJ.

JOHANNA: A NOVEL OF THE VAN GOGH FAMILY (Cooperstein*, Claire, Scribner, 1995), substantial adult biographical novel about Johanna van Gogh-Bonger (1862–1925), the widow of Theodoor* van Gogh, called Theo, and the sister-in-law of renowned painter Vincent* van Gogh. Set near Paris and Amsterdam, the story is related in the form of diary entries and letters written by Johanna to her relatives and friends and letters that she receives from them. Events start the day before Christmas in 1888, just before the party to announce the engagement between the cultured daughter of a prominent Amsterdam businessman, Anton Bonger, and Theo, the respected manager of a Paris art gallery. Theo misses the party, since his erratic brother, Vincent, has been hospitalized after mutilating his ear in a fit. The incident ushers in their tumultuous two-year marriage, in which Johanna struggles to maintain her individuality against her imperious, intrusive, controlling father, proves herself a devoted and industrious wife, and gives birth to a son, Vincent Willem, called Vinnie*. Increasingly, Vincent makes demands on the time, emotions, and finances of his loyal and dedicated younger brother, demands that many years later Johanna recognizes derive from intense posessiveness as well as ill health from syphilis. Since Vincent never recovers his health and remains under treatment, except for a brief and intensely productive period in the village of Auvers-sur-Oise outside Paris, Theo often neglects Johanna, although the two are loving and enjoy one another's company. Theo never recovers from his brother's tragic suicide by a gunshot to the abdomen in July 1890, and soon degenerates into madness, outliving his brother by only about six months. Johanna is left with Theo's small bank account, furniture, and some 200 of Vincent's paintings, which are generally regarded as the work of a genius but of little financial value. Confronted by the need to support herself and her infant son and advised by her loyal brother, Dries* Bonger, she successfully operates a boardinghouse near Amsterdam. Through Dries, she also meets Johan Cohen Gosschalk, artist, critic, and contributing editor to an Amsterdam paper who recommends boarders, advises her about Vincent's paintings, and helps her with the vast amount of work involved in exhibitions. Her boardinghouse becomes a center for intellectuals and artists. Her relationship with Johan ripens into romance, and in 1900 they are married and move into a new villa. The next years are almost idyllic for Johanna and Vinnie, both of whom adore Johan. When Vinnie is ready for more specialized education, they take a house in Amsterdam. Johanna continues with exhibitions, now that Vincent's work is being recognized, and starts to edit the considerable correspondence between Vincent and Theo. At the time that Vinnie is in engineering school, Johan falls ill with what turns out to be terminal tuberculosis and dies in 1912. Johanna continues to edit the letters, which are eventually published, and in 1913 arranges for Theo's body to be moved to Auvers to be buried next to Vincent's. In her diary, she writes, addressing Vincent, "You've won." A dozen years later she will be buried next to Johan. The novel suffers from defects often found in the genre—details supplied that either Johanna would not know or would probably not include. The impact of this compelling novel comes from the author's careful attention to the details of what is known about the lives of the principal figures, poignant depiction of Johanna's emotions, aspirations, and courage, and her complete loyalty and love for Theo in spite of Vincent's almost unreasonable claims. The picture of the times, especially from the woman's view, is strong, and there is a clear sense of what the art world was like. While Johanna is well drawn, Theo is less so, and Johan seems a knight in shining armor. Vincent, who barely appears, dominates the book, as he dominated Johanna's, Theo's, Johan's, and Vinnie's lives. The author provides a helpful epilogue and chronology of the later years and notes that diaries left by Johanna have never been made available for research by the van Gogh family. The letters and diaries of which the novel is composed are "faction." SLJ.

JOHNNY FOSTER (*While No One Was Watching**), solicitous widower-father of Earl*, Frankie*, and Angela*, who get into trouble after they have been abandoned by their Aunt Lula, in whose care Johnny has left them while he works on the Eastern Shore to make money to rent a house for them all to live in. Johnny is unaware that Lula has run off and that the children are in danger of starving. Laid off from work and facing foreclosure on his house, Johnny applied to Social Services for help but was rejected because the agency's resources were too limited. Hence, he lost his house and everything that he had. He writes home diligently to the children every week, enclosing money for Lula as he can, funds that she squanders mostly on drink. He demonstrates how easily working families can fall prey to misfortune, how close to the edge they may live.

JOHNNY RAVEN (*Far North**), aged great-uncle of Raymond* Providence, friend of Gabe Rogers, the narrator, and an elder of the Native-American Indian Slavey group in Canada. He speaks almost no English but is knowledgeable in the old beliefs and ways when the Indians lived closer to the land. He is largely responsible for the boys' managing to get through their wilderness ordeal alive. Some of the novel's best scenes revolve around him, for example, that in which he and the boys capture and kill beavers by invading their auxiliary and main houses. Johnny is a modest man who speaks in understatement. His last will and testament, written down for him in English by a nurse at the hospital in Yellowknife, is a poignant summary of his life and beliefs. His will is partly responsible for Raymond's decision to return to school.

JOHNSON, SCOTT (1952–   ), born in Chicago, Illinois; high school teacher of English and creative writing; writer of problem and growing-up novels for young adults; contributor of articles and stories to journals and magazines. After receiving his B.A. with honors from Indiana University and his M.F.A. from the University of Massachusetts in 1978, he began teaching in Pleasantville, New York. His observations of, and experiences with, his students form the substance of his books, which have been praised for their authenticity, understanding, quick pace, and hard looks at the choices that teens face in life. His first novel, *One of the Boys* (Atheneum, 1992), chosen as an American Library Association Best Book for Young Adults, deals with the effects of peer pressure. *Safe at Second** (Philomel, 1999), a choice of the *School Library Journal*, deals with handling adversity and making morally correct choices within a sports setting. Johnson has also published *Overnight Sensation* (Atheneum, 1994), which concerns similar themes. He lives in Mahopac, New York, with his wife and three sons.

JOSEPH KEYSER (*Running Out of Time**), father of Jessie, her brother Andrew, and her two sisters, Hannah and little Katie. A blacksmith, Joseph Keyser is one of the few adults at Clifton Village who really like living in 1840. He learned his trade in a historical village in Massachusetts but found little use for blacksmithing in the twentieth century. Although his wife, a nurse, is less enthusiastic, since nursing was not a recognized profession in the early nineteenth century, she loves him enough to agree to live in the village in the manner of the earlier time. After Clifton Village closes, Joseph becomes the caretaker, on the advice of a psychiatrist who thinks that he is denying the existence of the modern world and that a gradual transition may be helpful to his mental state.

JOY-IN-THE-DANCE (*The Arkadians**), spirited, clever young woman also known as the Woman-Who-Talks-to-Snakes. The daughter of the wisest woman in the land of Arkadia, Lady of Wild Things, and the leader of the horse tribe Sees-Far-Ahead, she is the oracular pythoness at the sanctuary that King Bromios* orders destroyed because he was not pleased with the prophecy that she gave him. She occasionally worries that she should have altered the prophecy in the best interests of the realm, but her mother assures her that her actions were correct. She teasingly calls Lucian* Aiee-Ouch, because when she first meets him he has just received a sword blow. When she tries to tend the wound, he says, "Aiee, ouch," in pain. She and Lucian fall in love and are married at the end of the story. She is installed as the resident wisewoman, healer, and oracular speaker at the capital of Arkadia. She is a pleasing, well-drawn character.

JUBILEE JOURNEY (Meyer*, Carolyn, Harcourt, 1997), sequel to *White Lilacs*, a novel telling of African-American Freedomtown, Texas, destroyed to make a park for the white community of Dillon. *Jubilee Journey* picks up seventy-five years later, in 1996, when Rose Lee Jefferson's great-granddaughter, Emily Rose Cartier, 13, comes at her invitation with her mother and two brothers for the celebration of Juneteenth Day, commemorating the day when news of the Emancipation Proclamation reached the slaves of Texas. Raised in Connecticut with a French-American father, Emily Rose and her brothers have always considered themselves *au lait*, neither black nor white but "doubles," some of each. Because their mother, Susan, has said almost nothing about her childhood, they are very naive about the prejudice that still exists in the South, even in the 1990s. Their visit is full of surprises, both good and bad. Rose Lee Jefferson, now called Mother Rose by the whole community, lives with her much younger cousin, James Price, in private quarters in his funeral home. Her Protestant church, center of the African-American community, is a surprise to the Catholic Cartiers. The hostility of the first girl whom she meets, Brandy Woodrow, annoys Emily Rose, but eventually she realizes that her precise northern speech is perceived as snobbishness, and, aided by the way Brandy, as well as all the other girls, want to get close to her handsome older brother Steven, 17, she is able to make peace and start a real friendship. Dark-skinned Steven provides the biggest culture shock. A good tennis player, at the Dillon courts he meets Marissa Plunkett, a girl with a fancy red convertible who offers to show him around. Naively, he doesn't realize that this is an unusual relationship in the South and that Marissa is deliberately flouting convention for a thrill. When the redneck foreman on her father's horse ranch sets him up to be arrested, Steven ends in jail, beaten up and charged with car theft and resisting arrest. Although Marissa's father insists that the young people never see each other again, he responds to pleas from Susan and contacts the sheriff, and eventually, largely because of the long history of the relationship between the two families, the charges are dropped. A far pleasanter surprise occurs when Mother Rose shows her great-granddaughter the paintings that she has done over the years of Freedomtown and its residents. Emily Rose is so impressed that she persuades the old woman to allow the paintings to be displayed at the church, where Mother Rose has been asked to give a talk on the old town for the Juneteenth celebration. Her pictures are a great hit, and in the end a drive has started to return the only still-standing house removed from Freedomtown seventy-five years ago to the park as a memorial to the African-American community and to put the paintings on permanent display there. Emily Rose, realizing that she still knows very little about the Texas side of her heritage, persuades her mother to let her remain the rest of the summer with Mother Rose. Although not as compelling as *White Lilacs* because the threats and dangers are not as severe, this is a clever way to bring the story into the modern period and show how deep-seated prejudices still trouble the town. As narrator of most of the chapters, Emily Rose is an attractive protagonist, but the chapters in the mind of Mother Rose depend on the earlier book to bring her character into focus. As before, the town itself, with its complicated relationships of the white and black families, is the center of interest. ALA.

JULIA HATCH (*Finn**), daughter of the tiny, beautiful Vietnamese woman and the big, blond Vermonter who live down the road from Finn's Gram's Riverview Farm. Since Julia had been a close friend of Finn's younger sister, Penny, who was killed in the plane crash that Finn survived, at first Finn is not sure that he wants to associate with her. Gram explains that Julia has been spending a lot of time at Riverview Farm working with Belle the horse and with Belle's filly. Julia is small but strong, has won trophies for riding, and loves dancing. Once she starts to come to the farm, Finn is glad that she is around. Becoming romantically fond of Julia makes him even more determined to help her when she is imprisoned in the well. Although the author's having Toq the dogwolf, who has fled to the wild to avoid domestication, help with the rescue strains belief, it works in the context of Finn and Julia's having saved Toq from certain death in the trap.

JULIAN (*The Shakespeare Stealer**), one of Widge's fellow apprentices in the Chamberlain's Men company. Julian falls afoul of surly, troublemaking Nick, who stabs him. Julian is then discovered to be a girl (Julia) and is no longer allowed to play parts because it is against the law for girls or women to do so.

As a result, Widge gets to play Ophelia before Queen Elizabeth. Julia becomes a "gatherer," money taker, for the company. At the end, she leaves for France, where women are allowed to be on the stage.

JUSTICE (Watson*, Larry, Milkweed Editions, 1995), episodic prequel to *Montana 1948*, set mostly in Bentrock, a town in Montana's far northeastern corner, in the years 1899 to 1937. In seven separate, but connected, pieces, the novel traces the two generations of the Hayden family, whose men have been sheriff of Mercer County for more than a third of a century and whose tragic conflict is the subject of the earlier book. Protagonist of the first and longest episode is Wesley Hayden, 15, younger son of Sheriff Julian Hayden, who starts off in the fall of 1924 on an ill-fated hunting trip with his brother, Frank, 17, and two of Frank's friends. When a snowstorm makes camping out impossible, they head for the tiny town of McCoy, North Dakota, with vague ideas of getting drunk and bedding local Indian girls. They do meet two girls from the Catholic high school, Sacred Heart, and Frank strikes up an acquaintance that seems promising, but when one of his show-off friends pulls out a battered pistol, the girls flee, and the boys are arrested. After subjecting the two friends to a humiliating punishment, the local sheriff lets the Hayden boys off and starts them back toward Montana. They meet their father waiting for them on the icy road, and he grimly follows their Model T back into Bentrock. Throughout the whole adventure, Wesley, two years younger and more sensitive than the other three, is apprehensive, and he alone thinks of the Indian girls as people whom he would like to know, not just have sex with. The next episode goes back to 1899 to the youth of Julian, their father, who at sixteen after the death of his father brings his mother from Iowa to Montana to homestead in Mercer County. They leave behind his timid sister to care for the children in the household of a minister. Although his mother is no help on the homestead and soon moves into town, Julian prospers by boldness and hard work. At one point he returns to Iowa and persuades the minister, with some violence, to stop exploiting his sister, then boards the train back to Montana without seeing the girl. This penchant for decisive action with little sentiment is Julian's strongest characteristic. Subsequent segments tell of the women in the family. Julian woos Enid Garland of Wild Rose, North Dakota, and organizes their wedding in Bentrock, an occasion almost ruined by the arrival of Enid's father, determined to take her home. Julian holds him off with a pistol while Enid drives the buggy as they leave on their honeymoon trip. In 1927 Wesley returns from college for Thanksgiving, a dinner to which his mother has invited his high school girlfriend with whom, to his fury, both his father and his brother, Frank, flirt. The last three segments concern Wesley's wife, attractive, spirited Gail Berdahl, the first about the hopeless and unspoken love for her of Len McAuley, the deputy sheriff of Julian's generation, and the other two about her not entirely happy marriage. Although the focus varies in the episodes, Wesley remains the most important character, a boy and young man not at ease with his position in the world or in the family, always trying to live up to what he thinks his father expects of him and what his own integrity demands, sometimes conflicting requirements. Julian is a memorable figure, dominant and domineering, scornful of weakness and dismissive of his wife and sons. The strongest element in the novel, however, is the picture of life in the raw prairie town of the early twentieth century where Indians and Russian immigrants are considered lesser breeds, where the sheriff is the law, not always with gentle means, and where the job is handed down in the family as in a royal dynasty. The deceptively simple style catches a reader into the complex emotions deeply felt, if not admitted, by the family members. SLJ.

JUSTIN BECK (*The Music of Dolphins**), teenage son of Dr.* Elizabeth Beck, research scientist who is studying Mila, the feral girl discovered living with dolphins. From the first, Mila, who is very sensitive to nuances of relationships, senses conflicting attitudes in Justin toward his mother, anger but something else, love or desire for love and attention. Justin is the first person who really listens to Mila and understands her need to return to the sea. He is able to compare her hurt at being removed from her environment and loving friends with his hurt when his parents separated. At first he is very antagonistic and unwilling to be touched by Mila or by his mother, but he gradually comes to sit in the room where Mila is playing music and seems to relax until in the end he lets his mother stroke him and kiss his hair, and, before Mila returns to the sea, he hugs her. She thinks of him as "the beautiful boy" and knows that if they were dolphins, they would mate, but since she can never be fully human, the hug is as much as they can have together.

K

KARR, KATHLEEN (1946–   ), born in Allentown, Pennsylvania. She did her undergraduate work at Catholic University of America and her graduate work at Providence College, with further study at Corcoran School of Art. She has been an English and speech teacher, curator of film archives, advertising director, director of public relations, and an instructor of film and communications at various institutions, screenwriter, contributor to journals, and editor of a book about American film history. She has written a half-dozen romance novels for adults and almost a dozen novels of light historical fiction for middle graders, among them a *School Library Journal* choice, *The Great Turkey Walk** (Farrar, 1998), a fast-action tall tale about walking a flock of turkeys from eastern Missouri to Denver in 1860, based on an actual incident. Her first novel for young readers, *It Ain't Always Easy* (Farrar, 1990), concerns late nineteenth-century orphans who seek a home in the West. This was followed, among others, by *The Cave* (Farrar, 1994), a Great Depression story set in South Dakota; a set of novels about the move westward, including *Oregon, Sweet Oregon* (Harper-Collins, 1998); and *Spy in the Sky* (Hyperion, 1997), about the use of balloons in the American Civil War. While critics have complained about her characterizations, they have commended her use of period details and her ability to keep a story moving along well.

KATHRYN CANDELARIA (*Confess-O-Rama**), mother of Tony Candelaria, the narrator. Since she has been married and widowed four times, her full surname is Candelaria-De Boom-Kidder-Katt, but she uses the name of Tony's father, who was an ambassador from Panama. When the story begins, she is grieving for Bill Katt and tends to be forgetful and tearful. Tony cares deeply for her and is an unusually tender and solicitous son. She reads books on handling grief and has had both Tony and herself in therapy. She knows that she must get out of the house but feels rejected when she does not get a job as a hostess at a restaurant. She takes a job as agent for Larry* Deluxe, whom she meets at a party and, when she does not do well at that, accepts a position with his ex-wife, Sheila Larson, who sells coffins. Since she is happier at book's end than she was at the beginning, there is hope that Tony will be eased out of his role of parenting his mother.

KEEPING THE MOON (Dessen*, Sarah, Viking, 1999), girl's growing-up novel set in the late 1990s in Colby, North Carolina. When her mother, Kiki Sparks, a highly successful and publicized fitness guru, leaves for a European tour, Colie (Nicole) Sparks, 15, goes to stay with her aunt, Mira* Sparks, in Colby, a little town on the coast, for most of the summer. There she is first embarrassed for, then amused by, and finally admiring of her eccentric, over-weight aunt, who wears outlandish clothes, rides an ancient bicycle, and avidly watches wrestling on television, paying more attention to her cat, Norman, than to Colie. The household also includes a young artist who lives in the basement, Norman* Carswell, known as Norman Norman to distinguish him from cat Norman. Almost by accident, Colie gets a job at the Last Chance Bar and Grill, where Norman is a cook and two twentyish girls, Morgan* and Isabel, who live next door to Mira, are waitresses. Although at first Isabel is critical, telling Colie bluntly that her lip-ring is repulsive and her hair is badly dyed, they soon become friends, the first she has really ever had, since she and her mother, both of them then grossly overweight, sometimes living in the car, drifted from one town to another where she was always the fat new girl in school, the butt of mean jokes. Since her mother started at Lady Fitness and discovered her talent for promoting aerobics, they have both lost weight, and Kiki has risen to prominence, but Colie is still haunted by the taunts and holds herself apart to keep from being exposed to new hurt. Isabel is a natural beauty, though a difficult personality. Morgan is tall, bony, and compulsively orderly, insisting on everything being lined up neatly, with all the fork tines facing the same way, the napkins folded just so. Although they quarrel frequently, they are dependent on each other, and Isabel tries to shield Morgan from the pain when her baseball player-fiancé doesn't show up as he has promised. Isabel takes Colie in hand, cuts and shapes her hair, applies makeup, and persuades her to remove the lip-ring for one night when they go to the beach to watch the fireworks. There an attractive high school-age boy named Josh literally bumps into Colie and is enamored. He invites her to join the crowd around his bonfire, and as she does, she sees Caroline Dawes, a girl who has been meanest to her at her school in Charlotte and has spread rumors that Colie is "fast" and "easy," a real slut. With newfound confidence, Colie faces up to her and tells her to forget it, then walks off with Isabel. Josh chases after them, apologizes for his cousin, and suggests dating when they are back in Charlotte, where he and Caroline are returning the next day. In her delight at having scored over Caroline, Colie forgets that Norman has suggested that he paint her portrait, starting after the fireworks. Prodded by some straight talk from both Isabel and Morgan, Colie apologizes to Norman for having stood him up and asks for a second chance. Somewhat reluctantly, he agrees, and they meet night after night in his basement and sometimes during the days beside the dumpster behind the Last Chance, while he paints but refuses to let her see the portrait until it is done. As she gets to know him, she appreciates his unusual qualities, and when he finally does show her the painting, she realizes that he has seen her as beautiful, not pretty like Caroline or even Isabel, but a very special girl. The plot of an ugly duckling finding herself could be trite, but good characterization and small-town details make this a convincing story. Colie's humiliation and shame at her former fat state and the taunts that it has inspired are well evoked, and her prickly personality, even after she has slimmed down, is psychologically sound. SLJ.

KERR, M. E. (MARIJANE MEAKER) (1927–   ), born in Auburn, New York; graduate of Columbia University; versatile author, popular mostly for her many contemporary problem novels for early adolescents and teenagers. Her novel about lesbians, *Deliver Us from Evie** (HarperCollins, 1994), in addition to being named to the *School Library Journal* list, has also been cited by the American Library Association and named to the Fanfare list. She has also published the novels *Hello, I Lied* (Harper, 1997), about a gay, possibly bisexual boy; *What Became of Her* (HarperCollins, 2000), about revenge; and *Blood on the Forehead: What I Know about Writing* (HarperCollins, 1998), nonfiction. For additional information about Kerr and other titles and entries, see *Dictionary, 1960–1984* [*Dinky Hocker Shoots Smack*; *Gentlehands*] and *Dictionary, 1990–1994* [*Deliver Us from Evie*; *Fell Back*].

KEVIN (*The Midnight Club**), one of the five teenagers with terminal cancer who gather every night at 12:00 in the hospice study to tell stories. Kevin has leukemia, a disease that he has hidden from his girlfriend, beautiful cheerleader Kathy, who thinks that his hospitalization is temporary and that he will soon be well and come home. A talented painter and former track star, he is imaginative and warm. Ilonka Pawluk is in love with him, although she is in as much denial about her love for him as she is about her impending death, matters that her roommate, Anya*, points out to her. Through the stories that Ilonka tells, in all of which Kevin figures in some form, she comes to terms both with her love for him and with the fatality of her disease. Kevin satisfies her need for belonging to someone by sleeping with her on the night, ironically, on which he dies.

THE KHATUN (*Shadow Spinner**), the mother of the Sultan, the most powerful woman in the harem. An immensely fat, bejeweled woman, she is intent on persuading her son falsely that Shahrazad* has taken a lover. She wants Shahrazad dead so that her tool, Soraya, can become the Sultan's wife. The Khatun pledges to Soraya that when the girl is queen, she will keep her well supplied with tales. Marjan* learns that Soraya does not want to marry the Sultan. Near book's end, Soraya is found dead, floating face-down in a palace pool, apparently murdered. The Khatun is an utterly self-seeking and evil woman, ambitious for wealth and power.

THE KIDNAPPERS (Roberts*, Willo Davis, Atheneum, 1998), mystery set in New York City in the late 1990s involving the abduction of a wealthy boy from the street in front of his private school. Joey (Joel) Bishop, 11, is terrified that Willie (William John Edward Groves III) is going to beat him up. By accident, Joey knocked his elbow into Willie's face, causing pain and a nosebleed, and Willie, taller and heavier than Joey, will accept no apology and is determined on revenge. At St. Bart's, their exclusive school where all the boys are picked up by parents or chauffeurs, Joey slips out the gate before Willie and hides in the lobby of the next-door apartment building, peering through the glass in the door to see either Ernie, his family's driver, or Willie's chauffeur arriving. Instead he sees a black Chrysler New Yorker with a distinctive enamel crest on the door pull up next to Willie, who has come out of St. Bart's gate looking for Joey. A man jumps out, grabs Willie from behind and drags him into the car, which then leaps forward and disappears from sight. Joey tries desperately to get Ernie, who drives up almost immediately afterward, to call the police or to let him stop at a phone, but because he has always had a wild imagination, neither Ernie nor Sherman, the doorman at their apartment building, nor his older brother, Mark, 15, nor his mother, preoccupied with arrangements for a party, nor his father takes his story seriously. Only his sister, Sophie, 12, believes him, and she persuades their father to call Mr. Groves. He does, only to be told that Mr. Groves is taking no calls. The next morning Joey, banished from the apartment so that he won't interfere with the caterers, meets his friend Pink Murphy, who accepts his story. Twice they are almost run down, once by a yellow cab and once by the Chrysler New Yorker, which they spot parked in their alley. A policemen comes and questions them, and later Joey's father takes them to the station to look at mug shots and to work with an officer to make a computer-generated picture from Joey's memory of his brief glance at the kidnapper. When Ernie takes them to get a video, to while away their time in Joey's room during the party, Pink spots the man in the picture, carrying a bag of groceries, but they lose sight of him. Later in the evening, Mark gets Joey to go pick up a math book from his classmate who lives in the same building. In the elevator, he runs into two men, one the pictured kidnapper. They grab him and drag him into an apartment, talk of "shutting him up," and shove him into a room where they are holding Willie. In these circumstances, Willie is no longer threatening. He does know some things about the kidnappers. One is the secretary of the man who owns this apartment, now in Paris for a month. The other is a chauffeur for a woman temporarily in Miami. Joey's vivid imagination tells him that they are not likely to be released alive, even if Mr. Groves comes up with ransom for his son. He sets about thinking of escape plans. In the bathroom connected to the room where they are locked, he finds a small hand mirror. By surrounding it with lamps, he amplifies its light and flashes SOS signals at the apartment house opposite, only to be ignored by the two people visible in the windows. To Joey's astonishment and horror, he recognizes Ernie's voice talking to the other men. While the kidnappers seem to be out of the apartment, Joey and Willie manage to loosen the bolts holding the door hinges, using a spoon and a wire coat hanger, until they can pry the hinge side of the door open and break the lock. As they dash out, Ernie, who has waited behind, stops them and discusses with one of the other bad guys how to get rid of the boys once the third has picked up the ransom. The boys' terror is interrupted by police, crashing in the front door of the apartment and, after a chase, rounding up the kidnappers. It turns out that residents of the apartment house opposite had called in about the distress signals, as had Mark, who noticed the flickering lights and got Sophie to interpret them. Although Willie and Joey don't end up best friends, they are no longer enemies. While the kidnappers come off as less than accomplished crooks, and coincidences play some part in the solution, the tension is well handled. Joey, whose frustration at not being believed is one of the strongest elements in the story, is a likable character. Poe Nominee.

THE KILLER'S COUSIN (Werlin*, Nancy, Delacorte, 1998), chilling mystery novel set in Cambridge, Massachusetts, in the late 1990s, involving the possibility of paranormal experience but not dependent upon it. As the reader learns gradually, David Bernard Yaffe, 17, the narrator, has been accused of killing his girlfriend, Emily, but acquitted, more because of highly paid lawyers than of innocence, as most people, including his own father, believe. Actually, Emily was killed by a blow that David aimed at her brother, Greg, formerly his best friend, who was abusing Emily in a quarrel after he had squandered their joint college money to support his cocaine habit. To help him pick up his life and prepare for college, his parents have sent him to live with his mother's brother, Vic Shaughnessy, and Vic's wife, Julia, and finish his last high school year at a highly selective and expensive private school. Consumed by guilt, David goes along with this plan but realizes immediately that neither Vic nor Julia wants him, and their daughter Lily, 11, is openly hostile. Their strange behavior increases his uneasiness. Vic and Julia do not speak to each other and converse, when necessary, through Lily. At first David thinks that his presence has caused their disagreement but begins to see that it stems from the death of their older daughter, Kathy, four years earlier or perhaps even before that, when Kathy dropped out of school and started acting wild. David lives in the small third-floor apartment that was Kathy's, having to reach it through the Shaughnessys' apartment on the second floor. The first floor is rented to an art student, Raina Doumeny. David begins seeing a strange, human-shaped shadow and hearing an unexplained hum in his room at night, a noise that Vic and Julia uneasily explain as normal old-house noises. Aside from the Shaughnessy family, David gets to know only two people, a strange boy with a shaved head named Frank Delgado in one of his classes, evidently as much of an outcast as David, and Raina, who treats him in a matter-of-fact way and even invites romance, which

David does not feel ready for. When his parents come for a very uncomfortable Thanksgiving dinner, David finds out more. Kathy's death, ruled suicide at the inquest, was in his apartment bathroom, where she drank half a glassful of cleaning solvent, slipped below the water, and drowned. Lily burst in upon her, tried to pull her from the water, cut her knees and hands on the glass, and at the inquest insisted that it was all her fault. He also learns that Julia has always resented his mother as interfering. In the ensuing months Lily's antagonism increases, manifested in all sorts of mean tricks: ruining all his CDs (compact discs) with glue, hiding in Raina's apartment, and jumping out at their only romantic moment, obviously trying to goad him into a violent reaction. In addition, the shadow in his apartment more clearly becomes Kathy, now whispering to him, "Help Lily, helplily, helplily." When he finally breaks, accusing Lily to her parents and trashing his own room hunting for her latest prank, Vic summons his father, thinking that David is mentally disturbed. His father takes him to a hotel and listens to his whole story, but with some reservations, not entirely believing what David knows is true, that Lily has admitted to him that she deliberately gave Kathy the glass of ammonia. That night, unable to sleep with Kathy's voice more insistently in his head, David gets up to run in the dark and circles back to find the Shaughnessy house going up in flames. Realizing that Lily is still inside, he dashes in, finds her in the half-filled bathtub in his apartment, and, after fighting to control her, wraps her in a soaking beach towel and carries her through the flames to safety. In the hospital, badly burned, he asks for Lily, who is in the psychiatric unit, and learns that she has asked for him, but her parents and the doctors have refused. Frank Delgado, disguised as an orderly, manages to bring her one night in a wheelchair. The cousins admit to each other that both fear their own impulses and promise that they will help each other in the years ahead. The story builds with increasing intensity, until it is easy to believe that David doubts his own sanity. The shadow of Kathy and her voice could be the result of his own disordered mind, although the reader is obviously expected to believe in them as David does. The scenes of Cambridge in winter and the claustrophobic Shaughnessy house are well evoked with strong sensory detail. Poe Winner.

KIM (*Wish You Were Here**), girlfriend of Jackson Watt's father, Oz. She works in a health club, where she directs bodybuilding exercises, and insists on a diet that includes large amounts of tofu, sprouts, and vegetable juices. Nearer in age to Jackson than to Oz, she dresses at work in glitzy briefs and talks like an airhead but proves to be less a lightweight than she seems. When Jackson and his mother, Ellen Harper, arrive in the hospital intensive care unit after Oz's accident, Kim and Ellen form a friendship in their common distress, but when the tube is finally removed from his throat, Oz, his face lighting up, totally ignores Kim and calls out to Ellen. Although badly hurt, Kim continues to be supportive and, after his release from the hospital, shares the care of Oz with Jackson. Their relationship falls apart, however, partly because of her protectiveness and partly because she comes in to find Layla Burton in bed with Oz one afternoon. Although Jackson, having seen other girlfriends in and out of Oz's life, foresees this end, he likes Kim and feels guilty and somehow responsible for his father's lack of appreciation.

KIM, HELEN, born in Korea; teacher of literature and creative writing at Montclair State College; resident of New Jersey. *The Long Season of Rain** (Holt, 1996), a young adult novel cited by *School Library Journal* and praised for its evocation of Korean family life in the late 1960s, tells of several months in the lives of a Seoul, Korea, family as they confront two main problems: what will happen to the boy whom the family is fostering and how will the family cope with their irascible, usually absent Father, an army colonel.

KINDL, PATRICE (1951–), born in Alplaus, New York; author of bizarre, but convincing, fantasies for children and young adults. *Owl in Love** (Houghton, 1994) is about a "wereowl," a girl in an ordinary high school who becomes an owl at night. Even stranger is *Woman in the Walls* (Houghton, 1997), in which the main character has disappeared into the spaces between partitions of an old house and lived there for years, eventually almost forgotten by her family. For earlier biographical information and a title entry, see *Dictionary, 1990–1994* [*Owl in Love*].

KINGDOM COUNTY (*Northern Borders**), remote county in northern Vermont next to the "Line," as the locals call the Canadian border. The county got its name when Sojourner Kittredge, Austen's great-great-great-great-great-grandfather, a Loyalist at the time of the American Revolution, fled Connecticut, heading for Canada. When he reached a small, icy river that he named the Kingdom, after his loyalty to England, he stopped, thinking wrongly that he had already crossed the border. A teacher, he established a sawmill and a school, which he called Lost Nation Academy. Although he never recognized the right of Vermont to govern the area, he ceded a 10,000-acre tract to the state for a college to educate white and Abenaki youths. The state eventually sold the land but honored its agreement that any graduate of Lost Nation Academy may attend the University of Vermont free of charge. It is partly for this reason that Austen's widowed father sends him to live with his grandparents and attend the school. The long winters, isolation, and primitive roads have kept the county in a frontier condition up to the 1940s, when Austen lives there.

KING, LAURIE R. (1952–), born in Oakland, California; author of mystery novels for both young people and adults. Although she grew up in the San Francisco Bay Area, she has lived in twenty countries on five continents with her husband, an Anglo-Indian professor of religious studies. They have also made their home in Freedom and in Watsonville, California. Among King's novels are several starring Mary Russell, who becomes an apprentice to Sherlock

Holmes after he has retired to the country, a series starting with *The Beekeeper's Apprentice** (St. Martin's, 1994). Another series has a lesbian heroine, Kate Martinelli. An unrelated crime novel is *A Darker Place* (Dell, 1999).

KING ORRIK (*Flight of the Dragon Kyn**), King of Kragland. Orrik is amiable, pleasant, and ruthlessly determined to retain his royal power by slaying the area's dragons, even at the cost of the life of his young ward, Kara, the farmer's daughter, who is believed to be able to summon dragons. Orrik has a loyal following among the Kragish warriors, but many soldiers defect to join his more assertive and openly hostile brother, Prince* Rog, who, like Orrik, hopes to marry Signy, the Princess of Romjek, and thus acquire her kingdom. After Rog is slain, and the dragons move to the remote, northern island, Orrik builds a fortress against the dragons' possible return and names it after Rog, a clever political move to appease his brother's defeated followers and win them to his side. Seeing that Kazan the trader is in love with Kara, Orrik allows Kazan to remain in Kragland if he agrees to oversee building a ship for Orrik. After things have settled down, Orrik becomes the stereotypical ruler, self-satisfied, paternalistic, and inclined to make wordy speeches.

THE KING'S SHADOW (Alder*, Elizabeth, Farrar, 1995), historical novel about events leading up to the Norman conquest of England in 1066. Evyn, 13, a young Welsh shepherd with a beautiful speaking voice, yearns to become a traditional storyteller. In 1063, at the annual Easter celebration in his lord's hall, his roguish Uncle Morgan drinks too much and kills a visitor. In revenge, the slain man's kin kill Evyn's father and cut out the boy's tongue. Uncle Morgan flees southward with the forlorn boy and sells him as a slave to Lady* Ealdgyth Swan Neck, the common-law wife of Harold* Godwinson, Earl of Wessex. Since the boy cannot speak or write his name, the Lady calls him Shadow from his rich, dark hair and, when soon he breaks his arm, sends him to recover at Aethelney Monastery. There the stoop-shouldered little herbalist named Brother Alfred teaches him healing with herbs. When Shadow is assigned to menial tasks in the scriptorium, bright, lighthearted Lewys*, a monk from Wales, becomes his friend and teaches him to read and write, a welcome gift for the downhearted boy. Shadow also is taught something about fighting, skills that will serve him well during the years that follow. Because Shadow knows the Welsh hill territory, Harold recalls him to assist with a campaign against intransigent Welshmen early in 1064. When Shadow saves Harold's life, Harold rewards him by giving him his freedom and soon makes him his squire. As squire, Shadow accompanies Harold on maneuvers on the Narrow Sea, the body of water between England's south coast and Brittany. Shipwrecked, they are taken captive by William*, Duke of Normandy, who solidifies his slim claim to the English throne by cunningly extracting an oath from Harold to support William for the English throne, if the present king, Edward the Confessor, dies childless. Back in England, they learn that the people of Northumbria have rebelled against Tostig* Godwinson, Harold's brother. When Harold refuses to support his brother, Tostig goes into exile, vowing revenge. When King Edward dies, Harold is chosen to succeed him and is crowned early in 1066. Evyn reveals his loyalty and love for Harold by telling him his real name. Now Harold's fate and Evyn's are bound up with the realm's. Tostig brings in a huge Norwegian army against Harold but is defeated in a terrible battle at Stamford Bridge. Barely recovered from that costly victory, Harold hears that William has landed at Hastings, attempts to repel the attack, and is defeated and slain at Senlac Bridge. Just before the encounter, Harold announces that he has made Evyn his foster son. Lady Ealdgyth claims him from William, treats his wounds, and sends him to Aethelney. There the youth who was known as the King's Shadow records in honor of his beloved master the historical events that he has seen, an account that will be included in the body of material known as the *Anglo-Saxon Chronicles*. The novel scores high on all counts: fine characterizations; plenty of well-delineated action; a somewhat formal style that captures the sense of important times long gone; a convincing, likable protagonist who suffers greatly but never lapses into self-pity; dramatic battle and political scenes; and carefully detailed views of life inside halls and monastery. The book presents a finely illuminated and credible picture of the period and the real-life people who made it significant from the vantage of a nonhistorical youth who might have lived the events. IRA; SLJ.

KIRK MADISON (*Brothers and Sisters**), head of lending operations at Angel City National Bank in Los Angeles, where Preston* Sinclair is president. Kirk covets a position at Humphrey* Boone's level and feels that his efforts at racial diversification entitle him. His resentment and anger at being passed over, in addition to his wife's scorn for his not achieving the success that her friends' husbands have, lead him to undermine Humphrey and to steal from dormant accounts about $300,000, money that he squanders, flashing cash and bestowing lavish gifts variously. When he offers an elegant bracelet to Mallory Post to secure sexual favors, she refuses and reports him. Kirk is both pathetic and despicable.

KISSIN' KATE BARLOW (*Holes**), legendary, notorious outlaw of the Old West. One hundred ten years before the novel begins, she was known as Miss Katherine Barlow, a respected teacher at the one-room school at Green Lake, Texas, famous for her fabulous spiced peaches. Courted by all the young men around, she refused the proposal of Trout Walker, son of the richest man in the county. When Sam, the black onion peddler, made much-needed repairs to her schoolhouse, she kissed him, not knowing that it was against the law for blacks and whites to kiss. The upshot was that Miss Katherine shot the sheriff, the schoolhouse was burned, Sam was shot dead, the lake dried up, and Miss Katherine became one of the most feared outlaws in the West. She held up the stage carrying Stanley Yelnats (the ancestor of the boy incarcerated at Camp Green

Lake) and stole his suitcase filled with valuables. Later, she returned to Green Lake to live in an abandoned cabin, where evidently she buried the suitcase. Being a descendant of Trout Walker, the Warden* seeks the now legendary treasure. She establishes the penal camp to get free labor and has the boy prisoners dig holes in the dry lake bed to look for the treasure.

KIT HANKS (*The Cuckoo's Child**), younger sister of Mia Veery's mother, Jess* Hanks. Kit is saddled with the care of Jess' three girls when Jess and her husband are lost at sea. Being unused to children, Kit has a very hard time with Mia. She vacillates between sympathy and anger, unable to understand Mia's rudeness and strange behavior. When Mia reports seeing Dan Flannery, Kit's lover, with another woman, Kit at first refuses to believe her and shuts her out of the house but then discovers that what Mia said was true and sends Dan on his way. With this breakup added to her injuries (both her arms are in casts after she tries to catch Mia as she jumps from the water tower), Kit is understandably depressed, unable to work, lonely, overwhelmed by her new responsibilities. On top of this, Mia has bitten Morse Cooper severely and is continually rude to him, an additional problem to Kit since Morse is clearly interested in her. At the end, Mia accepts the loss of her parents, and the prospects for a family unit, however unconventional, with Kit and Morse look good.

KLAUSE, ANNETTE CURTIS, born in Bristol, England; librarian and writer of science fiction and horror novels for teenagers. *Blood and Chocolate** (Delacorte, 1997), a *School Library Journal* pick, is a novel of werewolves and magic in which trouble ensues when Vivian, 16, violates werewolf Law and becomes romantically involved with a human boy. Although predictable and sensational, the book raises important questions about loyalty to self and to group. She has also published short stories and poetry and contributed articles and book reviews to professional journals. For additional biographical information about Klause and more title entries, see *Dictionary, 1990–1994* [*Alien Secrets*; *The Silver Kiss*].

KOERTGE, RON(ALD) (1940–   ), born in Olney, Illinois; professor of English at Pasadena, California, City College; resident of South Pasadena; writer of prose and poetry for adults and of popular and deftly amusing growing-up and contemporary problem novels for young adults. *Tiger, Tiger, Burning Bright** (Orchard, 1994), about a boy's efforts to keep his aging grandfather, a former cowboy, from being regarded as senile and taken to a nursing home, deals humorously with a serious personal and sociological concern. It was picked by both the American Library Association and *School Library Journal*. *Confess-O-Rama** (Orchard, 1996), also an SLJ book, tells of a boy, new in a California school seemingly filled with oddballs, who attempts to cope with school and family problems by contacting a call-in service called Confess-O-Rama. For additional information and earlier title entries, see *Dictionary, 1990–1994* [*The Harmony Arms*].

KOLLER, JACKIE FRENCH (1948–   ), born in Derby, Connecticut; writer of many books for both young people and adults. She is a graduate of the University of Connecticut, has taught writing in the Groton, Massachusetts, Center for the Arts, and has made her home in Westfield, Massachusetts. In addition to a large number of picture books, she has written several novels, including *A Place to Call Home** (Simon & Schuster, 1995), about a biracial girl who tries to keep her family together after her mother's suicide, and a historical novel, *The Primrose Way* (Harcourt, 1992).

KONIGSBURG, E(LAINE) L(OBL) (1930–   ), born in New York City; highly popular author best known for her humorous novels about contemporary life in family, school, or neighborhood and her lively fantasies, although she has also written picture books and is an accomplished illustrator. She burst onto the children's book scene when her first novel, *Jennifer, Hecate, Macbeth, William McKinley, and Me, Elizabeth* (Atheneum, 1967), was a Newbery Honor Book and her second, *From the Mixed-up Files of Mrs. Basil E. Frankweiler* (Atheneum, 1967), won the Newbery Medal, both in the same year. Since then she has written about twenty novels in a similar in-your-face vein, witty, lively, filled with surprises, polished in style, often complex in plot. Thirty years after winning the Newbery, she won the medal again, for *The View from Saturday** (Atheneum, 1996), a puzzle novel in which schoolchildren compete in an Academic Bowl. More recently she has published *Silent to the Bone* (Atheneum, 2000), about a mute boy who is accused of injuring his baby half sister. Konigsburg lives in Ponte Vedra Beach, Florida. For more biographical information, titles, and title entries, see *Dictionary, 1960–1984* [*About the B'Nai Bagels*; *From the Mixed-up Files of Mrs. Basil E. Frankweiler*; *Jennifer, Hecate, Macbeth, William McKinley, and Me, Elizabeth*; *A Proud Taste for Scarlet and Miniver*; *The Second Mrs. Giaconda*]; *Dictionary, 1985–1989* [*Up from Jericho Tel*]; and *Dictionary, 1990–1994* [*A Proud Taste for Scarlet and Miniver*; *T-Backs, T-Shirts, COAT, and Suit*].

KONRAD (*Zel**), young nobleman who falls in love with Zel* and, after suffering both physical blindness and emotional trauma, becomes the means of her redemption from her overprotective, scheming Mother*. When he is first met in the novel, having brought his horse, Meta, to the local smith, Konrad is proud and used to having his way. As time passes, and he endures many obstacles from his family as well as from Mother's magical powers, he becomes less arrogant and self-centered and much more likable. His best traits are his perseverance and his capacity to love single-mindedly. Count Konrad is the counterpart of the ill-fated prince in the folk tale "Rapunzel," of which *Zel* is a retelling.

KOSS, AMY GOLDMAN (1954–   ), writer of humorous novels of family life and friendship for middle-grade and early teen readers. Her first novel, *The Trouble with Zinny Weston* (Dial, 1998), was hailed as a truly funny story of friendship, and *How I Saved Hanukkah* (Dial, 1998) was also lauded for its gentle fun. *The Ashwater Experiment** (Dial, 1999), a *School Library Journal* choice, an amusing story of family life and friendship, describes problems that ensue when Hillary's near-hippy, gypsylike parents decide to settle down for a change, and Hillary enrolls in school in a yuppie community. *The Girls* (Dial, 2000) concerns a hurtful middle-school girls' clique. Koss lives in Glendale, California, with her husband and family.

KRESS, NANCY (1948–   ), born in Buffalo, New York; educator, copywriter, author of science fiction and fantasy. She received her B.S. degree from the State University of New York in Plattsburgh and two master's degrees from the State University of New York at Brockport. *Beggars in Spain* (Avon, 1994), which was first published as a novella, then expanded into a novel, is the opening volume of her trilogy set in the near future concerning a society that results from gene alterations to intelligence. The second and third volumes are *Beggars and Choosers** (Tor, 1995) and *Beggars Ride* (Tor, 1996). *Beaker's Dozen* (Tor, 1998) is a book of short stories. Kress, who has made her home in Brockport, New York, is the winner of both the Nebula and the Hugo Awards for science fiction.

KRISHER, TRUDY (1946–   ), born in Macon, Georgia; freelance writer and teacher. She has a B.A. degree from the College of William and Mary and an M.Ed. degree from Trenton State College and has taught at the University of Dayton. In addition to a chapter book for early readers and a college textbook on writing, she is the author of *Spite Fences**, a novel of a biracial friendship set at the period of civil rights sit-ins in a small Georgia town. A sequel is *Kinship* (Delacorte, 1997). Krisher has made her home in Dayton, Ohio.

KRISTIN HARPER (*Wish You Were Here**), stepsister of Jackson Watt, nine years old when their parents are married. A bright and self-contained child, she is determined not to be seduced by the goodwill offered on all sides in the new family alignment and feels betrayed when her younger sister, friendly five-year-old Amy, starts to fit in happily. Jackson, who suffered from his parents' divorce at about Kristin's age, makes friends with her by approaching her as one would a cat, which will creep toward you quietly and eventually leap into your lap but will skitter away if you seem to notice it. Amanda, the girl whom they meet in Jamaica, brings the fused family together, since both the little girls, as well as Jackson, love her, and the newlywed parents are pleased that their offspring are no longer antagonistic. After their return to Indianapolis, the accident to Oz, Jackson's father, occupies everyone's attention until their father takes the girls back to St. Louis, where they live with their mother. Although Jackson cannot bring himself to write to Amanda, she keeps in touch with Kristin, who manages to bring him up to date on her every time that she and Amy visit their father. From Memphis Jackson calls Kristin to get Amanda's address so he can write to her, and the little girl says, "Well, it's about time!," having long since decided that Amanda should be part of the family.

KYLE (*Tiger, Tiger, Burning Bright**), African-American youth in Norbu, California, who adopts Jamaican speech rhythms and is a classmate and best friend of Jesse. Kyle is a good student, well liked, and the son of a rancher who raises beef and has managed by intelligence and hard work to make a go of his business in spite of the prolonged drought and economic downturn. His pretty mother is a good friend of Jesse's single-parent Mom, Bonnie. At Kyle's mother's birthday party for the community, Bonnie learns that Pappy* claims to have seen a tiger print. Kyle sticks with Jesse, although he cautions Jesse against what seem to be excessive dissembling and evasion to protect Pappy.

L

LADY EALDGYTH SWAN NECK (*The King's Shadow**), strikingly beautiful, historical common-law wife of Harold* Godwinson, Earl of Wessex, and benefactress of the mute young protagonist, Evyn, called Shadow. A kind and gentle woman and an able household manager, she is admired and respected by everyone and much loved by Harold, who reigns briefly as King of England. Understanding Evyn's pain at being a slave and realizing that the boy is intelligent and good at heart, she sends him to Aethelney Monastery, where he will be with Lewys*, a young Welsh monk, and where she knows he can be trained in reading and writing. Ealdgyth stands by Harold even when he agrees to a political marriage to the sister of the earls Edwin and Morcar of Mercia. She is present at the battle in which Harold is killed and afterward begs William*, Duke of Normandy, for Harold's body but is refused. After the battle, she flees for safety to Ireland. She is the only developed female figure in the book, a strong and admirable person in her own right.

LAKE WINDSOR DOWNS (*Tangerine**), expensive new housing development in Tangerine County, Florida, where Paul Fisher's family moves so his father can be Deputy Director of Civil Engineering for the county. Their new house is large and like all the others in the development, handsome, but problems appear almost immediately. In the field beyond the wall that surrounds Lake Windsor Downs, a muck fire smolders continuously, filling the air with smoke. Because the area used to be citrus orchards, and the trees were plowed under before the houses were built, most are infested with termites, which will continue to breed and return, even though the houses are being covered with exterminator's tents and filled with gas to kill them. The Homeowners' Association has stocked the runoff pond now called Lake Windsor with koi, Japanese carp, and it is suspected that someone is stealing them. Only Paul realizes that the osprey nesting nearby are swooping down and carrying off the fish. The area has more lightning strikes than any other part of the country, and every afternoon about time for sports practice, rain deluges the playing fields. The worst problem, however, is a sinkhole that opens up in the middle-school grounds, burying a couple of the portable classrooms and splintering the board-walks that connect them. It soon is revealed that, because the county engineer is corrupt, the construction sites for the new developments, including Lake Windsor Downs, were never surveyed for possible problems. The revelation causes the ousting of the engineer, to whose job Paul's father succeeds, but that does not resolve the difficulties of the development, into which the residents have sunk a great deal of their money.

THE LANDRY NEWS (Clements*, Andrew, illus. Salvatore Murdocca, Simon & Schuster, 1999), school story set for a few weeks in the town of Carlton near Chicago about the time of publication. Intelligent, quiet, retiring Cara Louise Landry, 10, who lives with her mother, Joanna, still feels the pain of her parents' divorce. Although most parents of Denton Elementary School students think Mr.* Larson is the worst teacher there, Cara enjoys his fifth-grade, unstructured, open classroom, a place so cluttered with teaching materials that it is like "a giant educational glacier" out of which she can carve a little separate cubbyhole all her own, unobserved and ignored by the other twenty-two students and also Mr. Larson, who spends most of his time reading the newspaper. One October, she puts out the first of what will become nine editions of *The Landry News*, in which she editorially points out that, since Mr. Larson never teaches his class, leaving the students to teach themselves and one another, the students should divide his salary among them. Although at first he is very angry, Mr. Larson decides to make the incident into a lesson on reading the newspaper and sets the students to collecting stories and editorials from different papers to find out "what kind of heart" the papers have. Cara is sorry for having hurt him, defends telling the truth, and then thinks carefully about what her mother tells her about combining truth and mercy. She puts out another issue, this time aided by Joey DeLucca, a classmate, who helps her publish it on the computer in the school library. Articles appear on students' favorite teachers and on their least favorite cafeteria food, and Cara writes an editorial on what a paper is for—to tell the truth and to do it in the spirit of their new motto, Truth and Mercy. The paper is a big hit, all seventy-five copies being distributed in less than six minutes. One copy ends up on the desk of overly officious, self-important Principal P. K. Barnes, who dislikes Mr. Larson immensely. When he asks to review each edition before it comes out, Mr. Larson refuses, saying that since it is a class paper, the class alone has that right. Mr. Larson then gives the class a lesson on the Constitution, Bill of Rights, and freedom of the press. Trouble follows the publication of the ninth edition, which carries an article by student Michael Morton about his feelings when his parents got a divorce. Principal Barnes says disciplinary action is needed, because the family's right to privacy has been violated, and Mr. Larson must appear before the school board. Mr. Larson uses the issue as an experience for the class in the First Amendment and freedom of the press. Cara and the students put out another paper, the *Guardian*, which, although published and distributed completely off school property, infuriates Principal Barnes. The other teachers and parents rally around Mr. Larson and the class, the media pick up the matter, and numerous interviews for newspapers and television follow. Mr. Larson conducts discussions, and the class thinks that this is the most interesting subject they have ever studied. At the meeting, Mr. Larson says that the story appeared because divorce causes real problems for children, Michael reads his story for the record, the audience of more than 400 people breaks into applause, and the case is dismissed. Freedom of the press has prevailed. Only Cara and Mr. Larson have depth and dynamism, the student-written articles are unusually sophisticated and well written, and the book's didactic and polemic intent—to examine issues facing teachers at the end of the century—is cleverly masked as school lessons. Each chapter is introduced by a headline-like title, so that the whole book looks like a series of newspaper articles. The newspaper-like format, larger than usual print, and humorous full-page illustrations serve two purposes: they lighten the tone, and they remind the reader that such incidents have actually happened. SLJ.

LANSA, PETE (*Prophecy Rock**), Native-American Indian Hopi father of the main character, Will, and the chief of police on the Hopi Reservation in Arizona. After college in Flagstaff, Arizona, and police academy in Phoenix, Lansa served with the Denver Police Department and married a wealthy white Denver social worker. They lived on the reservation for a few years, where Will was born, and then were divorced. Will and his mother have been living in Aspen, Colorado. Because of his father's insights into tribal ways and involvement in tribal ceremonies, Will learns much about this dimension of his inheritance. Lansa is a careful man in his work and also in the way that he helps Will to learn about and appreciate Hopi culture. He never denigrates white culture, just deplores white inroads into Indian culture. He also takes pains to explain traditions to the boy and makes it possible for Will to be included in Hopi activities.

LARRY DELUXE (*Confess-O-Rama**), popular talk-show host for radio station KGAB, one of the many eccentric figures in the novel. He becomes a friend of Tony Candelaria, the narrator and protagonist. Tony describes Larry as looking like "the sixth runner-up in the Robert Redford look-alike contest," blond, rugged, and possessing a dazzling smile. Larry likes to host shows on controversial topics and suggests that, for the high school shows he intends to stage, they talk about such matters as school uniforms, birth control on campus, bilingual education, and censorship, and, when Rochelle, one of the students, suggests chastity, he adds that to his list of possible topics. He later airs the students' protest about censorship. Tony's mother, Kathryn*, becomes Larry's agent, but, when she does not get him the size contract she thinks she ought to, she gives up the job and accepts one from his former wife, Sheila Larson. Larry helps

Kathryn see that her deceased husband, who loved her, would not want her to grieve indefinitely. For a while Tony hopes that his mother and Larry will become sweethearts. Larry points out to Tony that he should not feel bad about his relationship to Jordan Archer, since she still wants to kiss Tony in spite of what he said on the Confess-O-Rama machine. He compliments Tony when Tony appears on the stage in an artichoke bra to back Jordan up in her censorship protest. Larry, like Drew* Archer, is a kind of temporary father figure for Tony.

LARRY KING (*Ironman**), television personality to whom Bo Brewster writes letters one school year, telling King of events that happen in school and lead up to his winning Yukon Jack's triathlon competition. Bo tells King that these letters are to constitute a memoir in connection with the publication of which Bo wishes an interview on *Larry King Live*. Bo never mails them. Before the big race, Shelly*, Bo's friend and also a member of the Nak Pack, sends the letters to King, without Bo's knowledge. King then records an encouraging segment on the tape that the Nak Pack prepares for Bo to listen to during the race.

LASKY, KATHRYN (1944–   ), born in Indianapolis, Indiana; writer of many books of both fiction and nonfiction for young people. She has also published novels for adults, using the name Kathryn Lasky Knight. *Beyond the Burning Time** (Scholastic, 1994) is about the Salem witch trials from the point of view of a girl whose mother is arrested. A lighter-hearted historical novel is *Alice Rose and Sam** (Hyperion, 1998), a mystery set in Virginia City, Nevada, in the early 1860s, involving much skulduggery uncovered by a girl and her friend, Sam Clemens, who later takes the name Mark Twain. For earlier biographical information and title entries, see *Dictionary, 1985–1989* [*The Bone Wars*] and *Dictionary, 1990–1994* [*Double Trouble Squared*].

THE LAST PIPER (Cavanagh*, Helen, Simon & Schuster, 1996), fantasy of reincarnation set in Scotland in the 1990s. Accompanying their mother, Julia, on a business trip, Christie Malcolm, 13, is not happy since she knows that the care and entertainment of her frail brother, Mikey, 5, will fall, as usual, entirely upon her. As they near Oxton, Mikey suddenly starts recognizing places and announces, "When I was bigger, I lived here." As they approach a turnoff, he goes into an uncharacteristic tantrum, insisting that they must go to his castle, and, when they come within sight of a small stone castle, begins wheezing with a severe asthma attack. Christie runs to the castle, where an elderly woman quickly phones a doctor and welcomes them in, her mother carrying the already recovering little boy. While Mikey naps, the woman, who introduces herself as Emma Lauder, gives them tea and persuades them to stay as her paying guests rather than going on to Oxton. This pleases both Julia, who finds that Castle Lauder is centrally located for her research on tartans for Pennington Textiles, and Mikey, who has treated both Emma and her cat, called alternately Sixtoes and Malkin, as old friends. Christie is less sure, especially when she starts having strange experiences, evidently leaving her bed and climbing a nearby hill to where a kilted figure is playing bagpipes. Em, as she tells the children to call her, is interested in the comments that Mikey makes about his past life and his claim that he was Firth, the name of her brother who was hanged by a vigilante group some fifty years earlier, having been accused of stealing the family treasures and killing his girlfriend, Calinda Douglas. In their rambles around the area, Mikey shows Christie a large, flat rock on the hill, where he says he used to like to sit, and he exhibits terror when they near a certain dead tree, where, Em later admits, her brother was hanged. One afternoon they have a visit from Dr. Ian Dalvercroft, Em's friend who holds a chair in parapsychology at the University of Edinburgh. He is interested in Mikey's memories, but Julia, whose husband died only seven months earlier and who is touchy on the subject of death, wants nothing to do with the matter and forbids Christie to talk or speculate about it. After another night of viewing the piper, Christie decides to force a more extended memory from Mikey, hoping to cure his asthma but putting his health and mental stability at risk. Having determined that the word that the piper seems to be mouthing, though she cannot hear it, is *broch*, not rock, as she orginally thought, and knowing that there are several small brochs in the vicinity, she takes Mikey up the hill and forces him to sit near the tree, where he trembles and seems on the point of another asthma attack but leads her to a broch where they dig and find not only the family valuables but records and Calinda's journal. The journal details her fear of Rab Hawlie, Firth's cousin, who is infatuated with her and wants to marry her, although she is engaged to Firth. It becomes clear that, after killing her, he has accused Firth and rounded up the three Douglas brothers to form a posse with him and hang his rival. With the papers that they have found, Em is able to retrieve some family money and predicts that Mikey will become the new Lauder piper, like Firth, whose ghost Christie has been seeing. Although the relationship between the hanging and Mikey's asthma is explained, and speculation on reincarnation, mostly in the voice of Dr. Ian, is supplied, the connections and Christie's role in solving the mystery of the lynching are not entirely plausible. The strongest element is Mikey's naive conviction of what happened, as he says, "Before I was born to Mommy." Christie's deep involvement is explained by her role as almost mother to the little boy, having taken care of him more than her own mother has since his premature birth on the same date that Firth was hanged. It is an appealing story, but not especially convincing. Poe Nominee.

LEE ANNE HARRISON (*The Magic and the Healing**), one of the four veterinarian students who travel with Sugar* Dobbs into the remote valley of Crossroads* to help ailing animals. Lee Anne is particularly good with large animals, because she worked with Clydesdales at home in North Carolina. Since she has helped birth foals, she assists Polyta, a centaur, in giving birth, a ticklish assignment. Afraid that her baby will not arrive safely, the mother centaur urges that they take the baby and let her die. The vets save both, but without Lee Anne's knowledge concerning horses and procedures, probably both would have died. The colt is named Sugarly, a combination of Sugar and Lee. Lee Anne grows in confidence from their assignments in Crossroads, and after receiving her degree, she accepts a position with a veterinary practice, whose owner thinks highly of her, rewards her with a large salary, and probably will offer her a partnership. Of the four students, she is the most financially successful. The practice that she joins ironically deals with small animals, since Lee Anne is tired of working with large ones.

LEVINE, GAIL CARSON (1947–), born in New York City; author best known for inventive retellings of stories from oral tradition. She was graduated from City College of the City University of New York in 1969 and since then has worked in various capacities for departments of the New York state government. Her first book for children, *Ella Enchanted** (HarperCollins, 1997), based on the Cinderella story with many charming embellishments, was named a Newbery Honor Book. In a series known as the Princess Tales, shorter, illustrated books for a slightly younger audience, she has retold other folk and fairy tales, starting with *Princess Sonora and the Long Sleep* (HarperCollins, 1999), based on "The Sleeping Beauty," and *The Princess Test* (HarperCollins, 1999), based on "The Princess and the Pea." *Dave at Night** (HarperCollins, 1999), is a very different, realistic novel of a boy who sneaks out of a Jewish orphanage in the 1920s and becomes involved with members of the Harlem Renaissance. Levine lives in Brewster, New York.

LEVITIN, SONIA (1934–), born in Berlin, Germany; teacher and for three decades a popular and versatile writer for children and young people, publishing more than thirty books. She immigrated to the United States with her family when she was four, a flight to escape the Nazis that is recreated in fiction form in her first novel, *Journey to America* (Atheneum, 1970). Chosen by both the American Library Association and *School Library Journal*, *Escape from Egypt** (Little, Brown, 1994) is a historical novel that retells the biblical story of the ancient Hebrews' escape from slavery. In a sharply contrasting genre is *Yesterday's Child** (Simon & Schuster, 1997), a mystery-detective story in which a young girl uncovers secrets of her mother's background. A tense and gripping mystery, it was nominated for the Edgar Allan Poe Award. *Dream Freedom* (Harcourt, 2000) revolves around slavery in present-day Sudan. For additional biographical information, titles, and title entries, see *Dictionary, 1960–1984* [*Journey to America*; *The No-Return Trail*] and *Dictionary, 1985–1989* [*Incident at Loring Groves*; *The Return*].

LEWYS (*The King's Shadow**), young Welsh monk who teaches the protagonist, mute Evyn, to read and write and becomes Evyn's dear friend and counselor. A lighthearted, laughing youth, who Evyn thinks looks something like a court jester, Lewys has common sense as well as skill with language. He helps Evyn look at his situation with greater objectivity and urges him to make the most of his lot in life and serve Harold* Godwinson, Earl of Wessex, well. At the end, when Evyn despises the earls Edwin and Morcar of Mercia because they have accepted the overlordship of the conqueror, William*, Duke of Normandy, Lewys points out that they are acting out of sincere concern for their war-torn land and people. As a character, Lewys is a worthy foil for Evyn. Both are fictitious figures.

LEXAU, JOAN M., born in St. Paul, Minnesota; author of many books for children and young people, published under both her own name and the pseudonyms Joan L. Nodset and Marie Seth. *Trouble Will Find You** (Houghton, 1994), a humorous mystery for younger readers, was a nominee for the Edgar Allan Poe Award. For earlier biographical information and title entries, see *Dictionary, 1960–1984* [*The Trouble with Terry; Striped Ice Cream*].

LIGHTHOUSE GEORGE (*Ghost Canoe**), young, highly regarded Makah Native-American Indian, the son of a chief. He and his wife, Rebecca, befriend Nathan MacAllister and his mother after they move to the Makah village for her health. Lighthouse George delivers mail and supplies to the Tatoosh lighthouse and takes Nathan fishing with him many times, teaching him how to row the dugout canoe and fish in the Makah way. Lighthouse George appears in many scenes, but the most memorable ones are the sea hunts, in one of which he suffers a severe blow to the head while hunting whales and is rescued by Nathan. For a long time, he remains in a coma. Nathan faithfully visits him, and at his mother's suggestion, sits by Lighthouse George's bed and speaks to his stricken, unconscious friend. Nathan is instrumental psychologically in Lighthouse George's full recovery. Nathan lives up to Lighthouse George's name for him, Yaw-ka-duke, which means partner. Nathan regrets leaving Lighthouse George to move to California and promises to return some day.

LIKE SISTERS ON THE HOMEFRONT (Williams-Garcia*, Rita, Lodestar, 1995), girl's sociological problem novel set in recent years, first in South Jamaica, Queens, New York, and then in a rural area near Columbus, Georgia. Selfish, barely literate, street-talking, African-American Gayle Ann Whitaker, 14, lives in a small, seedy apartment with her widowed Mama* (Ruth Bell) Whitaker, a maid; and brother, Junie, 18, a loafer and ne'er-do-well. When unwed Gayle's baby boy, Jose, is only seven months old and she gets pregnant for the second time, Mama hustles her off to an abortion clinic. She then puts Gayle, grumbling and protesting at being separated from her homegirls and the aborted baby's father, and Jose on a plane to Mama's brother, the Reverend Mr. Luther Gates, in Georgia. Uncle Luther openly disapproves of Gayle, but his wife, Miss Auntie (Virginia Gates), a college professor working for her Ph.D., and cousin Cookie* (Constance), 16, are welcoming. They remain sweet and nonjudgmental in spite of Gayle's sassing, snide remarks, and continual complaints about having to help about the house and care for Great*, the senile, bedridden great-grandmother, who is expected to die before summer is out. Gayle is awed by the grand, former plantation house, which is surrounded by a big yard and peach trees and has an old cemetery off to one side. She rebels by surreptitiously making some peach wine with Great's old recipe, which she also samples, searches Great's room for money, and coaxes Cookie into driving her into town, all the time yearning for her homegirls and sex. She would like to be homegirls with Cookie but looks down on Cookie for doing social service work, enjoying choir, where she is a soloist, and the spirituality of her religion, but Gayle's frank talk about sex embarrasses Cookie, as do her general rebelliousness and insensitivity to others' needs and concerns. Gayle learns from Cookie that Great will "Tell [sic] before she dies," that is, pass along the family history, and that she will "tell" to Cookie. Great seems to like Gayle and occasionally passes along bits of family history and old lore while Gayle sits with her. She predicts that Gayle will some day "lay down her deviling" and that Jose will join the long line of preachers in the family. Gayle learns that Cookie is sweet on Stacey Alexander, a handsome college freshman and football player who returns her romantic interest. Gayle is offended when Cookie decides to talk with her mother about her feelings toward Stacey instead of discussing them with Gayle, who considers herself an expert on sex because she is experienced and has had frequent discussions about sex with her homegirls. Angry and jealous and hoping to cause trouble, Gayle passes along to Cookie Stacey's remark that it would not be a normal Sunday for him unless Cookie sang a solo. On the Sunday that they have a guest preacher and a famous radio soloist, Sister Rebecca Lloyd, Cookie steps forward unbidden to impress Stacey and sings the same solo that Sister Lloyd does, shocking the congregation and causing Uncle Luther to ground her for displaying such pride. Cookie not available, Great "tells" to Gayle instead, going all the way back to slave-ship days, and then dies. Having heard the story, Gayle has a new appreciation for her family and their history. She keeps Cookie from sneaking out to join Stacey, saying that she wants to save her cousin and acknowledging that she needs the family to save her. From an epilogue letter that Gayle writes to an unnamed homegirl, the reader learns that Great has had a large funeral, that Mama and Junie are moving south, and that Gayle plans to return to school in the fall. The conclusion is abrupt and unconvincing, the often explicit sex talk may offend some, the contrast between Gayle's New York life and street talk and the Gateses' Georgia life and proper southern speech comes through strongly, the style employs street talk, dialect, and Standard English, Gayle whines and sasses too much and seems too self-absorbed and lazy, and the main characters are stereotypes. Great, however, arouses admiration and rises above the other figures. Fanfare; SLJ.

LILY BRIDGER (*Looking for Jamie Bridger**), thoroughly cowed wife of Cletus Bridger, who raises Jamie as their grandchild, although it is revealed that she is actually their daughter, born when Lily was forty-six and Cletus was fifty, a child conceived to be a replacement for the son whom they had rejected. When Cletus discovered that the boy, also named Jamie, was gay, he threw him out and led Lily through the house to clear out and discard everything belonging to him, then commanded her to forget that he ever existed. Evidently, Lily has succeeded in wiping the boy from her mind and in believing that their daughter is their grandchild. For years she has called Cletus "Daddy" and has obeyed him in every way. At his death she is devastated, her mind reverting to that of a child. Since he handled all the money, she believes that the food that they have on hand cannot be replaced, and she stops eating and later crouches in a closet. When their son, now called Bridge, returns, she accepts him but rejects Jamie, unable to cope with the idea that there are two of them. Her sister, Aunt Mary, explains that Lily was an old maid, twenty-nine, when Cletus came to town as a tent preacher, and she fell for him totally. Their son was born six months after their marriage, and Lily has accepted the guilt of leading Cletus astray. She is clearly a victim of his pathological hatred of sex, having tried to make amends by suppressing her own personality and obeying him implicitly. After hospitalization, she begins to paint and shows other hopeful signs, but there is no assurance that she will recover. Bridge and Jamie plant bulbs for the Resurrection Lily, that being her full name, a plant that seems to die, then blossoms with a beautiful flower, a development that they hope will be paralleled in her life.

LILY'S CROSSING (Giff*, Patricia Reilly, Delacorte, 1997), period novel with girl's growing-up story aspects set in Rockaway, New Jersey, in the summer of 1944 just after D-Day and skipping then to mid-1945. Half-orphaned hoyden Lily (Elizabeth) Mollahan, 11, has several problems: getting along with strict, demanding Gram, with whom she lives; yearning for her absent engineer-father, Poppy, who leaves for World War II; her admitted tendency to daydream, tell lies, and avoid responsibility; and her need for friends her age. After she and Gram arrive at the Atlantic for their annual summer vacation, she learns that the family of her longtime friend, Margaret Dillon, will be leaving for Detroit, where Mr. Dillon is to be a foreman in the B-24 bomber plant. Margaret leaves Lily a key to the Dillon house, and Lily often takes refuge there from what she thinks of as her "troubles," like picking up her room, helping Gram with household tasks, and practicing piano lessons. She grows curious about a thin, dark boy, new in the neighborhood, who is staying with the Orbans down the road. She watches him, because she thinks that he might be a spy. At dinner one night with the Orbans, she learns that he is Albert*, a Hungarian refugee. A friendship gradually develops between the two children after she and Albert rescue from the water a tiny, bedraggled, red-orange kitten. They take the forlorn creature to Margaret's house, dry it off, feed it, and name it Paprika. Lily begins teaching Albert to swim, although she despairs because he is obviously afraid of the water. She tells him that she intends to row out, catch a ride on a convoy ship, and join her father in Europe. Because he yearns for his little sister, Ruth, living somewhere with nuns in France, Albert practices diligently, with little success, and Lily fears to tell him that she is not really serious about catching a ship. They play on the rocks together and sneak into the local theater, among other activities. Feeling guilty because Albert has high hopes of catching a ship, she tells him that she knows that it is impossible to row and swim that far out. Albert confesses that he has lied, too. He tells her that he left Ruth behind alone in France and that he put his own safety ahead of staying with her, although he knew that she was ill, and that he did not even say good-bye. Lily also confesses that she deliberately did not say good-bye to Poppy because she was distraught over his leaving. When Albert stubbornly sets out in a storm to try to catch a ship, Lily rescues him. Gram eases their consciences by asserting that both are safely in Rockaway because they were loved, Albert by his parents and grandmother, now probably dead, and Lily by Poppy. In a few short chapters that serve as an Afterword, Poppy returns in 1945, with the news that he has found Ruth safe in a French convent. At Rockaway in the summer of 1945, Lily finds Albert back at the Orbans, his sister, Ruth, with him. Although some episodes in the disjointed plot seem forced, like Albert's attempted departure, Lily's behavior, musings, and fabrications seem typical of a preadolescent girl trying to find her place in life and identifying her values for herself in the midst of a major war. Albert as a character, however, has become a stereotype. The mass in the local church for Eddie Dillon and others lost in the war is the most poignant scene, and occasional humor lightens the tone. The sense of the war is strong: the radio programs, the entertainers, songs, movies, shortages, the ethic and worldview of the era—all these serve to point up Lily's personal problems and bring the times to life from a young person's perspective, clearly the book's best aspect. ALA; Boston Globe Honor; Newbery Honor.

LISLE, JANET TAYLOR (1937–   ), born in Englewood, New Jersey; journalist, novelist, noted for creating a wide variety of characters and settings. *A Message from the Match Girl** (Orchard, 1995) is third in a series of fantasy-mysteries known as the IOU Books (Investigators of the Unknown), the first being *The Gold Dust Letters* (Orchard, 1994). *The Lost Flower Children** (Philomel, 1999) is a touching novel of two little girls dropped off to live with an elderly great-aunt after the death of their mother. For earlier biographical information and title entries, see *Dictionary, 1985–1989* [*Sirens and Spies*] and *Dictionary, 1990–1994* [*Afternoon of the Elves*; *The Lampfish of Twill*; *Forest*].

LIZ COLES (*The Wedding**), elder daughter in the elite African-American family that summers on Martha's Vineyard. Liz has married Lincoln, a doctor, a man with a darker skin than hers, and has a nut-brown child, Laurie, whom she adores. When they were planning for her wedding, her mother, Corinne, graciously included Lincoln's parents among the invited guests but refused to add his aunt and uncle, who actually paid for his medical education, since they were of lower social status and darker-skinned than the Coles. Angered, Liz eloped. She is enough of a realist, however, to see that she is not much of a wife to Linc, choosing to spend the summer on the island instead of making a home for him in the city. He has refused to come to the wedding, and Liz sees that this may be the beginning of the end of her marriage. She also is a realist about her parents: she knows about the mistress of her father, Clark*, and she has pieced together the clues about her mother's various affairs, all with dark-skinned men. She tells her sister that Corinne, despite her apparent protest at her marriage to Linc, is actually jealous that she has married the sort of man whom she herself desires.

LIZZIE FRANCY (*Beggars and Choosers**), daughter of Annie Francy, the African-American woman loved by Billy* Washington in East Oleanta, New York. Through some natural genetic mutation, Lizzie is unlike other Liver chil-dren her age, being highly intelligent and curious about the world around her, full of an insatiable thirst for knowledge. Even before Diana* Covington comes to the village, Lizzie has reprogrammed the servoentrance door of the food service, so that her mother, who loves to cook, can enter, and she has taken the robotic apple-peeler apart to see why it no longer works. When Diana, now called Vicki Turner, gets her a handheld computer and crystal library, she takes off mentally, despite the opposition of her mother, who is suspicious of learning. Lively and a bit saucy, in many ways a typical girl entering her teens, Lizzie rebels in small ways, argues with Annie, and twists Billy* Washington, who dotes on her, around her finger, but she is also loving and perceptive beyond her years. To her own surprise, Diana becomes as devoted to the child as she would be to one of her own. Their joint desire to protect Lizzie binds Diana and Billy together and deflects Annie's opposition. Lizzie represents the possi-bilities among the ordinary people without gene modification to achieve great leaps in intelligence and ability. Like Billie, Annie, and the other Livers, Lizzie originally speaks in a pattern with frequent reflexive pronouns: "You promised, you. I heard you, me," but after she has learned more, she begins to adopt standard speech.

LIZZIE HARDWICK (*The Great Turkey Walk**), Elizabeth Hardwick, a young woman of sixteen, whom Simon Green, Jabeth* Ballou, and Mr*. Bidwell Peece find living all alone in a sod house on the high prairie. As they draw near, she rushes wildly out of her house, "screeching like a banshee," and begs to be saved from "this godforsaken place." Mr. Peece says that she is suffering from "prairie madness." The travelers learn that she lost to sickness all six members of her family, parents and siblings. Benefiting from their solicitous companion-ship, she soon calms down and contributes variously to the success of the en-terprise. She is described as having shiny dark hair and bright blue eyes. Simon is romantically attracted to her, and she to him. At the end, she becomes a partner in the the Great Turkey Five Ranch, but she and Simon decide to follow

Mr. Peece's advice and wait a couple of years to see whether they really like each other enough to get married.

LIZZIE MAG (*Spying on Miss Muller**), Elizabeth Margaret, named for the two British princesses, also called Lizard by her fellow students at Alveara boarding school. A genuinely sweet girl, Lizzie Mag is the least willing of the girls to indulge in the romantic game of spying on their half-German teacher, and she is moved to kindness when Miss Muller is splashed with the foul-smelling egg balanced on her door. She also stands up for Jessie Drumm when the prefect tries to shame her by reading aloud Jessie's note from Ian McManus. Since her parents are in India, and travel is impossible in wartime, Lizzie Mag is stuck at the school for the holidays. She keeps from the others her mother's letters describing how her father has taken off with another woman, but the maids read the letters and discuss the situation in Jessie's hearing. In the end, Jessie admits to Lizzie Mag her own secret shame, that her father drinks heavily, and she invites Lizzie Mag to spend the summer holidays with her anyway.

LONE WOLF (Franklin*, Kristine L., Candlewick, 1997), novel of a boy who has lived for four years, since his parents split up, in the isolated Minnesota north woods with his reclusive, almost silent father, home-schooled, seeing almost no one else until a family moves into an abandoned house nearby. Now eleven, Perry Dubois, the narrator, has become used to being alone with Rhonda, his German shepherd, while his father, who sells wood and drives a snowplow, is making a delivery or clearing roads. Once a week they drive to Grand Marais, to the grocery store, the library, and the post office, where there is always a letter for Perry from his mother, which he adds to the sack of unopened letters under his bed. He cannot forgive her for leaving without saying good-bye, even though he knows that life was intolerable for her after his little sister was killed in an accident, which both she and her husband blame on her. Perry spends much of his time at a cave that he has found high on a rocky hillside, a place that his father knows about but has never visited. When one day he sees a truck pull up to the unoccupied house down the hill, Perry watches secretly, seeing a skinny girl with glasses about his age, then three younger girls, all wearing glasses, and a toddler. The next day the oldest girl, hunting her cat, Tunafish, discovers the cave. When he accuses her of trespassing, she points out that it is her family's land, so *he* is the trespasser. Then she bargains with him: she will not tell anyone about the cave if they can have joint ownership. He learns that she is Willow Pestalozzi and that her parents are artists and, when she admires the charcoal pictures that he has drawn on the cave walls, that she is an artist, too. Together, they hear a wolf howl, the second time that he has heard it. In his mind, he has named it King. After staying away from the cave for nearly a month, Perry goes back one rainy day and finds it undisturbed except for a notebook that Willow has left for him full of very skillful drawings of birds and small animals and one wonderful picture of a wolf. Astonished and excited that she might have seen King, he pushes through the wet brush down the hill to her house, where her mother, a potter, is working clay in the kitchen with her little brother, Ian, in the high chair. He leaves his phone number, and when Willow calls, they arrange to go looking for the wolf. After that they often hike together as he shows her a beaver dam and other natural wonders, but although they do find a wolf track, they do not see King. After numerous invitations, Perry finally goes to the Pestalozzi house for dinner, a meal full of squabbling and hugging and good food, followed by an all-family game of Monopoly. After that he goes to their house every Saturday, gradually getting used to the noise and the younger children wanting to climb on his lap. He tries, unsuccessfully, to start conversations with his father and even buys some playing cards, thinking that they might have a game, with no response. One night, when his father is out plowing, Perry straps on his snowshoes and hikes to the cave, then builds up his fire against the increasing cold. Waking in the night, he hears a wolf howling and, he thinks, an answering howl and is too scared to start home. At first light he goes to the Pestalozzis, who have been alerted by Perry's father that he is missing. After retrieving him, his angry father grounds him for a month. To Perry's surprise, his father accepts an invitation to Christmas Eve dinner. A heavy snowstorm keeps him out plowing, and when he doesn't show up, they finally eat without him, but Perry is so worried that when the younger girls pity him for being an only child, he tells them about his sister and his mother leaving and for the first time breaks down and sobs but recovers by the time that his father, delayed by the storm, shows up. On Christmas Day, his mother calls, having been given permission by his father, who has sole custody and has refused before. Although Perry says almost nothing to her, the next day he takes the bag of letters from under his bed to the cave to read them. Perry's determination to be as tough and unemotional as his father vies with his need for love and friendship, which the Pestalozzi family offers in abundance. The picture of their almost silent, isolated life and the beauty of the woods is well drawn, as is the fascination that Perry shares with Willow for the wolf. SLJ.

THE LONG SEASON OF RAIN (Kim*, Helen, Holt, 1996), realistic novel of family life set in Seoul, Korea, for several summer months in 1969 as described by the second daughter, Junehee, 11, an intelligent, aware child. Junehee lives in a small, cramped house filled with women: her bossy, spiteful older sister, Changhee, 13; her likable younger sisters, Moonhee, 9, and Keehee, 6; her Mother*; and Father's* mother, imperious, disapproving Grandmother*, who owns the house. Providing cohesion for the mostly everyday episodes are two problems: what will happen to the boy whom the family fosters and how will the family cope with their irascible, usually absent Father, an army colonel. In late June, during the rainy season, Grandmother decides to take in Pyungsoo, 11, the grandson of her church friend, Grandmother Boksoon. The boy, who was orphaned when his family was killed in a mountain landslide, is very thin, poorly dressed, and frightened. Changhee treats him shabbily, as do most people because they regard him as lower class. Father wants to get rid of the boy immediately, and Grandmother agrees that they should soon find someone to take him. Kindhearted, moral Junehee befriends him, however, and Mother, who longs for a son in their patriarchal society, becomes increasingly attached to him. The girls are very close to Mother, who is always warm, solicitous, hard-working, and obedient to Grandmother. Mother is the center of their world, but they long for their father's approval, especially Changhee, who is an exception-ally good student. Father, however, on those rare occasions when he is home, treats the girls with disdain, barking orders and doling out military-type disci-pline. The children are aware that Father and Mother do not get along well. While they are vacationing on an island in Inchon harbor, Junehee first really notices how little time Father spends with his family and how he is often gone at night. She learns that some men have "bad women" and wonders whether her Father has one. She notices that Mother, who behaves uncharacteristically romantic around Father, pleads unsuccessfully with him to let her keep Pyung-soo. Just before they leave for home, Mother abruptly hacks off her hair, and, home again, she accepts the gift of a smart, green dress from her friend Mrs. Park, who owns a boutique. Grandmother disapproves of both, and Mother com-plains that she has to ask permission for everything. When they visit Grand-mother's sister, Great-Aunt tells Mother not to keep Pyungsoo and to try to have a son. Grandmother even brings the matter up to Father—tells him to try for a son—but when Mother says that she wants to adopt Pyungsoo, Father says that both ideas are ridiculous. Finally, without informing anyone, Grandmother takes Pyungsoo to live with her friend, Mrs. Kim, where at book's end he seems to be happy. Junehee is distressed, however, and angrily calls Grandmother "Devil Granny." Mother's self-esteem is severely damaged, especially when Grand-mother tells Auntie to check around to see if Father has a son somewhere, and walks out. Father is furious but relents and takes the girls with him to Grandma Min's, where Mother has gone, and persuades her to return home. Junehee is happier at book's end, because she occasionally sees Pyungsoo at school, but still worries that Auntie might find and bring home a son of Father's. The conclusion, though unsatisfying to Western readers, is probably true to the cul-ture and period. The descriptions of the house and furnishings, preparing food, working about the home, going to the bathhouse and church, doing homework, visiting relatives, traveling about the city on the bus, and the like are clear and revealing. It is hard to find redeeming features about Father as Junehee presents him, but the possibility that he might have a mistress and illegitimate children seems to be taken in stride by the mature women whose conversations she reports. This novel, which is primarily about adults, is all the more telling be-cause it is not only reported by a child with a child's eyes but also reveals the effect of adult dissension and worries on children. SLJ.

A LONG WAY FROM CHICAGO: A NOVEL IN STORIES (Peck*, Richard, Dial, 1998), delightfully humorous episodic, realistic novel, replete with local color and period flavor, set in a small railroad town in Illinois somewhere between Chicago and St. Louis from 1929 to 1942. Every August, narrator Joey* Dowdel, nine when the book begins, and his sister, Mary* Alice, 7, travel "by Wabash Railroad's crack Blue Bird" to spend the month with their imperious Grandma* Dowdel "in one of those [little] towns the railroad tracks cut in two." Grandma lives by herself at the edge of the Great Depression-hit town in a big house with an upstairs and an attic and a privy out back. Each of the seven episodes is a short story in itself, but taken together the episodes convey a vivid, eloquent picture of a bygone era and a tough, independent old woman. Joey and Mary Alice have never seen a dead body until Grandma, to spite certain townspeople and put one over on a nosy big-city newspaper reporter, decides that the town reprobate, Shotgun Cheatham, will have a hero's funeral, makes up an illustrious Civil War history for him, and buries him from her own front room. At midnight, while they sit up with the corpse, in a never-to-be-forgotten experience for the children, Grandma demonstrates her dexterity with her old twelve-gauge, double-barreled Winchester. In other episodes, Grandma puts a mouse in a bottle of milk to teach a lesson to the owners of the local dairy, the Cowgills clan, after the dim-witted youngest son blows her "mailbox sky high" with a cherry bomb. Grandma takes the children trap fishing (an illegal activity) on private property (also illegal), where they observe the sheriff and other town dignitaries in a drunken orgy (during Prohibition). On their return home, they cook the fish and feed Great Depression drifters passing through town (against the sheriff's orders), all activities that Grandma manages scot-free because of her skill with subtle blackmail. Joey rides on a barnstorming plane at the county fair because Grandma wins, or does not win (depending on the point of view), first prize with her gooseberry pie. Joey helps Grandma bring together two young lovers when he plays the role of the phantom brakeman of town legend. Grandma also manipulates the local banker into ensuring that an elderly citizen will be able to live out her days in her own house. In the final episode, which takes place in 1935, the last year that the children spend August with Grandma, Grandma's float upstages that of the banker's wife in the Centennial Celebration. Grandma's carries not only Mary Alice and Joey dressed in Grandma's and Grandpa's wedding clothes but, most outstandingly, Uncle Grady Griswold, "by far the oldest settler in the community," who had been wounded in the Mexican War and who gets into a brawling fistfight with the town's next oldest citizen, a Civil War veteran. An Epilogue finds Joey (now called Joe) on a 1942 troop train passing through on its way to Camp Leonard Wood. Joe sees Grandma standing at her door, waving. The episodes move rapidly with unexpected twists, and the children change and grow credibly. The focus of the hilarity and down-home atmosphere and values is Grandma, a well-drawn figure of depth, determination, and ingenuity. Hints of colloquial speech help establish place and times; the mix of small-town eccentrics is well concocted; and the smooth style never calls attention to itself. This is an all-ages book, in which young readers will savor the slapstick humor, while adults will respond to the ironies of character and plot, the Great Depression-period details, the vividly depicted small-town life, and the deftly controlled style. ALA; Fanfare; Newbery Honor.

LON PEREGRINO (*The Maze**), aloof, taciturn biologist who is reintroducing condors into the wilds of Canyonlands National Park in Utah and befriends frightened, runaway Rick* Walker. Lon is an obvious foil for the boy; his story is much the same as Rick's. He, too, was abandoned by his teenaged mother and adopted by a couple whose husband abused him, giving him the facial scar that he still bears. He was then placed in a series of foster homes, among them a veterinarian's. Rescuing an eagle that the vet treated aroused Lon's interest in birds and motivated him to go to college to become a bird biologist. A graying man nearing middle age, Lon is kind but still does not relate well to people. Rick grows to like, trust, and admire him during just the few weeks that they are together in the wilds. Lon's advice to Rick to forgive those who he feels have wronged him starts the healing process for the hurting boy.

LOOKING AFTER LILY (Bonner*, Cindy, Algonquin, 1994), western period novel set in Texas in 1884, sequel to *Lily*, which is based on the historical McDade Christmas Lynchings, the culmination of a feud between townspeople and a band of local outlaws, including the Beatty brothers. *Looking After Lily* starts with the release of the third Beatty, Woody (Haywood), 20, from jail after being acquitted of murder in the shoot-out that killed his older brothers, Azbury and Jack. His younger brother, Shot (Marion), who is sentenced to two years in prison for robbery, extracts a promise that Woody will take care of his very young, pregnant wife, Lily. Despite her youth, Lily, 16, proves more capable of taking care of herself than Woody is. The novel, narrated by Woody, traces his gradual maturity over the next two years. At first they head off in a light wagon pulled by a broken-down mule with Shot's horse, Mollie, for San Antonio, where Woody hopes to hire on as a cowboy for a cattle drive, although his experience has been mostly in holdups. His main idea is to get Lily settled some place so he can get on with his life. Lily has about $160, which Woody takes charge of and which doesn't last long. He meets two cowboys who let him finance a spree for all three. They do give Woody a lead on a ranch job, which turns out to be breaking wild horses for two dollars each. When he returns after nearly a month to the inn, where Lily now has a job cooking, he is surprised that she is upset that he didn't let her know where he was. While he waits for a cattle drive in the fall, he gets a job helping a blacksmith and sleeps in the dormitory at the inn, sharing a bed with a smelly drifter from Tennessee. One night he wakes to find the man gone and traces him to Lily's room, where he is starting to rape the girl. After a bruising fight, Woody kills him with his own knife, then rolls his body in a rug, hoists it onto Mollie, weights it with a rock, and dumps it in the river. As soon as possible they start off, heading south. A few days later, Lily's contractions start just as they run into a family of Mexicans. Although Woody distrusts them, they turn out to be friendly and honest, the women caring for Lily as she delivers a daughter named Emmaline Eliza and the men getting Woody drunk in the traditional man's role during labor. Figuring to head for Mexico, Woody takes off again, leaving Lily with the Mexicans. At a little wayside store he runs into one of the cowboys whom he met in San Antonio and, after a series of drunken adventures, ends in a crude, one-room shanty of a jail, where he is kept without trial for two months and is released with nothing but his ragged clothes, the city marshall having appropriated his saddle and fancy vest. He almost reaches San Patricio, where he left Lily, on foot before he is overcome by malaria. He wakes up in a nunnery, where he discovers Lily and Emmaline have been taken in and are great favorites. The nuns assume, as the Mexicans did, that he is Lily's husband, and they load the little family down with hand-made quilts and baby clothes. Woody decides they should head for Parker County, where his lawyer in McDade has a brother in need of farming help. He has also grown up enough to see that possibly Lily can keep him out of trouble. They have a hard trip, going far out of their way to avoid San Antonio and suffering a delay when his illness returns. When they reach Parker County, they discover that the job has already been given to Bob Stevens, old friend of Jack Beatty, best man at his wedding and now husband of Jack's wife, Estelle. At first Woody is furious, but soon Lily is keeping house for Estelle, who is far from competent, and Woody has taken over the blacksmith shop in nearby Brock. All this time Woody has become more and more in love with Lily, an attraction that he tries to deny, then conceal. Conditions change when Estelle dies in childbirth, Bob disappears, and Lily is afraid to stay in the house alone. Woody moves in, fighting against his interest in Lily, who nurses both babies until Estelle's snooty parents arrive and, with no thanks, take the baby, a move that Lily fights and grieves over. Then Lily's brother Dane shows up, having run away from his father and stepmother, and Woody moves back to his blacksmith shop, though he has begun to buy the farm and works it with Dane's help. He is continually confused by Lily, who sometimes flirts with him and shows affection but rebuffs him the only time he lets himself respond. When he returns after a few weeks cutting cedar fence posts in the hills, Shot has arrived, having completed his two-year sentence. He wants to try sheep farming in West Texas. Woody gives him Jack's horse, which he had acquired from Bob, and the mule and spring wagon and lends him some money, the start, he says "of all the money I would come to loan him through the years." Woody loses Lily and Emmy, to whom he has become devoted, but he has learned to get on with his life and make do. Also included are episodes of a revival meeting, at which he is briefly saved, of a girl who seduces him as he spends the night in a neighbor's barn, and of his shooting of another man, this time clearly in self-defense, for which he is not even brought to trial. What starts as a humorous chronicle of a naive young hellion develops into a touching story of deep love and renunciation. Woody's voice is convincing, a young, untutored western dialect, and details of life in Texas of the 1880s seem authentic. An author's note at the end says that she could not find out what happened to Marion Beatty but that Haywood, who never married, died a highly repected citizen in 1941 at the home of a niece. ALA; SLJ.

LOOKING FOR JAMIE BRIDGER (Springer*, Nancy, Dial, 1995), mystery novel of family relationships, set in the small coal-mining town of Dexter, Pennsylvania, at about the time of publication. Jamie Bridger, 14, is determined to find out, at last, something about her parents, a subject that her grandparents, with whom she lives, have never discussed. When she presses her grandmother, Lily*, for information, the timid, nervous woman, totally dominated by her husband, says convincingly that she does not remember. When Jamie tackles her grandfather, Cletus, he erupts in fury, and Jamie is saved from physical harm by Lily's ushering them in to dinner, where Cletus overeats and dies of heart failure. With Lily totally unable to cope, all the arrangements fall to Jamie, not an easy job since Cletus has made the family decisions and completely controlled the finances. Her best friend and next-door neighbor, Kate Garibay, is her only confidant and help. Together they find Cletus' will and, from the address on the envelope, learn that the town that they came from, only a faint memory to Jamie, is Silver Valley. Leaving Lily, who has reverted to a childlike state and refuses to eat, with Kate to watch over her, Jamie takes a bus to Silver Valley in hope of discovering some family. There she finds a house that she recognizes, now occupied by an eccentric woman, Shirley Dubbs, who welcomes her, shows her through the house, lets her spend the night, and even introduces her to the twenty-one box turtles that she has saved from becoming roadkill now living in her yard. Jamie also calls at the office of the lawyer listed on the will and finds that he has retired but that his daughter, Ian Lampeterson Russell, is not only there but remembers Jamie Bridger, a boy in her high school class, who Jamie assumes must be her father. She also talks to an old couple who remember her as a child and, by phone, to Ian's father, and with both she has a feeling that there is something that they are not telling her. Back in Dexter, she finds that Lily has regressed further, now hiding in a closet. Through Ian, who has a friend trace credit records, she gets an address for Jamie Bridger in New York City, and, with Kate again as backup caretaker for Lily, she takes a bus to the city. Just as she nears the building, she naively cuts across a vacant lot and is attacked by a mugger, who is driven away by a young man whom she recognizes from a yearbook picture that she has seen in Silver Valley. Battered and bleeding, she is taken by Bridge, as he says he is now called, and his partner, David, to their apartment, where he gently explains to her that she couldn't be his daughter, since he is gay and has never had sex with a woman. They clearly are related in some way, however, and the next day he accompanies her back to Dexter, where he lures Lily from her closet by acting like a hurt little boy. Ironically, when she accepts him, she rejects Jamie, treating her like a stranger, a friend of Bridge whom she has never met before. Pooling their limited family knowledge, Bridge and Jamie contact Lily's sister, Amaryllis Duncan (Aunt Mary), who hops in her car in Chicago and arrives the next morning. With her help, the relationships are cleared up. Both Jamie and Bridge are children of Cletus and Lily. Cletus, who had a pathological fear and hatred of sex, threw his son out because he was gay, then sired another child, Jamie, to replace him. His horror of the sexual act made him think that his son's orientation was punishment for the act of his conception and that Jamie's gender was further punishment for his carnal attempt to replace his son. When she was very young, he insisted that she be kept a secret in Silver Valley, but as she approached school age, he moved to Dexter, severing all ties with family and acquaintances, and insisted that Lily tell the girl that they are her grandparents. Bridge, who is a nurse, gets Lily into a psychiatric hospital before he returns to New York and David. Jamie goes to live with Kate and her family, who are moving to a new home near the state capitol. After some months, Lily is released to board at Shirley Bunn's house, where Jamie and Bridge both visit. Good characterization of Jamie makes this bizarre family believable and keeps the story interesting. The relationship between Bridge and David is treated tactfully and sympathetically. The explanation for Lily's submissive acceptance of Cletus' tyranny and her subsequent mental illness is expressed rather heavy-handedly by Aunt Mary but is acceptable since she is warning Jamie not to give up her own personality to please anyone else. Point of view is mostly Jamie's but shifts occasionally to Kate or Bridge. Poe Winner.

THE LOST FLOWER CHILDREN (Lisle*, Janet Taylor, illus. Satomi Ichikawa, Philomel, 1999), novel of the summer after their mother's death when two little girls live with a great-aunt who at first seems too old to be competent but proves to be wise and compassionate. Olivia, 9, takes good care of her little sister, Nellie, 5, foreseeing the compulsive "rules" that she follows—walking up and down stairs backward, never eating food that has more than two things mixed, putting on her socks and shoes first when she gets dressed—and forestalling the screaming tantrums that follow if the rules are broken. As they start on the two-hour drive to Aunt Minty's house, Pop at first refuses to take all twenty-three of Nellie's stuffed animals but backs down quickly when Olivia points out that they are Nellie's family, and she would never think of leaving them behind. Olivia, who listens in on phone and other adult conversations, realizing that it is the only way she will find out what is going on, knows that Aunt Minty is appalled at the thought of caring for two children all summer, but Pop, a salesman, has smooth-talked her into it and, after dropping them off, makes a hasty retreat before she can change her mind. Their first weeks are rocky. With all good intentions, little, wispy Aunt Minty keeps doing the wrong things, and Olivia has to work hard to keep Nellie's fury from erupting. The worst thing that Aunt Minty does is try to find them friends. After they have refused several suggestions, she invites a ten-year-old girl named Jill and her brother, Leo, just Nellie's age, for lunch without consulting Olivia, and the occasion is a disaster. Feeling left out, Nellie starts throwing stones at everyone, hits Olivia with a big one, and knocks her out. When she comes to, Nellie has disappeared. After a long wait, Aunt Minty allows Olivia to look for her, and she finds her in the overgrown garden where she has hidden all afternoon. Nellie is convinced that she has been one of the "lost flower children" from a story by Ellis Bellwether, an author who once lived in the house and whose book the girls have found and read, recognizing the garden from the descriptions and pictures. Olivia knows that it is fiction, a fairy tale about how the wicked Green-Skins impose a "Transferring Spell" on a party of children and change them into flowers, all except the youngest, who was on the porch at the time and was struck dumb by a second spell. She still goes along with Nellie in her quest to find the eight little blue cups and the teapot from the original party. If these are set back on the table, as they were before the spell, it will trigger a countercharm and restore the children to life. Earlier, they have come upon one cup, and gradually they find more, digging industriously in the overgrown garden that was once Aunt Minty's pride. Nellie has figured out that each cup is buried under or near a different type of flower, one for each child, she points out. She even corrals two boys in the neighborhood to help with the digging. Eventually, they find all eight cups and even, with Aunt Minty's help, a blue teapot. They drag an old picnic table from the shed, spread a lace tablecloth on it, and arrange the cups and teapot, making it all as close to the illustrations in the Bellwether book as they can. For a couple of days, as Nellie waits confidently for the countercharm, Olivia worries, afraid that she will be disillusioned and disappointed, but when children show up for a tea party, the digging boys, Jill, and Leo among them, Nellie is delighted. A little later, when their father calls and admits to Aunt Minty, with Olivia secretly listening on the extension, that he has lost his job and will have to leave the girls with her through the fall, neither girl is upset. Just who planted the eight little cups is never certain, possibly the Green-Skins, possibly Bellwether, possibly Aunt Minty. What is certain is that the girls have found a home and are happy, even though sometimes Nellie is still difficult and bossy, and some nights Olivia still aches with longing for her mother. Although the story is not in first person, the action is all seen through the eyes of Olivia, an overly conscientious older sister, coping with difficulty but determination in a situation too demanding for her age. The book is attractively illustrated with many small, black-and-white drawings, and one double-page spread of the garden with the lace-covered picnic table set for the party, but the children and Aunt Minty are shown in none of them. SLJ.

LOUIS CASELLI (*Bad Girls**), fifth-grade bully with whom Margalo* Epps and Mikey* Elsinger have trouble and who particularly picks on Mikey. Louis dislikes Mikey because she challenges his position as leader of the grade when she inspires the other girls to demand that they be allowed to play soccer on the fifth-grade team. This encourages the girls to think about having a team of their own. Louis almost gets kicked off the school soccer team for not treating girls as equal players. Although Louis resents having to play with girls, he also comes to see that they are effective players. One of the three Caselli cousins in fifth grade, he is described as having mean eyes and being a general nuisance. The other children, however, like him more than they fear him.

LOUIS LITTLEBIRD (*The Other Shepards**), ninth-grade boy on whom Holland Shepard has a crush. He is described as having streaked hair and wearing a leather jacket and motorcycle boots. He is a high school wrestler, and Holland has attended one of his meets without his knowing. Annie encourages Holland to invite Louis to visit her at her home, and Holland does. Holland's mother comes upon them kissing (Holland's first) and angrily orders him out of the house. She tells Holland that he is not the kind of boy whom she should be seeing. She wants Holland to associate with the son of family friends, also a ninth grader at Louis' school, whom the kids dislike and refer to as Aaron the Pious. Holland continues to see Louis on the way to school, and the two meet secretly and talk on the roof of Holland's house. Louis is the only figure in the novel who seems completely real.

LOWRY, LOIS (HAMMERSBERG) (1937–   ), born in Honolulu, Hawaii; prolific novelist, twice winner of the Newbery Award. A new addition to her Anastasia Krupnik series is *See You Around, Sam** (Houghton, 1996), in which Anastasia's little brother, Sam, decides to run away and is gently thwarted by his whole neighborhood. For earlier biographical information and title entries, see *Dictionary, 1960–1984* [*A Summer to Die*], *Dictionary, 1985–1989* [*All About Sam*; *Rabble Starkey*], and *Dictionary, 1990–1994* [*Number the Stars*; *The Giver*].

LUCIAN (*The Arkadians**), youth who accompanies Fronto*, the donkey-poet, and the pythoness, Joy-in-the-Dance*, across Arkadia to consult the wise Lady of the Wild Things. Feckless and garrulous, he becomes a hero in spite of himself and accomplishes their deliverance whole or in part on several tight occasions. In particular, he employs the slingshot that Catch-a-Tick* gave him as a parting gift to rescue King Bromios*. Lucian enjoys telling about his experiences and embroiders the facts in such a way as to make the stories dramatic and exciting. Fronto soon realizes that Lucian is a natural storyteller. Lucian falls in love with Joy-in-the-Dance, and they are married at the end.

LUIS CRUZ (*Tangerine**), Hispanic-American youth, older brother of the twins, Teresa and Tino, who are among the first kids whom Paul Fisher gets to know at Tangerine Middle School. Since the death of their mother, Luis has taken care of the twins, and he still picks them up in his old truck after every soccer practice, along with Victor, the team leader, and several other soccer players who live in their area. When he was just twelve, Luis fell from a tree where he was picking and damaged his knee, so he walks with a limp, but he has become a horticultural specialist and has developed the Golden Dawn, a new strain of tangerine resistant to the frequent cold snaps in the area that have destroyed much of the citrus industry. After Erik* Fisher and Arthur Bauer insult Tino at Paul's house, Luis confronts Erik at football practice, and, at Erik's direction, Arthur slugs him on the side of the head with a blackjack, causing an aneurysm that leads to his death. It is clear that Tino and Teresa adore Luis. Even though Tino resents Paul, he warms up after Luis welcomes him to their orchard. After his death, the family business is swamped with orders for the Golden Dawn, signaling a possible rebirth of citrus as a main product of the area.

LUTE MCNEIL (*The Wedding**), highly successful maker of fine furniture, who has rented a house on the Oval of Martha's Vineyard, where he lives for the summer with his three little girls. Dark, handsome, and sexy, he is almost the stereotype of the black stud, confident that he can seduce any woman as he has the three white women who are the girls' mothers, among many others. These three he has married because, illegitimate himself, he wants to sire no bastards, but he has treated the women badly, even the latest, Della, who is a potential heiress from a higher social stratum and whose contacts are a large element in his success. Lute craves to be included in the elite society of the Ovalites and sees Shelby* Coles as the way to gain entrée. He sets about seducing her, ignoring the fact that he has not yet divorced Della. Brutal when angered and heartless toward women, Lute does have the redeeming factor of being a devoted father, taking good care of Barby, 8, Muffin, 4, and especially Tina, 6, the child whom he really loves, seeing that they are clean and well dressed, even braiding their hair each morning. Tina's death, caused by his anger at Della and his own wild driving, is an irony perhaps too contrived.

LYNCH, CHRIS, author of novels of family relationships and growing up for middle-grade and early adolescent readers. A stay-at-home father and writer, he lives in Boston. He has won praise for his ability to handle potentially morbid subjects with a light touch but without lessening their seriousness. *Gypsy Davey** (HarperCollins, 1994) is a contemporary realistic novel of a twelve-year-old boy who must take care of both his irresponsible mother and increasingly irresponsible older sister. In *Iceman** (HarperCollins, 1994), a boy's growing-up and sports novel, Eric, 14, learns that he does not have to play dirty hockey in order to win. Both books were chosen by the American Library Association and *School Library Journal*. Recent novels include *Extreme Elvin* (HarperCollins, 1998), about the obese teenage boy introduced in *Slot Machine* (HarperCollins, 1995), and *Gold Dust* (HarperCollins, 2000), a sports story about a boy who befriends a Caribbean newcomer. For more information about Lynch, his other books, and a title entry, see *Dictionary, 1990–1994* [*Shadow Boxer*].

M

MACGREGOR, ROB, journalist; freelance writer of articles, novels, and books of nonfiction. He has published a dozen books that range widely in genre and subject, reflecting his interest in archaeology and the world of adventure, intrigue, mysticism, and romance. He has traveled extensively, exploring ancient Celtic, Greek, Aztec, Maya, and Inca ruins. His novels include seven about Indiana Jones; two of science fiction, *The Phantom* (Avon, 1996) and *Spawn* (Avon, 1997); and two that reflect his interest in Native Americans, *Prophecy Rock** (Simon & Schuster, 1995), an Edgar Allan Poe Winner, and *Hawk Moon** (Simon & Schuster, 1996), a Poe Nominee. Both are fast-paced murder-mysteries that feature Hopi-Caucasian high school-age Will Lansa and are particularly notable for their careful, sympathetic presentation of Native Americans and their ways and beliefs, in addition to telling good stories. He lives in southern Florida.

MAGGIE JOHNSON (*The Cage**), stringy black woman who drives the polar bear patrol car through the streets of Churchill every night. From Atlanta, she moved to northern Manitoba with her husband and two children, but he didn't last in the Arctic climate, which she had grown to love. She treats the discrimination that made it hard for her to get her job and the facial scars that will result from the bear mauling with wry humor, and she strikes up a warm friendship with Beryl* Findham after rescuing her from a stalking bear. The women share a fascination with the huge bears that they admit to each other is partly sensual.

THE MAGIC AND THE HEALING (O'Donohoe*, Nick, Berkley, 1994), fantasy novel in which people from present-day United States enter a mythological kingdom and interact with talking animals there. Having just failed Professor Truelove's small-animal medicine course, Western Virginia College of Veterinary Medicine student BJ* Vaughan empties out her locker and prepares to leave school. On her way out of the building, she is informed by sympathetic Laurie Kleinman, anesthesia technican, that Dr. Charles Dobbs, affectionately known as Sugar*, wishes to see her. Sugar shows her a long, elegant object that she recognizes as a broken horn, although she cannot immediately identify the animal from which it comes. Intrigued, she abandons her intention of dropping out of vet school and agrees to investigate the horn, using a book about unbiological species that he gives her, and to report on the object for the next large-animal rounds. On Monday, she and three other vet students, arrogant Dave* Wilson from tidewater Virginia, Lee* Anne Harrison from a Clydesdale farm in North Carolina, and shy, religious Annie* Taylor, pile into Sugar's truck, which is outfitted with medical equipment. While BJ explains what she has found out about the horn, which is a unicorn's, Sugar drives through the mountains into a remote valley, following a map that BJ recognizes is a xerox of one that she saw in a mysterious library book, *The Book of Strangeways*. The valley is the land of Crossroads*, a place of magic and exotic flora and such fauna as centaurs, griffins, werewolves, and rocs. They are greeted by a leering satyr named Mr. Field, who informs Sugar that trouble is brewing in Crossroads, since a certain, much-feared Inspector General has returned. Unknown to the vets, in another part of the kingdom, the king, Brandal, consults a seer, Harral, who informs him that heroes will come and save Crossroads. Brandal also bravely keeps tabs on the enemy, the beautiful, red-haired Morgan, by infiltrating her camp. On subsequent trips to the valley, each of the other three vet students takes a turn at presenting information about, and healing, injured Crossroads creatures: Annie tends to an ancient breed of sheep that are strangely dispirited; Dave checks over a huge, learned Griffin*, finally diagnosing gout; and in a particularly engrossing episode, Lee Anne helps a centaur give birth. On other visits, they also care for a flowerbinder, a kind of overgrown kitten, and a wyr (werewolf) and meet, among other unusual figures, a trader known as Owen* and an innkeeper called Stein*, whose establishment is the gathering place for the creatures. The students also learn that Sugar has been coming to the valley for some time to care for the inhabitants and is particularly interested in why such common human diseases as cancer do not occur. The final battle, a furiously fought cosmic conflict, takes place at Stein's inn and involves both humans and mythological beings. Among the elements that achieve triumph for the good side are the return of Owen the trader, who turns out to be King Brandal in disguise, and of the Griffin, who is the Inspector General, King Brandal's right-hand man. Since Morgan gets away, they know that peace is only temporary. Sugar remains interested in the valley for medical research, and BJ, her medical degree in hand, returns to the valley to serve the creatures as best she can. The book's main attraction arises from the great care with which Crossroads is depicted—its history, geography, population, economy, recreation, and worldview of peace, cooperation, and acceptance—and the extensive detail with which the medical procedures are described. Taken as a whole, this meticulously developed and credible tale of an otherworld and of its interaction with the real world to the betterment of both offers engrossing reading for those who enjoy broadly conceived, highly imaginative stories in the manner of J.R.R. Tolkien and C. S. Lewis. ALA; SLJ.

MAGUIRE, GREGORY (PETER) (1954–   ), born in Albany, New York; educator and freelance writer of fiction for children and adults, science fiction, and literary criticism and history. After completing his undergraduate work at State University of New York at Albany and his postgraduate work at Simmons College, he received his doctorate from Tufts University. He has been a staff member of the Center for the Study of Children's Literature and a professor at Simmons College and codirector of Children's Literature New England. He has published a dozen novels for the eight-to-fourteen range, among them, *Seven Spiders Spinning** (Clarion, 1994), a witty, amusing, fast-action fantasy of seven prehistoric spiders who make their way to the town of Hamlet, Vermont. An unusual school story chosen by both the American Library Association and *School Library Journal*, its companions in the Hamlet fantasy series are *Six Haunted Hairdos* (Clarion, 1997) and *Five Alien Eyes* (Clarion, 1998). Maguire has also written realistic novels like *Missing Sisters* (McElderry, 1994), about a girl in a Catholic orphanage; historical fiction like *The Good Liar* (Clarion, 1999), set in occupied France; and futuristic fiction like *I Feel Like the Morning Star* (Harper, 1989).

THE MAGUS (*The Thief**), the clever, knowledgeable scholar of King Sounis of Sounis. The magus organizes and leads the journey through the mountains of Eddis, the country to the north of Sounis, into Attolia. He alone knows the location in Attolia of the fabled stone called the Hamiathes' Gift, which ensures its holder of the throne of Eddis. The magus wishes to give the stone to King Sounis, so that the king can marry the queen of Eddis and thus also rule that land. When the magus brings Gen to the palace and tells him that he wishes him to steal the stone, Gen realizes that the magus is tough—the man will not hesitate to kill Gen if Gen refuses to help him—but he also realizes that the magus is fair. At the bridge over the river at the Eddisian border, the magus correctly suspects that Gen is recognized by the border guards as a fellow countryman. At the end, the magus has completed his responsibility but in a way other than he expected that he would, since it will be Sophos*, the king's heir, rather than the king of Sounis himself, who will marry the queen of Eddis.

MAKE LEMONADE (Wolff*, Virginia Euwer, Holt, 1993), contemporary realistic novel set in an unspecified American urban area and revolving around the problems of a teenage, single-parent mother. LaVaughn, 14, tells how she answers an ad for a baby-sitter and agrees to work for Jolly, a never-married mother of two, whose life LaVaughn is instrumental in turning for the better. The plot seems intentionally instructive, and authorities speak in textbook voices. Descriptions of Jolly's terrible living conditions, poverty, and near-helplessness; the simple, homely details of life with LaVaughn's own widowed Mom in their overcrowded apartment; and the plausible interactions between the leading characters are the book's best points. Josette Frank. Earlier the book won the following citations: ALA; Fanfare; and SLJ. A longer entry appears in *Dictionary, 1990–1994.*

MAKING UP MEGABOY (Walter*, Virginia, illus. Katrina Roeckelein, DK, 1998), essentially a case history of a middle-school boy who shoots Jae Lin Koh, the Korean proprietor of a liquor store in Santa Rosita, California, in the late 1990s. Each page gives a statement from a different person—his mother, his father, a television reporter, a witness, a teacher, his principal, various schoolmates, his victim's widow, his attorney—each seeing the incident from his or her own point of view and colored by his or her own self-interest or prejudice. All agree, however, that Robbie Jones, 13, is an unlikely child to have erupted in this sort of violence. He is quiet, inclined to daydream, interested mostly in drawing. Only his Mexican-American friend, Reuben, knows much about Robbie's obsession with a comic strip that the two are drawing together about Megaboy, an alien from another planet who masquerades as a regular American boy named Frankie Montalban but who, after consuming some of the megachips from the supply that he has brought with him, suddenly becomes powerful and able to rescue children and animals in trouble and right other wrongs. Reuben also knows about his crush on Tara Jameson, an attractive classmate who considers him "geeky," and about the handgun that Robbie's father keeps in his sock drawer, a weapon that Robbie once showed him. State-ments by Robbie's parents show his mother as indulgent yet out of touch with her son and his father as bigoted and unsympathetic, considering the boy some-thing of a sissy and concerned more about the cost of the lawyer whom he has engaged than his son's welfare. The reader is left to come to his or her own conclusion about why Robbie did the shooting and why he chose Mr. Koh. Although it is possible to blame his fantasy life as having divorced him from reality, it also seems that he was hoping to impress Tara and that he chose Mr. Koh as his victim because the storekeeper had once angered the girl and her friends by refusing to sell them cigarettes. The illustrations taking up at least half the pages dominate the book. Some are line drawings in blue ink, presum-ably those done by Robbie, mostly of spaceships and his comic-strip characters but some of Tara. Others are photographs, often pieced together into collages or expressionistic compositions, like the one of Tara's face in blue tones, set against a background of repeated pictures of her lips. The resulting brief novel is interesting but not entirely satisfying. ALA.

MALLORY POST (*Brothers and Sisters**), well-educated, blond, stylish white woman, 36, who comes from a posh part of Los Angeles and is a loan officer at Angel City National Bank. She becomes a friend and confidant of Esther* Jackson, although neither completely trusts the other because of race. Mallory's father was a cold, unfeeling man whose lack of validation of Mallory produced strong feelings of inadequacy toward men that have resulted in a series of affairs with wealthy, exploitative, married men. She finally takes control when Humphrey* Boone makes advances. The incident is reported to the bank hatchet man, who distorts her story into an accusation of attempted rape against Humphrey. Mallory is a sorry, but sympathetic, character, an effective foil for Esther.

MAMA LOGAN (*The Well: David's Story**), Caroline Logan, tall, big-boned, no-nonsense wife of Papa* Logan (Paul-Edward) and mother of David (who becomes Papa Logan in related stories and novels) and of Hammer* Logan. Caroline becomes Big Ma in the other books about the Logan family. Strong-minded, generous, staunchly Christian, she knows the danger of crossing the Simmses and other whites, but she also does not want her boys to be accused falsely by racially intolerant whites. She cleverly influences the sheriff by baking his favorite molasses bread when she knows he will be appearing soon at the Logan house to investigate the charge that her boys attacked Charlie Simms. When he arrives, the house is full of the aroma of molasses bread.

MAMA NAKAJI (*Under the Blood-Red Sun**), mother of Tomi and Kimi and wife of Taro*. Stern and proper, she is a good mother and wife and hardworking maid for the wealthy Wilsons, on whose land the Najakis' stilted shack stands. A picture bride, she came to Oahu from Japan when she was sixteen to marry, but before she arrived, her husband-to-be was killed in a gambling fight. When word got around the fishing boats of her plight, Taro, who was lonely, asked to marry her. He saved her from life as a bar girl or having to return home in disgrace. Mama is tough and persevering and encourages the children by reminding them that if they all work hard together, they will survive these bad times as she survived hers.

MAMAW (*The Window**), white grandmother of African-American Elgin* Taylor, mother of Marcella* Taylor and Aunt* Edna, and great-grandmother of Rayona Taylor, the eleven-year-old narrator. A heavyset woman, she wears her gray hair done up in a bun. She is a stickler for good manners and likes Rayona to address her as Ma'am. She loves to cook, feeds the household of women well, and is determined to teach Rayona how to cook. Mamaw's masterpiece is a special pineapple upside-down cake. Like the other two women, she pets and indulges Rayona, making the girl feel special.

MAMA WHITAKER (*Like Sisters on the Homefront**), Ruth Bell Gates Whitaker, Gayle Whitaker's mother. A widow, she supports herself, Gayle, her son, Junie, 18, and Gayle's baby son, Jose, by working as a maid. When unwed Gayle gets pregnant for the second time, Mama says that she allowed her one mistake, hustles her off to the abortion clinic, and then sends her south to Columbus, Georgia, to live with Mama's brother's family. After Gayle arrives there, she learns that, while Uncle Luther Gates opposed her coming, Miss Auntie (Virginia Gates, Luther's wife), who had been Mama's best friend when they were children, persuaded him to let her come. Gayle also learns that her mother had once been a fine singer in church and glee club and that she, Miss Auntie, and another girl had formed a singing group that everyone thought was Motown-bound. But Mama and Gayle's father, David, eloped right after graduation, Luther disowned them, and the two left for New York, where David lined up a recording contract. The recording company was shady, however, and David fell sick of tuberculosis and pneumonia and died. Miss Auntie, who tells Gayle about her parents, says that she always felt guilty about helping Mama and David sneak around. Later, Gayle prevents Cookie* Gates from running away to join Stacey Alexander.

MANDY O'DELL (*A Place to Call Home**), beautiful, golden-haired five-year-old half sister of Anna. Mandy has a complex personality, a combination of whiny childishness, astute manipulation, stoic acceptance, and stubborn spirit. She is devoted to Anna and trusts her, although she never lets her forget the one time that Anna promised to be home when she arrived from school and was not there. Mandy's understanding of their mother's problems is, in some ways, surprisingly mature, and, although her experience makes her sometimes cringe, expecting to be hit, she remembers the happier times and her mother's occasional cheering, if unrealistic, optimism. Mandy's forthrightness about their foster mother's unkindness is instrumental in getting her and their baby brother, Casey, into a better home. Although the three children presumably have different fathers, she and Casey look alike, and all three are emotionally close.

MA RACHEL (*The Well: David's Story**), grandmother of David and Hammer* Logan. Like Hammer, she feels that whites have no business setting foot on Logan land, just because they want to, and no right to use Logan water, just because they think they should. She is very old and is considered somewhat unbalanced. Whenever the Simmses or any other whites come, the rest of the family tries to keep Ma Rachel from finding out lest she cause trouble. Ma Rachel hates all whites because many years ago when she was born, her mother's white plantation mistress refused to let Ma Rachel's mother call her baby Rachel, because she had given that name to her own daughter. When Ma Rachel's mother persisted in calling her baby girl by that name anyway, the mistress had Ma Rachel's mother brutally whipped.

MARCELLA TAYLOR (*The Window**), white mother of Caucasian-African-American Elgin* Taylor and grandmother of narrator Rayona Taylor, whose mother, Christine, is Native American. Marcella meets Rayona at the airport in Louisville with a tremendous hug and a Raggedy Ann doll, delighted at finally meeting the granddaughter whom she has longed to see for so many years. Since she is not employed outside the home, she spends a lot of time with Rayona, taking the girl to Churchill Downs for the races and to Penney's for clothes. Rayona says that when the two of them receive inquiring looks from waitresses and salesladies because Marcella is white and Rayona brown, her grandmother never lets on that she sees. Marcella tends to stick to the familiar, even if it is incorrect. For example, she persists in calling Rayona Ramona, from a movie that she liked, even though she knows that it is wrong. She had loved Rayona's grandfather very much and thought him the handsomest man who ever lived. When she remarks that Rayona is very beautiful, too, her words embarrass the girl.

MARGALO EPPS (*Bad Girls**), one of the two fifth-grade girls to whom the title refers. Less bad than mischievous, she is manipulative and sneaky in getting her way, causing trouble, and seeing what trouble might be caused. She is seated in alphabetical order next to Mikey* Elsinger, who becomes her best friend. Margalo seldom confronts situations, seeming to go along with whatever is being said or done. She has learned this behavior from being in a large, blended family. She is a good speller and poor at sports, unlike Mikey, who is poor at spelling and great at sports. Margalo was named after the bird in E. B. White's *Stuart Little*.

MARICONDA, BARBARA, teacher, musician, and writer for middle elementary and early adolescent readers who makes her home in Connecticut. Nominated for the Edgar Allan Poe Award, *Turn the Cup Around** (Delacorte, 1997) tells how finding out who painted a cat on a rock on the Maine coast leads a twelve-year-old girl to learn the truth about her absent father. Mariconda has written board books for the very young, *Yes, Please!* (Modem, 1987) and *Looking Good* (Modem, 1987), and humorous chapter books about two adventurous witches, *Witch Way to the Country* (Dell, 1996) and *Witch Way to the Beach* (Dell, 1997).

MARISOL GUZMAN (*Hard Love**), high school senior who helps John Galardi, Jr., deal with several problems. She is petite, with short dark hair, a quick tongue, and a lively mind. John meets her through their common interest in zines (self-published literary magazines) and is romantically attracted to her, although he knows from her zine that she is a lesbian. She is Puerto Rican American, having been adopted by a white American social worker and a Cuban-American college professor. Her mother has difficulty accepting her daughter's sexual orientation, and Marisol resents that fact. She also resents her birth mother giving her up, abandoning her, Marisol calls it. Although on the surface she seems irritated that John asks her to the prom, and she appears to hate the idea of a formal dress and all the trimmings, she later confesses that she liked being able to have some of the things that had been denied her because of her lesbianism. She appears to have a lot of unresolved problems in her life. John tells her that his name is Giovanni, Italian for John, the name he publishes under, and she calls him Gio. Later, when she finds out that Gio is not his real name, she accuses him of lying to her, and that leads to his examining other aspects of his life.

MARJAN (*Shadow Spinner**), the "shadow spinner," or storyteller, of the title. Muslim, she becomes the foster daughter and servant of Jewish Uncle Eli and Auntie Chava, a most unusual situation for a Muslim. After Marjan was crippled when she was eight years old, she was given to them because they were known to be kind people. Marjan's personal problem in the novel is her inability to understand why her mother deliberately maimed her. She eventually realizes that her mother intended it for her good. Auntie Chava worries about her because in the Muslim society of that time Marjan is an outcast because of her physical deformity. Since she can tell stories well, Majran becomes a slave in the Sultan's harem, brought there by Dunyazad*, the sister of the Sultan's consort, Shahrazad*, in order to replenish Shahrazad's supply of tales. As Marjan tells her story, she fills it with details of palace life, the teeming city, and her own near escapes and close encounters, a vivid, lively, and suspenseful narrative that, in the final analysis, is a story about the power of story to enrich and change lives.

MARTIN, ANN M(ATTHEWS) (1955–), born in Princeton, New Jersey; received her B.A. from Smith College; former educator, editorial assistant, copywriter, and editor for publishing houses, most recently for Scholastic Books Services and Books for Young Readers; since 1985 a freelance writer and editor. Since 1983, she has compiled an impressive list of more than seventy books for children and young people, most them in such series as the Baby-Sitters Club, Baby-Sitters Club Super Specials, and Baby-Sitters Little Sisters. Although formulaic in plots and stereotyped in characters, these novels have been perennially popular with girls. Her other novels range more widely in subject matter, dealing with such matters as dyslexia, adoption, autism, and death of a parent. All have been praised for their authentic-sounding dialogue and their grounding in actuality. With Paula Danziger*, she has written *P.S. Longer Letter Later** (Scholastic, 1998), an epistolary novel of friendship and family life, in which two girls, who used to be classmates, reminisce about old times and share confidences. It was a choice of the American Library Association.

MARTINEZ, VICTOR (1954–), born in Fresno, California; poet and novelist. After studying at California State University at Fresno, he attended Stanford University on a postgraduate fellowship in creative writing. Named by the editors of *The Horn Book Magazine* to their Fanfare list, *Parrot in the Oven: Mi Vida** (HarperCollins, 1996), an episodic story about a Mexican-American boy growing up in central California amid poverty, prejudice, and violence, was praised in particular for its evocation of the culture. Martinez has at various times worked as a field laborer, welder, truck driver, firefighter, teacher, and office clerk. He has contributed to such periodicals as *Iowa Review* and *Blooms-bury Review* and published a book of stories and poems, *A la Conquista del Corazon* (with Juan Antonio Diaz; Uruguay: Tradinco, 1993).

MARVELOUS MARVIN AND THE PIONEER GHOST (Pryor*, Bonnie, il-lus. Melissa Sweet, Morrow, 1995), contemporary, realistic mystery-detective novel with family-story, ghost-story, and environmental-awareness aspects set in the small American town of Liberty Corners one recent April. Introspective Marvin Fremont, 9, his active twin, Sarah, and Mean Ernie Farrow, the biggest kid in fourth grade, solve the mystery that begins when Marvin reports seeing what he is sure is a ghost down by Liberty Creek. He remembers that the air grew icy and that the man wore ragged, old-fashioned clothes. Although Sarah is skeptical, she and Marvin go to the creek to hunt for clues, Sarah taking her camera along as a joke. Ernie arrives and suggests that the three of them start a detective agency, since they were instrumental in solving a mystery once before. Later that morning, they encounter old Mr. Dinkerhoff at his run-down plastics factory. Mr. Dinkerhoff introduces them to his nephew, Mr. Klinger, who has come to help him operate the place. Mr. Dinkerhoff also proudly shows them the new plastic finger puppets soon to be introduced for the Christmas trade. Back at the creek, the children discover dead fish and a slimy red sub-stance on the stones, of which Sarah takes pictures. They now decide that they have two mysteries on their hands—the ghost and the red substance and dead fish. Joined by a new girl in the neighborhood, Kyla Cross, they trace the red stuff upstream to a drain pipe from Mr. Dinkerhoff's factory. Since Mr. Dink-erhoff is known to be a kind, civic-minded gentleman, they are sure that he does not realize that dumping from his plastics factory is harming the creek. That evening while they camp out by the creek, Marvin senses the same unset-tled atmosphere that he felt when he spied the ghost. Later, when a heavy rain causes the tent to leak, and they run to Ernie's house for shelter, they see a ragged man by the creek. Mrs. Farrow says that maybe they saw the local legendary ghost. Various leads, clues, and assorted happenings occupy their attention for several days. They observe media reporters investigating the creek water, and there are more ghostly sightings. At the public library, they learn that a man (later identified as appliance-store owner Mr. Snyder) has also been inquiring about the local ghost, reputed to be reclusive Henry Jones of the early 1800s. Henry was thought to have murdered his brother, who mysteriously dis-appeared. When the children ask Mr. Dinkerhoff about the red substance, he says that one time the dye switch was not turned off when it should have been and that he is sorry if the dye fouled the creek. The children also notice Mr. Snyder and Mr. Klinger in deep conversation and learn that Mr. Snyder is cir-culating a petition to shut down the factory. Other untoward events occur, in-cluding the atmosphere turning icy at critical moments. The children decide that at these times Henry the ghost is warning them of impending danger. During a flash flood, they are pursued by someone down the creek and hastily take refuge in a cave, where they discover and later report a very old skeleton, apparently of the long-lost brother. The assumption is that the brother was not murdered but probably perished in a flash flood. Eventually, the children learn that Mr. Klinger has been in cahoots with Mr. Snyder to drive Mr. Dinkerhoff out of business by dumping red dye in the creek at night and playing ghost to scare people away. The two men have hoped to force Mr. Dinkerhoff to sell out to a national motel chain, a move that would have made them personally rich. Although clichéd in characters and plot, the book combines a winningly light tone; sprightly pace; gothic atmosphere and conventions; adults on the fringes (where children like them to be); plenty of action; and likable, active children in a club situation, features that appeal to the middle-grade set. A twist is that Sarah is the more outgoing, conciliatory, and athletic of the twins, while Marvin prefers reading and recording his observations in a notebook. Smudgy black and white, slightly comic illustrations picture incidents and add atmosphere. Poe Nominee.

MARY ALICE DOWDEL (*A Long Way from Chicago: A Novel in Stories**), seven at the book's start, thirteen when it ends, Joey* Dowdel's younger sister and granddaughter of Grandma* Dowdel. When she is younger, Mary Alice thinks life in Grandma's small town is boring, spends a lot of her time jumping rope, and hates having to use the privy. As Grandma requires, she and Joey help about the place, processing tomatoes and picking gooseberries for Grandma's famous pies, and she and Joey accompany Grandma on various jaunts. As she grows older, she takes up tap dancing, as do many girls during the Great Depression, and later she learns ballroom dancing so that she is ready for high school dances and mixers. Two scenes in which she figures strongly are the one in which she helps an abused waitress elope with her boyfriend (the episode in which Joey pretends to be the ghost of a deceased brakeman) and the one, at the town's Centennial Celebration, in which she and Ray Veech enchant the audience with their ballroom maneuvers. Even Joey is impressed with the way that she sweeps around the stage wearing Grandma's elegant, old-fashioned wedding dress with bustle and train.

MATTHEW SPICER (*Pigs Don't Fly**), merchant whose house Summer and her crew approach by accident, taking it for an inn. A kindly, rather shy and lonely man, Matthew welcomes them and treats them lavishly, getting his friend and associate in his trade to the East to treat Sir* Gilman with his advanced medical skills and keeping them with him as the knight recovers. With Summer he is courteous and interesting, telling her of his caravans that ply the spice trade and of the strange lands that they cross. Although she does not expect his proposal, still thinking of herself as grossly fat and ugly, she genuinely likes him and knows he would be a far better husband than she could normally expect, even though she has some education. Still, her infatuation with Sir Gilman makes her reject his offer, and later her great love for Wimperling*, now become

Jasper, the dragon, makes her leave the safe haven of Matthew's house in an effort to reach Cathay and find her love. Still, she writes Matthew a note saying that she expects to be back in a year and a day, ready to settle down if he still wants her. Matthew is a good, kind man. One small, but telling, gift from him is cloth for an outfit that he asks her to make, supposedly for his sister who is her size and build but actually intended for Summer herself.

MAURIZIO (*Stones in the Water**), Italian soldier whom Roberto encounters at the Black Sea and whom he at first fears. Roberto hides his identity and knowledge of the Italian language from the soldier because he thinks that the man may kill him or turn him in as a runaway. The soldier is tense and nervous and chatters away while they are fleeing. While he forces Roberto to do his bidding, he is kind to the boy and generous with his food. From him Roberto learns that the villages in Ukraine are deserted, the fields empty, and the few remaining people starving because Stalin has sent the farmers to Siberia. Maurizio knows the area around the Black Sea and heads toward the Mediterranean, where Roberto wishes to go. After Roberto realizes that he can trust Maurizio, he tells Maurizio his story. In turn, Maurizio tells him that he deserted because he has had enough of war and wishes to go home to join those who are protesting against the fighting. Maurizio is convenient for the plot but not entirely credible.

MAURY, JIM (*Cezanne Pinto: A Memoir**), the elderly coachman for the Canadian Ramsey family. Maury takes a special interest in Cezanne Pinto and continues to teach the boy proper English, picking up where Tamar* left off. He takes on the white stable boy, Bart, who baits Cezanne and calls him names like "nigger" and "darky," and forbids Bart to treat Cezanne disrespectfully again. Maury comforts the lonely boy, who soon sleeps behind a partition near Maury in the attic. Maury has a deep voice, loves to sing gospel songs, and has veterinary skills. Cezanne says that he has "a fine old face" and loves him very much. After Maury dies of a stroke or heart attack, Cezanne leaves Canada for the United States, hoping to join the Union forces in order to help those who are fighting to free his people.

MAYNARD GLENN (*While No One Was Watching**), Asian-Indian-born, adopted son of Dr. Glenn, about ten. His house is next door to that of the Johnsons, whose bikes and rabbit are stolen by Earl* and Frankie* Foster and Wayne* Bonner. A bright boy, Maynard is determined to trace the culprits and does so in true detective-story fashion, by deduction, observation, and computer techniques. His best friend and ally in crime-solving is Addie Johnson, a girl his age whose rabbit, Flag, Frankie stole and named Spot. Dr. Glenn punishes Maynard for wandering about without permission, an action that contrasts sharply with the lack of attention and supervision that the Foster children receive from their Aunt Lula. Through Maynard the Fosters are reported to Social Services and are reunited with their father. Maynard is one of the most interesting figures in the novel.

THE MAZE (Hobbs*, Will, Morrow, 1998), contemporary, realistic, sociological problem, boy's growing-up, and adventure novel set for about two weeks mostly in the Maze, a rugged portion of Canyonlands National Park in Utah. After the death of his beloved grandmother, his only relative, and a series of foster homes, angry, unhappy Rick Walker, 14, of California is sentenced to six months in a detention home in Las Vegas, declared incorrigible for throwing stones at a street sign and stealing a couple of CDs (compact discs). He runs away from the home to avoid a terrible beating for reporting personnel thefts to authorities. After hitching a ride, he ends up in the little town of Hanksville, Utah, where he hides inside a truck that carries supplies to a remote campsite in the Canyonlands. He meets a biologist, scar-faced, moody Lon* Peregrino, who is working on a condor-reintroduction project and simply accepts the cornered, frightened boy. Shortly after arriving, Rick observes Nuke* Carlile and a sidekick, Gunderson, surly, thuggish, big-talking men, and Nuke's pit bull, Jasper, arrive in a Humvee. They snoop around the campsite, spouting antigovernment talk and denigrating Peregrino's work. Rick also snoops around and, among other interesting discoveries, finds that Peregrino might not be the biologist's real name. The boy and the biologist get along well, however, and the previously taciturn man begins to open up as he explains his work and condor life to the boy. Rick finds that he likes Lon, enjoys learning about the birds and the sport of hang gliding, at which Lon is expert, and gains an appreciation for the rugged area, which he explores in a limited way. Lon is sure that the two surly men are pottery hunters out to steal Native-American artifacts and that they are afraid that he might expose their illegal activity. After the men kill Lon's favorite among the young condors, Maverick, tension builds. The two men steal and ruin Lon's equipment, including his radio. On one of his canyon jaunts, Rick observes them working with guns, ammunition, and materials that they seem to have stored in a cave, apparently to make bombs. Increasingly hostile, they refuse to help when Rick is caught in a storm in a canyon, leaving him to extricate himself from a very dicey situation, among other instances of antagonistic behavior. Matters come to a head when another bird is endangered. Lon rescues it and is also caught in a storm. Rick uses the hang glider to save him, and after great effort they get themselves and the bird back to camp. While these various activities are occurring, Rick tells his story to Lon, who, as it happens, has a similar background and has changed his name. Lon asks to be relieved of his duties temporarily, takes Rick back to the judge who sentenced him, and with the help of a friendly librarian at the detention center and Rick's social worker, persuades the judge to review the case. Rick is placed in a group home in Arizona, where he is to go to high school and is also to spend summers helping Lon with the condor project. The future looks brighter, since Rick seems to have found his way out of the literal and figurative mazes in which he has been caught. An exciting, action-filled plot; a likable, if stereotyped, protagonist; suitably functioning stock characters; enthralling details of setting and bird life; thrilling glider flights; and such well-handled, if obvious, parallels as fledgling birds and fledgling boy; the maze concept; the facial scars that Lon has and the one that the boy suffers in his escape; and the alluded-to myth of Icarus and Daedalus combine for a topnotch adventure novel. ALA; Poe Nominee.

MAZER, HARRY (1925–   ), born in New York City; long a popular writer of young adult novels, some with his wife, Norma Fox Mazer*. He served in the U.S. Army Air Force in World War II, receiving the Purple Heart and Air Medal, was graduated from Union College, and received his master's degree from Syracuse University. He held various jobs, among them teaching English, before becoming a full-time writer in 1963. He and his wife have four children and have made their home in Manhattan and Jamesville, New York. Although his work has been criticized as contrived and trite, he has been praised for his empathy in presenting the problems of growing up. Among the best known of his some eighteen books is *Snowbound* (Delacorte, 1973), about two teenagers caught in a blizzard, and *The Last Mission* (Delacorte, 1979), about a Jewish-American youth captured by Germans in World War II. The content of some books is evident from their titles: *I Love You, Stupid!* (Crowell, 1981), *Hey Kid! Does She Love Me?* (Crowell, 1985), and *The Girl of His Dreams* (Crowell, 1987). With his wife, he has written three books, the first of which received the most attention: *The Solid Gold Kid* (Delacorte, 1977). Individually, he published *The Wild Kid** (Simon & Schuster, 1998), a *School Library Journal* choice about a Down's syndrome boy of twelve who runs away to the wilds of Vermont, where he becomes friends with an almost feral youth. He has also published a book of short stories and edited a collection of stories about guns.

MAZER, NORMA FOX (1931–   ), born in New York City; writer best known for her many popular realistic problem novels for adolescents and the recipient of many honors and citations. She has written individually and also with her husband, novelist Harry Mazer*. *When She Was Good** (Scholastic, 1997), chosen by *School Library Journal*, is an almost plotless story of two sisters, the older of whom regularly abuses the younger. It excels in depicting Em's feelings of despair and her few short moments of joy. A recent book is *Good Night, Maman* (Harcourt, 1999), a historical novel about Holocaust refugees. For more information about Mazer and title entries, see *Dictionary, 1960–1984* [*A Figure of Speech*; *Saturday, the Twelfth of October*; *Taking Terri Mueller*] and *Dictionary, 1985–1989* [*After the Rain*].

MCCRUMB, SHARYN, born in North Carolina; recipient of many awards for her southern crime fiction and other writings set in Appalachia, although she has also written novels set in Scotland. Her two most prominent series are those starring Elizabeth MacPherson, a detective and forensic anthropologist, among them *Lovely in Her Bones* (Avon, 1985) and *Highland Laddie Gone* (Avon, 1986), and her "Ballad Series," whose main character is Sheriff Spencer Arrowood of Mitchell County, Tennessee, near the North Carolina border. Among these are *If I Ever Return, Pretty Peggy-O* (Scribner, 1990), *The Hangman's Beautiful Daughter* (Scribner, 1992), and *She Walks These Hills** (Scribner, 1995), all replete with Appalachian history, folklore, and local color, as well as a brooding tone of mystery and impending doom found in many folk songs. McCrumb is a graduate of the University of North Carolina and has her M.A. degree from Virginia Tech, where she has also taught journalism and Appalachian studies. She has made her home in Virginia.

MCGRAW, ELOISE JARVIS (1915–2000), born in Houston, Texas; artist and novelist who published outstanding books over a long period. Her moving fantasy *The Moorchild** (Simon & Schuster, 1996) was named an honor book for both the Boston Globe and the Newbery awards. For earlier biographical information and title entries, see *Dictionary, 1859–1959* [*Moccasin Trail*], *Dictionary, 1960–1984* [*The Golden Goblet*; *A Really Weird Summer*], and *Dictionary, 1990–1994* [*Tangled Web*].

MCKINLEY, ROBIN (1952–   ), born in Warren, Ohio; editor, novelist. Her retelling of the folktale "Beauty and the Beast" in a novel titled *Beauty** (Harper, 1978) was chosen as a Phoenix Award Honor Book in 1998. A second retelling of the same tale in a more complicated form, *Rose Daughter* (Greenwillow, 1997), was named to the American Library Association's Young Adult list. For earlier biographical information and title entries, see *Dictionary, 1960–1984* [*Beauty*; *The Blue Sword*] and *Dictionary, 1985–1989* [*The Hero and the Crown*; *The Outlaws of Sherwood*].

ME AND RUPERT GOODY (O'Connor*, Barbara, Farrar, 1999), realistic novel of family life, developing friendship, and growing up set one recent summer in the small mountain community of Claytonville, North Carolina, not far from Cherokee. Narrator Jennalee Helton, 11, regularly escapes her large, contentious, "ton-of-hell" family by going down the road to Uncle Beau Goody's country store. She takes pride in helping the gentle, arthritic, elderly man with such chores as stocking shelves and sorting fresh produce. One night after supper the "skinniest black man" Jennalee has ever seen appears. He says that his name is Rupert Goody and that Uncle Beau is his father. Jennalee is shocked and angry when Uncle Beau simply accepts Rupert and sends her home for the evening. In the weeks that follow Jennalee becomes more and more jealous of gentle-natured Rupert, who, although obviously slow-minded, gradually assumes tasks about the store. While some townspeople are skeptical that Rupert is Uncle Beau's son, others remember Hattie Baker, the pretty black woman who Uncle Beau says is Rupert's mother and who simply up and disappeared, taking "my heart with her." Uncle Beau tries to help Jennalee adjust to having Rupert around. He takes them ruby mining at Cherokee, where Rupert comes up with one that the man in charge says even in its raw state is worth $1,800. On the way home, Jennalee finds that Rupert has put the huge stone in her bag, perhaps as a gesture of friendship. When Uncle Beau asks Jennalee what about Rupert bothers her so and why she is so angry at the young man, she has no good answer. A late summer thunderstorm paralyzes Rupert with such fear that Jennalee rushes out to retrieve his bike. As Rupert hugs her in thanks, she notices that Uncle Beau, who has been sitting on the metal porch glider, has suffered some sort of attack. Later, she is relieved to learn that Uncle Beau is going to be all right but meanly tells Rupert that the attack was his fault. He runs away, and when she visits Uncle Beau in the hospital, she evades his questions about Rupert but realizes that she must find the young man. She leaves juice and a sandwich at the edge of the nearby woods, where she suspects he is hiding. The first night Uncle Beau is home, Rupert returns, dirty and wet but safe. He asks if Uncle Beau is angry at him for making him sick. When Uncle Beau says lightning did it, Rupert does not give Jennalee away, and she feels extremely ashamed. Rupert is generous toward her in other ways, too, among them choosing her favorite pound cake to celebrate Uncle Beau's birthday rather than his favorite fried trout. When, at vacation Bible school, a boy calls Rupert a "retard," she hauls off and slugs him, leaves abruptly for the store, and presents Rupert with the wallet that she has made. In August Uncle Beau yearns for pinto beans and starts them cooking on a hot plate that Rupert has repaired. While they are out taking a walk, they notice that the house is smoking. Rupert races home and carries out everything that he can, including Uncle Beau's cherished picture of Hattie. Uncle Beau hugs them both close to him, and for the first time Jennalee realizes that she and Rupert have something very important in common: both love Uncle Beau with all their hearts. Eventually, neighbors and friends rebuild the store and Beau's living quarters, but no one tells Rupert that the hot plate caused the fire. The whole community celebrates the opening, and Rupert and Jennalee realize that they are now friends. Jennalee tells her story in hill-country dialect and extensive dialogue. Her jealousy and anger are credible, and she is a sympathetic figure, even though she shades the truth to Uncle Beau and her family. Uncle Beau and Rupert are stereotypes but sufficiently individualized. Uncle Beau's concern for the biracial young man is understandable, and it is to the credit of the community and to Uncle Beau that everyone accepts Rupert. SLJ.

MEAN MARGARET (Seidler*, Tor, illus. Jon Agee, HarperCollins, 1997), gentle fantasy concerning small animals of the woods and fields, featuring two woodchucks and their interaction with one small, disagreeable human. Fred, a refined, careful bachelor woodchuck, lives in a tidy, meticulously kept burrow, where he can putter about as he wishes without ruffling his fur or exposing it to dew, resting in his antique chair in the soft light of a jar of glowworms. His only visitor is a striped snake who occasionally chases prey down the hole but doesn't stay for conversation. Fred's set routine is broken by recurring dreams, nightmares in which he is married, a prospect that makes him shudder. Although he has no desire for a wife, the dreams drive him to look for a likely female woodchuck, first at the greenhouse, where he is disgusted by one with dirty paws and another who chews with her mouth open. Eventually the snake, queried, recommends one who lives under the big stump, a young female with a nice smile who is in mourning for her mother. Fred finds a ravishing female named Babette, but he also discovers that she has many suitors, among them a mink, a raccoon, and an otter, and worse, she has three noisy children. Then he sees a young woodchuck less gorgeous than Babette but with a lovely smile, who is called "Aunt Phoebe" by the children playing nearby. Cautiously, Fred suggests that they go for a walk next Sunday, when she is not baby-sitting her sister's family. He shows her his burrow and, after another lonely week, fixes her Sunday dinner and proposes. Although Fred keeps his distance from his new wife for fear of ruffling his fur, they live happily for some time. Not far from the burrow is the home of a human family named Hubble, a grossly overweight couple with nine children, the youngest of whom is so obnoxious that her three next youngest siblings decide to do away with her. One night, stuffing a banana into her mouth to silence her constant howling, they cart her out of town and dump her in a ditch not far from Fred's burrow. The next morning, awakened by her bawling, the woodchuck couple find her. Overcome by maternal instinct, Phoebe pushes her into their burrow where she takes up most of the living room. Screaming, she rejects all the food that they try to give her. With helpful suggestions from the snake, a squirrel, and a goat, they feed her a bowl of milk, berries, and honey, after Fred follows a bear to a bees' tree and pries off a chunk of comb, getting well stung and sticky. Calling her Margaret, they soon are working around the clock to satisfy her, and she is growing bigger all the time. Trying to enlarge the burrow, Fred causes a cave-in, and they move to a cave shared by the snake, the squirrel, a skunk, and a couple of bats. Soon all the animals, in thrall to Margaret's appetite, are fully engaged in finding her food. Having been flooded out, Babette and her three children move into the cave, and the snake, the only one who hasn't welcomed Fred and Phoebe, falls under her charm. Margaret, however, only gets worse, throwing the young woodchucks around like handballs and stomping on the snake and the squirrel's tail. For revenge, snake whispers in her ear as she sleeps, "Stomp on skunk's tail." Acting on this suggestion, Margaret gets a direct spray from the skunk, stumbles into the fresh air, and runs off, howling. When they cannot find her, Fred, to comfort Phoebe, puts his arm around her and even cuddles with her at night. In the meantime, the Hubbles are so worried about their ninth child that both parents lose weight and start eating sensibly. Then Mr. Hubble's cousin, who runs the pig farm, arrives with a very fat, smelly child in his arms that he has found in the sty. At first, her siblings are terrified that she will tell on them, and they threaten to smother her, but she bargains with them to take her back to the ditch where they dumped her. She evicts a badger from Fred's burrow, crawls in and cleans it up, and sends word by the bats that it is now all better, and she even tells them to say thanks. The next day, Phoebe has a baby, a girl they name Patience. Although their old burrow is now inhabitable, she and Fred decide to stay with their friends in the cave. Since none of this is meant to be taken seriously, Margaret's conversion does not seem too unlikely. The strongest elements are descriptions of Fred's elegant living quarters and his frustrated efforts to get rid of Margaret without losing Phoebe. SLJ.

MELBA FOSS (*The Ornament Tree**), girl of about fourteen hired as replacement cook when the old one leaves in a huff. Melba is dirty, rude, and lazy, but she is an adequate cook. Audra and Winnie Devereaux, who found her at a settlement house where they do good works, plan to teach her to read and better herself, but Melba has other ideas. She takes up with James, the young handyman, and they both are reported by Clare* Harris, Audra's granddaughter, to ridicule the idea of education. Melba is especially disagreeable to Bonnie Shaster, but when Bonnie retorts with a disparaging remark about Melba's inability to add, Audra reprimands her young cousin, saying that one must never criticize those less privileged. After that, Bonnie bites her tongue rather than reply until she sees Melba with a man who approached her when she first arrived in Seattle and no one met her at the station. He seemed friendly and offered to find her a job in "a nice little hotel," but she afterward learns that he recruits waifs and newcomers as prostitutes. Audra sends him on his way but somewhat later finds that Melba is pregnant and will not, or cannot, name the father. Audra arranges that the girl go to a home for unmarried mothers in Portland. Bonnie is puzzled at the mores that keep her from helping with the cooking for the boarders because she is too young yet make it suitable to hire Melba. Since Bonnie has worked hard on her mother's farm and for her demanding Aunt Suze, far harder than Melba works, she does not understand the distinction. To Clare it is simple: "We come from a good family."

THE MELLOWER (*The Ear, the Eye, and the Arm**), Anthony Horsepool-Worthingham, Praise Singer employed by General Amadeus Matsika to calm and soothe the feelings of the family members, which he does by fulsome praise and some hypnosis. Of the English tribe, the Mellower is the son of Mrs. Horsepool-Worthingham, an unprincipled woman who holds the Matsika children in "quarantine" for chicken pox, refusing to notify their family of their whereabouts since she hopes that her son can persuade the General to offer a sizable reward. The Mellower himself has done most of the care of the children in his official role, but they often find him asleep when he is supposedly supervising them. He has a *shava*, or talent, for storytelling and has given them, especially Tendai, a love and appreciation of the world of the imagination and the history and culture of their country. Though a weak person, he has a basically good nature.

A MESSAGE FROM THE MATCH GIRL (Lisle*, Janet Taylor, Orchard, 1995), third in a series of fantasy-mysteries for middle-school children called collectively Investigators of the Unknown or IOU Books. When Walter Kew tells his friends, Georgina Rush and Poco Lambert, all about nine years old, that his mother is trying to talk to him, Georgina thinks that he is crazy, and Poco speculates that he may have some sort of built-in antenna to communicate with ghosts, since they both have been told that his parents were killed when he was an infant, before he came to live with his grandparents, the Dockers. The two girls, both introduced in the first book of the series, *The Gold Dust Letters*, are very different. Georgina is assertive, impatient, and practical. Poco is small, precise, and addicted to long pauses for conversations with birds and rabbits. They meet Walter, as he has requested, in Andersen Park near the statue of the Little Match Girl, which is isolated on a slight hill away from the other figures of fairy tale. A pale, overly polite, timid boy, Walter has finally insisted that his grandmother, now a widow, old, and very deaf, must have something of his parents to tell or show him, and she has produced a snapshot of a baby looking over the shoulder of a woman, his face and little arm, with a dangling mitten, and the back of the woman's head all that show, except that in the background is the statue of the Little Match Girl. This seems a slim bit of the story of his origins, which his grandmother claims she cannot remember, but Walter is hungry for any connection to his past and is sure that his mother has returned from death and is trying to get in touch with him. Poco understands his need, and Georgina suspects that there is something fishy about Mrs. Docker's defective memory, both reasons to investigate further. The waitress at the sandwich shop just outside the park gate seems to know a good deal about the children, and they notice that the Little Match Girl is visible from the shop window. Soon Walter begins getting messages from, he believes, his mother's spirit. The first comes through the regular mail, just a plain envelope addressed to him containing three matches. When he investigates the Little Match Girl, he finds in the statue's pocket another envelope holding a tiny blue mitten, just like the one dangling from the sleeve of the baby in the picture. From old Miss Bone they discover the real story of Walter's connection to Mrs. Docker: he was left in her large casserole dish after a church supper. She and her husband obeyed a note tucked in with the picture beside him, saying to tell no one but to keep him and that Walter was his name. Old Mr. Docker gave him the Kew surname, standing for Questionmark. In the next weeks, Walter gets other items—a newborn baby sweater; a locket with a picture of a soldier, the bracelet saying "Walter" from a hospital pediatric unit; and finally a lock of hair. Walter thinks that his mother's spirit has left each of these things with the Little Match Girl, and he is contented now, believing that she must return to the land of the dead. He has acquired new confidence, makes other friends, and, with the help of Mrs. Docker's new hearing aid, begins communicating better with his foster grandmother. Although the reader, like Georgina and Poco, can suspect that the waitress no longer at the sandwich shop was the real mother, returning to town for a glimpse of the son whom she gave up nine years earlier, some little fantasy mystery remains in the contributions to the story of Juliette, the old Siamese cat left by a friend in Poco's care, who seems to know what is going on and influences action at various points. While the plot is not complex, and the psychology is fairly obvious, humor and clever touches of characterization lift the book above the average offering for this age. Georgina's annoyance with the Andersen story (why doesn't the match girl hustle up some wood and use just one match to light a fire and keep herself warm, saving the rest of her matches to sell instead of freezing to death?) and Poco's defense of it (each match produces a beautiful picture that makes her so happy that they are worth sacrificing) give amusing and thought-provoking critiques of the literary work. SLJ.

MEYER, CAROLYN (1935–   ), born in Lewistown, Pennsylvania; teacher, author of many books of both fiction and nonfiction for young people. She is a graduate of Bucknell University, has taught at the Institute of Children's Literature, and was a lecturer at Bucknell at two different periods in the 1970s. Her novel *White Lilacs* (Harcourt, 1993) tells of the destruction of African-American Freedomtown to make a park for the white community of Dillon, Texas. *Jubilee Journey** (Harcourt, 1997) picks up the story seventy-five years later when the granddaughter and great-granddaughter of the protagonist come from Connecticut for the Juneteenth celebration to discover a different, but still prejudiced, town. Meyer has made her home in Denton, Texas.

MICK HARTE WAS HERE (Park*, Barbara, Knopf, 1995), sociological and psychological problem novel set in an unnamed American city in recent years. Narrator Phoebe Harte, 13, tells in an intimate tone and with ironic humor about how her brother, Mick, 12, dies of a head injury in a bicycle accident and about how her family copes with their loss. Phoebe early informs the reader that her beloved brother is dead, then traces the circumstances of his death, concentrating mostly on those of the month following the event. She ruefully describes the fight that they had the morning of the day that he died, over the toy in the cereal box. That afternoon Mick asks her to ride his bike home from school, since he is going to a friend's house, but she refuses. Later, she hears sirens and learns that he was knocked from his bike, and then Pop tells her that he is dead. Life loses meaning for the family—Pop goes around in slipper sox and does not shave, Mom is sedated, and Phoebe gets sick looking at family pictures. They do not discuss Mick, eat at the table together, or watch television. Condolence calls that refer to Mick's death as part of God's plan puzzle Phoebe, and she endures the memorial service and the interment. She turns rebellious and taunts her mother by repeating Mick's name, then hates herself for hurting her mother. She and her best friend, Zoe Santos, speculate on where Mick is and discuss the concept of heaven. Going back to school is hard because the kids avoid talking about Mick's death around her. Phoebe races out of school, goes home, and buries herself in Mick's bed, savoring the smell and feel of him there. Nana from Florida comes, prepares spaghetti, and gets the family to eat it at the table. When the school principal and a woman from the PTA (Parent–Teacher Association) ask her to say a few words about bike safety at an assembly, she says that Mick thought that the helmet made him look like a "dork" and would not wear it. Later she wonders whether what she said at the assembly will help someone, but she knows that the doctors said that an inch of styrofoam would have made the difference between Mick's living and dying. A month after the accident, Mom goes back to work for two days a week, and both parents, compulsive about schedules, appearance, manners, and order in the house and in their lives, have lightened up a good deal. Phoebe calls it "perspective," meaning that they view life and people differently now because of Mick's death. But Phoebe tells Pop that she feels guilty about not riding Mick's bike home, to which Pop responds that he is going to make a list of "if onlys," of which Phoebe's not riding the bike is just one of many that they might add but that cannot change what happened. Pop says that his "if only" is: if only he had made Mick wear his helmet. After soccer practice one afternoon, Phoebe notices wet cement near the field, in which with a stick she writes in large clear letters, "M-I-C-K H-A-R-T-E W-A-S H-E-R-E." She remarks that during his short life Mick was a really neat kid. The story seems tailor-made to promote bike safety, an attitude supported by an author's note at the end giving statistics about how helmets prevent deaths from head injuries and extending a plea to readers to wear theirs. Phoebe and her parents go through the different stages of grieving, and all grow expectedly as a result of the experience. When Phoebe and Zoe discuss where Mick might be in death, the answers seem to be in the author's voice instead of theirs. Best are Phoebe's feelings and her memories about Mick. He is the most interesting figure, a good-bad, big-little, life-loving boy whose needless death seems to be having a great impact on the community as well as on his family. SLJ.

THE MIDNIGHT CLUB (Pike*, Christopher, Simon & Schuster, 1994), contemporary romantic thriller set in Washington state with fantasy aspects and stories within a story. The tone is serious, for the most part, but not morbid. Five young people, all in their late teens and dying with cancer, become extremely close friends while spending their last days in a seaside mansion that has been converted into a hospice. Most events are seen from the perspective of once-pretty Ilonka Pawluk, who has abdominal cancer. Every night at midnight, Ilonka and four friends gather in front of the fire in the study and tell stories, which pass the time and function as a special, very personal counseling device: Sandra, Spence*, Kevin*, and Ilonka's roommate, Anya*. Anya's stories are horrifying in a ghoulish way, matching her acerbic and bitter personality. She tells of a girl named Dana, who makes a pact with the devil for a perfect double through whom she vicariously experiences all her baser desires. Spencer's stories are filled with violence and reflect his inner tension: one concerns a sniper who shoots from the Eiffel Tower, and another involves a young magician and a school cheerleader who set on fire a gymnasium filled with spectators. Kevin, a talented painter, tells a story in three parts about an artist at the Louvre who is really an angel and falls in love with a human girl who betrays him. Ilonka's stories are, she says, from her past lives in ancient Egypt and India and involve Kevin, with whom she is in love, in the form of different lovers. All the stories hold ironic twists and tragic events and reflect their tellers' longing for love. Sandra, who is too shy to contribute but listens avidly, is the first to leave the hospice, in health not in death, since it is discovered that she has been misdiagnosed. Privately, Anya tells Ilonka the story of her ill-fated love affair with handsome, orange-haired Bill, who happened on her in bed with another man and threw across the room the clay statue that she was fashioning of the two of them, breaking the right leg of the Anya part of the statue. Ilonka experiences two problems: she is sure that the herbs that she has been taking regularly are curing her cancer and is extremely disappointed to learn that her tumors have spread. Her other concern involves Kevin's girlfriend, Kathy, who visits Kevin regularly and who believes that he is getting well. Ilonka informs Kathy of his true condition, then suffers from guilt because she realizes that she acted out of spite and jealousy. Eventually, she confesses to Kevin. All four youths die: Spencer drugs Ilonka, so that he can spend the night in her and Anya's room. During the night, he smothers Anya, so that she can die with dignity. Spencer reveals to Ilonka that he is gay and has AIDS. Kevin and Ilonka declare their love for each other and spend the night together. In the morning, Ilonka discovers him dead beside her. Because she knows that Anya was sincerely sorry for being unfaithful to Bill, she asks that Bill be found, and when he learns of Anya's feelings of guilt, they discover that the statue has become whole again. Ilonka dies in her sleep. In an epilogue she awakens in another dimension on a spaceship to another planet with her young husband, who is the counterpart of Kevin. Although characters are a stereotypical and studied mix, language is occasionally crude with contemporary sex slang, melodrama and sentimentality abound, the discussions are filled with teen philosophical speculation, and the progression of the disease is clichéd—in spite of these drawbacks, the book has enough gothic mystery and tension to hold the interest throughout and provide satisfying escapist reading. Poe Nominee.

THE MIDWIFE'S APPRENTICE (Cushman*, Karen, Clarion, 1995), period novel set in a medieval English village following a girl's progress from a despised, homeless waif to a respected assistant to the midwife. One chilly morning, Jane, the midwife, finds a scrawny girl, perhaps twelve or thirteen, sleeping in the dung heap where she has burrowed to keep warm and, being greedy, gives her a little food for much work. The girl, variously called Brat or Beetle or Clodpole, stays around for the bit of security that this provides, her only friend being a cat that she has rescued from drowning. With her stomach full or at least not so painfully empty, the girl's wits sharpen, and by watching and listening, she learns something of the midwife's skill. Several incidents give her a sense of worth. When the midwife sends her to Saint Swithin's Day Fair for supplies, a man gives her a comb for her dark curly hair, and another mistakes her for someone named Alyce, who can read. Beetle adopts the name, and as Alyce she saves a red-haired boy named Will, who has fallen into the river, and gains her first friend. Later she helps Will with the birth of his twin calves and, feeling love for them, her first experience of the emotion, makes up a song. When she finds another waif, a boy pehaps six or seven, almost freezing in the cowshed, she feeds him, saves him from tormenting boys, and learns the name of the king, Edward, to give him for his own. She then sends him off to the manor, where she hopes he can get work helping with the harvest. Although she is successful in assisting with the childbirth of the bailiff's wife, whom the midwife has deserted for a more lucrative job at the manor, and gains some local reputation, she cannot bring the woman's sister to birth and must call upon the midwife to take over. Despairing, Alyce leaves the village, followed by the cat, and gets work at a crossroads inn some distance away. Grim-faced and heavy of heart, she works hard and pleases Jennet, the inn wife, but remains despondent. Three events begin to lighten her depression. A scholar, Magister Reese, who is wintering at the inn while he writes an "encyclopaedic compendium" of all the world's knowledge, unable to get her to speak to him, pretends to teach the alphabet to the cat, then simple words, then bits of information from his great work, all of which Alyce learns quickly as she sweeps nearby. One day in spring Will Russet, her red-haired friend from the village, delivers a load of wood to the inn, gives Alyce news, and reminds her of how well she helped in the birth of the calves. Jane the midwife appears one day to give Magister Reese information about her skills. As Alyce listens from the shadows, Jane asks if her apprentice came that way and, before she can get an answer, volunteers that the girl had promise but would not do, because she gave up. When the cow drops her first calf, Alyce is reminded of her joy at new birth and thinks again of Edward, who, she fantasizes, might become her adopted child. She walks to the manor and finds that the cook has taken Edward under her protection, and, while he welcomes Alyce, he is quite happy where he is. She stays to help with the sheep washing the next day and discovers how pink and white her own skin is under the dirt. When a rich merchant stops at the inn with his wife in great pain, devoured, he thinks, by a stomach worm, Alyce is the only one not frightened away and, applying all she remembers of the midwife's skills, delivers a healthy baby boy. Although Magister Reese, returning to Oxford, wants her to become a servant in his home, the merchant proposes that she be the baby's nursemaid, and Jennet even offers her a little pay to remain at the inn, Alyce gathers her few belongings and returns with the cat to the village. There, to her dismay, the midwife shuts the door in her face. At first devastated, she suddenly realizes that Jane is testing her resolve, and she returns to the cottage, demands to be taken in as apprentice, and is allowed to enter. Alyce's gradual change from despised urchin to a young woman with some self-assurance is believable and compelling, told in economical prose that is strong in evoking the attitudes, the physical features, and especially the dirt and misery and stench of medieval life. Descriptions of the lack of hygiene and the superstitious remedies employed by the midwife can make a reader accustomed to modern antisepsis wince, but Alyce's reliance on kindness and encouraging language gives some credence to her skill. An author's note at the end discusses midwifery as it was in the Middle Ages, how it fell into disrepute with the development of scientific medicine, and its reemergence as a viable alternative to hospital birth since the 1960s. ALA; Fanfare; Newbery Winner; SLJ.

MIKAELSEN, BEN(JAMIN JOHN) (1952–   ), born in La Paz, Bolivia; since 1985 a writer of adventure and problem novels for middle-grade and early adolescent readers. While his earlier award-winning novels involved adventure, *Petey** (Hyperion, 1998) is the moving story of a boy born in 1920 with cerebral palsy. His desperate parents make him a ward of the state, and the treatment that he receives during his lifetime reflects the medical and social-services thinking of the day. The skillful characterization of the plucky, indomitable Petey keeps the book from sounding didactic. It received the Spur Award. Mikaelsen has also written *Stranded* (Hyperion, 1995), about rescuing pilot whales, and *Countdown* (Hyperion, 1996), which presents parallel stories about the National Aeronautics and Space Administration's (NASA) first junior astronaut and a Masai herder boy. For more information and a title entry, see *Dictionary, 1990– 1994* [*Rescue Josh McGuire*].

MIKEY ELSINGER (*Bad Girls**), along with Margalo* Epps, one of the two fifth-grade girls of the title. Like Margalo, with whom she becomes friends, she is less bad, however, than mischievous. She tends to be more confrontational than Margalo, especially over her ability to play soccer (at which she is very good) and to lead (she was class president at her old school). She hates being called Michelle, her real name, and asks her teacher, Mrs.* Chemsky, to address her as Miss Elsinger, to aggravate the teacher and assert herself in front of her new classmates. She is the one to whom Louis* Caselli, the class bully, takes an almost immediate dislike, since she poses a threat to what he thinks are his authority and the established way of doing things at Washington Street Elementary School. He belittles her at every turn, makes snide comments about her size (she is overweight), and provokes her to fisticuffs. After he chops off her long braid, Mikey gains considerable attention by dyeing her hair green.

MILLER, DOROTHY REYNOLDS (1941–   ), born in Gap, Pennsylvania; author of novels for middle-grade readers. Her suspense novel *The Clearing** (Atheneum, 1996) won the Edgar Allan Poe Award. An eleven-year-old girl is sent to relatives who live in rural Pennsylvania in a clearing surrounded by woods, where she uncovers the identity of a mysterious stranger and also learns what happened to a little boy who disappeared ten years earlier. Miller also published *Home Wars* (Atheneum, 1997), a family problem novel in which a gift of antique flintlocks to the sons starts arguments between father and mother over guns. She and her husband, Donald, a professor of engineering at Pennsylvania State University, and their children live in Leola, Pennsylvania.

MIRANDA SHARIFI (*Beggars and Choosers**), leader of the twenty-seven Super-Sleepless, children of the Sleepless who have been gene-modified in vitro to such an extent that their intelligence is far beyond that of their parents, at the expense of their appearance. They have enlarged heads, and originally, because their metabolism is so speeded up, they twitch and stutter among other people and communicate most easily by a sort of telepathy among themselves. Miranda has developed a vaccination that eliminates the twitching and, to thwart her grandmother's megalomaniacal plan for controlling world finances, has asserted the power of the Super-Sleepless, who afterward leave Sanctuary and go to live on an island that they have made in the Caribbean. Because she is not beautiful like most of the gene-modified humans, Miranda has been rejected by most of the men whom she approached, and her love for Drew* Arlen, the Lucid Dreamer, is excessive and mostly one-sided. Drew eventually rejects her because he does not believe in her plan to control society and because he has long resented the way that she must simplify her thoughts and works so that he can understand. In spite of having almost everything—super intelligence, great technological ability, wealth—she in the end has lost most, because she wants only Drew's love.

MIRA SPARKS (*Keeping the Moon**), eccentric aunt of Colie, with whom she spends the summer while her mother leads a fitness tour in Europe. Mira is overweight, has red hair, wears outlandish clothes that she buys at rummage sales, and considers herself an artist, concentrating on designing greeting cards, mostly to be sent at a death—of a former love, the mailman, or a pet hamster. Almost nothing in her house works properly, their shortcomings noted with signs: "chair has one leg too short," windows are marked "painted shut." A light is labeled "works, but only sometimes." Since she inherited all her parents' money, her way of life is clearly by choice, not need, and she is generous, taking in a stray cat and Norman* Carswell, a young artist whose father evicted him. Other people in town laugh at her, but she blithely ignores their ridicule. At first Colie thinks that Mira is very good at pretending not to be hurt by their sneers, but she comes to realize that Mira is so self-confident that she really does not care what people say about her.

MISSING THE PIANO (Rapp*, Adam, Viking, 1994), boarding-school novel set in a brutal military academy near Oakfield, Wisconsin, in the 1990s. When his little sister, Alice, gets a part in a touring company of *Les Misérables*, Michael Tegroff, who has been expecting to start soon at Joliet, Illinois, Catholic High, has to stay in Chicago with his father and his father's new wife, Rayne, while his mother chaperones Alice in Boston. Alice, as Little Cosette, makes such a hit that she is asked to stay on for six weeks in Philadelphia. Michael's father balks at the prospect of driving him to Joliet every day, and Rayne, who dislikes having the boy live with them, insists that he should be sent to St. Matthew's Military Academy, where the son of one of her friends is a student. Without telling him where they are going, Michael's father drives him to the school and leaves him in a state of shock. Everything is foreign to his experience and inclinations—the phony cheer of the director of admissions, the spit and polish required, the hierarchy of student officers, the tradition of saluting the statue of the founder, the inferior academic standards, and a hundred details of everyday life for a new boy at the school. Especially galling is the hazing by the fat bully Staff Sergeant Hillcrest, in charge of Delta Company, to which he is assigned. Only a few people are civil or slightly friendly: a huge African-American junior from Detroit named Truvoy Shockley, who becomes his roommate; an older boy named John Warner, who explains some of the rules to him and whom he later comes upon masturbating in the shower; and Mr. Savery, the new basketball coach and English teacher who welcomes him to the team tryouts. Even at the basketball court, where Michael expects to be at ease since he is an accomplished guard, an older player named Hufford warns him not to compete for a place on the team, punches him out, and injures his ear. Truvoy tells him why he is at the school—because he and a friend robbed a money machine—and why he has been transferred to Delta Company—because he punched the Staff Sergeant of Echo Company for calling him a nigger. Truvoy, though a junior, treats Michael well, tries to teach him to dance, and might be a potential friend, but Nealy and Hilllcrest beat the black boy up while Michael is polishing his shoes in the shower, and though he knows what is going on, he is afraid to intervene. In horror at his own cowardice, he races across the campus in the rain to the chapel, where, having been deprived of food and sleep by the constant hazing, he faints in front of the organist. He wakes in the infirmary, where he is visited, briefly by his father, by Mr. Savery, and by Truvoy, who is battered but determined on revenge. By the time that Michael is released from the infirmary, Truvoy has caught up with Nealy, broken his collarbone, and been kicked out of the school. In despair, Michael walks out of the dorm, climbs over the high fence, and jogs down the road to a country garage, where he calls the hotel in Philadelphia. Alice answers, and they have a good conversation, the first since he has arrived at the school because new boys are not allowed phone privileges for their first six weeks. Michael gets her to sing her hit song for him, but he doesn't tell her what the school is really like. Reassured by her voice, he goes back, climbs over the fence, goes to his room, and changes for the gym. There he is taunted by Hufford again and, without thinking about it, punches the bully. Later he stops by Mr. Savery's apartment and listens to the teacher play the guitar. He has decided to stay at the academy and "tough it out." Just what this decision means is unclear. After hitting Hufford, he shouts, "I'm the cream of the crop!," a phrase that is often repeated at the school. That he is

ironic, or that he has joined the cruel ethic of the place both seem wrong conclusions, but what toughing it out will entail, and for how long, is not explained.
The novel's strongest element is the evocation of the helpless rage of a young
person against an abusive system where he has no recourse. Although some
details show that his father is not entirely insensitive, he is almost a stereotype
of the successful, middle-age man who has jettisoned his first family and found
a trophy wife. Michael's mother is treated sympathetically, though she could
easily be considered a typical, ambitious stage mother who abandons her son
for her more talented daughter. The many questions left unresolved weaken what
is otherwise a strong picture of the worst kind of school. ALA; SLJ.

MISS PRECIOUS DOOLITTLE (*Moving Mama to Town**), the most respected and probably the most feared person in the little South Carolina town
of Elderton. Miss Precious is the town dowager, the town's power center, so to
speak. Everyone defers to her, and everyone realizes that she pretty much controls the area and, in a certain way, the lives of everyone in the town. She lives
in a big yellow house, which is visible throughout the town, and has eyes and
ears everywhere. People go to her when they need help, but the implication is
that she may well exact some price in the future for previous services rendered.
She appears systematically to have made the town into a small empire for herself. When Freddy James Johnson visits her after Mama tells him that Miss
Precious sold their farm, Miss Precious gives him a cigar box with family photographs and eighty dollars, apparently left over from the sale of the farm, telling
him that she admires his gumption. Freddy puts the money away for some future
time of need. Miss Precious is a mixture of qualities, some admirable, some
quite the opposite.

MOLL GARFIELD (*The Apprenticeship of Lucas Whitaker**), part Pequot Indian "granny woman," revered by some as an effective herbalist doctor and
shunned by others as a witch. Doc* Uriah Beecher gets materials for his medicines from her and also keeps an eye out for her welfare since she lives alone.
He sends Lucas Whitaker to her to learn about herbs, barks, and the like. She
does not tell Lucas that she has no faith in the cure for consumption that Oliver
Rood and Mr. Stukeley feel is effective, but she does suggest that he "consider
the end of the story," that is, think carefully about what happens or does not
happen as a result of the cure. Moll is a stereotype of the wise old Indian woman.

MOM (*Iceman**), mother of Eric, 14, the narrator, and Duane*, 17, and wife
of Dad*. Mom is an ex-nun and very religious, going regularly every day to
mass. A saving-souls person, she no longer relates well to Dad, and Duane seems
to frighten her with his independent ways and quick tongue. She concentrates
on reforming and uplifting Eric. Occasionally, she tries to lay down the law to
her sons about what she calls their weird behavior, but neither pays much attention to her. While Dad is more conscious than she of the impression that

other people might form about his sons from things that they do, and general appearances are important to him, Mom is more intent on instilling moral and ethical behavior, which she sees as allied to religion. She is sometimes successful at getting Eric to attend church with her on Sundays. Mostly the boys just tolerate her.

MOM HERNANDEZ (*Parrot in the Oven: Mi Vida**), Rebecca Hernandez, mother of Manny, the protagonist, Nardo*, his older brother, and his sisters, Magda and Pedi, and wife of Dad* Hernandez. She is presented as a typical Mexican-American wife and mother, dominated, for the most part, by her husband and victim of his vagaries, solicitous of her children, whom she wishes strongly to have better lives, tense to the point of striking them almost unreasonably, and proud but almost powerless to control her life. Mom wants very much for Manny, who is bright, to go to a school that is less Mexican-American and hence has students who are more academically motivated than those in the school that he currently attends.

THE MOORCHILD (McGraw*, Eloise Jarvis, McElderry, 1996), fantasy novel of a changeling, a half-elven child rejected by the elven Moorfolk and left in exchange for a human baby in a society much like preindustrial England. Although she can remember little of her life as Moql in the elven Mound before she awoke in the home of Yanno*, the blacksmith, and his wife, Anwara, in the village of Torskaal, and soon forgets that little, Saaski is always a strange child, unable to fit into the normal pattern of the community. Even after she no longer screams and struggles when Yanno, with his iron belt buckle, approaches her truckle bed, she is given to night wandering and is attracted to the moor, where decent village people do not venture. Only Old* Bess, Anwara's mother, the Wise Woman of the village, realizes what Saaski is, but when she tries to tell her daughter, she only alienates both parents. On the moor Saaski meets Tam*, an orphan boy living with old Bruman, the drunken tinker, who summers in a hut beyond the village land, and they strike up a secret friendship, increased when Saaski finds the bagpipes that once belonged to Yanno's father and discovers that she can play on them tunes wild and different, melodies that no one in the village has heard before. As she grows older, the village children turn against her, encouraged by their mothers, who blame her for any ill fortune. Only Old Bess understands that Saaski sees the runes glittering on sheds and doors, marking where Moorfolk can steal milk from a cow or be warned away from danger. Although the Wise Woman cannot see the runes, she can interpret them when Saaski copies them in the dirt, and with the child guiding her hand she can scrub them off. She begins to teach Saaski to read from the books that she inherited with the monk's hut where she lives, and the two develop a warm relationship. Saaski's troubles culminate as Midsummer's Eve approaches. On the moor she pretends to sleep and is able to grab one of the Folk, Tinkwa, as he tries to steal her pipes, and his answers to her questions stir her memories of life in the Mound, of her rejection because she was unable to blink out and become invisible like the other young ones and therefore was turned into a baby and left in exchange for the child of Anwara. Old Bess confirms as true what Tam has once said to her, that he "suspicions" that she may be Folk. Determined to tell Anwara and Yanno the truth, Saaski starts home, only to be surrounded by village people who howl at her and beat her until she scampers up a wall and hides in the thatch, skills that she has always concealed before. Yanno chases the mob away and rescues Saaski, but it is clear to both of them and to Anwara that the girl cannot stay. In the middle of the night she leaves, taking only a small bundle that Anwara has left for her and Yanno's bagpipes. Just before dawn she remembers something else from the Mound, her Moorwoman mother saying that her father was a fisherman named Fergil, and she realizes that it is the strange old "lackbrain" who lives on the edge of Moor Water, a handsome twenty-year-old when he was lured into the Mound but fifty-five years older when he was thrown out in what seemed a short while later, since time goes differently there. Determinedly, Saaski walks to Fergil's hut and makes a bargain with him: she will help him get even with the Moorfolk by leaving the bag part of her instrument with him but taking the chanter, the pipe part. If anyone comes with the chanter, it will mean that she has been able to trick the Moorfolk by stealing back Anwara's child, and whoever comes is to be given the bag and the drones for his help. The rest is the thrilling venture of Saaski and Tam, who insists on going with her, as they enter the Mound on Midsummer's Eve—the only time that a human can do so—rescue the child who has been a slavey to the elves, and escape again, with the erratic help of Tinkwa, who claims the bagpipes as reward. In a bittersweet ending, Tam returns the child, now become a baby again, to Old Bess and leaves with Saaski, since Bruman followed them into the Mound and stayed, making Tam now owner of his cart and animals, for whom he has long cared. Told mostly from the point of view of Saaski, the story is one of the outsider, rejected by her first group and unaccepted by her second. The bafflement and hurt that she feels are the main emotional pull of the book. Her growth from a careless Moorchild, incapable of real emotion, to a brave, determined, and loving young woman is convincing and touching. There are strong scenes of village life, of the beauty and freedom of the moors, and of both the false glitter and the shabby reality of the interior of the Mound. ALA; Boston Globe Honor; Newbery Honor; SLJ.

MOORE, MARTHA (A.) (1950–   ), born in Canyon, Texas; received her undergraduate and graduate degrees from West Texas State University and the University of Dallas, respectively; teacher of English literature and creative writing in high school; resident with her husband and two sons of the Dallas-Fort Worth area; writer of young adult fiction. For years, she wrote plays, stories, and poems, which she shared mostly with her classes. Around 1985, she began to pursue publication seriously. Her first published novel, *Under the Mermaid Angel** (Delacorte, 1995), was cited by the American Library Association. A girl's growing-up novel in a school-story context, it is the loosely plotted, but affecting, story of a girl whose life changes for the better when she becomes friends with a flamboyant waitress new in her Texas town. She has published another young adult novel, *Angels on the Roof* (Delacorte, 1997), in which a mother tries to prevent her daughter from finding out about her father.

MORDECAI, SAMUEL (*Under the Beetle's Cellar**), fanatical leader of the Hearth Jezreelite religious cult that kidnaps a busload of schoolchildren and imprisons them in a bus buried under the barn in the cult compound. Mordecai blames technology for the corruption that he deplores in the world, especially evidenced, he maintains, in mothers' abandoning their children. Molly Cates learns that Mordecai was a foundling, abandoned by his birth mother and then again abandoned by his adoptive mother and left in the charge of his adoptive mother's mother, Dorothy Huff, a difficult, complaining woman. Then known as Donnie Ray Grimes, he ran away from home in his teens and later founded the cult. Molly learns that he tried unsuccessfully to trace his birth mother and that much of the imagery that appears in his rantings derives from details of his early years.

MORGAN (*Keeping the Moon**), tall, bony waitress at the Last Chance Bar and Grill, where Colie Sparks works during her summer in Colby, North Carolina. Morgan is compulsive about keeping things in order, but she is more friendly and sensitive than Isabel, the pretty blond waitress with whom she lives. Morgan is engaged to Mark, a baseball player whom Isabel dislikes because he treats Morgan badly, standing her up after saying that he will come, forgetting to call when he has promised. Because she has never been considered attractive, Morgan is pathetically grateful for his attention, even when he shows up with no warning and refuses to talk about plans for their wedding. After Morgan goes to Durham, where the team is playing, to surprise him and discovers that he has a pregnant wife there, she is devastated, crying for twenty-four hours straight and shutting Isabel, whom she blames because Isabel has always distrusted Mark, out of the house. When she finally comes to her senses, she turns music up loud, as Isabel always does, and dances wildly around the house, soon joined by Colie and Norman* Carswell, forgiving Isabel and preparing to make a new start in her life.

MORGAN CAMPBELL (*Driver's Ed**), 16, handsome, bright son of two affluent, successful lawyers and sweetheart of Remy* Marland. His father has gubernatorial aspirations and is well regarded in the community. Morgan is typical of youth his age. He has sexual fantasies, especially about Remy, and tops on his list of wants is a red sports car. He is so good-looking and nice that every girl about his age in school lusts after him. Although he has trouble communicating with his parents and has the usual sibling troubles with his sister, Starr, he appears to be a "good kid." He is an honor student, has never been in trouble, and goes to church. The thefts of the street signs are sexual turn-ons for him, and he kisses Remy for the first time while they are in Nickie's Buick. A good aspect of the book is how, while he agonizes over what he and Remy have done to cause Mrs. Thompson's death, his sexual desire for Remy diminishes, to be replaced by the wish to comfort and be comforted by her. At the end, he is the one who realizes that they all have to find some way of going on and of making the best of the future.

MOSHER, HOWARD FRANK (1943–   ), author of several novels and a book of short stories, all set in the fictional Kingdom County, Vermont. Mosher is a graduate of Syracuse University and has studied further at the University of Vermont and the University of California. A teacher and a worker in an antipoverty program, he is the recipient of prestigious honors, including a National Endowment for the Arts Fellowship, an American Academy of Arts and Letters Literature Award, and a Guggenheim Fellowship. *Northern Borders** (Doubleday, 1994) is a novel of a boy growing up with his eccentric grandparents in the 1940s in Vermont. Mosher lives in Irasburg, Vermont, near the Canadian border.

MOTHER (*The Long Season of Rain**), wife of Father*, a cold, surly, career Korean army colonel; mother of Junehee, who tells the story, and three other daughters; and daughter-in-law of Grandmother*, Father's mother, with whom the family lives. Mother is a strength in the household, a hardworking, solicitous wife and respectful daughter-in-law. She is Catholic, whereas Grandmother is Methodist, and she enjoys visiting with Father Cho, the priest, with whom she is relaxed and conversational. She regrets her plainness, longs for smarter clothes, chafes at always having to ask Grandmother for permission to do things, and often bites her hands and fingers, a sign that she has little self-esteem. She says that she will have nothing to live for in Grandmother's house after her girls marry and go to live in their husbands' houses. She yearns to keep the orphan boy, Pyungsoo, since she has lost two sons, but Grandmother and Father oppose the idea. When she walks out on Father, she stays with Grandma Min, her mother, a warm and accepting woman, the opposite of Grandmother. Mother is a sympathetic figure.

MOTHER (*Zel**), overprotective, domineering, single-parent mother of pretty, lively young Zel*, who falls in love with Count Konrad*. In her youth, Mother was like Zel, eager for life. Much in love with her young husband but unable to conceive a child, she sold her soul to devils in return for magical powers. She bargained with a young pregnant woman for the baby in return for a lettuce called rapunzel. She raised the child, a daughter whom she named Rapunzel after the lettuce, with deep love but has become so attached to the girl that she refuses to let her live a normal life. When it is obvious that the girl is of marriageable age and is falling in love with Konrad, Mother imprisons her for several years in a remote tower, telling her that danger imperils her. When she realizes that the girl is nearly mad from loneliness, Mother attempts to retain control by offering her magical power in return for physical freedom, a bargain that the girl refuses. Mother is the most interesting character in the novel, one both repugnant and sympathetic.

MOVING MAMA TO TOWN (Young*, Ronder Thomas, Orchard, 1997), realistic novel of family and community life set for a few weeks briefly in rural Georgia and mostly in the small South Carolina town of Elderton just following World War II. After his father, Big Kenny Johnson, takes off without a word, resourceful, determined Freddy James Johnson, the thirteen-year-old narrator, acts on his father's advice always to have a "Plan B" in mind. He persuades his mother, Eleanor, and little brother, Kenneth Lee, 9, to move from their middling farm into Elderton and sets about making a living for the three of them. He gets a job as boy-of-all-work for forty-five cents an hour at Fenton's Fine Establishment, a saloon/gambling hall/restaurant, which is a community fixture of dubious reputation. Proprietor Fenton* Calhoun proves to be a good friend to the boy, however. He sends him to Miss* Precious Doolittle, the town dowager, for a place to live. She refers him to Miss Susannah Doolittle, her adopted daughter, who runs an apartment house for Miss Precious on River Street and gives French lessons. Mama, Kenneth Lee, and Freddy make out fine in their tiny space and become good friends with Susannah. Kenneth Lee, who has a green thumb, soon has a garden growing in the backyard, the produce from which they all enjoy as the summer wears on. Freddy works willingly and hard and is liked and respected by his co-employees, among them Dorothea, the cook; Evelyn, the loud, orange-haired lady of shady repute, who Dorothea says has had a hard life; and Jacob, the "colored" man-of-all-work, who shows him how to construct a barbecue pit and then leaves to work on the railroad. Freddy builds the pit, cuts wood, polishes cars, which Fenton sells on the side, helps Dorothea select a pig for the barbecue, works at the serving table for the barbecue, and does whatever else needs to be done. Mama gets a job doing laundry and also sells her prize devil's food cakes, and the three get along. One big mystery lurks in the background: why did Big Kenny take off so abruptly? It seems that Freddy and Mama are late in finding out what the townspeople already know. Big Kenny, an inveterate gambler, had borrowed an enormous sum of money from Miss Precious and had given her the deed to the farm as collateral. Miss Precious sells the farm, leaving Freddy's family without a resource that they had counted on as a last resort. Then, unexpectedly, Custis Fullbright turns up, a sometime boyfriend of Mama whom Freddy heartily dislikes. Although Mama assures Freddy that everything is over between her and Custis, she accepts Custis' invitation to drive with him to Charleston, where he has business, to visit her parents. Freddy refuses to go along, and Mama and Kenneth Lee leave. Word soon arrives that an accident has left Mama dying and Kenneth Lee injured. Susannah departs immediately with Freddy in her car, and they arrive just after

Mama dies. Freddy spends almost all the money that they have on a headstone and heads back to Elderton with Susannah, determined to find a job that will enable him to care for himself and Kenneth Lee. The book's strong points lie in the characterizations, the picture of the community, and the first-person narration and use of present tense, a mode that vividly realizes people and events. Throughout, the careful reader is aware that there is more to the tale than Freddy, a naive speaker and observer, is able to relate. As a result, there is a depth to the novel not immediately apparent. One drawback comes from the otherwise effective style. Frequently, Freddy's thoughts and what he says appear to run together, with the result that one must often reread in order to determine what actually has been communicated and what lies behind it or expands upon it. On the whole, however, this is an engrossing account of a boy's assuming a man's responsibility and doing exceedingly well, though he is not without some justified resentment toward his ne'er-do-well father. IRA.

MR. BIDWELL PEECE (*The Great Turkey Walk**), drover on the turkey drive to Denver, organized by Simon Green. Town drunk of Union, Missouri, he accepts Simon's offer of a percentage of the proceeds upon selling the turkeys to be the skinner, or mule driver, and subsequently is responsible also for the horses that they acquire. He is also the cook. During the early part of the journey, he openly longs for a drink, but Simon keeps him away from towns and stores. Earlier in life he had his own successful mule train on the Santa Fe trail, "better'n twenty wagons strong," married, had three children, and lived most of the year in Santa Fe. On returning from a trip, however, he learned that his entire family had died from cholera, and in his grief he "took up the bottle." Mr. Peece is a kind, capable, wise man, from whose advice and hard work the entire party benefits.

MR. BIRKWAY (*Walk Two Moons**), English teacher of Sal Hiddle and Phoebe* Winterbottom. Sal thinks that he is strange and has a "few squirrels in his attic." He is very enthusiastic about his subject, jumps dramatically about his classroom, and is highly effusive with praise for his pupils. He has a strong sense of fairness and, when reading from their journals creates consternation among them, he apologizes. The two girls see him next door at Mrs.* Cadaver's house and are sure that he had a part in her husband's death. Later they learn that he is Mrs. Cadaver's twin brother and that her husband died in a car accident. Mr. Birkway is a colorful figure.

MR. FISHER (*Tangerine**), father of Paul and Erik, whose new job as Deputy Director of Civil Engineering for Tangerine County takes the family to Florida. Typically, Mr. Fisher has bought a house in Lake* Windsor Downs without looking beyond the attractive appearance and the prestige of the development, leaving the family to discover all the problems when it is too late to back out. He devotes his major energies to the Erik Fisher Football Dream, planning his older son's sports career, buttering up anyone who might be able to promote Erik's prospects, and keeping a running file on Erik's scholarship offers on his computer. When the incumbent Director of Civil Engineering is discovered to have been corrupt and to have approved developments without proper inspections, Mr. Fisher eagerly steps into his position and, when the man dies a short time later, doesn't even attend the funeral. This same cavalier attitude appears when Erik gets into trouble with the law. His father, no longer able to live vicariously in the football glory, abruptly drops his interest in Erik's future. While Mr. Fisher is not pictured as a bad man, only ambitious and self-centered, he has deliberately turned a blind eye to what Erik has done to Paul. Erik's problems seem to be similar to his father's, only magnified.

MR. HILLINGER (*Dave at Night**), art teacher who comes two days a week to teach the elevens at the Hebrew Home for Boys. He speaks in gasps, his mind going faster than he can speak. He earnestly tries to bring out the best in the boys, unlike Mr. Gluck (Mr. Cluck), who belittles the boys as being ignorant but never tries to teach them anything of substance. The first time that Mr. Hillinger comes after Dave Caros arrives at the home, he brings his sister as a model. He is pleased with Dave's drawings and compliments the boy by saying that Dave has the "beginnings of an eye." Later, he invites Dave to participate in special classes that he holds. Mr. Hillinger is one of the reasons that Dave is reluctant to leave the home, although living conditions are terrible. Mr. Hillinger does much to elevate Dave's self-esteem.

MR. HORATIO DRABBLE (*Beyond the Western Sea: Book One: The Escape from Home**; *Beyond the Western Sea: Book Two: Lord Kirkle's Money**), unemployed, grandiloquent Shakespearean actor who befriends Maura and Patrick O'Connell. He is a long, lanky, very thin man of about thirty, with a big smile, large brown eyes, and heavy, thick, straw-colored hair. He meets the O'Connell children when Ralph Toggs* brings them to Mrs. Sonderbye's miserable boardinghouse and helps them manage not to be cheated too much by the grasping landlady. He also helps the children get their medical exams before embarking, negotiate the masses of emigrants, and board the ship *Robert Peel*, bound for America. In return for his help, Maura offers him her mother's unused ticket. Given the chance to emigrate, Mr. Drabble decides to accompany them, especially because he has fallen in love with Maura. Maura rejects his suit, but he leaves with her and Patrick anyway. He also wishes to bring culture to the Americans. After they arrive in Boston, Maura dismisses him abruptly, an action for which she later apologizes, and he becomes the traveling companion and friend of Mr.* Toby Grout, now reformed, and of Sir Laurence Kirkle. He is extremely upset to be rejected when he applies for an acting position. He dies in the fire that Mr.* Jeremiah Jenkins sets. Mr. Drabble is one of the few kind and good people in the book with whom the O'Connell children and Sir Laurence Kirkle come into contact.

MR. JAMES HAMLYN (*Beyond the Western Sea: Book Two: Lord Kirkle's Money**), respected and well-liked owner of the boardinghouse in which Maura O'Connell lives. Mr. Hamlyn was a supervisor at the cotton mill where Mr.* Jeremiah Jenkins worked. One day, contrary to regulations, Mr. Jenkins appeared at work with his young son in tow. When a pulley broke, Mr. Hamlyn lost the use of his legs trying unsuccessfully to save the boy's life. Ever since, Mr. Jenkins has hated Mr. Hamlyn and has tried to stir up trouble for him, telling everyone that Hamlyn is Irish and bad for the country like all the other Irish immigrants who are taking jobs from Americans. In truth, Mr. Hamlyn came from Ireland with his family when he was two years old. Mrs. Hamlyn runs their home as a boardinghouse for young Irishwomen employed at the mills and is known to be especially kind, loving, and generous to them. Mr.* Nathaniel Brewster carries Mr. Hamlyn from his burning house just in time to save the man's life.

MR. JEREMIAH JENKINS (*Beyond the Western Sea: Book Two: Lord Kirkle's Money**), half-demented former worker at the Shagwell Cotton Mill in Lowell, Massachusetts, who heads a deeply patriotic secret society dedicated to preserving jobs for Americans by driving out immigrants, especially Irish. Mr. Jenkins particularly hates the Irish because he holds Mr.* James Hamlyn responsible for the death of his son and believes that Hamlyn is Irish. He hires a Boston writer to ghostwrite speeches, which he delivers to his followers with fiery passion. He often spies on Mr. Hamlyn, standing outside and in full view of the Hamlyn house and directing malevolent glares at Mr. Hamlyn's room. Mr. Jenkins dies in the fire that he has set, which destroys the Hamlyn house but from which Mr. Hamlyn escapes.

MR. LARSON (*The Landry News**), Karl Larson, teacher with nineteen years' experience, regarded as the worst in school because of his completely unstructured, open classroom practices and his general laziness. He spends most of his time reading the newspaper and drinking coffee, allowing the students to spend the day doing whatever they wish and earning the dislike of teachers nearby, who deplore the noise, and of Principal Barnes, who would like to fire him because of the numerous verbal and written complaints from parents. Ironically, Cara Landry, who appreciates the freedom of his room, learns that earlier in his career he had won three Teacher of the Year awards. Cara's article in *The Landry News* motivates him to take a serious look at himself, try to rise above self-pity at his struggles in life, and become a better teacher. The way in which he uses Principal Barnes' effort at censorship for a lesson in First Amendment rights shows that he has considerable teaching talent. He is both unsympathetic—for allowing self-pity and burnout to cause him to ignore his students' needs—and sympathetic—for drawing positive strength from Cara's critical article and for rising to the occasion against Principal Barnes.

MR. LEFTY LEWIS (*Bud, Not Buddy**), kind, concerned elderly gentleman who befriends Bud, not Buddy, Caldwell. Bud is walking along the road near Owosso, Michigan, on his way to Grand Rapids to try to find the man who he thinks is his father, Mr. Herman* E. Calloway, when a big car pulls up. At first, Bud is very suspicious of Mr. Lewis, because he is carrying a box marked blood (which he is transporting for a hospital) and Bud, who is often melodramatic, thinks that he is a vampire. Mr. Lewis lives with his daughter and her children. They feed Bud and clothe him in his first pair of trousers, and for the first time he gets a look at good family life. Mr. Lewis is a redcap at a Grand Rapids railroad station, where there is labor unrest, the union movement being under way in the United States. Mr. Lewis telegraphs Mr. Herman E. Calloway about Bud, so that when Bud arrives, Mr. Calloway has been apprised of Bud's existence and imminent arrival. Mr. Lewis' character is based, according to an endnote, on the author's mother's father.

MR. MATTHEW CLEMSPOOL (*Beyond the Western Sea: Book One: The Escape from Home**; *Beyond the Western Sea: Book Two: Lord Kirkle's Money**), round, portly man who operates a business on Bow Lane in London called Brother's Keeper, the purpose of which is to help brothers manipulate or even dispose of one another to their financial advantage. In Book One, Sir Albert* Kirkle engages Mr. Clemspool to make sure Albert's younger brother, Sir Laurence, a runaway, reaches America and never returns to England. Mr. Clemspool traces Laurence to London's Euston Station, manages to take a seat beside him on the train to Liverpool, and insinuates himself into the boy's confidence. In Liverpool, he takes Laurence prisoner and holds him for some time in a hotel, from which the boy cleverly escapes. Much of the time Mr. Clemspool and Mr.* Toby Grout, who says he is emigrating to America, are accomplices. When Laurence sees the two men conversing and because he is sure that Mr. Grout picked his pocket of £1,000 that Laurence stole from his father, the boy grows suspicious of Mr. Clemspool. Mr. Clemspool and Mr. Grout are responsible for most of the complications in Book One. In Book Two, Mr. Clemspool steals Laurence's money from Mr. Grout, intending to use it to swindle Mr. Ambrose Shagwell, owner of the Shagwell Cotton Mill in Lowell, Massachusetts, or to lure people to invest in a bogus business. He loses the safe-deposit box key, however, and the money eventually returns to Laurence's hands.

MR. NAKATANI (*Ironman**), Naboru Nakatani, also known as Mr. Nak, teacher of industrial arts and leader of the Anger Management Class, whose members are known to the students at Clark Fork High School as the Nak Pack. Mr. Nak is a short, wiry Japanese American from Texas who, according to Bo, talks "like Slim Pickens and dresses like his fashion guru is the Marlboro Man." Bo says that Mr. Nak "knows stuff" and exudes "confidence." His kind, astute comments to the students, delivered in Texas dialect, are often funny. Mr. Nak tries unsuccessfully to get Bo's father to see that denigrating and humiliating Bo and setting him up for failure are no way to build Bo's self-esteem and gain his love and respect. When Bo's father charges that Mr. Nak knows nothing except theory about raising children, Mr. Nak tells him how, while driving drunk, he got into an accident and killed his children, a story that he later tells the class.

MR. NATHANIEL BREWSTER (*Beyond the Western Sea: Book Two: Lord Kirkle's Money**), kind Maine farm boy of about twenty, who is the friend, fellow millworker, and roommate of Gregory O'Connell and who carries the news of Gregory's death to Boston to the O'Connell children, Maura and Patrick. He becomes their good friend and benefactor, helping them in many ways to survive in the city. He also saves Mr.* James Hamlyn's life when the Hamlyn house is set on fire. At the end, he, Sir Laurence Kirkle, and Mr.* Toby Grout (now reformed) head for the California goldfields, hoping to make their fortunes. Nathaniel asks Maura to wait for him, and, while she compliments him as a "fine young man," she says only that she will "not forget him." He is one of the most admirable figures in the story.

MR. OCAX (*Poppy**), the owl who tyrannizes Dimwood Forest and "looks like death itself." Since Mr. Ocax finds mice tasty, he lies to the mice who live in the area, telling them that he is their protector, especially against porcupines, and requiring that they not stray outside without his permission. He ferociously attacks and kills Ragweed, Poppy's rebellious and smart-talking boyfriend, attacks Poppy on several occasions, and follows her as she makes her way through Dimwood to New House. When he attacks Poppy at New Barn, and she stabs him, he ironically helps her to pay her debt to her benefactor, Ereth* the porcupine, who has enabled her to triumph against him.

MR. PHINEAS PICKLER (*Beyond the Western Sea: Book One: The Escape from Home**), the small, pot-bellied private investigator of about forty hired by wealthy Lord Kirkle to find and bring home his younger son, Sir Laurence, 11. Unknown to both Mr. Pickler and Lord Kirkle, Lord Kirkle's older son, Sir Albert*, has hired Mr.* Matthew Clemspool to make certain that Laurence arrives in America and never returns to England. Overhearing Mr. Pickler tell a constable at London's Euston Station that he is looking for a runaway, Laurence does his best to stay away from Mr. Pickler, although in so doing the boy falls into the clutches of Mr. Clemspool. When he fails to apprehend the boy, Mr. Pickler seeks the services of a Liverpool street gang, the Lime Street Runners, but still fails to find his quarry. When last seen, Mr. Pickler is swimming toward land, having been dumped, along with Ralph Toggs*, into the Liverpool harbor by Fred* No-name, in full sight of the *Robert Peel*, the ship on which Fred has helped Laurence stow away. The two watch helplessly as the ship steams off toward America.

MRS. CADAVER (*Walk Two Moons**), Margaret Cadaver, widowed, red-haired nurse who lives in Ohio and friend of Sal Hiddle's father, a farmer. Since Sal knows that her father thinks a lot of Margaret, she is jealous of her and ready to believe the worst—that Mrs. Cadaver murdered her husband and has buried him in her yard, an idea suggested by Phoebe* Winterbottom, who bases part of her theory on Margaret's last name. Sal learns from Mr.* Birkway that Margaret's husband died in an auto accident caused by a drunken driver, the same accident that took the sight of Mrs.* Partridge, Mrs. Cadaver's eccentric mother. The friendship between Mrs. Cadaver and Sal's father began when Sal's father visited her in the hospital after his wife died in the bus crash. Mrs. Cadaver had been Sugar* Hiddle's seatmate on the bus and was the only survivor. Mrs. Cadaver tells Sal that her mother was "one of a kind," words that help to relieve Sal's grief.

MRS. CARVER (*The Ornament Tree**), wife of the disagreeable boarder Mr. Bertram Johnson and a woman who has been in an insane asylum until Audra Devereaux's lawyer has her released. Because if his wife is granted the divorce that she seeks, he would lose control of her money, Mr. Johnson has had her committed, and she has been badly mistreated, a situation not unusual in Seattle of 1918. Although she has resumed her maiden name and is in Audra's supportive household with Mr. Johnson long banished, Mrs. Carver is very timid, almost never speaking. Blind Carson Younger realizes, from hearing her uneven step and stifled gasps, that she has something wrong with her foot. When Audra asks, Mrs. Carver denies it, but Bonnie Shaster insists on seeing the badly infected wound. Because Mrs. Carver is terrified of doctors, who certified her as insane and evidently mistreated her in the mental institution, Bonnie treats the foot herself, and it gradually heals. The experience reinforces Bonnie's interest in a medical career. When she is about to leave for the university, she urges Mr. Younger to get Mrs. Carver to read to him, knowing that the experience of helping someone else will be good for both of them.

MRS. CHEMSKY (*Bad Girls**), teacher of the fifth grade at Washington Street Elementary School, where Margalo* Epps, Mikey* Elsinger, and Louis* Caselli are enrolled. Her reputation as a tough, strict, serious teacher has preceded her, and most of this year's fifth graders are at least a little apprehensive. Although she tolerates no nonsense, she is kind and fair, and the children respect her. After Margalo starts the rumor that Mrs. Chemsky is a witch, the school receives complaints about her. She announces to the class in her defense that she is not a witch, that she is a Congregationalist, and that, if she were a witch and had witch's powers, some of the class would have been summarily dealt with by this time. She tells the two girls that Steven Chemsky, the garishly dressed young man who came for her one day, is her brother, not her husband, as they expected, refuses to answer questions about her husband for them, and tells Margalo to stop spreading rumors.

MRS. CORA BUNCE (*The Apprenticeship of Lucas Whitaker**), widowed sister and housekeeper of Doc* Uriah Beecher, the physician to whom young Lucas Whitaker is apprenticed. Mrs. Bunce is stereotypically described as a tall, thin, acerbic, stern woman with a pinched nose and tight lips. A stickler for cleanliness, she makes Lucas take a bath every couple of days, an activity almost unheard of in Lucas' times and one that displeases him greatly. Mrs. Bunce is protective of her brother and thinks people of the town take advantage of him, since they know that he feels duty-bound to help them even if they cannot, or do not, pay him. She also worries that there will not be enough money to keep their household going and thinks that Doc's new microscope is a ridiculous, extravagant gadget.

MR. SERBOUSEK (*Ironman**), also known as Mr. S [*sic*]. He is Bo Brewster's journalism teacher, swim coach, friend, and psychological support at Clark Fork High School. Mr. S persuades Bo to attend Mr.* Nakatani's Anger Management Class after Mr. Redmond has taken steps to get Bo suspended from school. Bo often confides in Mr. S, who enjoys Bo's company, sees his talent at the triathlon, admires his determination to excel, and encourages his writing ability. After Bo's father tells Bo that Mr. S is gay, something that he learned from Mr. Redmond, with whom Mr. S does not get along, Bo drops swimming. Later, ashamed of his bigotry, Bo apologizes to Mr. S and resumes swimming. Mr. S suggests that Bo form a training support group called Stotans (Stoics and Spartans), but he also warns Bo to be careful about whom he selects for the group. Bo picks his friends in the Nak Pack. Mr. S confides in Bo that he also had an abusive father, a perhaps too fortuitous matter.

MRS. HORSEPOOL-WORTHINGHAM (*The Ear, the Eye, and the Arm**), Beryl, woman of the English tribe, mother of the Mellower*. Although she does not have the malevolent intentions of some of their captors, she still keeps the Matsika children prisoners, hoping the Mellower can persuade the General to offer a substantial reward for their return. She bullies her son, underfeeds the children, and makes them work as soon as the worst of their chicken pox, which they have all contracted, is past. In a caricature of the horsey type of Englishwoman, she and her friends of the Animal Fanciers Society worship their pets, dead and alive, while treating children, theirs and other people's, with indifference and even hostility.

MRS. MADELINE GLADSTONE (*Rules of the Road**), wealthy, elderly owner of some 176 very successful shoe stores who hires teenage Jenna Boller to drive her Cadillac in Chicago and on their trip to a stockholders' meeting in Dallas, Texas. Imperious, elegant, and dignified, Mrs. Gladstone makes the trip with the dual pains of a hip badly in need of replacement and of the duplicity of her son Elden, who can't wait until she resigns as president and director to sell out to The Shoe Warehouse. During the trip Jenna learns about the growth of Gladstone Shoes, Inc., from a small Texas store started by Mrs. Gladstone and her husband, to its admired position in the business. Always dedicated to providing high-quality footwear, Mrs. Gladstone is hurt by the thought that Gladstone's will be selling shoddy merchandise. She encourages Jenna to pose as a customer to spy on the various stores that they visit on their trip. Sharp-tongued and strong-willed, she has nonetheless earned the loyalty of many of her best managers, and when she resigns, her valiant stand brings others to her side. After the owner of The Shoe Warehouse offers to keep the Gladstone chain as a separate entity with Mrs. Gladstone in charge of quality, she is not above gloating over Elden, reminding him that women in her family live long, active lives.

MR. TIPTOP (*While No One Was Watching**), old, blind, former musician and now owner of a small shoe repair shop who befriends the Foster children, especially Frankie*. He gives them food on occasion and tries to teach them morals. He once was a backup singer for Elvis Presley and often speaks with affection about the famous singer, who he asserts was the victim of the "almighty dollar." He deplores the ruin into which his neighborhood has fallen. He often sings with Frankie, harmonizing the melodies, and always prays before he eats. Frankie flees with Spot the rabbit for refuge to Mr. Tiptop's basement apartment when he thinks that Wayne* Bonner is moving into the house where Frankie and his siblings are living. Wayne attacks Mr. Tiptop for his money, and Frankie attacks Wayne and saves Mr. Tiptop's life. Mr. Tiptop represents the old school of neighborliness: allow others to remain as independent as possible, keep an eye out so you know what is going on, and help out if there is need. Mr. Tiptop is still in the hospital at book's end.

MR. TOBY GROUT (*Beyond the Western Sea: Book One: The Escape from Home**; *Beyond the Western Sea: Book Two: Lord Kirkle's Money**), the London thief who, impersonating an old, lame man and wearing a patch over one eye, picks Sir Laurence Kirkle's pocket of £1,000 that the boy took from the desk of his father, Lord Kirkle, when he ran away to America. When next seen, Mr. Grout is a young, powerfully built, one-eyed man of about twenty. Mr.* Matthew Clemspool engages Mr. Grout to help him make sure that Sir Laurence gets to America and never returns to England. With the stolen money, Mr. Grout buys better clothing and decides to emigrate himself. Although he dresses like a gentleman, his unschooled speech marks him as lower-class, a situation that he would like to remedy. Late in the novel, Mr.* Horatio Drabble agrees to teach Mr. Grout to read and speak well, a task begun in Book Two during the voyage, to make money for a new start in America. In Book One, Mr. Grout pops in and out of the action, complicating matters along with Mr. Clemspool. On the ship, Mr. Clemspool steals the money from Mr. Grout, thus setting up much of the story interest of Book Two. By this time, Mr. Grout thinks that Laurence is dead, and when he sees what he thinks is Laurence's ghost on the ship, he has a sudden conversion of character. He decides to mend his ways and soon becomes a staunch friend of Mr. Drabble and the O'Connells. When Mr. Grout informs Laurence that Mr. Clemspool told him that he had placed the stolen money in the bank, Laurence realizes that the key that has fallen into his possession is a safe-deposit box key and recovers his lost money.

MR. WAS (Hautman*, Pete, Simon & Schuster, 1996), complicated time-travel fantasy set mostly in the small town of Memory, Minnesota, with some vivid scenes of Marine battles on Guadalcanal Island in the South Pacific during World War II. The two main time periods of the action are the early 1940s and the early 1990s. The novel opens in 1993 in Skokie, Illinois, where Jack Lund, 13, lives with his alcoholic father and his abused mother, Betty*. When a call comes in the middle of one winter night, he learns that his Grandpa Skoro is dying and that he is to accompany his mother to Rochester, Minnesota, because his father is "not feeling well," her code phrase for "drunk." Since his grandfather has never wanted to see Jack before, he reluctantly approaches the bedside and is horrified when the old man grabs his neck and dies, trying to strangle the boy. Jack and his mother go to Memory for the funeral and stay in Grandpa Skoros' strange, isolated house known as Boggs'* End, for the family who disappeared from it years earlier. There Jack finds a door in a third-floor closet that leads him into a balmy autumn evening. He meets two young people, Scud* (Franklin Scudder) and Andie* (Andrea Murphy), about his age. Together they raid an apple orchard until, for a joke, Scud throws an apple at the door, and the farmer sets the dog on them. Jack returns to Boggs' End and, later, to Skokie, where his parents continue their dysfunctional marriage. Almost three years later, after a beating from Jack's father lands his mother in the hospital, she takes Jack and moves to Boggs' End. At first Jack avoids the time-travel door, but eventually he feels compelled to try it again and finds himself in September 1941. When he tries to buy a comic book at a local bar-general store, the date on his quarter sets off suspicions and, as he is running from pursuit, Scud drives by and picks him up. Together they visit Andie, who lives several miles up the road and has blossomed into a lively beauty with whom Jack immediately falls in love. Although he is able to get back through the door to the 1990s, life at Boggs' End is not happy. Jack's father appears, saying that he has stopped drinking, and argues with his wife about the house, which he wants to sell and she doesn't. As he starts to drink again, their conflict escalates until he kills her. In shock, Jack goes through the door to 1941 and walks to the Murphys' farm, where Andie's father, who recently injured his hand, puts him to work. For most of the winter Jack lives at the farm with motherless Andie and her suspicious father, often being thrown into the role of chaperone when Andie goes out with Scud, whom her father trusts even less than he trusts Jack. After Pearl Harbor, although he is not yet seventeen, he lets Scud talk him into enlisting. A large portion of the novel is told in letters written by Jack to Andie but never intended to be sent, on a troop ship in the Pacific and through the terrible Battle of

Guadalcanal. Cut off from their unit, Jack and Scud hole up in a cave surrounded by jungle filled with Japanese soldiers. There Scud reads Jack's letters, which reveal that he loves Andie and thinks that she reciprocates the feeling. Enraged, since he has always assumed that he has exclusive rights to the girl, Scud attacks Jack and leaves him for dead. The next section of the novel is made up of reports from army psychiatrists investigating a man found naked, disfigured, and unable to remember anything, even his name. Eventually, the man, known as Mr. Was, is sent to Salisbury Acres, a mental hospital in Virginia, where he stays in a semivegetative state until 1993, when a young orderly tries acupuncture on him, starting a gradual return of his memory. Jack walks out of the hospital, hitchhikes to New Orleans, steals a fat wallet, buys a car, and drives to Memory. There he runs into an old, sour man who is so shocked at his name that he has a heart attack. Jack figures out that it is Scud, who has adopted his mother's maiden name, Skoro, married Andie, separated from her, and, through the time-slip of the door, is Jack's own grandfather. Throughout the novel, Jack occasionally runs into Pinkus Boggs, who originally disappeared through the door to the 1890s. Through Pinky's help, Andie sends a letter to Jack, who goes through the door again and meets her in 1952. The convoluted plot is cleverly worked out, and many of the scenes are strong, especially those of the conflicts between Jack's parents and those of the horrors of Pacific island warfare. Poe Nominee.

MUSIC FROM A PLACE CALLED HALF MOON (Oughton*, Jerrie, Houghton, 1995), girl's growing-up novel set in the early 1950s involving anti-Indian prejudice in the small town of Half Moon in the North Carolina Smoky Mountains. When Horace Houp gets up in the church business meeting and says that the Vacation Bible School should be open to all the children of Half Moon, not just those of church members, much of the congregation is outraged. That will mean that the school will be full of half-breeds! The narrator, Edie Jo Houp, 13, doesn't know whether her father actually supports integration or just likes a good fight, but the fight is clearly what he gets. The church erupts in a torrent of argument, through which Edie's mother, Helen, stands up with her husband, but the disagreement goes on in the town and even in the Houp home. Family relationships, which have already been tense since Gramma* Houp's house burned down, and she moved in with her son's family, are further strained when Helen is refused credit and humiliated at the Truitt grocery store because of her husband's stand, and she stops speaking to him. Edie herself knows only one Indian, Cherokee Fish, who is in her class at school and whom she saw almost choke a boy who called him a half-breed. Since she has had to give up her bedroom to her grandmother, and her parents are fighting, Edie spends more time than usual at the sawmill site up the mountain from their semirural home, where she likes to read and write poems. Always fearful, partly because her older brother, Jonah, has made a sport of scaring her, she is terrified when she runs into Cherokee at the sawmill and astonished when he sits on a sawhorse and plays his harmonica. Her fear is intensified when, one night after taking her friend, Mary Grady Heldron, home, Jonah drives through Davis Bottoms, where most of the town's Indians live, and their car is surrounded by a group of young toughs. Although Jonah is able to gun the motor and back out, knocking some of the boys off the hood, they are both shaken by the encounter. Nevertheless, Edie goes back to the sawmill site and meets Cherokee, and when he asks her to read poems, he really listens, then plays her more music and, another day, brings her an arrowhead. She begins to dream of him romantically, but she keeps this acquaintance secret, worrying even more because a second house burns down, this fire killing Mr. Truitt, and because a jacket left in a drainage ditch behind Gramma's house has been traced to Cherokee's older brother, Sierra. In spite of her anger at Mrs. Truitt, Edie's mother makes a pound cake to take to the widow. A short time later, Edie and Mary Grady are hiking on the mountain and come upon Sierra and his friend Arlie quarreling with Cherokee, accusing him of calling the sheriff. As the girls listen, hidden in the rhododendrons, they hear about Sierra's fury at being insulted by Gramma's locking the screen door when he came on the porch and Cherokee's incredulous discovery that for this and some unnamed insult by Mr. Truitt, Sierra has burned down two houses and caused a man's death. When Cherokee says that he won't volunteer this information to the sheriff but that he won't take the rap for his brother if he is accused, Sierra attacks and kills him, then runs off. Edie forces Mary Grady to run to the Houp house for help, while she frantically tries to revive Cherokee with her T-shirt soaked in spring water. Surprisingly, her family is understanding. Her mother takes a pound cake to the Fish home with Edie, and they sit for a few uncomfortable minutes in the first Indian house that they have ever entered. Giving her deposition to the judge, Edie breaks down for the first time, but gradually she begins to recover. Finally, she takes her own first positive step toward healing by giving the harmonica, which she had taken from Cherokee's pocket, wanting something to remember him by, to his younger sister, Leona. The novel does a remarkably good job of exposing the emotions and unreasoning fear of difference in a small southern town of the period. Edie and Mary Grady's witnessing Cherokee's murder is too fortuitous a coincidence, but the subsequent scene in the Fish home rings true. Especially telling is the way that a fight between parents affects the whole family. Although there are two African-American families in the town, the prejudice centers on the Indians, especially on the mixed-bloods. An article reprinted from the local paper some five years later, saying that Edie and Leona are rooming together at college, strains credulity and is unnecessary. Josette Frank.

THE MUSIC OF DOLPHINS (Hesse*, Karen, Scholastic, 1996), novel of a feral girl "rescued" from her life with dolphins in the Caribbean. Most of the story occurs in the mind of Mila, a girl of about thirteen when she is found, naked, long-haired, encrusted with salt, seaweed, and even barnacles, on a small cay between Florida and Cuba. In long, lyrical passages printed in italics, Mila's thoughts are recorded in full sentences, short but not unsophisticated. A reprinted newspaper account tells of the surveillance mission helicopter crew spotting and capturing her. Narration then moves to extremely simple sentences, in large type, relating in English her lessons with Dr.* Elizabeth Beck, the research professor at Boston University who has won the disputed right to train and study Mila at her facility on the Charles River. Dr. Beck is studying another feral child, a younger, or at least smaller, girl named Shay, found in the Salmon River Mountains of Idaho, and it is thought that the girls may thrive in each other's company. At first Shay responds a bit to Mila's overtures, but she does not have the intelligence or the drive to learn. Mila likes to please Dr. Beck and her assistant, Sandy*, and she learns quickly, especially when she is introduced to music, both through tapes and by playing a recorder that a Dr. Peach begins to teach her. As her English and her understanding of human ways improve, the type becomes smaller and the sentences longer, but Mila does not give up her longing for the sea and for her dolphin friends. One night she lets herself out of the house, dives into the Charles River, and swims a long way, but the cold water is too hard on her, and she becomes very ill. When she returns from the hospital, her room and the house doors are always locked. Discovering this throws her into a panic, and she injures her hands beating on the walls and window. Only when Justin*, Dr. Beck's teenage son, yells at her does she stop. Convinced that if she tries hard enough to learn all that they ask, she will be allowed to return to the sea, she concentrates furiously. Finally, with the help of Justin, with whom she has developed a real friendship, she realizes that the more she does, the more they will want. With this newfound understanding, she demands that the doors be unlocked and stops eating until, nine days later, Dr. Beck capitulates. Mila has seen videotapes of her capture, only gradually realizing that they are of her, and has learned that she is probably a Cuban child lost with her mother and younger brother at sea years earlier. Little by little, bits of her predolphin memories surface, until she retrieves some Spanish words from her infancy. As she sees Shay retreat into an almost catatonic state, she realizes that she has to go back to the sea. With the support of Justin, then Sandy, and finally Dr. Beck, she is taken back to the Caribbean, where she finds her dolphin family and rejoins them. The moving story is made comprehensible by the clever typographic and stylistic changes that reflect the natural, partly telepathic communication that Mila has with the dolphins compared with the painfully acquired primer English. The novel is a protest against the scientific attitude that treats Mila as a subject, not an individual worthy of respect. Her character, sensitive, highly intelligent, and ultimately assertive, is memorable. SLJ.

MY BROTHER, MY SISTER, AND I (Watkins*, Yoko Kawashima, Simon & Schuster, 1994), autobiographical novel set in Japan shortly after World War II, sequel to *So Far from the Bamboo Grove*, continuing the harrowing survival story of the three siblings who escaped from their home in Korea only to find

Japan devastated by the war. Although their mother has died, Yoko, 13, the narrator, and her older sister, Ko, are reunited with their brother, Hideyo, 21, and live in a tiny room in a warehouse in Kyoto, where they eke out a bare existence from the sale of Ko's sewing, Hideyo's occasional day's work, and Yoko's enterprising scavenging. Both girls are in school, Yoko in snobbish Sagano Girls' School, where she is made miserable by the taunts and mean tricks of her schoolmates, and Ko at the university. Disaster strikes when the warehouse burns, and Ko, retrieving their mother's ashes and other treasures, is badly injured. Yoko and Hideyo move into Ko's room at the hospital, where they can care for her and cook what little food they have. Their predicament worsens when they discover that the kind couple who had owned the warehouse and allowed them to live there died in the fire, not from smoke or flames but from blows to their heads. Yoko and Ko are accused of the murder and of stealing the missing cash box. Yoko suspects a heavyset, hunched man whom she saw lurking near the warehouse the night of the fire, probably the same man whom Ko hit with a sharp stick when he jumped at her as she left the outhouse that same night. With the help of the doctor who treated this man's injury and some sleuthing on their own, Hideyo and Yoko eventually prove that the niece of the warehouse owner, to get the insurance, hired two local thugs to set the building on fire and that they are the murderers. When Ko recovers sufficiently, Hideyo builds a shack beneath a highway bridge among a rough crowd of home-less people, and they move in without running water or electricity. Ko, who remains partially crippled, is so terrified that she dares not sleep at night or when she is left alone during the day. One morning Yoko, discovering that Ko is feverish, runs all the way to the hospital for help. There she meets Mrs*. Minato, a woman whom Yoko befriended when she was in the hospital, now returned for a checkup. When she hears of Ko's new illness, she takes charge, helps get Ko to the hospital, invites them to live in a vacant room in her house, and has her husband bring his truck to transport their belongings. Ko survives an operation on her infected leg, Hideyo helps repair the Minato house, Yoko graduates from Sagano and enters an experimental English Village Program, learning conversational English at the expense of the government. Throughout their long ordeal, all three siblings keep hoping for news of their father, a Japanese diplomat captured by the Russians, and pursue all official avenues to learn of his fate. Finally, they receive a letter sayng that he is alive and will join them soon. When he does arrive, Yoko does not recognize the feeble old man who has been terribly abused during his six years of captivity, but when he calls her "Little One," the family pet name for her, she knows her kind, gentle father, and they rejoice to be together again. An Afterword tells how Yoko meets and eventually marries her American husband and summarizes the rest of their lives. Although presumably the novel follows the facts of their lives faithfully, the mystery of the warehouse fire and their part in discovering the culprits and the missing cash box sound fictionalized, far less convincing than the details of their day-to-day existence, in which a soup made of discarded greens from daikons, a kind of radish, is a delicious treat and a codfish head rescued from garbage is a bonanza. Yoko's suffering at the hands of her wealthy schoolmates, who sneer at her, throw her slippers into the toilet, and even accuse her of stealing, all incidents that she keeps from her brother and sister, ring true, and her occasional resentment of Ko's bossiness makes her seem like a real girl her age. ALA; SLJ.

MYERS, WALTER DEAN (1937–), born in Martinsburg, West Virginia; highly acclaimed writer of novels and biography about African Americans. His *Glory Field** (Scholastic, 1994) is an ambitious, multigenerational novel ranging from slavery times to the late twentieth century. In a different vein is *Slam!** (Scholastic, 1996), a sports novel about an inner-city high school basketball star. More recently he has published *At Her Majesty's Request: An African Princess in Victorian England* (Scholastic, 1999), a biography of an African orphan brought to England and taken under the protection of Queen Victoria. For earlier biographical information and title entries, see *Dictionary, 1960–1984* [*Fast Sam, Cool Clyde, and Stuff*; *Hoops*], *Dictionary, 1985–1989* [*Fallen Angels*; *Me, Mop, and the Moondance Kid*; *Motown and Didi*; *Scorpions*], and *Dictionary, 1990–1994* [*Somewhere in the Darkness*].

MY LOUISIANA SKY (Holt*, Kimberly Willis, Holt, 1998), girl's growing-up novel set in the semirural town of Saitter, Louisiana, in the late twentieth century. Although she loves them dearly, at twelve Tiger Ann Parker has begun to be embarrassed by her retarded parents, Lonnie and Corrina, and her old-fashioned grandmother, Jewel Ramsey, who directs their little family firmly. Tiger's best friend, Jesse Wade Thompson, whose father owns the nursery where Lonnie works and where occasionally Corrina, Granny, and Tiger pick peas and other vegetables, prefers playing baseball with Tiger to fooling around with other girls, but she longs for pretty clothes, a pink-and-white complexion, and yellow curls like Abby Lynn Anders instead of her homemade dresses, freckles, and lank red hair. When stylish Aunt Dorie Kay, who works in Baton Rouge, visits and gives them their first television, all except Granny are delighted. Soon Corrina is ignoring Lonnie and neglecting her simple household chores, and Granny puts her foot down, limiting television watching to two hours a day. When Abby Lynn gives a swimming party at her new pool and doesn't ask Tiger, she is deeply hurt, even after Jesse Wade, discovering she has not been invited, leaves, hunts up Tiger, and tries to comfort her with her first real kiss. This pain, however, is quickly overshadowed when Granny suffers a stroke and dies. Aunt Dorie Kay arrives and takes charge. Although Lonnie can read, learning to pay the bills is too much for him, and Aunt Dorie Kay makes a deal with the minister to handle this chore if Lonnie will cut his grass. Corrina, a slim, pretty woman, stays curled up in bed, refusing to bathe or change out of her nightgown, although she finally agrees to let Tiger wash her hair. Aunt Dorie Kay takes Tiger with her to Baton Rouge to get her cleaning woman, Magnolia, to manage the household and take care of Corrina. She invites Tiger to come live with her and go to school in Baton Rouge. She points out that she has changed her own name there to Doreen and suggests that Tiger use her middle name, Ann, in the city. She even reveals the never-mentioned reason for Corrina's mental condition. When Corrina was six and she was a toddler, she started up a ladder left leaning against a tree. Trying to rescue her, Corrina fell, broke her arm, and suffered brain damage. In Baton Rouge Tiger gets her long, red hair cut and is delighted with the excitement of the city and her aunt's attractive apartment, and they plan that at the end of the summer she will return and start school there. In Saitter, Magnolia finds a room in the Negro quarter, but she rapidly takes charge of Tiger's household and soon has Corrina cleaned up and peeling potatoes. Tiger starts working at Thompson's nursery, as does Jesse Wade, the first time that he has done any physical labor. Lonnie shows them both how to prepare and transplant cuttings of Mr. Thompson's specially developed Louisiana Lady camellias, which he has gone to Dallas to market. Lonnie, who understands signs of weather change in the behavior of birds and animals, realizes while the sky is still clear that a bad storm is coming, and he advises Mrs. Thompson to spread sheets and newspapers on the floors in the house, and he mobilizes Tiger, Jesse Wade, and the other workers to dig up plants in the field, take the cuttings in buckets, and the liners of seedlings inside. When one of the workers protests at her taking the advice of an idiot, Mrs. Thompson fires him. The others work frantically until the wind begins, and Lonnie sends Tiger home, staying himself to finish the work. On the way, Tiger pauses to pull a calf belonging to Abby Lynn's family out of a mudhole and drive her home. When she reaches their porch, Magnolia meets her with the news that her mother has started out on the shortcut to find her and bring her home. Tiger turns back through the woods and reaches Corrina, and together they make their way through the crashing branches and the hurricane winds, finally crawling across the yard to the porch steps. Corrina keeps looking out the window and finally dashes out, trying to retrieve Granny's sunbonnet, which Tiger has left on the clothesline. Just as she is about to be blown away, Lonnie drives up, kisses her, and in the quiet eye of the storm, Tiger joins them in the yard, her heart overflowing with love for them both and her realization that this is where she wants to be, not in Baton Rouge. When Aunt Dorie Kay comes to take Magnolia home, Tiger tells her that she is staying and will take care of her parents. A subtheme throughout the story is the treatment of the African Americans, a discrimination so deeply rooted that Tiger has never really been aware of it and only gradually realizes it from her acquaintance with Magnolia and with Otis, who works at the Thompson nursery. This theme could be intrusive, but it is introduced so naturally and with so little didacticism that it simply adds to the vivid picture of the small town and of Tiger's spunky and sensitive character. ALA; Boston Globe Honor.

N

NAPOLI, DONNA JO (1948–), born in Miami, Florida; received her B.A. degree in mathematics and her Ph.D. in Romance linguistics, both from Harvard University; head of the Linguistics Department at Swarthmore College; writer of books and articles on linguistics, poetry, and short stories and novels for children and young adults. Since her first juvenile book, *The Hero of Barletta* (Carolrhoda), a retelling of an Italian folktale, came out in 1988, she has published more than a dozen books for young readers, some of them fantasies like *Soccer Shock* (Dutton, 1991) and *Shark Shock* (Dutton, 1994) and many of them clever improvisations on old, originally oral stories. Among these are *The Prince of the Pond: Otherwise Known as De Fawg Pin* (Dutton, 1992) and its sequel, *Jimmy, the Pickpocket of the Palace* (Dutton, 1995), which rework the "The Frog Prince" story. *Zel** (Dutton, 1996), a young adult novel cited by *School Library Journal*, cleverly redoes the story of "Rapunzel," giving the mother more sympathetic attention than does the original. *Beast* (Atheneum, 2000) retells "Beauty and the Beast" from the viewpoint of the Beast. Chosen by the American Library Association, *Stones in the Water** (Dutton, 1997) ventures effectively into historical fiction, being the dramatic account of Italian boys who are captured and enslaved by the Germans during World War II. Napoli lives in Swarthmore, Pennsylvania, with her husband, Barry Furrow, a law professor, and their five children.

NARDO HERNANDEZ (*Parrot in the Oven: Mi Vida**), Bernardo Hernandez, later adolescent in age and older brother of Manny (Manuel) Hernandez, son of Dad* Hernandez and his wife, Rebecca, called Mom* by her children. Nardo is handsome, big, tough, lazy, and manipulative. Mostly he likes to hang out with his friends, avoid working, and defy his parents. His peers respect him only because he is big and smart. He and Manny get on variously, but on the whole Manny looks up to him, if not always wisely.

NATHAN (*Escape from Egypt**), rude, surly, hard-drinking father of Jesse*, husband of Devorah*. Nathan is an inherently practical man, a chameleon ready to compromise principles if he feels that it is in his or his family's interests. He accepts Moses' leadership because he thinks that Moses may possibly be right, but he questions Moses' authority and thinks Moses puts on airs. Nor does he have much faith in Adonai, the Hebrew god, feeling that people do best by helping themselves. Throughout most of the book, Jesse despises him, much preferring his mother's brother, Uncle Rimon*. Late in the story, Jesse learns that his father bought him the apprenticeship in In-hop-tep's jewelry smith's shop as a way of keeping his son from having to work in the much-dreaded quarries and that the jewels that Nathan uses to buy influence he acquired from Hebrews who sought his help in saving the lives of their children. Jesse learns late in the book that he is not really Nathan's son but that Nathan married Devorah when she was pregnant with Jesse and a widow, thus ensuring her a better life and saving Jesse's life. Nathan is one of the most interesting characters in the novel, a several-faceted, ambivalent figure.

NELL COOPER (*The Cuckoo's Child**), half sister of Mia Veery, like her sister, Bibi, a daughter of their mother's first marriage, to Morse Cooper. Nell is especially interested in medicine, with a romantic idea of becoming a surgeon and working for Albert Schweitzer in Africa. Nell and Bibi, both of high school age, consider themselves intellectual and sophisticated, far above the little Tennessee town where their mother grew up and where they have come to live with her younger sister, Kit* Hanks. They wear long, black skirts, sandals, and shawls and read French novels. When it becomes apparent that Mia's parents will not be found and that the girls will stay in Ionia with Kit, Nell and Bibi adjust and go off to register at the high school, still feeling superior, but they are stricken when Mia tells them that they are laughed at because of their airs and their odd clothes. Nell considers Mia a spoiled baby, but she loves her and occasionally tries to do things for her, like trimming her hair. To tell Mia that the search for their parents has been discontinued, she and Bibi persuade Morse to drive them to Ionia, but then they lack the courage to give her the bad news.

NELSON, THERESA (1948–   ), born in Beaumont, Texas; freelance writer since 1983 of novels for middle graders and young adults, which have won many awards and been praised for their characterization, lyrical style, and strong sense of place. *Earthshine** (Orchard, 1994), a contemporary problem novel, concerns a nontraditional family whose father is dying of AIDS. Highly regarded, it has received several awards and citations: American Library Association, Boston Globe-Horn Book Honor; Josette Frank Award (formerly Child Study); and *School Library Journal*. A more recent book is *The Empress of Elsewhere: A Novel* (DK, 1998). For more biographical information, titles, and title entries, see *Dictionary, 1985–1989* [*The 25¢ Miracle*] and *Dictionary, 1990–1994* [*And One for All*; *The Beggars' Ride*; *Earthshine*].

NEUFELD, JOHN (ARTHUR) (1938–   ), born in Chicago; Illinois raised in Des Moines, Iowa; educated at Phillips Exeter Academy and Yale University. After two years' service in the U.S. Army, he worked in New York City for various publishing companies. During this time he began writing novels, among them *Edgar Allan* (Phillips, 1968) and *Lisa Bright and Dark* (Phillips, 1969), which were hailed as innovative and daring reading fare for young adults. After living abroad for a while, he went west, where he taught, wrote more novels for young readers and also produced fiction for adults. Among his books for adolescents are *A Small Civil War* (Ballantine, 1982), about censorship; *Sherelle* (New American Library, 1983), about teen pregnancy; *Almost a Hero* (Atheneum, 1995), about a boy who volunteers in a homeless center; and *Gaps in Stone Walls** (Atheneum, 1996), a murder mystery set on Martha's Vineyard in 1880, which is strong in period details as well as in gripping suspense and an Edgar Allan Poe nominee. *Boys Lie: A Novel* (DK, 1999), tackles another issue: boys' harassing an eighth-grade girl thought "easy." For more information and a title entry, see *Dictionary, 1960–1994* [*Edgar Allan*].

NEVER TRUST A DEAD MAN (Vande Velde*, Vivian, Harcourt, 1999), comic fantasy novel with murder-mystery and thriller aspects, set for a few days in a fictitious, Wales-like land in which people believe in magic and witchcraft, mostly in the tiny, isolated village of Penryth. Convicted, kangaroo-court fashion, of stabbing to death Farold, presumably because his girl, Anora, had chosen Farold and because his knife was used in the killing, Selwyn Roweson, 17, is sealed inside the village burial vault to die there, along with Farold's shrouded corpse and countless other decaying bodies. Despairing, his imagination running amok with the smells of the corpses and the spooky noises of unseen vermin and flying creatures all around, Selwyn is surprised to detect a pale, but glowing, light slowly coming toward him and even more surprised to see that it is borne by a hooded, haggard, old woman who says that she is Elswyth* the witch. In return for Selwyn's promising to work ever-increasing lengths of time for her, the irritable Elswyth conducts a raising-of-the-dead ceremony for Farold, so that Selwyn can ask him who killed him. The ceremony goes awry, and Farold is reincarnated as a irascible, talkative bat who attaches himself variously to Selwyn throughout the rest of the novel, gives him mostly bad advice and suggestions, and usually addresses him as "dumb twit." Farold says that he has no idea who killed him, since he was stabbed in the back in the dark. Elswyth then disguises Selwyn as a pilgrim so that he and Farold can investigate in the village. At the tavern, the most likely place to pick up gossip or take advantage of a loose tongue, the two learn nothing of substance. When they request another disguise, Selwyn becomes the tavern keeper's daughter, Kendra, who is away presumably studying at St. Hilda's convent, and Farold becomes her caged goldfinch. No one in the village detects the impersonation, but the plan goes somewhat awry when Kendra's mother asks her where the baby is. It seems that Kendra had named Farold as the father of her out-of-wedlock child. He, now a bird, privately denies the role vigorously. Selwyn's investigations lead nowhere, except to verify his suspicions that almost everyone in the village disliked Farold and had reason to want him dead. Eventually, he learns that Farold's elderly uncle, Derian, killed Farold because he coveted Farold's inheritance, the village mill, and wished to claim Anora. The answer to the mystery is withheld nicely to the very end, the action being deliberately and engagingly overcomplicated, and except for Selwyn, who is a typical unfortunate, most characters are pleasingly overdrawn types. The dialogue is filled with patter, comic insults, and loads of silly bickering, and the transformations are accomplished with expected, amusing difficulties. The whole is of no great moment except good fun, but reemphasizes the age-old maxim of not jumping to conclusions. SLJ.

NICK OLSEN (*What Girls Learn**), owner of a house and limousine service on Long Island, New York, to which Frances* Burbank and her daughters, Tilden and Elizabeth*, move from Georgia. A thoroughly decent man, he has met Frances a year before at a wedding and is prepared to take on all three of them, with or without marriage. He has kept his house and run his business neatly and seriously, and he has the tact not to push his affections on the girls. Although he clearly does not approve of Uncle* Rand, Frances' younger brother who comes to stay with them, he understands Rand's need to be with the sister who really brought him up and is now dying, and he accepts the help that Rand can give Frances with cooking and other housework. A bit old-fashioned, he gets down on his knee at their Christmas celebration to ask Frances to marry him. While Elizabeth cheers, Tilden ungraciously says, "I don't care. Whatever you want," hating the idea of losing more of her mother than she already has. Not until after Frances' death is Tilden able to feel the depth of Nick's loss, as well as her own, and begin to love him. His is a rare portrait of a genuinely good, believable, and still interesting character.

NIGEL (*Tiger, Tiger, Burning Bright**), likable newcomer to Norbu, California, friend of Jesse and Kyle*. Since his father is a famous photojournalist, Nigel has lived in many places, some of them exotic, and, as Jesse learns from Mr. Wright, the English teacher, Nigel attended ten schools before he arrived in Norbu. He has a strong sense of self and a good mind, talks a lot, and is socially aware. He has an encyclopedic memory and often contributes more information about whatever is under discussion than the boys want to hear, ranging from rain forests and jungles to dementia, but his friends just good-naturedly order him to shut up. His father, Thomas, has come to Norbu to make a pictorial record of what he feels is the dying way of life on the high desert. Everywhere that Thomas goes, he carries his expensive Nikon and related equipment, although he is never intrusive or obnoxious, and Nigel often helps him with his work. Thomas takes a lot of pictures of Pappy*, whom he regards as a "living archive" and a "national treasure." Nigel's family live in an upscale house on the edge of town. Although financially above everyone in town, they are accepted for the nice people that they are. Nigel is one of the most attractive figures in the book.

NIXON, JOAN LOWERY (1927–   ), born in Los Angeles; resident of Houston, Texas; teacher, instructor in creative writing, and writer of nonfiction and fiction for children and adolescents. Since 1967, she has published more than 100 books and is an acknowledged leader in mystery and suspense books for young readers. She is the only author to receive four Edgar Allan Poe awards for juvenile mysteries, and several others of her books have been nominated for the award, including *Shadowmaker** (Delacorte, 1994) and *Spirit Seeker** (Delacorte, 1995). She has also written period books in her Young American Series and basic reading mysteries in her Thumbprint Series. Nixon's books move fast, are carefully plotted, and always tell a good story. For earlier biographical information, titles, and title entries, see *Dictionary, 1960–1984* [*The Kidnapping of Christina Lattimore*; *The Mysterious Red Tape Gang*; *The Seance*]; *Dictionary, 1985–1989* [*The Other Side of Dark*; *The Ghosts of Now*]; and *Dictionary, 1990–1994* [*The Weekend Was Murder*; *The Name of the Game Was Murder*].

NO EFFECT (Hayes*, Daniel, Godine, 1994), third in a series of novels starring Tyler McAllister, 13, and his lumpish friend Lymie Lawrence, eighth graders in Wakefield, New York. The first, *The Trouble with Lemons*, is a mystery; the second, *The Eye of the Beholder*, is a series of domestic adventures; and *No Effect* is mostly a school and sports novel, concerning Tyler's experience on the wrestling team and his infatuation with his new science teacher, Miss Williams. When the high school team cannot fill its quota of lightweight wrestlers, a call is put out for eighth graders, and Tyler, egged on by Lymie's scorn of his scrawny frame, responds. To his surprise, so does Lymie, who, although bigger and heavier than Tyler, is more interested in eating than in exercise. At first the macho, pain-is-great workouts exhaust both boys and fill Tyler with fear, but after Coach Robilatto injures his back demonstrating an exercise and is out of school for the year, his place is taken by Chuckie Deegan, groundskeeper for Tyler's mother. Tyler is astonished to learn that Chuckie was a state champion wrestler, since the young man, who has become part of the family, has never mentioned it. The boys' enthusiasm for the sport increases under Chuckie's more encouraging coaching. At the same time, Tyler experiences his first love, a severe crush on the young woman who has taken over his earth science class since the death of their termagant teacher, Old Lady Waverly. After shyly helping Miss Williams put away equipment after class for some weeks, Tyler gradually begins talking to her and learns, to his surprise, that she is interested in his wrestling attempts. She agrees to come to his first meet, and he begins to worry that he might be badly beaten and disgraced. When he learns that she has no family in the area, he impulsively asks her to join his family, which includes his mother, their housekeeper, Mrs. Saunders, and Chuckie, for Thanksgiving dinner. He is elated when she accepts. He tells his mother that he has invited a guest but doesn't have nerve enough to say that it is his teacher. Predictably, she arrives with Chuckie, as his guest, and Tyler is humiliated, though he realizes that she has thought that his invitation was simply reinforcing Chuckie's earlier suggestion. Although he avoids her at school, she sends him to a counselor, a man so enthusiastic about preventing teenage suicide that he all but offers Tyler a weapon so that he can save the boy. Appalled, Tyler tells Chuckie the whole story, and with his intervention Miss Williams has an understanding talk with him. Tyler finds that he is free from his obsession and feels great relief to be just a friend of his teacher, who clearly likes him. In his first meet his opponent, known as The Slug, throws him out of the ring and is disqualified so that Tyler, after he regains consciousness, is declared the winner. Although Tyler's mother and older brother's being in the movies is mentioned briefly, nothing is made of it in this book. There are a flashback to his father's funeral and some mention of Tyler's asthma attacks that prompted their move from Los Angeles, but mostly the novel is independent of the earlier ones in the series. Tyler is a sensitive, hyperactive kid, inclined to worry excessively but still head recklessly for trouble. Lymie is slower, unimaginative, and prone to use his fists to compensate, but he is goodhearted. The humor of Tyler's infatuation is painful but may amuse readers of Tyler's age. ALA; SLJ.

NOLAN, HAN (1956–   ), born in Birmingham, Alabama; raised near New York City; teacher of dance and novelist for young adults. She received her undergraduate degree from the University of North Carolina at Greensboro and her master's from Ohio State University, both in dance. Because she wished to stay home with her children, she turned to writing as a career. She published her first book in 1994, *If I Should Die Before I Wake* (Harcourt, 1994), a fantasy about an American neo-Nazi girl who travels back in time and experiences the Holocaust firsthand. *Send Me Down a Miracle* (Harcourt, 1996) explores a girl's relationship with her domineering preacher-father; *Dancing on the Edge** (Harcourt, 1997), a *School Library Journal* choice, focuses on the descent into mental illness of an Alabama girl in a dysfunctional family of eccentrics; and *A Face in Every Window* (Harcourt, 1999) tells of a boy who must care for his mentally challenged father. Han has been praised for her characters, daring subject matter, and ability to create humorous situations that advance the plot and also keep the stories from becoming morbidly serious.

NORMAN CARSWELL (*Keeping the Moon**), sweet-tempered, gentle young artist who lives in Mira* Sparks' basement. Norman first appears as a collector of weird junk—mannequin torsos, bicycle gears, sunglasses—which he incorporates into artworks, but eventually he is revealed to be working on a series of very skillful portraits for his art school portfolio, among them one of Isabel and Morgan*, the young women who work at the Last Chance Bar and Grill where he is a cook, and one he paints of Colie Sparks, all of them wearing sunglasses. He is the third son of the owner of a prominent auto dealership, in which his older brothers became salesmen. When Norman was seventeen and began applying to art school, his father was furious, declared that he wouldn't pay for it, and made life so miserable that Norman moved out and lived in his dilapidated truck parked by the dumpsters behind the Last Chance. Although he wins a scholarship to art school, his father does not relent. Mira Sparks has taken him in, letting him live in her basement room crowded with his found-art materials, and declares him invaluable because he opens jars for her. While he is painting Colie's portrait, his phone rings every night, but he never picks it up, and no message is left on the answering machine. Finally goaded by Colie to answer it once, he talks briefly with his father, who has not relented but keeps calling to insist that the boy comply with his plans. Norman finally shows Colie a portrait that he has painted of his father as a young man from a photograph of the day when he opened his first dealership, a radiantly happy picture. The book's title comes from a childhood memory of a lunar eclipse, when Norman slept in the backyard with his brothers and was terrified that the moon was gone forever.

NORTHERN BORDERS (Mosher*, Howard Frank, Doubleday, 1994), novel of a boy growing up in the late 1930s and 1940s in an eccentric family of northern Vermont. Lost Nation Hollow, part of Kingdom* County, is isolated, and life there is still much like that at the turn of the century when Austen Kittredge III, the narrator, is a six year old, sent by his widowed father to live with his grandparents, who are among the last of the traditional hill farmers of New England. Little Austen is catapulted into the middle of what is known locally as the Forty Years' War between Gramp* (Austen Kittredge Senior) and Gram* (Abiah), both proud, fiercely independent old people who vie for blue ribbons at the Kingdom Fair and for control of the family and who seldom speak to each other, directing their remarks to the boy ("Austen, ask Mrs. Kittredge to pass the butter along if it isn't too much trouble"). Their children have all left home, Austen's father to attend college and become a schoolteacher in White River, his two sisters, Freddi (Nefertiti) and Klee (Cleopatra), known as the little aunts, both of whom attend the University of Vermont and in the summer work at a furniture factory and board in the village, and Rob Roy, who has just graduated from high school. They return frequently for tumultuous family gatherings, which usually end by everyone storming away from the dinner table. There are other relatives nearby, notably Great-Aunt* Maiden Rose, known as a "big aunt," who lives farther down the hollow, and two cousins, W. J. (Whiskeyjack) Kittredge, a moonshiner and bootlegger, and his brother, J. W. (John Wesleyan) Kittredge, a strict lay preacher. Into this contentious group young Austen fits with delight. Both Gramp and Gram expect him to work hard, but he thoroughly enjoys it, loves the rugged country, and steers his way between their demands for his loyalty with very little unease. The visit, which starts with a trial month, lasts until he is ready for college. In ten episodes, often hilarious, sometimes touching, he recounts incidents in those twelve years, all tinged with the special flavor of a bygone era. At the Kingdom County fair, Gramp buys a mistreated elephant, getting the money by conning the carnival con men, and employs the beast for several years on his remote farm. When a logjam keeps the raw material from reaching his water-powered sawmill, he proposes raising the level of his mill pond. Since this would flood her orchard, Gram takes him to court, much to the entertainment of the community. One episode concerns the Lost Nation Atheneum, a tough country school where teacher after teacher is run off until Mrs. Armstrong arrives, a husky, heavy-drinking widow who sneers at learning and keeps order by freely wielding her heavy cane. Another is about Uncle Rob, who, fancying himself a great hunter, bets and loses his new car to a sharpshooter from an ammunition compay. When Austen is fifteen, his Great-Aunt* Liz returns to a family reunion unexpectedly. She enlists Austen to help her find the proceeds of a bank heist, locally assumed to have been her own work. In August of Austen's seventeenth year, Gram dies. The next summer, Gramp takes him on a long-promised expedition into an uncharted part of Canada known as the Great Lost Corner, a trip that tests all the physical reserves of the boy toughened by twelve years of hard farmwork and that he fears will be too much for his seventy-two-year-old grandfather. Several times it promises to be fatal as they haul their canoe up icy rivers, plow through deep snow up mountains, and narrowly escape a forest fire. To Austen's astonishment, at an island in No Name Lake beyond where the country has been surveyed, they come upon a new cabin and an Inuit guide whom Gramp has had flown in, with the agreement that the two of them will be partners in a trapline after Austen has been flown by a bush pilot back to start college in Vermont. This is a fitting culmination to the story of the unsentimental old man and his hard, rough life. Despite the stormy relationships, the novel is a story of family love, which young Austen never doubts. The writing is spirited and humorous and gives such a feeling of authenticity that it is easy to forget that it is not autobiographical. It is also a picture of a way of life that began to die with the coming of electricity and better roads to the area about the time Austen was in high school and a change in the economy that made the isolated hill farming, already forty years out of date by that time, truly a thing of the past. SLJ.

NUKE CARLILE (*The Maze**), surly, vicious, U.S. government–hating owner of a gas station in Hanksville, Utah, the little town near the Maze, the area in Canyonlands National Park where Lon* Peregrino's condor-reintroducing camp is located. Rick* Walker encounters Nuke in Hanksville before he steals the ride to the camp and thus recognizes the man when he prowls around Lon's camp. Although Nuke is presented almost as faceless evil, enough of his story is given for the reader to understand his motivations. Once a prosperous rancher, he was forced to withdraw his herds from the areas that he had once grazed freely when the region was made a national park. Lon reports Nuke's vicious behavior and bomb-making activities to officials, who presumably will keep tabs on him. His also vicious pit bull, Jasper, perhaps named after the now off-limits canyon by the same name that Nuke once grazed, is killed in a fall in the canyon trying to pull down a fledgling condor.

NYE, NAOMI SHIHAB (1952–   ) born in St. Louis, Missouri, her father Palestinian, her mother American; lived for a year in Jerusalem during high school before moving to San Antonio, Texas, where she still lives; freelance writer, editor, and speaker; visiting writer at the universities of Hawaii, Alaska at Fairbanks, and Texas at Austin. Best known for her poetry for adults, of which she has published eight books, and her poetry anthologies and translations for young readers, among them *This Same Sky: A Collection of Poems from around the World* (Four Winds, 1992), *I Feel a Little Jumpy around You: A Book of Her Poems and His Poems Collected in Paris* (Simon & Schuster, 1996, with Paul Janeczco), and *The Space between Our Footsteps: Poems and Paintings from the Middle East* (Simon & Schuster, 1998). She has written the stories for three picture books and published a novel for young adults, *Habibi** (Simon & Schuster, 1996), about a Palestinian-American family in Jerusalem, which reflects her own experience. It won the Jane Addams Award and was an American Library Association choice. Nye has also contributed stories, poems, and essays to journals and periodicals.

O

O'CONNOR, BARBARA, born and raised in Greenville, South Carolina; writer of novels and biographies for middle-grade readers; resident with her husband and son of Duxbury, Massachusetts. Her first novel was *Beethoven in Paradise* (Farrar, 1997), a mixture of humor and poignancy about a musically talented boy whose father wants him to play baseball. This was followed by *Me and Rupert Goody** (Farrar, 1999), a *School Library Journal* selection about a slow-developing friendship between a young girl and a mentally challenged, biracial young man set in the Smoky Mountains. Her novels are engaging, made up of real-seeming characters, and reflect the mountain communities in details of setting and in style. She has published biographies for children on Katherine Dunham, Louis Braille, Ernie Pyle, Isadora Duncan, and Maria Montessori.

O'DONOHOE, NICK (NICHOLAS BENJAMIN) (1952–   ), born in Charles City, Iowa; writer of fantasy, science fiction, and mystery novels that appeal to both adults and young people. With a B.A. degree from Carleton College and a Ph.D. from Syracuse University, he is a professor at Virginia Polytechnic Institute and State University in Blacksburg, Virginia, where he lives. He is best known in young adult literature for his Crossroads Series, the first of which was cited by both the American Library Association and *School Library Journal*: *The Magic and the Healing** (Berkley, 1994). BJ Vaughan and her fellow Western Virginia College veterinary students venture the backroads of Virginia into a fantasy realm called Crossroads, populated by unicorns, satyrs, centaurs, and the like. Although derivative of the work of such novelists as C. S. Lewis and J.R.R. Tolkien, Crossroads is meticulously developed and memorable. *Under the Healing Sign* (Berkley, 1995) and *The Healing of Crossroads* (Berkley, 1996) continue BJ's adventures in the remote mountain realm. *Wind Chill* (PaperJacks, 1985) and *Open Season* (PaperJacks, 1986), both set in Minneapolis, feature the fictional detective Nathan Phillips, and *Too, Too Solid Flesh*

(TSR, 1989) blends genres with a murder mystery involving a theater troupe of androids.

OLD BESS (*The Moorchild**), Wise Woman of Torskaal village, mother of Anwara and apparently grandmother of Saaski. She is the first person to suspect that Saaski is a changeling and suggests that the way to get the Moorfolk to take her back is to throw her into the fire or the pond or to beat her badly, but when she has a chance to drown the child, she resists and later becomes her strongest defender, even teaching her to read. Old Bess herself was a foundling, picked up by gypsies when she was a newborn left at a crossroads and later abandoned by them when she was a child in front of the house of the miller in Torskaal. Long a widow, she lives in the house once occupied by Brother Oswic, a monk who taught her much about plants and healing herbs and how to read and left her his books. It is to her that Tam* and Saaski take Anwara's child, whom they have stolen back from the Moorfolk.

OPAL McCLOY (*Dancing on the Edge**), ex-husband of Gigi* McCloy, father of Dane* McCloy, and grandfather of the narrator and protagonist Miracle Mc-Cloy. He and Gigi split up before Miracle was born because they disagreed about how to raise their prodigy son. Opal insisted that the boy be raised learning at least some practical skills. When Miracle gets to know Opal, he is a thin, lively, elderly man who makes a living delivering newspapers and doing odd jobs. He lives in a dilapidated house filled with tattered furniture. Opal frightens Miracle for a while, especially when he informs her that since she was not born in the usual way, she really does not exist. He is kind to her in his peculiar way, however, and Miracle grows fond of him. He buys her a bicycle and teaches her how to work on it. He also arranges for her to have dancing lessons, mainly because he wishes to spite Gigi, but the girl loves him for it. He suffers a heart attack during the tornado because he rushes home to save the manuscript of Dane's first book. Although he is not well, he visits Miracle in the hospital.

OPS (*The Arkadians**), king of an area of Arkadia that has fallen on hard times because of the edict of King Bromios* and who is made its scapegoat, or pharmakos, for all the woes that have befallen the Arkadians. Due to be sacrificed, he leaves, becomes stuck in a tree, is rescued by Lucian*, and joins the group on their way to consult the Lady of Wild Things at Mount Panthea. In several ways, his story recalls that of Oedipus of Greek mythology. At the end, he becomes king of Arkadia in Bromios' place and marries the Lady of Wild Things' servant, Laurel-Crown.

ORGEL, DORIS (DORIS ADELBERG) (1929–   ), born in Vienna, Austria; editor and author and translator of children's books. During her long and varied writing career of more than forty books, her most highly acclaimed novel has been *The Devil in Vienna** (Dial, 1978), which tells in fiction form the story of her family's escape from Vienna after Hitler came into power in Austria. It was a Phoenix Award Honor Book of The Children's Literature Association. In addition to single titles, Orgel has written extensively for the Bank Street Ready-to-Read series, West Side Kids series, and Trumpet Book Club. She has also published fictionalized retellings of Greek myths, among them *The Princess and the God* (Orchard, 1996), about Cupid and Psyche, and *We Goddesses: Athena, Aphrodite, Hera* (DK, 1999). Some of her books have been translated into other languages, and some have been issued in paperback. She has made her home in Connecticut. For more information about Orgel, her books, and a title entry, see *Dictionary, 1960–1984* [*The Devil in Vienna*].

THE ORNAMENT TREE (Thesman*, Jean, Houghton, 1996), historical novel and understated love story set in 1918 in Seattle, Washington. After the death of her widowed mother and a summer of drudging at the farm of carping Aunt Suze, Bonnie Shaster, 14, travels to the city to live with elderly Audra Devereaux, her mother's cousin, in the house where her mother grew up. When no one meets her at the station, she is shaken, but she is found by voluble Winnie Devereaux, a cousin of Audra's late husband, who also lives at the family home. They arrive at the large white house set in a yard of big trees to find a young, blind man being escorted by his mother and the iceman shouting at a girl who snitches slivers of ice from his wagon. In the ruckus, Bonnie helps out by paying off the iceman and learns that the girl is Clare* Harris, 12, Audra's granddaughter, that the blind man is Carson Younger, the newest roomer, a soldier injured in the war, and that Audra, Winnie, and Audra's daughter, Sally, are disapproved of locally because they pass out pamphlets discussing birth control and urging votes for women. Into this unusual establishment, Bonnie fits happily, welcomed by everyone except Clare, who remains standoffish. The boarders are a surprise, since Bonnie has believed Audra to be well off, but learns that she needs money to pay interest on mortgages. Two of the other three roomer-boarders are pleasant gentlemen, but the third is abrasive Mr. Bertram Johnson, whose wife is in an insane asylum. In the yard an old apple tree has strips of paper tied to it. Audra explains that it is an ornament tree, where messages are sometimes tied to honor deeply loved ones and sometimes contain wishes or troubles to be blown away, all of them private so no one ever reads another's message. Bonnie ties on a slip saying, "Please let me find a way to be of help." Audra will not accept any of the money that Bonnie inherited or let her help the cook, Mrs. Marshall. Audra runs the establishment with great kindness and tact, but when Mrs. Marshall quits in a huff, only Bonnie knows how to start the stove and cook a simple breakfast. Though Bonnie loves Miss Delaney's Academy for Young Ladies, which both she and Clare attend, various incidents and near catastrophes complicate her life. Sally's husband, Jacob Harris, who has been gone for most of Clare's life, turns up making demands. A new cook, Melba* Foss, no older than Bonnie, does not last long and creates new problems. Jacob Harris comes and goes, involving Mr. Johnson in a fraudulent scheme and then disappearing, only to show up again. Audra banishes Mr. Johnson from the house and retrieves his wife, now called Mrs.* Carver, from the mental institution to which he has had her confined so he could control her money. Bonnie begins to think seriously of a career in medicine, which Mr. Younger once suggested to her. Of all the new people in her life, Mr. Younger is the most puzzling. He is only twenty-one, but seems very old to Bonnie. He insists on eating alone at a small table in the parlor but listens to conversation from the dining room and often shouts comments. By turn, he is friendly to Bonnie and then bitterly sarcastic. When Sally contracts Spanish influenza, which has raged across the country and through Seattle, Mr. Younger insists on walking with Bonnie for the doctor, since a general strike has knocked out all telephone service. A riot drives them off the street, and she steers him into a shed in an alley, where they wait, shivering, until the street is quiet again. On their way home Bonnie reacts to his critical comments about her lack of purpose by shouting at him that he should get some purpose himself and start by learning braille. Some days later, Audra tells her that he is enrolling in a day school for the blind. Bonnie is with him when they witness a suicide as a young woman steps into the path of a streetcar. In the next year he studies braille and becomes a teacher in the school, his spirits improving markedly. The morning that Bonnie announces her plans to attend the university in Los Angeles so she can prepare for a medical degree, she sees Mr. Younger waiting for the streetcar and deliberately stepping into its path. She runs, knocks him out of the way, and steers him back to the house, roundly scolding him all the way. Then she begs him to take care of everyone in the house for her while she is gone. Not until Audra has shepherded him inside and Bonnie starts for school again does she suspect that he might care about her romantically. After she leaves for Los Angeles, he makes his way to the tree and ties on it a strip of paper that says, "Bonnie, Bonnie, Bonnie." The way that this well-behaved, but spirited, girl affects and helps the lives that she touches is the main point of the novel. Although the action is minimal, involving mostly the conflicts and problems in the house, it beautifully evokes the period, the derogatory attitudes toward veterans and workers as expressed in dinner table conversation, the difficulties of independent women imposed by both society and their upbringing, and the emotions of a girl thrust into a new environment as she finds her way toward maturity. Both major and minor characters are well developed. Jefferson Cup.

THE OTHER SHEPARDS (Griffin*, Adele, Hyperion, 1998), realistic psychological problem and family novel with fantasy and growing-up aspects set in Manhattan, New York, not long ago. In speaking about the effect of her dead, much-older brothers and sister on the lives of her younger sister, Geneva, and herself, organized, solicitous Holland Shepard, 13, says that "the problem with living in a house full of angels is that each year they soar just a little bit higher." Holland says that Geneva has a "phobic little brain." She is often ill or fears that she is becoming ill, awakens at night with terrible fears that she compulsively tries to wash away, and loses control in school so that Holland must bring her home. Their parents, Quentin, a research scientist, and Lydia, a buyer for Macy's, seem obsessed with the loss of their older children in an auto accident caused by a drunken driver, or at least it seems that way to the two girls, especially Holland, who thinks that her mother regards her as inferior to those who died eighteen years earlier, before Holland and Geneva were born. Arriving home one day after buying a gift for their mother's birthday, they discover a bright-blond, upbeat young woman named Annie in the kitchen, preparing to paint a mural for their mother's birthday. Although they are never sure who Annie is—possibly a new therapist hired by their parents—they develop a friendship of sorts with her. Annie says that Mom and Dad are lucky to have them and encourages them to drink coffee (a grown-ups' drink) and develop various interests. Mom and Dad seem to accept their talk about Annie as routine. Holland becomes friends with Louis* Littlebird, a ninth grader whom she has noticed on the way to school, a relationship not pleasing to possessive Geneva. Annie takes them on excursions—to a thrift shop and Geneva to Annie's fortune-teller friend, Miss Pia, who predicts that she will go on a journey. The girls go by themselves to the Metropolitan Museum of Art, where they encounter Annie, whom, strangely, other museumgoers do not appear to see. During these episodes, the girls become more self-assured. Increasingly, Holland regards their historic old house (an obvious symbol) as a "house of silent disapproval," where the girls never seem to measure up to the deceased siblings whose pictures adorn walls and whose furniture still occupies their long-empty rooms. One day, two tickets to Saint Germaine in the Caribbean arrive by mail. Holland gets herself and her sister to the airport, and they make their way to the house that their parents own, now rented to the Hubbards, old family friends. They thoroughly enjoy their visit, since Ryan and Dana Hubbard are supportive and affirming. The girls had spotted Annie on the plane and feel that she helped them get to Saint Germaine, but the morning after they arrive, Annie is gone. They come to feel close to the lost siblings who enjoyed the house but also feel that they have made the place theirs, too. They return home to parents grateful that they are safe, have a new confidence in themselves as able people, and plan to visit the Hubbards again at Christmas. They wonder about Annie, whom their parents regard as figments of their imagination, Annie being a version of dead sister Elizabeth's confirmation name. Whether Annie was a ghost or made up is never clear. Whoever or whatever she is, she voices advice and suggestions that echo those of the girls' counselors. The girls' psychological problems and those of the parents who cannot let go of the past are presented in detail but without sentimentality or blame. A surreal quality contributes to the sense of intense family trauma. ALA; SLJ.

OUDEIS (*The Arkadians**), burly, capable mariner on whose ship Lucian*, Fronto*, and Joy-in-the-Dance* attempt to reach the island of Callista, where the wisewoman lives who can help Fronto regain his human form. Oudeis is usually careful to pour a libation of wine to Earth-Shaker, the god of the sea, before embarking on a voyage but neglects to do so on the occasion when he is distracted by one of Lucian's stories. As a result, a huge storm comes up, and the group is shipwrecked on the southwest coast of Arkadia. Oudeis has already told the group his life story, a tale filled with remarkable happenings and exotic adventures much like those of Odysseus, including the aspect of the left-behind sweetheart, here known as Mirina. When the shipwrecked group arrives at Metara, the capital of Arkadia, Oudeis finds his Mirina running a tavern. Although she informs him that she has had many suitors in his absence, she agrees at the end of the book to marry him. He agrees to direct the rebuilding of Metara, which has been destroyed by fire.

OUGHTON, JERRIE (1937–   ), born in Atlanta, Georgia; teacher, reteller of Navajo legends in picture-book form. Her novel *Music from a Place Called Half Moon** (Houghton, 1995) is also concerned with Native Americans, these a marginalized group in a small town in the Smoky Mountains. She is a graduate of Meredith College and has worked in North Carolina public schools for much of the last forty years.

OWEN (*The Magic and the Healing**), a traveling trader in the land of Crossroads*. The four veterinarian students learn about him from the Griffin* when they inquire about how they will get prescriptions to him if he needs them. The Griffin tells them that Owen is an "interesting" man who can find anything. When they ask if Owen is wicked or cruel, the Griffin responds that he is quite the opposite, overly kind. After the battle at Stein's* inn, they learn that Owen is really King Brandal, whom the Griffin serves in his capacity as Inspector General, and that King Brandal is sometimes too lenient and goodhearted to make the hard decisions needed to foil the forces of evil. Owen adopts different disguises as he goes about the country gathering information about what is going on. Unknown to the students, Brandal has consulted the seer Harral, who has informed Brandal that heroes will enter Crossroads and save the realm from the danger that will soon confront it because of the evil Morgan.

OWEN FOOTE, FRONTIERSMAN (Greene*, Stephanie, illus. Martha Weston, Clarion, 1999), amusing, realistic chapter book set in recent years in an unidentified American semirural or suburban area, third of the domestic-adventures novels starring Owen Foote, second grader, whose hero is Daniel Boone. Assertive, inventive Owen and his best friend from kindergarten, over-weight, diffident Joseph, plan to spend a night in the tree fort that Owen has built in old Mrs. Gold's woods and of which he is exceedingly proud. To their great consternation, they discover inside two big boys, Jake and Spencer, who they learn are Mrs. Gold's visiting grandsons and who trash the place. Angry, remembering Daniel Boone's words, "Act brave and you are brave," Owen declares "war." He adopts Wolverine as his secret code name, because wolverines are "ferocious," and assigns the name Badger to Joseph, because the badger is a "formidable adversary." He plots revenge: they will scatter animal poop on the floor, cut through the bottom rung of the ladder, smear pitch on them all, and release a snake in the fort—a can't-fail plan that Joseph, wary as always, finds many problems with. Both know that if the big boys catch them, it will go hard for them. Complicating matters more, Owen's mother announces that Mrs. Gold has phoned that she is going to stop by with her grandsons that afternoon so they can get to know Owen. Owen angrily runs off to booby-trap the fort, soon joined by Joseph, who suggests that they prepare a pit trap along the path to the fort. The two work through the time of Mrs. Gold's visit, and when Owen gets home, Mrs. Foote is perturbed with him for not showing up. At dinner, Owen tells his story, pleased at the end by the sympathy that he gets from his family, even from his usually snide older sister, Lydia, whom Mr. Foote joins in suggesting that Owen should be allowed to solve the problem in his own way. The next day, when the big boys come intending to finish ruining the fort, they tumble into the pit trap, get pitch all over their hands, notice the broken rung in time but flee in fright when Owen, who is lying in wait on the floor of the fort, releases the snake on top of them. When, the next day, Owen and his mother encounter Mrs. Gold, Jay, and Spencer at the grocery, Owen greets the boys as though nothing has happened, informs Mrs. Gold that he has built a tree fort in her woods (she says she is delighted), and says that it is too bad there is no time for Jay and Spencer to visit it. Later, Mrs. Foote tells Owen he put on "quite a performance." That night, Owen and Joseph, wearing their cherished coonskin caps, enjoy a peaceful overnight in the fort. Extensive, real-sounding dialogue, broadly foiled characters, accurate point of view, and a well-defined conflict of the David-Goliath, underdog-conquers variety combine with a plucky hero, a small moral problem, and rapid action to produce splendid entertainment for those who are just beyond very easy books. Black-and-white drawings add interest by picturing settings, situations, and characters, and the large print and good leading make for reading ease. SLJ.

OWL IN LOVE (Kindl*, Patrice, Houghton, 1993), unusual and compelling fantasy about a girl who becomes an owl at night, though otherwise she seems almost like other fourteen-year-old girls in her late twentieth-century New York town. The novel was earlier named to the ALA Notable Books list. SLJ. For a longer entry, see *Dictionary, 1990–1994.*

P

PAGE, KATHERINE HALL (1947–   ), native of New Jersey; teacher of English and history, director of programs for special-needs adolescents, educational consultant, and writer of mystery-suspense novels for adults and for middle graders and early adolescents. After her undergraduate work at Wellesley, she received her master's from Tufts University and her doctorate from Harvard in education. She has published eight novels for adults in the acclaimed series about detective Faith Fairchild and introduced a set of schoolgirl sleuths, who first appeared in *Christie & Company* (Avon, 1996). Three mixed-ethnic, boarding-school classmates join forces to discover who is stealing at their school. In *Christie & Company Down East** (Avon, 1997), a nominee for the Edgar Allan Poe Award, the intrepid threesome address themselves to problems that occur in and around an inn off the coast of Maine. The girls have more adventures in *Christie & Company in the Year of the Dragon* (Avon, 1997). Page has been praised in particular for the distinctive characterizations of the three girls.

PA GILMORE (*Sun & Spoon**), gentle, kind, perceptive grandfather of Spoon and Joanie* Gilmore. A former history professor at the University of Wisconsin, he is a bony, pale man in his seventies. His son's family has taken a closer interest in him since his wife, Gram, died, and he often comes for meals, or they send food from their garden to him, so that he knows that they are concerned about him. When he realizes that Spoon has a deep-felt need to be close to Gram in memory and to him as he and Spoon once were, he starts to spend more time with the boy. The book shows well how different family members handle grief.

PALE PHOENIX (Reiss*, Kathryn, Harcourt, 1994), fantasy novel involving time travel set in the small town of Garnet, Massachusetts, not far from Boston, for a few weeks in the late twentieth century. On a cold, snowy January morning,

Mandy (Miranda) Browne, 15, only child of Helen, a gynecologist and obstetrician, and Philip, the assistant curator and research director of a museum in Lexington, and Mandy's boyfriend, loyal Dan Hooten, 16, look forward to the flea market that their high school is holding. The school is raising funds to restore the Witch House, also known as the old Prindle House. The oldest building in Garnet, it was built in 1692 by Nathaniel Prindle, an avid witch-hunter, variously used down the years and sorely in need of repair. Among the items that Dan is contributing is a small stone whistle in the shape of the legendary phoenix, which his mother found in a jumble of stuff donated to the Garnet Museum and which later Mandy buys. As Helen is driving them to school, Mandy blows the whistle just before a young girl suddenly steps off the sidewalk into the path of the car. Small, thin, and exceedingly pale, with long, wispy, blond hair, she refuses treatment and walks on. Mandy sees her again at the flea market, where, though aloof, she says that her name is Abby Chandler. Abby's strange behavior continues. Although she does not select in the cafeteria food line, Mandy sees that her pink beaded bag is filled with food. When Abby leaves school, Mandy follows her and hears a grocer accuse her of stealing food. Abby then simply vanishes from Mandy's view, her footprints in the snow stopping abruptly. Matters come to a head when Helen and Phil catch Abby trying to steal groceries from their car and bring her home for an explanation. Abby says that she is an orphan, ran away from her dead grandfather's house, and has been living hand-to-mouth in the Prindle House. Helen and Phil invite her to move in until social workers can straighten matters out. Mandy doubts Abby's story and dislikes her "weird" behavior, and tension between the girls builds. Abby plays the piano incessantly; sobs, which only Mandy can hear, emanate from her room; she vanishes occasionally; and photographs, which she carries in her bag, appear to show her in different time periods. Pressed for an explanation, Abby says that the true story is that she was born in 1680 in Garnet, where, at the age of thirteen she lost her fiancé, William, and her family, except for an older brother, Thomas, in a house fire. Abby survived as a kind of ghost, but since she is forever thirteen, she has been forced to move from family to family, leaving before they discover that she never grows older. She wishes, above all, to be with her family and marry William. Eventually, Abby wishes Mandy, Dan, and herself back to 1693, hoping that Mandy and Dan can help her remain in that dimension. They discover that that is impossible but also learn that the phoenix whistle, which was given to Abby by an Indian woman, probably enabled her to survive. Back in the twentieth century, Mandy persuades Abby to derive another meaning from the phoenix. She suggests that, like the legendary bird, she may be able to claim another life in this dimension. Mandy urges her to resist yearning for the past and concern herself with the here and now. After reflection, Abby agrees. The book ends with Mandy's suggesting to her parents, with Abby's consent, that they arrange with social workers that Abby become a part of their family permanently. All elements work together to produce a top-notch tale of magic and ghosts—a carefully worked out, detailed plot; interesting characters; convincing, detailed setting; and controlled, slowly escalating tension, with the reader always being kept aware of the historical New England witch-hunts. Except for the school principal, who is thoroughly disagreeable, adults are presented sympathetically and are liked by the young people, another good feature. The romantic feelings that Dan and Mandy have for each other are handled with restraint. Poe Nominee.

PAPA LOGAN (*The Well: David's Story**), African-American Paul-Edward Logan, husband of Mama* Logan (Caroline) and father of David and Hammer*. Calm and hardworking, he is respected for his common sense, generous nature, and industry. He urges his sons not to borrow trouble by provoking the whites. Hammer refuses to heed his advice, and after Papa returns with his two older sons to the Natchez Trace, Hammer beats up Charlie Simms. The incident leads to the fouling of the Logan well. Paul-Edward's father was a white man, and Paul-Edward looks white. He was born a slave, and after the Civil War, although free, Paul-Edward, his mother, and his sister were still treated by his father as though they were his slaves. Paul-Edward tells the story of how, once when he was a boy and his half brother by his father's white wife hit him, he hit back. His father whipped him in front of the white son in order to impress upon Paul-Edward that, no matter how white he looked, he was still "a Negro and a Negro couldn't go around hitting white folks. Said that whipping was for my own good." Paul-Edward says that he is glad now that his father whipped him because he started to use his head, and as a result he worked hard and acquired the 200 acres of land that the Logans now own. He tells the story to his sons in order to impress upon them, in particular upon Hammer, how they are to behave with respect to the white Simms boys. The story stands out among the several vignettes in the novel.

PAPERQUAKE: A PUZZLE (Reiss*, Kathryn, Harcourt, 1998), mystery-detective novel with girl's growing-up, family-story, and fantasy aspects set in the San Francisco area at the time of publication. Short, dark-haired Violet Jackstone, 14, the youngest, frailest, and plainest of triplet sisters, feels neglected, dominated, and completely overshadowed by her two sisters, tall, blond, boisterous Jasmine and Rose, and overprotected by her parents because of the heart problems that she experienced in early childhood but has completely overcome. She particularly resents having no room of her own and being Baby. During an earthquake at school, she has a vision of shadowy children fleeing from a fire, the first of several such manifestations. While helping her sisters clean a former hat shop on Chance Street, which her parents plan to reopen as a florist shop, she finds in an upstairs room secreted in the wall letters to a someone called V written by a man named Hal, in which references sound much like herself—V is Baby, and she is frail, has heart problems, and is much protected—and in later letters and in diary entries Vi finds other similarities, among them mention of a vision/dream of children fleeing flames. Mr. Koch, her science teacher, assigns Vi the 1906 earthquake as the topic for her next paper and lends her several books, in one of which she finds another letter. Mr. Koch explains that the letter is a family treasure, that Hal, whose last name was Emerson, was a newspaper reporter. Hal and a certain Laela Baublitz were his grandparents, and Verity was his mother, named after Verity Stowe, a dear friend of both Laela and Hal. With the help of her sisters, Beth Madigan, her supportive classmate, and Sam, a nice, dark-haired boy with a foghorn voice whose house is across Chance Street and whose father gets them information from his newspaper's archives, they gradually learn about V and Hal, but not entirely before Violet prevents a tragedy. Certain that the Golden Gate Bridge is in danger from an earthquake, not knowing how else to warn authorities, she phones to report a bomb threat to the bridge. Authorities seal off the bridge, and thus many lives are saved when the quake comes. The shock of the quake uncovers more written communications in the Chance Street shop, and the girls are able to piece together the puzzle from the past. As a favor to Hal, whom she loved, Laela Baublitz had taken the job of companion to Verity Stowe, Hal's sweetheart and the sickly daughter of the Stowes, who owned the hat shop. Verity dictated letters for Hal to Laela, which Laela dutifully recorded and smuggled to Hal, also carrying letters from Hal to Verity. Before Verity died of her "wasting sickness," about the time of the big 1906 quake, Laela forged a note for Hal over Verity's name urging Hal to marry Laela after her (Verity's) death, because Laela loved him. Book's end finds Violet more self-assured. She no longer wants to be a carbon copy of her sisters and understands that she has gifts of her own. She now has a boyfriend, Sam, with whom she goes to the Halloween Ball, a room of her own in the attic, and an appreciation of her ability to take charge of her life. Although only Violet has dimension, the other main characters are sufficiently differentiated. Details about the past come out gradually and believably, and bolstering the mystery are brief philo-sophical discussions about such matters as personal responsibility and intergen-erational connections. Occasional humor lightens the tension, and the morality of the forgery, among other matters, is addressed. The letters and diary entries are romantic enough, as well as Violet's need to be appreciated and respected, to connect with the intended audience of teenage girls. This is a detailed, sub-stantial novel that occasionally outruns itself but addresses issues and respects the minds of its readers. Poe Nominee.

PAPPY (*Tiger, Tiger, Burning Bright**), eighty-two-year-old grandfather of Jesse and father of Bonnie, Jesse's mother. Pappy is the old man about whom the novel revolves. Jesse says that Pappy, an ex-cowboy, has legs that are "honest-to-God bowed from seventy-plus years of riding." Pappy wears a bleached Wrangler shirt, and his long gray hair is pulled back in a "Willie Nelson ponytail," which is held in place by a silver Zuni clip. Pappy is range-wise and people-smart and knows more about what is going on in town than most people think. For example, when he tells Jesse about seeing the tiger print in the high desert, he also says that he needs to talk to Bobby* Yates, evidently suspecting that Bobby is secretly conducting big-game trophy hunts. Jesse loves Pappy dearly and tries to keep Bonnie from learning how forgetful Pappy has become, although Jesse does not always know whether Pappy has really forgotten something or is just teasing him. Neither Bonnie nor Jesse likes Golden Shadows, the nursing home that they visit. Bonnie is turned off, among other aspects, by the director's negative reaction when told that Pappy likes to watch skater Dorothy Hamill's behind. Pappy is drawn with depth and sympathy.

PARABLE OF THE SOWER (Butler*, Octavia E., Warner, 1995), futuristic fantasy set from July 2024, to October 2027, beginning near Los Angeles and then gradually moving to northern California. The people of the United States live under conditions of tremendous social and economic stress. Extremes of wealth and poverty divide the nation. Unemployment is rampant, and megacorporations pay such poor wages that people become debt slaves in order to survive. Food is scarce, and water has become more expensive than gasoline. People live in small, walled communities for protection against marauding gangs of poverty-stricken homeless seeking to survive. The book starts on the fifteenth birthday of African-American Lauren Olamina, who keeps a journal of events as they happen. She describes how her steady, highly respected father, Mr. Olamina, a college professor and minister, attempts to ensure the safety and well-being of the handful of families within their walled enclosure by, for example, taking the young people out for target practice on weekends, mounting patrols, and urging his people to help and watch over one another. Lauren assists her tense, frightened stepmother, Cory, a teacher, in the little school that Cory runs, since the children, for safety's sake, are not allowed outside the little community's walls. Lauren has three main traits: a toughness that suggests that she will survive whatever terrors arise; hyperempathy syndrome, sometimes called sharing, a condition that means that she can physically feel other people's pain; and the need to define God for herself and record her ideas about God and life in her journal as her "Earthseed" philosophy. Lauren describes the last days of the community, a terrible time in which friends and neighbors are robbed and raped, everyone in her family dies or disappears, and the complex is set afire. Lauren plunders what remains of their house for clothing, money, and usable items and heads north, intending to travel until she finds a place where she can found a religious and social community called Earthseed. Passing herself off as a black man, she is accompanied by two young people who soon become lovers, white Harry Balter, who was also a member of her community and black Zahra Moss. With them as they travel are "shuffling hordes of people on the move," some of whom are also unfortunates and others who are predators against whom the little band must constantly be on guard. Lauren killed a man on the night of the complex fire and is ready to kill again if need be, even though she will suffer horrible physical pain herself from the act because of her syndrome. Gradually, other people join their little, racially mixed troupe, among them an elderly black man, Taylor Franklin Bankole, a widower and doctor who eventually becomes Lauren's lover. After various frightening encounters, they decide to go to Bankole's "safe haven," a remote property in the mountains occupied by his sister and her family. They arrive to find his relatives dead but decide to stay anyway. They are pessimistic about their chances but will do their best to survive. The plot moves with surprisingly little buildup for suspense. Characters are individualized but never seem really alive. The book's strengths lie in spunky Lauren's ability to capitalize on whatever circumstances bring and in the vast amount of detail that she provides about the times and conditions. The biblical influence is strong, but the sower aspect of the title appears only at the end and then abruptly. Lauren's frequent mention of buying and using condoms for safe sex seems an overly obvious instruction to young readers. ALA; SLJ.

PARK, BARBARA (1947–   ), born in Mount Holly, New Jersey; writer of amusing novels for middle-grade and early adolescent readers. Almost twenty years after *The Kid in the Red Jacket* (Knopf, 1987) was cited by *School Library Journal*, Park published *Mick Harte Was Here** (Knopf, 1995), also chosen for the *School Library Journal* Best Books list. It concerns the devastating effect on his family of the death of a son in a bicycle accident, as told by his just-older sister. Gentle humor keeps this very serious, poignant story from becoming morbid or maudlin, although its emphasis on bike safety gives it a didactic thrust. For more information about Park, more titles, and a title entry, see *Dictionary, 1985–1989* [*The Kid in the Red Jacket*].

PARROT IN THE OVEN: MI VIDA (Martinez*, Victor, HarperCollins, 1996), boy's growing-up novel set in central California among Mexican Americans. Each chapter contributes an episode that fleshes out a picture not only of an early adolescent boy's sometimes tempestuous life but also that of the community in which he and his close-knit family live. Diffident Manny (Manuel) Hernandez, the first-person narrator, enjoys good times and endures bad ones with his older brother, tough-guy Nardo* (Bernardo), his alcoholic, unemployed Dad*, his house-conscious Mom*, who is always worried about money, his pretty big sister, Magda, and cute little sister, Pedi. To get money for a baseball glove, Manny accompanies Nardo to the chili pepper fields, where he witnesses immigration agents round up illegals. When Mr. Hart, a teacher who recognizes Manny's ability as a student, gives the boy twenty dollars for school expenses, Dad appropriates the money, blows it on liquor in Rico's Pool Hall, goes on a rampage with his rifle, gets arrested, and is briefly jailed. Shortly after Manny and Nardo clean the yard and do chores for their Grandma, at Dad's orders, the old woman dies, and the two boys join the mourners at her house. When Magda leaves Manny to baby-sit Pedi while she steals out to be with her boyfriend, Manny fondles Dad's rifle, which accidentally discharges, almost hitting Pedi. Mom finds out about Magda's liaison and warns her not to ruin her life with precipitous behavior, her words provoking a blowup with Magda. Manny realizes that he is having romantic thoughts about girls and also toward a teacher, pretty, provocative Miss Van der Meer. He acts as equipment manager and trainer for a boxing tournament that his tough-guy schoolmate, Lencho, puts on to elevate esteem about La Raza, the Mexican Americans in the area, with terrifying consequences for the boys who participate. When Magda suffers a miscarriage, Manny helps Mom take her to the hospital for treatment. Mr. Giddens, the pharmacist for whom Nardo delivers, invites Manny to a birthday party for his daughter, where a red-haired white boy makes it clear to Manny that he is not wanted and where Manny realizes that he is not yet "smooth" with girls. He takes a terrible beating to pass the Test of Courage for initiation into the Callaway Projects gang, so he can "make out" with a girl named Rita, a privilege that he does not invoke. After he observes Magda's boyfriend rob a woman of her purse, he returns home disquieted and appreciative of his home and people, flawed as they are. The book is unified by characters and community, which is so strongly depicted that it seems a character in its own right. The ending is so abrupt that the reader wonders why the book closes when it does. Strengths derive from the sense of pride in heritage and family that form the core of the Mexican-American culture and from the well-drawn main characters. The title comes from a statement of Dad that implies that Manny is too trusting. Fanfare.

PATERSON, KATHERINE (WOMELDORF) (1932–   ), born in Tsing-Tsiang, China; twice winner of the Newbery Medal. Her *Flip-Flop Girl** (Lodestar, 1994), which was earlier recognized by the *School Library Journal* as a best book of the year, was named to the American Library Association list of Notable Books, as was *Jip His Story** (Lodestar, 1996). In addition, *Jip* was named to the *School Library Journal* list and won the prestigious Scott O'Dell Award for Historical Fiction. It is a sequel to *Lyddie* (Dutton, 1991), although the connection is not apparent until late in the novel. For earlier biographical information and title entries, see *Dictionary, 1960–1984* [*Bridge to Terebithia*; *The Great Gilly Hopkins*; *The Master Puppeteer*; *Of Nightingales That Weep*]; *Dictionary, 1985–1989* [*Come Sing, Jimmy Jo*; *Park's Quest*]; and *Dictionary, 1990–1994* [*Of Nightingales That Weep*; *Flip-Flop Girl*; *Lyddie*].

PAULIE ROY LOCKWOOD (*Safe at Second**), high school junior, 16, who helps his best friend, Todd Bannister, 17, return to baseball after Todd loses an eye. Whenever he feels like abandoning the self-pitying and self-destructive star pitcher, he remembers how Todd often helped him when they were kids. He does not realize that much of the attention that Todd gives him is to ensure that Todd will always have someone to whom he can play second fiddle. To his credit, Todd does try to get Paulie to pay more attention to his studies, but at that point Paulie does not intend to go to college. He even disregards his father's frequent efforts to help him get ready for his SATs (Scholastic Aptitude Tests). Later, Paulie discovers that Todd persuaded the baseball coach to put Paulie on the team, which turns out also to be more to Todd's advantage than to Paulie's. He also learns that Todd applied for college without informing Paulie. When Paulie starts to write for the school paper edited by Melissa Donovan at her request, Todd derides his work, perhaps because writing baseball columns was Melissa's idea, not Todd's. Paulie initiates a popular column known as "The Hot-Stove League." He also begins to think romantically of Melissa. At the end, realizing that he is never going to be the personal assistant of a Big League star, because Todd will never have a Big League career, Paulie thinks about his own future, perhaps in journalism, alone, on his own, without Todd, for the first time in his life. Paulie grows up a great deal in the novel.

PAULSEN, GARY (1939–   ), born in Minneapolis, Minnesota; educated at Bemidji State University in Minnesota and the University of Colorado at Boulder; popular and prolific writer of more than 130 books, which range widely in subject and form—adventure, mystery-suspense, western, problem, ethnic, nature, survival, historical, picture-book stories, nonfiction, autobiographical—for adults, children, and young adults. He is one of the most highly honored of American writers, more than a dozen of his books being variously cited, among other awards, to the Newbery Honor, Spur, International Reading Association, American Library Association, and *School Library Journal* lists. *Soldier's Heart: A Novel of the Civil War** (Delacorte, 1998) is the deeply moving story of a Minnesota boy in the Union army, based on an actual figure and real events. It received the Jefferson Cup Award for Historical Fiction. For more information about Paulsen, titles, and title entries, see *Dictionary, 1985–1989* [*Dogsong*; *Hatchet*] and *Dictionary, 1990–1994* [*The Cookcamp*; *Nightjohn*; *The Voyage of the "Frog"*; *The Winter Room*].

PECK, RICHARD (1934–   ), born in Decatur, Illinois; educated at Exeter University in England and at DePauw and Southern Illinois universities; teacher and highly acclaimed writer of more than two dozen books for middle readers and young adults in several genres and a variety of tones, although he is best known for his contemporary problem novels for young adults, a genre in which he pioneered. A Newbery Honor book, selected for the Fanfare list, and cited by the American Library Association, *A Long Way from Chicago: A Novel in Stories** (Dial, 1998) is an amusing episodic novel, overflowing with local color, Great Depression flavor, and positive family relationships. It tells of two Chicago children who travel by train to visit their grandmother somewhere in Illinois. Other recent publications include *Strays like Us* (Dial, 1998), about a girl and her great-aunt, and *Amanda Miranda* (Dial, 1999), about two look-alike girls on the *Titanic*. For additional information, titles, and title entries, see *Dictionary, 1960–1984* [*Are You in the House Alone?*; *Dreamland Lake*]; *Dictionary, 1985–1989* [*Blossom Culp and the Sleep of Death*; *Princess Ashley*; *Remembering the Good Times*]; and *Dictionary, 1990–1994* [*Bel-Air Bambi and the Mall Rats*].

PENANCE (Housewright*, David, Foul Play, 1995), realistic series mystery-detective novel set in St. Paul, Minnesota, about the time of publication. The opening scene introduces the plot problem and sets the tone for the novel. Ex-policeman Holland Taylor, private detective and narrator, is being interrogated by the police with whom he formerly served. They are investigating the shooting death of ex-convict John Brown, the drunk driver whom Taylor had threatened when Brown was sentenced to prison for killing Taylor's wife and young daughter and who was recently released from prison. At the end of the interview, Taylor is admonished to find out who killed Brown. Taylor's investigations take him from local bars and back alleys to the highest levels of government in the Minnesota state capital. His investigations lead him to Cynthia* Grey, who had been Brown's lawyer; a man named Sherman, who served nine years for the vehicular homicide of a candidate for the Minnesota House of Representatives and was Brown's friend; and C. C. (Carol Catherine) Monroe, who was elected to the House when the candidate was slain. C. C. hires Taylor to contact an ex-boyfriend, Dennis Thoreau, and offer him $10,000 in return for a compromising videotape, with which he has been blackmailing her. Taylor discovers the man shot dead, his house thoroughly ransacked, finds the tape still in the camera, takes the tape home, hides it when he discovers that it was obviously staged, and keeps its existence secret. For some time Taylor believes that C. C. and her people are responsible for Thoreau's murder. Complicating matters even more is Taylor's relationship, among others, with Randy Sullivan, a gambler who insists that Taylor collect from a hustler, Heather Schrotenboer, a pretty college student intent on using her charms to bend Taylor to her will. Cynthia locates the absent Sherman, who says that C. C. and Marion framed him for the candidate's murder and are doing the same for Brown's. Then Sherman is found dead, murdered, Taylor thinks. After still more complications, Taylor discovers that C. C., Thoreau, and Thoreau's ex-wife had together staged the compromising videotape to ruin C. C.'s gubernatorial campaign and latch onto remaining campaign funds. He learns that a campaign security guard, Conan Pivec, who is in love with C. C., perpetrated the murders and then was killed by security guards. C. C. informs the media that she was an innocent victim of a psychotic villain. Taylor discovers that Thoreau was killed by a close friend of C. C.'s secretary, because Thoreau had made the girl drunk, filmed a pornographic movie of her, and blackmailed her over it. Since Taylor has both a heart and a conscience and feels that he himself has plenty of sins to account for, he decides not to turn Thoreau's killer in but to allow the police to continue to investigate. Thoroughly disillusioned by C. C.'s behavior and her general lack of ethics, Taylor mails the videotape done by and about her to a reporter who deals in sleaze. The reporter releases the tape to the public, dooming C. C.'s candidacy, and one of the opposing candidates, although also shown to be morally lacking, is elected. Taylor remarks that he, like most other voters, stayed home on Election Day, no candidate seeming worthy. Although the book is pessimistic about the electoral process and not sanguine about the behavior of either the police or the media, and the cast is overly large, the plot is complicated by skillfully planted red herrings, fleshed out with careful detail, never flags, and is credibly advanced by Taylor's ability on the job and occasional good luck. He is a sympathetic protagonist about whose sad life the reader learns gradually and whose budding romance with Cynthia Grey, it is hoped, will develop into a satisying relationship for both. Poe Nominee.

PENN WEBB (*Crash**), sometime neighborhood playmate and middle school classmate of Crash Coogan. When Penn's Quaker family move into the Coogan neighborhood, Crash thinks that Penn is a funny-looking little runt. Penn never takes offense at the mean tricks that Crash plays on him; takes Crash home to dinner, where the vegetarian diet puts Crash off and gives him more fuel for teasing; tells him about his great-grandfather back in North Dakota who named Penn after the Penn Relays that the old man won when a youth in 1919; and says that he is never allowed to play with guns because his family is Quaker. His family and Penn are also attuned to ecological concerns and to the disadvantages of strip mall development and participate actively in addressing such socioeconomic concerns. Only late in the novel does Crash appreciate Penn's fine qualities of loyalty, forgiveness, and dedication to cause.

PETEY (Mikaelsen*, Ben, Hyperion, 1998), realistic sociological problem novel and story of friendship set in Montana during most of the twentieth century. Petey Roy Corbin, born in 1920 with cerebral palsy and a severely deformed body, is made a ward of the state at the age of two by his desperate parents and then committed to Warm Springs Insane Asylum, where he is placed with other "idiots," as is the practice. When he is seven, a young Mexican man, Esteban, new at the institution, notices that Petey can comprehend, is convinced that the boy is no idiot, makes the effort to relate to him, takes offense when Petey and others are called "freaks," and then suddenly "disappears," that is, is dismissed, leaving Petey to wonder what has happened to him. At twelve, Petey is moved to the Men's Ward, where he is even more neglected and despised. So starved is he for companionship that he makes friends with several mice. The only other child in the ward is Calvin Anders, a foundling with deformed feet who is a little younger than Petey, also wheelchair-bound, and considered "retarded." Gradually, Petey learns to communicate by groans and gestures with Calvin, who can speak, but the incident that binds them in friendship is the need to save the mice from an attendant who intends to poison them. A big attendant named Joe takes an interest in the boys, especially Petey, and when Petey becomes chilled and feverish, and the doctor is reluctant to treat him, saying that idiots do not live long anyway, Joe insists that Petey is no idiot. He also brings the boys gifts at Christmas, including toy pistols with which they play shooting games, and takes them to movies at the institution. When Joe leaves, too ill to work, Petey, now twenty-two, is befriended by pretty nurse Cassie Graber, to whom Petey is romantically attracted but who leaves to join her soldier-husband in New York. Twenty years later, in 1965, the institution now called a State Hospital, Calvin suffers from depression for lack of intellectual stimulation and becomes withdrawn, but Owen Marsh, a new, elderly attendant, is sure that the responses that he sees in Petey are not merely "conditioning," as medical and administrative personnel assure him. Angry at the administrator for refusing to provide a wheelchair for the now bed-bound Petey he modifies an old wooden one to fit Petey and takes the two boys for excursions to movies and dances. In 1973 Owen finds the work too much for him and sadly departs, leaving Petey stunned and tearful. Two years later, without having the opportunity to say good-bye to Calvin, Petey is abruptly moved to Bozeman Nursing Home, where life is monotonous, and care is painful, since the aides and nurses do not understand his needs. He feels bitter; it seems that every time he loves someone or something, it is taken away from him. In the spring of 1990, Trevor Ladd, a school-boy of thirteen and new in town, sees three bullies throwing snowballs at the shriveled-up old man lying defenseless in his rickety wheelchair, interposes himself between Petey and the boys, and takes the snowballs meant for the old man. This is the beginning of Petey's last friendship. Although his parents object to his spending so much time with Petey, associating with the old man arouses in Trevor a sense of self-worth and purpose. Doggedly persistent, Trevor gets Petey a new wheelchair and takes him fishing and shopping—incidents, among others, that open a whole new world for Petey. Trevor brings Calvin and Owen back into Petey's life and arranges for them all to go on an outing to Palisades Falls. In February Petey develops a raging fever and is hospitalized with pneumonia and a bleeding ulcer. The doctor decides not to operate but is persuaded to by Trevor and other friends and by Petey himself. Petey never recovers, however, and Trevor is at his side when he dies. Sissy Michaels, Petey's nurse, points out that Petey has set an example for all of them in how to make the most of life—she says, "Petey's whole life has been about living." The novel is most notable for two features: the callous way in which people with cerebral palsy were treated throughout most of the twentieth century and the credibility of Petey's character. Point of view is sometimes the author's, sometimes Petey's friends, sometimes Petey's. Petey is always remarkable for his pluck, persistence, and indomitable spirit. Spur.

PHOEBE WINTERBOTTOM (*Walk Two Moons**), Sal Hiddle's friend and classmate in the eighth grade. Phoebe has a tendency to be condescending, melodramatic, and overly precise, even prissy, but she is loyal to her friends and family, and Sal enjoys her company. Phoebe misses her mother so much after her mother disappears that she lies to her friends, saying that she is on a business trip to London, and she is sure that her mother has been kidnapped and murdered. Phoebe has mixed feelings when she learns that her mother is coming home, having seen her kissing and hugging the lunatic, whom Phoebe does not know is her half brother, Mike Bickle. At first she rejects her mother and Mike, even though her father welcomes both of them. Later, after Mrs.*

Partridge arrives at the Winterbottoms with another white-envelope message, a repeat of the one about not judging someone until you have walked two moons in his moccasins, Pheobe thinks about the situation, walks to the street, into which she spits heartily, invites Sal to do the same, and then walks into her house. Sal thinks that this is the exact right thing for Phoebe to do.

PHOENIX RISING (Hesse*, Karen, Holt, 1994), futuristic novel of survivors of a nuclear disaster, set on a marginal sheep farm in Vermont near North Haversham, presumably in the late 1990s or early years of the twenty-first century. The grandmother with whom Nyle Summer, 13, lives takes in two evacuees from Cookshire, where a leak in the nuclear plant has destroyed Boston and much of New England. At first reluctant to have anything to do with Ezra Trent, 15, who is suffering from radiation poisoning, Nyle gradually becomes attached to the boy, rejoices at his seeming recovery, and grieves over his inevitable death. The grim theme concerns the way that the country and particularly the neighbors resent and fear the refugees, close their eyes to nuclear dangers, both before and after the leak, and seem to forget the disaster. The book earlier was named to the SLJ Best Books list. ALA. For a more detailed entry, see *Dictionary, 1990–1994.*

PIGS DON'T FLY (Brown*, Mary, Baen, 1994), picaresque fantasy set in a preindustrial land that corresponds roughly to late medieval Europe. When Summer's mother, the town whore, dies, and she discovers that all the regular customers are claiming not only the goat, chickens, and furniture but even their hut itself, the girl sets the place afire and leaves in the middle of the night, taking with her only what she can carry, including coins from many lands left for her dowry by her long-dead father, a mercenary, and a transparent ring that she learns is made of unicorn horn. She is soon joined by a scruffy, flea-ridden dog whom she calls Growch* and a swaybacked, half-starved mare named Mistral, which she rescues from the brambles that have enmeshed and trapped it. Because of the ring she can understand their speech. At the first good-sized village, she comes upon a crowd tormenting a blind, nearly naked man in the stocks whom she recognizes with shock as the wonderfully handsome knight who had spoken kindly to her a day or two before. By claiming that he is her simple-minded brother and bribing the bailiff, she secures his release and takes him to the stable that she has rented for the night. With fear Mistral says he is Sir* Gilman, the leader of a band of gentry for whom she has been a pack-horse. They were set upon and mostly slain the day before. A blow on the head has robbed him of his sight and his memory, but not of his haughty airs. Infatuated, Summer overlooks his scorn and grouchiness, proposing that they pose as siblings and that she call him Gill. She makes him a tunic from one of her two blankets and leads him away before first light, being careful to stay far enough away from him so that he will not discover that she is grossly fat, the main reason that the village mayor did not impress her into her mother's job. Before they get much farther, she has rescued three other creatures, a wounded pigeon being stoned by boys, a tortoise chained in a yard and abandoned, and a strange, piglike animal with vestigial wings that was being exhibited and mistreated at a fair. The bird she calls Traveler*, the tortoise Basher, and the pig Wimperling*. As they travel south, they have a variety of adventures. In these Summer is guided by her ring, which burns when there is danger, and by the increasingly astute advice of Wimperling. As a snowstorm and Gill's increasing weakness threaten to defeat them, by chance they find a safe haven, mistaking the sign to the warehouse and home of Matthew* Spicer, Merchant, for the Martlet and Swan Inn. Matthew, a widower, not only takes them in as welcome guests but also has Suleiman, his friend from the East who has a wide knowledge of medicine, treat Gill's pneumonia. The weeks slip by pleasantly as he recovers. To Summer's astonishment, since she does not realize that she has lost her excessive weight and has a pretty face, Matthew asks Gill's permission to propose to her, and the travelers admit that they are not brother and sister. Summer tells Matthew about her infatuation with the knight, and they soon are again on their way, heading south toward what they hope is Gill's home, though his memory returns only in tantalizing scraps and scenes. After a number of other adventures, some threatening their lives or their freedom, they arrive at the seashore. Traveler, Basher, and Mistral all find and join some of their own kind. Finally, after a chance meeting with a singer at a fair gives them a clue, Summer and the rest of her crew find the manor house that was Gill's home, where his betrothed, Rosamund, is in residence. When he hits his head upon a low lintel, his sight and the rest of his memory return. He declares his love for Summer, his disaffection with Rosamund, and his desire to take to the road again. Before she can decide what to do, Summer overhears a conversation between Rosamund and Gill's father, Sir Robert, by whom she is two months' pregnant. They plot that she will seduce Sir Gilman and pass the baby off as his child and that Summer will suffer an "accident." Summer, Growch, and Wimperling escape and head for the circle of standing stones where Wimperling was hatched and where he undergoes dramatic changes, first into a full-scale dragon and then, because three times Summer has impulsively kissed him, into a marvelous man who makes passionate love to her, only to return again to dragon form and fly off. Summer and Growch struggle back in winter storms to Matthew's house, where he proposes again, and she accepts. The memory of Wimperling, now named Jasper, haunts her, however, and soon, accompanied by the dog, she is on the road again, headed for Cathay, the true home of the dragon kind. The wealth of action carries the rollicking story along at a good pace. Summer is a hardworking, capable girl whose naive goodness is endearing. All the characters are well developed and interesting, and while the reader knows early in their adventures that Wimperling is a dragon, his final transformation is dramatic and exciting. ALA; SLJ.

PIKE, CHRISTOPHER (KEVIN CHRISTOPHER MCFADDEN) (1961 ?–), born in Brooklyn, New York, raised in Los Angeles, where he now lives; popular author of about sixty horror, suspense, crime, mystery, and science fiction novels, mostly for high school readers but a few for adults. Nominated for the Edgar Allan Poe Award, *The Midnight Club** (Simon & Schuster, 1994) involves five teenagers, all dying with cancer, who meet every night at midnight and tell mostly gory stories to pass the time and provide emotional support for one another. For additional information, titles, and a title entry, see *Dictionary, 1990–1994* [*Remember Me*].

A PLACE TO CALL HOME (Koller*, Jackie French, Atheneum, 1995), girl's growing-up novel set in the 1990s in Westbridge, Connecticut, about a dysfunctional family that the half-black older daughter tries desperately to hold together. When her mother disappears, Anna O'Dell, 15, is distressed but not surprised, since it is not the first time that she has been left to cope with her little blond half siblings, Mandy*, 5, and Casey, seven months. In some ways, life is easier without her alcoholic mother verbally and physically abusing all three, but there are problems of Anna's schoolwork and money for necessities. She solves the first, temporarily, by forging a note to the school and getting the closest neighbor to their deteriorated semirural home, red-haired Nate Leon, to bring her assignments, and she shops warily and argumentatively at Mel's Convenience Store, where prices are high but to which she can hurry while Casey naps. Just as the money runs out, she finds an envelope in the mail, postmarked Sunnydale, Mississippi, containing $200 but no note. About that time, taking Casey for a walk in the nearby game preserve closed for the winter, she sees a place where a car has driven into the lake and recognizes her mother's station wagon submerged in the deep water. Panicky, because when Mandy was a baby social workers once took her away, Anna moves the children to a tumbledown cabin on the mountain that she thinks is an abandoned pioneer home but learns, when Nate arrives with a sleeping bag, that it is actually his, built by his great-grandfather and left him by his dead father. Against his better judgment, Nate helps her, and they manage for a week in the cold, rainy weather, but when Casey develops an ear infection, Anna gives up and takes him to a doctor. The social worker, Mrs. Romero, finds a foster home to take all three, but it is not the pleasant place that it appears on the surface. The woman, Mrs. McCallum (Auntie Roe) is house-proud and insensitive, and her husband, Uncle Elvin, is hostile. For a month they stick it out, with Anna worrying as Mandy gets withdrawn and Casey distrustful, but then Anna overhears a conversation in which Mrs. Romero says that they have found her mother's suicide car and Auntie Roe declares that she might keep Casey, but she doesn't want the other two. Anna prompts Mandy to say that she went off with a boyfriend in a red car and enlists Nate's help again, although he is leery from her frequent rejections. Dressed in boys' clothes with her hair cut short, she takes a bus to Sunnydale, Mississippi, where the money came from, hoping to find relatives. There she looks up in the phone book and goes to see a Mrs. O'Dell, who looks so much like her mother that Anna knows she must be her grandmother. Instead of the welcome for which she has hoped, she gets frigid rejection. She learns enough to realize that her mother was sexually abused by both her father, a police chief, and her older brother, to get the name of her own father, James Hughes, and, since she needs bus fare back to Connecticut, to take the wad of bills that Mrs. O'Dell thrusts at her to bribe her to leave. Almost by accident, she runs into an African-American garage owner who knew her father and can show her his picture in a high school yearbook. He confirms that her mother was abused sexually, a fact that Mrs. O'Dell has denied too vigorously, and that James was run off the road and killed by a police car, presumably her grandfather's. Back in Westbridge, Mrs. Romero tells her that Mandy has admitted that Auntie Roe is mean and that she and Casey have been moved to the home of a young couple who hope to adopt them. At first Anna, whose whole life has been wrapped up in caring for the little children and in keeping the family together, is devastated, but after she meets the prospective adoptive couple and sees how happy and well cared for Mandy and Casey are, she agrees and accepts the offer of a home for herself from Mel, the owner of the convenience store, and his wife, Annie Theopolis, whose own six children are college graduates and who have admired Anna's intelligence and spirit even when she argued with them about prices. In the end, she has Nate for a boyfriend, frequent visits with Mandy and Casey, and contact lenses bought by Mel to replace her Coke-bottle glasses. Essentially a picture of a child of an alcoholic forced by circumstances into an adult role, the novel does a good job of showing Anna's often conflicting emotions: both love and hate for her mother, devotion and irritation for her siblings, romantic desire and suspicion for Nate. While her African-American paternal side has some function in the plot—most foster parents don't want a black child, and her grandmother is horrified that the neighbors might see her—it seems to be an element heaped on top of her other troubles unnecessarily and leaves some questions unanswered, for instance, how Nate's mother feels about her racial background. Told entirely in the present tense, the novel is written in a convincing and compelling style. ALA.

PLUMMER, LOUISE, author of several well-received books for young adults, including *The Unlikely Romance of Kate Bjorkman** (Delacorte, 1995), a novel that is as much a spoof on romances as a serious story of a girl's first love. For earlier biographical information and a title entry, see *Dictionary, 1990–1994* [*My Name Is Sus5an Smith. The 5 Is Silent*].

POISON (Ferguson*, Alane, Bradbury, 1994), mystery of detection and suspense, featuring a teenage girl who must come to terms with the disappearance of Diane, her elegant, much admired stepmother, and her wealthy father's apparently irrational rigidity in refusing to talk about it and insisting that she spend her seventeenth summer working in his office. When Jon Smythe, owner of the very upscale Smythe Towers office complex in an unidentified small city, finds his daughter, Chelsea, talking on his office phone to her friend, Amber Farrington, he angrily demotes her from receptionist to the Communications Room in the bowels of the tower, a move that pleases his longtime secretary, Nola Pierce, who with some relish instructs Chelsea about her duties in the cheerless, windowless room full of wires, computers, and other electronic equipment off the parking ramp. One item that Nola tries to hide but Chelsea insists on knowing about is the "goat," a yellow, telephone-like handset to check that the system is working but also making it possible to eavesdrop on any phone in the building without detection. Although Nola angrily denies it, Chelsea is sure that the secretary has used the device to keep up on office gossip, and as soon as possible she and Amber try out the goat, justifying their curiosity by saying that it may reveal something of Diane's whereabouts, since she kept a small law office in the building. To their astonishment, they hear an angry conversation between a whining young man and a gravelly-voiced older man who is berating him for leaving "it" in the back of Dover Cave where anyone might find it at the risk of millions of dollars. Feeling no obligation to stay on the job, which she views as unjust punishment, Chelsea insists that Amber accompany her to Dover Lake Park and explore the cave. Amber refuses to go in with Chelsea, bringing to a head their argument about the morality and sense of their search and Amber's assertion that Chelsea has changed under the influence of Diane, becoming more self-centered and inconsiderate, a perception that Chelsea attributes to Amber's jealousy that Diane warned her about. Armed with her flashlight, Chelsea proceeds alone and discovers, under a blanket at the far back of the cave, Diane's dead body. The girls, united now in their horror, drive to the police station, agreeing not to mention the goat, and report the finding of the body. Detective Fayette, obviously suspicious of her story, talks to Chelsea, while another detective grills Amber, getting her to admit to their eavesdropping on the phone line. Before they are released, officers have checked the cave and report that no body is to be found. The girls' story is considered a hoax or, at best, a delusion of a hysterical teenager. Chelsea's father, who has been summoned to the police station, is furious, fires her, and retrieves her keys to the tower, but that night, rather drunk and uncharacteristically weepy, he comes to her room and apologizes. The next morning Chelsea and Amber "borrow" her father's extra keys and let themselves into the Communications Room. While Chelsea tries to relocate the lines that she previously tapped with the goat, Amber, more technically skilled, attempts to get a printout from the computer of the calls from Diane's office. When Amber ducks out for Cokes, words appear on the screen saying, "I know you are down there," calling Chelsea by name, warning her not to go to the police, and ending, "I'll be watching you." Terrified, the girls rush to the police station. Detective Fayette seems more inclined to take them seriously, but he warns them, in no uncertain terms, that by using the goat they may poison the investigation, that is, get illegally information that would therefore be inadmissible in court. Before he lets them go, word comes that a crew dredging Dover Lake has dragged up Diane's body, and Chelsea's father, whom she has phoned, arrives and is arrested for murder. At home Chelsea gets a call from the same gravelly voice, warning her not to return to the Smythe Towers. When she reports the call to the police, she is clearly disbelieved. Deciding that they must do just what they are told not to do, she and Amber go to the Towers, mostly deserted on Friday evening, use duplicate keys that they have made to enter Diane's office, and find evidence in the files that she has been involved in an extremely lucrative insurance fraud aligned with a Dr. Marcroft in the same building. They are interrupted by Marcroft, who herds them with a gun to the Communications Room, where he plans to electrocute them by shorting out the high-voltage wires with the parking ramp hose. Thinking quickly, Chelsea sets off the smoke detector, flooding the Communications Room with foam and allowing their escape. Loose ends like why Jon Smythe has insisted that Diane leave—he discovers a huge balance in her checking account that she refuses to explain—and how she died—trying out their scam with Pete, the helper who created the accidents on which they collected insurance—are tidied up neatly. Through the whole novel, hints that Diane was not the perfect role model that Chelsea took her to be are interwoven with red herrings like Nola's crush on Jon, which, with her access to the communications network, makes her a likely suspect. Although the pattern of a bright, attractive girl and her somewhat jealous sidekick investigating on their own, an authoritarian, but truly loving, father, and police detectives who doubt them is repeated from Ferguson's earlier novel, *Show Me the Evidence*, the action and tension are sufficient to produce an exciting story. Poe Nominee.

POL (*The Thief**), skillful, loyal, tough soldier who accompanies the magus*, Gen, Ambiades*, and Sophos* on the journey to find the stone known as Hamiathes' Gift. Gen early realizes that Pol requires obedience and attentiveness but is also kind and helpful. For example, Pol gives Gen valuable advice about handling his horse. Gen eventually learns that Sophos' father had refused to let Sophos accompany the magus unless Pol went along, too. Pol's most important duty is to guard Sophos, who, unknown to Gen until the end, is the heir to the throne of Sounis. Pol's next most important responsibility is to bring back the Gift. Thinking that Gen has been killed, Pol pushes Ambiades over a cliff during the final fight against the Attolians, because he knows that Ambiades is a traitor. Pol then throws himself over the cliff, taking two Attolian soldiers with him as he commits suicide. Sophos weeps over Pol, because Pol has been a faithful friend and retainer and leaves a wife and two children. Alone of the group, Pol had noted that Gen is Eddisian-trained in swordfighting and mentioned his observations to the magus. It is a sign for the attentive reader that Gen may be much more than he seems to be.

POPE JOAN (Cross*, Donna Woolfolk, Random House, 1996), adult historical novel with a strong feminist slant set in the ninth century in what is now France and in Rome and revolving around the only woman pope. Joan's two-year reign is denied by the church but is supported by tradition and accounts in more than 500 manuscripts. Born in 814, the only daughter and youngest of the three children of an obscure Frankish village canon* (priest) of English birth and his Saxon wife, Gudrun, Joan early reveals the qualities of independence, courage, and high intelligence that distinguish her life, cause her trouble on occasion, and win her admiration, love, and loyalty. Her older brother, Matthew, a kind, bright boy, secretly teaches her to read in response to her pleadings. The Greek scholar Aesculapius*, assigned to the cathedral school at Mainz, recognizes her ability and insists on teaching her Greek, Latin, theology, and logic. Eventually, Joan is given a scholar's position in Dorstadt, to the disappointment of Odo, the teacher, who is unusually hard on her. She is assigned to live in the household of Gerold*, a respected, married knight a dozen years older than she. Now thirteen years old, Joan thrives in the school and wins the admiration and eventual love of Gerold, although at that time their love is unconsummated, and the hatred of Gerold's conventional wife, Richild, as well. While Gerold is away on business, Norsemen raid the area, leaving everything in smoking ruins. Joan survives by hiding behind the reredos of the church. When she finds the body of her brother John, also a student, she assumes his garments and identity, becomes a novice at a nearby monastery, calling herself John Anglicus, and henceforth lives as a man. At the age of twenty-seven, after twelve years in the monastery and some disputes with the abbot, she becomes a priest and heads for Rome. She enters the Schola Anglorum, where her education, humanity, skill at logical argument, and knowledge of medicine set her apart. Her reputation as a healer brings her into the household of Pope Sergius, a good, but sickly, man, and plummets her into the intrigues that rage around the office as well as into the larger political arena and the rivalry between Lothar, king of the Franks, and the church. Things so fall out that, when Lothar descends on Rome with a mighty army, Gerold is in charge of his rear guard and thus after fifteen years comes in contact with Joan. Having promised Sergius to serve as his priest/physician, Joan refuses to leave with Gerold and become his wife. When the Saracens ravage Rome, the people turn against Sergius, who soon dies, and Joan, now thirty-three, can no longer deny her love for Gerold but chooses to continue in the church. Under Pope Leo, Gerold becomes the commander of the pope's militia, and Joan is given the high post of nomenclator. Years pass as Leo rebuilds Rome, a program in which Joan has a great deal of responsibility. When Leo dies, Joan succeeds him by will of the people. As pope, she shows a special concern for the poor and downtrodden, rebuilds the aqueduct that serves the poor, improves the education of the clergy, and starts hospices and a school for women. When Gerold is wounded fighting a terrible flood, Joan saves him. They make love, and other times of intimacy follow. Disaffection, however, against the "people's Pope" arises and spreads among the institutionalized clergy. When Gerold is assassinated, the shock causes Joan to give birth prematurely to their stillborn child. Joan dies at the age of forty-one, revealed in death as a woman. Although the plot is predictable, melodrama abounds, characters offer no surprises, and the large cast is hard to keep straight, the novel exudes color and movement and is enthralling from start to finish. It is most notable for the picture that it gives of the status of women—considered inferior and held subject to the men in their lives—and of the organized church—made up of cruel, hard, self-seeking, venal men bent on using any person and every means to advance their own interests and perpetuate the status quo. An author's note at the end about Joan and the period is helpful. SLJ.

POPPY (Avi*, illus. Brian Floca, Orchard, 1995), action-filled, lighthearted animal fantasy set in a rural area in recent years involving a family of field mice. After Mr.* Ocax, the much dreaded, voracious horned owl who dominates Dimwood Forest and its environs, devours her golden mouse sweetheart, Ragweed, sensible, orange-brown deer mouse Poppy returns from Bannock Hill, where the mouse-murder occurred, to find her father, Lungwort, conducting a family council. Lungwort officiously informs his wife, Sweet Cicely, and their twelve children that a dwindling food supply necessitates that they move to New House across Dimwood. He says, furthermore, that they must ask permission of Mr. Ocax, who has said that he protects them from the ferocious creatures that inhabit the forest, especially porcupines, and that they must never go out of the area without his permission. Lungwort also says that Poppy must accompany him to confer with Mr. Ocax. Carrying a white flag, Poppy and Lungwort meet Mr. Ocax at his huge old dead oak and return dejected because the owl has refused to let them leave. Suspecting that Mr. Ocax has an ulterior motive, Poppy decides to travel to New House to investigate. Her perilous journey takes her through the woods, where she heroically meets numerous dangers, including an attack by Mr. Ocax and a threatening red fox, which she eludes by diving into a hollow log. The stench in the log, which almost overwhelms her, comes from a scary, irascible creature who says he is a porcupine, Erethizon Dorsatum, Ereth* for short. After he chases the fox away, Ereth informs her that Mr. Ocax lies when he says that porcupines eat mice. Poppy promises Ereth that if Ereth helps her get to New House safely, she will secure for him his heart's desire, the salt lick for deer that stands near New Barn. Ereth takes Poppy through Dimwood past Old Barn and a lush cornfield until they arrive at New Barn. When she sees that the salt block sits atop a pole, Poppy almost despairs. She also discovers that Mr. Ocax's reason for not wanting them to be near New House is a larger than life-size owl under the overhang of the barn roof, which gives her anxious moments until she learns that it is a wooden image put there to frighten Mr. Ocax away. The more Poppy sees of New House, the more she realizes how the old owl has contrived to keep her family under his control. When Mr. Ocax attacks just as she is starting home, Poppy stabs him in the claw with her porcupine-quill sword. The wound ironically causes him to crash into the salt lick. The crash kills him, knocks the salt lick down, and breaks the block into pieces of a size that she can carry. After she arrives home with the good news of his death and the rich supply of food, her family moves to New House cornfield. Thirteen moons later, Poppy and her husband, Rye, are living free from worry on Bannock Hill with their litter of eleven babies because Poppy has had the ingenuity and courage to confront evil. Although the reader never fears that dauntless Poppy will triumph in this takeoff on the heroic quest of folklore, tension abounds. Characters are pleasing, appropriate types: the staunch heroine; her father, Lungwort, a pompous fool who refuses to think for himself; Mr. Ocax, a menacing, deceitful villain; Ragweed, a smart-talking adolescent mouse; and Ereth, the accommodating helper. Snappy, extensive dialogue; a clearly delineated setting augmented by a map and realistic black-and-white drawings; a mice history and philosophy of sorts; and just enough gentle, witty humor—these make this novel a top-notch David and Goliath story for middle-grade readers. ALA; Boston Globe Winner; SLJ.

POP RILEY (*Flyers**), lawyer-father of Gabe and Ethan* Riley, in his sixties. Voluble and easygoing, Pop is well known throughout New York state for defending the indigent or near-indigent or those whose cases are unpopular. For example, he defends Mr. Lindstrom, who is alleged to have abused his daughter when she was a child. There is some social commentary involved in the brief descriptions of his cases, for instance, the speed with which people accused of certain acts are automatically assumed to be guilty. Pop likes to cook huge brunches for the boys on Sunday, listen to CDs (compact discs) of Irish music, engage in philosophical discussions with Gabe, and spin lengthy yarns. He occasionally drinks too much, and when he does, Gabe drives him home. Although Gabe is too young for a license, the local police always look the other way. Pop is the epitome of the trusted town professional, tough as nails but with a heart of gold, respected and valued by all his neighbors.

PORTE, BARBARA ANN (1943–   ), born in New York City; librarian, author of picture books, retellings from oral tradition, and novels for young adults. She attended Iowa State University, was graduated from Michigan State University, and received her M.S. degree from the Palmer Graduate Library School of Long Island University. Her writings include a series about Harry, starting with *Harry's Visit* (Greenwillow, 1983), and two novels starring biracial girls, *I Only Made Up the Roses* (Greenwillow, 1987) and *Something Terrible Happened** (Orchard, 1994). Among her many picture-book titles are *Chickens! Chickens!* (Orchard, 1995) and *"Leave That Cricket Be, Alan Lee"* (Greenwillow, 1993). She has also retold Chinese stories in *Hearsay: Strange Tales from the Middle Kingdom* (Greenwillow, 1998). Porte has made her home in Arlington, Virginia.

POWER, SUSAN (1961–   ), born in Chicago, Illinois; enrolled member of the Standing Rock Sioux. She was educated at Radcliffe and received her law degree from Harvard and an M.F.A. from the Iowa Writers' workshop. She has published short fiction in such periodicals as *Atlantic Monthly* and *Paris Review* and in anthologies. She is currently a Bunting Institute Fellow in Cambridge, Massachusetts. *The Grass Dancer** (Putnam, 1994), written for adults, was cited by *School Library Journal* and the American Library Association. An episodic period story of Native-American Sioux in North Dakota, the novel employs a complicated structure that moves backward in chronologically uneven segments from 1981 to 1864 and then forward again. Cultural texture is high, and satire on the ways of both Indians and whites and some hilarious scenes set the story in relief. She has also published *Strong Heart Society* (Putnam, 1997), another adult novel.

PRESTON SINCLAIR (*Brothers and Sisters**), president of Angel City National Bank in Los Angeles. His attempts to capitalize on affirmative action and mount a diversity program in his bank to impress the community and advance his professional and political ambitions result in the hiring and subsequent firing of African-American Humphrey* Boone and the ironic establishment of Solid Rock National Bank. Preston has been so involved in his selfish ambitions that he hardly knows his wife and teenage sons. When one of them, Pres, is severely injured in an accident, he comes to understand what is really important in his life, to reaffirm his belief in God, and to want to do better by everyone around him. He agrees to serve on the board of directors of Solid Rock. Circumstances cause him to grow and change in a credible way.

PRINCE ROG (*Flight of the Dragon Kyn**), surly, ambitious brother of King* Orrik of Kragland. Although Rog is almost unctuously pleasant to Kara and her family when he comes to their farm to fetch her for his brother, he changes abruptly and treats her roughly and disrespectfully as soon as they depart, a clear sign of his duplicitous nature. Although he is always a pain in Orrik's side with disparaging and snide remarks, his real objectives do not come out until after Kara returns from the dragons' cave with the plan for sending the creatures to the far north. The scene in which he is most despicable is that in which he begins to drown the little girl Myrra in order to force Kara to call the dragons so that he can kill them. He is a consistently unsympathetic figure.

PROPHECY ROCK (MacGregor*, Rob, Simon & Schuster, 1995), realistic murder mystery-detective novel with boy's growing-up story aspects set on the Native-American Indian Hopi Reservation in northeastern Arizona about the time of publication. Will Lansa, 16, flies to Arizona from Aspen, Colorado, where he has been living with his white mother since she and his Hopi father, Pete Lansa*, now Hopi chief of police, were divorced when Will was three. Will is to stay for the summer with his father while he works at the Public Service Hospital as an orderly to explore the possibility of going into medicine as a career. Will is apprehensive about spending so much time with the father whom he barely knows and about being plunged into a strange culture. He gradually learns to appreciate both as his father enlists him in the annual Home

Dance, the ceremony to send the kachinas (spirits of ancestors and nature) home to their dwellings on the peaks of the San Francisco Mountains in northwestern Arizona, and father and son combine to solve a murder that occurred just before Will arrives. Aaron Carlyle, a young white research assistant to ethnologist Professor Arneson, who has been working on the reservation, is found gruesomely murdered near Prophecy Rock, a Hopi sacred place. The body is brought to police headquarters by the Reverend Shulpa, a fundamentalist minister bent on eradicating traditional Hopi beliefs. To complicate matters for Will, he is immediately attracted to pretty Hopi Ellie Polongahoya, a hospital coworker whose grandmother Abbey Polongahoya, a highly respected tribal elder and seer, opposes their friendship because Will is only half-Hopi. The plot speeds up when Abbey is found severely assaulted, her rude house in old Oraibi is thoroughly ransacked, and she is later murdered in her hospital room. Suspicion points to several people: Reverend Shulpa; Danny Tsotsie, a Navajo youth also interested in Ellie and vehemently ordered by Abbey to keep away from Ellie; Professor Arneson; Doctor Haaz, a physician at the hospital; and George Koottewa, a half-Hopi hospital maintenance man. The point of view alternates among Will (although the story is mostly his), Ellie, and a character called Pahana, the murderer, who is introduced early into the narrative. Pahana believes himself to be the incarnation of the legendary savior of the Hopi, the figure also known as the Elder White Brother. Pahana has committed these murders, he believes, at the will of Masau, the extremely powerful Hopi kachina who rules the upper and lower worlds. Pahana believes that he is to reunite the two sacred tablets of the Hopi, bring about the end of the current Fourth World, and usher the Hopi into the next or Fifth World. Pahana also slashes Will's tires, so that Will's jeep plunges over a cliff into a canyon, and kidnaps Ellie to hold in exchange for the sacred tablet that the Fire Clan possesses. Pahana (the murderer) is unmasked at the Home Dance as Koottewa. He flees in a pickup truck through a wash and is swept to his death by a flash flood. The summer now almost over, Will has begun to think of himself as Hopi and expects to return to the Reservation next year. Although the shifts in point of view cause some confusion, the device increases the suspense. Will's little romance with Ellie is sweet and credible, and Will's father becomes more likable as Will grows to understand and appreciate him as a person and officer. The mystery grips, and Hopi ways and beliefs are worked well into the narrative. Even Will's dreams about Masau are believable under the conditions in which they occur. The physical setting is well realized and also plays an important part in the story. The author does not indicate the source of the details of the kiva (underground religious chamber) sacred ceremony. Although spellbinding and informative of Hopi ways, the book is less convincing than the detective novels set in the same area by Tony Hillerman. A glossary at the end of the book helps with Hopi words and phrases. Poe Winner.

PROTECTING MARIE (Henkes*, Kevin, Greenwillow, 1995), realistic contemporary novel of family life focusing on a girl's relationship with her father and set in Madison, Wisconsin, for a couple of months beginning just before Christmas. Emotional, imaginative Fanny Swann, 12, the only child of older parents, sometimes longs for the "amiable chaos" of a household like that of her closest friend, Mary Dibble. Fanny relates well to her mother, Ellen Cross, an elegant professional woman, but faces problems with her demanding, temperamental father, Henry Swann, a prominent gallery painter and professor of drawing and painting at the University of Wisconsin. Henry, who is having trouble coping with turning sixty, stands up Fanny and her mother at his own birthday party. To spite him, since he hates fast food, they go to Burger King, then return home to discover that he has left Christmas presents for them along with a note that he will spend the night in their cabin. Fanny's present, a glass statue of a dog, evokes memories of Nellie, a wiggly black Lab mix that Henry gave her but then adopted out because he considered the dog too lively and lacking good habits of personal hygiene. Fanny recalls other instances of his excessive fastidiousness, as when she loses items dear to her when they clean her room, except for a paper cutout doll called Marie that she hides in a filing cabinet. The next day he telephones Ellen with the news that he will be home that evening and will bring dinner with him. Ironically, dinner turns out to be a dog, a soft, creamy tan, spotted, three-year-old part German shepherd. Fanny immediately fears that she will lose Dinner as she lost Nellie. Fears also afflict her from an external source. While walking the dog, she several times spots a boy with a red cap and assumes that he is Dinner's former owner, spying on her in order to get his dog back. Eventually, she discovers that he is a new boy and happens to be attracted to her. A parting remark on New Year's Eve by Stuart Walker, a dear friend of the family, that if "Henry can't handle this dog," he (Stuart) will gladly take her, arouses agonies of fear that this might be an easy way out for Henry. Her fears increase even more when she discovers that, while she is at school, Dinner has been in her father's attic studio. Fanny realizes that she is attempting to protect Dinner as she once tried to protect Marie the doll. More harrowing moments ensue until Fanny realizes that Henry is putting Dinner in a painting. She panics when Henry takes Dinner for a ride in his car, tears Marie to pieces (a symbolic act), and then is relieved to learn that Henry took Dinner to Stuart to make photographs of the dog. Henry apologizes for upsetting her and asks her to trust him. She summons the courage to tell him that he is simply too fussy, accuses him of trying to take Marie away, tells him that she is afraid of him sometimes, and is astonished to hear him say that he occasionally feels the same way about her. He presents her with a photo of Dinner that depicts Dinner wearing a crown like the Snow Queen. They hug and kiss, and for the time being at least Fanny feels safe and happy. Most of the book describes scenes of family life, like skating in the park, or remembered events that point up the difficulties of life with father. Interspersed among the episodes of the loosely knit plot are school scenes and passages with Mary Dibble and the red-capped boy, Timothy Hill, with whom Fanny is seen at the end, talking about his becoming a scientist and she a linguist, happy, content, and optimistic. Sensory details, mostly visual, make the book into a latter-day family portrait and create more than just a run-of-the-mill story about how two well-drawn figures, a temperamental father and a sensitive daughter, learn to get along with one another. Dialogue is important in getting at themes: for example, Ellen cautions Fanny against wanting things to be perfect to her standards. SLJ.

PRYOR, BONNIE H. (1942–   ), born in Los Angeles, California; resident of Gambier, Ohio; public speaker, owner of children's bookstores in Ohio, and since 1985 the author of thirty books, some novels, some picture books, of amusing domestic adventures and light fantasy for middle-grade and younger readers. *Marvelous Marvin and the Pioneer Ghost** (Morrow, 1995), a well-paced, lighthearted mystery-detective novel with ghost-story and environmental-awareness aspects, was nominated for the Edgar Allan Poe Award. *Joseph: A Rumble of War* (Morrow, 1999), in her American Adventure Series, is set at the beginning of the American Civil War. *Luke on the High Seas* (Morrow, 2000), a clipper ship story, is another in the series. She has also contributed to such periodicals as *Woman's World* and *Writer*.

P.S. LONGER LETTER LATER (Danziger*, Paula, and Ann M. Martin*, Scholastic, 1998), epistolary novel of friendship and family life set for one school year about the time of publication. The story is told entirely in letters exchanged by Tara*Starr (Tara-Starr) Lane, 12, and her former classmate, Elizabeth Richardson (whom Tara soon addresses as Eliza*Beth), after Tara*Starr's family has moved to Ohio. The girls speak of how much they miss each other, reminisce about old times, encourage each other in troubling situations, describe their family and school life, become interested in boys, tell about new friends, and describe their feelings about their parents. As they do, they characterize themselves and reveal their growing maturity. Ebullient Tara*Starr is a witty, outgoing, assertive preadolescent with a good sense of fun and the desire to become "a great American writer." Eliza*Beth, on the other hand, is shy, pleasant, and more introverted. Tara*Starr, who has dubbed her parents, still in their twenties, the Charents (Childlike Parents), tells how they assume responsibilities about the house that they used to leave to her, have found reasonably well paying jobs, intend to enter college, and, to her disgust, decide to have a baby. While Tara*Starr's parents are coming together and getting their feet on the ground, Eliza*Beth's seemingly happy home—her father, mother, and sister, Emma, 4— is breaking up. At first, she has no idea of what is going on between her parents; she just knows that something is wrong and that her mother is uneasy and would like to get a job outside the home. Then she learns that her father's large corporation, of which he is a vice president enjoying a $250,000 annual salary, is being downsized and that the family is in danger of losing their elaborate $600,000 house. Her father begins to drink, orders expensive gifts at Christmastime, and runs the family into debt until they are forced to sell the house and most of their possessions to pay off bills and move to an apartment. On the day that they move, he announces that he will no longer be living with his family and in about a month asks for a separation. Life in school for both girls follows a parallel pattern. At first, Tara*Starr has no friends, but at Eliza*Beth's urging she tries out for Drama Club and wins a part in *Cheaper by the Dozen*. After that, her sense of fun and intelligence gain her friends and a greater part in school life. Her social life grows, she dates, does well in her classes, and even writes a humor column for the school paper. While Eliza*Beth takes her family problems hard, she follows Tara*Starr's advice and discusses them with her English teacher, who asks her to initiate a poetry journal. She also grows closer to her mother as they work through their fears and sense of loss and abandonment. Eliza*Beth also finds that some of her classmates live in her apartment building, and she makes friends with them. She is able to bring friends home for the first time, since her father was, in Tara*Starr's word, "snobby" and discouraged her associating with those financially less advantaged. At the end, Eliza*Beth looks forward to a visit with Tara*Starr and her parents, Barb and Luke, who also have encouraged her with her problems. The girls' voices are distinct, and their letters are vivid with details, more elaborate than letters of most girls their age would probably be, and the disintegration of the Richardson family is credible. Some scenes are especially vivid, but the prattle gets tedious, at least for the adult reader, although probably most preteen girls would savor it. Probably the book's greatest drawback, in addition to that intrinsic to the epistolary form—the need to fill in for the reader details that the letter writers would not need to communicate—is that the whole seems dated in tone, substance, and especially form. Today's teens, even the generally less computer-literate girls, would be more likely to communicate by email. ALA.

PUT NELSON (*Jip His Story**), Putnam Nelson, mentally ill older man who is brought to the poor farm screaming and struggling against the ropes that truss him and rub his wrists and ankles raw. Mr. Lyman, the manager, has had Jip and Sheldon* Morse build a cage, about six cubic feet, to confine him. Only Jip thinks and has the courage to cut his bonds and bring him ointment to sooth his rope burns. When he is not in one of his raving spells, Put is a kindly, educated man, helping Jip learn to read and willingly singing endlessly the hymn that little Toddy Wilkins loves and calls "the blood-washed frong." Although dark and winter weather brings on his bad spells, in good weather Put works happily on the farm, where he is kept mostly because Mr. Lyman does not want to pay the fees to send him to the lunatic asylum. When Jip must escape and wants to take Put with him, the old man does his best to make the journey cross-country to the Stevens farm, but his age and his confinement in the cage have weakened him. Ill and confused, he makes one last effort to save Jip at the quarry, where the slave catchers have seized the boy, and is shot as he approaches, singing his hymn. The book ends with the music and text of the hymn "All Is Well."

Q

QUALEY, MARSHA (RICHARDSON) (1953–   ), born in Austin, Minnesota; writer of a number of novels set in the upper Midwest. *Come in from the Cold** (Houghton, 1994) is about protests during the Vietnam War. Her Poe Nominee mystery novel, *Thin Ice** (Delacorte, 1997), is concerned with a girl's conviction that her older brother and guardian has not been the victim of an accident but has staged his own disappearance. For earlier biographical information and a title entry, see *Dictionary, 1990–1994* [*Revolutions of the Heart*].

QUEEN ELIZABETH (*The Shakespeare Stealer**), Elizabeth I, Queen of England at the time that Widge associates with the Chamberlain's Men, William Shakespeare's company, at the Globe. When the players are invited to present *Hamlet* at Whitehall, the entire cast is thrilled and works hard to do a good job. Widge plays Ophelia, because Julian* has been discovered to be a girl and hence is banned by law from acting. Widge does well and wins compliments from the company and the Queen. Although he is impressed by the monarch, he is surprised by her appearance. From a distance, he thinks that she looks far too young to have worn the crown for forty years. Up close, however, he sees what he calls a "ghastly mask" of white face paint, that her red hair is clearly dyed, and that her teeth are black with decay.

R

THE RAMSAY SCALLOP (Temple*, Frances, Orchard, 1994), episodic period novel with growing-up aspects set in England, France, and Spain in 1300. Leisurely in pace, long, and filled with detail, the story describes the pilgrimage of two young English nobles, Lady Elenor* of Ramsay Castle, 14, and her betrothed, Thomas* of Thornham, twenty-one or twenty-two, a returned Crusader, on behalf of their people. They intend to lay a record of the sins and contrition of residents of the castle and estate at the shrine of Saint James in Spain on the orders of their priest, Father* Gregory. Neither young person wishes to marry the other, since they are nearly strangers, Thomas having just returned from seven years on Crusade and Elenor having been a child when he left. Both know that their marriage is inevitable, however, since it has been arranged by their fathers, and they are the last of their lines. Elenor, small, high-spirited but capable and dutiful, fears giving herself to the hulking Thomas and dying in childbirth, while Thomas dreads assuming the duties laid on him by his father and taking to wife the girl whom he inwardly thinks of as a child and calls the Brat. Both young people mature in mind and spirit as a result of their experiences on the approximately ninety-day foot-journey, gain respect and affection for each other, and are married at the Spanish shrine before returning to England by ship. With minimal supplies and money, they leave home on their cherished horses, Thomas on Daisy and Elenor on Mab, and ride to Yarmouth, where they take a small ship to France, join other pilgrims overland to Paris, and then head south. Along the way, they camp out, sleep in hostels, and stay in churches, rest houses, and monasteries, associating with all sorts of pilgrims, among them some rough characters, learning about features of the countryside, attending fairs, and dealing with problems as they arise. Among the people with whom they become acquainted are Adam, a troubadour, whose songs Elenor loves; gentle, unpretentious Brother Ambrose, on his way to Amiens to visit his sister, now an old woman, and to view once again the cathedral whose construction was begun in his childhood and is still under way; Marthe and her three small children, one a baby in arms, on their way to Bordeaux to be reunited with their husband and father; Etienne, a student with whom they have philosophical conversations and who helps Elenor buy a book of Bernard of Chartres' writings as her first present for Thomas, who, she subsequently discovers, cannot read; Martin McFeery, a Scotsman who buys a puppy, Greatheart, for Elenor; Pierre Maury, a young shepherd who finds and cares for Elenor after she falls down a mountainside while searching for runaway Greatheart; and Hassad, the Saracen (Muslim) shepherd who is Pierre's good friend, whose questions and comments prod Elenor to think about what as a Christian she really believes and whom, to her surprise, she admires. Temporarily losing Elenor makes Thomas realize how much she has come to mean to him. Along the way, various pilgrims, Thomas, and Elenor tell stories, all of which have some application to the places or situations in which they find themselves. For example, before they arrive at Roncevalles Pass in the Pyrenees, Elenor tells the story of Roland, the French hero who was slain there. Near the end of the journey, Thomas is attacked by a wild boar. During his slow recovery, Elenor realizes that she admires and has grown fond of him, too. At Santiago, they deposit the packet of sins, Thomas buys a scallop shell from among the religious artifacts, and they prepare to return home to assume the responsibilities that they know await them. The story follows the pattern of the oral-tradition story of the helpful traveling companions, the outcome holds no surprises, and the book's chief attributes are its picture of the hustle and bustle of the castle, the motley assortment of pilgrims who give a strong sense of the times, and the growing maturity of the two central figures. ALA; SLJ.

RAPP, ADAM, born in Chicago, Illinois; playwright, novelist. His work for the theater has won prestigious awards and been produced in New York, Chicago, Los Angeles, and Washington, D.C. Among his novels are two about boys in abusive situations, a rigid, unenlightened military academy in *Missing the Piano** (Viking, 1994) and a brutal reform school in *The Buffalo Tree** (Front Street, 1997). Among his other titles is *The Copper Elephant* (Front Street, 1999). Rapp lives in New York City.

RATS SAW GOD (Thomas*, Rob, Simon & Schuster, 1996), realistic, psychological problem and boy's growing-up novel set in San Diego at the time of publication. The narrator, Wakefield High School senior Steven York, is caught in physics class high on drugs and sent to the school counselor, Jeff DeMouy*. Curious because Steve had compiled a perfect academic record for five semesters straight at Grace High School in Houston, Texas, before moving to San Diego and was recently named a National Merit Finalist, DeMouy tells Steve that he cannot be graduated unless he restores his failed English credit. Steve can do this, he says, by producing 100 typewritten pages of any single literary form. Steve turns the assignment into a kind of therapeutic exercise by describing his life in Houston from the time of his parents' divorce, when his famous, ex-moon-walker, astronaut father, Alan*, received custody of Steve, to the present.

Interspersed among the Houston passages about life with Alan and Steve's friends at Grace High are those about San Diego with his mother, stepfather, and younger sister, Sarah*. In Houston, Steve lives in a large, well-appointed house in an upscale neighborhood, avoiding as much as he can the busy Alan, whom he resents as an overachiever whose expectations Steve can never live up to and as the one whose actions and attitudes broke up the marriage. Thus disaffected, Steve spends his after-school time at his job at the local cinema or studying. At school he falls in with Doug Chappell, dedicated iconoclast and aspiring musician who organizes the Grace Order of Dadaists, or GOD*, a group of about a dozen rebels who intentionally flout school rules for clubs (as Dada did for art). Since he is on the fringes, Steve's relationship with Doug and the other club males is mostly lukewarm but satisfactory. He manages, for the most part, to evade the girls who lust for him but gradually becomes close to club member Dub* (Wanda) Varner, then falls in love with her. The two consummate the relationship one night in a torrid and innocently humorous love scene, in which they clumsily but satisfyingly lose their virginity. Soon they are known in school as a couple. Because the club gets in trouble with school authorities, they enlist as adviser the most nonconforming teacher in school, Sky (from Luke Skywalker) Waters, who teaches creative writing. All goes well until Dub grows jealous because Steve wins a writing contest. When he returns from a visit to San Diego, he finds her in bed with Sky. He angrily quits creative writing and moves to San Diego as soon as he can. Although his senior year at Wakefield is rocky, he forms a friendship with the school's other National Merit Finalist, Allison* Kimble, moves his grades up, learns from Sarah that their mother was at least partly to blame for the divorce, and, when Alan marries again, begins to see his father in a better light. He receives his diploma and leaves for the University of Washington and possibly a career in counseling. Although the story-within-a-story device is awkwardly motivated, the book stands out as a late twentieth-century slice of home and school life. The central problem is common in teen stories, but Steve's angst is mercifully never belabored, and the reader is spared repeated instances of son-father acrimony. The school and club scenes are credible, attitudes and behavior of teens caught with sometimes excruciating exactness, and the diction and dialogue have the realism of transcriptions from tapes. The sex scenes are explicit but not erotic, safe-sex procedures are not overlooked, and teen obsession with sex is not glossed over. While most of the book is serious, certain scenes, like those in which Steve invites and takes Dub to the prom, are funny, and some, like that in which he gives her $600 earrings, are disturbingly poignant. Outstanding are the warmth and understanding that the writer apparently holds for teens, teachers, and parents, all caught at stages in life that probably always have been critical but that the peculiar pressures of the end of the millennium have undoubtedly increased. The kids are familiar, late-twentieth-century youths, headstrong, pampered teenagers, young people not completely out of control but with too much money and too much free time. SLJ.

RAYMOND PROVIDENCE (*Far North**), Native-American Indian youth of the Slavey group who is the roommate of white Gabe Rogers at the boarding school in Yellowknife, Northwest Territories, Canada. Raymond, 15, arrives at school carrying a red electric guitar and a hockey stick. Shy and inclined to be withdrawn, he makes few friends and has a hard time with algebra. He says that the school will not let him play the guitar, and he is reluctant to try hockey, although he is evidently very good at the game. Gabe encourages him with his classes and helps him with math in return for Raymond's teaching him to skate. But Raymond misses his friends in Nahanni Butte and, after two months, elects to go home. He has some knowledge of woods lore, is tougher physically and steadier in mind than Gabe, has confidence in Johnny* Raven, his old great-uncle, and in Indian ways and beliefs, and knows a little Slavey language so that he can communicate with Johnny. After Johnny's memorial potlatch, Raymond decides that he will return to school, influenced by Johnny's will, in which the old man stressed the importance of education.

REACHING DUSTIN (Grove*, Vicki, Putnam, 1998), novel of a girl's growth in understanding through a school assignment to interview a classmate. When the narrator, Carly Cameron, draws Dustin* Groat to interview in Ms. Aspen's sixth-grade class, she is disgusted, especially when she finds that the other students have secretly traded until each is interviewing a best friend. Dustin Groat sits slumped in the back of the classroom, unkempt, his boots dirty, paying no attention to what is going on. In addition, Carly has had run-ins with Dustin since third grade, when he began kicking furniture, head-butting the other children on the slide, and spitting on the desks. Moreover, everyone in the small Missouri town of Cooper's Glade knows about the Groat compound down on the bottomland by the river, an area fenced in with padlocked gates where they are rumored to manufacture methamphetamine and to warn trespassers off with guns. However, since the writer of the best interview is to be the editor of the class newspaper, a post that Carly covets, she pushes on in her attempt to pry some information from Dustin. She gets little directly from him but gradually she learns that the year when they were in third grade his mother drowned herself, his sister, Julie, was forced to drop out of school to take care of him, and the Groats have become involved with right-wing survivalists called Patriots whom they met at gun shows. Since the farm where Carly lives with her parents, her brothers, Noah, 17, and Luke, 6, is just across the soybean field from Koshkanong Woods, where the Groats sometimes cut wood, Carly's father knows them better than most of the townspeople and is one of the few people whom they trust enough to talk with, yet even he is afraid of their fascination with guns and violence. By doing some research, Carly learns about Quantrill's Raiders, a guerrilla band fighting for the Confederacy in the Civil War, a group that earlier Groat men were part of, and how they had escape tunnels from their headquarters in the swamp to nearby woods. She also discovers that Noah used to go with Julie and is still interested in making contact with her. After the music teacher issues all the sixth graders recorders and starts to teach them simple tunes, Carly begins to hear music, far more complicated, coming from Kosh Woods at night. She sneaks out across the bean field and sees Dustin sitting at the mouth of a tunnel, playing to his pet frog. By accident, she discovers that Dustin often hides out from bullying classmates under the bleachers in the gym. One day when Carly is watching her friends, Randi and Alicia, practice a dance routine, he suddenly darts out from under the bleachers and runs in front of Alicia, making her trip over him and fall. Everyone is so concerned with her injuries, a broken arm and minor scrapes, that they blame him and pay no attention to his disappearance. That night Carly returns to the woods to warn Dustin to come back to school to defend himself, but he shuts her out, saying that he is through with all that. In the middle of their conversation, helicopters, which have been more and more frequent in the area, come over, and a great blast of noise and flame erupts from the river bottom as the drug lab blows up. When Alicia and Carly realize that Dustin was chasing his frog, not deliberately tripping Alicia, they go to the principal but are told it is too late, that the Groats have taken Dustin out of school, saying he would be home-schooled from now on and that his recorder would be retrieved from the compound. Little Luke, to whom Carly has been telling a long fantasy about the "Goatboy," who plays the music that they hear at night, realizes that Dustin will no longer have a recorder. He goes to the woods at night and climbs the biggest oak tree, hoping to see the goatboy and give him a whistle carved by his grandfather. Carly discovers Luke's absence, rushes across the bean field, and comes on ambulances and paramedics loading him onto a stretcher. He has been shot in the heel and suffered a concussion in a fall from the oak. A week later, when she hears the music of Luke's whistle coming from the woods, Carly goes to the tunnel opening, finds Dustin, and asks him to come and play for Luke, who has finally regained consciousness. She also tells him that she did a mean thing to him in third grade, that she is sorry, and that her parents think that they can help get both him and Julie back into school since there is no record that they have ever been taught at home. Carly's gradual turn from hostility to interest and eventual sympathy for Dustin is well drawn, reinforced by her very decent father's confession that he could have been nicer to Dustin's uncles when they were in school with him, her mother's concern for the Groat children balanced by her worry over the wild shooting so near her home, and Noah's desire to see Julie again, even to the point of being shot at from the compound as he drives by. Carly's conflicts with her best friends, Alicia and Randi, are typical of young teenage girls and trite, but the novel does not dwell on them except to advance her exploration of Dustin's life. SLJ.

RED DRESS (*The Grass Dancer**), ancestor of several characters in the novel. She possesses malevolent magical powers, which are later inherited by Anna Thunder and also used for malevolent purposes. Red Dress loves Ghost Horse, a warrior and sacred clown or heyoka. She leaves him to go to Fort Laramie, where she works as a secretary for Reverend Pyke. There she uses her magical stones to make spells that induce the fort soldiers to commit suicide. When Pyke discovers what she is doing, he shoots her. Ghost Horse marries her spirit and then seeks death on the battlefield. The Reverend Pyke section gives a vivid picture of what life must have been like at the fort in those days.

REISS, KATHRYN, holds degrees from Duke University and The University of Michigan in creative writing; lives in Oakland, California, with her husband and three children; is a teacher of creative writing and novelist for teenagers. Honored with several awards, she has published *The Glass House People* (Harcourt, 1992); *Dreadful Sorry* (Harcourt, 1993); *Pale Phoenix** (Harcourt, 1994), a time-travel fantasy back to colonial New England and the witch hunts, which was nominated for the Edgar Allan Poe Award; *PaperQuake: A Puzzle** (Harcourt, 1998), a mystery with fantasy aspects in which diary entries help a girl prevent an earthquake in San Francisco, also a Poe Nominee; and several books in the Dollhouse Series, among them *Dollhouse of the Dead* (Scholastic, 1997). Reiss has been praised not only for her gripping plots but for her characterizations as well.

REMEMBERING MOG (Rodowsky*, Colby, Farrar, 1996), contemporary, realistic novel of the psychological effect on a family of their elder daughter's murder by a thief interrupted as he breaks into her boyfriend's car. Two years after the event, the narrator, Annie Fitzhugh, 16, is still suffering from the death of her sister, Mog, especially as she approaches her graduation from St. Kit's (St. Christopher's), the private Baltimore girl's school from which Mog had been about to graduate. The wealthy family of her friend, Erin McNabb, gives a graduation party reminiscent of the one that Mog and her boyfriend, Bobby Ritter, attended on the fateful night before they drove to Fell's Point to walk and talk and ended with Mog dead and Bobby in the hospital. Erin's understanding mother gives Annie the name of a counselor, Harriet Jeffers, knowing that the girl needs help. Even she does not realize how dysfunctional the Fitzhugh family has become, with Annie's father withdrawn and aging visibly, her mother in total denial, as if she has a plastic shield around her, and even her younger brother, Cricket, disoriented by the catastrophe and its continuing pall on family life. Only Reilly, an older distant cousin of her father who lives with them, is stable and able to keep a semblance of normality in the household. Annie has been bullied by the school guidance counselor to apply to several colleges, and she has received acceptance letters but has never bothered to respond. Most of her friends are working and living at the beach for the summer, but Annie didn't make arrangements and has ended up, almost by accident, as lifeguard at a neighborhood swimming pool. When she decides to follow up on Mrs. McNabb's suggestion, she calls Harriet Jeffers and begins seeing her but doesn't even mention, at first, the original cause of her troubles, Mog's death. Her father responds positively to Annie's start of therapy, but her mother's reaction shocks them all, a wild, hysterical storming through the house restoring Mog's room to the way it was when she was a small child. By accident, Annie runs into Bobby Ritter, who has recovered after several operations, and he often stops by the pool to take her home after work. Annie knows that Mog was planning on breaking up with Bobby the night of the graduation party and is relieved to find that they had not discussed it before the murder. Although the counselor suggests that seeing Bobby might not be a good idea for either of them, Annie begins to fall in love with him. Gradually, Annie sees that although she has always followed Mog's lead, now she must strike out on her own. She arranges to visit Mount St. Mary's College at Emmitsburg, is accepted, and feels comfortable there. She realizes that Bobby's attraction to her is mostly his desire to have Mog back, and she gently breaks off with him. In the end she is starting her freshman college year. Her mother, who has buried herself in her job of arranging and putting on wonderful fantasy parties for children, is still not facing reality, but her father is hopeful that she may recover. Cricket is getting help from his lacrosse coach at school. Reilly promises to pick Annie up the first weekend that she wants to come home for a visit. The story of Annie's childhood closeness to Mog, her death, her funeral, and all that has happened in the past two years is told in a series of flashbacks. Annie's psychological difficulties and those of her family ring true, and although there is not much action in the plot, and most of the characters are merely functional, the book is absorbing. ALA.

REMY MARLAND (*Driver's Ed**), Rembrandt Marland, 16, high school girl who, with her romantic interest, Morgan* Campbell, steals a STOP sign and causes the death of a young mother. Remy is presented as typical of contemporary high school girls. She yearns for the rites-of-passage driver's license and for the affection of Morgan, the handsomest boy in school. She comes from what is commonly regarded as a good home with responsible, middle-class parents who try to keep track of what she does and take her to church and Sunday School. She wants the MORGAN ROAD traffic sign as evidence that Morgan is hers and helps to steal the other signs for thrills. After the death of Mrs. Thompson, Remy realizes that the death is indirectly her fault. One of the book's good aspects, in addition to depicting her moral growth, is how her feelings for Morgan go from sexual desire to the deeper comfort that comes from having his arms around her and knowing that he shares her agony.

THE REVENGE OF THE FORTY-SEVEN SAMURAI (Haugaard*, Erik Christian, Houghton, 1995), historical novel set at the beginning of the eighteenth century in feudal Japan. It is based on an actual, well-remembered incident told from the point of view of a humble servant boy, Jiro, 14, the son of a lowly cook in the household of Oishi Kuranosuke, one of the chief retainers of Asano, lord of Ako in the province of Harima. When Kira Kozukenosuke, grand master of ceremonies for the shogun who rules Japan, insults Lord Asano repeatedly, Asano draws his sword and wounds Kira slightly. For this the shogun commands that he commit seppuku (slit his belly open), a suicide that makes all his lands forfeit and his 200 samurai retainers *ronin*, masterless soldiers with no regular means of support. Because Oishi is highly respected and also has control of the "clan money," some funds saved out of the estate, he becomes leader of the samurai who want to avenge this unjust death of their lord. At first, although they move from Ako castle to a small village near Kyoto, Oishi persuades the more hotheaded young samurai that they must wait until the shogun acts upon their request that Ako castle be given to Asano's brother, in which case they would become the brother's retainers. When the request is denied, Oishi counsels more patience, pointing out that they must lull Kira into a sense of security and attack when his guard is down. Because a servant boy attracts little notice and because Jiro is quick-witted and loyal, Oishi employs him to gather news and to spread false information, telling the boy to say that his master has retired from active life and turned to tending peonies and studying the lotus sutra. Several times Jiro is stopped and questioned by samurai as he does errands for the household, once even being cut on the forehead, marked, the samurai says, so that he will be known again. Oishi decides that he must do more to convince Kira's spies that he is no threat, and he starts visiting "the floating world," the disreputable district of women and sake for sale, and Jiro accompanies him to wait with other servants and light his master's staggering steps home, though Oishi is never as drunken, Jiro notices, as he pretends to be. One of Asano's younger retainers, Otaka Gengo, takes a liking to Jiro and often talks to him, a very unusual friendship between a samurai and a servant. Of the 200 original Asano samurai dedicated to revenge, the number gradually shrinks to forty-seven. When the appointed time for their attack on Kira approaches, they travel in small groups to Edo, since any large number passing a checkpoint would be suspect. Jiro goes as servant to Oishi, and they are accompanied by a former horse keeper at Ako castle, a slow-witted giant named Uma, to carry their baggage. Although Oishi has told Jiro to leave in the morning and has given him a small purse for food on the trip home, curiosity to know the end of the story makes Jiro follow the conspirators and observe their assassination of Kira, an old man in his nightclothes. Although Oishi has given him a pass that should get him a place as a servant in the household of a samurai, and Otaka has advised him to become a merchant, Jiro has already decided that when the forty-seven have committed seppuku, as they will be commanded to do, he will become a "riverside beggar," a term for the traveling actors of the day, since he has learned, finally, that his father was such an actor, and he has fallen in love with the idea on his only visit to the theater. The novel cleverly describes the code of honor subscribed to by the samurai while at the same time, through Jiro's thoughts, questioning the value of such an ethic. Jiro is cleareyed in his appraisal of those around him. He understands that his mother is greedy and lazy and that she would have been sent to the fields to work if he had not covered for her many times, but he feels some responsibilty for her. He sees that Oishi's kindness to him is genuine but that it is the same kindness that he would show to a favorite dog or horse. His great affection for Otaka is based not on the gifts that the young man occasionally bestows on him or the money that the young samurai has given a monk to teach the boy to read and write but on the way that Otaka treats him as a real person whose thoughts are worth considering. The novel's picture of life in feudal Japan is rich and detailed with scenes set in the great Ako castle, the small house near Kyoto, the Buddhist temple that adjoins it, the pleasure district of the floating world, the inns, and the road itself as they travel. Jiro's position as a junior spy is dangerous, since any samurai may kill with impunity any person of a lower class simply for suspicion of disrespect or even just to test the sharpness of his sword. The style is compelling without sensationalism. A list of characters, telling the role of each in the story, and a Preface about Japan of that period are very helpful. ALA.

THE REVEREND MR. GIDEON BARTHOLOMEW (*Beyond the Western Sea: Book One: The Escape from Home**), kindly Protestant cleric who operates the chapel boat, the *Charity*, at Queen's Dock in Liverpool, which serves runaways and indigents. He takes in both Patrick O'Connell and Sir Laurence Kirkle when they have lost their way on the harbor, feeds them, and gives them shelter for the night. Certain that Laurence has run away from a wealthy home and that his people will be searching for him, Bartholomew writes a note to the police informing them of his suspicions and unwittingly gives the note to Fred* No-name to deliver, not knowing that Fred belongs to the Lime Street Runners Association street gang. Hence, the note does not get to its intended destination. With the best of intentions, Bartholomew drags Patrick off to the Catholic Society for the Protection of Abandoned Irish Boys, much against the boy's will. On the way, Patrick breaks loose, runs, and happens to encounter his sister, Maura, and Mr.* Horatio Drabble, whom he has been seeking. Meanwhile, Laurence, who now just wants to go home and get away from these frightening characters, is lured off the chapel boat by Fred, who informs the boy that he is being sought by police, Mr.* Matthew Clemspool, and various others. Bartholomew acts out of noble, if somewhat misguided, motives and is one of the admirable people in the book.

REYNOLDS, MARILYN (1935–   ), author of problem novels for teenagers. Reynolds works in an alternative high school, where the experiences of the students often inspire her novels, many of them in her True-to-Life Hamilton High Series. Among those dealing with unwanted pregnancies are *Detour for Emmy* (Morning Glory, 1993) and *Too Soon for Jeff** (Morning Glory, 1994). Others deal with abusive partners, failure at school, sexual molestation by the father of the children for whom a girl baby-sits, and death in an auto accident after a party with alcohol. Reynolds makes her home in Southern California.

RICK WALKER (*The Maze**), boy, 14, who escapes from a detention home in Las Vegas and makes his way into the wilds of Canyonlands National Park in Utah, where he encounters Lon* Peregrino, a condor biologist who befriends him and changes the boy's life for the better. Born in California and abandoned by his fifteen-year-old mother, Rick was raised by her mother. When his grandmother died at an early age, Rick was placed in a series of foster homes. After he got in trouble with the law by destroying a street sign and stealing a couple of CDs (compact discs), he was remanded to a detention home in Las Vegas, from which he ran away because he feared for his life. One factor that persuades the judge to send Rick to a group home rather than back to finish the remaining six weeks of detention is that details of unlawful behavior by the guards there have been made public, substantiating Rick's story of why he fled from the place.

RIMON (*Escape from Egypt**), uncle of Jesse* and brother of Devorah*, Jesse's mother. He is a devout, pious man, a staunch follower of Adonai, the Hebrew god, and a solid supporter of Moses, until late in the story, when he begins to have doubts about Moses' authority and is punished by Adonai with death. Jesse loves and admires him greatly and wishes that Rimon were his father instead of Nathan*. Rimon urges Jesse to strengthen his faith in Adonai and always to remember that he and Talia* have a responsibility for leadership when the Hebrews arrive in Canaan.

RITTER, JOHN H., writer and lecturer. He was born into a baseball-loving family whose father was a sportswriter in Ashtabula, Ohio. Just before John was born, the family moved west to San Diego and shortly thereafter settled in rural San Diego County along the Mexican line. This family history provides background for Ritter's critically acclaimed first novel, *Choosing Up Sides** (Putnam, 1998). Winner of the International Reading Association Award, it tells of a left-handed boy whose desire to play baseball brings him into conflict with his Baptist preacher father, who adamantly opposes using one's left hand and all sports. It has been praised for its astute handling of the subject of discrimination. After high school, Ritter attended the University of California at San Diego, where he met his wife, an elementary teacher. The Ritters live in San Diego and have a grown daughter. Ritter operated his own custom painting contracting business for twenty-five years. In addition to writing and lecturing, he is writer in residence for the Oceanside, California, Unified School District. He has also published *Over the Wall* (Philomel, 2000), about violence in sports, religious hypocrisy, and the Vietnam War.

ROBERTS, WILLO DAVIS (1928–   ), born in Grand Rapids, Michigan; prolific writer for both adults and children. Most of her novels for young people are mysteries, ranging from the essentially humorous *The Absolutely True Story . . . How I Visited Yellowstone Park with the Terrible Rupes** (Atheneum, 1994), to the scary *Caught** (Atheneum, 1994), to the highly improbable, but fast-moving, *The Kidnappers** (Atheneum, 1998). For a slightly older audience are two set in Michigan summer colonies, *Twisted Summer** (Atheneum, 1996) and *Secrets at Hidden Valley** (Atheneum, 1997). For earlier biographical information and title entries, see *Dictionary, 1960–1984* [*More Minden Curses*], *Dictionary, 1985–1989* [*Megan's Island*], and *Dictionary, 1990–1994* [*To Grandmother's House We Go*].

ROBINET, HARRIETTE GILLEM (1931–   ), born in Washington, D.C.; African-American writer of realistic and historical fiction for children and young adults. After completing her undergraduate work at the College of New Rochelle, she received a doctorate from Catholic University of America. She has held various positions as a medical and research bacteriologist and instructor in biology. Her first two publications, picture books for younger readers about handicapped boys, *Jay and the Marigold* (Children's, 1976) and *Ride the Red Cycle* (Houghton, 1980), were inspired by her own son's cerebral palsy. Her next books, all historical and period novels about African Americans for older readers, show evidence of careful, extensive research and good plotting: *Children of the Fire* (Atheneum, 1991), about the Chicago fire of 1871; *Mississippi Chariot* (Atheneum, 1994), about a boy's efforts to free his father from the chain gang in 1936; *If You Please, Mr. Lincoln* (Atheneum, 1995), about an unfortunate expedition to relocate freed slaves to an island off Haiti in early 1864; *Washington City Is Burning* (Atheneum, 1996), about the British attack on Washington in the War of 1812; *The Twins, the Pirates, and the Battle of New Orleans* (Atheneum, 1997), also about the War of 1812; and *Forty Acres and Maybe a Mule** (Atheneum, 1998) about freed slaves' problems during Reconstruction at the end of the American Civil War, a book that won the Scott O'Dell Award for Historical Fiction.

ROCKLIN, JOANNE (1946–   ), born in Montreal, Quebec, Canada; psychotherapist and writer of lighthearted problem novels popular with middle-grade and adolescent readers. Her first, *Sonia Begonia* (Macmillan, 1986), concerns an ill-conceived effort to capture neighborhood robbers. Also among her nearly dozen books are *Dear Baby* (Macmillan, 1988), *Strudel Stories* (Delacorte, 1999), and *The Very Best Hanukkah Gift* (Delacorte, 1999). She has also published several first readers and a picture book. Learning about Langston Hughes' work in encouraging young writers inspired her to write *For YOUR Eyes Only!** (Scholastic, 1997), a *School Library Journal* Best Book, about two sixth graders, one a fairly typical girl, the other an angry, abused boy who record their daily experiences in journal entries that will be read only by their enterprising substitute teacher. Rocklin received her undergraduate teaching degree from McGill University and an M.A. and a Ph.D. from the California School of Professional Psychology. She lives in Los Angeles.

RODOWSKY, COLBY (1932–   ), born in Baltimore, Maryland; teacher and author of both picture books and problem novels for young adults. Two novels of the mid-1990s are both concerned with family disruptions. In *Hannah In Between** (Farrar, 1994) the problem is the mother's alcoholism, a condition denied or ignored by most of the other adults. In *Remembering Mog** (Farrar, 1996) an older sister has been murdered, and the surviving daughter watches the disintegration of her family under the strain. For earlier biographical information and a title entry, see *Dictionary, 1990–1994* [*Sydney, Herself*].

ROSASHARN (*Flyers**), Billy Rose, high school-age pal of Gabe and Ethan* Riley, Bo* Michaelson, and Jeremy Wulfson. A large, tubby teenager, clumsy and oafish, he provides comic relief. Although not eager to do so, he accommodates Gabe and Bo by playing the part of Green Guy in the film that they are making. No one knows it at the time except Ethan, but Andy Foster is the shadow that Ray McPherson sees when, dressed as Green Guy, Rosasharn jumps on the hood of Ray's Buick.

ROSEN, MICHAEL J(OEL) (1954–   ), born in Columbus, Ohio; received a bachelor's degree from Ohio State University and an M.F.A. from Columbia University; college instructor, lecturer, participant in poets- and artists-in-the-school programs, among other positions; writer of nonfiction, poetry, novels, and short stories for adults and children and editor of collections of poetry and short stories. He has received many awards, in particular, for his poems. Among his publications are the illustrated novelettes *Elijah's Angel: A Story for Chanukah and Christmas* (Harcourt, 1992) and *A School for Pompey Walker** (Harcourt, 1995), an American Library Association selection, a period story about an ex-slave who builds a school for black children in Ohio. Others are *Home* (HarperCollins, 1992), writings and drawings by children's authors; *Speak! Children's Book Illustrators Brag about Their Dogs* (Harcourt, 1993); and *Purr . . . Children's Book Illustrators Brag about Their Cats* (Harcourt, 1996). Proceeds from some of Rosen's books benefit charities for animals and for the homeless.

ROXANNE (*Under the Mermaid Angel**), young woman in probably her late twenties who moves into the trailer next door to that in which Jesse and her family live in Ida, Texas, and helps her to a stronger self-image. Roxanne wears her dark, brick-red hair long, miniskirts, tight sweaters, and push-up bras, making her the sort of person that Jesse's Mama says she does not want her daughter to spend much time with. Roxanne tells Jesse that she married very young—at sixteen—a boy whom she dearly loved. He died in a fall, leaving her pregnant. She left town, moved to another town to have her baby, and gave it for adoption to a wealthy family who could not have children. Later she married again but lost the baby that she was carrying and discovered that she could have no more children. After she divorced her husband, who was abusive, she came to Ida, where she had had her baby, to find her son, who turns out to be Franklin* Harris. In Jesse's view, she looks much like the mermaid angel that Mr. Arthur has hung over the Last Supper exhibit in his wax museum. Roxanne comes through as a woman for whom life has been hard but who has never lost her ability to hope for the best and do what she can to make life better for those around her.

ROYBAL, LAURA (1956–   ), born in Des Moines, Iowa; writer, worker with children and teenagers. Recently she has helped run a youth wilderness camp in Pecos, New Mexico, where she has made her home. She attended the University of New Mexico and received her B.A. degree from New Mexico Highlands University. Her first novel, *Billy** (Houghton, 1994), is the story of a boy kidnapped years earlier by his own father. When this comes to light, he is faced with having to leave his happy New Mexico life and return to his adoptive family in Iowa, whom he hardly remembers, to save from prosecution his father, whom he loves. It was named to both the American Library Association Notable Books list and the *School Library Journal* list of Best Books for Children.

RULE OF THE BONE (Banks*, Russell, HarperCollins, 1995), adult, picaresque novel of a boy's growing up set for about eighteen months in recent years in Au Sable in upstate New York and in Jamaica. After Chappie, the self-obsessed narrator, is caught stealing valuable family heirloom coins to support his marijuana habit, the disaffected fourteen-year-old walks out on his mother and his stepfather, who has molested him since he was seven. He moves in with his best friend, Russ* Rodgers, 16, also a school dropout, and Russ' several older, drugging motorcycle friends, the Adirondack Iron. Chappie lives all winter with Russ and the unpredictable bikers, dealing drugs to satisfy their habits as well as his own. After some harrowing experiences with the usually high bikers, Russ and Chappie steal a truck and live in an abandoned school bus with a pair of drugged-out, ex-college students, whom Chappie calls the Bong Brothers and to whom they sell the truck for $100 and then take off. They adopt new identities; Russ takes the name Buck, while Chappie acquires his first tattoo, a crossbones, and calls himself Bone. They hop the bus to Keene, New York, and occupy an empty summerhouse for the winter, generally trashing the place. In the spring, Russ moves in with an aunt. Bone steals a gun, camping gear, and outdoor clothes, shoots the gun out a window, yelling, "The Bone rules!," and hitches a ride to Albany. He gets picked up by a van whose driver turns out to be a "porn dude" and pedophile who calls himself Buster Brown and has with him a little girl of seven he calls Froggy (real name Rosie). During a fracas with the surviving members of the Adirondack Iron, Bone takes the girl and hurries back to the school bus, which is now occupied by a "grinning little black dude," I-Man*, an elderly Jamaican with imposing dreadlocks who says he is Rastafarian, has a drug habit, and grows marijuana. The three live happily as a family for a while, but Bone thinks that little Rosie should go home and puts her on the bus to her mother in Milwaukee, Wisconsin. Bone then leaves with I-Man for Jamaica, where he learns that I-Man is both a major drug dealer and a respected religious leader. The now dreadlocked Bone discovers his real father in Jamaica, a doctor called Doc who is also often stoned and has a Jamaican family and a mistress known as Evening Star. She lives in a big house called Mothership, which is the center for high-living, usually drugged-out tourists. I-Man arranges for Bone to be initiated into his Rastafarian sect, a process during which the boy has a vision of the slave experience on Jamaica. After I-Man is shot to death for trying to cheat an American drug dealer, and Bone persuades Evening Star to have sex with him, Bone decides to go home and live a normal life. He has come to live by the rule of bone, that is, to make decisions for himself, and says he wants to get an education and leave behind the marginalized life (although he admits that he may be lying). As Chappie/Bone tells his story, the plot is jam-packed with often happenstance incidents. An honest, articulate, and likable fellow for the most part, in spite of his self-absorption, Chappie tells the reader of his seamy life in very long, run-on sentences and occasional humor, but the almost 400 pages of his account have so much trash and sex talk that the style becomes tiresome, and the reader yearns for real action. I-Man is an intriguing and also likable character, in spite of his faults. His end is expectedly brutal and emotionally unsatisfying, although his death paves the way for Chappie's emancipation and entry into a more normal adult world. Bone's sexual initiation is an overly obvious, literal symbol, the vision seems unnecessary and also obvious, very little is made of the childhood molestation except as an excuse for his leaving home, and Bone's rejecting Russ, who also comes to Jamaica to live on the edge, is entirely appropriate given recent events in his life. The book is a troubling slice of life and leaves one unclear about themes, ambivalent about characters, and bothered by the writer's apparent sense that readers need shock appeal and a plethora of four-letter words to remain attentive. SLJ.

RULES OF THE ROAD (Bauer*, Joan, Putnam, 1998), quirky career novel of a girl who gains enough self-confidence during an unusual summer to speak up for her eccentric boss at a stockholders' meeting and later, with more difficulty, confront her drunken father and insist that he sober up or get out of her life. The narrator, Jenna Boller, 16, is tall, red-haired, and inclined to be ungainly, but she does one thing well. She sells shoes. She likes her boss, Murray Castlebaum, and she loves her job at Gladstone's Shoe Store in Chicago, until one day when Mrs.* Madeline Gladstone, president of the large chain of high-quality shoe stores, is present when Jenna's father, whom she has not seen for nearly three years, appears, loud and drunken. Jenna maneuvers him out of the store, finds out where he is staying, gets him in a cab, and gives the driver the address and ten dollars, then returns to work, shaken and humiliated but determined to hide her feelings. Impressed by her attitude, Mrs. Gladstone hires her as a driver, first to chauffeur her around Chicago in her Cadillac, then to drive her to her home in Texas, stopping along the way at various stores to surprise the managers and check on how things are going, ending in Dallas in time for the stockholders' meeting at which she plans to resign in favor of her son, Elden. On the trip

Jenna learns a great deal, in addition to skill in driving, at which she has been a novice. Elden has been firing good managers and replacing them with flunkies who are willing to push the cheap and poorly made shoes from The Shoe Warehouse, a huge firm that wants to buy out Gladstone Shoes but continue to use the more prestigious name. Despite being in pain constantly from a bad hip, which needs a replacement, Mrs. Gladstone is determined to make the trip and preside with dignity at the stockholders' meeting. Afraid that she won't resign, Elden has been acquiring stock and promises from other stockholders, planning to force her out. In Springfield, Illinois, Mrs. Gladstone's hip is so bad that Jenna calls a doctor, who puts her in the hospital overnight. Jenna also calls Harry Bender, manager of the flagship store in Dallas, and gets advice from him on how to deal with Elden, who flies in, determined to see and bully his mother. Jenna, as Bender advises, meets Elden, tells him sweetly that his mother is too ill to see him and, despite his verbal abuse, continues to smile and be polite but firm. He leaves in a huff. Jenna and Mrs. Gladstone are joined in St. Louis by Alice Lovett, a retired shoe model who matches her friend Mrs. Gladstone in toughness, if not in elegance. In Dallas they stay at Mrs. Gladstone's lavish home, again fend off Elden's attempt to influence his mother, and learn that Harry Bender is organizing resistance to The Shoe Warehouse takeover. Jenna learns that Bender is a recovered alcoholic who sponsors and counsels many others trying to give up drink, and she wishes he were her father. The news of Bender's death in a car accident shortly before the stockholders' meeting hits her hard. Alice has taken Jenna in hand, cut her hair stylishly, supervised her purchase of good-looking clothes that fit her well, and given her confidence in her appearance. After she has dropped Mrs. Gladstone off at the meeting and gone to park the car, she is waylaid by Elden, who takes the car keys, fires her, gives her a one-way ticket to Chicago, and puts her in a cab for the airport. Stunned at first, Jenna soon recovers, tells the cabbie to turn around, and returns to the meeting, which, as the holder of a few shares of stock that Mrs. Gladstone has given her, she has a right to attend. Although Elden's henchmen try to evict her, she gains a supporter in a friend of Bender, and at a crucial point in the proceedings, she struts to the platform and gives a brief speech in favor of attention to high quality and the retention of Mrs. Gladstone. In the end, Mrs. Gladstone's resignation as president is accepted, and the takeover by The Shoe Warehouse is approved, but the founder and president of that company agrees to keep Gladstone Shoes as a separate entity with Mrs. Gladstone as director of quality control. Back in Chicago, Jenna finds courage to arrange a meeting with her father, confronts him for the first time about his drinking, and insists that he either get help to stop or stay out of her life and that of her younger sister. Although the girl-growing-up aspect of the novel is predictable, the passionate interest in shoes, details of selling techniques, and information about the corporate takeover, all told with contagious enthusiasm, make this an unusual and engaging story. ALA; SLJ.

RUNNING OUT OF TIME (Haddix*, Margaret Peterson, Simon & Schuster, 1995), mystery novel of an 1840s town of Clifton, Indiana, which turns out to be actually a tourist site with the residents constantly on display through an elaborate system of mirrors and video cameras. At first it seems benign to the volunteer families but gradually changes into a prison camp, where no one is allowed to speak freely or to leave. The crisis occurs when several children come down with what Jessie Keyser's mother, who was a nurse before coming to Clifton, recognizes as diphtheria. Since the doctor is one of a group now known as "Clifton's men," those who report, beat, and might even kill anyone who questions the system, she knows she can get no effective modern medicine from him. Because she would be missed and also can no longer fit into the clothes that she secretly saved from her past life, she cannot try to escape, but she can conceal the absence of her daughter by saying that the girl is ill. In desperation, she takes Jessie, 13, to the woods at night, whispers to her the true story of the town, which none of the children knows, has her change into blue jeans, a T-shirt, and windbreaker and shows her a manhole hidden by brush that leads to a tunnel into the world of 1996. The most daring of the four Keyser children, Jessie is still terrified of starting out in the unfamiliar clothes into a world more than 150 years in the future. In the tunnel she mingles with a tourist group of schoolkids, and after several narrow escapes she makes her way out to the entrance gate of Clifton Village, a park that is surrounded by a high fence topped with constantly swiveling cameras. After almost giving up, she manages to stow away in a bread truck. Although in her hurried departure her mother told Jessie a bit about the modern world, almost everything is new to her— electric lights, automobiles, flush toilets, radios, refrigeration. She knows that she must find a telephone and call the number of Isaac Neeley, a man who protested the idea of an "authentic" village and who may give her help. Her first efforts at using the phone are frustrating, and she is almost abducted by a couple of young hoodlums, but after walking most of the day, she finally contacts Neeley, and he picks her up. At his second-story apartment he provides a glass of water, but since a man whom she met on the road warned her not to drink from the stream because the water is poison, she pours it out the window. When he looks in on her later, she pretends to be asleep, and then she hears him telling someone on the phone that he has drugged her, but if she knows too much, they will have to kill her. She escapes out the window to a ledge and works her way down the building. After a number of other adventures in the world where everything is strange to her, she finds herself at the state capitol. Her mother told her that Mr. Neeley would probably call the health officials and then a news conference. She tries calling the Department of Health but is rebuffed as a prankster. So she calls all the newspapers and television stations that she can find in the phone book and announces a news conference on the capitol steps about "terrible problems at Clifton Village" and the possibility of a murder. Since rumors that the village might be closed have been circulating, a few newspeople show up. At first they don't believe her, but when she collapses with a high fever that turns out to be diphtheria, they are convinced. Jessie wakes up some days later in a hospital with her little sister, Kate, 6, in the next bed. Soon other Clifton Village children come to her room, and she finds that they are all being kept there while their parents are jailed and questioned. The conspiracy of the village is finally unraveled. Isaac Neeley died a few years previously, but one of the Clifton executives impersonated him and picked Jessie up. The whole enterprise has been an experiment in creating a disease-resistant gene pool, with the tourism as a cover. The diphtheria was deliberately introduced so that the weaker children would die, the adults gradually would be removed, and the remainder would establish a strong gene pool. In the end, Jessie and her family are back in Clifton, temporarily, since her father, Joseph* Keyser, has been appointed caretaker while the legal disposition of the land is decided. The complicated plot with its double betrayal is neatly handled, with all the loose ends tidily tied up, so that it seems possible, if implausible. Interest is maintained by good characterization of Jessie, an intelligent and brave girl persisting despite modernisms that baffle her at every turn and the real danger that she faces. ALA; IRA; Poe Nominee.

RUSS RODGERS (*Rule of the Bone**), marginalized, drugging high school dropout, 16, pal of equally marginalized Chappie, the narrator. When Chappie first walks out on his mother and stepfather, he depends on Russ, but after his experiences in Jamaica, Chappie is able to think matters out for himself and rejects Russ' suggestion that they do Jamaica together. Russ steals with no compunctions from the video store where he works, from his motorcycle friends, and from the owners of the summerhouse where he and Chappie stay for the winter. For a time, feeling that the wayward life is not for him, Russ lives with his aunt, leaving Chappie feeling abandoned and angry. Very late in the story, Chappie finds a phone credit card and calls Russ, who tells Chappie that Chappie's grandmother has died and that his father and mother have left town. He also tells Chappie that he is coming to Jamaica. When he arrives, Chappie spots him but does not go to meet him. Later, Chappie observes Russ with Evening Star, who, Chappie knows, will lead Russ into a dissolute life of sex and drugs.

RYLANT, CYNTHIA (1954–   ), highly acclaimed writer of more than seventy books of short stories, picture books, poetry, and novels mostly for elementary and middle-school children, many in series, like the popular early reading Henry and Mudge and Mr. Putter sets. Among other prestigious awards, she received the Newbery Medal for *Missing May* (Orchard, 1992). She has published the fantasies *The Van Gogh Cafe** (Harcourt, 1995), a short, episodic novel about a magical cafe that brings out the best in whoever enters, an American Library Association choice; and *The Islander* (DK, 1998), about a boy and a mermaid. *The Blue Meadows* (Harcourt, 1997) consists of realistic short stories about family life. She lives in Oregon. For more information about Rylant, titles, and title entries, see *Dictionary, 1985–1989* [*A Blue-Eyed Daisy*; *A Fine White Dust*; *A Kindness*] and *Dictionary, 1990–1994* [*Missing May*].

S

SACHAR, LOUIS (1954–   ), born in East Meadow, New York; attorney and highly popular, critically acclaimed writer of some twenty humorous, inventive novels for middle-grade readers. He received an undergraduate degree in economics from the University of California at Berkeley and a law degree from the University of California in San Francisco, the city in which he now lives. Winner of the Boston Globe-Horn Book, Newbery, and Christopher awards, named to the Fanfare list, cited by the American Library Association and *School Library Journal*, and nominated for the Edgar Allan Poe Award, *Holes** (Farrar, 1998) is an often ironically funny novel of friendship and mystery that stretches the envelope of realism. Boys in a detention camp are forced to dig holes in the desert under the incredibly hot Texas sun and find a surprising prize. Sachar has also written the popular Wayside School titles, the first of which was *Sideways Stories from Wayside School* (Follett, 1978), about happenings in a school built sideways. Other well-liked titles are *There's a Boy in the Girls' Bathroom* (Knopf, 1987), *Dogs Don't Tell Jokes* (Knopf, 1991), and the Marvin Redpost books, including *Marvin Redpost: Super Fast, Out of Control!* (Random, 2000).

SAFE AT SECOND (Johnson*, Scott, Philomel, 1999), sports novel with boy's growing-up aspects set for one school year in Edgeview, a small town north of Albany, New York. Narrator Paulie* Roy Lockwood, 16, describes himself as a scrawny, jittery kid with reddish hair and admits that he is not motivated academically. From childhood, he has enjoyed being in the shadow of his best friend, Todd Bannister, who has always looked after him. Paulie says that Todd, now a six-foot-three, good-looking, laid-back high school senior, is not only the best player for the Panthers but the "best high school pitcher in the universe." He is so good that he is being courted by big-league scouts and college coaches. Although he himself is a poor player, Paulie loves baseball, unlike Todd, who does not really enjoy the game, just being good at it. Paulie studies baseball history and can spout statistics about any player whom one names. Todd revels in the adulation that goes with being a star and tends to be haughty and arrogant. He also at times still looks after Paulie, for example, without Paulie's knowledge persuading the coach to keep Paulie on the team, even though he consistently makes bonehead plays. In the last scrimmage game of fall training, with five scouts watching in the stands, Todd takes a hard line drive smack in the eye. The next weeks are touch-and-go, as the doctors try unsuccessfully to save the eye. In due time, Todd is fitted with a prosthesis. Realizing that his professional career is probably over before it even started, Todd becomes bitter, angry, and discouraged, neglects his classes and friends, and drinks, but he avoids the party scene after excessive alcohol makes him very ill one night. Throughout all this, Paulie tries to bolster his increasingly distant and disconsolate friend, remembering the many times that Todd helped him. Paulie notices warning signs— various memorabilia and awards are missing from Todd's bedroom walls, Todd's reading about a ballplayer who commits suicide on the field, Todd's taking solitary walks—and thinks maybe he should tell either Todd's or his own parents that Todd may be contemplating suicide. When he follows Todd to the park one evening, he finds to his surprise that his friend has rigged up an apparatus by which he can practice pitching. Thereafter, the two work out together, and when spring training begins, Todd is on the team. He no longer has his former excellent control, however, and when he hits a batter, he loses confidence, does poorly, is for the first time in his baseball life taken out of a game, and is seldom used thereafter. Paulie, who has also been practicing with the team, has become a good defensive fielder. In a big game, Paulie is playing second base when the Panther pitcher is thrown out of the game for swearing. The Panther coach calls on Todd to save the game, Todd struggles, then suggests that the coach put him on second and let Paulie throw his crazy "knurve" (combination of curve and knuckleball), for the first time thinking about the team and not just about himself, and the strategy saves the game. Todd looks forward to college in the fall and Paulie to continuing to write for the school paper, a task at which he has found that he excels. This is less a sports story than a study in how two teenagers deal with adversity and decide what to do with their lives. Both boys and Todd's former girlfriend, Melissa Donovan, as well end up with a better values system. Because the story is told by Paulie, it is limited to what he knows and deduces. Thus, facts about why Todd and Melissa have broken up and exactly why Todd decides to emulate a certain 1950s pitcher who lost an eye but made a brief comeback do not appear. Although the conclusion is expected and the main characters are too carefully foiled, excitement rules, and the sports scenes and interactions among players are well done. SLJ.

SALISBURY, GRAHAM (1944–   ), born in Philadelphia, Pennsylvania. He was graduated from California State University and received an M.F.A. from Vermont College. He has held a number of jobs, as the captain of a glass-bottomed boat, deckhand on a deep-sea boat, rock musician, elementary school teacher, and manager of an apartment building in Oregon, where he has made his home. His first book, the episodic novel *Blue Skin of the Sea* (Delacorte, 1992), about a young boy growing up in Hawaii, received several awards, among them the Parents Choice Award and a *School Library Journal* citation. *Under the Blood-Red Sun** (Delacorte, 1994), a dramatic and substantial historical novel about the Japanese attack on Pearl Harbor as experienced by a Japanese-American family and their friends, was chosen by the American Library Association and *School Library Journal*. *Shark Bait* (Delacorte, 1997), *Jungle Dogs* (Delacorte, 1999), and *Lord of the Deep* (Delacorte, 2001) also involve mixed-ethnic American boys in Hawaii. Salisbury is descended from some of the first missionaries to arrive in the Hawaiian Islands and grew up on Oahu and on Hawaii.

SAMMY KEYES AND THE HOTEL THIEF (Van Draanen*, Wendelin, illus. Dan Yaccarino, Knopf, 1998), realistic mystery-detective novel set in an unnamed American city at the time of publication, one in a series about the intrepid girl detective and narrator Samantha Jo Keyes, called Sammy, 12. Abandoned by her mother, feeling cooped up in Gram's tiny apartment in a subsidized senior high-rise in a mixed residential-light business neighborhood, Sammy scans the area with binoculars, observes a bushy, brown-haired, bearded, gloved thief pawing through a purse in a fourth-floor room in the ironically named Heavenly Hotel across the street and, when spotted by the thief, saucily waves at him. The rest of the book involves Sammy's efforts to catch the thief, all the while uneasy in the realization that he probably knows who she is. When she sees police at the hotel, she enters, overhears that $4,000 was stolen from a lady gaudily dressed in silver, Gina, an astrologist who calls herself Madame Nashira, and then boldly tells the officers what she saw. On the first day of seventh grade, when snotty Heather Acosta meanly sticks a pin in her rear, she socks Heather in the nose and is suspended for a day. She spends the day and a few more hunting for the thief and pursuing personal diversions, some of which rouse her suspicions about certain people. She goes to Maynard's Market with her close friend Marissa McKenze, where she overhears T. J., the owner's son, on the phone discussing his need for money to cover losses on the stock market; buys ice cream from Oscar, the blind street vendor, whom she once observes cleaning his glasses; visits her friend Hudson Graham, an older gentleman who informs her there have been six burglaries in the area in the last two weeks, tells her he has a new renter, reclusive Bill Eckert, and cautions her that appearances are not always what they seem; spies on the area from the roof of the mall; and increasingly suspects that the thief is someone whom she knows. Acting on a hunch and her powers of deduction, she borrows $18 in paper money from Marissa, whose parents are well-off enough to be quite generous, and scatters the bigger bills along the path that she knows Oscar will follow. Just as she expected, he stops and picks up the money. Oscar the blind ice cream vendor is a fake. She reports to Sergeant Jacobsen, the policeman whom she privately calls Tall 'n' Skinny, who takes her seriously. It is found that Oscar is really a small-time thief whose real name is Larry Daniels, employs various disguises, and is currently being hunted by his probation officer. The pace is fast, the reader can play detective alongside Sammy, and the cast includes a variety of one-dimensional, but effective-in-context, figures: snoopy neighbor Mrs. Graybill, who confronts Sammy and Gram about Sammy's living with Gram illegally; warm and understanding Gram; Marissa, the little rich girl poor in parental attention, not unlike Sammy, whose mother has dumped her on Gram; crotchety Officer Borsch, who thinks she is a snoopy, lying kid; seemingly introverted Bill Eckert, who turns out to be the popular disk jockey, Rockin' Rick of station KRQK, Hudson's proof that appearances sometimes deceive; thoroughly despicable Heather Acosta, who is suspended from school for three days for having lied about the extent of her nose injury; and eccentric Madame Nashira, among assorted others. Always winning is overdramatic, talkative, impulsive Sammy, enterprising, persistent, alert, and bold, a character worthy of starring in a series of books. She reports in colloquial, conversational style, and the episodes that she describes are sometimes humorous, sometimes scary, sometimes just plain adventurous but always full of action and always in motion. Poe Nominee.

SANDY (*The Music of Dolphins**), research assistant to Dr.* Elizabeth Beck, who is studying Mila, the feral girl found living with dolphins in the Caribbean. From the first, Sandy is more sensitive to Mila's feelings than Dr. Beck is, and, although she doesn't always credit the girl with her real understanding, she shows affection and tries to help her in the difficult transition to human life. Sandy senses, long before Dr. Beck, that Mila needs her freedom, and she stands up to her superior in insisting that Mila be returned to the sea. Mila thinks of her as her friend.

SARAH YORK (*Rats Saw GOD**), younger sister by two years of Steve York. She lives with their divorced and married-again mother in San Diego, while Steve lives with their father, Alan* York, in Houston, Texas. Because their father held Steve back in school so that he might have an advantage athletically, Sarah is only one academic year behind Steve. She is a highly aware young woman experientially, socially, and politically. Well organized and articulate, an outgoing mover and shaker, she is president of the student council her junior year and an active proponent of numerous causes. Sarah advises Steve on such matters as purchasing condoms and taking Dub* Varner to the prom. She enlists Steve's help in persuading their mother to allow her to accompany several friends of both sexes to a Pearl Jam concert and stay overnight in a hotel room together. For Steve's help, she gives him two tickets, and he invites Allison* Kimble to go along, their first real date.

A SCHOOL FOR POMPEY WALKER (Rosen*, Michael J., illus. Aminah Brenda Lynn Robinson, Harcourt, 1995), novelette set in Madisonville, Ohio, in 1923, related by an aged African American concerning his escape from slavery and work in building a school for black children. When an Ohio school is named in his honor, ninety-year-old Pompey Walker addresses the children and their teacher, Mrs. Gilbert, telling them the story of his early life and of how the school came to be. Born a slave on the Georgia plantation of Charles Bibb, Pompey's earliest memories are of crows flying around him, while the mother whom he hardly knows toils picking cotton near by. When he is about seven and big for his age, he becomes a stableboy, caring for Starbright, the beautiful mount that belongs to Bibb's son-in-law, Jeremiah Walker. He also remembers overhearing the lessons that Jeremiah's wife teaches the plantation's white children. After Mrs. Walker dies with the birth of her first child, Pompey is taken to auction, where, now about fourteen years old, he is purchased by Jeremiah, because Jeremiah abhors Bibb's brutal ways and the institution of slavery. Although not a member of the abolitionist movement, Jeremiah is from the North and wishes simply to give Pompey his freedom. Persuaded by Pompey that emancipation is out of the question, since the boy will only be captured and returned as a runaway, Jeremiah gradually travels northward with him, Pompey hidden under the false bottom of their buggy. When their money runs out, they sell Pompey at auction, and then Jeremiah helps him escape from his new masters. In Ohio Jeremiah finds Pompey a black family with whom to live, but the boy wants an education and is disappointed that no school will admit blacks. When he is about sixteen, Pompey persuades Jeremiah to help him create a school for blacks. For years, to raise money, they employ the same deception that they used to pay for the trip north—Jeremiah sells Pompey into slavery at auctions and then helps him escape. They continue doing this for some years throughout the South, employing various ruses and disguises, knowing full well the danger that they run, until they have enough money to build a school in Ohio. At this point, Pompey asks Jeremiah to give him his name, and henceforth Pompey is known as Pompey Walker. Sweet Freedom, their four-room school, stands for sixty years, when it is enlarged and named Pompey Walker Elementary School. Pompey's account, related in modern educated, but not formal, language, is understated in its picture of the brutal, dehumanizing aspects of plantation life, the terrors of the journey, and the repeated forays into slavery. What lifts this book above others of its kind is its emphasis on the importance of education and on the combined efforts of a white man with a conscience and an enterprising black youth. Pompey's experiences were inspired by a brief newspaper story about one Gussie West, who built a school, and were elaborated upon from other ex-slave recollections. Robinson's patterned, deep-palette paintings skillfully picture incidents, extend details of character and setting, and produce a highly attractive book. ALA.

SCHULMAN, AUDREY (1963–), born in Montreal, Canada; writer; computer consultant, designer of software. She attended Sarah Lawrence College from 1981 to 1983 and was graduated from Barnard in 1985 with a degree in psychology. Her first novel, *The Cage** (Algonquin Books, 1994), is a gripping adventure story of a young woman who joins an expedition to film polar bears on the shores of Hudson Bay. It was named to both the American Library Association list of Notable Books and the *School Library Journal* list of Best Books for Children.

SCOOTER (*Crash**), Crash Coogan's maternal grandfather. A colorful figure, Scooter is an ex-navy cook whose visits Crash and his sister, Abby*, thoroughly enjoy. The two children are overjoyed when Scooter moves in because his health has deteriorated and he can no longer live alone. They enjoy his cooking, which is as distinctive as he is, and especially the mildly outrageous stories that he tells when they are huddled up on his bed, alone with him in his room. When Scooter suffers a stroke just before Christmas, Crash worries greatly, and as Christmas draws near, he realizes to his horror that he has no gift for his grandfather. With the irrational fear that if he does not get the old man a gift, Scooter will die, Crash races out and buys the first handy item: a pair of high-heeled, red women's shoes. He later gives Scooter a more appropriate gift but hangs on to the shoes. When Scooter returns from the hospital, he is unable to walk or talk. This understanding of the preciousness of life is probably a factor in influencing Crash to throw the big footrace and allow Penn* Webb to win.

SCUD (*Mr. Was**), Franklin Scudder, boy whom Jack Lund meets the first time he goes through the time-slip door at thirteen, when Scud is perhaps fifteen. Their lives beome entwined through several meetings and their mutual love for Andie* Murphy, who is Jack's age. Scud is a complex character, charismatic with a streak of wildness and viciousness that Jack recognizes even before they are on the transport ship in the South Pacific. As Andie tells Jack, "Scud will take care of himself. It's all he cares about." When Scud reads Jack's journal, full of letters declaring his love for Andie, he becomes murderously jealous and, after beating Jack, abandons him for dead in the jungle cave. Surprisingly, Scud survives, returns to Memory, and marries Andie, who believes that Jack is dead. Because he hated his father, Scud changes his name legally to his mother's maiden name, Skoro. Although he never dares to go through the time-slip door that he learned about from Jack's journal, Scud does have a 1996 newspaper that Jack once brought into the 1940s and so is able to make a lot of money in the 1940s and 1950s by investing in the stocks that would prosper in the 1990s. When they are both old men, he meets Jack Lund and is so shocked to find him alive that he has a heart attack. Then when Jack, as a thirteen-year-old boy, shows up at his bedside, Scud tries to strangle him and dies in the attempt. Andie has long before left him, but their daughter, Betty*, has become Jack's mother, so Scud, besides being his buddy and near-murderer in the 1940s, is his grandfather in the 1990s.

SEBESTYEN, OUIDA (1924–   ), born in Vernon, Texas, author of historical and contemporary novels for young people. Her *Words by Heart** (Atlantic/

Little, Brown, 1979) was chosen an honor book for The Children's Literature Association Phoenix Award, which goes to books published twenty years earlier that have stood the test of time. For earlier biographical information and title entries, see *Dictionary, 1960–1984* [*Words by Heart*] and *Dictionary, 1990–1994* [*Out of Nowhere*].

SECRETS AT HIDDEN VALLEY (Roberts*, Willo Davis, Atheneum, 1997), mystery novel set at a third-rate Michigan trailer park in which a girl learns about the causes of a longtime rift between her recently deceased father, a stuntman in movies, and her grandfather and at the same time discovers secrets that keep several park residents wary of being found by police. Because her aspiring actress-mother has second lead in a B-western and must go on location, Steffi Thomas, 11, has been sent by bus from Southern California to Hidden Valley Trailer Park owned by her paternal grandfather, Victor Thomaschek, whom she has never seen and who, it soon becomes apparent, has not even known of her existence. The irascible old man does not welcome her, but since she has nowhere else to go, and he doesn't send her away, she settles in, cooking meals that he eats without comment and helping out when she can, getting comfort from his friendly black Labrador, Buddy. She soon makes friends with Casey Chapman, a boy just a little older than she is, and other park residents: Casey's affable father, Bo, who brings their groceries from the store where he works in a nearby town; Helen Riska, a woman in her nineties who always hides from newcomers, and her dog, Barkley; Oliver Mandell and Elwood Grisham, both elderly bachelors who fish together; the cheerful Montoni family; and others. Less friendly are Burt Taylor, 16, who works at a local gas station, and his father, Chester, a brutal man with an ostensibly injured back, although he has been seen lifting heavy objects with ease, both of whom are inclined to steal from the small park store if not carefully watched. When a new tenant, Kurt Vail, starts asking questions about the others, Steffi notices that not only Helen and the Taylors are nervous but also Casey and his father. Casey, who works as handyman to pay their site rent, joins Steffi in a project of cleaning out and refilling the long unused swimming pool and also helps her clear out a back bedroom long used for storage. Steffi comes upon a box of family pictures, the first that she has seen of her grandmother or her father as a child, and later a family Bible, which shows that she has cousins near her age. After a fall from a ladder disables Vic, Steffi takes over as much of the work as possible, renting out sites, cleaning the office and rest room, and waiting on her bedridden grandfather, though she resents his surly attitude and the way that he calls her "girl," refusing to use her name. He tells her that he quarreled with his son over the boy's desire for an acting career, an occupation he thinks useless. The various other mysteries culminate when Mr. Vail drops his identification that shows he is an FBI (Federal Bureau of Investigation) agent. Casey admits to her that he has run away from his mother, who has legal custody of him, because of her drinking and men friends, and he and his father have been hiding ever since. Helen faints when Mr. Vail tells her that he has gone into her trailer, not waiting to hear that something was burning on her stove. When she comes to, they discover that she has been using an assumed name and hiding from her daughter, who wants to put her in a nursing home. The only ones who have real reason to worry about a federal agent are the Taylors, who, it turns out, have robbed a bank and plan, when enough time has passed, to take the money to Canada. When Chester tries to escape, using Steffi as a shield, Vic hobbles into the office and clobbers him with the heavy end of his crutch, even though, or perhaps because, a few minutes before, fed up with the overwork and his demands, Steffi has told him what a disagreeable, thankless old man he is. That evening he refers to her, for the first time, as his granddaughter and even thanks her and, when she asks about cousins, says that they are living in Cadillac and Petoskey. While solutions are suggested for the Chapmans' problem and for Steffi's future, it is not clear what will happen to any of them. The strongest element in the novel is the picture of life in the run-down campground, the hard work, the frustrations, and the camaraderie among the long-term residents. Steffi is an independent youngster, a survivor. Poe Nominee.

SEEDFOLKS (Fleischman*, Paul, ill. Judy Pedersen, HarperCollins, 1997), novel in thirteen brief, first-person chapters, each narrated by a different person whose life had been affected by the development of the Gibbs Street garden in a formerly trash-filled vacant lot in Cleveland, Ohio. This unlikely neighborhood project is started by Kim, 9, a Vietnamese girl who wants to plant something that the spirit of her father, who died before her birth, might recognize from his own life as a farmer and understand that she is his daughter. She clears a small spot in the junk-filled lot and plants six lima beans, vowing to take care of them and make them thrive. Her action is watched from a window by Ana, an older woman who has lived there since 1919 and seen the neighborhood change as her own Romanian people moved out to be supplanted in turn by Slovaks, Italians, Negroes, Mexicans, Cambodians, and others. Suspecting that the child is burying a gun or drugs, she takes her cane and hobbles down three flights to the jungle of junk, where she digs up three of the beans, then, ashamed of her suspicions, replants them carefully. She alerts Wendell, a school janitor, the only other white person in her building, who examines the wilting plants, tells her that it is too early to plant beans but that the heat reflected by an old refrigerator has warmed up the soil. He waters the beans and decides to clear a little plot to plant something himself. A boy from Guatemala, who is assigned to baby-sit his great uncle, Tio Juan, hunts frantically when the old man has wandered off and finds him in the garden trying to communicate with Wendell. Since Tio Juan speaks no English or Spanish but only an Indian language that the boy does not know, young Gonzalo cannot interpret. His mother, the next day, buys a trowel and some seeds and has Gonzalo take Tio Juan back to the garden to help him plant them. An African-American woman, thinking of planting a little goldenrod to make the tea that her mother considered a cure-all, surveys the lot and, since she is wise in the ways of city activists, takes a bag of the foul-smelling trash from the lot to the Public Health Department and demands a cleanup. Another sort of social activist, Sam, a retired Jewish man, starts a contest for children with a prize for the best idea for getting water to the gardens, won by a little black girl who suggests putting garbage cans under the drainage spouts on the sides of the surrounding buildings. Sae Young, a timid Korean woman, traumatized by an assault in the dry cleaning shop where she used to work, comes out of her self-imposed shell to buy funnels to aid in dipping the water into containers. Virgil, a boy from Haiti, works reluctantly to plant a large plot of lettuce, which his taxi-driving father plans to sell to restaurants. Curtis, a bodybuilding African American, plants tomatoes to persuade his girlfriend, Lateesha, that he has interests beyond muscles and fights. When some are stolen, he hires Royce, a homeless teenager, to sleep by his plot and guard it at night. Soon Royce, who is lonely since his father threw him out, is helping other people in the garden. Nora, a British nurse, wheels her patient, a stroke victim named Mr. Myles, past the garden and sees his interest. She buys a plastic trash barrel, cuts holes in the bottom, fills it with dirt to a level that he can reach from his chair, and offers him a choice of vegetable and flower seeds. He plants hollyhocks, poppies, and snapdragons. Maricela, a pregnant Mexican sixteen-year-old, is forced by her teacher to start a garden, and her resentment gradually subsides when Leona gives her some goldenrod and talks to her in a humane way. Amir, from India, plants eggplants, and soon people are talking to him, asking about the strangely colored vegetables. When a woman is attacked down the street, he runs with Royce and two other men to her rescue and realizes that it is the first time that he has joined in any community effort. Even Florence, a black woman from Colorado so afflicted with arthritis that she can't garden, watches the others and is pleased, the next spring, to see a little Vietnamese girl again planting beans. The novel is simple and unpretentious, making no claims for larger, permanent improvements in the city caused by the garden. Each person has a distinctive voice, and, though their diversity may seem overstudied, each has an interesting story suggested succinctly. SLJ.

SEES BEHIND TREES (Dorris*, Michael, Hyperion, 1996), personal-problem novel set among an unspecified group of woodlands Native-American Indians in the sixteenth century and combining realism and mysticism. Although his mother works diligently with him, partially sighted Walnut, about twelve years old, is unable to hit a moving target with his bow and arrow. He knows, however, that he will not receive his man's name and take his place among the male members of the group unless he does. Accepting his limitations, his mother blindfolds him and urges him to learn to "see" with his ears those things that she and most others cannot. At the coming-of-age shooting contest, Otter, the weroance, or ruling female elder, says that the group has need for someone "to see what can't be seen." When, blindfolded, Walnut quickly identifies Gray Fire, the limping old man who was once the fastest runner in the group and is now their respected artist, Otter rewards the boy with an adult name, "Sees Behind

Trees." Although now highly regarded, Sees Behind Trees feels both grown up and at the same time a child. He struggles inside himself: What does being grown up mean? One day at Gray Fire's place, the artist tells him how once, while in the countryside with his twin, Otter, he discovered a "land of water" within a remote gorge, a place so beautiful that he did not want to leave it and where he lost two toes that became caught between stones and acquired his limp. Sees Behind Trees agrees to help Gray Fire try to find that extraordinary place. They travel for two days, during which they have discussions about the relationship between instinct and logic. Gray Fire informs the boy that the body itself can retain information. They encounter strangers, Karna and Pitew, a husband and wife who have a baby called Checha. As they draw nearer the gorge, Gray Fire walks more easily, and when they arrive, to his amazement Sees Behind Trees can see. The place is a deep gorge with a white-water river and a whirlpool. Gray Fire sinks in the pool, merging with the land of water for which he had longed. Lost without Gray Fire, who is either drowned or reunited with that part of himself that had never really left the place, telling himself that he is now a man, the boy climbs out of the gorge. His vision blurry again, he makes his way back to the strangers' camp, where he finds their shelter burned and their possessions scattered and ruined. His keen hearing locates the baby, and, the child in his arms, he follows the path home, finding his way by touching the moss on rocks and trees and following other signs that Gray Fire identified. Once home, he encounters Otter, who confesses her part in Gray Fire's laming. Jealous of her twin's ability as a runner, she took him to the land of water that she had stumbled upon while hunting and prepared the trap in which he lost the toes. Realizing that she has now lost her brother forever because of her selfishness, she weeps uncontrollably, and Sees Behind Trees understands that, when he "received . . . [his] new name, . . . [he] had no idea how many trees there were, and how much there was to see behind each of them." Questioned by friends and family about what happened on the trip, the boy realizes that he cannot explain what he himself does not understand, and so he simply says that Gray Fire was not strong enough to return. Checha is adopted by Sees Behind Trees' family, and Sees Behind Trees hopes that some day he and his new brother will be able to find the baby's lost parents and "make the circle whole" once again. Sees Behind Trees tells of his coming-of-age in keenly sensory language. Although his first-person narrative conveys little evidence of the culture, and the pieces of the plot do not mesh well, the two elders are well, if minimally, drawn, and the boy is a credible figure. SLJ.

SEE YOU AROUND, SAM (Lowry*, Lois, illus. Diane de Groat, Houghton, 1996), humorous novel of contemporary family life in the popular Anastasia Krupnik series. This book stars Anastasia's little brother, Sam, 4, who asserts his independence by running away but learns that home is the best place, after all. At nursery school, Sam promises a friend his Etch-a-Sketch in exchange for vampire fangs that, he is sure, make him as scary as Dracula. His mother, however, is not pleased. She has, she tells him, fangphobia, and forbids him to wear them in the house. Sam decides to run away from his home in a Massachusetts neighborhood to Alaska, where there are walruses among whom, he is sure, fangs will be acceptable. He collects his treasures—his fireman's badge, his stuffed bear, mittens (in case it should get cold), some Band-Aids—in his father's Harvard University gym bag and starts off. First, he decides, he will need provisions, so he detours to the home of his elderly neighbor, Gertrude Stein, who always has cookies on hand. There he samples a few cookies and discusses his journey with the African-American postman, Lowell Watson, who tells him the zip code for Sleetmute, Alaska, a destination that Sam adopts. As he starts off again, he needs a drink of water and stops at the home of Mrs. Sheehan, where he plays for a while with her baby, Kelly. Mrs. Sheehan suggests that he might want to call his sister, who has just come home from school, to say good-bye before he leaves for Alaska. Anastasia, now fourteen, is quite matter-of-fact about his plans but does drop over to the Sheehans to tell him about how she almost ran away when she was his age. She goes with him to say good-bye to Mr. Fosburgh, who drives a motorized wheelchair and often lets Sam sit in his lap and steer it. And so it goes. At each place he learns that his mother is inviting the neighbors for a dinner of lasagna and banana cream pie, and each one gives him some indispensable item for his journey, until he can hardly drag the heavy bag after him. Anastasia points out that it is getting dark and remarks that it is a very grown-up thing to change one's mind. Sam announces that he has changed his mind, and they get home in time for a neighborhood party for which his father has brought joke favors for all of them, plastic lips for the ladies, mustaches or fake glasses for the men, and a new set of fangs for Sam. His mother says that she has changed her mind, and he can have them. Sam, who has found the fangs uncomfortable, says that he has changed his mind, too, and trades them for a fake nose. The slight story is warm and amusing, with all the family and neighbors obviously fond of Sam and going out of their way to help him maintain his self-respect at the same time that they are keeping close track of him and reporting his moves to his mother by phone. The relationship between Sam and Anastasia is especially attractive. While a reader can see the whole picture, the narration sticks carefully to Sam's point of view. He was also the protagonist in earlier books, including *All About Sam* (*Dictionary, 1985–1989*). SLJ.

SEIDLER, TOR (1952–   ), born in Littleton, New Hampshire; writer of text material for children and of novels for children and young adults. His gentle fantasy *Mean Margaret** (HarperCollins, 1997) features two woodchucks and various other small animals of woods and fields and one small, disagreeable human. For earlier biographical information and a title entry, see *Dictionary, 1990–1994* [*The Wainscott Weasel*].

SEVEN SPIDERS SPINNING (Maguire*, Gregory, illus. Dirk Zimmer, Clarion, 1994), amusing fantasy and school novel set in recent years from early September through late October mostly in the small Vermont town of Hamlet. Seven poisonous, prehistoric Siberian Snow spiders, frozen in a block of ice thousands of years ago, are discovered in an ice floe in the Atlantic, taken to Canada, and then shipped by refrigerated truck to Harvard University. On the way, their crate splits open, and the spiders thaw. One enters the truck cab and frightens the driver into a heart attack. Released in the ensuing accident, the spiders make their way to Hamlet, where they overhear seven schoolgirls, classmates in Miss Earth's room and members of the club called the Tattletales, discuss plans for defeating their archrival classmates, the Copycats, in the annual Josiah Fawcett Elementary School Halloween Pageant of Horrors. The spiders bond with the girls, each with a different girl. Pearl Hotchkiss happens onto the spiders and takes one for show-and-tell. Each of the other spiders subsequently makes its way to the school and meets a violent end while attempting to connect with its girl. One spider is impaled on the tip of a pencil, thrown out a schoolroom window, and run over by a school bus. The next gets caught in an egg sandwich and is tossed by the school janitor into his portable trash masher. The third gets squashed when the Halloween pumpkin in which it is hiding is smashed, another is crushed when the school door closes on it, another clings to an apple floating in a tub and is thrown to smithereens against a wall, and the sixth is mashed when a forty-pound sandbag falls on it during the pageant but not before it has bitten Miss Earth. Prior to the pageant, most of the scenes occur in the classroom, where the youngsters engage in such activities as spider-centered spelling bees. Subplots focus on Meg Snoople, a pushy television investigative reporter, intent on ferreting out why the seven spiders did not arrive at Harvard, and the romance between Pierre Montrose, the stricken truck driver, and his hopital nurse, Prudence Lark. Nurse Lark falls in love with Pierre, who is in a coma, and brings him back to consciousness by reading him torrid romance novels. Her efforts are strongly opposed by Head Nurse Crisp until Pierre proposes marriage to Prudence, which appeals to Nurse Crisp's sense of romance. When Pierre hears that Meg is centering her investigations on Hamlet, he and Prudence go there, accompanied by Head Nurse Crisp, who delivers a lecture at the school on what to do in case of spider bite. The pageant provides the grand climax, uniting the different story strands. Time constraints force the rival clubs to combine their skits, and thus the rift between them is healed as Miss Earth wished. Meg Snoople helicopters to Harvard the spider remains that Pierre scoops up. Spider expert Professor Williams suggests that they consult the ancient "The Epic Verses of Hubba the Magnificent." The old tale provides a clue for an antidote for Miss Earth's spider bite, which they concoct from Halloween trick-or-treat sweets. Miss Earth recovers, the sweethearts marry, Nurse Crisp resigns her hospital position to become the school nurse, and Pearl Hotchkiss' spider, the only one left alive, is donated to Harvard for research. The children are an ethnic mix, Meg Snoople affords opportunities for jabs at the media, the romance will appeal to some segments of the intended middle grade audience, and the children's repartee and sexist putdowns will catch the interest of others. Most middle graders will find the characters' names happily silly and the abundant squishing and squashing of spiders satisfyingly gross. The theme of cooperation cannot be missed, and the contemporary turns of phrase and wisecracks will garner attention but soon date the book. The children's liking for school and deep affection for the motorcycling, doughnut-munching Miss Earth are pleasant features in this lightweight, consistently amusing, fast-moving story, one of a series set in Hamlet. ALA; SLJ.

SHADOW (Sweeney*, Joyce, Delacorte, 1994), fantasy novel of family conflict set in contemporary Coral Springs, near Fort Lauderdale, Florida, in which disaster is averted by a girl's extrasensory perception (ESP) and the spirit of her dead cat. The only one in the family of Sarah Shaheen, 13, who has much sympathy for her grief over the death of her cat, Shadow, is her brother Patrick, 17, and even he fails to understand why she feels that the cat is somehow still present months later. Her friend Julian Lopez, 14, has a scientific mind and tries to explain away her intuitions. The newly hired young housekeeper, Cissy Champion, who cheerfully volunteers that she is psychic, recognizes Sarah as someone with special powers, but Sarah's mother, a journalist, has no patience with such nonsense, and her father, a doctor, thinks only of the impending return of his older son, Brian, from his first university year at Gainesville. Brian's return triggers an explosion of resentments and problems. Dr. Shaheen, who counts on Brian's following him in a medical career, dotes on the big, good-looking boy, blind to the way that he bullies Patrick and mistreats his girlfriend, Karen. Sarah, who realizes that Brian is flunking out of college and drinking too much, is apprehensive when Karen starts flirting with Patrick and going out with him to make Brian jealous. Their rivalry erupts one night when both parents are out, and Patrick brings Karen into the shawdowy living room to make love. Sarah, who has been sitting in the dark and has slipped behind the sofa to avoid being seen, is too embarrassed to emerge until Brian charges in, obviously drunk, and starts to beat up Patrick. Half naked, Karen flees, and the fight grows vicious, as Brian starts to strangle his brother. Suddenly, in answer to Sarah's mental summons, a shadow cat flies into his face, momentarily blinding him and scratching his cheek, and lands on Patrick's chest, where it also leaves scratches but enables him to get away and lock himself into his bedroom. The fight brings long-festering problems into the open. Brian has harbored a pathological jealousy of Patrick, who is much smarter and more sensitive, and he has taunted the younger boy as gay, a wimp. Patrick admits that he has been using Karen to get back at Brian and prove him wrong. Dr. Shaheen realizes that his hopes for Brian have blinded him to reality and made him discount Patrick's abilities. Sarah knows that Shadow's spirit has accomplished what it was lingering for and has now departed. With help from Cissy, whom her mother has fired, she begins to come to terms with her gift. Julian, who loves Sarah, is willing to keep an open mind about her ESP. Although the cat-as-savior is a bizarre plot element, the highly charged emotions of the dysfunctional family have credibility, and Sarah's earnest worry about her brothers gives the novel some weight. Throughout, the tone of impending doom is well sustained. Sarah's low-key romance with Julian seems likely to proceed happily, but her doubts about whether Brian can carry out the reforms that he has vowed and her suspicion that her father is having an affair with his patient, a young single mother to whom he takes her to choose a replacement kitten for Shadow, presage more family problems. ALA; SLJ.

SHADOWMAKER (Nixon*, Joan Lowery, Delacorte, 1994), mystery novel set in recent years in the small town of Kluney in eastern Texas. Pretty, red-haired, blue-eyed Katie (Katherine) Gillian, the fifteen-year-old narrator, and her widowed mother, Eve, move from their apartment in Houston to a small beach house left to Eve by her Uncle Jim so that Eve can complete a novel. A syndicated reporter of considerable renown, Eve has recently been investigating why babies in Brownsville are being born with serious birth defects. Shortly after they arrive in Kluney, they are awakened one night by the sound of barking neighborhood dogs and then spot shadowy intruders on the beach house grounds. Big, easygoing, literature-quoting Sheriff Granger assures them that only petty crimes are the norm in Kluney but warns Eve that local residents, aware of who she is, oppose her pursuing investigations of any sort in Kluney. Katie, who already misses her ballet classes very much, wants her mother to complete the novel as soon as possible so that they can return to Houston. At school, the students are also less than welcoming, but Mrs. Walgren, her English teacher, likes her journal entries and pairs her with Lana Jean Willis, who can benefit from her coaching. A friendship of sorts blossoms between Katie and Lana Jean, a skinny girl with bad skin, dirty blond hair, and untidy clothes. Lana Jean has a crush on classmate Travis Wyman, a local stud, and has been spying on him, hoping to attract his attention. She says that she has overheard that he is part of a group of male students called the Blitz. Eve is visited by a local woman, Anita Boggs, who says that she has just lost her unborn baby and that her five-year-old son is sickly. She thinks that her house may be located on a toxic-waste dump and hopes that Eve will investigate. She urges Eve not to let anyone know that she has contacted Eve since her husband works for a large local employer, a toxic-waste disposal business run by the Hawkins brothers. Two plots take center stage, one revolving around Eve's investigations of the Hawkinses' business and the other involving Lana Jean's crush on Travis, whom she continues to follow around. Disturbing events occur. A traveling carnival worker is found shot dead, and then Lana Jean's body is found strangled in a clearing in the woods at the edge of Kluney. Eve's investigations eventually reveal that the Hawkins brothers have been disposing of wastes illegally and that the land on which Anita's house stands is seeping poisons. Travis romances Katie, who enjoys his company and kisses but is wary, since he shows an unusual interest in Lana Jean's journal, some pages of which are in Katie's possession. It comes out that B. J., a relatively new boy in town, had formed the Blitz group, which demanded of its several members ever more dangerous and illegal acts for membership. The group has been perpetrating petty thefts, the spoils of which they have stored in the beach house. B. J. killed the carnival worker in a robbery that went awry and then strangled Lana Jean because she had learned more about the group than B. J. considered desirable. Characters are familiar types, and the conclusion is rushed and demands rereading for clarity. Red herrings and gothic thrills abound, and the pace is fast and relentless. The book offers splendid escapist entertainment and a schoolgirl heroine of intelligence, common sense, and considerable courage. Poe Nominee.

SHADOW SPINNER (Fletcher*, Susan, Atheneum, 1998), realistic novel, with fantasy aspects, of political intrigue and the power of story set in an ancient, fictitious, Persia-like kingdom, a clever improvisation upon the tale of Scheherazade. The narrator, Marjan*, 13, has been living with foster parents, a once-prosperous merchant family. Since Marjan is crippled in one foot, Auntie Chava despairs for her future in this culture where physical deformities make a girl an outcast. Marjan's life changes abruptly, however, when she accompanies Auntie Chava to the Sultan's palace to sell jewels and fine cloth to the ladies of the harem. There, to pass the time and draw attention away from her disability and drab, cheap garments, Marjan tells stories, doing what Auntie Chava calls "spinning shadows," for the children. She is observed by Dunyazad*, about fifteen, younger sister of Shahrazad*, the Sultan's current consort, and taken to Shahrazad. Marjan learns that Shahrazad has been telling stories each night for the Sultan to keep from being killed and also to keep the Sultan from killing other girls, as he had done before he encountered her. After 989 nights, however, Shahrazad is running out of stories. A tale Marjan shares with her about a mermaid pleases the Sultan, and Marjan is summoned to live in the palace. The book's main complication ensues when the Sultan demands that Shahrazad tell him the rest of the mermaid story. Since Marjan knows only the part of the story she has already told, they must find the old, blind, marketplace storyteller from whom Marjan heard the tale originally to tell them the rest. The storyteller proves elusive, however, and another problem involves evading the clutches of the Khatun*, the Sultan's powerful, imperious mother, who wishes to replace Shahrazad with her tool, beautiful, copperhaired Soraya. The pot of intrigue thickens, involving also a strange old woman named Zaynab, who keeps the Sultan's messenger birds and who rescues Marjan on occasion, and several mysterious deaths. Eventually it is learned that the storyteller was the Sultan's father's vizier, Abu Mulem, a sort of Robin Hood who has been smuggling girls and women out of the country for their safety and hence is considered the Sultan's enemy. Marjan asks to be taken to the Sultan, to whom she tells the entire story (as though it were just a tale) and persuades him that Shahrazad loves him dearly. The marriage of the Sultan and Shahrazad is celebrated with much rejoicing; Dunyazad and the Sultan's brother are wed; and Marjan, the storyteller-vizier, and their friends depart for the foreign country of Samarkand, where they will live happily ever after in peace and splendor. Marjan tells the story with vigor and insight into the power of story to affect lives. Characters and situations are largely cliche but skillfully combined to keep the reader enthralled. An additional mystery involves how Marjan's foot became crippled— her own mother maimed her to keep her from being summoned to the palace for the Sultan's harem. Shahrazad and Dunyazad have the most dimension, and the Sultan is presented as a proud, self-centered man who ironically is tormented by the thought of how much blood he has shed. Best are the descriptions of the bustling marketplace and city streets; the complex palace, a warren of passages, squares with fountains, flowers, and shadowy areas, plenty of places for spies to hide and schemes to be hatched; harem life—pulling and hauling for favor and bickering and backbiting; tiny value placed upon human life; vanity and conspicuous consumption; class distinctions; and velvet-footed eunuchs slipping about, serving interests both good and evil, interests known only to themselves and those who instruct them. An author's note about the Scheherazade tales concludes the book. ALA; SLJ.

SHAHRAZAD (*Shadow Spinner**), for two and one-half years the beautiful young consort of the Sultan of an ancient, Persia-like kingdom. To remain alive and to save the lives of other girls, every night Shahrazad has told stories to the Sultan, the agreement being that as long as the Sultan feels entertained, he will allow her to live. Because one of his previous wives had taken a lover, he killed her and every one of his wives before Shahrazad. When the novel begins, Shahrazad, about twenty, has borne him three sons and has held his interest for 989 nights. The problem that she faces, however, is tremendous and frightening—she is running out of stories. The novel's narrator, Marjan*, is brought to the palace to replenish Shahrazad's supply of tales. At the end, Marjan, by telling the story of events that have been happening at the palace, persuades the Sultan that Shahrazad has always been true to him, loves him, and would never harm him. Shahrazad is presented as a brave and intelligent young woman. Marjan admires her spunk and perseverance.

THE SHAKESPEARE STEALER (Blackwood*, Gary, Dutton, 1998), picaresque historical novel set in Yorkshire and London, England, in 1601. Orphaned Widge, 14, the narrator, tells how in 1594 at the age of seven he was taken from the orphanage in which he grew up and apprenticed to Dr. Bright in the hamlet of Berwick, Yorkshire. Dr. Bright teaches him to read and write and also a kind of shorthand, which Dr. Bright developed and calls "charactery." When Widge is fourteen, a tall, black-bearded, scarred, hooded, menacing stranger called Falconer buys his apprenticeship for ten pounds and takes him to his new master, Simon Bass, in Leicester. Bass orders him to accompany Falconer to London, where Widge is to copy in charactery and later transcribe into English William Shakespeare's new play, *The Tragedy of Hamlet, Prince of Denmark*, currently being performed by the Chamberlain's Men at the Globe. Knowing that Falconer will deal harshly with him if he does not succeed, Widge makes his way into the theater, where he surreptitiously begins his work, only to find that he gets so caught up in the play that he forgets to copy it. On the way out, he and Falconer encounter cast members who seem to recognize Falconer. After other unsuccessful attempts, he meets one of the players, Mr. Thomas Pope, and says he is there because he wants to become a player. He is taken at his word and introduced to other boys who are being trained for the stage, among them Sander, with whom he soon becomes fast friends. He gets on well with a boy named Julian*, who plays Ophelia, but not with Nick, a surly sort who frequents alehouses and is often late. He makes friends also with such historical figures as players Mr. Heminges, Mr. Phillips, and Mr. Shakespeare, who acts the part of the ghost. As he becomes more familiar with the ways of the stage and the players and other boys, he grows more fearful about Falconer, who threatens him, and also guilty about not being honest with his new friends, especially when Sander asks him why he seems so nervous. He tries unsuccessfully to steal the playbook after he fills in for Sander at prompting, gets a small part, and learns that Simon Bass was once part of this company but left in disgrace. When the company plays for Queen* Elizabeth, he acts Ophelia so well that she compliments him. Seeing Nick with Falconer one day, Widge is sure that they are conspiring, confesses to Sander, spots Nick in the property room, where the playbook is kept, and reports what he has seen. The chase is up—Falconer and Nick are pursued, Falconer is killed in a swordfight and unmasked as Simon Bass, and Widge recovers the playbook from Falconer's bags. Widge's part in the company is ensured, and he feels good at finally having a home and friends. Except for Widge, characterization is subordinated to plot and life in the theater. Descriptions of the lives of apprentices, stage practices, and preparation for playing; numerous forays about London, which give a good sense of the congestion and danger of that overcrowded city; cliff-hanger chapter endings; just enough information about publishing practices of the day and political events, like the beheading of the Earl of Essex; selectively used country dialect; a few glimpses of real historical figures—these combine with the little mystery about Falconer's identity and a plucky, intelligent protagonist who pops in and out of scrapes and tight spots to produce a first-rate adventure story built around the historical practice of pirating plays. ALA; SLJ.

SHAZAM (*Bat 6**), psychologically scarred girl who plays centerfield for the Barlow Road sixth-grade girls' softball team and who deliberately injures the Japanese-American, Bear Creek Ridge first-base player in the big Bat 6 game. Shazam has frequent flashbacks to the Japanese raid on Pearl Harbor, during which her sailor-father was killed. Her "fire dreams" and "stomach squeezes" are particularly sharp when she is around a Japanese person. Her antipathy toward Japanese people is detected occasionally by the girls and even on occasion by an adult, but no one speaks about it. After the accident, they all wish that they had shared their observations. Shazam needs a great deal of help in handling her feelings about Japanese people and also with community sentiment about her illegitimacy.

SHE ELEPHANT (*The Ear, the Eye, and the Arm**), huge, crude woman who controls the abandoned toxic-waste dump called Dead Man's Vlei in the middle of the city and manages the shadowlike Vlei people who work as virtual slaves, mining the ancient trash for anything valuable or usable from earlier times. Although she has the children abducted with the intention of selling them to the terrible Mask gang, she does have her good points: she feeds her people and the children well, and she is kind to Trashman*. She makes, sells, and drinks *kashasu*, a potent illegal liquor, and only because she is drunk and asleep can the Matsikas escape her the first time. After she recaptures them and sells them to the Masks, she is so infuriated at the gang's mockery and refusal to pay her that she wrecks their powerful fetish and helps bring about their destruction. In the end, after she serves two years in prison, she returns to Dead Man's Vlei and starts her slave empire again.

SHELBY COLES (*The Wedding**), younger daughter whose wedding on Martha's Vineyard promises to be the big event of the season for the elite African-American community of the Oval. Blond and fair-skinned, Shelby has never dated dark men and is still a virgin on the night before her marriage. Three people have aroused her doubts about her choice of Meade, a white jazz musician. One is her sister Liz*, who married a dark man, has a nut-brown baby, and tells Shelby that she might do well to experiment with sexy Lute* McNeil, who has been pursuing her all summer, before she commits forever to Meade. Another is her father, who fears that the family snobbery about skin color and his own poor example as a father may have prejudiced her against black men. The third is Lute himself, who uses all his vast experience in seduction to shake her faith in her choice and turn her attention to him. Shelby's ambivalence about her race goes back to her early childhood when she was lost on the island and wandered all day, seen by many people but not recognized as the "colored girl" for whom they know a search is out, because she has yellow hair and a fair skin. It is not until she comes upon Lute and his white wife, Della, after he has accidentally run down and killed his six-year-old Tina, that she realizes that love, not race or color, matters in marriage. Just why the scene leads her to that particular conclusion is not entirely clear.

SHELDON MORSE (*Jip His Story**), called the idgit, a young man with a strong back and a weak mind, the only able-bodied worker besides Jip at the poor farm. Always obliging, Sheldon is devoted to Jip and looks to the boy for direction and approval in everything. When Mr. Lyman, the farm manager, decides to rent Sheldon out to the quarry, Jip has grave misgivings, knowing that Sheldon needs constant supervision. Sheldon, however, is proud to be doing man's work and carrying a lunch pail, the only poor-farm resident earning cash money. When he is killed, Jip is heartbroken and later blames himself for treating Sheldon like a child when what he wanted most was to be a man.

SHELLY (*Ironman**), only girl in Mr.* Nakatani's Anger Management Class at Clark Fork High School and sweetheart of Bo Brewster. Shelly is big, strong, tough, and a fine athlete, excelling at basketball. Her ambition is to become a woman warrior on the *American Gladiator* television show. Adopted in very early childhood, she was never really accepted by her new parents. Her mother repeatedly told her that she was no good because her birth mother was a prostitute and drug addict. When Shelly traced her birth mother, she discovered that her adoptive mother had lied and that her real mother was a college student who gave Shelly up because she could not care for her. Angry and hurt about her adoptive mother's lie, Shelly went berserk and trashed the house. Regarded as incorrigible, she was placed in a succession of institutions and foster homes. Attitude improved, she went out for basketball at Clark Fork but was dropped from the team by Mr. Redmond, who seems to be "down" on her just as he dislikes Bo Brewster.

SHERIFF TOM (*Billy**), Thomas Jonathan Liebenguth, Caucasian, chief law officer of Banes County, Mississippi, a post that he has held for twenty-eight years. He occupies the office in 1937–1938, when African-American Billy Turner, 10, is executed for killing a white girl. A strong, thick-necked man, intensely realistic and pragmatic, the sheriff is aware that he is sworn to uphold the law for everyone, but he also knows that under the circumstances it is the white community to which he will be most answerable because they hold the balance of power. He shows personal compassion for Billy, however, and even remarks to the local examiner/coroner that Billy is just a boy and was sorely provoked. He is ruthless in attacking Cinder, Billy's mother, brutally knocking her around in his quest for information about where Billy is hiding. He is a well-drawn, if generally unlikable, figure.

SHE WALKS THESE HILLS (McCrumb*, Sharyn, Scribner's, 1994), suspense mystery set in Mitchell County, Tennessee, near the North Carolina border. In the Appalachian community of Hamelin and the surrounding Smoky Mountains, rural citizens and local law enforcement officials are alerted by the escape of Harm* (Hiram) Sorley, 63, from the prison at Mountain City, where he has served thirty years for murder. The novel shifts point of view from one character to another. Harm, who has lost most of his near-term memory through an alcohol-related syndrome, is making his way back to his trailer on Ashe Mountain, where he expects to find his wife, Rita, and his toddler, Charlarty (Charlotte), whom he thinks he left a few weeks earlier to go logging, though he cannot remember for sure. Martha Ayers, probationary deputy under Sheriff

Spencer Arrowood, sees the apprehension of Harm as a way of proving herself, since she is determined to succeed, despite Spencer's doubts and the active resentment of her lover, Deputy Joe LeDonne. Henry Kretzer, disc jockey and host to a call-in radio program where he is known as Hank* the Yank, starts by treating the elderly escapee as a geriatric joke but becomes fascinated by the story when a number of his callers say that in his ax murder of the local wheeler-dealer, Claib Maggard, Harm did the county a welcome service. Peripherally drawn into the hunt for Harm are Sabrina, teenage wife of Tracy Harkryder, one of a violent, isolated hillbilly clan, and mother of an infant whom she threatens to murder to get even with her gallivanting husband, and Jeremy* Cobb, a young lecturer at Virginia Tech, a graduate student from Long Island. He romantically starts on a hiking trip to retrace the path of Katie Wyler, who, in 1779 after being captured by Indians, escaped and made her way hundreds of miles back to Mitchell County, a story that he has come across in research for his dissertation on ethnohistory. Two new murders are initially credited to Harm, that of his ex-wife, Rita, who has been married for nearly thirty years to conservative, highly respectable Euell Pentland and whose body is found in the ruins of the trailer high in the mountains where she lived with Harm, and the Harkryder baby, who Sabrina says was stolen by the convict. The paths of all these people intersect: Hank the Yank, investigating leads for his show, comes upon the battered body of Rita Pentland; Jeremy Cobb, thoroughly lost on a mountain trail, runs into Harm, who walks off with the student's backpack and supplies, having forgotten the encounter while Jeremy goes for water; Martha successfully talks Sabrina out of knifing her baby but discovers that LeDonne has been spending his nights with a local floozy named Crystal; Charlarty, now a graduate geology student, hoping to find her father before a trigger-happy posse shoots him, returns to the trailer and, to keep it from becoming a mecca for the curious, lights it afire; Jeremy, nearly starving and suffering from injured feet, runs into Sabrina, who has reported her child missing, then stolen a car from a search party with a confused idea that if she finds Martha, her life can be straightened out. Together they reach the mountain home of Nora Bonesteel, an old woman with "the sight" who has seen Katie Wyler running through the woods at various times and is expecting Sabrina and Jeremy. Spencer, the low-key, patient sheriff, actually solves both the recent murders and learns, from an analysis of the liquid oozing out of the ground around the trailer, that Harm had good reason to murder Claib, who had dumped toxic chemical waste onto Harm's land. This discovery, however, is not in time to help the old man, who arrives at his blazing trailer and dives into the fire in a vain effort to save the baby girl whom he left there. The various strands of the story are neatly woven together without the appearance of contrivance, and the solutions are logical. Even the elements of Nora Bonesteel's extrasensory perception and Katie Wyler's ghost are treated matter-of-factly, with no sensationalism or feel of fantasy. The strongest element in the book is the sense of place, of the mountain com-

munity, with its pockets of old-time families coexisting with the 1990s townspeople, and of the wild beauty of the country. SLJ.

SHIPWRECK SEASON (Hill*, Donna, Clarion, 1998), boy's growing-up novel
set on the rugged New England coast of Cape Cod in 1880, concerned with the
rescue crews in the early days of the U.S. Life-Saving Service. Against his will,
Daniel Stafford, 16, has been sent by his widowed mother to spend the summer
with his uncle, Elisha Alder, captain of the Perkins Hollow lifesaving station,
because he has been expelled from school for poor grades and is consorting
with boys in an "athletic club," which seems to honor drinking and gambling
as much as physical fitness. Before they reach the station, his uncle makes it
clear that Daniel will obey orders without question, address him as "sir" or
"Captain Adler," and train with the other men, although he will not be officially
enlisted. Although Daniel's manners are imperious and rude, he is treated well
by the six surfmen, especially the youngest, Will Ryker, a bright, eager boy,
and Obed Woolsey, a slow-minded but powerful and gentle man who loves to
cook. The only real opposition that he gets is from Ross Ogilvie, who makes a
joke of almost everything that he says or does. Even Jonathan Pilgrim, a giant
Indian who has attended Harvard, is polite to Daniel after the boy has deliberately insulted him. A secret that Daniel tries to hide but that almost defeats him
is his pathological fear of heights. Since he has no experience in the actual
rescue drill, he is assigned the role of victim and required to climb the forty-
foot wreck pole to a crow's nest, catch the line shot from a cannon below, jump
into the breeches buoy, and ride it down to the beach. The first time, though he
gets to the top, he has to be rescued by Will, his arms pried from the mast, and
he vomits when he finally reaches the beach. For a while he is relieved of that
duty, but as the summer wears on, and he comes to admire the men, he decides
to try to do his part, especially when the Perkins Hollow crew is challenged by
the Parmet River crew to see who can complete the drill in the shortest time.
With Will's help, he goes to the pole early each morning, climbing a little farther
each time until he can make it to the top without feeling faint. At the actual
contest, he panics at first but manages his part so that not much time is lost,
and the two teams tie at exactly the same number of minutes and seconds. In
the first real rescue of the season, Daniel is one of the rowers because Will has
broken his collarbone. When Ross is entangled in the lines and dragged down,
Daniel dives, cuts him loose, then, with great difficulty, drags him to shore.
Although Ross does not survive, the men praise Daniel for his courage and
effort. In a subordinate plot, Daniel mends the romance of Will and Rachel
Beckers, the daughter of one of the other surfmen. At the end of the season,
Daniel returns home to restart school, having caught up on his studies at the
rescue station, a much improved young man. Although the plot is predictable,
the surfmen and even minor characters are well differentiated and interesting.
The work of the rescue crews is explained without the research seeming to be

inserted heavy-handedly, and action scenes are exciting. The forbearance of the men at the station in the face of Daniel's insufferable ego at first, however, is hard to believe. Christopher.

SHOUP, BARBARA (1947–   ), novelist, writer in residence at a high school center for humanities and performing arts, and coordinator of a summer arts workship for high school students at the Children's Museum of Indianapolis, Indiana. In her first novel for young adults, *Wish You Were Here** (Hyperion, 1994), she explores the mental turmoil of a boy facing the loss of his best friend, who has run away, and the remarriage of his mother to a man with two young daughters. In *Stranded in Harmony* (Hyperion, 1997) the main character, a high school senior, struggling with the claustrophobia that he feels with his small Indiana town, his parents' expectations, and his fear that his girlfriend is pregnant, turns to an older woman, who helps him sort out his life. Shoup has also written books on art and education. She received her B.S. degree from Indiana University in 1972 and her M.S. degree in 1976 and has made her home in Indianapolis.

SHUJA (*Ironman**), only African-American member of the Nak Pack, the students in Mr.* Nakatani's Anger Management Class, which includes Bo Brewster. Shuja is a big, strong, good-looking youth whom teachers, he says, accuse of having a "'tude." Shuja is quick to take offense at any remark or action that even hints of racial discrimination. His anger at the world comes, he says, from, having to take on "all of history." Shuja is the one who suggests that as a project the class "get behind the Ironman," that is, Bo Brewster, and thus they become Bo's Stotans or support group.

SINCLAIR, APRIL (1953–   ), born in Chicago, Illinois; teacher, worker in community service programs, and author of three widely read novels. Her first, usually considered her most popular and successful, is *Coffee Will Make You Black** (Hyperion, 1994), a growing-up story of an African-American girl in Chicago at the time of the civil rights movement. Its sequel, *Ain't Gonna Be the Same Fool Twice* (Hyperion, 1996), takes the main character to San Francisco, where she experiments with the lesbian lifestyle. The third, *I Left My Back Door Open* (Hyperion, 1999), is again set in Chicago with a somewhat older woman as the main character. All have been commended for lively incidents and a witty style. Sinclair has lived in Chicago, Florida, and Oakland, California.

SINGER, MARILYN (1948–   ), born in New York City; resident of Brooklyn, New York; for a quarter of a century a versatile and prolific author of more than forty picture books and novels for children and young adults. After a year at the University of Reading in England, she was graduated from Queens College of the City of New York and received her M.A. from New York University.

She has been an editor for a literary agency and a magazine, a high school teacher of English and speech, and since 1974 a full-time writer. She has written two series of mysteries and a dozen mystery-fantasies for young adults, among them a nominee for the Edgar Allan Poe Award, *Deal with a Ghost** (Holt, 1997), about a girl's encounters with the ghost that haunts her high school. Singer's books have won several honors, including the American Library Association's young adult citation for *The Course of True Love Never Did Run Smooth* (Harper, 1983) and for *Several Kinds of Silence* (Harper, 1988). She has also written short fiction and nonfiction about films, birds, and animals, among other topics.

SIR GILMAN (*Pigs Don't Fly**), young knight who speaks courteously to Summer, a rare occurrence in her life as the grossly fat daughter of the village whore. Later, when she comes upon the carnage left by an attack on his company, she finds a scrap of his standard, which she carries with her as a memento, fearing that he is dead. In the town where she and her animal companions spend the night, she sees him, almost naked, being tormented in the stocks, and without hesitation she claims him as her demented brother and bribes the skeptical bailiff to release him to her. Since he has lost his sight and his memory, she cares for him devotedly, overlooking his complaints and superior airs. After he regains his vision, he is astonished at Summer's beauty, which has emerged as their hard journey and shortage of food have slimmed her down, and he compares his betrothed, the fair Rosamund, unfavorably with her. Summer does not attempt to tell him that Rosamund is pregnant with his father's child, knowing that his training as a knight and sense of honor would keep him from denouncing his betrothed and that he will raise the child as his own more happily not knowing that he has been tricked. He is shallow and somewhat spoiled, but he matures during their journey and is basically a good man.

THE SKULL OF TRUTH: A MAGIC SHOP BOOK (Coville*, Bruce, illus. Gary Lippincott, Harcourt, 1997), lighthearted fantasy of magic that examines the nature of truth and of telling the truth. To save Tucker's Swamp, whose mysterious atmosphere he loves, Charlie Eggleston, 11, circulates a story about classmate Mark Evans' father, a developer who wants to turn the area into an industrial park, and incurs the anger of Mr. Evans' bully son, Mark. Fleeing through the swamp from Mark and his thuggish pals one day, Charlie encounters a strip of land that he has not seen before and soon finds himself in an isolated little shop filled with magicians' paraphernalia and operated by a crotchety little old man. Among the store's items is a skull, labeled The Skull of Truth, which Charlie steals and hides in his garage. That night two talking rats, Roxanne and Jerome, appear at his window and give him a note from the magic shop owner, Mr. S. H. Elives, which warns him to be careful of what he says and not to let the skull out of his possession. The skull, an articulate, witty speaker, says that he is what is left of Yorick, the jester of the King of Denmark, Hamlet's father.

He also says that he was present when "Bill" Shakespeare wrote the play. The skull soon affects the behavior of Charlie and his family and eventually the lives of everyone whom Charlie contacts. Charlie finds that he tells the truth even when he does not want to. He tells Mark that his father is a "nature-destroying capitalist swine" and gets punched in the stomach; tells Gilbert Dawkins, a bald-headed classmate suffering from cancer, that he looks terrible, to the disgust of both; and tells classmate Karen Ackerman that he loves her, which is all right. He later renews his friendship with Gilbert by shaving his head, an action soon imitated by most of the boys at school, the principal, and even Karen. He learns from unusually frank dinner conversation that his Gramma Ethel was once a striptease dancer, that his Uncle Bennie is gay and has a boyfriend, and that his mother had been married before. Various difficulties arise before Charlie gets the idea of taking the skull to the public meeting about the industrial park project and thus forcing Mr. Evans to tell the real truth about the project, which is canceled as a result. Charlie is instructed by Mr. Elives via the rats to take the skull to the cemetery at midnight. There in a series of surrealistic scenes, he is introduced to a mystical woman in white named Truth, who leads him into an underground passage, changing shapes various times (the symbolism is obvious). Charlie deposits the skull as instructed and then finds himself back in the magic shop, where he agrees to run errands for Mr. Elives to pay for the skull. Charlie feels more comfortable with himself now and is better liked by family and friends. Except for the sequence with Truth, which seems highly anomalistic in both substance and tone, the book is adventurous, funny, fast paced, and often very witty. Yorick's portions are delightfully amusing, although probably more so for the adult reader than for the intended audience of middle graders. This is one of a series about Mr. Elives' magical store. SLJ.

SKURZYNSKI, GLORIA (1930–   ), born in Duquesne, Pennsylvania; author of a wide variety of books for young people. With her daughter, Alane Ferguson*, she wrote *Wolf Stalker* (National Geographic, 1997), a story of the antagonism to the reintroduction of wolves into Yellowstone Park, one of a series of National Park Mysteries. Her *Virtual War* (Simon & Schuster, 1997), for young adults, is a futuristic novel in which life is confined to a few highly regulated domed cities. For earlier biographical information and title entries, see *Dictionary, 1960–1984* [*What Happened in Hamlin*] and *Dictionary, 1985–1989* [*Trapped in Slickrock Canyon*].

SLAM! (Myers*, Walter Dean, Scholastic, 1996), sports novel set in Harlem in the 1990s, following part of the junior year of basketball player Greg "Slam" Harris, 17, during which he gradually comes to terms with his resentment at real and supposed slurs against his abilities and his race in the mostly white school. Because he has transferred to Latimer Arts Magnet School, he has left behind his old friends at Carver, including his longtime buddy Benny "Ice" Reece and Mtisha, the girl whom he likes. At first he has difficulty adjusting.

His teachers point out that he is behind the other students and seem to scorn him for not trying or possibly not having the brains to compete. More disturbing to Slam, Coach Nipper will not let him be a starter, putting him in games only when the situation is desperate. Among the other players, only Ducky, a red-haired guitar player with earnest, but minimal, basketball skills, is friendly to Slam. The other African American on the team, Jimmy, is closer to the best player, Nick, than to Slam. Only the assistant coach, Goldy (Mr. Goldstein), understands Slam's insecurity, which he masks with a truculent attitude, and he tries to help. Several subplots add complications. Slam's family life is loving but tense because his grandmother is in the hospital, probably dying of cancer, and his out-of-work father is drinking too much. Mtisha suspects that Ice has begun selling dope, and she tries to get Slam to confront him. When Slam lets his brother, Derek, 9, use the school video camera with which he is making a documentary about his life and neighborhood, the little boy leaves it briefly on the stoop, and it is stolen. Several games are described in detail, the strongest element in the novel, culminating in the crucial game between Latimer and Carver, in which Slam and Ice go up against each other. Latimer, mostly because of Slam's play, wins, paving the way for a rematch in the upcoming citywide tournament. Ice congratulates Slam and invites him to a party that night, but the good time is spoiled when an incident makes it clear that Ice really has been dealing, and Slam breaks with him. Although he is badly hurt, Slam has learned to deal with life as he deals with his game, taking the bad, like losing his best friend and his grandmother's illness, along with the good, like the success of his video and the recognition of his basketball skill. At the end Slam seems to be gaining control of his emotions, is possibly in line for a basketball scholarship to college, and is beginning to understand the tactless, but sincere, advice that adults on all sides are giving him. The novel avoids some of the clichés of inner-city stories. Mtisha is a sensible girl, not trying to push him into premature fatherhood. As his video shows, his neighborhood has roaches and drug addicts and poverty, but it also has good people like the secondhand store man who gets the video camera back for him and a sense of community that most of the people at Latimer don't understand. The mostly street-smart language gives a strong sense of place without being overdone. The disparate elements do not meld together into a tight-knit plot, but the randomness may be an asset, since it reflects Slam's own confusion and ambivalence about his life. C.S. King Winner.

SOLDIER'S HEART: A NOVEL OF THE CIVIL WAR (Paulsen*, Gary, Delacorte, 1998), historical novel of a Minnesota farm boy in the American Civil War, based on an actual figure and real events. In early June 1861, Charley Goddard, 15, moved by gallant spirit and desire for excitement, walks from Winona, Minnesota, to Fort Snelling, where he lies about his age and enlists in the Minnesota Volunteers. After a brief period of training and certain of victory, the recruits are loaded on a steamboat and transported to St. Paul, Minnesota, and to La Crosse, Wisconsin, and then are put on a train to Maryland, crowds hailing them along the way. All this is thrilling to a boy who has never before been more than five miles from home. In Maryland, Charley sees his first "coloreds" and also is revolted by the way that the southerners treat blacks. He sees his first action at Bull Run (Manassas Junction), where the bullets are like "horizontal hail" and "death was everywhere." Charley is terribly frightened. He screams, "Make it all stop now!" and "feels his very soul would leave him." Later, he remembers the terrible fear, an intense emotion that accompanies him through the rest of the war, a terrible fear and the certainty that he will die. It rides him through "farming," that is, foraging for food and supplies; at encampments getting ready for the next skirmishes and battles; and at the Battle at Gettysburg, after which of the 1,000 Minnesota Volunteers only 47 are left standing. Charley is not one of the standing. He takes a hit and another and finally goes down, sure that he been killed. In the last chapter, set in Minnesota in 1867, Charley is old, not in years, being only twenty-one, but in body. He is deeply tired, broken in body and spirit, and moves laboriously with a cane. He lives alone in a shack at the edge of Winona and almost yearns for death. He has a Confederate revolver that he brought back, taken from a soldier whom he shot, a coveted trophy. He cocks the "pretty" thing, then sits back and looks out over the river. The book ends abruptly at this point. The real Charley died at twenty-three of "soldier's heart," what today is known as posttraumatic stress disorder. The lean, laconic style and bleak tone emphasize the horror of the conflict and make the short narrative extraordinarily vivid and heartrending. A Foreword about "soldier's heart," a map, a note at the end about the real Charley Goddard, and a bibliography of selected sources add to the book's impact and ground the story in reality. Some scenes are unforgettable—Charley's helping a fellow soldier, who has a fatal stomach wound, commit suicide; Charley's night conversation across a river with a Rebel soldier; and the horrors of a field hospital in which Charley helps—in addition to the monstrous defeat at Bull Run. Although reminiscent of *The Red Badge of Courage* and similar war narratives, the book projects its own unique pain. It makes personal war experiences that probably cannot be repeated too often. Jefferson.

SOLLY GRUBER (*Dave at Night**), grandfatherly old Jewish man with a talking parrot named Bandit. Solly takes Dave Caros to the party where he introduces the boy as his grandson and tells fortunes, having instructed Dave when to groan and otherwise assist him in entertaining his customers and making a few cents. Dave would like to live with him permanently and asks to do so, but Solly refuses, since he is old, in failing health, and lives by himself. Solly is ultimately instrumental in improving conditions at the Hebrew Home for Boys. He also helps Dave to think better of Gideon, helping the boy to see that he has been adopting an "alrightnik" or judgmental attitude toward Gideon. Solly sprinkles his speech with Yiddish words, calls Dave "Daveleh" and "boychik," and refers to himself as a "gonif," a kind of crook or con man. He is described as wearing a long, gray beard, a green tie with orange polka dots, and a sagging black suit—a kind of shabby Rip Van Winkle.

SOMEONE LIKE YOU (Dessen*, Sarah, Viking, 1998), novel of a friendship that helps two teenage girls face problems in their high school junior year and, as a result, to grow in understanding. The narrator, Halley Cooke, 15, is summoned home from a summer camp that she despises by a phone call from her best friend, Scarlett Thomas, who reports the motorcycle accident death of their classmate, Michael Sherwood, whom Scarlett has been quietly dating all summer. Since Scarlett's mother, Marion, is a flaky type, disorganized and inclined to sleep with a new fellow every couple of months, Halley becomes her friend's strongest support, reversing their roles in which Scarlett was always the leader and decision maker. To Halley's surprise, Macon Faulkner, a friend of Michael, notices her, and gradually they start going together, although her parents, Julie, a therapist and expert on adolescent behavior, and her father, Brian, a radio talk-show host, are doubtful about the relationship. Halley herself wonders about Macon, who never comes into the house for her and who seems to have another life and a social group that doesn't include her. Still, since she has never gone with any boy except dull Noah Vaughn, son of her parents' friends, she is thrilled at Macon's attention and begins sneaking out to meet him. She is stunned when Scarlett tells her that she is pregnant from the only time that she and Michael had sex. Halley supports her when she tells her mother and picks her up at the abortion clinic where Marion deposited her. Scarlett has decided to keep her baby, against her mother's wishes, and even ignores Marion's insistence that she put it up for adoption. The novel follows the progress of these relationships through the school year, as Marion becomes involved with Steve, an accountant who is a medievalist, dresses in costume, and participates in festivals on weekends; as Scarlett's condition becomes apparent and she endures curiosity and scorn at school; and as Macon with increasing insistence presses Halley to have sex with him. When she decides that she will, they go to a sleazy party where she drinks too much and is extremely sick at the critical moment. Furious, Macon drives wildly on their way home and runs a red light, and Halley wakes up in the hospital, with multiple, but not life-threatening, injuries. Macon, unhurt in the crash, does not come to see her, but after she is home, he drives by and lingers every night, waiting, as she rightly suspects, for her to come out to meet him. Although forbidden to see him again, Halley does sneak out quietly one night, finds him in the yard, and tells him that she is through and wants nothing more to do with him. The novel concludes with the prom, to which Halley goes with Noah because Scarlett wants to go, even nine months pregnant, with Cameron Newton, an artistic boy, a bit nerdy but bright and decent, who has been nice to her. It is a disaster. Noah is drunk, tries to assault Halley, and rips the back out of her dress. She is in the rest room trying to fasten it together with bobby pins when a girl bursts in saying that Scarlett is having her baby.

Halley takes charge, helps Scarlett outside, commandeers Macon to drive them to the hospital, and stays with Scarlett, telling the nurse that she is Scarlett's sister, until the baby, a girl, is born. Parallel to this plot is the story of Halley's relationship with her mother, once very close but badly estranged not only by Macon's presence but more basically by Julie's effort to direct all Halley's activities and even thoughts, since she is sure that she is the expert on adolescence. At the end Halley has asserted herself, and they are tentatively building a new understanding. Although most of the characters are either stereotyped, like the catty girls at school, or merely functional, like Cameron, the three main figures, Halley, Scarlett, and Macon, are individualized and interesting. Halley's brittle mother and her genial, peacemaking father, who thoughtlessly humiliates his daughter by telling embarrassing stories about her on the air, are well drawn, and the teenage angst, painful to read about as it is for the girls to endure, is convincing. SLJ.

SOMETHING TERRIBLE HAPPENED (Porte*, Barbara Ann, Orchard, 1994), growing-up novel of a girl whose African-American mother contracts AIDS and dies, leaving her with the family of her white father's older brother in Oak Ridge, Tennessee. Although her father died of a drug overdose before she was four, Gillian Hardwick at ten is ideally happy with her mother, a stylish teacher, singer, and actress in New York City. Her grandmother lives nearby, and even her great-grandmother, Gigi-ma, from Trinidad, is close enough to visit often. When her mother becomes ill, all her family are in denial at first. In a wild and hopeless effort to find a cure, her mother takes Gillian to Florida, where they live at first in a shabby motel and eventually on the street, until she is so weak that, the day before Christmas, Gillian calls her grandmother, who sends money for plane fare home. Gillian is shocked when her grandmother arranges that she go to Tennessee to live with her Uncle Henry, whom she met once when she was about five, his wife, Aunt Corinne, and their child, DeeDee, 5, neither of whom she has ever seen before. Although they are welcoming, and Gillian tries to be polite, the arrangement is a strain for everyone except DeeDee, who adores Gillian. At first Gillian tells herself that it will be just a few weeks until her mother is well again or that her grandmother will send for her to come back to New York, but the months stretch out. In August, her mother comes to Oak Ridge to see her and is much more ill than Gillian has expected, and the girl sets her sights on returning to New York for Christmas. In mid-December her mother dies, and Uncle Henry flies with Gillian to the funeral. Despite her pleas, her grandmother refuses to have her stay in New York, and she returns to Tennessee. The rest of the book is about her gradual adjustment to Oak Ridge and the family. At first she is plagued by nightmares. The therapy group that her aunt arranges that she join is a disaster; she is horrified by the dreadful experiences that the other members report. Her only real comfort is DeeDee, who has sympathetic bad dreams and needs the comfort that Gillian provides. Oak Ridge has only one other African American, an auto body shop owner, who encourages the black young people from nearby Scarboro to hang around his shop. Although they are older than Gillian, they treat her as a little sister and provide some social life. The best therapy comes when Cousin Antoine visits. Although Gillian knows that he is several years older than she is, she is astonished to see that he is of Asian descent. Actually, he is Filipino, adopted when he was six by Aunt Corinne's sister. He helps in several ways. He firmly tells her to stop feeling sorry for herself, relates some of the story that he has gleaned of Uncle Henry's even more traumatic childhood, and, before he leaves, organizes the family in a memorial service for Gillian's mother, which helps to ease the feeling that she has that she was never allowed to say good-bye. A new relationship develops with Uncle Henry, who, though of few words, is understanding and assures her that her mother's AIDS came not from her father but from some other man, information that helps her forgive the white side of her family. She does well in school and is chosen for a special program at Oak Ridge National Laboratory. In December she looks forward to a visit from her grandmother, who has been facing her own loss by taking up running and returning to graduate school and who announces that she has been offered a teaching job at the University of Tennessee in Knoxville. Gillian is glad not only that her grandmother will be within easy visiting distance but also that her new life in Oak Ridge will not be disrupted. Gillian's progress toward maturity and acceptance of her new life is believable, but the book is told in a strangely disjointed way, partly through narration by Isabelle Ramos, a friend of Gillian's grandmother who never appears as a character, partly by letters from Gillian to Mrs. Ramos, and partly by imagined passages that Gillian might have narrated if asked, and it is continually interrupted by stories told to or by Gillian, all with some moral or other connection to the main action. Although Gillian is drawn as a girl especially interested in stories, they tend to disrupt the narrative. At the end are notes about the stories, both fact and folklore, used in the novel. The problems of Gillian's mixed West Indian and white heritage, though central to her feeling of alienation, are never explored at length. ALA; SLJ.

SOPHOS (*The Thief**), the younger of the two apprentices of the magus*, the scholar of King Sounis of Sounis. Sophos accompanies the magus, Gen, Pol*, and his fellow apprentice, Ambiades*, to find the fabled stone known as Hamiathes' Gift. Of the two apprentices, he is the less skilled at almost everything, especially swordfighting. He is far more pleasant to travel with, however, than Ambiades. He is the son of a duke of Sounis and, it is learned at the end, the heir of the king to the throne of Sounis. Although Gen thinks that Sophos and Ambiades are both generally useless, Sophos proves capable, helpful, and loyal. At the end, it is expected that he will marry the queen of Eddis, thus uniting Sounis and Eddis.

SPARROWS IN THE SCULLERY (Wallace, Barbara Brooks, Atheneum, 1997), Dickensian novel of suspense and mystery set in Victorian times in a coastal city, presumably in America. When Colley Trevelyan is nearly eleven, his parents are killed in an accident, and he is kidnapped from the lavish family estate, wrapped in a rough blanket so he cannot see, and brought to a grim orphanage, the Broggin Home for Boys, run by Obadiah and Quintilla Crawler, both despicable and terrifying. They give him the name of a recently deceased boy, Jed Broggin, and his old cot in a cold, dark room with five other boys. The only sense that he can make of his abduction is that his kidnappers must be holding him for ransom until his uncle and stepaunt return from their travels. He thinks that he recognizes the voice of one of them as that of Cark, the new butler. The other boys, led by Marty, ridicule Colley's ruffled nightshirt and treat him as an outcast. The horrors mount the next day. Breakfast porridge is inedible, but his uneaten portion is returned at supper and each meal thereafter. He is sent with other boys to the glass factory led by a burly, murderous-looking foreman named Gorp. Exhausted by his work there and further duty in the scullery, Colley still can't sleep and is amazed to see the boys with a dim lantern disappear beneath one of the beds and later return. At supper the next evening, Mrs. Crawler suddenly demands that the boys empty their pockets. Marty, standing next to Colley, throws down the contents of his pocket, including a bent and discolored penny that lands halfway between them and that Mr. Crawler thinks is Colley's. Under the baleful questioning of Mr. Crawler, Colley claims that he found it in the street. For the crime of not turning it in to the Crawlers, he is shoved into a narrow, moldy pit in the cellar with a grating padlocked across the top. Later that night first Marty and Noah, with a gift of a gummy bun, then the other three boys from their room, visit secretly and whisper apologies through the grating. For the first time in his life, Colley has friends his own age. This undoubtedly saves his life the next day, when he is shoved from behind by Gorp and saved from falling onto red-hot bottles in the glass factory by one of the boys whom Marty has told to watch out for him. That night the boys show him their secret room, reached by a trapdoor under one bed, a hideaway furnished with scraps of carpet and broken chairs salvaged from the streets. The room leads into a passage that ends in a graveyard, sheltered by windowless buildings on all sides. They also introduce him to Abigail, the rat that they found wandering in the graveyard and adopted as a pet. When a group of well-dressed people, patrons of the Broggin Home, visit the next day, the boys have been ordered to be reading from a strange assortment of books handed around. To the surprise of the Crawlers, one of the women, Miss Dorcas, suggests that the boys read aloud to her and first chooses Marty, who is illiterate. He makes up a ludicrous sentence. Then Colley, asked next, reads a long, complicated sentence from the ancient medical book that he has been handed. When Colley's turn comes to visit the graveyard during their "play" period, as the boys secretly do one at a time, he is astonished that Miss Dorcas and a friend enter. They recognize him as the boy who read so well and question him gently. On one night expedition, Colley and Marty are nearly caught in the reception room, but they learn that while most of the boys are bought by the Crawlers, whoever brought Colley paid them to take him. As the mystery thickens, Colley becomes ill, and Marty, who was fond of the original Jed and doesn't want this one dying, too, hides him in the underground room and arranges to steal blankets and occasionally food for him and to leave a door unlocked, so the Crawlers will think he escaped that way. As Colley recovers, he spends more time in the graveyard, and one day he hears the Crawlers, who have discovered the room and the tunnel, emerge into the cemetery and speculate on whether he is dead in a ditch somewhere. They nail the trapdoor under the bed shut and plan to similarly nail the one to the graveyard, but Colley first rescues Abigail. As he sneaks out of the cemetery, hoping somehow to make his way to his old home, he is grabbed by a man whom he recognizes as Cark whom he assumes first kidnapped him. Cark takes him, however, to a young naval captain, introduced as Colley's cousin, Jeremy, who long ago ran off to sea. To Colley's consternation, they go the next day to the Broggin Home, where three lawyers, Miss Dorcas, Colley's uncle and stepaunt, and another sea captain await them. There the whole story comes out, how Colley's uncle, wanting to inherit the estate, had him kidnapped and, with the help of the dishonest lawyers, put him in a situation where he could be expected to die soon. Jeremy and Miss Dorcas, daughter of the other sea captain, are to be married. At Colley's request, the five boys from his room come to live with him, and the Broggin Home will have new management, real teachers, and no more work in the glass factory or similar sweatshops. In the tradition of Victorian novels, the villains are thoroughly evil, the setting of the Broggin Home grim and terrifying, the plot convoluted, and the orphaned hero, at first pampered and sickly, made of sturdier stuff than expected. The novel, in many ways reminiscent of those by Joan Aiken, although not as outrageously exaggerated, is excellent fun. Poe Winner.

SPEAK (Anderson*, Laurie Halse, Farrar, 1999), psychological problem novel set almost entirely in a school in a suburb of Syracuse, New York, in the late twentieth century. Melinda Sordino, 13, starts ninth grade at Merryweather High ostracized by her circle of friends from middle school because she called the police at Kyle Rodger's drunken end-of-the-summer party, and some of the revelers got into trouble. No one knows, because Melinda is unable to tell anyone, that she called 911 because she had been raped by Andy Evans, a senior. All this comes out gradually in the novel, which is presented in brief, first-person chapters giving ironic pictures of school classes and happenings and is divided into the four marking periods with her report card of falling grades at the end of each. At first Melinda attempts to reach out to old friends and a new girl, "Heather from Ohio," who is determined to break into the rigid social structure, with Melinda as a partner. When Heather makes it with a group called the Marthas, she drops Melinda abruptly. As the school year progresses, Melinda's depression increases until she stops speaking completely. Her preoccupied parents, never very interested or sympathetic, are more exasperated than concerned. Melinda starts skipping school or escaping into an unused janitor's closet that she has cleaned out and decorated as a hideout. There are a few rays of hope. David Petrakis, her intellectual lab partner in biology, finds her interesting. Mr. Freeman, the eccentric art teacher, the only adult who makes any effort to understand her, consistently gives her As and quirky encouragement, although he is never satisfied with her attempts to make an artwork of a tree, her semester assignment, always finding her efforts too literal and stiff. Toward spring Ivy, an artistic girl from her past circle of friends, begins to talk to her again. Melinda is concerned when her former best friend, Rachel (now "Rachelle"), starts to go with Andy Evans (whom Melinda now can call by name, whereas she earlier referred to him as "IT"). She tries to warn Rachel, is shunned, and ends by writing an anonymous note. In the rest room with Ivy, she pens a graffiti, "Guys to Stay Away From" and starts the list with Andy Evans. Later, in the library, she tries again to warn Rachel and this time gets as far as admitting, in a note, that she was raped at the party. Shocked and penitent, Rachel asks who did it, but when Melinda writes "Andy Evans," Rachel flares up in fury and calls her a jealous liar. Ivy finds her stunned and leads her to the rest room, where her list still has only one member, but under Andy Evans many have written comments agreeing and expanding on her assessment of him. Beginning to feel some interest in life again, Melinda starts raking up her yard and even gets her father into the project. Just as she feels that she has no more need for her janitor's closet hidey-hole and goes to clear out her pictures, Andy Evans, furious that Rachel dropped him at the prom, follows, hits her viciously, and starts to assault her sexually. She screams and grabs a piece of broken mirror, holding it to his neck until she is rescued by the lacrosse team. At semester's end, she finally completes a sketch of a tree that satisfies Mr. Freeman, who has been supportive all year and has told her that she can talk to him if she needs to. He gives her an A-plus, and she begins to tell him what happened in August, the first time that she is able to talk about it. Besides being a moving study of the psychological trauma experienced by a rape victim, the novel is a scathing picture of social life in a modern high school and an ironic look at a school's self-deluding way of handling problems, from choosing a name for the team mascot to the conferences with difficult students, like Melinda, and her parents. Hurt and depressed, Melinda still is more clear-sighted than most of the people with whom she deals, and she has an ironic, mocking voice that keeps her interesting. SLJ.

SPENCE (*The Midnight Club**), one of the five teenagers with terminal cancer who gather every night at midnight in the hospice study to tell stories. Cadaverous in appearance with unsightly facial scars, he tells stories of violence and killing that reflect his inner rage. He had hoped to become an actor, and, more creative and outgoing than the others, he always goes first in the storytelling. He spends a lot of time writing letters to his girlfriend, Caroline, according to Kevin*, his roommate. Near the end of the book, he confesses to Ilonka Pawluk that he is gay, has acquired AIDS from an early lover, has no girlfriend, and feels angry and guilty because he infected his latest lover, Carl, who has died.

He tells her that there is no Caroline and that he has been writing the letters and mailing them to himself. When Ilonka tells him that she is willing to stand before God and take some of the burden of his guilt upon herself, he gains a measure of relief.

SPENSON, BLORE (*Stranger at the Wedding**), good-humored young man in his mid-thirties who is engaged to marry Alix* Peldyrin, the beautiful younger sister of Kyra Peldyrin. At first Kyra finds him repulsive—heavy, overdressed, red-faced, a kind of buffoon. Later she thinks him kind, gentle, helpful, a true gentleman. He feels trapped in a marriage arranged to please his father and pursued by aggressive, manipulative mothers seeking a wealthy marriage for their daughters. Since Kyra is mageborn and hence unable to marry and because, in any event, she wishes to complete her mage's training, he gives up his position as his father's shipmaster and moves to a town not far from the Citadel of Wizards, from which he can travel often to visit her, and they can continue their relationship, apparently with Kyra as his mistress. While this solution to their romantic problems provides a conclusion to the novel, it is neither entirely plausible nor appropriate to the plot and the characters as presented.

SPINELLI, JERRY (1941–   ), born and raised in Norristown, Pennsylvania; magazine editor and writer of middle-grade humorous novels that draw upon his own life with six children for situations and characters. He is best known for *Maniac Magee* (Little, Brown, 1990), which won the Newbery Medal and several other awards and citations. A *School Library Journal* choice, *Crash** (Knopf, 1996) involves a slowly developing friendship between a football hero and a pacifist Quaker boy. *Wringer** (HarperCollins, 1997), named to Fanfare and the Newbery Honor list, tells of a small-town boy who dreads the town coming-of-age rite, wringing the necks of pigeons. *Stargirl* (Knopf, 2000) concerns the tensions of popularity, nonconformity, and first love. Spinelli's books are fast moving, hyperbolic, and sometimes crude but always entertaining. His wife, Eileen Spinelli, is also a noted writer. The Spinellis live in Phoenixville, Pennsylvania. For more biographical details, titles, and a title entry, see *Dictionary, 1990–1994* [*Maniac Magee*].

SPIRIT SEEKER (Nixon*, Joan Lowery, Delacorte, 1995), contemporary, realistic detective novel set for five days in Houston, Texas. Police detective Jake Campbell, father of narrator Holly, 16, is often late in coming home from work, seemingly obsessed with solving cases to such an extent that his marriage to Lynn, a fourth-grade teacher, is endangered. Holly resents his frequently abstracted behavior and inattention to Lynn and their ordinary family life. Domestic matters worsen when, at 2:00 A.M. one Saturday morning in September, Jake arrives and informs his family that he has been working on a disturbing case. The parents of Cody Garnett, Holly's boyfriend, whom she has known since junior high, were murdered Friday night. All the evidence in the brutal knife slaying points to Cody. Cody insists that he spent the night at the Garnetts' Lake Conroe house, then changes his original story, admitting that he had words with his parents over a new car and that he did not spend the night at the Conroe place but rather in a sleeping bag near by. Since the evidence is circumstantial, and no witnesses or weapon is found, the police do not arrest him. Jake insists that Holly stay away from Cody, maintaining that in such instances a family member is often the murderer. Holly angrily asserts that she will prove Cody innocent. Neighbor Glenda Jordan, who claims to be clairvoyant, says that if she and Holly can get into the Garnett house, she may be able to re-create the crime scene. She says that she can see what happened but cannot visualize the face of the murderer. Holly confers at different times with Cody, who is scared, and Sara, her best friend, who insists that Holly is foolishly unobjective. The two girls go to the Garnett house, using a key that Cody tells them is in the garage, and open Mr. Garnett's computer files. They discover that Mr. Garnett seems to have been involved in some shady deal. Holly later goes back to the house with Glenda, who carries a tape player to record what goes on. Glenda chants to invoke the spirits so that she can visualize the murder and, when they hear a mysterious click, says that evil is in the house. When Cody phones one morning, highly distraught, Holly goes to his Uncle Frank's house, where Cody is staying, and finds that Cody is preparing to run away. Jake arrives just after Cody leaves and spots what turns out to be the murder weapon among Uncle Frank's kitchen knives. He also finds goods stolen from the Garnett house hidden in Uncle Frank's house. Holly returns to the Garnett house, where she sits in the living room as she and Glenda had done, after putting a blank tape in the entertainment center. Cody arrives, and shortly thereafter Uncle Frank. In a grand climax, it comes out that Uncle Frank killed his sister and her husband, his own business deals having gone sour, and put the blame on Cody, whose inheritance he would control since Cody would be in jail. The police arrive just as he is about to shoot the young people, but Holly can prove that he is the murderer because his comments to them are on the audiotape. Cody is exonerated, Holly's faith in him is vindicated, and Holly now understands her father's intense need to solve his cases, because she has felt similarly obsessed to prove Cody innocent. Jake resolves to pay more attention to Lynn, and the future looks brighter for the Campbells. Characters and events are common to murder mysteries, the conclusion is predictable, and style and incidents are frequently melodramatic. The story moves rapidly with plenty of action and carefully placed clues and red herrings. Holly's faith in her boyfriend, stubborn will to clear him, and courage to go to the scene not just once but several times will appeal to young readers. Poe Nominee.

SPITE FENCES (Krisher*, Trudy, Delacorte, 1994), historical novel of the early civil rights movement in the small Georgia town of Kinship, narrated by a poor white girl. Although Maggie (Magnolia) Pugh, 13, has known all her life that whites and "coloreds" don't mix, she still thinks that big Zeke Freeman is one of the nicest people whom she knows, and she admits to herself that most of the best things in their home come secondhand from Zeke's trading cart. Especially precious to her is a camera that Zeke gave her, with which she has practiced taking pictures without film until her eye is trained to view the world around her as a series of subjects to be recorded. She also has a secret reason for knowing Zeke, since she saw him, along with some out-of-town African Americans, enter the white rest room in the drugstore and be mistreated and arrested. After Zeke filed suit against the sheriff and his attackers, she was hiding in the big horse chestnut tree at the edge of Negro Park when six men, including her redneck neighbor Virgil Boggs, drag Zeke from the back of a pickup truck, his hands tied behind him, and strip and beat him viciously, then urinate on his unconscious body, a scene that is a waking nightmare to her and that she has never told anyone. Naively thinking that Zeke's problem is that he is illiterate, she seeks him out and offers to teach him to read, so he can tell the difference between the words "white" and "colored." Although he assures her that he knew which rest room was which, he takes her up on her offer and learns quickly, wanting especially to read the biblical chapter of Ezekiel. Still, she is surprised when he offers her a job because she is a good worker and can keep a secret, the main criterion being to follow the direction, "Don't ask." He directs her to a small house nearly hidden by trees and Spanish moss, where she is to clean and occasionally mail or deliver letters and packages. Her employer, she learns from his stationery, is George Hardy, Ph.D., professor of mathematics, but he is not present while she works. It is a shock to her when she first sees George Hardy and discovers that he is an African American, since whites don't clean for coloreds, but she continues because she likes him, and she knows her family badly needs the money that she earns, with her father out of work. Her own life is complicated not only by poverty. Her mother, Izzy*, bullies her quiet, ineffectual father, greatly favors her beautiful, delicate younger daughter, Gardenia, 7, over Maggie, and lashes out at the older girl with the back of her hand, belts, sticks, even suckers trimmed from their rose bushes, which leave deep scratches across her cheek. Lecherous Virgil Boggs peeps through her bedroom window, tries to corner and rub up against her, and waylays her and attempts to rape her as she delivers the laundry that Izzy takes in for well-to-do whites. Izzy's response to this last outrage is to make her husband build a high fence around their yard, intensifying the antagonism of the Boggs family. Maggie and her adventurous friend, Pert Wilson, hide in the tree at the edge of Negro Park to watch the African-American Independence Day celebration and hear George Hardy speak. When Pert falls out of the tree, they are welcomed by George and others, and Maggie takes pictures of the event, ending with a picure that Pert snaps as George lifts her up to reach a flower on the tree. The prints are swiped from the drugstore by Hazel Boggs, who works there, and the next day they are nailed to the fence, with "Nigger lover" and other rude graffiti painted in red around them. Maggie's father goes berserk, shooting at the fence, and her mother pelts Maggie with her prized collection of jelly glasses. Then they make Maggie paint the entire fence red, while half the white population of Kinship comes by to gape and jeer. Trying to copy the quiet dignity of the African Americans, Maggie tells her mother that she is leaving, moves into the Wilsons' trailer, and gets a job baby-sitting a retarded boy. She just happens to be at the drugstore, with her camera, when a sit-in erupts into a riot, which she records in pictures. After biking to Troy to get them developed, she sells them to *Life* magazine. She finally admits to him that she witnessed Zeke's beating in the park. He asks her to think about testifying, an idea that terrifies her, but later she knows what she has to do. While the events in the novel are compelling, they do not entirely ring true. No one in the African-American community seems to resent or even question Maggie for spying on them. Her ability to take publishable pictures with no real practice is questionable. She is Johnny-on-the-spot for all the major action, mostly by coincidence. Despite the abuse that her mother heaps on her, she never seems to resent her spoiled little sister, who acts more babyish than her age would justify. The social tensions in Kinship, both racial and economic, are the most convincing part of the book. ALA; IRA; SLJ.

SPRINGER, NANCY (1948–   ), born in Montclair, New Jersey; educator, novelist for both adults and children. She is a graduate of Gettysburg College and has made her home in Dallastown, Pennsylvania. In addition to teaching high school in McSherrystown, Pennsylvania, she has been personal development–plan instructor at the University of Pittsburgh at Johnstown and special-programs instructor at York College of Pennsylvania. Besides many fantasy novels, she has written realistic books for young people, including two mysteries that have won the Edgar Allan Poe Award, *Toughing It** (Harcourt, 1994) and *Looking for Jamie Bridger** (Dial, 1995), both well-developed novels concerned with tracing what has happened to brothers.

SPYING ON MISS MULLER (Bunting*, Eve, Clarion, 1995), boarding-school novel with mystery aspects set during World War II in Belfast, Northern Ireland. Four fourth-form girls, all thirteen, share the small Snow White dormitory: the narrator, Jessie Drumm; bookish Ada Sinclair; Maureen Campbell, who thinks mostly about boys and her appearance; and sweet-natured Lizzie* Mag, who is stuck at Alveara school for the duration because her parents are in India. Their dorm mistress is Miss Muller, a half-German whom they have loved and ad-mired for her kind understanding and her beautiful face and figure, but now their patriotic duty seems to require them to be suspicious of her. When Jessie discovers that Miss Muller gets up at night and makes her way through the dark halls to the stairs to the roof, the girls decide to follow her, imagining that she could be signaling to German planes. An air raid on a night that she has left the dorm seems to confirm their suspicions. As the reader expects, they even-tually discover that Miss Muller goes to meet the Latin teacher, Mr. Bolton, their favorite instructor. The girls from Snow White are ashamed of their spying and pledge not to tell about the teachers' tryst. Unfortunately, Jessie has mentioned their suspicions to Greta* Ludowski, a Polish Jew whose parents have been killed by Nazis, and Greta is determined to get revenge on Miss Muller. Although Jessie, fearing that Greta means physical harm, is able to retrieve the razor-sharp nail file that the refugee girl has stolen from her, Greta still destroys Miss Muller by reporting to the headmistress, Miss Rose. Miss Muller is dismissed, and Mr. Bolton resigns and joins the army. Despite its predictability, the plot has impact because of the harm that the girls' spying does, a game that they regret but cannot take back, especially hurtful because Miss Muller is supporting her mother and will not be able to find another job in wartime Ireland. The strength of the novel, however, lies in the details of life in the boarding school: the arcane rules (girls and boys sit separately in class and at meals and are not allowed to speak to each other); the physical discomfort (icy baths, unheated dorms, musty, damp blankets in the air-raid shelter); the terrible food (one girl finds a well-developed chick in her breakfast egg); the nurse's invariable medication (milk of magnesia for the insides, iodine for the outsides); even the toilet paper (so scratchy that the girls refer to it as Last Resort and bring their own from home). All these the girls put up with as a matter of course. What bothers them more is the absolute lack of privacy, since phone calls are permitted only rarely and then in Miss Rose's parlor, with the headmistress sitting a few feet away, and letters and diaries, even when hidden, are routinely found, read, and discussed by the maids. Still, there is a camaraderie among the girls. In one scene they band together to defeat the dictatorial study-hall prefect who tries to read Jessie's note from Ian McManus aloud to shame her. The most memorable occasion is the night of the first real air raid, when boys and girls all troop down to the bomb shelter, and the lights go out, allowing for a thrilling and unprecedented mingling, during which Ian gives Jessie her first kiss. Jessie's own private worry is not about her cousin Bryan, serving in France, since she envies him the excitement until he becomes a prisoner of war. She is much more concerned that someone may find out that her father, whom she loves deeply, is an alcoholic, coming home gentle and cheerful but drunk night after night in their County Derry village of Ballylo. Despite their ignorance of all things sexual compared with thirteen-year-olds today, the characters are real and believable, far better developed than the typical mystery-novel figures for this age group. Poe Nominee.

STARPLACE (Grove*, Vicki, Putnam, 1999), novel of an interracial friendship that opens a girl's eyes to the bigotry of her small Oklahoma town in the early 1960s and to the failures of her own well-meaning, but culture-blinded, parents. Frannie Driscoll, like most of the others at Quiver Junior High, has never questioned that African Americans, called Negroes or colored people at the time, live in Minetown, a dusty suburb of Quiver, and go to Carver Junior High until Celeste Chisholm starts at her previously all-white school. Frannie has already met Celeste's father, a university professor from St. Louis, and has been impressed by his immaculate appearance, his obvious wealth, and his beautiful manners. She is also uneasy knowing that the manager of the real estate office where her mother works has told him that there are no houses for sale in upscale Foxgrape Woods and called him "boy." She is mostly preoccupied, however, by decorating her patio for the back-to-school party on the Hawaiian luau theme that she and her friends are planning. In a perfunctory way she invites Celeste to the party and is relieved when she thanks her but says that she will not be coming. Later, after listening to the mean things that some girls in the rest room are saying about Celeste and suddenly realizing that they know that she is in one of the booths, Frannie feels compelled to repeat the invitation and say that she and her friends really hope Celeste will come. As it happens, the party is a debacle, mostly because of the uproarious behavior of the junior high boys, and Frannie flees to the platform of the space needle left in the center of a nearby field when a playground was dismantled, a place where she sometimes hides out to be by herself. There she finds Celeste and has her first real talk with the girl, and they decide to try out together for a special girls' double trio being organized by Miss Cantwell, the music teacher. Together they go back to the Driscoll patio to clean up, and Celeste meets the other girls, horsey Kelly, bossy Nancy, and pretentious, fake-French-speaking Margot, as well as the three nerds of the class, Theodore C. Rockman, Maximillian, and Jason, all of whom like her. The eight of them become a group, walking with Celeste in the halls and eating with her in the cafeteria. The Chisholms have bought the old Teschler place, known as the haunted house, and Celeste confides to Frannie that it does have a mysterious past and that her father, on sabbatical leave, is writing a book about it and "other things in Quiver." At the vocal tryouts, Celeste, who has a lovely, trained voice, is chosen first soprano and Frannie the soprano alternate of the group, to be called the Ladies of Harmony. The double trio becomes locally popular and is even invited to perform at the Chamber of Commerce banquet at the Foxgrape Country Club. "The irony is exquisite," Theodore observes, and Celeste explains that the country club is restricted and that she will probably be the first colored person to eat there except in the kitchen. Frannie begins to pay attention to the news of Vietnam, read up on the civil rights protests, and even question her parents, who change the subject or tell her to accept the way that things are. One evening, when Celeste's father is out, she takes Frannie to the third floor of the old house they have bought and, without explaining the meaning of it, shows her mysterious rooms with strange markings on the walls and an altarlike table, all hidden until her father found a stairway blocked off and plastered over. The prejudice in the town is brought to a head when the Chamber of Commerce and local businessmen offer to pay the entrance fee and buy the very expensive gowns for the Tulsa competition that the Ladies of Harmony hope to enter, and Miss Cantwell, obviously prompted by the donors, decides that the voices will "blend" better if Celeste is replaced by another girl. A few days later Frannie, Kelly, and Celeste ride Kelly's horses to a cave that Kelly knows and about which Celeste is intensely curious. Deep in the cave they come upon a pair of manacles hanging from the ceiling. Curious, Frannie sticks her hand in one and snaps it shut, realizing too late that she has locked herself up. She panics, but Celeste sensibly tells Kelly to get her father, explain what happened, and ask him if he has found a key to a lock like this. To calm Frannie, Celeste locks her own wrist in the other manacle, and as they wait for rescue, she tells the story of what her father's research has uncovered, the history of Ku Klux Klan lynchings in Quiver in the early days of the century, of the upper rooms of their house where the Klan met, of the death of her own great-grandfather at their hands, probably in this very cave, and of the burning alive of the baby daughter of the brave judge who tried to bring the perpetrators to justice and his hanging, along with his little son. Celeste's father finds the key and releases them, and a few days later he and his daughter go back to St. Louis, where she plans to study vocal music seriously. An Epilogue set in 1986 has Frannie, a reporter for the *St. Louis Post Dispatch*, writing a review of Celeste's stunning performance in *Aida*. A related subplot concerns Frannie's mother, who, energized by gender discrimination, starts her own firm. Although the situation is simplified and the end predictable, Celeste is too mature and dignified to be entirely believable, and it seems unlikely that Frannie would be as naive about racial bigotry as she is, her gradual growth in understanding is interesting and moving. The other characters are mostly flat, just adequate for their roles. SLJ.

STEIG, WILLIAM (1907–   ), born in New York City; humorous artist and writer. His Robinsonnade starring an elegant Edwardian mouse, *Abel's Island** (Farrar, 1976), was chosen by The Children's Literature Association as an honor book for the Phoenix Award, which goes to books published twenty years earlier that are deemed to have lasting literary merit. For earlier biographical information and title entries, see *Dictionary, 1960–1984* [*Dominic*; *The Real Thief*; *Abel's Island*].

STEIN (*The Magic and the Healing**), Jewish man in his sixties, survivor of the Warsaw ghetto during the Holocaust of World War II who built and operates the inn in Crossroads*. The inn is the social center of the valley and runs under strict rules to ensure that everyone is respected and accepted regardless of religion, race, or ethnic origin. After the war he made his way to Crossroads and never left the place. Reading material and whatever else that he feels he needs are brought to him from the outside. At his inn the veterinary students gain most of their information about, and insights into, the inhabitants of Crossroads. He is a friend of Owen* the trader, who turns out to be King Brandal.

STEVENSON, JAMES (1929–   ), born in New York City; writer of almost 100 novels for adults and picture books and novels for children. After graduating from Yale University, he saw service in the U.S. Marine Corps. He has been a reporter for *Life*; cartoonist for the *New Yorker*; and illustrator of his own books and those of other writers. He has received many awards and citations, chiefly for his self-illustrated picture books, among them *"Could Be Worse!"* (Green-willow, 1977), *What's Under My Bed?* (Greenwillow, 1983), and *Oh No, It's Waylon's Birthday!* (Greenwillow, 1989). *The Bones in the Cliff** (Greenwillow, 1995), nominated for the Edgar Allan Poe Award, is a suspense novel for middle readers about a boy and a girl who become involved in a mystery surrounding the boy's father. It has been praised for its fine plotting and for its crisp, de-scriptive, and sharply visual style. Its sequel is *The Unprotected Witness* (Green-willow, 1997). Other recent publications include *The Mud Flat April Fool* (Greenwillow, 1998) in the Mud Flat Series, *Sam The Zamboni Man* (Green-willow, 1998), and *Popcorn: Poems* (Greenwillow, 1998).

STOLZ, MARY (SLATTERY) (1920–   ), born in Boston, Massachusetts; res-ident of Florida; highly honored writer of sixty books for a broad age range and in several literary forms. *Cezanne Pinto: A Memoir** (Knopf, 1994), selected by both the American Library Association and *School Library Journal*, is a sub-stantial historical novel for teen readers about a young slave's flight to freedom in Canada, his service in the American Civil War, and his life as a cowboy thereafter. Among other awards, Stolz received the Kerlan Award for excellence in children's literature and the George G. Stone Center Award for the total body of her work. For additional biographical information, titles, and title entries, see *Dictionary, 1859–1959* [*Because of Madeline*; *In a Mirror*; *To Tell Your Love*]; *Dictionary, 1960–1984* [*Belling the Tiger*; *The Bully of Barkham Street*; *A Won-derful, Terrible Time*; *Cat in the Mirror*; *A Dog on Barkham Street*; *The Edge of Next Year*; *The Noonday Friends*]; and *Dictionary, 1985–1990* [*Quentin Corn*].

STONES IN THE WATER (Napoli*, Donna Jo, Dutton, 1997), historical novel of World War II with boy's growing-up and survival-story aspects. Except that food and supplies are growing scarce and his older brother, Sergio, a schoolboy, has to train with the local unit, events of the war raging in Europe have little impact on fun-loving Roberto, about thirteen, the son of a gondolier in Venice, Italy. One afternoon as Roberto, Sergio, and their pals Memo and Samuele are sitting in a theater about to view an American western movie, German soldiers unexpectedly enter, round up all the boys, march them out of town, and herd them onto trains, destination unknown. When three boys protest, they are sum-marily shot to death. When the Germans divide the boys into several groups in order to separate them from their friends, Samuele manages to stay with Roberto. Grateful for Samuele's company, Roberto also recognizes that being with Sa-muele may be dangerous, since Samuele is Jewish. They decide that Samuele will call himself by the Italian name of Enzo*, and Roberto gives him his St. Christopher medal to wear around his neck. At Munich, the boys are put to work digging in fields with pickaxes, then building a tarmac runway for planes. There follow weeks of extremely hard labor, short rations of bread, sausage (a problem for Enzo because of dietary laws), cheese, and potatoes, and brutality, since the soldiers often beat the boys with gun butts. Both boys are homesick, always hungry, and, inadequately clothed, often cold with the oncoming winter. To help his friend get to sleep at night on their hard, earth beds, Enzo tells Roberto stories, some of them biblical, others original. Roberto is horrified when it turns out that a pen that they have been forced to construct contains Jewish prisoners. He soon detects that these people are much worse off than are the boys and are also frequently brutalized or tormented. Roberto passes food to two starving girls, one a baby, sometimes in broad sight of the soldiers, who either ignore his behavior or overlook it. In gratitude, the older girl gives Roberto a round stone with one flat side, which he carries henceforth. Conditions worsen after the boys are taken to Ukraine to build an airstrip. Some boys freeze to death, and others die of respiratory infections in the extreme cold. The remaining boys always take the dead boys' clothes and blankets and often steal food from one another. After Enzo dies, Roberto runs away, heading south toward the Black Sea, following streams, foraging for food, always afraid and on the lookout. He arrives at a strangely deserted town, where a little boy of seven or eight, a single survivor, gives him food. The two leave, dragging a sled with a few meager supplies, but part later outside another town. Roberto's solitary journey continues by boat to the Black Sea, where he falls in with a tense and nervous soldier who calls himself Maurizio*. Roberto identifies the man as Roman but conceals his own identity at first. The soldier shares his food with the boy and tends him when he falls ill of a fever. After they survive several tense encounters, Roberto realizes that the soldier is a deserter. They decide to make their way back to Italy and join the *partigiani* (partisans) against the Axis. They carry with them stones as tokens of the building that they intend to do (a rather obvious symbol). The plot proceeds much as expected, and, by the end, Roberto has become a sturdy, sober, and enduring young man, far from the lighthearted, almost silly early adolescent who he was. Although Enzo is credible as a character, Maurizio seems too convenient a deus ex machina. The German soliders are presented as cruel but not entirely without feelings for their captives. The horror of the boys' kidnapping, however, and the servitude that they suffer dominate the book—the novel's most telling features. The story is based on known facts about Italian boys whom the Germans enslaved. ALA.

STONE WATER (Gilbert*, Barbara Snow, Front Street, 1996), realistic boy's growing-up and personal and sociological problem novel set for about a year in Oklahoma City at the time of publication. Sturdy, steady Grant Hughes, 14, is the only child of Allison Taylor Hughes, a respected judge, and William* Henry Hughes, a highly successful lawyer. Grant has been very close to his Grandpa Hughes, a rancher, since William is heavily engrossed in his work. When Grandpa has a stroke and is moved to the "Other Wing" of the nursing home, Grant recalls that Grandpa left an envelope with him two years earlier with instructions to open it if he entered the "Other Wing." Inside, Grant finds an audiotape and a letter in which his Grandpa tells him that the tape contains a story from Grant's great-great-grandfather and that if Grant understands the story, he will know what he is to do. Grant finds that the tape tells of an Indian youth who gives an ill old chief a drink that he has made from poisoned berries in a bowl at the center of which lies a small stone. Grant is confident that Grandpa does not want to linger or be kept alive artificially. Grandpa lies almost comatose for many months. Grant visits him faithfully, helping to feed, change, and generally care for the old man, whose increasingly wizened body he sees as a stark contrast to the vigorous outdoorsman of his happy memories. With the help of his father's law secretary, Grant investigates the penalties for assisted suicide and premeditated murder in Oklahoma. On the surface, his life goes on as before. He remains an almost straight-A student and performs well with the swim team. Grant has good times with his neighborhood chum, clownish Avery, and becomes interested in Avery's pretty cousin, Randi. These ordinary, every-day events point up the dilemma that he must confront not long after his fifteenth birthday in April. Grandpa worsens but lingers; exactly what the old man feared appears to be happening. Grant agonizes about what to do. He even goes into a church and discusses the matter anonymously with a priest. He knows that he and Grandpa have always been partners and that partners always help each other out. His decision made, he steals his father's bottle of sleeping capsules and places the contents in a small film can, which he puts in his backpack along with a trail cup that had come down in the family. His first attempt to give the drink with dissolved pills to the old man fails when the glass slips and breaks. Wrapping his grandfather's fingers around a small stone, Grant then tries with the trail cup, which Grandpa holds and drinks from by himself. Continuing to emulate the Indian youth of the taped story, Grant climbs into bed by the old man, holds him close, and strokes him as he falls asleep. After the funeral, Grant accompanies the body to Oregon, where it will be buried beside his grand-mother's. His parents both too busy to take time off, Grant has asked the funeral home people to place the stone in Grandpa's hand, where it will keep the old man company forever. The book's central problem strains belief. Since Grandpa, although hard-bitten, seems to have been a highly moral man, it is hard to believe that he would place such a burden upon the grandson whom he so dearly loved. The mother's resentment toward her husband for leaving the decisions about his father up to her and not visiting regularly is credible, but the father is too obviously the stereotypical ambitious, selfish, corporation lawyer. The one saving grace to his characterization is that Grandpa, too, had been preoccupied with his work and thus was not a good role model. The dilemma revolving around assisted suicide to end a loved one's suffering is simplistically, but mem-orably, dramatized, and Grant is an admirable young man. SLJ.

STRANGER AT THE WEDDING (Hambly*, Barbara, Ballantine, 1994), fan-tasy novel of wizards and magic set in the land of Angelshand in the Kingdom of Ferryth at a time when society and economics resemble those of England at the turn of the eighteenth century. When plain, sharp-tongued Kyra Peldyrin,

24, a wizard in training at the Citadel of Wizards, called Kyra the Red for her luxuriant, tawny hair, observes the water in her divining bowl turn to blood, she realizes that her beautiful sister, Alix*, 18, is doomed to die on her wedding night. Alix is soon to marry Blore Spenson*, the new president of the Guild of Merchant Adventurers and one of the wealthiest men in Angelshand. Forbidden by witches' law from meddling in human concerns, Kyra nevertheless causes the Bishop to break his ankle, the church to be infested with mice, and, after the wedding has been rescheduled, the church to be flooded by water from burst pipes in the building next door. Although at first she scorns Spenson as gawky and too old in his mid-thirties for her sister, she gradually comes to appreciate him for his finer qualities of gentleness and clear-headedness, and the two grow fond of each other. When it becomes obvious that Spenson and Alix's wedding is off, Kyra and Spenson unite to discover who intends Alix's death. Then Alix and the handsome pastry maker and lovelorn poet Algeron Brackett, who have been madly in love all along, elope, and it is imperative that Kyra and Spenson find them before Alix dies. Several complications later, Kyra discovers that a spell has been placed inside Alix's wedding dress for reasons of revenge by the laundry maid, Gyvinna, the widow of Tibbeth, the dog wizard (an uninstructed, uninitiated wizard) who had been Kyra's early teacher and who was burned at the stake for misbehavior at the instigation of Kyra's father. In an action-filled sequence of events involving pursuit by, among others, the Inquisition, whose task is to ferret out witches and wizards for the church, Kyra and Spenson track the lovers down and fend off the evil forces that would destroy them. Because Kyra is mageborn and hence cannot marry and because she values her profession of wizard, she and Spenson decide not to wed, and she returns to the Citadel to complete her training. Primarily gothic in structure, tone, and narrative conventions, the book presents through a wealth of detail a convincing picture of life and thought inside the Citadel and especially in the teeming, bustling city streets and among the pretentious, social-climbing, moneyed class. The plot is sometimes overwhelmed by detail of setting and inhibited by overly long, complex sentences, and some features seem forced: Kyra is altogether too clumsy and must be too frequently rescued from falls by Spenson. Characters are distinctively drawn, if anticipatory, and Kyra's occasional visions and flashbacks are satisfactorily introduced. Figurative language, touches of humor, and gentle caricature add to the pleasure, and, while the book belongs to the formula-romance genre, it has more substance than most of its counterparts. Kyra's deep love for her sister, the ethical problem that results from her decision to meddle in human affairs, and her romance with Spenson, if clumsily resolved, are good aspects. ALA; SLJ.

SUGAR DOBBS (*The Magic and the Healing**), veterinary medicine instructor of BJ* Vaughan at Western Virginia College of Veterinary Medicine. He is the means by which BJ becomes involved in healing the creatures in the mythical world of Crossroads*. Since he is a handsome man in his mid-thirties and is careful not to compromise himself with female students, BJ is surprised when he asks her to enter his office and shut the door. He then shows her the broken unicorn horn, which precipitates the expedition that she and three other students make to Crossroads. Sugar has been going to Crossroads for some time and is trusted there for his expertise. He has also grown interested in finding out why certain human diseases like cancer do not occur there. He is instrumental in arranging for BJ to embark on her career as a veterinarian in the remote valley. Sugar serves as the catalyst by which the best characteristics in each of the students are brought out and their lives changed for the better. Once a rodeo rider, he occasionally projects an air of brashness.

SUGAR HIDDLE (*Walk Two Moons**), Chanhassen Hiddle, Sal's mother. Her name is Native American and means maple sugar. It was given to her by her grandmother in honor of her Indian ancestors. Sugar feels inferior to Sal's father, for some reason, and loves the out-of-doors, where she spends a lot of time. She often kisses trees, a behavior that Sal remembers with particular fondness. Sugar and Sal's father had wanted a houseful of children, but after Sal's mother loses the baby and discovers that she can have no more children, she runs away to a cousin in Idaho, on the way dying in a bus crash. Only when Sal sees her mother's grave does the girl really accept the fact that her mother is never coming home.

SUN & SPOON (Henkes*, Kevin, Greenwillow, 1997), realistic novel of family life, set in recent years in a middle-class neighborhood in Madison, Wisconsin. Joanie* Gilmore, 6, and her big brother, Charlie, 12, seem to have adjusted well to the death of their paternal grandmother, Gram, but Spoon (Frederick), 10, called Spoon from a baby spoon that his mother found while she was pregnant with him, has trouble coming to terms with Gram's absence. Among other matters, he misses the games of triple solitaire that he, Gram, and Pa* (grandfather) frequently played together. Spoon also yearns to have something of Gram's so that he will not forget her, something special but not a photograph. One Saturday, partly to avoid having to help his parents weed the garden, he walks, Joanie tagging along, over to Pa's house. When he sees Pa cleaning the garage, Spoon hopes to find among the discards the exact special something that he wishes. Finding nothing, he pokes around inside Pa's house. He thinks maybe one of the many representations of the sun in all shapes, sizes, and materials, which Gram collected and tacked up all over the house, will do. Then he remembers the deck of cards with which Gram always played, the one with suns on the backs of the cards. He slips the deck out of the breakfront, hides the cards in his pocket, and takes them home. He feels good about the cards; they bring Gram close again. Then Spoon learns that Pa has been consoling himself on the nights that he cannot sleep by playing solitaire with Gram's sun cards. When Pa says that, although he has hunted all over the house, he cannot find them, Spoon feels guilty and later surreptitiously returns them. When Pa turns up for breakfast the next day and says that he found the playing cards, Spoon confesses, explains why he took the cards, and tells Pa that he misses their card games. The next time that Spoon visits Pa, Pa gives him a photograph of Gram when she was ten and a tracing of her hand that she made at the same age. The tracing clearly shows an M on the palm. Underneath the tracing, Gram had lettered "M is for Martha." When Spoon notices Ms on his parents' palms and also on Joanie's, he takes them as a sign: M is always for Martha, his Gram. He has the special something he needs. A couple of days later, Pa drops by with the playing cards for Spoon. He says he is pleased that Spoon wanted them so much and wishes Spoon to have them. Spoon refuses and says that he has the photograph and the tracing, and they are all that he needs. Pa says he loves Spoon very much and suggests that they resume their games of solitaire. Spoon is satisfied; he has both his Gram and his Pa back again, each in a different, but special, way. The story is simple: a boy learns to handle his grief. Subsurface meanings, however, give the book a complexity not immediately evident: coming to terms with death, confronting guilt, and working out delicate interpersonal relationships within the family and between generations. Spoon's emotions are gently handled, without condescension, trivializing, and melodrama, and his differences with, and adjustments to, tagalong Joanie actualize the home environment well. Scenes are created with visual detail, for example, Gram's suns "hung all around, orbiting the tables like colorful planets in some fantastic solar system." Best is the close, warm relationship that exists between the boy and Pa. ALA; SLJ.

A SUNBURNED PRAYER (Talbert*, Marc, Simon & Schuster, 1995), realistic boy's growing-up novel with animal-story aspects set mostly one recent Good Friday near and in the mountain village of Chimayo, New Mexico, not far from Santa Fe. Hispanic-American Eloy, 11, is determined to emulate the feat of his *abuelo* (grandfather) years earlier and join the Good Friday pilgrimage of seventeen miles from his village of Pedernal to Chimayo. He wishes to get dirt from the Santuario (church) to heal the terminal cancer of his *abuela* (grandmother). His mother has to work that day, and his cynical father disparages pilgrimages and prayer. They forbid him to go, unless someone in the family accompanies him. His older brother, Benito*, whom Eloy regards as tough, silent, hard, and interested only in girls and cars, is unwilling to oblige, and his *abuela* tells him to obey his parents and stay home. Determined to make the journey, Eloy fills his deceased grandfather's canteens with water, packs a little lunch of salami and cheese tortillas, and leaves Pedernal early in the morning before his parents are up and can object. He cuts across the foothills of the Jemez Mountains to the highway, where he joins the procession of pilgrims. While he is still in the hills, he notices that he is being followed by a medium-sized, grayish, spotted female dog just beyond the puppy stage. Eloy dislikes dogs intensely, because once he saw older dogs tear apart and chew up a puppy. As the journey proceeds, however, he warms to the spirited, loyal, companionable creature and names her Magdalena. One of the book's strengths is its fidelity to Eloy's point of view. He questions the nature of God, bargains with God, even threatens God. He worries about the propriety of thinking "dirty" thoughts and of using curse words. When he remembers that *abuela* says they must fast on Good Friday, he forgoes his lunch. Remembering that she prays often, he says his rosary, not well, he knows, but avidly. He associates the acute tension that has developed between his parents with his grandmother's failing health and decides that his pilgrimage is also for them and Benito, to restore their previous warm family life. When he realizes that he has grown fond of Magdalena, he thinks that the price of his grandmother's healing may be that he must relinquish the animal, since she dislikes pets. As the day wears on, he becomes hungry, hot, thirsty, and footsore and tears off his shirt to cool his overheated body. He shares his small supply of water with the dog and also with an aged Indio (Indian). At one point, an old, low-slung car pulls up, which he identifies as Benito's. Although he is extremely tired, he contemptuously gives the car the finger, and it pulls away. When he finally arrives at Chimayo, his village priest, Father Ribera, spots him and ushers him inside the Santuario. There to his surprise he finds Benito and *abuela*. Along with his grandmother, he prayerfully eats a few pinches of the holy soil. His grandmother compliments him on his perseverance, emphasizing how what he has done cannot change things—she will die soon—but makes it easier for her to die, since she knows that he is becoming a good man. She also tells him that he can keep the dog. At home again, his back uncomfortable from sunburn, Eloy thinks of himself as a prayer walking on two legs, a sunburned prayer. The sense of time on the journey is vague, an element that supports the boy's increasing weariness and disorientation and also his intense determination to finish. The sense of Hispanic-American working-class life is vivid, as are the strong Catholicism and close family connections. The third-person viewpoint is strictly focused and projects the impression of first person, giving the narrative intensity. The occasional humor and poignancy set the essential seriousness in relief. The style is effectively economical, almost minimalist. This is a moving account of a boy's gaining new insights into life and of his efforts to act upon and define his faith through his relationships to those whom he loves the most. A glossary gives definitions of the numerous Spanish words and phrases. SLJ.

SUNNY RICO (*Finder**), female cop who recruits Orient to help find the killer of Bonny Prince Charlie, a minor thug whom she suspects of being a distributor of a new, gene-altering drug reputed to change humans to elves and actually produces in its users some elflike characteristics, although it has proved fatal before any have changed completely. Sunny's hope is that Orient can lead her to the mastermind behind the drug, and she uses her knowledge of his past in the World to blackmail him into working with her. He retaliates by pressing her to reveal her past. Reluctantly, she finally lets him know that, as an adolescent, she learned that the father whom she had idealized and admired tremendously because he was a policeman was actually a bad cop, on the take. In reaction she fled to Bordertown, where, after doing various other things, she joined the police, determined to prove herself incorruptible. Although much more loosely organized than police forces in the World, the profession has suited her, and she has become a good cop, trusted and well liked by her elf partner, Detective Linn. When she realizes that the head of the drug ring must be on the police force, her past makes her even more shocked and desperate to uncover the truth. She and Orient indulge in a single night of sex, but, although he is very attracted to her, she puts him off, insisting that they stay apart for six weeks and then talk it over at dinner. An eventual relationship between the two is a possibility.

SWEENEY, JOYCE (1955–), born in Dayton, Ohio; freelance book critic and novelist. She received her B.A. degree from Wright State University and did graduate study in creative writing at Ohio University. She has written numerous novels for young adults, mostly realistic stories dealing with family relationships, including *The Dream Collector* (Delacorte, 1989), *Piano Man* (Delacorte, 1992), *Free Fall* (Delacorte, 1996), and *The Spirit Window* (Delacorte, 1998). Her *Shadow** (Delacorte, 1994) also concerns family relationships, a bitter rivalry between two brothers, with disaster averted by the spirit of their sister's recently deceased cat. Sweeney lives in Coral Springs, Florida.

SYKES, SHELLEY (1955–), newspaper correspondent and columnist. Her first novel, *For Mike** (Delacorte, 1998), which was a nominee for the Edgar Allan Poe Award, is a haunting mystery with paranormal elements, concerned with the disappearance of a high school boy's best friend and the clues that he gets in dreams that lead to an explanation. Sykes lives in Arendtsville, Pennsylvania, in orchard country.

T

TALBERT, MARC (1953–), born in Boulder, Colorado; resident of Santa Fe, New Mexico; writer of more than a dozen books of children's fiction and nonfiction. After receiving his degree from Iowa State University, he taught in elementary schools in Iowa, then was a columnist for papers in Iowa, a writer and editor for the Los Alamos National Laboratory, a speechwriter for the National Science Foundation, and instructor in children's literature at the University of New Mexico. *A Sunburned Prayer** (Simon & Schuster, 1995) is a poignant, occasionally funny boy's growing-up novel set one recent Good Friday in New Mexico of a Hispanic-American boy's pilgrimage to heal his grandmother's cancer. It was cited by *School Library Journal*. He has also published *The Trap* (DK, 1999), about a girl's attempt to trap a coyote that goes awry; *Star of Luis* (Clarion, 1999), about a Mexican-American boy's discovery of his Jewish heritage; and *Small Change* (DK, 2000), about terrorists in a Mexican town.

TALIA (*Escape from Egypt**), pretty, gentle, warmhearted, young Hebrew woman of fifteen or sixteen, who, the concerned families understand, is to become the bride of Jesse*. She seeks earnestly to please him, waiting on him and looking after his needs as best she can and still remain modest. Jesse thinks highly of her and occasionally embraces and kisses her, but when he pays attention to her, he also often thinks of Jennat*, the half-Egyptian, half-Syrian girl whom he had met in his Egyptian master's house. Although not formally betrothed, Jesse and Talia sometimes talk about getting married and about where they might live when the Hebrews arrive in Canaan. Talia and Jennat have an argument over Jesse, and Jennat leaves the group, later to return with information about a potential attack from a hostile tribe, the Moabites. Eventually, things so fall out that Jesse marries Jennat, and Talia marries someone else in the tribe. She is a sad, forlorn figure.

TAM (*The Moorchild**), orphan living on the moor with old Bruman, the drunken tinker who suffers from a game leg and lets the boy do most of the work and care of his goats. With the old dog, Warrior, a pony, and a two-wheeled cart, they travel to King's Town for the winter, stopping at villages and towns on the way to do a bit of tinkering or leather work, skills at which Tam has become almost as good as Bruman. He is also a juggler and can play a shepherd's pipe well enough to pick up the elvish tunes that Saaski plays on the bagpipes, so they often entertain the goats with duets on the moors. Open and frank, Tam is totally without prejudice, even though he suspects that Saaski may be Moorfolk. He is also protective and determined. When he realizes that Saaski plans to enter the Mound to try to steal Anwara's baby back, he insists on going with her, although he fears the place. At first dazzled by the illusionary riches and sumptuous food there, after Saaski touches one eyelid with ointment he sees from that eye as the Moorfolk see the shabby reality. Before they leave, he spots Bruman, who has craftily followed them into the Mound, "eatin' and drinkin' with both hands" and laughing with delight. Although Tam realizes that Bruman is under an enchantment and will be thrown out when the Folk tire of him, he still feels a bit wistful at the sight of the lavish food and rich beauty that he can see with his left eye. Still, he starts off cheerfully with Saaski, now owning the cart and the animals but responsibly figuring to return in a year and a day to see whether Bruman reappears. Saaski realizes that Tam is an outsider, just as she is, and that he likes it that way.

TAMAR (*Cezanne Pinto: A Memoir**), slave cook of forty who runs away from the Gloriana plantation in Virginia with the slave stable boy, Deucy. Very tall, muscular, imperious, Tamar learned to read and write when she served as nursemaid to the children of a widowed woman in Maryland. Tamar knows the Bible almost by heart and speaks a finer English than her new masters, Mr. and Mrs. Clayburn, do. She teaches the Clayburn slaves when she can, and of them all Deucy is her favorite. Tamar guides their flight to freedom, using the map that she copied from Harriet Tubman, via the Underground Railroad to Philadelphia, Pittsburgh, and then Canada. In Canada, she becomes the cook for neighbors of the Ramseys, and when she learns that Mrs. Ramsey has been teaching Deucy, then known as Cezanne Pinto, she is a little jealous. Her ambition is to attend college and become a teacher, and eventually she does, attending Illinois State and teaching in Chicago. Cezanne never loses track of her and always honors her for the help that she gave him in learning to read and speak proper English and for inspiring him to a better life.

TANGERINE (Bloor*, Edward, Harcourt, 1997), sports novel in the form of journal entries, concentrating on high school football and middle school soccer, but with focus more seriously on family relationships and a strong element of mystery. Although he is legally blind, seventh grader Paul Fisher can't remember the accident when he was about five that impaired his eyesight. According to his brother, Erik*, seventeen or eighteen, he looked too long directly at a solar eclipse, a story that Paul has begun to think implausible. He has always feared Erik and resents what he ironically refers to as the Erik Fisher Football Dream, which consumes his brother and, even more, their father. When the family moves from Texas to central Florida, they immediately start to implement the Dream at Erik's new school, Lake Windsor High in their Tangerine County development, Lake* Windsor Downs. A skilled field-goal kicker, Erik soon is one of the stars of the team and plans to replace decent Mike Costello as his holder with his new sidekick, scummy Arthur Bauer. Shortly afterward, lightning, which strikes more often in the county than anywhere else in the country, hits and kills Mike during practice. Paul, who now also fears Arthur, is horrified at the way that he and Erik joke about Mike's death. Paul, who actually sees quite well with his thick glasses and sports goggles, is a great soccer goalie, a skill that his father has never noticed. He tries out for the middle school team and seems assured of a place until the school authorities insist that he be dropped, since a visually impaired player will not be covered by the school's insurance. Before his depression at this development sets in too deeply, a sinkhole, caused by unusually heavy rains, opens in the middle school grounds, splintering the board sidewalks, swallowing a couple of portable classrooms, and damaging the others. Most of the middle school kids are put on two shifts, but Paul seizes the opportunity to be transferred to tough Tangerine Middle School, where his mother has not told anyone in charge that he is handicapped, and he can be accepted on its first-class soccer team, made up of both boys and girls. Although he takes some jibes at his heavy glasses and generally nerdy appearance, he sticks it out and soon has some friends, in particular, the twins Teresa and Tino Cruz and, eventually, even Victor, the undisputed leader of the team. In advanced science class, Paul joins Teresa and Tino in a project to research local tangerine production, which has been greatly reduced by cold weather, focusing on the Golden Dawn tangerine, a new variety highly resistant to cold developed by their older brother, Luis*. Paul visits the Cruz nursery a couple of times, welcomed by Luis, but when the science group comes to his house to design the report on his father's computer, Erik insults and then attacks Tino. The next day Paul sees Luis confront Erik, and, from his position beneath the bleachers, he sees Erik motion to Arthur, who slugs Luis on the side of his head with a blackjack. A few days later, when a sudden cold snap hits, Paul and a teammate, Henry D., go to the Cruz groves and spend a long, arduous night helping spray and smudge the orchard, an effort that saves most of the older trees and all of the little Golden Dawn tangerine treelets. Paul takes the opportunity to tell Luis that he saw Arthur hit him with the blackjack, and Luis lets him know that he and friends plan to retaliate, but before they do, Luis is found dead in the orchard, evidently the victim of an aneurysm caused by the blackjack blow, though the authorities assume that he was hit by a falling branch. His friends and family know, however, and Tino and Victor show up at the senior awards ceremony and attack Erik and Arthur. The coach grabs Tino, but Paul leaps from the stands onto his back, freeing Tino, and then escapes and runs for home. He is waylaid by Arthur and Erik, and for the first time Paul stands up to his brother. As they drive away with threats of future retaliation, Paul finally remembers the incident when he was a young child and Erik, seething from some imagined affront, held him and got his sidekick to spray paint in Paul's eyes. At a neighborhood meeting the next day, Paul's mother announces that she has discovered that the recent thefts from "tented houses," those covered by exterminators' tents and pumped full of noxious gas to kill termites, were perpetrated by Arthur in a gas mask, with Erik acting as lookout. Mr.* Fisher and Mr. Bauer propose to make good all the losses if the neighbors agree not to press charges. As the meeting breaks up, Arthur is arrested in connection with the death of Luis Cruz, and as Mr. Bauer protests that it was self-defense, Paul finally speaks up and admits that he saw the incident and that Erik and Arthur were at fault. Paul is expelled from the county school system for the remainder of the year for attacking a teacher and has to go to a private school that he despises, but he is determined to return the next year to Tangerine, where he now has real friends and an assured place on the soccer team. Much of the conflict in the novel is motivated by the class differences between the residents of Lake Windsor, a new, expensive development, and the Tangerine County locals, mostly Hispanics. The descriptions of sports, both practices and games, are detailed and compelling, with no real attempt to sound like the journal entries of a twelve-year-old, the form being used mostly to establish time progression. Fanfare; Poe Nominee.

TARO NAKAJI (*Under the Blood-Red Sun**), hardworking Japanese-American father of Tomi and Kimi and husband of Mama*. A fisherman, he is a proud, law-abiding family man. His racing pigeons are his sole recreation, and Tomi is especially saddened and angered because the soldiers force him and Grampa* to kill the racers, which have been reported to the authorities, viciously and erroneously, by Keet Wilson as messengers. Although Tomi would like to fight Keet for his many bullying acts, Taro insists that such behavior would disgrace the family and that everyone would think that they were troublemakers. Taro is shot in the leg by American planes, imprisoned on Sand Island in Pearl Harbor, and then sent to a prison camp for Japanese Americans in Texas.

TAYLOR, MILDRED D., born in Jackson, Mississippi; teacher and author of many highly acclaimed and honored books for children and young adults, most noted for her stories about the Logans, the African-American family during the Great Depression that she first told of in her Newbery Award-winning novel *Roll of Thunder, Hear My Cry* (Dial, 1976). *The Well: David's Story** (Dial, 1995) continues the series, centering on a troubled summer in the lives of David (who grows up to become Papa in *Roll of Thunder*) and David's brother, hotheaded Hammer. This short novel received the Jane Addams Award and was cited by the American Library Association. For more information about Taylor, titles, and title entries, see *Dictionary, 1960–1984* [*Roll of Thunder, Hear My*

Cry]; *Dictionary, 1985–1989* [*The Gold Cadillac*; *The Friendship*]; and *Dictionary, 1990–1994* [*Let the Circle Be Unbroken*; *Mississippi Bridge*; *The Road to Memphis*].

TAYLOR, THEODORE (1921? 1924?–   ), born in Statesville, North Carolina; journalist, film producer, and writer. Taylor adds to his list of highly praised books for young people *The Bomb** (Harbrace, 1996), a historical novel about the testing of the atomic bomb on Bikini Atoll of the Marshall Islands in 1946 and the events leading up to this disaster. For earlier biographical information and title entries, see *Dictionary, 1960–1984* [*The Cay*; *The Odyssey of Ben O'Neal*; *Teetoncey*; *Teetoncey and Ben O'Neal*] and *Dictionary, 1990–1994* [*Sniper*; *The Weirdo*].

TEACHER (*Jip His Story**), college-educated woman who takes over the one-room school for its three-month term. A woman of unusual understanding and sensitivity, she sees that Jip is a boy with potential, and she goes out of her way to gain his interest, choosing *Oliver Twist* to read aloud to the children and to ensure his continued attendance by calling at the poor farm. At the end of the novel it is revealed that she is Lyddie Worthen of *Lyddie* (*Dictionary 1990–1994*), now graduated from Oberlin College and returned to the Vermont community where she grew up. Readers who know the earlier book will realize that the cabin where Jip hides is the one that belonged to her family and that the friend whom she mentions and to whom Jip flees in Canada, Ezekial Freeman, is the runaway slave whom she aided when she was a girl. When Jip is in jail, she proposes that she will swear in court that he is her child, the result of an indiscretion when she was a mill girl in Lowell. Her friend, Luke Stevens, is the son of the Quaker neighbor who bought her family's cabin. Having loved her since she was young, he volunteers to claim to be Jip's father, to keep the white slave master from claiming the boy and to save her from the worst of the scandal. Since Jip escapes and reaches Canada on his own, this proves unnecessary, but the last italicized page reveals that the two married anyway and are parents.

TED HARPER (*Wish You Were Here**), stepfather to Jackson Watts, father of Kristin* and Amy. A solid, thoroughly nice man, he realizes that in some ways Ellen is still in love with Jackson's father, Oz, but he nevertheless wants to marry her and take care of her unconditionally. His main concern is that his little girls become happy with the new arrangement, and he is grateful to Jackson for breaking through Kristin's reserve and making friends with her. When Jackson is arrested for drunken driving, Ted is understanding, and when Jackson calls to tell him of his spur-of-the-moment trip with Brady, he warns the boy to be careful and gives him permission to get money on his charge card. Although almost too good to be true, Ted's determination to have a happy life with Ellen is explained party by his confession to Jackson that his artistic first wife made him feel like a worthless nerd, a real loser despite his business success.

TEMPLE, FRANCES (NOLTING) (1945–1995), born in Washington, D.C.; elementary teacher, Peace Corps volunteer in Africa, VISTA volunteer in Virginia, writer of methods articles and books, some with her husband, Charles Temple, a professor of education, and acclaimed author of novels for middle graders and teenagers. *The Ramsay Scallop** (Orchard, 1994), a period novel set in the Middle Ages of the pilgrimage of two young English nobles to France and Spain, was chosen by the American Library Association and *School Library Journal*. Her last book, *The Bedouin's Castle* (Orchard, 1996), another historical novel, is set in North Africa. For additional information, titles, and title entries, see *Dictionary, 1990–1994* [*Taste of Salt*; *Grab Hands and Run*].

THEODOOR VAN GOGH (*Johanna: A Novel of the van Gogh Family**), Theo, historical younger brother of the renowned Dutch artist Vincent* van Gogh and husband of Johanna van Gogh-Bonger, the title figure. Theo is a respected art critic and manager of a gallery in Paris when he and Johanna are married. For years, Vincent has made claims upon Theo's time, energy, emotions, and resources, taking the money, for example, that Theo provides him as his due. Theo is devoted to the Impressionists and insists on displaying them in the mezzanine at his gallery, in spite of his employers' skepticism and retains all his brother's paintings, which, because of Johanna's hard work, become recognized after Vincent's and Theo's deaths. After Vincent dies, having shot himself in the abdomen, Theo becomes unbalanced and eventually dies in an asylum. Johanna honors Theo's wishes that his brother's paintings be retained and displayed. In the novel, many of Johanna's diary entries are addressed to Theo, whom she had loved dearly. These entries not only reveal their romantic relationship but also convey information about the customs and ethic and artistic culture of the late nineteenth century in the Netherlands and France, in particular, attitudes toward the Impressionists and the Symbolists.

THESMAN, JEAN, author of both mass-market series novels and more highly commended young adult novels. Her *The Ornament Tree** (Houghton, 1996) is a historical novel and girl's growing-up story set in Seattle in 1918, giving a strong picture of the place and period. It was awarded the Jefferson Cup for Historical Fiction. For earlier biographical information and title entries, see *Dictionary, 1990–1994* [*Rachel Chance*; *The Rain Catchers*; *When the Road Ends*].

THE THIEF (Turner*, Megan Whalen, Greenwillow, 1996), engrossing adventure-mystery and fantasy novel set for a few weeks in Sounis, a mythical land much like ancient Greece, and in adjacent kingdoms. Gen, perhaps eighteen or twenty, is in a Sounis prison because he bet a man that he could steal the king's seal ring, steals it, and then displays it as proof of his prowess the next day in a wine shop. After Gen has spent enough time in his miserable cell to stink from the filth and suffer from malnutrition and the sores caused by his shackles, the king's scholar, known as the magus*, has Gen mysteriously brought to the palace. The magus proposes that Gen accompany him on a journey, during which Gen can verify his boast that he can steal anything. The little party includes a soldier named Pol* and two young apprentices to Pol whom Gen thinks of together as the Uselessnesses, Ambiades* and Sophos*. Throughout most of the trip, Gen is disagreeable, filches food, and needles the magus as much as he thinks he can get away with. The little group travels on horseback over the mountains into the country of Eddis, which lies to the north, and eventually into Attolia. Along the way, Gen learns that the magus wishes him to demonstrate the validity of his boast by securing the ancient Hamiathes' Gift, a fabled stone dipped in the water of immortality, which entitles the holder to the throne of Eddis. The magus intends to present it to Sounis, King of Sounis, who will then use it to prove that he is the rightful King of Eddis and can marry the current queen. Gen sees immediately that what the king really wants is control of the pass into neighboring Attolia. Gen also learns about his traveling companions: Ambiades is the grandson of a duke; Sophos is the son of a duke; and Pol is a brave soldier sent along to watch over Sophos and teach him swordplay. The journey through mountainous Eddis into Attolia is difficult and hard on everyone (and the slowest part of the book), but once they have arrived, the pace accelerates as Gen acts on the instructions that the magus gives him for acquiring the Gift. The fabled stone lies somewhere inside a temple maze of rock, which can be entered only when the river by which it stands is low. Once inside, Gen has only six hours to find the stone and get out with it before the river rises. In highly suspenseful episodes, Gen enters two times without success, with great physical difficulty and growing panic as the hours pass. The third time, he discovers a hidden room filled with statues of gods, receives help from Eugenides, his namesake god, and returns with the unpretentious gray stone to the entrance, where the rising water hits him and carries him away. He survives miraculously and is found by the magus and Sophos. The long flight out of Attolia is filled with close encounters, among them a fierce battle with Attolian soldiers. Gen unexpectedly proves his worth as a soldier, elevating himself in the esteem of both the magus and Sophos. Pol and Ambiades are killed, Ambiades having turned traitor and sold out to the Attolians, and the rest are imprisoned. By picking locks, Gen gets them out, and eventually they arrive in Eddis. There it is revealed that Eddis is Gen's homeland. His father is the minister of war, and Gen himself is known as a scholar, a far cry from the near-boob that he has presented himself as being. The Queen's Thief, he possesses the Gift, having lifted it from the magus in the fight with the soldiers. His theft of the king's seal and his boasts were clever ruses to impel the magus, who alone knew the location of the stone, to initiate the journey so that Gen could gain the stone for the Queen of Eddis, who is his cousin, and thus make the throne secure for her. The novel is a whiz-bang adventure story, with plenty of action and fine pacing. The writer sets the reader up to believe, along with the magus, that Gen is a lowlife, ignorant pickpocket, only here and there dropping little hints for the attentive reader that Gen may not really be as stupid as he seems. The plot makes the most of inventive twists and turns, and the settings, whether interior or exterior, are clearly detailed and convincing. The tales that Gen and the magus spin along the way about the origin of the world and the activities of gods point up happenings and provide elegant texture. The loyal, true, and stalwart magus and especially the brave, resourceful Gen, however, steal the show. So engaging are they that they deserve a sequel. ALA; Fanfare; Newbery Honor.

THIN ICE (Qualey*, Marsha, Delacorte, 1997), mystery novel of the disappearance of a girl's older brother, who has been her guardian for twelve years, in what looks at first like a snowmobile accident on a frozen river near Penokee, Wisconsin. Arden Monro, 17, and her brother, Scott, have lived together since their parents were killed in a plane crash when Arden was six and Scott was in college. Considered by everyone who knows him to be a very careful and responsible young man, he returned home to care for her and has worked as a mechanic since then, his strongest passion restoring a 1970 Plymouth Barracuda. Arden's chief interest is ArdenArt, a picture-framing business that she has built, though she spends a good deal of time with their next-door neighbors, the Drummond twins, Jean and Kady, high school seniors who have a juggling act. Scott and Arden have a good relationship, respectful of each other's privacy, so that Arden doesn't even know the names of the women whom Scott dates. When he loses his snowmobile and nearly loses his life in an accident on the frozen river, he begins to brood uncharacteristically, then takes various trips to look for a new snowmobile. A second accident, when he is alone on the river at night, appears to be fatal, though his body cannot be found. Arden gets to know Clair Poole, the woman whom he has been dating, and her little daughter, Hannah, and learns that Clair is pregnant with Scott's child. Thinking back on his recent actions and going through his things, Arden realizes that, overwhelmed by the prospect of more responsibility, he has carefully planned his disappearance. Arden gets permission to live as an emancipated minor, though Mrs. Drummond and half the town keep a close eye on her. Most of them think that her insistence that Scott is still alive is misguided, at best, and crazy, but Jace Dailey, an old boyfriend who has moved away but gotten back in contact, is willing to help her hunt for evidence. For several months she flails around, tracing down false leads and worrying her school mentors and Mrs. Drummond, even hiring a detective, but at last she gives up. In the Barracuda that she has adopted, she drives the twins to juggle at a festival in Madison, Wisconsin. They see an announcement of a performance of a world-famous juggler in Chicago and persuade her to take them there, although she has never tried city driving. While the twins attend the juggling show, Arden goes to the Art Institute and suddenly realizes that she is interested in art, not just frames. Afterward, in a lakeside park where the twins do an impromptu juggling act, Arden suddenly spots Scott watching them in amazement. Before he can slip off, Arden pounces on him, hitting him and yelling at him, torn between relief at finding him and fury at the way that he tricked them. After she cools down, they talk, Scott explaining how the scam worked, with money he got by selling a photography collection belonging to their parents that he found stashed in the basement, and Arden telling him how she figured out his disappearance by the way everything in his room and his life was so perfectly in order. After roaming around the South, he has come to Chicago to see an artwork newly put on display, a mobile of their parents' hands cast in bronze, done by an artist friend who recently died of AIDS. In a brief last part, Arden, Hannah, and the baby visit the museum and, with special permission from the curator, see and touch the bronze hands, thereby connecting them all to the past and to each other. The strongest part of the novel is Arden's frantic search for clues about Scott and her efforts to prove herself responsible enough to live alone. The end is something of a letdown. Presumably, Scott returns to Penokee, is put on probation for endangering law enforcement officers, and later returns to live in Chicago, where Clair seems to be planning to join him. Arden is now in, or will soon enter, art school in Chicago. She understands her brother's need to get away and has forgiven him as, presumably, has Clair. The ethics are somewhat murky. Poe Nominee.

THE 13TH FLOOR: A GHOST STORY (Fleischman*, Sid, illus. Peter Sis, Greenwillow, 1995), humorous time-travel fantasy with period aspects set in San Diego, on the Atlantic high seas, and in Boston. Orphans Buddy Stebbins, 12, the narrator, and his sister, Liz, 23, a feisty feminist lawyer, fear that they may lose their house because their recently deceased parents left them with many debts. The big, old stucco place has been in the family ever since their great-grandfather came from Boston in 1910 and opened a law office in the Zachary Building on India Street. He built his house on a hill above Old Town with views of San Diego Bay. There he would often use a family heirloom, a copper speaking trumpet, to try to contact an ancestor, a pirate called Captain Crackstone, who was reputed to have buried a treasure before he was hanged. For fun, Buddy walks through the house shouting through the trumpet, pretending that he is trying to contact the pirate. To his and Liz's surprise, a voice with an English accent speaks to them on the telephone message machine, says her name is Abigail Parsons, and urges them to rush to the thirteenth floor of the Zachary Building and rescue her from some unspecified calamity. The family "death book" reports that Abigail was an ancestor who had been tried as a witch when a child. When Liz disappears the next day, Buddy hurries to the Zachary Building and, taking the elevator, manages to locate the thirteenth floor (although officially there is none), steps out, and finds himself on a ship on the high seas in the late seventeenth century, the *Laughing Mermaid*. A privateer whose skipper is Buddy's pirate ancestor, John Crackstone (real name Captain* John Stebbins), the ship is bound for Boston bearing a Red Sea treasure in jewels. The ship is boarded by the *Bloody Hand*, a privateer captained by Harry Scratch, who seeks the treasure. Another pirate, not very bright, unsavory Gallows Bird, is made captain of the *Laughing Mermaid* and given the name Captain Crackstone. The real Captain Crackstone, John Stebbins, and Buddy are set adrift in the ship's boat with a minimum of supplies. Two days later, they reach Boston Harbor, where Buddy discovers Liz and learns that she entered this dimension through the Stebbinses' barn. She is preparing to defend Abigail Parsons, a 10-year-old girl accused of being a witch. When, at the trial, Liz is prevented from serving as Abigail's lawyer because she is a woman, Buddy takes over, and Liz tells him what to say. Each of the charges is proved false by clever reasoning, and the jury acquits Abigail. Buddy joins the Captain on another ship, the *Sea Arrow*, which pursues the *Bloody Hand* and recovers the *Laughing Mermaid*. Captain Stebbins sails to a vast bay, where on a small island he buries the treasure, a large cache of jewels, which has been hidden in the *Laughing Mermaid's* figurehead. He inscribes the location on a sheet of copper, which he affixes to his speaking trumpet. He also seals a silver coin between the sheet of copper and the trumpet. When they return to Boston, they learn that Gallows Bird (calling himself Captain Crackstone) has been hanged as a pirate and that Liz has been imprisoned for witchcraft. Buddy contrives her release with a clever ruse using his tape recorder. Since the *Laughing Mermaid* is leaking badly, Liz and Buddy hurry below and find the door back to the twentieth-century elevator. They discover from the map on the trumpet that the treasure was buried on Bedloe's Island and now lies beneath the Statue of Liberty. Although disappointed at not recovering the treasure, they are able to pay their debts with the money that they get from selling the antique coin. The inventive plot has good fun with Massachusetts history concerning witches and piracy and takes a few good-natured swipes at gender discrimination and sex roles. Unflagging action; vigorous dialogue; hyperbolic characters, style, and incidents; twentieth-century technology and attitudes contrasted with seventeenth—all these combine in typical Fleischman fashion for outrageous, lively entertainment. The names alone are a treat for the ears and the intellect. Concluding the book is a historical note that gives information about the period. Poe Nominee.

THOMAS OF THORNHAM (*The Ramsay Scallop**), young noble of twenty-one or twenty-two who returns from a Crusade to learn that he is to marry Elenor of Ramsay Castle, a marriage arranged by their fathers. He is deeply unhappy about his experiences in Europe, the Crusades having degenerated into terrorism and marauding rather than the religious wars that he expected. He is also unhappy at being made the master of Thornham in title only, his father, Sir Robert, fully intending to retain control of the manor. Lastly, he has misgivings about Elenor herself, whom he remembers as a child and thinks of as the Brat. As the pilgrimage to the shrine of Saint James in Spain wears on, however, he becomes less gloomy in spirit, realizes that Elenor has many fine qualities and great strength of character, and assumes the responsibilities of leader and protector of the pilgrims with whom they are traveling.

THOMAS, ROB (1966?–), attended the University of Texas at Austin, where he still lives. He taught high school journalism for five years, advised the University of Texas student magazine, worked for *Channel One*, a Los Angeles-based television news show for teens, and toured the country with rock bands. His first novel, *Rats Saw GOD** (Simon & Schuster, 1996), published before he was thirty, is a high school senior's slice-of-life account of his school relationships and his relationships with his divorced parents. A *School Library Journal* selection, it projects humor, warmth, clout, and a thoroughly end-of-the-century tone. *Slave Day* (Simon & Schuster, 1997) revolves around a high school fund-raiser; *Doing Time: Notes from the Undergrad* (Simon & Schuster, 1997) is a book of short stories; *Satellite Down* (Simon & Schuster, 1998) follows a young television intern as he discovers corrupt journalism practices on the national network; and *Green Thumb* (Simon & Schuster, 1999) concerns a botanical trip to the Amazon rain forest. Thomas has been hailed as a fresh and vivid voice in young adult literature.

TICK-TICK (*Finder**), mechanically gifted female elf who has rescued Orient from a destructive life addicted to River water and has become his partner in a business using his incredible talent for locating things and her far greater practical skills to serve community members with unusual needs. Beautiful ("like the bust of Nefertiti, only more daunting") and brilliant, she usually wears oily coveralls and drives a souped-up Harley-Davidson with a sidecar. Although they are partners and close friends, Orient knows little about her past until her death, when her brother from Elfland shows up and tells him about her rebellion against their autocratic father, who forbade her to fool with mechanical and electrical things of the World, a prohibition that would have made her deny her inherent genius. The Ticker, as Orient refers to her, defies even the loose conventions of Bordertown, where pure-blood elves seldom have close ties to humans, and, as the crowd at her funeral shows, is well loved by a widely diverse group.

TIGER, TIGER, BURNING BRIGHT (Koertge*, Ron, Orchard, 1994), contemporary novel of family life set in the central California, economically depressed, desert town of Norbu and revolving around a boy's close relationship with his aged, forgetful grandfather. The narrator, Jesse, 13, enjoys the company of Pappy*, the eighty-two-year-old former cowboy who helped raise Jesse after Jesse's father walked out when he was a baby. Jesse and Pappy have a warm, joking relationship, have gone on numerous camping trips and outings, and have had untold numbers of man-to-man talks. Recently, however, Pappy has been unusually forgetful, and daughter, Bonnie, a chiropractor and Jesse's mother, thinks that they will soon have to put him in a nursing home, maybe Golden Oaks. After one of their frequent camping trips into the high desert, Pappy informs Jesse that he saw a tiger track up there. The next morning, Pappy forgets and burns the beans with which he always starts the day, and as usual Jesse covers for him. That afternoon on the way downtown to take in rancher Bobby* Yates' ostrich races, Jesse confides in his best pal, Kyle*, about the tiger print. After listening to Bobby's pitch about farming ostriches and watching the fiasco of a race, Jesse and Kyle join the three classmates who have been assigned to their final exam study group, Nigel*, Walter*, and fat Paul, at their cave hideout. After discussing their assignment for Mr. Wright, their English teacher, they decide that the next day they will ride up into the hills to search for the tiger print but find none. At Kyle's mother's birthday party a few days later, Mr. Wright says that Pappy is like the tiger in William Blake's poem, "still burning bright" in spite of aging, and Thomas, Nigel's photographer-father, calls Pappy a "national treasure." Shortly thereafter, Pappy falls asleep with a cigarette, which catches some newspapers on fire and burns up the living room couch, drapes, and carpet. Bonnie calls Golden Oaks, finds that it has a long waiting list, and heads for another place called Golden Shadows, which neither she nor Jesse likes. While Bonnie attends a chiropractors' seminar, Pappy gets slicked up and goes downtown to gamble at the Long Branch Saloon. Uneasy, Jesse and Kyle follow and observe him win well against Bobby Yates, who gives him an IOU, and two strangers, brothers, one fat and the other thin, who pay up. Early the next day, Pappy takes off. Jesse and Kyle trail him to the Yates ranch, where he tells them that Bobby has a tiger in his barn. Inside the boys find a big, seedy-looking, declawed animal in a cage. A fracas ensues with Bobby Yates, shots ring out, and Pappy, who just wants to collect his IOU, falls and hits his head on the ranch-house step. The tiger, which was to be a trophy hunt for the brothers, is taken to a sanctuary in Los Angeles. The sheriff kicks the brothers out of town and warns Bobby against repeating this behavior. Jesse and Bonnie decide that they will do the best they can with Pappy as long as they can, although Bonnie reserves a place at Golden Oaks. The story, really two stories neatly knit, is mostly dialogue and employs snappy, contemporary diction and an intimate tone, with witty turns of phrase but without teen trash talk. The reader must pay close attention because the narrative works something like a jigsaw puzzle in which even little pieces count. Details of the family, neighborhood, and town come out gradually, as they would if readers were to visit the area. Although the book's main problem—how to care for and keep the elderly safe while respecting their dignity and freedom of choice—is a serious and delicate sociological concern, many light moments keep the mood upbeat and entertaining. The sense of community in the sleepy, dying town is a good aspect and ironically parallels what Pappy is trying to do—make the most of the time that he has left. ALA; SLJ.

TOGGS (*Beyond the Western Sea: Book One: The Escape from Home**), Ralph Toggs, one of the young members of the Lime Street Runners Association, a gang of pickpockets and con artists assembled and ruled by fat, ruthless Sergeant

Rumpkin, who takes a percentage of all that they accumulate. Toggs is described as a "ruddy-faced, bright-eyed young man" with a wry and cocky smile. He wears a seaman's hat, striped shirt, and wide britches. He first enters the story when he accosts Maura and Patrick O'Connell, just off the boat from Ireland in Liverpool, informs them untruthfully that the place where they are to lodge, the Union House, has burned down, and offers to take them to a better place, which turns out to be an unsavory dive run by grasping Mrs. Sonderbye. She acquires almost all the O'Connell children's money, feeds them only a little watery soup, and virtually imprisons them. Toggs pops up in the story repeatedly to influence their lives and also that of Sir Laurence Kirkle, whom he wishes to apprehend, mostly to prove that he contributes more to the gang than Fred* No-name, his rival. To his credit, Toggs feels a little guilty, but not much and not for long, about deceiving the O'Connells. His slight shame revolves mostly around his perception that Maura is spirited and pretty, with her dark brown hair and blue eyes.

TOO SOON FOR JEFF (Reynolds*, Marilyn, Morning Glory Press, 1994), realistic novel of the effect of a teenage pregnancy on the father, who at first blames his girlfriend and is resentful but eventually assumes responsibility and strives to be a good parent. In Hamilton High of contemporary Los Angeles, Jeff Browning, 17, has just about brought himself to break up with Christina Calderon, 15, because he feels stifled by her constant need for his attention, when she tells him that they are going to have a baby. Although he has always told himself that he would be a better father than his own, who left him and his mother when he was five, Jeff knows that he isn't ready to be a parent. He wants to go to college and has a good chance at a debating scholarship. He also blames Christy for lying that she is on the Pill, so he felt safe in no longer using condoms. His efforts to get her to consider an abortion or adoption appall her. She has cherished the idea of moving in with Jeff's mother, who has been studying to be a nurse, because her own parents do not get along, and her Hispanic father is authoritarian and sometimes abusive. When her father arrives at Jeff's house, demanding furiously that he marry Christy, Jeff's mother stands up for him, saying that he is not ready for marriage, but she sensibly insists that Jeff make his own decision about what to do. At first, angry and full of resentment, Jeff goes out with his two best friends, serious, intelligent Jeremy and carefree Benny, and gets drunk, is arrested, and is turned over to his mother and his mother's brother, Uncle Steve. At school, Christy's friends have banded together to treat him as a pariah. His debate coach, not knowing the whole story but sensing the antagonism, lights into the other team members, and the situation eases somewhat. At the big debate meet in San Diego Jeff does well enough to be offered a full scholarship to small Brooker University in Texas, and he looks forward to the national competition in New Orleans, where he and Jeremy are to team up in the Policy Debate. On the morning when he is to leave, however, he gets a call telling him that Christy's condition makes an emergency Cesarean necessary. When his mother promises to respect his decision but leaves it to him, he calls his debate coach, who is distraught but substitutes Dashan, an African-American teammate, and Jeff goes to the hospital to await the birth of his son. Several weeks premature, the baby is scrawny. Christy rejects him and refuses even to discuss a name, so Jeff insists that Browning be his surname and chooses Ethan Calderon for his given and middle names. The sight of the real baby and the feel of its tiny hand clutching his finger wake in Jeff love and paternal feelings. When the baby can leave the hospital, Jeff insists on helping take care of him at the Calderon house, and Christy gradually becomes more interested. In September Jeff leaves for college, which he finds small and unsophisticated compared with his large urban high school, but he likes it, and he soon has a girlfriend, Nicole, from the college debate team. After a trip home at Thanksgiving, however, he decides that he must return to California and become a more constant influence in Ethan's life. Nicole is committed to Brooker but agrees to visit him next summer. Jeff regains his job at the Fitness Club, which he had during high school, attends community college, and keeps Ethan about half of the time. Christy has been going out with Dashan and even Benny, who was home on leave from the army, but she also has grown up and become more responsible. The novel is so contrived to teach a lesson that it reads almost like a case history. It is saved, partially, by the characterization of Jeff, who is a convincingly angry and upset boy at first and a more serious young man through his experience. Christy is drawn as immature and Jeff's mother and uncle as supportive, but they are essentially stock figures. The difficulties ahead for Jeff and Ethan are not minimized, and the end is clearly not happy-ever-after, but there is no discussion of how much harder the situation would be if both Jeff and Christy were not middle class with a safety net of caring parents. ALA; SLJ.

TOSTIG GODWINSON (*The King's Shadow**), historical brother of Harold* Godwinson, Earl of Wessex and the King of England, who was defeated by William*, Duke of Normandy, in 1066. A large, red-haired, ill-tempered man, Tostig grows angry at Harold when Harold refuses to support him against his people, who rebel because he imposes high taxes. Outlawed, Tostig allies himself with King Harald Hardrada of Norway, but both die when Harold defeats them at the Battle of Stamford Bridge. Shortly thereafter, Harold meets William at the Battle of Hastings, and Harold and two other brothers, Gyrth and Leofwine, die. Tostig serves as a foil to Harold, who is presented as a gentler, fairer man who feels that a ruler should respond to the will of the people.

TOUGHING IT (Springer*, Nancy, Harcourt, 1994), mystery novel set in some unnamed river town in contemporary times that concentrates not on the question of finding a murderer but on the survivor, who is devastated, at first raging for revenge, then gradually pulling his life together again. When Shawn (Tuff) Lacey, 16, rides up Sid Mountain on the back of his brother's dirt bike, they hit a trip wire, and a shotgun fastened to a tree blasts Dillon, 18, in the head, killing him immediately. Bleeding and in shock, Shawn gets help but remembers little until a police car drops him at the rusty riverside trailer where he lives with his mother, Candy, her current man, and their five little kids. Candy, drunk as she often is, seems unable to take in Dillon's death or is indifferent to it. In fury, Shawn throws his few belongings into a paper bag and heads off, bent on revenge. His mother shouts after him that he should look up Penrose Leppo, adding, "He's your father." Since Shawn has spent much of his life speculating on who fathered him and Dillon, this revelation astonishes him. After he has returned to the site of the killing, been shot at, and plunged through brush back to the road, he looks up the name in a phone book, walks more than ten miles to Dam Shame, a river community, and finds, well after midnight, a shacky bait store at the address. Unable to rouse anyone with his knocks, he bashes his fist through the display window. This brings a pudgy man in undershorts, pointing a gun at him. When Shawn repeats his mother's words, Pen's only comment is, "Well, she must have some reason for saying that." He has already heard of Dillon's death. He takes Shawn in, bandages his hand, and puts him to bed on his sofa. Though hardly the blond athlete of whom Shawn has dreamed, Pen quietly assumes control, insisting on accompanying Shawn when the boy is determined to go back up the mountain and saving him by his quick action from being bitten by a copperhead planted in the bag that he had dropped the day before. In the days that follow, Pen collects money for a funeral, buys Shawn some decent clothes for the occasion, and runs interference for him with the police, who seem to consider the boy a suspect. Alerted that the boy is not in school by a girl named Monica, who helped Shawn the day of the murder, Pen even follows him up the mountain again to where he has rousted out a recluse named Al Quigg, whom he has decided must be responsible for the killing. In a dramatic scene, while Shawn points the gun that he stole from Pen at the unkempt, whimpering man, Pen tells him that Quiggy is possibly his father, since he, Pen, was rejected by Candy, while Quiggy was a basketball star. Shawn is unable to shoot. A rifle shot cracks, and all three are pinned down, first by someone shooting from higher on the mountain, then by police returning fire from below. Later, after Shawn, who as Tuff never cried, has sobbed until he is exhausted, Pen tells him that he loved Candy, her wild, free-spirited beauty, but married a different sort of woman and had a good life until she died. He offers to be a father to Shawn. At the funeral, Shawn seeks out Monica, gets her to sit with him and his mother, who is for once entirely sober and looking her age. The strength of the book lies in its evocation of Shawn's emotions, his lonely, rejected childhood, his dependence on Dillon, his rage at the murder, his blind desire for revenge, his tentative acceptance of Pen's help, and with it his return to reason. Although Pen's heroics and the revelation that he was a Green Beret in Vietnam seem overly fortuitous, the characterization of the minor figures is convincing: Shawn's gone-to-seed mother, the overworked, abrasive, but concerned police officer, Monica, not the flashy sort of girl whom Dillon attracted but one with whom Shawn can talk and learn to love. The solution to the shooting, a gang of small-time drug dealers protecting their marijuana crop and supplies stashed on state land, brings closure but is not important to the impact of the novel. ALA; Poe Winner; SLJ.

TRASHMAN (*The Ear, the Eye, and the Arm**), childlike derelict who wanders the city, welcomed by such diverse characters as the She* Elephant, who manages the slavelike Vlei people, and the villagers of Resthaven, who originally found him as an abandoned infant at their gate. About twenty years old, he is strong as an ox, with a mind of a four-year-old. Although his words sound like a meaningless babble to most people, Kuda Matsika understands him, and soon they share a strong affection. When Kuda, frightened by the idea that they might be sold to the Masks, starts wailing for his Mama, Trashman picks him up and carries him out of the Vlei to an airbus platform, with Tendai and Rita Matsika panting after him, and then on to Resthaven, where he is welcomed, and the Matsika children are warily allowed to enter. He is instrumental in their escape from there and devotedly follows them to the home of Mrs.* Horsepool-Worthingham, where he hangs about despite her great efforts to be rid of him. He is, however, also responsible for the She Elephant's finding them again, when she spots him sitting outside the gate. The Masks knock him out with chloroform, but he is later rescued by General Matsika's men. To the end he remains a free spirit, sometimes sleeping in the yard at the Matsika compound, sometimes wandering the city streets, sometimes disappearing, possibly back to Resthaven.

TRAVELER (*Pigs Don't Fly**), beautiful, white homing pigeon with an iridescent pinkish tinge rescued by Summer from a gang of boys who are stoning him. Summer, aided by understanding the language of all her creatures, splints his broken wing and nurses him back to health. Several times Traveler aids the little group of wayfarers by flying ahead and scouting the road or the situation. When they reach his home, and Traveler has delivered the message that he carries to the lady, he makes the mistake of thanking Summer affectionately in front of her, inciting her jealousy. As she is about to wring his neck, Summer rescues him again, and they escape. Later they spend the night in the ruined tower of an old chapel inhabited by wild pigeons, and there Traveler opts to stay. While not the most important member of the group, he is the first to leave and foreshadows the departure of all the others except Growch*, the dog.

TREE OF HEAVEN (Binstock*, R. C., Soho, 1995), historical novel of a strange love between a Japanese junior officer and his captive, a Chinese woman, set in 1938 in a garrison town somewhere west of Nanking. There is very little overt action in the plot. Kuroda, a captain trained as a botanist, is left behind in charge of the outpost, with no indication of what he is supposed to do and no clue as to what is going on in the war, the Japanese invasion of Manchuria.

One morning he comes upon several of his men who have pulled a woman from under a barnyard porch where she has been sleeping and are preparing to rape her. Against all precedent and against what he knows to be good policy, he orders them to stop, and he takes the woman to his quarters, where she becomes his servant and, eventually, his lover. In the end, he is stabbed by a guerrilla and dies of the wound. The woman, Li, gets away and heads west, after being beaten and raped by several soldiers. The depth of the novel lies in the relationship between Kuroda and Li, in what goes on in their minds, and in the changes in their understanding. In the present tense, except for their memories, the first-person narration alternates chapter by chapter between the two characters, gradually revealing something of their backgrounds and their attitudes. Kuroda has joined the army mainly in an effort to please his father, who is intensely patriotic but now is dying or, very likely, dead. A student rather than a fighter, Kuroda has been appalled and sickened by the wanton brutality, rape, and torture in the taking of Nanking, but this horror does not translate into sympathy for the Chinese, whom he sees as contemptible, a filthy mob, not even fighting back with any discipline. He cannot reconcile with his own sense of what is right and orderly the realization of what happens to Japanese men when they are away from the restraints of their own communities and societal restrictions. Li is also educated, the daughter of a doctor whose mother was Japanese. She was married but rejected by her husband because she was barren and had returned to her father's house, a figure of scorn to their neighbors, before her parents were killed and the village burned by the attacking Japanese. Hungry, cold, and filthy, she has managed to exist without becoming prey to the soldiers until the morning when Kuroda saves her, but she has almost lost hope and any sense of herself in the ordeal of day-to-day survival. At first, in the two-room schoolhouse that has become Kuroda's quarters, she is grateful for the warmth of his stove, the food that he shares without any thought, and the chance to be clean again, but she still hates him as one of the "dwarf beasts," as her people call the invaders, and she is very wary of telling him anything, even that she can speak Japanese. In his fear that he will lose control of his men and in the boredom of the isolated post, Kuroda finds that the wife and daughter whom he left in Japan have grown increasingly remote. He can see no purpose in the war and even questions his former reverence for the Emperor. Among the men in his group, there is no one with whom he can talk; and Li does not respond to his attempts to know her better. When their proximity and need finally bring them together, Li volunteers to go to his bed, although they both know that he could have ordered her to at any time. Kuroda, however, is the one who falls in love first, deeply and, it seems to him, astonishingly. He proposes to send her to Japan, to friends who would protect her and not let his family know. More realistic than Kuroda, Li knows that this would never work, but she does not try to dissuade him, simply existing from day to day. Not until he is dying does she admit to herself and tell him that she loves him. Despite the lack of action, the novel holds a reader's attention through the development of two compelling characters, both out of place in the world where they find themselves. At the end, Li knows that she is pregnant. While this can only add to her predicament, and there is no assurance that she will survive, it is a hopeful sign. Life has a chance of going on. The title comes from the common name for Ailanthus, a tree that roots, the world over, in unlikely places and manages to grow and reproduce against heavy odds. The novel is touching and haunting. SLJ.

TRILLO, CAL (*Cezanne Pinto: A Memoir**), brash young cavalry corporal in the Union army with whom Cezanne Pinto falls in when he goes to Washington to fight on the side of the North. Out of conviction, Trillo, the Mex-Texan son of a Mexican *vaquero* (cowboy), joined the Union forces in spite of the opposition of his brothers and goes home after the war with apprehension about how he will be received. When he and Cezanne arrive at the BoxK and meet Cal's brother Jacob, who has lost an arm fighting against the North, feelings run high for a little while, but the brothers decide to let bygones be bygones. Cal and Cezanne help Jacob get the ranch back on its feet by rounding up cattle and driving them to northern markets. Although Jacob wants to learn to read and write, Cal has no interest in anything beyond the ABCs, although he enjoys hearing the novels of Charles Dickens when Cezanne reads them aloud.

TROUBLE (*Guests**), village girl of another clan who shares Moss' dissatisfaction with life and also runs away. Moss associates with her, even though he realizes that, according to tribal custom, such contact is forbidden. When Moss encounters her in the forest, she is wearing boys' clothes, an obvious symbol of rebellion against the woman's role that her mother and sister are urging her to assume. She tells Moss the story of Running Woman, a great-aunt of hers who defied custom and was forever ostracized. When Trouble decides to run away for good, after having been struck by her mother, Moss intercepts her and takes her to his mother, who comforts her and presumably helps her to accept the inevitable.

TROUBLE WILL FIND YOU (Lexau*, Joan M., ill. Michael Chesworth, Houghton, 1994), humorous mystery for early readers set in a small town or suburb in contemporary times. Desmond Aster, probably seven or eight, known as Dis Aster, lives up to his name, despite his good intentions. When his father says that he can have a dog if he can spend one full day without getting into any trouble, he is delighted, but his parents are pretty sure that it is a safe bet. Still, Dis has high hopes as he starts out for the home of his baby-sitter, Mrs. Rooney, with his little sister, Megan. He is determined not to fight with Piper Rooney (known as Pepper for her hot temper) no matter how bossy she acts and thinks he will stay inside all day to keep out of trouble's way. Before they reach the Rooneys, a puppy shoots out of some bushes, a sock in its mouth and a tattooed man in hot pursuit. Dis is able to get the sock but refuses to give up the puppy, since the man clearly means to hurt it. After some threats, the man and the woman with him pull away in an old green van. Pepper and Dis find that in the sock is a gold pin with a red stone, which Pepper pins on Yellow, her stuffed cat that rides in her backpack. Together they make signs about the lost puppy and take it on a rope to try to find its home. Before they go far, the mystery deepens with the addition of three more puppies similar to the first, all reportedly dumped by someone earlier in the morning, and the return of the man in the van, who wears a shirt saying, "Stan, the TV Man," and seems to be picking up televisions for repair and tries to get the gold pin back. Before they straighten everything out, Dis and Pepper have been accused of burglary, Dis has broken his glasses (again!), the police have cleared up the mystery of daytime house break-ins and arrested the tattooed man who is, as Dis has been saying, a crook, newly hired as an assistant to Stan, the children have found homes for three of the little dogs, and the Aster parents, proud of Dis despite the trouble that always seems to find him, have decided that he can keep the first puppy he saved from the crook. In twelve brief chapters and simple style, the lively story captures the frustration of a young boy whose best efforts always seem to backfire and whose adventures, amusing to others, are often truly disasters to him. Poe Nominee.

TROUT SUMMER (Conly*, Jane Leslie, Holt, 1995), novel of mystery and adventure, set on the Leanna River in Pennsylvania in the 1990s. After the departure of their feckless father to find adventure or satisfaction in studying art history, the narrator, Shana Allen, 13, and her brother, Cody, 12, move from their semirural home in Warrensburg, Virginia, to LaGlade, Maryland, where their mother has a job with the phone company. Both the young people hate LaGlade, missing their friends, their Uncle Mike, and, most of all, the river that ran through the field behind their house. When an office friend of Mama offers them the use of an isolated, run-down cabin on the Leanna, they are delighted to get away from the town and persuade their mother to let them stay there for the summer, although it is some distance from the road end and has no phone, running water, or electricity, and she will have to drive to work every morning and be gone most of the day. The river is small and fast, quite different from their familiar Castle, and they soon discover that casting for trout is not like fishing for bass, but they love the place and willingly clean the cabin, do makeshift repairs on the roof and windows, and promise to obey all the rules that their mother sets down. Almost at once they break the first rule to stay together whenever they leave the cabin. Shana, who has received a letter from her father, now in New York City, wants to keep it a secret and answer it privately, while Cody wants to explore. Later she hears him scream and comes upon him fleeing from an old man wearing a khaki uniform and pointing a gun. Shana confronts him, points out that they are not trespassing, and, in exchange for a promise not to tell their mother, helps him retrieve the gun that he dropped. He insists that he is the ranger, that they have no right to be there, and that he will issue a citation. In the next weeks they encounter the ranger a number of times, and Shana realizes that he is disabled, evidently from a stroke. She picks him a bucket of raspberries, at which he is surprised and pleased, if not polite. He commands her to bring him groceries, which she manages to buy without her mother's knowledge the next time they go to town, in exchange for a survey map of the river. To their surprise, he decides that Cody should learn to navigate the river in his canoe and starts him on a rigorous training schedule. Soon it is apparent that Cody is naturally talented and, though small, soon becomes proficient enough to go down some of the less demanding rapids and takes Shana once, scaring her thoroughly. Throughout the summer, Shana worries about whether her father will return and also about her mother's friendship with a coworker named Phil. At the end of the summer the ranger, whom they now call Henry and know is not really the government employee as he claims, decides that he and Cody should run the canyon, even the very dangerous series of rapids just up river from a number of summer homes. When Cody refuses, Henry starts off by himself, and the young people, knowing he can never make it, go after him along the river edge and find him where he has lost control of the boat, hit his head on a rock, and been thrown halfway out of the water. Cody retrieves the canoe while Shana does what she can for the semiconscious ranger. Since the only possibility of help is from the summer cottages below the rapids, Shana and Cody dare the river in a thrilling, death-defying race in which Cody injures his wrist so that Shana must control the boat through the last two drops. A rescue helicopter takes Shana back to where they left Henry and they find him still alive, but barely. He makes Shana promise to try to protect the river when he is gone. He dies on the way to the hospital. Shana's mother is furious when she finds that they have been leading a secret life all summer without ever telling her about Henry, and she blames Shana. Cody decides to go back to Warrensburg and live with Uncle Mike. Shana finally admits to herself that her father will probably not return and that even if he does, her mother has grown to love independence and will not live with him again. A sheriff brings them a sheet of paper on which Henry has written a will, leaving his house and land to the two Allen children. The summer has given Shana good things, but it has a bittersweet ending, having taken away her father and Henry and split her from Cody. The most interesting figure is cantankerous old Henry, but both Cody and Shana are believable individuals, and the descriptions of the river itself, in particular the trip down the canyon, are compelling. The father, who never actually appears, is a constant presence, and his flawed character adds depth to the story. ALA.

TUCK EVERLASTING (Babbitt*, Natalie, Farrar, 1975), thought-provoking fantasy set in the American village of Treegap in 1880, dealing with the ramifications of eternal life. Winnie Foster, 10, falls in with the Tuck family, whose members have drunk from a magical spring and have not aged since. Seeing both the joys and, in particular, the pains of their condition, Winnie decides not to drink from the spring herself. The fantasy is completely convincing and the characters well developed, with Winnie far more than an adequate child character and the Tucks individualized and memorable. Phoenix Honor. Earlier citations are Christopher; Fanfare; and Lewis Carroll. A longer entry appears in *Dictionary, 1960–1984*.

TURNER, MEGAN WHALEN (1965–   ), born in Fort Sill, Oklahoma; graduate of the University of Chicago; children's book buyer in Chicago and Washington, D.C., and writer of fiction for middle graders and teens. Her first book, a collection of short fantasies, *Instead of Three Wishes* (Greenwillow, 1995), was well received by critics and public. A trip to Greece with her husband, a professor of English, inspired *The Thief** (Greenwillow, 1996), an engrossing adventure-fantasy novel with an ancient Greece-like setting that offers humor, plenty of action, unusual characters, twist and turns, and a surprise conclusion. The novel was a Newbery Honor Book and chosen for Fanfare. The story continues in *The Queen of Attolia* (Greenwillow, 2000). Turner is considered a turn-of-the-century writer of promise.

TURN THE CUP AROUND (Mariconda*, Barbara, Delacorte, 1997), realistic mystery novel in a family context set in Maine in recent years. Overly conscientious, take-charge Evie Johannsen, 12, longs for the love of her mother, who died in childbirth when Evie was six, and of her father, hospitalized with some mysterious malady. She and her two mischievous and adventurous brothers, Kirby, 8, and Jemmy, 6, live on a rugged coastal cove with Gram, their mother's mother, in Cozy Cove Bed and Breakfast, which caters to summer visitors. Several occurrences lead to Evie's gaining a stronger sense of self and learning about her father. The book opens during a nighttime storm, during which Evie glimpses a peculiar shadow flit across the yard. Then Gram reads soomp (coffee grounds), predicting the need for extra caution and responsibility, and Evie discovers an extraordinarily vivid oil painting of a white cat with mismatched green and blue eyes in a crevice among the rocks into which she has slipped, a painting signed with the letters C A T. (This scene, in which Evie just escapes the rising waters, is the book's most exciting.) The novel's big question, which solves Evie's personal problems, is: Who painted the cat, and why? Was it Julia, the hippy-dressing artist? Was it Gram, who does seascapes? Was it Bill McAllister, the professor with vivid blue eyes, who has taken a room for the summer, is interested in both art history and beliefs about cats, and becomes romantically involved with Julia? Was it the white cat itself? Evie's curiosity and the white cat, which the boys catch and name Robinson, lead Evie back to the crevice, where she discovers a remarkable landscape, also signed C A T, then to a rude lean-to where she discovers artist's paints and cloths that she identifies as Gram's, and soon to a man with watery blue eyes whom she thinks of as the "madman." Later, she discovers a painting of herself holding the cat on the crevice wall, also signed C A T. When she writes a letter secretly to her father but fails to stamp it so that it is returned, Gram decides that it is time to tell Evie the truth about her father. On the way to the New Hampshire hospital, she tells Evie that her father began drinking excessively and then had a nervous breakdown after his wife died. At the hospital, Evie is shocked by Jerry Johannsen's appearance, his shrunken face and body, and watery-blue eyes, and feels, to her shame, that he might be better off dead. In a hurricane, she and a summer visitor her age, Michael Elliot, and Pop the handyman race after Jemmy, who is hunting for Robinson. They find the cat in the pine tree by the crevice. The madman saves the cat but is himself drowned. He is identified by authorities as Clive Aaron Thompson, a renowned painter turned recluse who always signed his work with his initials. He was responsible for the paintings. Gram suggests that Evie read soomp, and when she does, to look for the good in it and in life henceforth, because what she looks for will probably be her lot. The story exudes gothic conventions. Gram is a strong figure, as overprotective and controlling in her way as Evie is in hers. Red herrings keep the reader guessing, and tight spots follow one upon another. The first chapter sets the tone (although a knowledgeable reader at first suspects satire) with the dark and stormy night and a surfeit of tension-building metaphors, which might be excused as intended to indicate Evie's not always rational state of mind. Although the various elements are not well knit, the book moves fast and provides an adequate introduction to the genre for middle-grade readers. Poe Nominee.

TWISTED SUMMER (Roberts*, Willo Davis, Atheneum, 1996), mystery novel of detection and suspense, set at Crystal Lake in Michigan in the late 1990s. Because her father's business took the family to California the previous summer, Cici (Cecelia) Linden, 14, the narrator, hasn't been to the large cottage owned by her stepgrandfather, Judge Baskin, for two years and so has missed the startling news of the murder of Zoe Cyrex, a flirtatious girl a little her senior, or the arrest, trial, and imprisonment of Brody Shurik, son of Lina, the longtime cook for the Judge and Grandma Molly. Because Cici has always been fond of Lina, no longer in the Judge's employ, and has long had a crush on Jack, 17, Brody's younger brother, she sets out to find the truth behind the unlikely circumstantial evidence that convicted Brody. She learns that Zoe was coming on to all the older boys and also some of the married men, that she was also seeing a drifter named Carl Trafton, and that Jack has been ostracized by the other young people at the lake, although formerly he and Brody had both been part of the group that made no distinction between the cottage owners and the help. Her preoccupation with this mystery is interrupted by her grandmother's stroke, hospitalization, and death. Quite by accident, while looking for paper to write a note, she comes upon the Judge's bank statements in his desk and, curiosity overcoming her propriety, examines them enough to learn that he has been writing checks to "cash" for $1,000 once a month for fourteen months. After her grandmother's funeral, she walks by herself along the shore path and is almost hit by a shot coming from the woods. Since Jack has warned her to be careful and not to get caught snooping, Cici is terrified, especially when her parents go off for a few days, leaving her with the extended family. The final revelation comes in the middle of a night when Cici hears the Judge leaving the cottage, follows him, and is in the back room of the deserted house where Zoe was strangled when Trafton shows up and threatens the Judge for stopping the blackmail payments. The Judge, saying that it doesn't matter anymore, refuses to continue forking over the money. The blackmailer forces him and Cici, whom he discovers, to the dock and into a rowboat, saying that they would have an accident on an early morning fishing trip. Jack shows up with a rifle to save the day and to hear the Judge's confession that Trafton was blackmailing him because he knew Grandma Molly had killed a pedestrian along the country road and driven off. Zoe, learning of the scam, had tried to horn in, and Trafton had killed her. The serious question of the Judge's culpability in remaining silent while Brody is sent to prison is not skirted, but it is trivialized by Cici's preoccupation with wanting to be considered one of the big kids in the summer lake crowd. There are plenty of red herrings to complicate the plot and creepy scenes to add to the tension, but the strongest element is the picture of life in a summer colony where, because everyone knows everyone else, children are pretty much on their own, and ordinary ranks by family money or prominence do not apply. Poe Winner.

TYRONE CARTER (*Brothers and Sisters**), young black Western Express deliveryman who services Angel City National Bank where Esther* Jackson is a regional manager. His warm and gentle ways and lively personality attract her, and they become lovers. He is always conscious of being much less educated than she and knows his unschooled speech embarrasses her. For a while he is content with just being her lover, although he suspects that he is merely a temporary convenience. He is active in Solid Rock Baptist Church and returns to college with the encouragement of Reverend Rice. Tyrone is a likable foil for the suave, well-educated Humphrey* Boone.

U

UNBROKEN: A NOVEL (Haas*, Jessie, Greenwillow, 1999), realistic period novel with girl's growing-up and family-life aspects set near the upland villages of Barrett and West Barrett, Vermont, in the late spring and summer of 1910. Newly orphaned narrator Harriet Gibson, 13, adjusts to the death of her mother and to life with her disapproving, rigid, uncompromising Aunt Sarah Hall, her dead father Walter's sister. After her widowed mother (Ellen), a seamstress and former schoolteacher, dies of injuries from a buggy accident, trusted Dr. Andy Vesper, named executor of the estate in Mother's will, sends the girl, now almost penniless and accompanied by her cherished pony, Kid, also orphaned in the accident, to live with Aunt Sarah, who has always disliked Mother. Aunt Sarah and retiring Uncle Clayton, much Aunt Sarah's senior, make a hardscrabble living on their stony mountain farm. Tension soon builds between the sturdy, assertive girl and her unyielding, controlling aunt. Harriet makes friends with one-armed Truman Hall, Clayton's brother and a Civil War veteran, who once courted Sarah, lives in the tiny hillside house in which Harriet was born, and often helps Sarah and Clayton with farm chores. When Sarah says that Harriet can no longer attend the Academy because there is no money, the two argue, and Harriet learns that Sarah hated her mother because she thinks that Ellen became pregnant, enticed Walter into marriage, and ruined his life. Harriet wonders why Mother specified that she should live with Sarah, a woman so different from Mother in her attitudes toward life and education. The girl decides to train Kid to the saddle so that she can ride to and from school and somehow find the money to pay the school fees. The Mitchells, a town family, offer to let her stay with them so that she can take Academy end-of-the-year exams, and John Gale, the man whose car caused Mother's horse to spook, pays her fees for the next three years, both situations that Aunt Sarah accepts with poor grace. The turning point in her relationship with Aunt Sarah comes when Harriet pushes the colt too hard. He bolts and drags her, causing severe rope burns to her hands. Aunt Sarah, uncharacteristically almost distraught, rushes her to Dr. Vesper. By this time, the girl has learned that Aunt Sarah was left an orphan at Harriet's age, too, and raised her four siblings. Sarah's resentment toward Mother came from losing her brother to Mother in marriage and from having had to give a large portion of her life to her siblings so that she could not enjoy the opportunities that Mother had. When Sarah views a picture that Harriet has of her parents newly married, Sarah realizes, evidently for the first time, that Walter was already ill with the consumption that took him shortly after his marriage. Having learned more about her family, Harriet understands her aunt better. She realizes that Mother knew that Harriet would be well raised and that several people, Truman, Clayton, Dr. Vesper, and villagers, would be there to take up the slack. Harriet also knows, too, as do the others, that life with Sarah will probably always have tense moments because they appear to be made of the same stern, unyielding stuff. Much of the book is given over to Harriet's grieving, fine descriptions of farmwork, and visits to, and discussions with, Truman and her best friend, Luka Mitchell. The writer makes the most of the moment and uses language distinctively, and there are many arresting turns of phrase. The interpersonal relationships between the principals are subtly drawn. One drawback is that Harriet gains too much essential information via overheard conversation, but a neat touch is the parallel between the girl, the colt, and the aunt. In spite of tough times, all three remain unbroken. SLJ.

UNCLE HOB (*Getting Near to Baby**), Hobart Hobson, husband of Aunt Patty, who takes Willa Jo Dean and Little Sister to live with her after the death of their baby sister. Gentle and sensitive, Uncle Hob does not argue with his wife, who has directed his life relentlessly, but he retains a sort of independence in his quiet way. When he joins the girls on the roof, he doesn't try to persuade them to go back in or to explain why they are out there. He points out roofs on which he worked before Aunt Patty made him quit that business, and he sings simple arithmetic problems that Little Sister quickly figures out and answers with her hand signals. When Aunt Patty from the yard below asks whether he has lost his mind, he tells her mildly that he'll be down directly, as soon as the girls are ready. When a neighbor questions his sanity, he stands, does a careful, graceful barefoot dance on the roof, and bows to her. He tells the girls that the summer when he was thirteen he was sent to live with his grandfather after his grandmother had died, the idea being that caring for him will bring the old man out of his grief. Instead, they both grieved for the grandmother, letting the housekeeping go and their hair grow long, eating peanuts and hard-cooked eggs, singing sad songs and telling sadder stories. He sees now that it was one way they both coped with their loss. He shows the girls how to make a human chain to retrieve the umbrella that has fallen into the roof gutter. When he learns that Noreen is coming to pick up the girls, he says, "It's time. Time for her to concentrate on the living." He gives Willa Jo her first nudge toward understanding Aunt Patty by saying that she acts as she does because her feelings are hurt. Despite her fussiness and directiveness, he seems genuinely fond of his wife.

UNCLE MICAH BARNES (*Choosing Up Sides**), Luke Bledsoe's rakish uncle, the brother of Luke's mother. Uncle Micah loves life, chewing on his cigar, drinking, sometimes to excess, fishing, baseball, and dancing. Worst of all in the eyes of his brother-in-law, preacher Zeke* Bledsoe, Uncle Micah is left-handed, using what Zeke calls the "hand of the Devil." A big "walrus" of a man with a "Gatling-gun voice," Micah takes Luke fishing and to a ball game, a charity event organized by Babe Ruth. The occasion helps Luke see that baseball, indeed, all sports, are not necessarily evil pursuits and can serve good purposes. Uncle Micah encourages Luke to follow his heart with respect to what he wants to do with his life. Uncle Micah is a sportswriter and the sports editor for the *Ashtabula (Ohio) Star Beacon* and has come to Crown Falls to do an article on star hitter Skinny Lappman, the boy who teaches Luke to pitch.

UNCLE RAND (*What Girls Learn**), brother of Frances* Burbank, younger by about a dozen years, a feckless, aimless man who drinks too much and has other undesirable habits but is sincerely devoted to his sister, who mostly raised him. When he shows up on Long Island, Nick* Olsen asks him casually how long he plans to stay, and he replies, "As long as you'll have me." Nick thinks of letting him drive for his limousine company, Trans-Alt, but Rand admits that he has lost his license for drunk driving. Tilden, whose room has a balcony with a stairway to the yard, knows that he does occasionally drive, sneaking a car out at night, and she is well aware that he drinks almost every night, then comes into her room, and, ostensibly rubbing her with lotion, fondles her in ways not quite sexually abusive but still not acceptable. Once, when he goes a little too far, he is ashamed and contrite. At the same time, he is outraged to discover that Elizabeth*, Tilden's younger sister, is experimenting with beer and sex in the garage with a neighbor boy. Before Rand leaves, Tilden discovers that he has been having an affair with the flamboyant dispatcher Lainey DeWitt.

UNDER THE BEETLE'S CELLAR (Walker*, Mary Willis, Doubleday, 1995), mystery-thriller with detective-story aspects set for about four days in Austin, Texas, at the time of publication. Although the perspective alternates between Walter Demming, Vietnam veteran and school bus driver, and Molly Cates, middle-aged crime journalist for the *Lone Star Monthly*, the plot is easily summarized. Walter and eleven schoolchildren, all firstborns ranging in age from six to twelve, were kidnapped forty-five days before the action begins by the fanatical religious cult leader Samuel Mordecai* and his followers, the Hearth Jezreelites, and incarcerated in a school bus buried somewhere on the Jezreelite compound. There the Jezreelites believe that the children will be purified by the earth in preparation for the apocalypse, which, according to Mordecai's interpretation of Revelation and his own Rapture of Mordecai, will arrive in five days and destroy the world now corrupted by technology. Walter's main problems are to allay the children's fears and meld them into a group for common survival, which he does by telling them in installments a story that the reader soon recognizes arises from his war experiences. It concerns a vulture named Jacksonville who triumphs against the enemy with the help of Lopez, an ant-eater. He must also prepare the children for either an FBI (Federal Bureau of Investigation) invasion or sacrificial murder, which he does by teaching the children to use the bus seats as barricades and care for little Josh, who dies of an asthma attack before release comes. He must calm down and encourage the children after Mordecai's frequent religious harangues. Molly, who once wrote about Mordecai in an article on cults, methodically and courageously assists authorities in tracking down clues about Mordecai that will help them in securing the children's release through diplomacy or, failing that, in executing an attack on the compound. She comes into contact with a series of colorful characters, including Dorothy Huff, Mordecai's grandmother, who knew him as Donny Ray Grimes; Jake Alesky, Walter's Vietnam buddy; and Samuel Asquith, also a preacher; and Mordecai's ex-wife, Annette Grimes, both of whom are subsequently horribly murdered by the Sword Hand of God, Mordecai's extracompound thugs. Molly herself barely escapes the same fate through the intervention of Copper, an ex-police dog given her by her ex-husband and current sweetheart, police lieutenant Grady Traynor, with whom she must resolve personal problems. Events so fall out that Molly and Rain Conroy, a sharpshooter police-woman disguised as the birth mother whom Mordecai has never met, enter the compound ostensibly to confer with Mordecai. Molly enables Rain to shoot Mordecai and thus precipitate the assault that releases the captives. The book's title comes from a line in Emily Dickinson's poem #949, which is quoted in a hurried phone conversation between Walter and the FBI commander and alerted authorities about where on the compound the children are being held. Most elements are familiar from formula fiction; violence abounds; Molly, Walter, and other characters are stock; the inevitable sex scenes appear, but in restraint; and Mordecai is an exaggerated, but otherwise typical, psychoreligious fanatic. The reader identifies early with Molly and Walter and cares about the children, who are drawn one-dimensionally and sympathetically—organized Kim, religious Conrad, tough-guy Hector, depressed Philip, sickly Josh, and others. Tension accelerates gradually and relentlessly, and welcome relief comes with the final scenes. Walter's death at the hands of the Jezreelites as he defends the children is presented as both a personal release and a redemptive conclusion to his Vietnam experiences. The book is more mature in its psychological ramifications than most books of its genre for the teen trade, and the psychological ramifications and police and FBI methods, social service work, and cult details are equally as enthralling as the action, which echoes the events at Waco. SLJ.

UNDER THE BLOOD-RED SUN (Salisbury*, Graham, Delacorte, 1994), historical novel of the Japanese attack on December 7, 1941, on Pearl Harbor in Honolulu, Oahu, Hawaii. The first half of the book sets the social and political milieu, and the last half tells about the bombing and the events leading out of it as they affect one Japanese-American family and their friends. The main concerns in late 1941 of narrator Tomi (Tomikazu) Nakaji, 13, are school; his mixed-breed dog, Lucky, and her puppies; being the man of the family while his fisherman-father, Taro*, is out on his sampan; taking care of Taro's prize racing pigeons; baseball and the progress of the Brooklyn Dodgers; hanging out with his best friend, Billy* Davis, a haole (white) boy his age who lives near-by, and the Portuguese-American Corteles cousins, Rico and Mose, who also attend mixed-ethnic Roosevelt School and are on the Rats baseball team; and staying out of the reach of the bullying haole kid Keet Wilson, on whose wealthy father's lands the Nakaji shack stands and for whose mother Mama* is a maid. Tomi and his friends are barely aware of the wars that are raging in Europe and the Far East, but they know that anti-Japanese sentiment has increased consid-erably. Tomi is often embarrassed and even frightened by Grampa's* great pride in being a first-generation Japanese immigrant—the old man's love for the Jap-anese flag, which he likes to wave, and his affection for the family samurai sword and similar heirlooms. Starting with that fateful Sunday morning, life gets tough for the Nakajis. Tomi is catching Billy's practice pitches when the boys become aware of many planes zooming overhead, which they think at first are American, then realize that the planes bear the blood-red sun emblem of Japan. Tomi remembers that Taro is out there in the harbor fishing. Frightened, Mama insists that all Grampa's Japanese heirlooms be buried immediately. From the radio belonging to Charlie, the Wilsons' Hawaiian gardener, they learn that the region is under martial law and that they must black out their windows. The next weeks are filled with uncertainty and turmoil. School is canceled indefi-nitely, and soldiers force Grampa and Tomi to kill Taro's pigeons, because it has been reported (by Skeet, Tomi later learns) that the birds are messenger pigeons. They learn that Taro was shot in the leg, his helper, Sanji, killed by strafing U.S. planes, and the fishing boat scuttled. Tomi discovers that Taro is being held prisoner on Sand Island in the harbor and bravely swims out to visit him, after which Taro is interned somewhere on the mainland. Tomi's little sister, Kimi, cowers in a closet until enticed out by Tomi with the offer of one of Lucky's puppies. Without Taro's income and with food and supplies like kerosene running low or unavailable, times get very hard. They play a little baseball, beating their archrivals, the Kaka'ako Boys, and their superpitcher, The Butcher, and have problems with a street gang, so some aspects of their life remain the same. Two FBI (Federal Bureau of Investigation) agents arrest Grampa and take him away somewhere. Near the end of January, a postcard comes from Taro, and Mr. Davis finds out that Taro is in Crystal City, Texas, but cannot learn where Grampa is. Mama bravely assures Tomi and Kimi that they will be strong and survive, and Tomi is sure that, while his family are ashamed of what Japan has done, some day he will bring Grandpa's heirlooms out and display them with pride again. Characters are well drawn, even minor ones like Mr. Ramos, the law student who became a teacher because he feels that he can do more good as a teacher and who discusses with his students such issues of the war as freedom of choice. Tomi's narrative, with Tomi always and credibly at the center, moves steadily. Best is the sense of chaos and tension that the bombing arouses among the unsuspecting, ordinary people and the irrational actions of some citizens and authorities. An epilogue with historical background adds information. ALA; O'Dell; SLJ.

UNDER THE MERMAID ANGEL (Moore*, Martha, Delacorte, 1995), realistic girl's growing-up novel in a school-story context. Jesse, 13, the narrator, thinks that she is very plain and a misfit; that life in small-town Ida, Texas, is boring; and that her not saying prayers for him caused the death of her younger brother, William III. Life picks up somewhat when red-haired, bosomy, flamboyant, romantic Roxanne*, a waitress, moves into the trailer next door. Although Mama disapproves of Roxanne, she nevertheless lets Jesse and her little sister, Doris Ray, 5, sleep outside overnight in Roxanne's yard to watch the meteor shower. This is the first of several adventures that Jesse has with Roxanne and that will elevate her self-esteem, make her less prickly, and prompt her to think and behave more charitably. Among others, they visit Mr. Arthur's Wax Museum, where they especially enjoy his version of the Last Supper, remark on the mermaid angel that hangs overhead, and learn that the old man, who suffers from Alzheimer's, will soon be moved to a home. At school, Jesse becomes involved with a new student, intelligent, red-haired, scar-faced Debbie Bartacelli, whose face and arms bear terrible scars from the auto accident that also took the lives of her parents. Debbie starts a school paper, which she calls *The Icon*, on whose editorial board Jesse sits and for which disagreeable, contentious Franklin* Harris, called Frankenstein, draws clever cartoons. Complicating Jesse's life more is troublesome Doris Ray, who, costumed as an angel, falls from the tree outside their trailer, breaks her leg, and suffers a concussion. Jesse is surprised and grateful when Doris Ray says that she herself caused the accident instead of that the fall was provoked by Jesse, as it really was. Jesse learns that Roxanne came to Ida to look for the son whom she gave up for adoption years before. Not unexpectedly, the boy turns out to be Franklin, Jesse's nemesis. A farewell party for Mr. Arthur is the book's climax, for which, among other decorations for the Hawaiian theme, Roxanne hangs the mermaid angel over the dance floor. Although she had said that she wished to dance with Franklin, Roxanne never appears that night, leaving Jesse to deliver the tribute to Mr. Arthur and dance with Franklin. A note found that night from Roxanne informs Jesse that she has left town and that she has placed a special gift—a plaster cast of his dead father's hand—in a bag for Jesse to give to Franklin when she thinks that the time is right. Later a postcard arrives from Roxanne that informs Jesse that she now lives in Pensacola, Florida, and has a job on a cruise ship. Jesse gives Debbie, who will soon leave for Europe to spend the summer with her professor-father there, a bottle with a note to William III telling him that she loved him and really wanted him to get well. She asks Debbie to throw the bottle into the ocean, thus relieving her conscience about his death.

The plot seems curiously fragmented, overforeshadowed, and heavily reliant on coincidence, and such symbols as angels are too obvious and frequent. Although the most vividly depicted of the cast, Roxanne never completely convinces, too overdrawn for believability and given too many romantic and sententious speeches. They suit the rather sentimental story but depict Roxanne as a kind of angel who, like those in the television show *Touched by an Angel*, pass through and miraculously change the whole area. Franklin mends his mean ways too abruptly, and Debbie's speeches seem more adult than those of the usual thirteen-year-old, even though she is exceptionally bright. Best are the family scenes, the vividly described small town life, and the gentle humor that pervades the book and leaves the reader with the feeling that life is good but could be better if everyone would only emulate Roxanne and try a little harder to be kind, charitable, and understanding. ALA.

THE UNLIKELY ROMANCE OF KATE BJORKMAN (Plummer*, Louise, Delacorte, 1995), romance novel set in St. Paul, Minnesota, that makes fun of the genre while conforming to its basic pattern. The narrator, Kate Bjorkman, 17, comes home from an errand to find that her brother, Bjorn, married the previous summer, has arrived from Stanford with his bride, Trish, for a surprise Christmas visit, bringing with him his old buddy, Richard Bradshaw, and Richard's friend, Fleur St. Germaine. Although Kate is four years younger than Richard, she has always had a secret crush on him. Kate is torn by envy of Fleur (who is petite and beautiful in contrast to Kate, who is six feet tall and wears thick glasses), and by a natural liking for the tactful, friendly girl. Their holiday proceeds with various conflicts and discoveries. Bjorn and Trish have a disagreement over whether to choose a spruce or a piñon pine for the Christmas tree, a fight that makes the whole household uncomfortable. The chief thorn in Kate's holiday is her friend Ashley Cooper, who cannot resist adding any new man to her collection and quickly tries to annex Richard, even inviting him to be her escort to the annual New Year's Eve dinner dance given by Kate's aunt. Since Kate has invited her debate partner, Helmut, an exchange student, she is easily outflanked, but on early Christmas morning she and Richard go skating. After a bump in the ice causes them both to fall and breaks Kate's glasses, Richard kisses her, and they both realize that they are in love. During the next week Fleur flies back to California to attend her mother's third or fourth wedding, a decision that she has reached after seeing how important the Bjorkman family members are to each other. Richard and Kate are enraptured with each other but know that they must go to the dinner dance with other partners. At the dance Ashley, dressed like a real siren, disappears with Richard for some time. Kate comes upon them embracing in the kitchen. When Richard follows her, trying to explain, Kate slugs him and gets Helmut to take her home. The next day she refuses to speak to Richard. The following morning, when the visitors are about to leave, Richard decides to stay, and Bjorn and Trish drive off without him. Kate threatens to leave home if he stays, so he builds a snow cave and camps out in the backyard. Finally, after he holds up a sign that says, "Will Work For Food," Kate has to laugh at his antics, and she goes out to make up their quarrel. The charm of the book lies not in the simple romantic story but in the analyses that introduce and follow each chapter, describing what should happen according to the pattern of romance novels and the Romance Writers Phrase Book, which Kate is attempting to follow, and the revision notes that explain why her story isn't quite working to plan. In the end Richard has transferred to the University of Minnesota, but Kate has applied to Columbia. Although she plans to go with him to visit his parents in California, she admits that the novel doesn't have the proper ending with a lasting commitment. Still, she has learned to value her supportive family and to understand them better. The humor is light but genuine. SLJ.

V

VAIL, RACHEL (1966–), born in New York City, writer of novels starring young teenagers. Vail grew up in New Rochelle, New York, and received her B.A. degree from Georgetown University in 1988. Her novel of a girl's experience at summer camp, where she is determined to change her image, *Daring to Be Abigail** (Orchard, 1996), was chosen for the *School Library Journal* list of Best Books for Children. Among her earlier titles are *Wonder* (Orchard, 1991), *Do-Over* (Orchard, 1992), and *Ever After* (Orchard, 1994). More recently, she has published several novels in The Friendship Ring Series, starting with *If You Only Knew* (Scholastic, 1998). She lives in Cambridge, Massachusetts.

VANDE VELDE, VIVIAN (1951–), born in New York City; attended the State University of New York at Brockport and Rochester Business Institute; writer of humorous parodies and thrillers. Since her first novel, *A Hidden Magic* (Crown, 1985), which fetchingly subverts the classic tale with its plain princess and vain, spoiled prince, Vande Velde has written almost a dozen more books of short stories and novels in a similar vein. In *User Unfriendly* (Harcourt, 1991), a computer game goes terribly awry; in *Dragon's Bait* (Harcourt, 1992), the dragon helps the princess instead of devouring her; *Tales from the Brothers Grimm and the Sisters Weird* (Harcourt, 1995) offers thirteen more or less fractured fairy tales; *Companions of the Night* (Harcourt, 1995) looks at vampires differently; *Never Trust a Dead Man** (Harcourt, 1999), a *School Library Journal* selection, is a comic mystery-thriller in which a presumed murderer is sealed inside the tomb of the man whom he is supposed to have killed and meets there an irritable, but helpful (at a stiff price!), witch; and *Magic Can Be Murder* (Harcourt, 2000) features mother and daughter witches. Vande Velde has also contributed short stories to such magazines as *Cricket* and *Highlights for Children*. Her writings have been hailed as fresh, engaging, and simply good fun.

VAN DRAANEN, WENDELIN, computer science instructor, wife, mother, and a part-time singer in a rock band. She enjoys writing funny stories about smart, determined young women and lives in Santa Maria, California. She is best known for her several books for middle-grade readers about Sammy (Samantha) Keyes, the intrepid girl detective. In *Sammy Keyes and the Hotel Thief** (Knopf, 1998), Sammy observes a theft in progress and sets out to bring the culprit to justice. Humorous, scary, adventurous, with an attractive protagonist, the book was nominated for the Edgar Allan Poe Award. Others in the series are *Sammy Keyes and the Skeleton Man* (Random House, 1998) and *Sammy Keyes and the Sisters of Mercy* (Knopf, 1999). She also published *How I Survived Being a Girl* (Scholastic, 1997).

THE VAN GOGH CAFE (Rylant*, Cynthia, Harcourt, 1995), short, episodic, contemporary fantasy novel set in the town of Flowers, Kansas, notable for its warm, whimsical tone, its forthright, unadorned style, and the care with which the fantasy elements are worked into the realistic aspects. The Van Gogh Cafe, known to be magical because it is located in a Main Street building that was once a theater, is owned and operated by an earnest young man named Marc and his daughter, Clara, 10, who believes in magic. The cafe always brings out the best in whoever enters, from the regular town clientele, who become involved in the magical occurrences, to those from out of town who also participate and even contribute new magic to it. One Saturday, an opossum hangs upside down in the tree outside the cafe window, attracting the attention of the customers, causing those who have not been getting along to make up, including a young husband and wife who have had a yelling spat, and helping a man whose wife has recently died to gain new purpose in life. In March, lightning strikes the cafe, creating perfectly cooked food for days and inspiring Marc to write helpful prediction poems. In October, a glamorous woman dressed in lace and pearls stops for a 7Up and leaves a little foil package that contains two tiny magic muffins. These mysteriously multiply until there are exactly enough to comfort fourteen preschool children whose bus has been caught in a sudden snowstorm. Near Christmas, an elegant stranger drops in, an elderly man whom Marc recognizes as a star of silent films. He tells them that he is awaiting the arrival of an old friend and stays in the cafe for the night. In the morning they find him dead, holding a newspaper clipping that indicates that the friend died many years ago. A wayward gull takes up residence on the cafe roof and provides some humor when Emerald, the cafe cat, falls in love with him, and then some consternation when the cafe is besieged by photographers, and other representatives of the media turn up to celebrate the happening. Eventually, the gull is joined by some fifty other gulls, all of whom leave town and the limelight together by hitching a ride on a moving van bound for California. In the last episode, a failed writer absorbs the cafe's magic, remembers that the painter after whom it is named sold only one painting in his lifetime, and leaves with renewed inspiration and the determination to write a book entitled, *The Van Gogh Cafe*. The gentle humor and understated poignance support the theme of the importance of the imagination and simple compassion in making life happy and worthwhile. ALA.

VICKY LEE (*Christie & Company Down East**), beautiful Chinese-American roommate of Christie* Montgomery and Maggie Porter at The Cabot School in Massachusetts, who with Christie is visiting Maggie at Maggie's parents' Blue Heron Inn. All three girls are expected to help the Porters at the inn by waiting tables and entertaining children, but only Vicky gets up early in the morning to help Mrs. Porter in the kitchen with breakfast. Vicky is experienced at food service, since her parents own a popular Cantonese restaurant in Brookline, Massachusetts. Vicky has long, heavy, dark hair, is always carefully dressed, and projects an air of elegance. Like the other two girls, she loves reading mysteries. She is a clear thinker and gets right to the point of whatever is under discussion.

THE VIEW FROM SATURDAY (Konigsburg*, E. L., Atheneum, 1996), light-hearted, amusing, contemporary, realistic novel of school and home life set for about a year mostly in Epiphany, New York, with some scenes in Florida and some elsewhere in New York state. Paraplegic Mrs. Eva Marie Olinski, sixth-grade teacher, returns to teaching at the beginning of the school year after ten years away. Four of her students, three boys and one girl, who call themselves the Souls, participate successfully in the state's Academic Bowl, beating the odds to win against a team of eighth graders. At the beginning the novel poses the question: "Why were these four students chosen?" which is answered gradually in the rest of the story. The novel's structure is complicated. The bowl scenes, in which the questions posed happen to connect with the experiences of the students to whom they are directed, and the events surrounding the bowl scenes are in third person and mostly feature Mrs. Olinski. The remaining chapters, in first person, are related by the students. In each, a student gains some knowledge that helps him or her answer the questions correctly. Noah Gershom tells how he happens to be best man at the wedding of Izzy Diamondstein and Margaret Draper, friends of his Gershom grandparents in Century Village (a retirement community) in Florida, and learns calligraphy (the target of the first question posed in the Bowl). Red-haired Nadia Diamondstein, Izzy's grand-daughter, helps Izzy and Margaret rescue threatened nesting turtles so that they can make their way to the Sargasso Sea (the answer to another question). Also involved in turtle rescue is Ethan Potter, Margaret's visiting grandson. Ethan tells of his growing friendship with a new boy in school, Asian-Indian-American Julian Singh, who is picked on by other boys and whose father has bought a historic house and turned it into a bed-and-breakfast (B and B). Julian tells how he foils a plot to keep Nadia's dog, Ginger, from successfully playing the part of Sandy in the school's musical, *Annie*. The four youngsters meet regularly on Saturday at the B and B (hence the book's title), soon to be joined by Mrs.

Olinski. She chooses them because of their qualities of teamwork, persistence, tolerance, and willingness to practice and practice even more. While the pieces of the clever plot come together gradually like a puzzle, the characters are mostly on the surface, although they do have connections, as do the plot pieces, that are not immediately apparent. The style is fresh, even saucy, and often wise-cracking, while striking metaphors, witty authorial intrusions, double meanings, and paradoxes provide many surprises. In a manner reminiscent of Konigsburg's first Newbery winner, *From the Mixed-up Files of Mrs. Basil E. Frankweiler*, Mrs. Olinski is a catalyst for bringing the children together. Margaret Draper, who turns out to have been Mrs. Olinski's principal before her accident, is also a mechanism by which the children make connections. Although the book is sometimes too clever and outruns itself, it demonstrates Konigsburg's remark-able skill with words and her ability to produce plots that are not all on the surface and project an intellectual appeal that goes beyond mere sequence of events. ALA; Newbery Winner; SLJ.

VINCENT VAN GOGH (*Johanna: A Novel of the van Gogh Family**), his-torical brother of Theodoor* van Gogh, brother-in-law of Johanna van Gogh-Bonger, the title figure of the novel, and renowned Dutch painter of the late nineteenth century in France and the Netherlands. Although Vincent, presented as a mad, demanding, selfish genius, contributes only a couple of letters in this epistolary novel, he dominates the book as he evidently dominated the lives of Johanna and Theo. Theo supported him throughout most of his later life, while Johanna retained and brought to the fore his paintings at great financial and emotional cost. She spent much of her later life sorting and editing the corre-spondence between Vincent and Theo.

VINNIE VAN GOGH (*Johanna: A Novel of the van Gogh Family**), Vincent Willem van Gogh, historical only son of Johanna van Gogh-Bonger, the title figure, and Theodoor* van Gogh, and nephew of the renowned Dutch artist Vincent* van Gogh. Vinnie was born after Vincent committed suicide and shortly before his father's death. He is presented as a lively, intelligent boy and eager adolescent, a good student, and a loving son and grandson. He very much wants his mother and Johan Cohen Gosschalk to marry and looks up to his stepfather, who becomes an excellent role model. Vinnie becomes a successful engineer. The author informs the readers that all that is known for certain about Johanna appears in a nine-page memoir written by Vinnie after her death and published as the introduction to the English edition of the letters between his father and Vincent, which Johanna had gathered together, arranged, and edited.

VOIGT, CYNTHIA (1942–   ), born in Boston, Massachusetts; teacher and for two decades the highly acclaimed writer of more than twenty contemporary novels for children and young adults. The best known involve the Tillerman family and their friends, including the Newbery Award-winning *Dicey's Song*

(Atheneum, 1982). *When She Hollers** (Scholastic, 1994) is an American Library Association selection about a girl who is sexually abused by her stepfather. Named to the Fanfare list is *Bad Girls** (Scholastic, 1996), a humorous school novel that takes place entirely within a present-day fifth-grade classroom. *Bad, Badder, Baddest* (Scholastic, 1997) and *It's Not Easy Being Bad* (Atheneum, 2000) continue the series. For additional information, titles, and title entries, see *Dictionary, 1960–1984* [*The Callendar Papers*; *Dicey's Song*; *A Solitary Blue*]; *Dictionary, 1985–1990* [*Building Blocks*; *Come A Stranger*; *Izzy, Willy-Nilly*; *Sons from Afar*]; and *Dictionary, 1990–1994* [*Seventeen Against the Dealer*; *When She Hollers*].

W

WALKER, MARY WILLIS (1942–   ), born in Foxpoint, Wisconsin; resident of Austin, Texas; graduate of Duke University with a degree in English; former high school teacher, writer of popular mystery-suspense novels for adults. Her third novel, *Under the Beetle's Cellar** (Doubleday, 1995), an adult thriller filled with suspense and emotional appeal featuring middle-aged crime journalist Molly Cates, who assists authorities in tracking down clues to the kidnapping of a busload of schoolchildren by the leader of an apocalyptic cult, was cited by *School Library Journal*. Her first novel, *Zero at the Bone* (St. Martin's, 1991), received numerous accolades, and her second, *The Red Scream* (Doubleday, 1994), introduced the intrepid, persistent Molly Cates. She has also published *All the Dead Lie Down* (HarperCollins, 1998), contributed essays and book reviews to periodicals, and written the script for a documentary. Her novels have been translated into seven foreign languages.

WALK TWO MOONS (Creech*, Sharon, HarperCollins, 1994), novel combining personal-problem and mystery elements, set in the mid-1990s on an automobile trip from Euclid, Ohio, to Lewiston, Idaho, and involving several stories within the frame story. In response to their request that she "spin us a yarn" to pass the time as she and her Gram* and Gramps Hiddle travel west to visit the grave of her deceased mother, Sal (Salmanaca Tree) Hiddle, 13, tells about how her best friend, Phoebe* Winterbottom, lost her mother, at the same time conveying a keen sense of her inability to come to terms with her own mother's death. After Sal's mother, Sugar*, leaves home after her baby dies at birth, Sal and her father move from their farm near Bybanks, Kentucky, to Euclid, Ohio, where her father's friend Mrs. Cadaver*, a widowed nurse, lives. Next door to Mrs. Cadaver's place live the stiff, correct, very respectable Winterbottom family, including Phoebe, Sal's age. Sal dislikes Mrs. Cadaver, because she thinks the woman and her father are sweethearts. Since Phoebe, especially, is inclined to overdramatize matters, the two girls soon believe that Mrs. Cadaver murdered

her husband. Mrs. Winterbottom seems unhappy and on edge but keeps a sparkling house and serves only healthful food. One day, a young man, a stranger
of about eighteen, appears at the Winterbottom door and asks for Mrs. Winterbottom. The girls become convinced that he is a lunatic and that he has left a
series of white envelopes on the Winterbottom doorstep bearing cryptic messages, including "Don't judge a man until you've walked two moons in his
moccasins." Shortly thereafter, Mrs. Winterbottom disappears. The girls go
twice to the police with what they feel are clues that something dreadful happened. The second time Sal sees on the sergeant's desk a photograph of the
lunatic standing beside the sergeant. They follow up on this clue, which leads
them to a nearby university where the lunatic is enrolled and are amazed to see
him and Mrs. Winterbottom embracing. When Mrs. Winterbottom returns, she
explains that the lunatic is Mike Bickel, her illegitimate son, who was put up
for adoption before she married Mr. Winterbottom, was adopted by the sergeant
and his wife, and recently traced his birth mother. The messages were not left
by the lunatic but by Mrs. Partridge, Mrs. Cadaver's blind, eccentric mother.
The Hiddles' trip west is eventful: they visit such landmarks as Pipestone National Monument, the Black Hills, and Yellowstone National Park and are accosted by a young man who attempts to rob them but, when Gram is bitten by
a water moccasin, saves her life by sucking out the poison, among other incidents. At Coeur d'Alene, Idaho, Gram suffers a stroke and is hospitalized. Fearing that she will not reach the grave by her mother's birthday and given money
and the car keys by Gramps and thus his implicit approval, Sal takes off with
the car and drives over the mountains by night to where her mother died in a
bus accident, a fact only now revealed to the reader. Returning to Coeur d'Alene,
Sal discovers that Gram has died, and she and Gramps return to Bybanks, where
they bury Gram and where Sal's father and Sal also return to live. Sal now
realizes that her mother is really dead. The several story strands are sometimes
hard to keep track of, since they are intermingled and complicated by coincidence, by Sal's reflections (it is hard to tell sometimes whether they are spoken
or unspoken), by the gradually revealed details of Sal's life, and by several
unusual characters: the loud, unruly Finney family, who contrast with the prim
Winterbottoms and include Ben* Finney, a cousin on whom Sal grows sweet;
the children's English teacher, lively, iconoclastic Mr.* Birkway, who is the
focus of arresting, humorous school scenes; and Mrs. Partridge. While most of
the figures are one-dimensional and functionary, Gram and Gramps are fully
rounded and almost steal the book from Sal, who is earnest, brave, and easy to
like. The style is crisp, often strikingly sensory, and replete with dialogue. Although the Native-American aspects involving Sal's family seem gratuitous, they
also do not detract. The abundant gentle humor, restrained seriousness, and
genuine interpersonal relationships add to the book's effectiveness as a picture
of contemporary family life. The title has specific application to the trip: Gram
and Gramps feel that Sal needs a chance to walk in her mother's tracks before
she passes judgment. ALA; Newbery Winner.

WALLACE, BARBARA BROOKS (1922–), born in Soochow, China; author of many books for young people, the best known being Dickensian melodramas set in the Victorian period. *Cousins in the Castle** (Atheneum, 1996), which moves from England through an ocean voyage to New York City, is a novel of an innocent, but brave, young girl, betrayals, and evil relatives, all turning out happily in the end. *Sparrows in the Scullery** (Atheneum, 1997), an Edgar Allan Poe Award winner, is an even darker story of an exploitative "school" where the boys are underfed, ill-treated, and sent to work in sweatshops and dangerous factories. For earlier biographical information and a title entry, see *Dictionary, 1990–1994* [*The Twin in the Tavern*].

WALTER (*Tiger, Tiger, Burning Bright**), son of the town mechanic in economically depressed Norbu, California. A member of Jesse's final-exam study group at school, Walter is small and hyperactive. He hires on as one of Bobby* Yates' ostrich jockeys in order to help out his family's finances. In the town ostrich race, Walter's mount is Big Bad John, who gets away and pursues Bobby down the street. Walter has low self-esteem and constantly seeks approval from the other boys. When fat Paul suggests that each boy hold a frog in his mouth to prove he is a real man, Walter not only holds the frog but also swallows it. Walter provides humor for Jesse's story. Walter's father has little work and to make ends meet is the weekend boxer at the Long Branch Saloon.

WALTER, VIRGINIA, associate professor in the Graduate School of Education and Information Services at the University of California at Los Angeles and writer for children. *Making Up Megaboy** (DK, 1998) is the strange novel of a boy who, in the person of a cartoon character that he invented, murders a Korean storekeeper. Without sustained narrative, it is composed of documents and thumbnail sketches of various figures who know or interact with the protagonist, pieces that, fitted together, give a picture of a troubled youngster but provide no definite explanation for his action. Earlier, she published a fanciful picture book, *"Hi, Pizza Man!"* (Orchard, 1996). Walter lives in Venice, California.

THE WARDEN (*Holes**), vicious, sadistic woman who runs the Camp Green Lake juvenile detention facility in the Texas desert to which Stanley Yelnats is sent. Tall, red-haired, freckled, she wears a black cowboy hat and black cowboy boots studded with turquoise stones. The boys are certain that she has microphones and tiny cameras hidden around the facility, by which she is able to keep track of them. When angered, she becomes violent. For example, she rakes Mr. Sir's face with her long fingernails, which she says are painted with polish made of rattlesnake venom. She works the boys hard in the attempt to find what Stanley is sure is a hidden treasure. As it happens, her name is Walker. She is apparently a descendant of the Trout Walker who unsuccessfully courted the outlaw Kissin'* Kate Barlow and then sought Kissin' Kate's hidden treasure, rumor of which must have come down in the Walker family.

WATKINS, YOKO KAWASHIMA (1933–   ), born in Asmori, Japan, and raised in Manchuria and northern Korea; Japanese-American whose first autobiographical novel, *So Far from the Bamboo Grove* (Lothrop, 1986), tells about her escape across Korea to Japan in the last days of World War II. Its sequel, *My Brother, My Sister, and I** (Simon & Schuster, 1994), continues the story of the siblings' difficult survival in Japan. She has also published a book of folktales, *Tales from the Bamboo Grove* (Simon & Schuster, 1992). For earlier biographical information and a title entry, see *Dictionary, 1985–1989* [*So Far from the Bamboo Grove*].

WATSON, LARRY (1947–   ), born in Rugby, North Dakota; college teacher and writer. He grew up in Bismarck and received his B.A. and M.A. degrees in English from the University of North Dakota and his Ph.D. degree in creative writing from the University of Utah. He is the author of a suspense novel, *In a Dark Time* (Scribner, 1980), and a chapbook of poetry, *Leaving Dakota* (Song Press, 1983), as well as the best-selling novel *Montana 1948* (Milkweed, 1993), set in Bentrock in northeastern Montana and concerned with conflicts of family loyalty and the requirements of the law for the sheriff of the small community. *Justice** (Milkweed, 1995) is a prequel, tracing in episodes two generations of the Hayden family for whom the position of sheriff is handed down like a royal dynasty. *White Crosses* (Pocket Books, 1997) is also set in Bentrock and concerns the efforts of the sheriff to prevent a scandal from erupting in the wake of two deaths. Watson teaches English at the University of Wisconsin at Stevens Point and lives in Plover, Wisconsin.

THE WATSONS GO TO BIRMINGHAM—1963 (Curtis*, Christopher Paul, Delacorte, 1995), situation-comedy, episodic family novel with period aspects, set mostly in a middle-class neighborhood in Flint, Michigan, in the first six months of 1963. African-American Kenny Watson, 10, looks back and describes those months for the "Weird Watsons," his warm, happy, active family: Dad, Daniel, a good-natured, solid-citizen autoworker; his solicitous, loving Momma, who with Daniel emigrated from Birmingham, Alabama, ten years before events begin; his sweet, pretty, kindergarten-aged sister, Joetta; and his older brother, Byron* (By), as Kenny presents him, a mean, self-centered bully, "just turned thirteen so he was officially a teenage juvenile delinquent." The chapters in the first half of the book are largely self-contained but linked by the same characters. Some deal with Kenny's problems: LJ [*sic*] Jones cheats him out of most of his dinosaur collection; he feels guilty about making fun of Rufus Fry, a new, poor boy from Arkansas; and he himself is teased because he has a "lazy eye" (one that refuses to focus) and excels at his studies. Most events involve Byron, of whom both good and bad sides are seen. When the family scrapes the ice off the Brown Bomber, their 1948 Plymouth, on a "super-duper" cold Saturday, Byron's lips get stuck on the rearview mirror, because, being vain, he kisses the cold glass. Byron and his bullying pal, Buphead, "teach" Kenny how to survive a blizzard by almost freezing him to death in a snowbank. The oldest kids in school, having been held back for obvious reasons, By and Buphead generally terrorize the other students. In the book's most hilarious scene, By plays with matches, in spite of Momma's repeated warnings, and, when he is caught setting fire to the parachutes of his toy Nazi soldiers, Momma furiously burns his fingers to teach him a lesson. The escapade that precipitates the family trip to Birmingham, during Dad's vacation, is By's getting a "conk," that is, bleaching and straightening his hair. After Dad angrily shaves By completely bald, he and Momma decide that By is intractable and should live with Grandma Sands in Alabama. Momma plans the entire trip down to the last penny and minute, and they set out down I75 in the Brown Bomber, which Dad has outfitted with a brand-new Ultra-Glide record player. They arrive ahead of schedule, Dad having decided that he can drive straight through, nonstop. Since Grandma Sands, although frail from a stroke, has a "Wicked Witch of the West" tongue and attitude, By behaves, for the most part. His most memorable act is saving Kenny from drowning in the Wool Pooh (whirlpool) in the river near by. The family leaves for Flint when the Baptist Church to which Joetta has gone for Sunday School is bombed, and four girls are killed. In Flint, Kenny is so distraught by what he saw at the church when he went to look for Joetta after he heard the explosion that he can find solace only in hiding in the "World-Famous Watson Pet Hospital" behind the living-room couch, until By sternly informs him that it was Kenny whom Joetta followed to safety and that the Wool Pooh creature that Kenny thinks was after her was a figment of his overwrought imagination. Although the action is disjointed and the conclusion abrupt, the family's decision to return to Flint, bringing By with them, seems reasonable under the circumstances. Since only a few aspects of racial discrimination are mentioned and then only briefly, the reader is not prepared for the bombing, and the book's title does not fit with what happens in the bulk of the book. Characters have dimension, and the family might live next door, so real do they seem. By often uses trash talk, and the children's behavior seems true to their ages. Whether or not By mends his antisocial ways is left open, but, since he exhibits positive behavior at the end, the expectation is that he will improve. A disturbing aspect is the idiosyncratic use of commas, which produces ungrammatical comma splices. An Epilogue summarizes some events in the civil rights movement to establish the setting for the bombing, which is historical. ALA; Fanfare; Josette Frank; Newbery Honor.

WAYNE BONNER (*While No One Was Watching**), mean, surly, older cousin of Earl*, Frankie*, and Angela* Foster, at seventeen a younger model of his ornery, often drunk father. Even his mother no longer wants him around, he is so disagreeable. Wayne has involved Earl in stealing various items, usually pickup pieces, but gradually those that are more valuable and can easily be sold, like bikes from yards and tools from construction sites. He decides that it would be lucrative to steal cash from homeless people who sleep under bridges, especially those who have some physical disability. Wayne is sure that the government will soon replace their stolen funds. It is his idea to steal from old Mr.* Tiptop. At the end he is on the way to jail. As the younger children illustrate one kind of fate that awaits those who get into trouble "while no one is watching," he represents another kind of unfortunate child.

THE WEDDING (West*, Dorothy, Doubleday, 1995), novel of family relationships through five generations, culminating with the wedding of Shelby* Coles at the Martha's Vineyard enclave of the elite African-American community called the Oval, in the 1920s or early 1930s. Although Shelby and her sister, Liz*, are both fair-haired and light-skinned, and there are both whites and blacks in their ancestry, they are considered black. Liz has married an African-American doctor, but of a darker skin and lower social class than her mother, Corinne, approved. Shelby* is engaged to a white jazz player, Meade, an even more controversial choice in the Oval and one his parents have refused to sanction. To complicate the situation, Lute* McNeill, an almost uneducated, but highly successful, maker of fine furniture, who is spending the summer on the Oval with his three little girls, each by a different white wife, has decided that Shelby will be his fourth wife. Confident of his ability to seduce any woman, he has set out to win her, although he is not actually divorced from his last marriage. The novel, which starts with the preparations for Shelby's wedding, swings between generations and time periods, going back to the Civil War, when Gram*, white great-grandmother of the Coles girls, then Miss Caroline Shelby, lost her family's plantation and fortune. Gram's daughter, Josephine, undernourished, now an old maid, marries Hannibal, the son of a slave who was a child with Gram, a young man educated more through persistence than brilliance, who becomes the first black president of the leading Negro college in Washington. Although devastated by the marriage, Gram rallies to raise Corinne, their child whom Josephine, now a recluse in her bedroom, will not touch. Corinne marries Clark* Coles, a doctor with a white forebear, Old Sir, who took a slave girl to bed after his wife was dead and his children grown, built a house for her, and lived with her as his wife after the Civil War. On the Coles side of the family, as with Hannibal and his ex-slave mother, there is a strong push for upward mobility. Through the help of a white old-maid schoolteacher, Clark's father, Isaac, finds his way north and becomes a doctor. The action culminates the morning of Shelby's wedding, when Clark learns that his longtime mistress, to whom he looks for love and comfort and whom he expected to marry when his daughters are off his hands, is marrying another man. He confronts Shelby, agonizing about his failure as a father and wondering if she has chosen a white man because he has given her a model of a black man as inadequate. Liz also tackles the racial problem with Shelby, pointing out that she will never know whether a black man could satisfy her more than Meade because she has never made love to one. Confused and uncertain, Shelby almost succumbs to Lute's seduction, but before she can keep her tryst with him, his current wife, Della, shows up. In his fury he beats Della, pushes her into his car, and zooms off to return her to the airport, not seeing his own six-year-old Tina, the darling of his heart, until he has struck and killed her. The tragedy brings Shelby to her senses, and she sees that race is a false distinction but that love is not, and she is sure of her love for Meade. The novel is badly overwritten in places, particularly in explaining in elaborate language emotions of the characters that could more effectively be shown. The major focus of the story, however, the way the twin, but distinct, concerns, race and color, haunt the people of the Oval, brings up important and often hidden questions. Because the Coles family has wealth, social status in the African-American community, and skins as light as most of the white summer residents of Martha's Vineyard, there is added irony in their preoccupation. A family tree showing both sides of Shelby's ancestry is very helpful in keeping the many figures straight. SLJ.

THE WELL: DAVID'S STORY (Taylor*, Mildred D., Dial, 1995), short historical novel set in rural Mississippi during the hot, dry summer of 1910, another in the cycle of novels and short stories about the African-American Logan family, the best known of which is the Newbery Award-winning *Roll of Thunder, Hear My Cry*. Polite, timid David Logan, 10, who grows up to become the much-respected Papa in *Roll of Thunder*, looks back on this summer of his childhood and starts his story: "Charlie Simms was always mean. . . ." Charlie, a neighboring white boy of fourteen, son of sharecroppers, and proud, self-assured Hammer*, David's brother, 13, are the catalysts for the trouble that afflicts the landowning Logans that summer. A prolonged drought has dried up most of the area's water. The only well with sweet water belongs to the Logans, who generously share it with everyone, white as well as black. Papa* Logan (Paul-Edward) and David's older brothers, Mitchell and Kevin, are away lumbering along the Natchez Trace for money to pay taxes and acquire more land. One dawn Charlie and his younger brother, Ed-Rose [*sic*], come for water. Hammer stands proud, refusing to behave obsequiously because the Simmses are white. Mama* (Caroline, also known as Big Ma) intervenes before there is trouble, but like Hammer, Ma* Rachel, David's grandmother, feels Mama is too generous. After breakfast, David and Hammer take cows to the Creek Rosa Lee, a shared watering place. They meet several youths, black and white, including the Simms boys and Joe* McCalister, an older, slow-minded black youth. Words are exchanged about the water, the white boys are racially insulting, and tension accelerates. Later that week, the Logan boys encounter Charlie by the side of the road, his wagon hanging over the ditch, one of its wheels off. Charlie orders the "niggers" to give him a hand. While Hammer stands back, his fists clenched, David quickly agrees, to keep the peace, although he is on a crutch from a broken leg. Over Hammer's protests, David tries but cannot hold the wagon up long enough for Charlie to replace the wheel. When the wagon falls, Charlie angrily knocks David down. Temper flaring, Hammer attacks Charlie, who hits his head against a stone. The Logan boys leave, afraid that Charlie is dead, rush home, and tell Mama. Even though a neighbor reports seeing Charlie up and about, they know that trouble will follow. When the white sheriff comes, Mama tells him what her sons told her happened. Although he is sympathetic, because he respects the Logans and also likes the molasses bread that Mama bakes for him, he realizes that the Simmses and other whites must be placated. He arranges that the Logan boys work that summer for Mr. Simms, and Mama whips the boys to satisfy Mr. Simms. For the rest of the summer, even after Papa returns, the boys labor for Mr. Simms, Hammer's resentment increasing all the while. After Papa and the brothers head back to the Natchez Trace, Hammer goes deliberately to the Simms place and knocks Charlie down. Charlie threatens that Hammer will pay. A couple of days later, the Logan well is found fouled with dead animals. Hammer accuses the Simms boys, and eventually on the witness of Joe McCalister it is proved that Charlie and Ed-Rose are guilty. They are forced to clean the well, but the water is spoiled for weeks. Based on stories told in the author's family dating back to the early part of the twentieth century, the book's strongest point is its picture of racial tension deriving from the whites' attitude that they are inherently superior to blacks and, in particular, from their resentment of landowning, independent blacks. Several short anecdotes about slave and just-post-slave days appear within the larger story. Although Hammer is too prickly and Charlie too mean, independent, resourceful Mama and sensible, sturdy Papa are good figures. Many of the characters appear in the other Logan books, and encountering them here lends depth to the other stories. Addams; ALA.

WELL WISHED (Billingsley*, Franny, Atheneum, 1997), fantasy novel of magic set in an unidentified country and unspecified period in the village of Bishop Mayne. It is just before Christmas, and red-haired, lively Nuria, 11, an orphan, has been living happily for about a year with her grandfather, the Avy, a clockmaker, in his small mountaintop house above the village. Although she loves the old man dearly, and he indulges her in simple ways, letting her win when they play games, for example, and encourages her to use her imagination, she yearns for a friend her age, but, except for her, the village is childless, all of them having disappeared months ago. In the village is a magical Well, whose guardian, crotchety old Agnes, warns her is dangerous, as does the Avy. Agnes is fond of repeating the rules: to make a wish there must be a coin; only one wish is permitted in a lifetime; and it may be called back in one month, provided that its contents have not been divulged. To Nuria's delight, Agnes informs her that Catty Winter, also eleven, and her father have moved back. Nuria's joy is somewhat tempered when she discovers that Catty is confined to a wheelchair, but, although Catty is a prissy child, spoiled, and considerably better off financially, the girls have fun together. Various happenings portend trouble, among them, a smoky face that follows Nuria and then appears in her dreams and the Well's freezing. Nuria and Catty argue over who will act whom in the play that they plan, *The Snow Queen*, and Catty wants Nuria to wish that Catty can walk again. When Catty visits Nuria's house, and the Avy seems to favor her, Nuria gets angry at the Avy, visits the Well, and, to spite the Avy by flirting with danger, wishes that "Catty had a body just like mine!" Immediately, Catty inhabits Nuria's body, and Nuria Catty's, even to being confined to the wheelchair. The problem then for Nuria is to get Catty to help in undoing the wish before the month is up and before the Winter family move back to the city where they had been living and to which the governess, Miss D'Estuffier, insists on returning. After a good deal of detail transpires, and some bad wishes are discovered and set straight, Nuria maneuvers Catty into playing Gerda in the story at the Revels and thus to sing unwittingly a song that undoes the spell. Each girl becomes herself again, but Catty is no longer handicapped. Characters are one-dimensional, except for Nuria and Catty, who are somewhat better fleshed. The fairy-tale atmosphere is effectively created, supporting well the old folk idea that one must be wary of what one wishes for. The tone throughout seems strained, as though the writer is trying too hard to play by the rules. As the book proceeds and comes to the expected conclusion, the reader must strive to keep the various wishes and related details straight. SLJ.

WERLIN, NANCY (1961–   ), born in Salem, Massachusetts; software technical writer and author of novels for young adults. She is a graduate of Yale University. Her first novel, *Are You Alone on Purpose?* (Houghton, 1994), is about Jewish teenagers with family conflicts. Her chilling mystery novel *The Killer's Cousin** (Delacorte, 1998), set in Cambridge, Massachusetts, won the Edgar Allan Poe Award. She has also published a thriller, *Locked Inside* (Delacorte, 2000). Werlin has made her home in South Boston and in Summerville, Massachusetts.

WEST, DOROTHY (1907–   ), born in Boston, Massachusetts; youngest member of the Harlem Renaissance writing group, author of one novel and numerous short stories. She studied journalism and philosophy at Columbia University and also attended Boston University. Founder of the magazine *Challenge*, which published the Harlem writers, she also worked as a relief investigator in the 1930s and on the Federal Writers Project, experiences reflected in some of the stories in *The Living Is Easy* (Houghton, 1948; revised, 1987). In 1932 she went to Russia with a group, among them Langston Hughes, to make a film, which was never produced. As a privileged daughter of a well-educated family, she grew up aware of the distinctions between the elite and the working class in the African-American community, but not until she was nearly ninety did she publish *The Wedding** (Doubleday, 1995), set on Martha's Vineyard, which explores the little discussed tensions and prejudice between the established and the newly rich and between those of lighter and darker skins. A long, multi-generational novel, it became a best-seller.

WHAT GIRLS LEARN (Cook*, Karin, Pantheon, 1997), novel of a girl's growing up and learning about death set on Long Island in the early 1980s, where the narrator, Tilden Burbank, 12, comes with her mother, Frances*, and her sister, Elizabeth*, 11, to live with Nick* Olsen, a man who runs Trans-Alt, a limousine service. Though this is not the first move that they have made, and Nick is not the first man whom her mother has brought into their lives, he is the first to threaten to become permanent. Tilden, serious and reserved, is cautious about accepting Nick into what has been their tight little triangle of a family, but Elizabeth, lanky and fearless, jumps at the idea of a father figure. There are surprises. Nick's house is large, and for the first time in their lives, the girls have their own rooms, preselected by Nick, who has been corresponding with Frances for a year since they met. There are a nice yard, a large space for parking Trans-Alt vehicles, and a garage that serves as office, where the dispatcher, Lainey DeWitt, a woman with long, painted nails, big, frosted hair, and greenish-blue eyeshadow, rules. Gradually, Tilden begins to adjust to the new life, to sixth grade at Brooklawn Elementary, to having a friend, Samantha Shaptaw, the first Jew whom she has ever known, and even to having her mother's attention often diverted from them to Nick. Then Frances discovers that she has breast cancer. After a mastectomy, she starts chemotherapy, which makes her frequently feel sick, but she seems hopeful. The rest of the novel traces her increasing illness and its effect on all of them. Frances' younger brother, Uncle* Rand, who has worked as a chef, among many other temporary jobs, shows up, moves in, and takes over the cooking. He also is material in the introduction to sex for both girls. At Christmastime, Nick formally proposes to Frances, and they plan a spring wedding. Since the impending British Royal Wedding is much in the news, the girls want fancy dresses and a big affair. Frances prefers just the family, with no special fuss. They compromise on a wedding in the Trans-Alt yard, attended by the drivers and mechanics, some of the neighbors, and a few friends. By then Frances is thin and weak, wearing a wig to cover her hair loss. Almost immediately her health becomes worse. Both girls are at a picnic at Dove Island when Jamie Sanders, a high school boy employed by Nick, is sent to bring them home. Frances has survived a suicide attempt. At last the girls must face the realization that she will not live, and in the next few days they alternately try to ignore the subject and to crowd all their questions for her into the remaining time: "How will you know when I get my period?" "What are your favorite names? You know, for children?" "How do you feel about living with someone before marriage?" "What do you want me to be?" "What's going to happen to us?" Tilden spends the night beside her bed but is briefly away to rouse Elizabeth when she dies. Uncle Rand leaves, to return to his family home in Atlanta. Nick wanders about, seemingly lost.

When he whispers to Tilden, "I miss her," she sees for the first time that she could love him and accept him as a father. But her mother's death leaves a hole in each of their lives that they struggle to fill or at least to come to terms with. While the problems and emotions that they face are universal, the novel deftly avoids stereotypes. Each of the five main characters is well rounded and individualized, and although the action is seen through Tilden's perspective, the others are plausible and complex enough to be interesting, as are several of the minor characters. The strongest element is the use of effective details, which are often unexpected but immediately recognizable. Despite their mother's devastating illness and death, much of the novel is amusing. It presents a convincing picture of family life and love. ALA.

WHAT JAMIE SAW (Coman*, Carolyn, Front Street, 1995), short, realistic, contemporary, sociological problem novel set for a few weeks and involving domestic abuse. Events unfold from the standpoint of Jamie, 8. The book opens with a disjointed sentence that conveys his conflicted mental state after he has just seen Van, his stepfather, pick up Jamie's baby sister, Nin, Van's daughter, and throw her across the room, fortunately into the arms of Patty Beauville, the children's mother. As Van stands stolidly, arms hanging limply, Patty packs up the children and essentials, including a sack of Jamie's toys and his magic book. They move to the apartment of her trusted friend, Earl, who drives them to his trailer house, which sits like a big silver toaster at the base of a mountain near Stark, New Hampshire. Although Earl remarks that they are "sitting ducks," Jamie is happy, "away from how things had been for a long time." Brief remarks like this inform the reader that Van is abusive, often ugly, frequently set off by even small matters. In fact, Jamie recalls that giving him the magic book was the only nice thing that Van ever did for him. Since Jamie is eager to attend the Christmas Carnival at the high school gym, Patty takes him, although money is tight. The boy enjoys himself, but then they spot a man who they think is Van and hide behind a snow cone stand until they realize their mistake. Although he likes his teacher, Mrs. Desrochers, he resents it when she turns up to see why he has not been attending. She promises Patty that if Jamie returns to school, she will see to it that he is safe. She offers to keep him at school on Tuesday afternoons so that Patty can attend a support group. Tough times continue. Jamie decides that he will do magic tricks for Nin as his Christmas present to her but yearns to give his mother something really good. He is grateful when Mrs. Desrochers gives him a small Christmas cactus for her. Earl, warm and caring, continues to bring them groceries and generally watches over them. In a particularly pleasant scene, he brings Jamie skates for Christmas, takes him to the pond nearby, and teaches him to skate. On Christmas Eve, while Patty is shopping for groceries, Van drives up. When Jamie sees him coming, he grabs Nin and hides her in the blankets on his bed. Van seems so forlorn and alone that Jamie takes pity on him and has started to show him a magic trick when Patty drives up, bursts into the house, and demands to know where Nin is. She orders Jamie to take Nin and leave, but Van says that he will leave. Jamie feels sorry for him, because it seems that no one wants him, but Patty makes it clear that Van is never to come back. Later, after their tension and fear have diminished, Jamie does a magic trick for Patty and his sister. The reader is never so directly informed, but Jamie's and Patty's thoughts and behavior reveal that Van has been regularly abusive of both of them, both physically and psychologically. The reader is inadequately prepared for Jamie's acceptance of Van at the end, unless his behavior is to be taken as typical of a conflicted child's desire to placate an adult in power. Patty's assertiveness also seems sudden and, perhaps dangerously, conveys the impression that a short period with a support group can so embolden an abused wife. Her emotional swings ring true, however. Earl's connection with Patty and Jamie is also left open. He is an attractive figure who might usefully have been developed. While the book is emotionally engaging, such gaps tantalize the thinking reader, who is left to ponder what thematically one is to carry away from the book. ALA; Newbery Honor.

WHEN SHE HOLLERS (Voigt*, Cynthia, Scholastic, 1994), contemporary novel of sexual abuse set one school day in an unnamed, present-day American city. At breakfast, Tish, 18, takes a knife and confronts Tonnie, her stepfather, who has abused her sexually since childhood. During the day, Tish's personality progressively disintegrates, but she manages to find her way to a sympathetic lawyer. That evening, school over for the day, Tish arrives home, the door to her house opens, and the reader is left to imagine what follows. Remarkably effective characterizations and short, often fragmentary sentences produce a novel that seems horrifyingly real and believable. ALA; SLJ. Earlier the novel was cited in *School Library Journal*. A longer entry appears in *Dictionary, 1990–1994*.

WHEN SHE WAS GOOD (Mazer*, Norma Fox, Scholastic, 1997), contemporary novel of family life involving alcoholism and domestic abuse set briefly in a rural area of New York state near Lake Ontario and then in Syracuse, New York. After the death of Pamela, her ugly, obese older sister, Em Thurkill, 17, the narrator, thinks back on her life with Pamela and to some extent with her parents, her abusively alcoholic father, Ray, and her meek, dispirited, over-worked mother, Veronica, who died when Em was thirteen. As she does so, she begins to clarify her values and aims in life and develop an internal strength that she never dreamed she could. Since she has always attempted to do what her mother repeatedly told her—be a good girl—she realizes that she can share with no one what Pamela was really like—misanthropic, possessive, controlling, and consistently physically and verbally abusive; that the last four years, in which they lived together on their own, have been horrible; and that she is glad that her sister is dead. She recalls how, from the time that they were very young, her drunken father beat their mother; how Pamela broke up all her (Em's) friend-ships and tore up the notebooks in which she had written the poetic words and phrases that she found so fulfilling and that her teacher praised; how after Ve-ronica died, Ray married a woman employed at the gravel pit where he worked; and how Pamela soon ordered Em to leave with her for the city. Most of the book occurs inside Em's head, dealing with her memories and reflections on life with domineering Pamela, interspersed with actual scenes. When they arrive in Syracuse, they take a cheap room from which they are soon evicted for nonpayment of rent. They sleep in the bus station, where they are found by a kind social worker, Mr. Elias, who says that Pamela has emotional problems and can qualify for disability payments; tells Em that she must get a job; helps them find an apartment; praises Em for her pleasant demeanor; and encourages her to be less timid. For Em there follows a succession of very short-term jobs. After each of them, Pamela beats Em black and blue for no longer being em-ployed. Immediately, as always, she asks for forgiveness but soon resumes her disagreeable attitude toward Em and her "couch potato" way of life. The few times that Em stands up to Pamela, Pamela finds another way of punishing her, for example, squeezing her face so hard that the imprints of the fingers linger. Regardless of Pamela's treatment, Em holds fast to her mother's words. When she is almost without resources, she applies for a job with a kindly man who runs a resale shop and who trusts her enough to advance her money. Although she knows that Pamela died of a stroke, Em has felt guilty about her sister's death. She informs the reader that Pamela was extremely angry over the tele-vision set's not working, called Em names, hit Em with a pan, and then fell out of her chair onto the floor. Em knows that she delayed calling 911 and realizes that although she is sorry that Pamela is dead, she is not sorry that Pamela is gone. She knows that she has the ability to make positive events out of the sordid happenings of the past. She is free to claim her own life. The narrative is highly internalized, filled with deep emotion, almost plotless, and almost to-tally engrossed with Em's emerging from her dark cocoon. Occasional humor lightens the bleakness, but overall this is a serious look at what happens to children when family life goes awry. Best of all is the style—the use of run-on sentences, brief phrases, and scrappy fragments to convey Em's usual feelings and short lyrical passages to convey her few moments of happiness. The title comes from an old rhyme: "When she was good, she was very, very good." ALA.

WHEN ZACHARY BEAVER CAME TO TOWN (Holt*, Kimberly Willis, Holt, 1999), novel of a small Texas town at the time of the Vietnam War and how a freak show affects its inhabitants. Everyone in Anther in the Texas Pan-handle knows that Opalina Wilson, mother of Toby, 13, has gone to Nashville to try out in a competition for the Grand Ole Opry, but they don't know that, win or lose, she plans to stay. Toby, the narrator, roams Anther and the vicinity on his bike with his friend and next-door neighbor, red-haired Cal McKnight, helps his father, Otto, in his worm-farming business, and tries to pretend that his mother will be back in a few days. One major distraction is the arrival of a house trailer containing the freak attraction, Zachary Beaver, "The Fattest Boy in the World," at whom one can get a look for two dollars. Toby and Cal, along with most of the other townspeople, file through the trailer and stare at the pale, obese boy, who studiously ignores them. In the next few days Toby and Cal watch the trailer from their favorite spot, the roof of Ferris Kelly's Bowl-a-Rama Cafe, and notice that Paulie Rankin, the young man who is barker, exploiter, and Zachary's manager, has unhooked the car from the trailer and abandoned it. They wonder about Zachary, worry about whether he has enough food, and begin dropping off bags of vegetables from the garden of Toby's father on the doorstep, knocking, then running. When a group of boys surround the trailer and bang on its sides, Toby and Cal drive them off by pelting them with pebbles from the roof, accidentally breaking one of the trailer's windows. They are terrified when Sheriff Levi Fetterman asks them to accompany him to the trailer, but his whole purpose is to see whether Zachary is all right and thinks that the presence of two boys will put him more at ease. Zachary is surly and demanding and tells them wild stories about his life in Paris and London, which they suspect are lies, but gradually they get to know him. They worry then that if Paulie does not return, the sheriff will have Zachary sent to Juvenile Hall. Cal, inclined to be nosy, has discovered that the fat boy has never been baptized, though his mother had planned it and given him a Bible before she died. Always full of ideas, Cal decides that they should take Zachary to a drive-in movie. He and Toby build a set of steps, so that Zachary can get into the back of McKnight's truck, talk Cal's older sister, Kate, into driving them, then try to persuade Zachary to go. To their surprise, when he sees Kate, he agrees. Emboldened by this success, Cal and Toby decide that they should get Zachary baptized. This takes even more organization than the night at the movie. In trying to learn about the procedure, Toby unwittingly gives the local minister the idea that he is feeling religious, an amusing misunderstanding that causes the boy great embarrassment. They decide that it will have to be done by Ferris, who once studied for the ministry but became an alcoholic instead. They also recruit Malcolm Clifton, the strongest boy in town, and Kate again. The McKnight truck, however, refuses to start, and their project seems doomed until crippled, almost mute Wylie Womack offers them the golf cart that pulls his snow-cone stand. With Kate driving and the other boys walking, Zachary rides in the golf cart to Gosimer Lake, an artificial pond that is mostly a mudhole. At the last minute Ferris, who has repeatedly refused to perform the baptism, turns up, recites the baptism ceremony, and they dunk Zachary. They are almost unable to pull him up again, but Malcolm's muscles do the trick. At their return, the sheriff tells them that Paulie has called to say that he will be back in a couple of days. As a last episode, they take Zachary to the McKnight cotton farm, where each year they release thousands of ladybugs. This time they are accompanied by both McKnight parents, Toby's father, and even Miss Myrtie Mae Pruitt, a fussy maiden lady who comes to record the event in photographs. Three parallel plots accompany Zachary's saga. One is Toby's longing for Scarlett Stalling, who is in love with Juan, from the Mexican side of town. After Toby helps patch up their romance, they both say that he's the nicest boy in town, a small comfort. Another is the much more serious event, the funeral of Cal's brother, Wayne, killed in Vietnam. The third is Toby's reconciliation with his mother, who has left the family for good but wants to keep in touch with her son. The main focus, however, is the town, set in the flat, dry land, small enough so that everyone's business is common knowledge, but underneath the eccentricities is genuine concern. The sheriff has the trailer's broken window repaired and sends a doctor to attend to Zachary's foot, cut on the broken glass. Miss Myrtie Mae cares for her demented brother, the Judge, and drops off her special Chicken Delight casserole at the trailer. Toby writes a letter to Wayne, since Cal is too lazy, signs it "Cal," and then worries that he'll be found out. After it is sent back with Wayne's things, Cal thanks him. The Norman Rockwell-like kindness might be cloying were it not for the many convincing, often amusing, and original details. SLJ.

WHILE NO ONE WAS WATCHING (Conly*, Jane Leslie, Holt, 1998), realistic sociological problem and family novel, with detective-story aspects, set for a few days in an unnamed urban area, which appears to resemble that of Baltimore, Maryland. After their widower father, Johnny* Foster, loses his house and leaves with his girlfriend, Beth-ann, for the Eastern Shore to earn money for a new house by picking vegetables, his children, red-haired Earl*, 11, willful Frankie*, 7, and imaginative Angela*, 6, live with Johnny's sister, irresponsible, alcoholic Lula Bonner, in her run-down brick rowhouse, until Lula simply takes off with her boyfriend, leaving the children to fend for themselves. For some time, her mean-spirited son, Wayne*, about seventeen, has been inducing Earl to accompany him on bike-stealing expeditions, sharing some of the proceeds with his younger cousin. One day, the two boys walk to Walnut Hill, an affluent part of the city, tagged by Frankie, and steal two bikes. They also help Frankie, who has yearned for a pet, steal a little rabbit from an unlocked hutch. Their action sets in motion events that cast into stark relief the differences in lifestyles and life-attitudes of the two regions of the city, bring social workers and police into the children's lives, almost cause a death, and finally reunite the children with their father. Asian Indian-born Maynard* Glenn, who lives next door to fellow fifth grader Addie Johnson, to whom the rabbit belongs, mounts a detective-style effort to locate the thieves. By chance encountering Angela in the park not far from her home, he soon learns where the family live. Wayne gets Earl involved in more thefts from local street people and construction sites and gives Earl money from the illegal take, money that now Earl desperately needs to feed his siblings. When Earl learns that Wayne intends to leave his drunken father and move back into his mother's house and fearing that Wayne will kill the rabbit, Frankie flees to the nearby home of old blind Mr.* Tiptop, a former musician and now shoe repairman who has taken a grandfatherly interest in the children. Wayne decides that Mr. Tiptop is a likely target for theft and attacks the old man, but Frankie comes from hiding just in time to bash Wayne in the head and save the old man's life. Maynard, who has arrived with Angela seeking Frankie and the rabbit, observes events and calls for help. Maynard's adoptive father, a physician, has already alerted Social Services about the children. At the end, the children are on the bus traveling to join their father. The book's strongest features lie in the detailed and convincing picture of the way that the children are forced to manage. Although Wayne's parents are almost unbelievably callous, irresponsible, and blind to the children's plight, the finger of blame is leveled at no one. Rather, the book points out how, in spite of Johnny's sincere efforts to provide for his children, the whole family has fallen through society's safety nets. They are the working poor who are not quite poor enough for help. The third-person narrative focuses on the three siblings and Maynard at different times, reporting their actions and feelings so that their stories shed light upon one another. Although the shifts sometimes make it hard to keep track of the action, they also enlist the reader's sympathies and contribute to the sense of confusion, uncertainty, and social and economic disparity. The novel demonstrates what can happen to a family while no one is watching, or even cares to watch. Boston Globe Honor; Fanfare.

WHIRLIGIG (Fleischman*, Paul, Holt, 1998), unusually constructed, realistic novel illustrating the wide-ranging effects possible from a person's acts. After a party at which Brent Bishop, newcomer to a private school in the Chicago area where he is a junior, is deliberately humiliated, he drives away drunk, depressed, and furious. His attempt at suicide, however, results not in his death but in that of Lea Zamora, a senior honor student active in the Filipino-American community. After he is sentenced to probation for manslaughter, Lea's mother meets with Brent and his parents and makes a strange request: that he make four whirligigs like the one that Lea's grandfather made for her years ago that has given many people pleasure and that he set them up in Washington, California, Florida, and Maine. She provides a picture of Lea, since the original whirligig had her face on it, and a bus pass good for the next forty-five days. Although his parents protest, Brent agrees to do it, glad to separate himself from them and from the scene of the tragedy that haunts him. In his backpack he carries some wood, tools, and a book on whirligigs that he has found in a Chicago used-book store. His first attempt is in a campground near Mt. Vernon, Washington, north of Seattle, where he shares a site with a cyclist from British Columbia. Not being skilled or trained at woodwork, he is clumsy in his first attempt to construct an angel. After he breaks off a wing, he decides that it is just a harp player, with propeller-like arms seeming to strum the strings. Although the face looks little like Lea, and the entire figure is crude, he mounts it on a tree branch and is proud of the result. The second, more ambitious whirligig is a whale, with a mermaid riding the top of its spout, which goes up and down. He has stayed several days in a hostel in San Diego for foreign youth, pretending that he is from Canada, toured the city with a German boy, learned to play simple tunes on a harmonica, and found some peace. With permission, he mounts the whirligig on the front porch of the hostel, and positions it so that it will catch the wind. After a long, boring cross-country bus ride, he ends up at a motel in a small town on Florida's Gulf Coast. He finds a boarded-up beachfront ice cream stand where he can work in privacy and starts a marching-band whirligig, with four figures all moving at different times. After several days a group of eight or ten African-American children discover him and swarm around his project. A few days later, when he is almost done, four of them return. As he mounts the band on the empty building, he discovers that at least one of the youngsters has recognized the principle and is trying to make his own propeller. Brent builds his last and largest whirligig in a campground near Weeksboro, Maine. It is a woman's figure made almost entirely from wood and other things that he salvages from the beach or the town dump, with a face that actually resembles Lea and glittering glass pieces in the hair. He mounts it on a pole that previously held a birdhouse near the cabin of a woman whom he has met on the beach. Without even knowing each other's names, they feel a community of spirit, and for the first time he tells the story of what happened after the party, thereby finally coming to terms with it. Interspersed through this story are chapters, not in chronological order with each other or with the main narrative, each showing how one of the whirligigs affects other lives. An eighth-grade girl in Maine gains self-esteem and finds a boyfriend. A Puerto Rican street sweeper from Miami, fleeing his hectic life, finds some peace looking at the marching band and returns to his family. An adopted Korean boy in Bellevue, Washington, escapes from his mother's ambitions and controlling schedule for him when he botches a recital, and his music teacher points out that even a whirligig like the one of a harp player that his mother has photographed and posted to encourage him, needs to rest sometimes. A teenage girl in San Diego is coerced by her grandmother, who is a Holocaust survivor and now a victim of Alzheimer's, to take her on a tour of places where she once lived or that she associates with a happy period of her life. They end their journey parked across from a house that has a whirligig of a whale and a mermaid mounted on its porch, while the grandmother gently explains that though terrible things happen, it is important that some things can still make one smile. The unusual structure is at first confusing, especially because the girl in Maine has her adventure before Brent is introduced, but the connections soon become clear and make the novel more intriguing. Brent's atonement that gradually brings him peace is convincing, though his skill in designing and building whirligigs may develop too fast. Descriptions of the four corners of the country are full of good sensory detail. SLJ.

WHITE, RUTH (1942–), born in Whitewood, Virginia; teacher, librarian, novelist. She received her A.A. degree from Montreat-Anderson College, her A.B. degree from Pfeiffer College, and her library media specialist degree from Queens College, Charlotte, North Carolina. For ten years she taught English at

Middle School, Mount Pleasant, North Carolina, and has been librarian at Albany, Georgia, Junior High since 1981. Her novel of two cousins who both discover unhappy truths about their parents, *Belle Prater's Boy** (Farrar, 1996), was highly acclaimed, being named honor book for both the Newbery Medal and the Boston Globe Award. Among her other titles are *Sweet Creek Holler* (Farrar, 1988), *Weeping Willow* (Farrar, 1992), and *Memories of Summer* (Farrar, 2000). She has also published under the name Ruth White Miller. White has made her home in Albany, Georgia, and Virginia Beach, Virginia.

THE WILD KID (Mazer*, Harry, Simon & Schuster, 1998), realistic survival and boy's growing-up novel set in the wilds of Vermont in recent years. Half-orphaned Sammy Ritchie, 12, mentally challenged with Down's syndrome, is reprimanded by his mother for using a "bad word" toward her boyfriend, Carl Torres, and put out of the house to think things over. Angry, he observes his bike being stolen, sets out to retrieve it, and gets lost in the thick woods. He tumbles into a deep ravine and finds himself lying next to a pile of brush with, surprisingly, a window. He is soon taken captive by an almost feral boy a little older than he, a tall, skinny youth with an animal-like face, the occupant of the small, uncomfortable, but effectively secluded room behind the window. The boy ties him up, takes Sammy's money, grumbles about what to do with him, releases him, takes a grudging responsibility for him, and becomes his friend. Kevin, who calls himself K-Man, has run away from a neglectful home and social workers. He has been living in the wilds for some time, in this damp, chilly rustic shelter that he built of brush and found materials. Sammy grows to like and respect the tough, aware youth, who is woods-wise and lives by snaring rabbits, raiding garbage cans, and stealing. Kevin wonders why Sammy wants to go home, says people are bad, teaches him to tie his shoes, helps him with counting, and finally suggests that he stay on, be his brother. Sammy, however, longs for home and suggests that Kevin return with him, be his brother there, an idea that Kevin consistently resists. On an expedition to the pond where Kevin washes himself and his clothes, Sammy, a Special Olympics swimmer, saves Kevin from drowning. One day, Kevin suggests that they dress up in black T-shirts and jackets. He leads them to a cemetery, where he steals mourners' wallets, and then to a mall, where they indulge themselves in food. When an orange-haired woman identifies Sammy as the lost boy being hunted, Sammy lies, says that his name is Mike and that they are brothers, and the two flee immediately. Sammy persists in his plan to take Kevin home with him, says that he has it all worked out that Kevin can live with him in his room, but Kevin remains adamant. Early the next day, Sammy leaves the shelter and climbs laboriously up a cliff, intending to reach the highway above, but gets stuck in a tree. Kevin searches until he finds him, tells him to tie himself to the tree with his sweater so that he will not fall, and then calls authorities, who soon release Sammy and take him home. A newspaper article fills in the gaps for the reader. Sammy has been missing thirteen days in rugged Middleburg

State Forest Preserve, is in surprisingly good health, and is praised by everyone for his calm demeanor and resourcefulness. His story about being helped by, and living with, Kevin is explained away by psychologists as a survival mechanism. When his family tell him that Kevin was bad for not bringing him home, his response shows a surprising maturity and a new confidence: "Just because you're not always good doesn't make you bad." Carl Torres responds that he could not have said it better himself. Sammy continues to yearn for Kevin; fixes up his room to accommodate his friend; writes him a note, which, of course, is never sent; and insists that his overprotective mother no longer "baby" him. Last seen, he is standing at his window at night, searching the darkness for his friend and instructing him to "Take care," using the words that Kevin had used with him. So closely is the book tied to Sammy's point of view that it seems almost to come entirely from inside Sammy's head. He is inclined to be literal, but he often is also amazingly and poignantly philosophical. At the end, the reader is left to ponder the meaning of the title: just which boy is "the wild one?" And what does the term mean? The very short chapters add to the tension. Fanfare; SLJ.

WILLIS, PATRICIA, writer of novels for children and young adults set mostly in Ohio. Her historical novel *Danger along the Ohio** (Clarion, 1997) is set in the 1790s, when three children, traveling west on a flatboat, become separated from their father and must survive and make their way through hostile Indian country. It was given the Spur Award by the Western Writers of America. Willis grew up on an Ohio farm, an experience reflected in three of her other novels, *A Place to Claim as Home* (Clarion, 1991), *Out of the Storm* (Clarion, 1995), and *Barn Burner* (Clarion, 2000), all concerned with farm life in the 1930s and 1940s. She lives in Canton, Ohio.

WILLIAM, DUKE OF NORMANDY (*The King's Shadow**), historical duke who defeats Harold* Godwinson, Duke of Wessex and King of England, in 1066 and assumes the throne, ending the Anglo-Saxon period in England. William is presented as a cruel, hard, manipulative man, the foil of the kind, fair, good-minded Harold. Harold once rescues a retainer of William's who is drowning in a river, while William stands casually by, uncaring of the man's fate. William cunningly extracts an oath of loyalty from Harold and later assembles a massive army of men and ships and attacks the English at Hastings. After Harold is killed, Harold's common-law wife, Lady* Ealdgyth Swan Neck, asks leave to look for his body. William gives permission, but when she finds it, he takes it from her, intending that Harold's burial place will forever remain unknown.

WILLIAM HENRY HUGHES (*Stone Water**), father of Grant Hughes, the protagonist, and son of Grandpa (Henry) Hughes, the old man whose impending death establishes the book's central dilemma: whether or not Grant should assist his aged, ailing Grandpa to commit suicide. Ambitious and hardworking, William is abstracted from his family, busy until all hours with his work, which often takes him on business trips. He attempts to compensate by giving them lavish gifts, which he often has his secretary secure for him. Grant's mother, who is also far too busy to be a good parent, occasionally takes time to listen to Grant and is kind and generous in holding him to family rules, but William seldom pays attention to the boy, expects him to be a leader, and is quick to point out how moral ambiguities might be of benefit. For example, he tells Grant that if one is liked and trusted, one can "get away" with almost anything. Grant capitalizes on the latter idea when he says that he gave Grandpa the sleeping-pill water only because he thought that that particular liquid was what the old man wanted. Grant's mother seems suspicious since Grant used the trail cup that had belonged to Grandpa's grandfather but voices no doubts about the boy's story. It is unclear why at the end Grandpa is also revealed to have been an abstracted father. Is this information offered as an excuse for William's not being a good father? Is it intended as a warning to Grant or the reader? At any rate, William is an unattractive figure, the stereotypical overachiever and uninvolved father.

WILLIAMS-GARCIA, RITA, born in Jamaica, Queens, New York, where she still lives; raised in California and Queens; graduate of Hofstra University, with further study in creative writing at Queens College; dancer (studied under Alvin Ailey and Phil Black), reading teacher, manager of software systems, acclaimed writer of novels about African Americans for young adults in which black, urban adolescents cope with difficulties produced by racial prejudice and poverty. *Blue Tights* (Dutton, 1988) recounts the difficulties of a talented black girl prevented from dancing because the white instructor believes that her body is not suited for ballet. *Fast Talk on a Slow Track* (Dutton, 1991) concerns a bright black boy who finds that college life holds more challenges than high school did. In *Like Sisters on the Homefront** (Lodestar, 1995), a Fanfare selection, Gayle, 14, pregnant for the second time, develops a sounder sense of values and of self through taking care of her aged great-grandmother in Georgia. *Every Time a Rainbow Dies* (HarperCollins, 2000) concerns rape. Williams-Garcia received a special citation from the PEN/Norma Klein Award for Children's Fiction Committee.

WILLNER-PARDO, GINA, born in California; attended Bryn Mawr College and received her master's degree from the University of California at Berkeley. She began to write for children after the birth of her first child. Since then she has published more than a dozen short novels and picture books about everyday things that happen to children, simulating the thinking and speech patterns of ordinary children of today and doing her research via overheard conversations and observation. The books include *Daphne Eloise Slater, Who's Tall for Her Age* (Clarion, 1997); *Jumping into Nothing* (Clarion, 1999), about diving; *When*

Jane-Marie Told My Secret (Clarion, 1999); and several other illustrated short novels about the misadventures of third grader Spider Storch. *Figuring Out Frances** (Clarion, 1999) is a story of friendship gone awry and growing up, for which Willner-Pardo received the Josette Frank Award (formerly Child Study). She lives in the San Francisco Bay Area.

WIMPERLING (*Pigs Don't Fly**), strange, piglike creature with vestigial wings that Summer steals from a brutal sideshow exhibitor who is mistreating him. Throughout their travels, Wimperling grows and changes, but most people still see him as a pig, which is what they expect to see. He also grows in astuteness, often giving Summer good advice and several times saving her from disaster, once by flying with her on his back from a castle tower where they are imprisoned and another time setting the woods afire to thwart pursuers. His own explanation for his piglike appearance when he is young is that he was hatched too early from his egg, in 99 instead of 100 years, because some farmer had built a pigsty in the circle of standing stones, a place of power, where he had been laid, and the heat of the litter of pigs brought him from his egg before the proper time. Since he was among piglets, he assumed their shape and mannerisms until the time was ripe for his true birth as an impressive dragon, now named Jasper. His travels with Summer have not left him unaffected, however. Since she kissed him three times, causing increasingly explosive reactions, he briefly becomes a man and returns her passionate love. Whether she can ever find him again and continue their relationship is left unresolved in the novel.

THE WINDOW (Dorris*, Michael, Hyperion, 1997), contemporary sociological-problem, girl's growing-up, and family-life novel set in Tacoma, Washington, and Louisville, Kentucky. When Native-American Christine Taylor's "hard nights" with alcohol keep her away from their small apartment for several days at a time, and the refrigerator stands bare, her daughter, Rayona, 11, the self-possessed narrator, reports that Elgin*, her African-American father, steps in. Separated from her mother and an unsteady, but personable, substitute mail carrier, he tries several possibilities, then takes Rayona by plane to stay with Marcella* (his mother), Aunt* Edna (Rayona's great-aunt), and Rayona's grand-mother, Mamaw*, in Louisville. All three women are white and have never seen Rayona. She is met with hugs and kisses, and her early feelings of strangeness soon disappear. She feels very much at home with this "army of women," independent and self-sufficient, worthy forebears. Rayona learns that her grand-father, Marcella's husband, was African American and that a cousin of her grandfather, a black woman also named Marcella, lives nearby and wishes to meet her, an encounter that is pleasing to both. She also learns that her white relatives descend from a woman named Rose who came from Ireland. When Elgin phones with the news that Christine has completed treatment, joined Alcoholics Anonymous, and moved into another apartment, his mother and Aunt Edna drive Rayona the 2,000 miles to Tacoma, stopping off at several landmarks along the way and enjoying one another's company. Since Elgin tells them that the counselors feel that Christine is ready to receive Rayona but not other visitors, the two women return to Louisville without meeting her. Rayona concludes that this time her mother really intends to make a good life with and for her. While the window through which Rayona saw life at the beginning of the book was very small, her view of the world has broadened. She has become acquainted with relatives whom she did not know existed, she knows that her father and mother love each other after a fashion but are unable to live together, and she decides that, unless Christine asks her directly for information, she will not betray her father's secret—that his mother is white and his heritage is Irish—since everyone is entitled to have secrets. Rayona's perceptions of her parents are astute, suitably so for an intelligent young-old child, and her ambivalent feelings toward them and other adults seem appropriate and credible. Elgin's women relatives are well drawn, lively, and individualized but nondynamic. The writer catches scenes well with sharp pictorial language. The novel seems foreshortened, however, and underdeveloped, a tantalizing "prequel" to the life of the triracial young woman whose story is more adequately explored in Dorris' adult novel *Yellow Raft in Blue Water*. ALA; Fanfare.

THE WINDOW (Ingold*, Jeanette, Harcourt, 1996), contemporary novel of family life with physical-problem, time-travel, and school-story aspects. Mandy's mother was recently killed in an automobile accident, the same one in which the fifteen-year-old girl was blinded. Shortly after the school year begins, Mandy, who tells the story, goes to live with her Great-Aunt Emma and Great-Uncles Gabriel (Emma's husband) and Abe. The girl gradually learns to cope with her disability, grows to love these relatives whom she had never known, and understands more about the events that led up to the tragic accident. After unpacking her clothes in the attic bedroom of the big, old Texas farmhouse that has been in the family for generations, Mandy hears a voice outside the window, a little boy calling for a girl called Gwen. The voice, that of Abe, her now elderly great-uncle, and other relatives' voices occur periodically, especially when Mandy is in a kind of reverie and approaches or gazes out of the window. Mandy is able to both see and hear what is happening in their lives and also experience what Gwen, her age, undergoes in mid-1950 at the beginning of the Korean War. Restless and yearning for excitement and affection, Gwen falls in love with a traveling salesman named Paul. They are married just before he leaves for the war. He is soon killed, and when Gwen finds that she is pregnant, she writes to her mother, a cold, unforgiving woman, who has been abandoned by her husband and who refuses to have anything to do with Gwen. She tears up the letter, which she later tries unsuccessfully to piece together. Gwen puts the baby, a little girl, up for adoption. That child becomes Mandy's mother, who is seeking to locate her mother (Gwen) when a delivery truck hits her car, and she is killed. Most of this Mandy learns from her visions or her traveling-backward-in-time experiences, information unknown to her relatives, who did not know that Mandy existed until they were traced by persistent social workers. When Mandy arrives, she is defensive as well as apprehensive about her disability. She is afraid of making mistakes, of their thinking her a burden, and of enrolling in school. All things work together for good, however. Her aunt and uncles are kind and understanding; the school arranges for her to have a high school aide, Hannah* Welsh, with whom she becomes best friends; and the students in the special education classroom are helpful, especially deaf Ted, a smart, outgoing young man who becomes her boyfriend. Mandy shares Gwen's story with Hannah, and Hannah takes her to a football game and encourages her to invite Ted to the Girl-Ask-Guy Dance. As Mandy gains confidence in school and learns more about her family, she becomes less prickly and more content and sure of herself. While Mandy's situation and disposition improve, Hannah's home life deteriorates, and when Hannah's unhappy mother leaves, Hannah runs away, too. Mandy enlists Ted's help in finding Hannah and persuades her that she needs to come back for Mandy's sake. Mandy also suggests that Hannah may be judging her parents too harshly, as some have judged Gwen and her mother without knowing the circumstances. Christmas morning is perfect, and Mandy and her relatives exchange gifts, items that are just right for each person. Mandy knows that they love her, and they know that she loves them. Although most characters are types—overly solicitous Emma, the kindly, generous uncles, nearly-perfect Ted, headstrong Gwen, sweet-talking Paul, Gwen's judgmental, unhappy mother, the blind girl who gains confidence and helps the kind, capable, sighted girl in her time of need—they nevertheless serve the plot adequately. Hannah's problems, as well as Mandy's familial ones, support the theme too obviously: the importance of family and the need for understanding and forgiveness for families to function. Modes of helping the handicapped are carefully but unobtrusively worked in. ALA.

WISH YOU WERE HERE (Shoup*, Barbara, Hyperion, 1994), novel of a boy's struggle to come to terms with his best friend's running away and to find his own identity in the middle of traumatic events of his senior year in an Indianapolis high school. Since the divorce of his parents when he was nine, Jackson (Jax) Watt has depended on his friend, Brady Burton, who treats life as a joke and delights in doing unconventional and even crazy things, bringing some lighthearted fun to Jackson's overconscientious personality. Pushed finally into a rage by the scorn of his long-divorced, uptight father, Brady trashes his father's apartment and takes off in his car. Jackson feels deserted. His own life develops complications. His mother, Ellen, is about to marry decent Ted* Harper, although she still loves Jackson's father, Oz, an aging hippie who works rigging sound systems for rock concerts and caroms from one live-in girlfriend to another. When Oz signs Jackson up for bodybuilding at a health club where his newest girl, Kim*, works, Jackson is humiliated by his skinny physique and secretly lifts weights at the club at times when he knows that his father won't be there. No one hears from Brady, not his flaky, but fond, mother, Layla, not his somewhat freaky girlfriend, Stephanie Carr, and not Jackson. He feels disoriented by the move that he and his mother make to the new, upscale home that she and Ted have purchased, and he goes through the wedding in a daze. Ted's daughters, Kristin*, 9, and Amy, 5, are still upset by their parents' divorce and are determined not to enjoy the occasion or the honeymoon at a Jamaican resort, to which Ted takes all of them. On the beach the first day Jackson sees a beautiful girl, way out of his league, he thinks, but effervescent Amy gets to know her, discovers that she is on vacation from her exclusive school with her elderly parents, and that her name is Amanda Clark. Soon more reserved Kristin and Jackson are drawn into the friendship. For the rest of the time in Jamaica Jackson revels in his first real and requited love, which does not lead to sexual intercourse but to genuine affection and understanding. He flies home still in a glow, but they are met at the plane by his weeping grandmother with the news that Oz has fallen from stage rigging and is badly injured. For the next weeks Jackson virtually lives at the hospital until Oz is released from intensive care and then moves in with his father to help Kim care for him. The romance disintegrates, however, and Kim moves out. Jackson is distracted by Stephanie, who flirts with Oz, hangs around his house, and seduces Jackson. Soon they are having sex at every opportunity, a situation that fuels Jackson's guilt, since he doesn't love her. Nor has he written to Amanda, and he finds it harder and harder to try. Two postcards arrive from Brady, neither saying anything informative except that he is following the Grateful Dead. Jackson cannot bring himself to mention the cards to Stephanie. He starts drinking frequently, and his grades plummet. Then he learns that Oz and Brady's mother, Layla, have married, a union that at first astonishes and shocks him but that he decides may have some chance of success. He tells Stephanie that they have to stop seeing each other. She drifts off with a motorcycle type and drops out of school, but on graduation night she dies of a deliberate drug overdose. Overwhelmed but pretending that he is all right, Jackson attends a Grateful Dead concert and comes upon Brady, as he has expected to. At first their reunion seems wonderful, but Jackson has grown up a lot in the past year, and Brady, too, has changed. At the concert he is clearly high on something. Jackson gets him into his bus and drives him back to Indianapolis, where Brady refuses to see Layla but opts to visit Steph's grave. There he blames her for her own problems and suddenly decides that they should go to Graceland in Memphis, because Elvis was "the biggest screwup of them all." Still hoping that he may somehow rescue Brady, Jackson agrees. There follows a nightmarish encounter with a family of devout Elvis fans, whom Brady parodies mercilessly while pretending to be also a fellow Elvis worshiper. Completely disillusioned and disgusted, Jackson decks him and refuses to fall under his spell again. The next morning Brady is gone, having taken Jackson's money. At last Jackson feels free and confident of his own judgment. He sends a card to Amanda, promising a full letter to follow, and for once is sure he can write it. While the story covers a year full of troubling events, there is not much action. Mostly it is a hashing over in Jackson's mind of his sense of responsibility, his self-doubts, and his memories of Brady and of happier times in his life. Although his self-absorption is sometimes annoying, it is convincing, and he emerges as a likable and potentially positive young man. The complications of broken homes and meshed families are explored with sympathy and understanding. ALA; SLJ.

WITTLINGER, ELLEN (1948–), born in Belleville, Illinois; completed her undergraduate work at Millikin University and received an M.F.A. from the University of Iowa; children's librarian and writer of poetry, plays, short stories, and young adult novels. After publishing a book of poems for adults in 1979 and then writing and preparing two plays for production, she published her first young adult novel, *Lombardo's Law* (Houghton, 1993), about two loner early teens who become romantically attracted to each other. In *Noticing Paradise* (Houghton, 1995), her second novel, teens find romance on a Galapagos tour. *Hard Love** (Simon & Schuster, 1999), selected by *School Library Journal*, relates how a friendship with a Puerto Rican-American girl and producing a literary magazine help a sixteen-year-old boy through tough times. Its crisp style, controlled diction, and not unpleasing hard edge hold the attention and seem appropriately turn-of-the-century. In *What's in a Name* (Simon & Schuster, 2000), teenagers are affected when a town changes its name, and in *Gracie's Girl* (Simon & Schuster, 2000), a girl befriends an elderly homeless woman.

WOLFF, VIRGINIA EUWER (1937–), born in Portland, Oregon; graduate of Smith College, with further study at Long Island University and Warren Wilson College; teacher of English; poet and novelist. *Make Lemonade** (Holt, 1993) is a much-honored book, having won several awards before receiving the Josette Frank (formerly Child Study) Award. It concerns the problems of a single-parent, teenage mother. *Bat 6** (Scholastic, 1996), a selection of both the American Library Association and *School Library Journal*, is a girl's sports novel set in Oregon just after World War II involving prejudice against Japanese Americans. Wolff has also contributed stories and poems to magazines. Her novels have been praised as lively in pace and sensitive to the feelings of the early adolescents and young adults for whom she writes. For more biographical information and title entries, see *Dictionary, 1985–1989* [*Probably Still Nick Swanson*] and *Dictionary, 1990–1994* [*Make Lemonade*; *The Mozart Season*].

WOLF STALKER (Skurzynski*, Gloria, and Alane Ferguson*, National Geographic Society, 1997), mystery novel set in Yellowstone Park, concerned with the difficulties of the Wolf Restoration Program. Jack Landon, 12, has come with his sister, Ashley, 10, and his parents, Steven, a photographer, and Olivia, who works at the Elk Refuge in Jackson Hole, Wyoming, to the park to help investigate a report that a wolf killed a dog near Slough Creek, near the park's northern border with Montana. The big problem for Jack is the presence of a short-term foster child, Troy Haverson, 13, whose mother has disappeared and who has been assigned to the Landons temporarily. They visit Old Faithful and Mammouth Hot Springs, neither of which impresses sullen Troy, on their way to meet Mike, the head of the Wolf Restoration Program. Unfortunately, Mike was unaware that the youngsters were to be with Steven and Olivia and has provided only two horses. He arranges that the kids wait in a parking area and will be picked up by a ranger who will take them to Roosevelt Lodge until their parents return. Jack realizes that it is up to him to keep Troy in line, although the older boy does not recognize his authority. Almost immediately Troy does take off, saying that he wants to see some wolves. Jack and Ashley follow, trying to persuade him to return, and see a beautiful wolf shot by someone hidden in a distant grove of trees. Jack takes some pictures of the wolf and also of the grove, but he has an inexpensive camera with no zoom lens so the quality is in doubt. Troy runs after the wolf, following the blood drops. After some quarreling, Jack and Ashley again follow and after the sun sets find him, with the wounded wolf, which he has begun to call Silver. When Troy refuses to come back with them Jack starts a fire and they tell stories, Troy's being about his nomadic life with his mother, who disappeared some days ago but who he is confident would not have abandoned him. They settle down for the night, the two Landons fairly comfortable in warm parkas but Troy in a thin plastic jacket. Once during the night Jack hears a plane, and he piles all the wood that they have gathered onto the fire as a signal. In the morning, their parents and Mike arrive and carry the wolf out. Steven develops Jack's pictures, some great shots of Silver but not much of the shooter except a curious red spot showing from the grove of trees. Because Silver's radio collar has been shattered, evidently shot sometime before he was hit, and some hair, not wolf or deer, is caught in the shards, Mike drives them all to the dilapidated ranch of George Campbell, a militia type who has been loudly complaining that a wolf killed his valuable golden retriever. Thinking that they are reporters, Campbell expansively elaborates on his story and convicts himself on the tape recording, explaining about his laser sight on his rifle, which Troy recognizes as the cause of the red dot in Jack's pictures. They discover that he has been illegally collecting antlers and letting a dog run loose in the park and has shot at Silver at least twice. When they get back to Mammoth, a phone call alerts them that Troy's mother has been found, trapped in her car, which went off the road, but is in good condition. The contrived plot is layered between heavy doses of information about Yellowstone Park, the Wolf Restoration Program, the concerns of ranchers, life patterns of wolves, and other natural history, mostly introduced as conversation, interesting in itself but heavy-handed in a novel. Jack is pictured as bossy, Troy as surly, Ashley as clever, all one-dimensional, and the adults are merely functional. This is the first of a projected series of National Park Mysteries. Poe Nominee.

WOODSON, JACQUELINE (1964–), born in Columbus, Ohio, raised in South Carolina and Brooklyn, New York; graduate in English of Adelphi University, with further study in creative writing at New School for Social Research; teacher of creative writing at several colleges and writer in residence for the National Book Foundation; since 1997 a freelance writer. Winner of several awards, herself African American, Woodson has published some dozen books, mostly novels for middle graders and early adolescents, about African Americans and such other marginalized groups as homosexuals, the poor, and abused. *I Hadn't Meant to Tell You This** (Delacorte, 1994), about the friendship between an African-American girl and two poor white sisters who are the victims of sexual abuse from their widower father, was selected by the American Library Association and *School Library Journal*. In *From the Notebooks of Melanin Sun* (Blue Sky, 1996), a black youth learns that his mother has a woman lover. *Last Summer with Maizon* (Delacorte, 1990), first in a trilogy, tells of a gifted black girl's encounter with discrimination at a predominantly white boarding school. *If You Come Softly* (Putnam, 1998) deals with an interracial romance. Woodson has also written stories for picture books and a novel for adults, edited collections of short stories and poems, and contributed to story collections and to periodicals.

WORDS BY HEART (Sebestyen*, Ouida, Atlantic/Little, 1979), historical novel of prejudice and discrimination against an African-American family in Texas of 1910. Bright, bookish Lena Sills, 12, inadvertently causes a situation that enrages the son of a shiftless, poor-white family, who rides to the remote place where her father, Ben, is working and shoots him but is thrown and dragged by his horse, scared by the noise. Lena, going out to find her father, brings them both back in the wagon, but Ben dies. Though heavy-handed in its treatment of race relations, the story has a strong protagonist and has been a favorite of many. Phoenix Honor. For a longer entry, see *Dictionary, 1960–1984*.

WRINGER (Spinelli*, Jerry, HarperCollins, 1997), realistic animal and personal-problem novel with domestic-adventure features set in a small, unnamed American town about 1990. Palmer LaRue, 9, a quiet, polite boy, dreads becoming a wringer. Wringers are boys ten years of age and up, who kill, by wringing their necks, pigeons wounded in the organized shoot on Pigeon Day during the town's annual Family Fest in August. Five thousand pigeons, shipped in crates from cities, are released for the men of the town to shoot, the proceeds going to maintain the town's well-appointed park. Palmer also hates his first name, which the kids make fun of, and he hates not being one of a group. Until his ninth birthday, his only real friend is Dorothy* Gruzik, who lives across the street in his middle-class neighborhood. He invites for his birthday three fellows his age, boys whom his mother regards as hoodlums, Beans*, the tough-guy leader, Mutto, and Henry*, and snubs Dorothy. He is delighted when they give him such insider gifts as a crusty, holey sock and, most special of all, a nickname, Snots. He is less pleased when they go to the park, where he knows that in a month's time the annual Pigeon Day shoot will be held. Without uttering a sound, he endures The Treatment, a painfully knuckled left arm meted out to him by the legendary Farquar, the big boy who is the town's champion wringer. Palmer is now in a gang and ignores his mother's complaints about their boor-ishness and poor treatment of Dorothy. Although he knows that his father was a wringer, is now a champion shooter, and expects that Palmer will follow suit, Palmer plays sick on Pigeon Day. That winter after a terrible Christmastime snow, Palmer awakens to a scratching at the window of his second-floor bed-room. It is a cold and hungry pigeon, which he tries to ignore but eventually feeds, makes into a pet, and names Nipper. While he hangs out with the boys, plagues Dorothy with them, and joins them in deriding pigeons, he privately worries that they will find out about Nipper and harm the bird. When Nipper seeks Palmer during the day, the boy's fears accelerate with sometimes humor-ous side effects. When the three boys depart after his tenth-birthday party, he notices that someone has written TONIGHT on the cake, realizes that Henry is warning him to guard Nipper, and protects the bird by sleeping downstairs that night. When he sees Panther, Beans' terrible yellow cat, hanging around the house, he realizes that he must get rid of Nipper. He and Dorothy bike to the country and release the bird, but it soon returns. He then gives the bird to Dorothy to release at the seashore when the family vacations there. On the next Pigeon Day, he cringes at the stacks of cages but feels fairly confident that Nipper is not among the birds, until Dorothy remarks that they released Nipper in a city with railroad yards, a prime source of birds. He sees Nipper killed thousands of times that day before he spots a bird that he knows is Nipper, a "miracle bird," one who seems to have escaped. It circles, looking for a chance to descend onto Palmer's head. Beans, now a wringer, grabs it and places it in front of a shooter. Before it is shot, Palmer screams and runs over to rescue it. The crowd boos him, but Palmer overhears one little boy begging his father for a pigeon to have as a pet. The message of this morality tale cannot be missed. The boys are one-dimensional bully types, and Dorothy, who stands up for her beliefs, is a sad and lonely figure. The sense of small-town life is strong. Com-munity pride and history sanction the shoots, in which sharpshooters win cov-eted golden trophies. What does a boy like Palmer do when there are so few boys his age with whom to be friends in a place where killing is associated with being a real man? Augmenting Palmer's psychological difficulty is the point of view, a strictly limited third person that makes his thoughts and feelings pain-fully poignant as he struggles to do what he knows is right for him and still have friends among the boys. This is a serious book, an examination of indi-vidual and collective morality and of early-youth gang life only occasionally lightened by humor. Fanfare; Josette Frank; Newbery Honor; SLJ.

X

XUCATE (*Indio**), girl a year older than the protagonist, her cousin Ipa, both Otomoacoan Indians in southwestern Texas who are taken captive by raiding Spaniards and enslaved in northern Mexico. Xucate is established early as proud, insolent, pretty, and determined to be a power in her tribe. While she is often jealous of Ipa, she is admirable in that she defies the Spaniards and adheres to her ways and beliefs, unlike Ipa, who capitulates. Her insolence and refusal to yield, in particular, to accept Christianity, lead to her being given by the friars as a servant to the cruel overseer, Juan Diestro, who rapes and impregnates her, as he has done several Indian girls before her. Although she asks, before she dies, that Ipa kill the baby, Ipa takes the little boy back to their village.

Y

YANNO (*The Moorchild**), blacksmith of the village of Torskaal, father of the child stolen by the Moorfolk and supposed father of Saaski, the changeling left in her place. Although continually annoyed and frustrated during Saaski's infancy, since she screams and flails away when he approaches her because, being half-elvish, she cannot stand the nearness of iron, Yanno eventually finds a common interest with Saaski in her ability with the bees that he keeps. At first furious when she finds his father's bagpipes and demonstrates untutored ability to play them, he listens to his wife, who points out that his drunken father is dead and that Yanno himself cannot play a note, and he allows Saaski to keep them. When the villagers attack Saaski, Yanno rescues her and seems to feel stronger emotion than his wife at the realization that she must leave. Although his life is simpler with his real daughter growing up, he sometimes regrets that she is so timid around the bees.

YEP, LAURENCE (MICHAEL) (1948–   ), born in San Francisco, California; editor of story collections; reteller of stories from oral tradition; often honored author of novels of science fiction, fantasy, mystery, realistic fiction, and historical fiction, noted chiefly for his books about the Chinese-American experience. *Dragonwings** (Harper, 1975), which tells of a young boy's experiences in immigrating to California in the early twentieth century, was the winner of the 1995 Phoenix Award of The Children's Literature Association. Recent additions to Yep's long and varied list of more than forty books include *The Khan's Daughter: A Mongolian Folktale* (Scholastic, 1997) and *The Dragon Prince: A Chinese Beauty and the Beast Tale* (HarperCollins), 1997). For more information, titles, and title entries, see *Dictionary, 1960–1984* [*Child of the Owl*; *Dragonwings*] and *Dictionary, 1990–1994* [*The Star Fisher*; *Dragon's Gate*].

YESTERDAY'S CHILD (Levitin*, Sonia, Simon & Schuster, 1997), realistic mystery with detective-story aspects set in the very late twentieth century briefly in Mill Valley, California, and in Toronto, Canada, and mostly in and near Washington, D.C. Still grieving over the recent unexpected death of her mother, Jasmine, only child Laura Inman, 16, the narrator, enters her mother's room and discovers, among other items, a photo of a prominent Canadian political figure and his equally well known wife, Jacob and Megan Meistrander of Toronto, and a recently written, but unmailed, letter to Megan from Jasmine, in which Jasmine talks about their mutual hometown and the need for forgiveness. Laura decides to visit Jasmine and Megan's hometown of Birch Bend, Virginia, while on her class trip to Washington to gather what information she can about her mother, an aloof, abstracted woman whom she hardly knew. She, her best friend, Kim, and two boys in whom they are interested, Ryan and Jordan, respectively, leave Washington by bus for Birch Bend, where ironically they discover a high school reunion in progress. Oddly, no one in the class of 1974 or about that time has heard of Jasmine Rogers. Later, on another trip, Laura and Kim find in the 1972 yearbook in the high school library a duplicate of one of the photos that Laura had found in her mother's room, under which are the names Jenny Rouseau and Megan Wynant. On still another trip, Laura and Ryan find the Rouseau house, whose owner said that she bought the place from the Rouseaus (who would be Laura's grandparents) eight years earlier, but Laura remembers that Jasmine had said that her parents died in a car crash. They also learn that two people died when the Wynant house on the corner burned but that a child was saved. Determined to get to the bottom of the mystery, Laura prevails upon Kim to cover for her once more with their chaperones, flies to Toronto, and looks up Megan. An elegant, imperious, secretive woman, Megan says that she knows nothing about Jenny's parents, except that Jenny hated them and ran away to go on the stage. Laura falls in love with Megan's handsome, intelligent, decent-appearing son, Thomas, who mentions that his maternal grandparents died in an auto accident, the same story that Jasmine had told Laura about her parents, both stories since shown, by the statement of the current occupant of the family home, to be untrue. Back again in Birch Bend, Laura and Kim find old news articles telling how Megan and Jenny had set fire to the Wynant house, "seeking revenge and freedom." The fourteen-year-old Megan put the blame on Jenny and received juvenile detention until she was twenty-one, while Jenny, a year older, served seven years in prison. Devastated by what she has learned, Laura breaks off with Thomas to spare him the truth. The novel now takes a melodramatic, almost unbelievable turn—Megan lures Laura to the Lincoln Memorial and tries to kill her but is repulsed by Laura and captured by police. The conclusion finds Laura in contact with her grandparents, closer to her previously aloof, elderly father than she has ever been, and more sympathetic toward the mother whom she had always thought cold, unloving, and disapproving. After release, Jenny had changed her name, gone to Europe, and carved out a new, very low-keyed life for herself. Yesterday's child, a convicted murderer, she could never resume her former life. Laura realizes that she, too, can never be a child again now that she knows her mother's past. She knows, too, that she can refrain from making unhealthy demands upon Kim, who has been a truly good friend. The story is completely engrossing, holding the reader close at Laura's side as she plays detective. Some gothic elements appear—bad dreams, old houses, voices from the past, secrets, and frequent mention of the power of evil. The cast, though large, contains mostly functionary or choral figures. Laura grows greatly in understanding of self and of people, as well as of the importance of friendship— true friendship is priceless, yet the price of friendship may be too high. The most interesting figure, of course, is Megan—mean, manipulative, and socio-pathological to the end. She had as the price of friendship maneuvered Jenny into perpetrating murder for her, and she got away with it. An abrupt shift from Laura's discourse to Megan's thoughts describing the attempted murder jars. Poe Nominee.

YOLANDA'S GENIUS (Fenner*, Carol, McElderry, 1995), light, contemporary, girl's growing-up novel in a family context. Since African-American Josie Blue, a widowed paralegal, is fed up with Chicago's drugs and violence, she moves her family, straight-As, inventive, fifth grader Yolanda and sweet, thin Andrew, 6, to the small town of Grand River, Michigan. A loner by nature, tall, heavy, strong Yolanda is slow to make friends and is often the butt of jibes about her size and shape. When some kids call her "whale," she responds with a discourse of information about that mammal, arousing the admiration of white classmate Shirley Piper, who wonders if she is a genius. Yolanda investigates the word's meaning and decides that the term applies to Andrew. She feels that his ability to capture the essence of people and rich sounds on a small wooden pipe and in particular on the Marine Band harmonica that his deceased policeman-father gave him is truly exceptional. Her sometimes humorous, occasionally poignant efforts to get his musical talent recognized drive the meager plot. Momma, who thinks Andrew will follow his father into law enforcement, has little regard for his music and is more concerned by his lack of progress in school. Only one teacher, Mr. Watts, recognizes that the boy wishes only to learn to read music (to read the "Mickey Mouse feet") and arranges it. After some big boys, the neighborhood gang called the Dudes, ruin the harmonica, Yolanda beats them up and then manages to buy Andrew a suitable replacement. Andrew's playing, however, is not the same; he has lost spirit. Late in the school year, hefty Aunt Tiny, wealthy from a string of hair salons, visits, and then after school lets out, the Blue family return the visit during the blues festival at Chicago's Grant Park. Determined to get Andrew recognized by the topflight stars, Yolanda arranges to get both him and herself "lost" and thus on the stage, where they meet the famous B. B. King, among other stars. After listening to Andrew's music, King calls him a "little dude" who is a "mean harp man" and encourages him to continue playing. A subplot revolves around Yolanda's relationship with Shirley, with whom she would like to be friends. She bullies the thin, man-voiced girl, however, and lies to her, asserting that she can do Double Dutch in jump rope, although she really cannot because of her ungainliness. At

478 YOUNG, RONDER THOMAS

the end, she resolves to tell Shirley the truth, but the reader never learns whether or not she follows through. Yolanda dominates the book, not always sympathetically or credibly; Aunt Tiny is a likable figure of near-caricature proportions; Momma is too remote from Andrew to seem credible; and Andrew is a winning child one-dimensionally developed. The book's best section revolves around the festival. The noise, crowds, and confusion of the situation come through strongly and believably. The title has an obvious double meaning. ALA; Newbery Honor.

YOUNG, RONDER THOMAS, born in Anderson, South Carolina; graduate of the University of South Carolina in Columbia; resident of Norcross, Georgia; writer of short stories and essays for journals and periodicals and novels for later elementary and early adolescent readers. *Moving Mama to Town** (Orchard, 1997), recipient of the International Reading Award, is a family novel of the efforts of a boy to move his mother and little brother to town from their farm after his father takes off. The book is strong in characterizations and local color. An earlier novel is *Learning by Heart* (Houghton, 1993), another story of southern family life. For additional information about Young and a title entry, see *Dictionary 1990–1994* [*Learning by Heart*].

Z

ZACHARY MACALLISTER (*Ghost Canoe**), former captain of clipper ships and father of Nathan, the protagonist. He is the keeper of the lighthouse near which the ship foundered, setting into motion the events that lead to the unmasking of the murderer of the ship's captain and the discovery and loss of the Spanish treasure. In addition to being a good professional, worthy husband, and caring father, Zachary is the one who receives the letter from the slain captain's brother about the carved bone pieces. He shares the information with Nathan, who then gets the pieces from the ghost canoe that eventually enable Jack Kane to find the treasure.

ZEKE BLEDSOE (*Choosing Up Sides**), a country-town Baptist preacher, father of Luke Bledsoe, the narrator. Luke describes him as a "little steel rod of a man" who is determined to be a good pastor to his little flock and a good father and husband, even though he is cruel and unfeeling in the process. Zeke thinks that sports are as sinful as dancing and movies, all of which are the "Devil's playground." He despises his wife's brother, Uncle* Micah Barnes, also a left-hander, who smokes, is a sportswriter, goes dancing, and even drinks a little too much sometimes. Zeke often regrets his rages, sometimes apologizes, and also often yearns for the close relationship with his son that Luke and Uncle Micah enjoy. Zeke, like Luke, is a character in conflict with himself.

ZEL (*Zel**), daughter of overprotective Mother*, who confines her in a remote, abandoned tower to keep her from marrying. Zel is a shortening of Rapunzel, a proper name derived from a species of lettuce. Zel is a loving, lively girl of almost thirteen when the story begins, eager to be with people and very close in spirit to Mother. In town she meets Count Konrad*, son of the area's nobleman, who later searches for her. She falls in love with him and bears him twin daughters. In the several years that she lives in the tower, having only the company of Mother and the wild creatures that she tames, she becomes frustrated and lonely and nearly loses her mind. Although the pivotal figure in the novel, as in the old folktale "Rapunzel," Zel is less interesting as a character than either Mother or Konrad.

ZEL (Napoli*, Donna Jo, Dutton, 1996), fantasy novel set in mid-sixteenth-century Switzerland, which retells the folktale "Rapunzel." In early July, lively, curious, warmhearted Zel*, almost thirteen, joyfully accompanies her devoted single-parent Mother* as they leave their isolated mountain-dwelling for their semiannual trip to town. Zel begs, and Mother reluctantly grants permission for Zel to watch the smith at work. While Mother shops for such birthday gifts for Zel as paper, ink, a quill, and material for a new dress, Zel gentles Meta, a remarkably beautiful horse, while the smith removes a tick from the animal's ear. When Meta's owner, a handsome, willful youth of about fifteen, asks what she would like in payment, she asks only for a warm, fertilized egg to place under the alm goose. The youth, Konrad*, son of the local count, searches for, and brings, the egg to the smithy (a clear foreshadowing of the zeal and diligence with which he will later search for Zel), only to discover that the girl is gone. He also learns that his father wishes him to marry a duke's daughter, an arrangement that he resists because he is much taken with Zel. Back at the alm, Mother sews the birthday dress, while Zel's thoughts dwell upon the regal-appearing youth. Fearing that she will lose her daughter, Mother takes her to a remote, abandoned tower, orders her to let her golden hair grow long, and leaves the girl there. Her magic keeps Zel prisoner by blocking ways out of the tower room. At first Mother enters and leaves the tower room by climbing up and down a magical tree just outside. Later she uses Zel's thick golden braids as a ladder. Count Konrad, who turns fifteen on July 6, the same day that Zel becomes thirteen, discovers her name but searches unsuccessfully for her. Two years pass, and Zel, almost mad from loneliness, relieves the tedium of the tower by making friends with various wild creatures, painting, and drawing. Konrad, assuming Zel is probably married by now, agrees to wed a young countess from the south. Restless one day, he goes for a ride on Meta in a wild part of the country and happens to arrive at the tower just in time to see Zel launch from the window a beautifully fashioned, painted paper bird. He watches as Mother arrives and overhears as she instructs Zel to lower her hair so that she can climb the tower. After Mother leaves, Konrad ascends by the hair ladder, and he and Zel make love. While Konrad is away arranging to release Zel, Mother returns, learns about Konrad, cuts off Zel's braids, and uses them to raise Konrad into the tower. She then catapults him from the tower to the ground, where his eyes are blinded by brambles. Zel is transported to a far-off land, where she gives birth to twin daughters. Although blind, Konrad searches and, when the twins are two years old, discovers his lost love and their children. Zel's tears of joy restore his sight. Thus far, the plot follows the pattern of the familiar folktale closely. It deviates at this point, where all three parties reconcile, even Mother. As is usually true with retellings of old stories, the bones of the plot are unchanged for the most part, but heightened emotion, psychological ramifications, here focusing on Mother's personality and motivations, greater attention to setting, and expanded background mark the story as fiction. The point of view alternates between the third-person accounts of the girl and her noble suitor and the girl's mother's first-person story, a technique that contributes additional depth, particularly to Mother's character. The plot often approaches movie-type romance and melodrama. Strongest is the style, which is crisp, visual, and sensory. Use of the present tense makes events and emotions vivid and implicitly underscores the theme, which comments on relationships between parents and children. SLJ.

ZERO (*Holes**), Hector Zeroni, boy of about twelve, a prisoner, along with Stanley Yelnats, at Camp Green Lake. Illiterate, he asks Stanley to teach him to read and write, and the two boys becomes friends. While they are trying to survive at Big Thumb, Zero confesses that he took the sneakers for the theft of which Stanley was sentenced to Camp Green Lake. From a homeless family, Zero remembers that when he was a child he had a yellow room and his mother sang to him. Zero cannot remember why they moved to the streets. After his mother disappeared, leaving him alone to fend for himself, he simply took whatever he needed, including the sneakers. Zero is a descendant of the Madame Zeroni who placed a curse on the Yelnats family. In carrying Zero up the mountain, Stanley lays the curse.

LIST OF BOOKS BY AWARDS

The following novels have been cited for the awards indicated and appear in this dictionary. Nonfiction books and collections of short stories are not included.

JANE ADDAMS PEACE ASSOCIATION CHILDREN'S BOOK AWARD

Bat 6
Habibi
The Well: David's Story

AMERICAN LIBRARY ASSOCIATION NOTABLE BOOKS FOR CHILDREN

The Apprenticeship of Lucas Whitaker
The Arkadians
Bandit's Moon
The Barn
Bat 6
The Beekeeper's Apprentice or On the Segregation of the Queen
Belle Prater's Boy
Beyond the Burning Time
Beyond the Western Sea: Book One: The Escape from Home
Beyond the Western Sea: Book Two: Lord Kirkle's Money
Billy (French)
Billy (Roybal)
The Cage
Catherine Called Birdy
Cezanne Pinto: A Memoir
Coffee Will Make You Black
Come in from the Cold
Dakota Dream

Deliver Us from Evie
Driver's Ed
The Eagle Kite
The Ear, the Eye, and the Arm
Earthshine
Ella Enchanted
Escape from Egypt
The Examination
Falcon's Egg
Far North
Fig Pudding
Finder: A Novel of the Borderlands
Flight of the Dragon Kyn
Flip-Flop Girl
A Girl Named Disaster
The Glory Field
Go and Come Back
The Grass Dancer
Guests
Gypsy Davey
Habibi
Hannah in Between
Holes
Iceman
I Hadn't Meant to Tell You This
In the Time of the Butterflies
The Iron Ring
I See the Moon
It's Nothing to a Mountain
Jip His Story
Joey Pigza Swallowed the Key
Jubilee Journey
Lily's Crossing
A Long Way from Chicago: A Novel in Stories
Looking After Lily
The Magic and the Healing
Make Lemonade
Making Up Megaboy
The Maze
The Midwife's Apprentice
Missing the Piano
The Moorchild
My Brother, My Sister, and I
My Louisiana Sky
No Effect
The Other Shepards
Owl in Love

Parable of the Sower
Phoenix Rising
Pigs Don't Fly
A Place to Call Home
Poppy
P.S. Longer Letter Later
The Ramsay Scallop
Remembering Mog
The Revenge of the Forty-Seven Samurai
Rules of the Road
Running Out of Time
A School for Pompey Walker
Seven Spiders Spinning
Shadow
Shadow Spinner
The Shakespeare Stealer
Something Terrible Happened
Spite Fences
Stones in the Water
Stranger at the Wedding
Sun & Spoon
The Thief
Tiger, Tiger, Burning Bright
Too Soon for Jeff
Toughing It
Trout Summer
Under the Blood-Red Sun
Under the Mermaid Angel
The Van Gogh Cafe
The View from Saturday
Walk Two Moons
The Watsons Go to Birmingham—1963
The Well: David's Story
What Girls Learn
What Jamie Saw
When She Hollers
When She Was Good
The Window (Dorris)
The Window (Ingold)
Wish You Were Here
Yolanda's Genius

BOSTON GLOBE–HORN BOOK **AWARD HONOR BOOKS**

Belle Prater's Boy
Dragonwings
Earthshine

The Folk Keeper
Jericho
Lily's Crossing
The Moorchild
My Louisiana Sky
While No One Was Watching

BOSTON GLOBE–HORN BOOK AWARD WINNERS

Holes
Poppy

CHILD STUDY CHILDREN'S BOOK COMMITTEE AT BANK STREET COLLEGE AWARD

See The Josette Frank Award

CHRISTOPHER AWARD

Frindle
Glennis, Before and After
Holes
Shipwreck Season
Tuck Everlasting

CORETTA SCOTT KING AWARD WINNERS

Bud, Not Buddy
Forged by Fire
Slam!

THE HORN BOOK MAGAZINE FANFARE LIST

Abel's Island
Bad Girls
Beauty
Catherine Called Birdy
The Cuckoo's Child
Deliver Us from Evie
The Devil in Vienna
Dragonwings
Frindle
A Girl Named Disaster
Go and Come Back
Holes

I Am the Cheese
I Hadn't Meant to Tell You This
Ironman
Jericho
Like Sisters on the Homefront
A Long Way from Chicago: A Novel in Stories
Make Lemonade
The Midwife's Apprentice
Parrot in the Oven: Mi Vida
Tangerine
The Thief
Tuck Everlasting
The Watsons Go to Birmingham—1963
While No One Was Watching
The Window (Dorris)
Wringer

INTERNATIONAL READING ASSOCIATION CHILDREN'S BOOK AWARD

Choosing Up Sides
Don't You Dare Read This, Mrs. Dunphrey
Dragonwings
The King's Shadow
Moving Mama to Town
Running Out of Time
Spite Fences
Words by Heart

JEFFERSON CUP AWARD FOR HISTORICAL FICTION

The Ornament Tree
Soldier's Heart

THE JOSETTE FRANK AWARD (Formerly the Child Study Children's Book Committee at Bank Street College Award)

The Cuckoo's Child
The Devil in Vienna
Earthshine
Figuring Out Frances
Glennis, Before and After
Make Lemonade
Music from a Place Called Half Moon
The Watsons Go to Birmingham—1963
Wringer

THE LEWIS CARROLL SHELF AWARD

Abel's Island
Dragonwings
Tuck Everlasting

JOHN NEWBERY MEDAL HONOR BOOKS

Abel's Island
Belle Prater's Boy
Catherine Called Birdy
Dragonwings
The Ear, the Eye and the Arm
Ella Enchanted
A Girl Named Disaster
Lily's Crossing
A Long Way from Chicago: A Novel in Stories
The Moorchild
The Thief
The Watsons Go to Birmingham—1963
What Jamie Saw
Wringer
Yolanda's Genius

JOHN NEWBERY MEDAL WINNERS

Bud, Not Buddy
Holes
The Midwife's Apprentice
The View from Saturday
Walk Two Moons

SCOTT O'DELL AWARD FOR HISTORICAL FICTION

The Bomb
Forty Acres and Maybe a Mule
Under the Blood-Red Sun

THE CHILDREN'S LITERATURE ASSOCIATION PHOENIX AWARD HONOR BOOKS

Abel's Island
Beauty
The Devil in Vienna
The Disappearance
Tuck Everlasting
Words by Heart

THE CHILDREN'S LITERATURE ASSOCIATION PHOENIX AWARD WINNERS

Dragonwings
I Am the Cheese

NOMINEES FOR THE EDGAR ALLAN POE AWARD BEST JUVENILE MYSTERY

Alice Rose and Sam
The Bones in the Cliff
Caught
Christie & Company Down East
The Clearing
Cousins in the Castle
Deal with a Ghost
Finn
Flyers
For Mike
Gaps in Stone Walls
Harvey's Mystifying Raccoon Mix-Up
Hawk Moon
Holes
In the Middle of the Night
The Kidnappers
The Last Piper
Marvelous Marvin and the Pioneer Ghost
The Maze
The Midnight Club
Mr. Was
Pale Phoenix
PaperQuake: A Puzzle
Penance
Poison
Running Out of Time
Sammy Keyes and the Hotel Thief
Secrets at Hidden Valley
Shadowmaker
Spirit Seeker
Spying on Miss Muller
Tangerine
Thin Ice
The 13th Floor
Trouble Will Find You
Turn the Cup Around
Wolf Stalker
Yesterday's Child

WINNERS OF THE EDGAR ALLAN POE AWARD BEST JUVENILE MYSTERY

The Absolutely True Story . . . How I Visited Yellowstone Park with the Terrible Rupes
Ghost Canoe
The Killer's Cousin
Looking for Jamie Bridger
Prophecy Rock
Sparrows in the Scullery
Toughing It
Twisted Summer

SCHOOL LIBRARY JOURNAL BEST BOOKS FOR CHILDREN

The Apprenticeship of Lucas Whitaker
The Ashwater Experiment
The Ballad of Lucy Whipple
Bat 6
The Beekeeper's Apprentice or On the Segregation of the Queen
Beggars and Choosers
Belle Prater's Boy
Beyond the Burning Time
Billy (French)
Billy (Roybal)
Blood and Chocolate
Brothers and Sisters
Bud, Not Buddy
The Buffalo Tree
The Cage
Catherine Called Birdy
Cezanne Pinto: A Memoir
Coffee Will Make You Black
Come in from the Cold
Confess-O-Rama
Crash
The Cuckoo's Child
Dakota Dream
Dancing on the Edge
Daring to Be Abigail
Dave at Night
Deliver Us from Evie
Driver's Ed
The Eagle Kite
The Ear, the Eye and the Arm
Earthshine
Escape from Egypt
The Examination

The Facts Speak for Themselves
Falcon's Egg
Finder: A Novel of the Borderlands
Flight of the Dragon Kyn
Flip-Flop Girl
The Folk Keeper
For YOUR Eyes Only!
Francie
Getting Near to Baby
The Ghost of Fossil Glen
A Girl Named Disaster
The Glory Field
Go and Come Back
The Grass Dancer
The Great Turkey Walk
Gypsy Davey
Hannah in Between
Hard Love
Holes
Iceman
I Hadn't Meant to Tell You This
Ironman
It's Nothing to a Mountain
Jip His Story
Joey Pigza Swallowed the Key
Johanna: A Novel of the van Gogh Family
Justice
Keeping the Moon
The King's Shadow
The Landry News
Like Sisters on the Homefront
Lone Wolf
The Long Season of Rain
Looking After Lily
The Lost Flower Children
The Magic and the Healing
Make Lemonade
Me and Rupert Goody
Mean Margaret
A Message from the Match Girl
Mick Harte Was Here
The Midwife's Apprentice
Missing the Piano
The Moorchild
The Music of Dolphins
My Brother, My Sister, and I
Never Trust a Dead Man
No Effect

Northern Borders
The Other Shepards
Owen Foote, Frontiersman
Owl in Love
Parable of the Sower
Phoenix Rising
Pigs Don't Fly
Pope Joan
Poppy
Protecting Marie
The Ramsay Scallop
Rats Saw God
Reaching Dustin
Rule of the Bone
Rules of the Road
Safe at Second
Seedfolks
Sees Behind Trees
See You Around, Sam
Seven Spiders Spinning
Shadow
Shadow Spinner
The Shakespeare Stealer
She Walks These Hills
The Skull of Truth: A Magic Shop Book
Someone Like You
Something Terrible Happened
Speak
Spite Fences
Starplace
Stone Water
Stranger at the Wedding
Sun & Spoon
A Sunburned Prayer
Tiger, Tiger, Burning Bright
Too Soon for Jeff
Toughing It
Tree of Heaven
Unbroken
Under the Beetle's Cellar
Under the Blood-Red Sun
The Unlikely Romance of Kate Bjorkman
The View from Saturday
The Wedding
Well Wished
When She Hollers
When Zachary Beaver Came to Town
Whirligig

The Wild Kid
Wish You Were Here
Wringer
Zel

WESTERN WRITERS OF AMERICA SPUR AWARD

Danger Along the Ohio
Far North
Indio
Petey

GEORGE G. STONE CENTER FOR CHILDREN'S BOOKS RECOGNITION OF MERIT AWARD

The House on Mango Street

WESTERN HERITAGE AWARD

Alice Rose and Sam
Daughter of Suqua

INDEX

Names and titles in ALL CAPITAL LETTERS refer to the actual entries of the dictionary, and page numbers in *italics* refer to the location of the actual entries in the dictionary.

free friend, 409; on flatboat, by Indians, 84;
on house parent, 50; on junior officer, by
guerilla, 423; on knight's company, 381; on
war protestor, 69; sexual, in janitor's closet,
390; woman on street, 367. *See also* battles;
conflicts; fights; rivalry; wars; war novels
attendants, asylum and hospital, 323
attic, farm house, with special attic window,
466
Attolia, 251, 329, 413
Attolians, battle with, 10
Attorney General, Texas, 182
attorney, white, defends black youths at
murder trial, 36, 46. *See also* lawyers
Audra Devereaux, 64, 265, 285, 307
Augustine Butler, 134
au lait, term for biracials, 209
AUNT CASEY DAWSEY, *15,* 83, 148
Aunt Chava, 256, 373
Aunt Chipo, 10, 148
Aunt Corinne Hardwick, 386
Aunt Dorie Kay Ramsey, 293
AUNT EDNA TAYLOR, *16,* 253, 465
Auntie Roe, 326
Aunt Lula, 259
Aunt Mary Cormac, 103
Aunt Mary Duncan, 235, 244
Aunt Minna, 194
Aunt Minty, 245
Aunt Pat, 120
Aunt Patty Hobson, 144, 432
Aunt Queen, 129
aunts: alcoholic, abandons children, 459;
Alzheimer's victim, 195; boy's, judgmental
about father's AIDS, 103; carping, 307;
controlling, judgmental, 104; depressed, 222;
dictatorial, fussy, 144; disappearing, 28;
eccentric, 214, 272; foreign correspondent,
160; great, 245, 424, 465; helps girl with
dragon's egg, 116, 160; lover of, married
and unfaithful, 78, 222; mother's, 129;
mother's younger sister, 78; of girl who
raises dragon, 136; raised four siblings, 432;
really mother, 37; rigid, controlling, 431;
stingy, bullying, 25; stubborn, difficult, 161;
university students, 301; wealthy, 477; well-
meaning but baffled by girl, 78; white, of
triracial girl, 16; wild, 150
Aunt Sally, 65
Aunt Sarah Hall, 431
Aunt Suze, 265, 307
Aunt Tiny, 477
Aunt Wanda, 150

Au Sable, New York State, 353
Austen Kittredge, Senior, 156, 301
Austen Kittredge III, 155, 156, 160, 161, 219,
301
Austin, Texas, 433
Austria, Vienna, 92
autistic persons, man called Spook, 65
autobiographical novels, 291
auto body shop owner, only African American
in Oak Ridge, 386
AVI, *16,* 22, 32, 34, 331
aviation, beginnings of, 97
the Avy, 452
award books. *See* Appendix
awards ceremony, interrupted by middle-school
kids, 409
"away time," boy's coming of age, 164
Axis league, World War II, 399
Ayers, Martha, 201, 377
Ayortha province, 108
Azbury Beatty, 242

BABA JOSEPH, *17,* 149
BABBIT, NATALIE (ZANE MOORE), *17,*
426
Babe Ruth, 433
Babette the woodchuck, 264
babies: abused, 455; adopted, 136, 154, 194,
352, 466; almost shot by accidental gun
discharge, 318; birth of, 166, 207, 336; born
dead, 191; born with birth defects, 372;
death at birth, presumed, 128; death of, 30,
143, 202, 402, 445; delivered from mother's
dead body, 83; discovered, 368; illegitimate,
233; Indian, dies of diarrhea, 154; rejected
by mother, 419; said stolen by convict, 378;
sickly, lead poisoning, 166
Baby (*PaperQuake: A Puzzle*), 315
Baby, pet name by sister, 189
Baby Dean, 144
baby-sitters: for lively boy, 424; for retarded
boy, 394; girl, eleven, 4; girl, fourteen, 251
Baby-Sitters Club series, 256
Baby-Sitters Club Super Specials series, 256
Baby-Sitters Little Sisters series, 256
BACON, KATHARINE JAY, *17,* 123
Bad, Badder, Baddest, 443
Badger, code name, 311
badgers, evicted from woodchuck burrow, 265
BAD GIRLS, 18, 443
"bad word," mentally challenged boy says,
462

Big Ma Logan, 253, 451

bigotry: by red-neck Georgia neighbor, 393; scorn for gay video filmer, 51; small Southern town, 395. *See also* discrimination; prejudice

Big Thumb, mountain peak, 182, 481

Big Wind Coming, 109

Bikini Atoll, 42

Bilal, Muhammad, 152

Bill Eckert, 361

BILLINGSLEY, FRANNY, *35,* 127, 452

Bill McAllister, 427

Bill Melendez, 37

Bill of Rights, 228

BILLY (French), *35,* 137

BILLY (Roybal), *36,* 353

Billy Calico, bandit, 21

BILLY DAVIS, *38,* 435

Billy Lee Turner, 35, 46, 377

Billy Melendez, 36

Billy Rose, 352

Billy Rupe, 4

BILLY WASHINGTON, 27, *38,* 92, 237

binoculars, girl observes thief at work, 361

BINSTOCK, R. C., *39,* 422

biographical novels: bandit Joaquin Murieta, 20; Dominican sisters, 190; Johanna van Gogh-Bonger, 206; Pope Joan, 329

biologists, bird, 242, 260, 350

biracials: boy, Hopi-white, 177, 333; boy, Indian-white, 289; children, French-African-American, 209; children, Native American-white, 159; girl, African-American-white, 178; girl, West Indian-white, 387; half-elf, half-human child, 275; young man, African-American-white, 262

Birch Bend, Virginia, 476

birds: condors, 242, 260, 302, 350; girl named after, 255; paper painted, 480

Birdy, 57

Birmingham, Alabama, 52, 449

birth control, 307

birthdays: gift of eagle kite, 103; girl's, 172; ninth, 25, 471; pound cake for, 263; tenth, 472

birth defects, babies born with mysterious, 372

births: after labor starts at prom, 386; baby woodchuck, 265; healthy baby boy, 270; of centaur, 250; of girl, 201; of half-Indian, half-Spanish boy, 188; of sister's baby, 195; of two boy babies, 115; premature, 420; twin calves, 270

Bishop, Brent, 460

Bishop family (*Christie & Company Down East*), 62

Bishop family (*The Kidnappers*), 216

Bishop Mayne, 452

bites, girl inflicts on half-sisters' father, 78, 222

Bitte, 194

B.J., 373

Bjorkman family, 437

Bjorn Bjorkman, 437

BJ VAUGHAN, *39,* 163, 249, 401

Blackbeard's Cove, 44

The Black Cauldron, 8

Black Elk, 82

Black Hills, 446

blackmail: by female cop, 404; of House of Representatives member, 321; of Jewish boy for food, 110; of judge, to silence him about murder, 429

Black Sea, World War II, 399

blacksmiths: cowboy becomes, 242; father of changeling, 275; in 1840s tourist village, 208; in mining town, 19; ship's, 32; village, 475

BLACKWOOD, GARY L., *39,* 374

Blake, William, quotation from poem of, 418

blame, for theater disaster, focused on 16-year-old assistant manager, 189

blankets, damp in airraid shelter, 395

Bledsoe family, 61, 433, 479

BLIND BENNY, 29, *40*

blindness, near, from paint sprayed into eyes, 110, 410

blind persons: fake, 361; from birth, 40; girl, fifteen, 173, 466; in one eye, 60; knight, 324, 381; old, former musician, 287, 459; old woman, 284, 446; young noble, 223, 480; young World War I veteran, 64, 307

Blitz, gang of schoolboys, 372

blood: comforting like chocolate, 41; for transfusion for the Griffin, 163; Nile River runs red with, 111; stains on window sill, 58; water turns to, 401

BLOOD AND CHOCOLATE, 40, 222

Blood Child, and Other Stories, 51

Blood on the Forehead: What I Know about Writing, 215

Bloody Hand (ship), 416

Bloomburg family, 115

BLOOR, EDWARD, *41,* 408

Blove Spenson, 401

Blossom Culp and the Sleep of Death, 320

cholera, 10, 148
CHOOSING UP SIDES, 61, 350
Christianity, *Vaspostori* sect, 17, 149
CHRISTIANSEN, C.B., *62,* 194
Christie, Agatha, 63
Christie Malcolm, 230
CHRISTIE MONTGOMERY, 62, *63,* 441
Christie & Company, 313
CHRISTIE & COMPANY DOWN EAST, 62,
   313
Christie & Company, girl detectives, 62
Christie & Company in the Year of the
   Dragon, 313
Christina Calderon, 419
Christine Taylor, 107, 254
Christmas: 99, 336, 455, 467; arguments over
   tree type, 437; brings mother's alcoholism
   to head, 173; 1888, Amsterdam, 206; gift for
   grandfather, high-heeled shoes, 364;
   occasion for proposal, 298, 454; school
   program, 203
Christmas Eve, 95, 239
The Christmas Rat, 16
Christmas Tree on the Mountain, 119
Chronicles of Prydain, 8
Chrysler New Yorker, black, 216
Chuckie Deegan, 299
churches: Baptist, bombed, 52, 449;
   congregation prejudiced against Indians, 289;
   meetings, 289; suppers, baby left in
   cassarole, 266
Churchill, Manitoba, 31, 53, 199, 249
Cici Linden, 428
cigar box, contains family photos and eighty
   dollars, 274
cigarettes, storeowner refuses to sell to minor,
   252
cigar-smoking man, 44
Cincinnati, Ohio, 129
Cinderella, 107
Cinder Turner, 36, 46, 377
circumcision, 110
circuses: confidence man, 162; strong man,
   162
CISNEROS, SANDRA, *63,* 183
Cissy Champion, 371
Citadel of Wizards, 9, 391, 401
cities, unnamed, United States, 99, 176, 251,
   267, 336, 361, 387, 456
citrus industry: almost destroyed by cold
   weather, 248, 409; possibly reborn by new
   variety, 248
City family, 131

civil rights: commentary on African-American
   quest for, 60; demonstrations, 153;
   movement, 392, 449; protests, 396; workers
   for, 187
Civil War: American, 59, 131, 152, 204; hero,
   bogus, 241; period, Virginia City, Nevada, 8
Claib Maggard, 175, 378
claims, farm, 22
Clair Poole, 414
clairvoyant, woman, 392
Clancy the cat, 57
"clan money, " 348
Clara (*Danger Along the Ohio*), 84
Clara (*The Van Gogh Cafe*), 440
Clara Sutton, 195
CLARE HARRIS, *64,* 265, 307
Clarissa Montgomery, 134
CLARK COLES, *64,* 237, 450
classics, Chinese, phenomenal knowledge of,
   112
class pictures, holding frindles, 138
classrooms: fifth grade, 18; open, unstructured,
   228, 282; swallowed by sinkhole, 228, 409
Clayburn family, 59, 408
Claymore, Brother Clyde, 19
Claytonville, North Carolina, 262
cleaning women: girl of thirteen, 393;
   managing household, 293. *See also*
   housekeepers; maids
cleaning solvent, kills girl who drinks it, 218
THE CLEARING, 65, 271
clearing, in the woods with a few houses, 65
Cleaver, 162
Clemens, Sam, 8
CLEMENTS, ANDREW, *66,* 137, 228
Clempool, Mr. Matthew, 7, 33, 34, 200, 283,
   284, 287, 349
Cleopatra Kittredge, 301
clergyman, Protestant, operates chapel boat at
   Liverpool, 349. *See also* ministers; preachers;
   priests
Cletus Bridger, 234, 244
Cleveland, Ohio, 366
Cliff Abernathy, 120
Clifford Allyn Abernathy III, 120
CLIFFORD (ROSENBERG), ETH(EL), *66,*
   176
cliffs, Indian bones protrude from, 44
Cliffsend, island, 128
Clifton, Malcolm, 458
Clifton's men, treacherous, 356
Clifton Village, 208, 356
clinics: abortion, 233, 253; veterinary, 250

New York, 386; to return to sea, 212, 291, 362; to return to the United States, 77; to sell shoes, 354. *See also* ambitions
desk, old with secret compartment, 147
Des Moines, Iowa, 37
Desmond Aster, 424
desperadoes, boarder suspected of being, 19
DESSEN, SARAH, *92*, 214, 385
Destiny, 164
Detective Fayette, 328
detective novels: abduction of schoolchildren, 433; attempted theft and kidnapping in motor home, 4; bizzare family relationships, 244; campground residents, 365; clues to boy's identity, 266; counterfeiting, 176; ecology, 257; embezzling, 57; kidnapping schoolboys, 216; knife slaying, 391; letters and diaries about mysterious "V," 315; murder, extortion, 321; murder in mining town, 8; mysterious happenings, 62; paranormal clues to murder, 130; reincarnation, 230; search for missing stepmother, 327; Sherlock Holmes and an American girl, 25; snowmobile accident, 414; spreading disease, 122; stolen rabbit, 459; summer colony murder and blackmail, 428; theft, 361
detectives: brother and young sister, 292; boy, eleven, 259; boy, sixteen, 93; boy, seventeen, 109, 177, 297; girl and two boys, all nine, 257; girl, twelve, 361; girl, fourteen, 315; girl, sixteen, 476; girls, three, all fourteen, 62, 63; hired to find brother, 414; mutants with special skills, 14, 105; nineteenth century, shady London, 33; police, overly involved in work, 391; private, ex-police, 80, 321; private, London, 284; youthful, 58, 266
detention facilities: in Texas desert, 181; conditions almost inhumane, 182; for boys, 49, 260, 349
Detour for Emmy, 349
Detta, 8
Deucy, 59, 408
developments: housing, planned, 147; housing, prestigious, 280, 410; industrial park, 381; resort on island, 62
Devereaux, Audra, 64
Devereaux family, 265, 285, 307
devil, girl makes pact with, 268
THE DEVIL IN VIENNA, 92, 306
DEVORAH, *92,* 111, 202, 296, 350

devotion; to sister-in-law and her baby, 243; uncle to Alzheimer's victim aunt, 195
Devotions group, vacation Bible school, 78
DeWitt, Lainey, 433, 454
Dexter, Pennsylvania, 244
Deza Malone, 48
dialects. *See* style, use of language
dialogue. *See* style, use of language
dharma (honor), 193
Diamond Lil the ostrich, 42
Diamondstein family, 441
DIANA COVINGTON, 27, 38, *92,* 237
Diana Rodriguez, 38
Diana Tree, 174
Diane Griffith, 63
Diane Smythe, 327
diaries: about van Gogh family, 206; of dead girl, 315; of dead girl, red leather cover, 147; of Dominican sister, 191; sister's, steamy, 67. *See also* journals; style, structure
Diaz, Juan Antonio, 257
Dibble family, 335
Dicey's Song, 442
Dickens, novels of, read by ex-slave, 424; read by teacher, 203
Dickensian novels, 73, 387
Dickinson, Emily, poem of, "I'm Nobody," 83, 434
dictators: petty, study hall prefect, 395; right wing, 190; of toxic waste site, 376
diction, lessons in, 375
dictionaries: newly published, 138; teacher's obsession, 137
didactic novels: AIDS, 106; atomic bomb tests at Bikini, 42; promoting bike safety, 268; social, ecological, 76; teenaged parenthood, 419; wolf reintroduction in Yellowstone Park, 469
Diestro, Juan, 188, 473
dilemmas: about mother, 93; about sharing discovery, 65; about "wringing" and shooting pigeons, 472; whether to assist a suicide, 400, 464
Diller Drug Store, 134
Dillon, Texas, 209
Dillon family, 235
Dillon, Lacey, 421
Dime Show, at fair, 142
Dimwood Forest, 110, 284, 331
Dinkerhoff factory, 257
Dinky Hocker Shoots Smack, 215

Five, 40

Five Alien Eyes, 251

Flagra the dragon, 125

flags: blood-red sun, of Japan, 435; Japanese, old man loves, 156, 435

Flannery, Dan, 78, 222

flares, ignored by plane, 54

flatboats, Ohio River, 84

Flatfoot Fox, 66

flattery: hypnotic and fulsome, 104; tool of Praise Singer, 265

flea market, school fundraiser, 314

FLEISCHMAN, PAUL, *124,* 366, 460

FLEISCHMAN, SID (ALBERT SIDNEY), 20, *124,* 161, 415

FLETCHER, RALPH, 120, *124*

FLETCHER, SUSAN (CLEMENS), *124,* 125, 373

Fleur St. Germaine, 437

FLIGHT OF THE DRAGON KYN, 124, *125*

flights: in motorhome to Canada, 5; to Hudson Bay, 53

Flint, Michigan, 48, 448

Flintlock, 49

FLIP-FLOP GIRL, 126, 319

Floating Lily (boat), 113

"floating world," disreputable district, 348

Floca, Brian, 331

floods: China, 113; flash, children caught in, 257; flash, kills murderer, 334

floors, 13th, avenue to past time, 415

Florence, 367

Florenz Deets, 152

Florida, late 20th century: 115; Century Village, 441; Coral Springs, 371; Gulf Coast small town, 461; Tangerine County, Lake Windsor Downs, 409; unspecified town, 96, 386

flowerbinder, 250

Flowering Talent, 113

Flowers, Kansas, 440

flowers, stroke victim chooses to grow, 367

flu, 1918 epidemic sweeping country, 308

Floyd Rayfield, 22, 60, 81, 91, 94

FLYERS, 126, 179

flyers: advertising bank, 48; symbol of striving for better life, 44

"flying," (levitation), 44, 126

flying pigs, 465

Flyilng Solo, 124

Folk: The Folk, 128; moor elves, 276

THE FOLK KEEPER, 35, *128*

Folk Keeper, 128

Folk Record, 128

folktales, basis for novel, 25, 107

food: absorbed through skin from mud, 39; dropped off at freak-show trailer, 458; freeze-dried, jettisoned by hiker, 175; inedible, 388; Japanese, distributed to islanders by Americans, 42; rejected, 264; smuggled to starving Jewish prisoners, World War II, 399; terrible at boarding school, 395

foot, Indian boy's maimed, 188

football: blind girl attends games, 467; high school, 408; player, girl's handsome sweetheart, 234; player, star, 177; records, boy makes six touchdowns in one game, 75; sport, 178

Foote family, 310

footprints, disappear in snow, 314

Fords, Model T, 211

foreman: murderous, 388; ranch, redneck, 210

foresight, essential for arctic survival, 199

Forest, 236

forests: Dimwood, 110; mentally challenged boy lost in, 462

FORGED BY FIRE, 97, *129*

forgeries, note to school, 326

FOR MIKE, 130, 405

Forrest family, Quakers, 59

Fort Kittredge, 161

Fort Laramie, 345

Fort Lauderdale, Florida, 371

Fort Snelling, Minnesota, 383

forts: Spanish in Pacific Northwest, 146; tree, in woods, 310

fortune: go on a journey, 309; made from time-slip information, 364; teller, old Jewish man, at parties, 88, 384; telling, in Colonial Salem, 31; telling, with soomp (coffee grounds), 427

FORTY ACRES AND MAYBE A MULE, 131, 351

forty-seven, number of dedicated samurai, 348

Forty Years Domestic War, 156, 301

FOR YOUR EYES ONLY!, 132, 351

Fossil Glen, 146

fossils, searching for, 146

Foss, Melba, 265, 307

foster children, sullen, 469

Foster family (*Flyers*), 112, 127, 352

Foster family (*Tuck Everlasting*), 426

Foster family (*While No One Was Watching*), 11, 104, 135, 208, 259, 287, 449, 459

boy, 388; four sixth graders, 441; girl dropped for higher-status girl, 78; girl/ elderly storekeeper, 262; girl new in school/ resident, 372; girl of eleven/more mature girl, 65; girls at camp, 86; girl's aunt/ ornithologist, 136; girls, dissimilar fifth graders, 271; girls/next-door neighbors, 244; great-grandmother/rebellious great-granddad, 234; handicapped boys, 322; high school boy/girl, close, helpful, 9; high school boys, close, 126; homesick boy/fat boy, at camp, 86; interracial, possibility denied, 157; Irish immigrant boy/Maine farm boy, 283; Israeli boy/Palestinian-American girl, 170; Italian boy/Italian army deserter, World War II, 259; Japanese-American boy/*haole* (white American) boy, 38, 435; Jewish girl/ Catholic girl, pre–World War II, 92; killed in World War II, 121; Makah Indian man/ white boy, 233; mentally challenged boy/ feral boy, 462; Mexican American/Anglo boys, 252; new bright girl/klultzy girl, 14; normal girl/handicapped girl, 453; northern girl/Texas girl, 209; nosy boy/small town buddy, 458; of grandmother, narrator and recipient of letters, 387; orphan boy/blind derelict, 40; orphan boy/chngeling, 275; ostracize girl for calling police to drunken party, 389; poor farm boy/new girl at farm, 203; schoolgirls, 335; servant boy/samurai, 348; shy boy/outgoing girl, 44; sixth-grade boy/sixth-grade girl, 147; southern girl/ Jewish girl, 454; teenaged girl/young waitress, 436; teenaged girls, African-Americans in Chicago, 1960, 56; teenaged girls, supportive, 385; teens, dying of cancer, 268; toddler/mentally ill man, 203; transient girl/popular girl, 15; two boys in juvenile camp, 481; two boys interested in baseball, 61; two dissimilar fifth-grade girls, 18, 255; village boy/army general, 113; waif/ boy she saves, 270; wealthy English boy/ poor Irish emigrant, 33, 35; well-to-do, turned condescending, 67; worldly, 67; young monk/mute boy, 232

The Friendship, 410

friendship, novels of: African-Ameican girl and two white girls, 186; boy and girl, 121; fifth-grade girls, 18; handicapped persons, 322; interracial, 395; orphans, aged eleven, 88; teenaged girls, 385; two boys in detension facility, 181; two girls who communicate by mail, 336; white girl and young African-American man, 262

friendships: imaginary, 309; marred by racial tension, 112, 252; new, made, 337; price of, high, 476; unusual, 126

Friends of Egg, 116

FRINDLE, 66, *137*

frindles, name for pens, 138

Frogge, Amos, 19

frogs: boy swallows, 447; pet, 101, 345

Froggy, 353

From the Mixed-up Files of Mrs. Basil E. Frankweiler, 223, 442

From the Notebooks of Melanin Sun, 471

frontier conditions, persist into 1940s, 219

FRONTO, 13, *139,* 247, 309

frostbite, necessitates toe amputation, 54

fruit picking, fall damages knee, 247

fuel tanks, eaten by bears, 54

Fugitive Slave Law, 59

fugitives: aided by girl, 135; tyrant king, 13

Fullbright, Custis, 279

fundraisers, school, 314

funerals: brother's, 421; father's, 300; for town reprobate, 241; grandfather's, 288; grandmother's, 185; great-grandmother's, 234; mother's, 107; unconventional, 122, 417; Vietnam victim, 459

funnels, bought by timid woman, 367

furniture: from old, empty house, 147; makers, 248, 450

future, girl escapes into, 356

futuristic novels: gene alteration, 26; nuclear leak, 324; 21st century, Califonia, 317; Zimbabwe, 104

Gabe Riley, 44, 112, 126, 352

Gabe Rogers, 117, 208, 344

GABRIEL, 6, 40, *141*

Gag-Me, 147

Gagney, Raymond, 147

Gail Aimsley, 93

Gail Berdahl, 211

Galardi family, 174, 255

Gale, John, 431

Gallows Bird, 56, 416

gamblers: cousin addicted, 74; father, 166, 279; friend of detective, 321; grandfather, 418

games: dice, 193; harmful, 395; softball, big annual girls', 23; solitaire, 313, 402

gaming pieces, Makah carved some, 145

Gandillon family, 5, 40, 141

Ganesh, 96

religious, 190; resentful, mischievous, 89; responsible for family, 244; responsible for younger brother, 95; romantic, 191; rude, 222; sassy, disobedient, 234; saucy, underachieving, 89; seeks to prove boyfriend innocent of murder, 392; self-destructive, 83; selfish, self-indulgent, barely literate, 233; serious, reserved, 454; sexually abused by father, 187; sexually active, with older man, 115; shy, intelligent, 228; silver-haired, green-eyed, strong-willed, vindictive, 128; singleton, 15; sister of five brothers, 120; sisters leave home, 187; sixth grade, sniping, 147; sixth grade softball teams, 6, 23; small, high-spirited, capable, 341; snotty, pricks new girl in rear, 361; social butterfly, 15; socks snotty girl in nose, 361; speaks at school assembly on bike safety, 268; spirited, independent, 109; spoiled, prissy, 452; spunky, 20, 173, 317, 373, 392, 431; stranded at boarding school for war's duration, 238; street, 233; strong, heavy, 477; strong, lifts 30-pound stone, 142; strongly attracted to the sea, 128; suspended from school, 362; sweet-natured, 394; tall, red-haired, ungainly, 354; taught to read and write by older brother, 330; teenaged sisters, on their own, 456; thought to be able to summon dragons, 220; tormented by bullies, 96; triracial, 16, 253, 254, 465; troublemakers in fifth grade, 18; turns rebellious after death of brother, 267; tutored in math by girl, 15; typical high school "good kid, " 347; unusually responsible and capable, 115; very good at math, 15; Vietnamese-American, 210; wears boy's clothes, 424; youngest of nine children, 264 *The Giver,* 247
"gizmos," handcrafted items, 14
Gladness, 131
Gladstone family, 286, 354
Gladstone Shoes, Inc., 286, 354
glasses: crystal, broken, 93; eye, broken, 425; young boy discovered to need, 5
The Glass House People, 346
Glenda Jordan, 392
Glenn family, 11, 259, 459
GLENNIS, BEFORE AND AFTER, 55, *150*
Glennis Reilly, 150
Globe Theater, 189, 339, 375
Gloria Brant, 172
Gloriana, Virginia plantation, 59
THE GLORY FIELD, 152, 293

goalies, soccer, 409
GO AND COME BACK, 3, *153*
the "goat," listening device, 328
Goatboy, fantasy character, 345
goat people, 13, 56
The Goats, 68
goats, boy cares for, 408
GOD (Grace Order of Dadaists), 100, 154, 343
God: boy ponders nature of, 404; boy tries to bargain with, 404; His will questioned, 191
Goddard, Charlie, 383
godmothers: fairy, 107; throws rent party for girl, 153
gods: ancient, Eugenides, 413; Egyptian compared, 200; Hopi, Masau, 177; statues of, inside temple, 413; Stepfather God, 77
Godwinson family, 175, 220, 227, 233, 420, 463
Godwinson, Harold, Earl of Wessex, 175
goggles, sports, prescription, 409
The Gold Cadillac, 410
Gold Dust, 248
The Gold Dust Letters, 236, 266
golden calf idol, 112
Golden Dawn tangeine, 247, 409
Golden Gate Bridge, 316
The Golden Goblet, 262
Golden Oaks, nursing home, 417
Golden Promise Whipple, 19
goldenrod tea, 366
Gold family, 310
goldfinch, dead man reincarnated as, 297
Goldie Paige, 152
Golding, David, 31, 51, 53, 89
gold nuggets, given girl by grandmother, 10, 150
gold rush, California, 19, 20
gold, Spanish, 146
Goldy, 383
golf carts, for obese boy, 458
gondolier, father is, in Venice, 398
Gondwanna, 106
Gondwannan Embassy, 14
Gonzales, Pedrito, 191
Gonzalo, 366
Good-bye, My Wishing Star, 164
Good family, 31
Good Friday, 30, 404
The Good Liar, 251
Good Night, Maman, 261
Goody Dawson, 31
Goody family, 262
Goody Hall, 17

gooseberry, nickname, 155
gopi (cowherd), 194
Gordam Peldyrin, 401
gorges: remote, very beautiful, sought, 368; river, 113
Gorilla, Gorilla, 119
Gorp, murderous foreman, 388
Gosimer Lake, 458
Gosschalk family, 442
Gosschalk, Johan Cohen, 99, 207
gout, Griffin suffers from, 250
government: haters, 302; investigators, 78
governor, woman candidate for in Minnesota, 321
Governor Phips, 32
Grab Hands and Run, 412
Grace High School, 100, 154, 342
Grace, Holly, 134
Grace Order of Dadaists (GOD), 154, 343
Gracie's Girl, 469
Gracious Living Magazine, 62
graduate students: geology, 378; ethno-history, 378
graduations, from girl's high school, 346
Grady Traynor, 434
graffiti: "Nigger lover," 393; warning about rapist, 390
Grafton family, 199
Grafton, Jeb, 34
Gram (*Finn*), 123, 210
Gram (*Jericho*), 201
Gram (*Turn the Cup Around*), 427
Gram (*The Wedding*), 450
GRAM AND GRAMPS HIDDLE, *155,* 445
Gram Gilmore, 313
GRAM KITTREDGE, *155,* 301
Gramma Ethel, 382
GRAMMA HOUP, *156,* 289
Gram Mollahan, 235
Gram Murray, 89
GRAMPA NAKAJI, *156,* 410, 435
GRAMP KITTREDGE, 155, *156,* 160, 161, 301
Gran, 157
Granddad Brant, 172
grandfathers: carpenter, 83; close to grandchildren, 75, 364; close to grandson, 399, 402, 417; completed Good Friday pilgrimage, 403; curmudgeonly, 48, 179; disavows grandson, 48; dominating, bad-tempered, 244; dying, 288; eccentric, 306; ex-Navy cook, 75, 364; forgetful, 316, 417; former cowboy, 417; former history

professor, 313; former miner, 178; girl's foster father, clockmaker, 452; great-great, 182; great, accepts girl into family, 149; great, opens law office, 415; great, visiting for races, 75; has stroke, 75, 364; invalid, 364; irascible, 365; journalist, 172; killed by maurading whites, 85; much loved, 156; police chief, 327; rancher, 399; range-wise, people-smart ex-cowboy, 316; religious, 42; rescued Indian's, 85; taciturn, hard working, 156; tells outrageous stories, 364; trailer park owner, 365; very ill, 463. *See also* old persons
Grandfather Skoro, 42
Grandma Annie, 120
GRANDMA DICKENS, 67, *157*
GRANDMA DOWDEL, *158,* 205, 241, 258
Grandma Hernandez, 318
Grandma Min, 158, 240
Grandma Molly, 428
Grandma Pigza, 205
Grand Marais, Minnesota, 238
Grandma Sands, 52, 449
grand master of ceremonies, 347
Grandma Van Fossen, 121
GrandMin Walters Dutton, 201
GRANDMOTHER, 118, *158,* 239, 278
grandmothers: African American, strongly anti-white, 254; affectionate, supportive, 10; businesswoman, successful, 157; cares for her infirm mother, 201; carping, 57; deaf, 266; death of, 185, 313, 318, 402; dislikes pets, 404; eccentric and controlling, 148; fosters granddaughter, 361; great, bedridden, 234; great, demented, 15; great, infirm, aged, 201; great, passes along family history, 234; great, very old, 160; great, white of triracial girl, 253; guardian, 45; has ADHD, 205; has cancer, 403; has "Wicked Witch of the West" tongue, 449; hit-and-run killer, 429; Hopi, elder and seer, 334; hospitalized, 383; imperious, disapproving, 239; imperious, tough, eccentric, frugal, 158; loving, 157; maternal, 10; maternal, dead, 95; megalo-maniac, 272; Methodist, 278; old-fashioned, 293; painter, seascapes, 427; Palestinian, 170; pharmacist, 89; plans visit for grandsons, 311; possessive, 60; rejecting, 327; rule-oriented, 89; runner and graduate student, 387; sheep farmer, 324; sold as girl for three blankets, 87; spiritualist, 83, 148; step, eccentric, 126; step, supportive, 172; suffers stroke, 428; supportive, 148; timid,

399; volunteer families in 1840s town, 356; war, cousin Bryan, 395. *See also* captives

prisons: activist sisters in, 191; castle tower, 465; escapes from, 172, 182; in Texas desert, 182 life in, forgotten, 175; teenage girl sent to, 476

thirty years served in, 175; two-year terms, 376. *See also* jail; reform schools

prison scenes: 150; in juvenile facility, 182; in Deep South, 36; in Sounis, 412

prison sentences, two years for robbery, 242

privacy: lacking at boarding school, 395; violated, 228

privateer, late 17th century, Atlantic Ocean, 415

Private Eye series, 147

private investigators, 33, 321

prize-winning idea, catching drain water in garbage cans, 367

Probably Still Nick Swanson, 469

problem novels: abandoned children, juvenile delinquency, 260; ADHD (attention deficit hyperactivity disorder), 205; alcoholism, 172; alcoholism and domestic abuse, 456; assisted suicide, 399; bias towards Quakers and ecological concerns, 75; blind girl, 466; boy mute since death of parents, 123; broken family, 342; caring for aged, 201, 418; cerebral palsy, 322; death of child in bike accident, 267; death of father from AIDS, 103, 106; death of mother, 445; death of older siblings traumatizes family, 308; disintegrating family, 459, 465; domestic abuse, 132, 455, 456; homosexuality, lesbianism, 91; irresponsible teenage drivers, 99; mental illness, 83; morality of killing pigeons, 471; partially sighted boy, 367; psychological, 36, 172, 389; racism, 47; rape, 115; sexual abuse, 186, 456; star pitcher loses eye, 359; teenage pregnancy, 194; teenagers in hospice with cancer, 268; teenage, single mother, 251; unwed teenage pregnancies, 233; widower raises family, 201 working poor, 460

prodigy: child, boy, 83, 84, 306

producer, film, for high school boys, 44

professional women: African-American, 47, 71, 112, 233, 252; chiropractor, 417; lawyer, 415; pharmacist, grandmother, 89; professor, 71; 233

Professor Arneson, ethnologist, 334

Professor Moriarty, 26

professors: African-American, called "boy," 396; college, African-American woman, 71, 233; college, African-American father, Ohio University, 186; mathematics, 393; mother, 233; of drawing and painting, 335; research, Boston University, 290; summer visitor at inn, 427

Professor Williams, 370

prohibitions: against eating certain foods, 78; against reading assigned journal, 95; against refusing a direct order, 107; against talking to other passengers on ocean liner, 73; against unpacking clothes, 78; against wandering around the house, 74; against wearing fangs in house, 369; against working with mechanical and electrical things, 417; not to answer phone, 189

promises: islanders can return to Bikini in two years, 43; look after brother's wife, 242; protect river, 426; return in year and a day, 259

proms, high school, 343, 362, 385

property, of accused witches seized, 32

PROPHECY ROCK, 249, *333*

Prophecy Rock, Hopi sacred place, 334

proposals of marriage: accepted, 370; declined, then accepted, 128; formal, 298, 454; permission asked for, 325; second, accepted, 325; to female woodchuck, 264; unexpected, 258

prospectors, California gold rush, 19, 51

prosthesis, eye, 360

protagonists (by sex and age)

—boys, men: three, 129; four, 368; six, 301; seven, 310, 459; seven or eight, 424; eight, 97, 455; nine, 22, 241, 266, 471; nine or ten, 205, ten, 35, 48, 402, 448, 451; eleven, 4, 33, 34, 44, 84, 88, 120, 152, 203, 216, 238, 381, 388, 403, 459; twelve, 11, 28, 33, 34, 35, 49, 59, 75, 131, 166, 176, 195, 367, 408, 415, 462, 469; twelve (about), 164, 181; thirteen, 61, 104, 220, 252, 272, 279, 288, 299, 398, 417, 435, 457; thirteen or fourteen, 318; fourteen, 42, 103, 145, 185, 260, 347, 353, 374, 399; fifteen, 70, 81, 117, 123, 152, 161, 383; sixteen, 36, 93, 99, 111, 126, 174, 189, 333, 359, 379, 420; seventeen, 131, 158, 177, 192, 217, 297, 342, 382, 419, 460, 467; high school senior, 69, 130; eighteen or twenty, 412; twenty, 242; twenty-one or twenty-two, 341; boyhood to old age, 322; ninety, 363;

46, 247, 306; timely, several, 21; tortoise, 325. *See also* escapes
research assistants: 362, murdered, 334
resemblances, boy to slave master, 203
resentments: against half-sisters' father, 78; at brother's getting attention, 126; subsiding, 367
reservations: Sioux/Dakota, 81, 158; Hopi, 178, 333
resignation, from bank because of rape accusation, 253
resorts: Christmas in, 120; Jamaica, 468; Maine coastal inn area, to be expanded into, 62; planned for family land, 153
responsibility: assumed by teenage father, 419, 420; boy assumes for protecting half-sister, 129; boy feels for mother, 93, 348; child takes for little sister, 245; girl takes for decisions after grandfather's death, 244; girl takes for vandalism, 126; individual need for, 23; teenage mother's increases, 420; teenager takes for family, 326
Resthaven, 14, 106, 422
restrooms, white, entered by African Americans, 393
Resurrection lilies, 235
Resurrection Lily Bridger, 235, 244
"retard," African-American boy called, 263
retellings: of Biblical story from Exodus, 111; of "Cinderella," 107; of "Rapunzel," 480
retreats: religious, 191; to catatonic state, 291
The Return, 232
returns: of stolen hood ornaments, 50; to dolphin family and sea, 291
Reuben, 252
reunions: family, 153, 160, 161, 233, 302; high school, 476
Revelation, Book of, 433
revenge: desired by retainers of lord, 348; desired on half-German teacher, 162; for parents' murder, 395; on straying husband, murder of infant, 378; plotted, secured against vandals, 311; sought by former employee, 34; sought by schoolmate, 216
THE REVENGE OF THE FORTY-SEVEN SAMURAI, 177, *347*
Reverend Ezekial Freeman, 204
REVEREND MR. GIDEON BARTHOLOMEW, 33, 137, *349*
Reverend Mr. Luther Gates, 71, 233
Reverend Pyke, 346
Reverend Shulpa, 334
Reverend Sims, 36

revival meetings, 243
revolutionaries, son and priest, revealed as, 191
Revolutions of the Heart, 339
rewards: for bandit's head, 21; magnificent ruby, 194
REYNOLDS, MARILYN, *349,* 419
Rhonda the German shepherd, 238
rhyming ability, called The Last Word, 128
Rhysbridge Home, 128
Richard Bradshaw, 437
Richard Paul Weineman, 122
Richardson family, 336
Richild, 143
RICK WALKER, 242, 260, 302, *349*
Rick Whitman, 130
Rico Corteles, 435
Rico, Sunny, 122, 404
Ridder, Corey, 178
The Rider and His Horse, 177
Ride the Red Cycle, 351
ridicule, at sisters' clothes, 296
rifles: boy's, upsets adoptive family, 37; discharges accidentally, 318
Riley family, 44, 112, 126, 332, 352
Riley Sutter, 195
RIMON, 111, 202, 296, *350*
Rimwalkers, 164
Rinamu family, 42
rings: drug, 178; enables girl to understand animal speech, 324; iron, symbol of obedience owed, 193; keepsake from dragon, 117; king's seal stolen, 413; of unicorn horn, 324; retrieved from dry well, 160; signal danger, 325
Rio Grande, Indians along, 188
riots: after Rodney King beating, 47; almost caused by mixed-race couple, 67; averted by woman owner of fried chicken stand, 67; in Seattle streets, 308; response to civil rights sit-in, 394. *See also* protests
Riska, Helen, 365
Rita Matsika, 104, 422
Rita Sorely, 172, 175, 377
Ritchie family, 462
rite-of-passage ceremony, for dragon, 116, 136
Ritter, Bobby, 346
RITTER, JOHN H., 61, *350*
ritualistic behavior, 78
rivalry: basketball player friends, 383. *See also* arguments; conflicts; fights
rivers: course, changed by dam, 149;

otherworld fantasies, 250; ugly duckling story, 215; underdog conflicts, 311

style, setting: blues festival vividly described, 478; carefully delineated otherworld, 250; city life, in Jerusalem, well-depicted, 170; cultural detail of Indians well evoked, 165; descriptive of community life and beliefs, 24; descriptive of cross-country geography, 162; descriptive of geography and way of life of Israel, 170; descriptive of London stage, 375; descriptive of palace conspicuous consumption, small value placed on human life, 374; descriptive of 17th century London, 375; fine details of Korean life and attitudes, 240; fine period details, World War II, 235; flavor of Ohio hills and upper South, 62; good details of farm life, 124; good details of mountain area and people, 196; good picture of medieval institutional church, 331; descriptive of mid 19th century period in Ireland, England, and Massachusetts, 34; Hopi reservation setting well drawn, 334; keen sense of small town and farm community, 91; medieval-period attitudes and beliefs, 401; mountain and farm life shown well, 432; post–American Civil War setting especially well depicted, 132; rugged wilderness palpable, 261; strongly created Martha's Vineyard, 142; strong sense of small-town life, 472; understated description of slavery, 363; very descriptive of desert town, 418; vivid Depression-era small-town life, 242; vivid description of painter's times, 207; vivid small-town life, 437; vivid 11th century life in halls and monastery, 221; vivid life among Indians at home and in captivity at Spanish mission, 188; vivid countryside and daily life, 14th century, England, France, Spain, 341; vivid life on Harlem streets, 93; vivid Hispanic-American family life, 404; vivid Sealmaiden and Folk Keeper duties, convincing, 128; vivid wolf life and culture, 41; well-depicted Mexican-American setting, 319

style, structure: afternote, 19; afterword, 162; alternating chapters narrated by sisters, 190; author's note about bike safety, 268; author's note on background, 146, 363; based on actual wilderness survival experiences, 118; based on family stories, 452; based on author's grandfather's experiences, 13; based on folktale, 25, 107,

480; based on legend, 373; bibliography on Martha's Vineyard, 143; book in form of journal, 317; book simulates series of newspaper articles, 229; brief vignettes, 183; broad canvas, 14, 194; chapters preceded by factual paragraphs, 43; clever narrative construction, 185; commentary on nature of poetry and story, 14; complicated circular narrative, 158; complicated structure of first and third persons, 441; contrasts way of life and attitudes of Indians and Spaniards, 189; diary entries, 191; diary entries and letters, 316; diary entries and letters addressed by Johanna van Gogh to husband, Theo, 206, 412; disjointed, 121, 387; endnote with historical background, 21; endpaper map of Martha's Vineyard, 143; epilogue, 397; epilogue and chronology included, 207; epilogue contains background information, 449; epilogue, letter to New York City homegirl, 234; epilogue, narrated by ship's captain, 32; epilogue set long after escape, 111; epilogue shows a fantasy sequence in another dimension, 269; epilogue shows kingdom at peace, 126; epilogue with historical background, 436; episodes based on actual classroom events, 229; episodes based on actual turkey walk, 162; episodic, 301; "faction," 207; flashbacks, 59, 65, 104, 115, 144, 267, 300, 347, 363, 375, 401, 457; foreword gives important background information, 384; frame story, 187; glossary of Hopi words, 334; glossary of Spanish terms, 404; improvises on Asian-Indian epics, 194; introspective ruminations, 457; italicized dreams, 124; journal entries, 57, 132, 408; last chapter related seventy years later, 23; letters and flashbacks, 92; letters, novel entirely in, 336; letters to grandmother's friend, 387; map of Canadian Northwest Territories, 118; note about hereditary deafness on Martha's Vineyard, 143; occasional notebook entries, 15; parallel between spunky girl, enduring aunt, and unbroken colt, 432; parallel stories told alternately, 201; preface gives sources, 189; present tense heightens dramatic effect, 481; proverbial sayings, old Kragish, 126; quest pattern, 108, 193, 412; reports, psychiatric, 288; stories within story, 11, 82, 165, 268, 315, 342, 343, 414, 434, 445, 452; story moves in circle, 158; titles, chapter, as headlines, 229; told partly in letters, 288;

Ireland, England, and Massachusetts, 35; vivid depiction of geography and social life, 63; vivid depiction of magic, ghosts, and time travel, 314; vivid picture of art world, 207; well-depicted childhood attitudes and activities, 66

style, use of language: African-American adolescent girl's voice convincing, 68; African-American and West Indian dialects, 93; almost entirely in dialogue, 19; appropriately rambling discourse, 206; arresting diction and turns of phrase, 14; articles, unusually sophisticated for fifth graders, 229; avoids clichés, 383; awkward dialogue, 165; biblical resonances, 318; biographical details compelling, 207; boy adopts Jamaican speech rhythms, 225; colloquial, deliberately ungrammatical dialogue, 162; colloquial unschooled speech of Illinois town, 241; colloquial unschooled speech of Ohio hills and upper South, 62; contemporary diction, intimate, witty tone, 418; contemporary teen talk, 70; contemporary, wisecracking narrative, 75; contemporary wisecracks and idioms, 371; contrast between New York life and street talk and genteel Southern ways and speech, 234; credible teenage boys' diction, 186; crisp, controlled, late 20th century in attitude, 175; crisp, sensory, 446; crisp, visual, sensory, 481; diction reveals boy's stress, 455; dialogue bantering, bickering, full of silly insults, 298; dialogue effective, sounds authentic, 127; dialogue extensive, 147; dialogue extensive, authentic, 311; dialogue incongruous, 196; dialogue in Jamaican dialect, 187; dialogue of children's insults and trash talk, 371; dialogue, street talk, 234; dialogue with trash talk, 449; dialogue with trash talk and sex slang, 269; disturbing use of commas, 449; excerpts from zines, from pop/rock lyrics, 175; explicit sex and trash talk, 234; extensive dialogue, 446; flamboyant, 21; formal diction, 221; fresh, saucy, wisecracking, 442; fragmentary sentences effective, 456; gentle, credible handling of boy's emotions, 403; high diction dialogue, 194; highly pictorial, 45, 466; hill-country dialect and extensive dialogue, 263; keenly sensory language, 368; lean, laconic, 384; letters too detailed for credibility as letters, 337; lots of specific details, 75; Makah/Chinook Indian words,

146; many references to nature, 104; meaning of title obscure, 463; minimalist, economical, 404; mostly dialogue, 132, 418; naive narrator, 280; narrative ungrammatical, 23; narrators' voices distinct, 337; Native-American Indian allusions, 446; overuse of metaphors, 428; pattern of reflexive pronouns, 237; present tense, 144, 327, 423; racial epithets, sexual references, earthy language, 36; restrained sex scenes, 434; run-on sentences and fragments, 166; run-on sentences, self-absorbed narrative, trash and sex talk, 354; seemingly taped teen dialogue, 343; sensory, 54, 204; sexist putdowns, 371; short simple sentences, no quotation marks for dialogue, 115; sign-language dialogue enclosed in wave signs, 143; slightly archaic speech, 126; snappy dialogue, one-liners, quick cracks, 71; snappy, extensive dialogue, 332; staccato style emphasizes emotional turmoil, 457; street jargon, 50; street-smart, 383; street talk, African-American dialect, and standard English, 234; teenage "angst" restrained, 186; teen romance handled with restraint, 315; teen talk, 193; trash talk restrained, 186; unschooled, colloquial speech seems forced, 49; variation on style of folktale, 481; vivid details of curing scenes, 12; voice convincing, 243; Western dialect, 243

scientific, girl treated as, 97

substitutes, debate teammate, 420

suburban area, unidentified American, late 20th century, 310

Successful Women, Angry Men: Backlash in the Two-Career Marriage, 55

SUGAR DOBBS, 11, 39, 89, 163, 231, 250, *401*

SUGAR HIDDLE, 285, *402,* 445

Sugarly the centaur, 232

suicides: after committing murder, 115; assisted, 400, 464; attempts, 134, 308, 454, 460; because face is disfigured, 29; boy assists girl in committing, 11; commanded by shogun, 348; contemplated, 41, 127; dancer-mother committed, 84; cousin's death, ruled, 218; drug overdose, deliberate, 468; father commits, 115; hanging, 31; in campus bombing, 69; Japanese soldiers, Bikini Atoll, 42; mother, 326, 344; of forty-seven conspirators, 348; planned, 131; planning of, suspected, 360; reform school

About the Authors

ALETHEA K. HELBIG, Professor, and AGNES REGAN PERKINS, Professor Emeritus, both of English Language and Literature at Eastern Michigan University. They are the authors of a series of encyclopedic works on fiction for children published by Greenwood Press: *Dictionary of American Children's Fiction*, *Dictionary of British Children's Fiction*, and *Dictionary of Children's Fiction from Australia, Canada, India, New Zealand*, and *Selected African Countries*. Helbig is also past president of the Children's Literature Association. They have also both published *This Land Is Our Land and Many Peoples, One Land* on multicultural literature for children and young adults, *Myths and Hero Tales*, a critical reference on myths and hero tales from around the world (all Greenwood), and numerous articles on children's literature.